SUSTAINABILITY ASSESSMENT OF URBAN SYSTEMS

Our world is becoming more urban. More than 50 percent of the global population now lives in cities, which poses new challenges for sustainable development. This book integrates theory and methods of sustainability assessment with concepts from systems science to provide guidelines for assessing the sustainability of urban systems. It discusses different aspects of urban sustainability, from energy and housing, to mobility and health, covering social, economic, and environmental factors, as well as the various stakeholders and actors involved. The book argues the need to find models and solutions in order to design sustainable cities of the future in light of the complexity of urban social life. Including diverse case studies from the developed and developing world, this book provides a useful reference for researchers and students from a broad range of disciplines working in the field of sustainability, as well as for environmental consultants and policy-makers.

Claudia R. Binder is Professor and Head of the Laboratory for Human-Environment Relations in Urban Systems at École Polytechnique Fédéral de Lausanne (EPFL), Switzerland. She holds the Swiss Mobiliar Chair for Urban Ecology and Sustainable Living. She is a leading researcher in the field of sustainability assessment. Her interests lie in inter- and transdisciplinary research to analyze, model, and assess scenarios and policies for transitions of urban systems toward sustainability.

Romano Wyss is a research scientist at the Laboratory for Human-Environment Relations in Urban Systems at EPFL, Switzerland. He also works as an independent consultant in the field of regional development and sustainability. Romano's research focuses on sustainable development, resilience theory, and energy transitions, linked to social network analysis and transdisciplinary research.

Emanuele Massaro is a scientist at the Laboratory for Human-Environment Relations in Urban Systems at the EFPL, Switzerland. He received his doctorate in Complex Systems from the University of Florence in 2014 and thereafter he conducted postdoctoral research at Carnegie Mellon University and MIT. His research interests span the areas of computational epidemiology, urban sustainability, and big data analytics.

SUSTAINABILITY ASSESSMENT OF URBAN SYSTEMS

Edited by
CLAUDIA R. BINDER
École Polytechnique Fédérale de Lausanne

ROMANO WYSS
École Polytechnique Fédérale de Lausanne

EMANUELE MASSARO
École Polytechnique Fédérale de Lausanne

CAMBRIDGE
UNIVERSITY PRESS

CAMBRIDGE
UNIVERSITY PRESS

University Printing House, Cambridge CB2 8BS, United Kingdom

One Liberty Plaza, 20th Floor, New York, NY 10006, USA

477 Williamstown Road, Port Melbourne, VIC 3207, Australia

314–321, 3rd Floor, Plot 3, Splendor Forum, Jasola District Centre, New Delhi – 110025, India

79 Anson Road, #06–04/06, Singapore 079906

Cambridge University Press is part of the University of Cambridge.

It furthers the University's mission by disseminating knowledge in the pursuit of education, learning, and research at the highest international levels of excellence.

www.cambridge.org
Information on this title: www.cambridge.org/9781108471794
DOI: 10.1017/9781108574334

First published 2020

Printed in the United Kingdom by TJ International Ltd. Padstow Cornwall

A catalogue record for this publication is available from the British Library.

Library of Congress Cataloging-in-Publication Data
Names: Binder, Claudia R., editor. | Wyss, Romano, editor. | Massaro, Emanuele, editor.
Title: Sustainability assessment of urban systems / edited by Claudia R. Binder, École Polytechnique Fédérale de Lausanne, Romano Wyss, École Polytechnique Fédérale de Lausanne, Emanuele Massaro, École Polytechnique Fédérale de Lausanne.
Description: Cambridge, United Kingdom ; New York, NY : Cambridge University Press, 2020. | Includes index.
Identifiers: LCCN 2019030551 (print) | LCCN 2019030552 (ebook) | ISBN 9781108471794 (hardback) | ISBN 9781108574334 (epub)
Subjects: LCSH: Sustainable development. | Cities and towns – Growth. | Sustainable development – Social aspects. | Sustainable development – Economic aspects.
Classification: LCC HC79.E5 S864555 2020 (print) | LCC HC79.E5 (ebook) | DDC 307.1/416–dc23
LC record available at https://lccn.loc.gov/2019030551
LC ebook record available at https://lccn.loc.gov/2019030552

ISBN 978-1-108-47179-4 Hardback

Contents

Preface

The idea to edit a volume on the sustainability assessment of urban systems emerged quite a while ago. Even though several books on sustainability assessment have been written in the last decade, and some of them refer to urban systems, in my view there was still a need for a book that brought together different strands of thought, methods, and fields of application. Currently, sustainability issues are approached in completely different ways, ranging from developing diverse indicator sets, which should make it possible to monitor and assess the current state of a system, to models that focus on very specific issues or sectors. When digging deeper into the question of sustainability assessment, we found that some aspects needed to be considered in more depth. For example, the questions: When does an indicator show that a system is really sustainable? What does sustainability mean and for whom? Who are the relevant actors? Who has the decision-making power?

Our personal experience has shown that it is very unlikely that different actors or a group of actors can agree on specific values or points at which a system is sustainable. They are, however, more likely to agree on a range within which an indicator can be regarded as being sustainable; thus, we might be looking at a space rather than a specific threshold. This space might depend on context, legal constraints, and the goals a city has set itself. Thus, determining what a sustainable urban system is, and what a sustainable space could look like, is a complex task that goes well beyond developing indicator sets. There is a need to become aware of different theoretical perspectives and to develop integrative assessment tools that include these perspectives.

Having done research on sustainability and sustainability assessment in urban systems and beyond for at least fifteen years, we decided to take on the task of editing a book focusing specifically on these issues. Thus, we conceived this book, which first presents the theoretical aspects of sustainability assessment, addressing different perceptions of sustainability, power relations, and systemic issues. In addition, we present a first conceptualization that can move us toward a dynamic and transition-oriented approach. In the second part, the book provides a set of methods that can be applied depending on the data available and the stakeholder involvement required. These methods, which cover the normative, systemic, and procedural aspects of sustainability assessment, range from purely qualitative methodologies that can be applied in very specific case studies and contexts, to data-driven methods that allow for benchmarking and cross-comparisons among cities. The third part deals with a major challenge in sustainability assessment: the conceptualization of the objects relevant for the assessment. It introduces concepts and methods for defining urban systems, and looks in depth at key problems of the sustainability of urban systems and the assessment of key functions of urban systems. In the last part of the book, we show practical solutions in which different methodologies are applied to different scenarios. This part argues for the need to find models and solutions in order to design the urban sustainable cities of the future, taking account of the complexity of urban social life. The goal, therefore, is not to be as complete as possible, but to provide insights into how sustainability and sustainability assessment in urban systems can be addressed.

We hope that this book will inspire scientists and practitioners to take a critical and comprehensive view of the sustainability assessment of urban systems and to develop policies leading to more sustainable urban systems in the future.

Claudia R. Binder

Acknowledgments

It is not possible to write and edit such a book without the support of many people. We would like to thank all the wonderful people who have helped make this book become a reality. First and foremost, we would like to thank all the authors for providing innovative chapters that offer outside-the-box thinking. Furthermore, we would like to thank all the reviewers for supporting us in critically developing, revising, and shaping the book's content and giving feedback to the authors of the chapters. The people involved in reviewing include (in alphabetic order) Marta Giulia Baldi, Michel Bierlaire, David N. Bresch, Susanna Burghartz, Elena Cogato-Lanza, Bert deVries, Pay Drechsel, Ursula Eicker, Daniel Favrat, Giuseppe Feola, Livia Fritz, Katharina Gapp, Pekka Halla, Niko Heeren, Vincent Kaufmann, Christopher Kennedy, Jan Landert, Igor Linkov, Patrizia Lombardi, Kevin G. Mac Adams, Franziska Meinherz, Albert Merino-Saum, Susan Mühlemeier, Vinicius Netto, Anna Pagani, Jessen Page, Stefan Paulik, Thorsten Schilling, Flurina Schneider, Anna Scolobig, Matthew Skjonsberg, Volker Stelzer, Sara Torabi Moghadam, Nuno Videira, Anne von Streit, Daniel Wachter, Robert Webb.

A special thank you goes to Stefanie Krauth for her early engagement in writing the proposal for the book, Charlène Ruppli for supporting us in keeping to deadlines and formatting, and Lorenzo Donadio for supporting with indexing the book. Deep thanks also go to Hannah Roberson for carefully editing all the chapters, and to Marta Giulia Baldi for looking into the final details and providing consistency across chapters and within the book. Finally, we thank Swiss Mobiliar for the financial support allowing us to devote our time to this book project.

Contributors

Dr. Aristide Athanassiadis
Chair of Circular Economy and Urban Metabolism, Université Libre de Bruxelles (ULB), Brussels, Belgium

BATir – Building, Architecture and Town planning, Université Libre de Bruxelles (ULB), Brussels, Belgium

Dr. Marta G. Baldi
Independent Researcher and Consultant on Sustainability, Lausanne, Switzerland

Prof. Claudia R. Binder
Laboratory for Human-Environmental Relations in Urban Systems (HERUS), École Polytechnique Fédérale de Lausanne (EPFL), Lausanne, Switzerland

Ms. Anne Boesch
Laboratory for Human-Environmental Relations in Urban Systems (HERUS), École Polytechnique Fédérale de Lausanne (EPFL), Lausanne, Switzerland

Multi-topic Monitoring Group, Environment, Sustainable Development, Territory Unit, Swiss Federal Statistical Office, Neuchâtel, Switzerland

Dr. André de Montmollin
Multi-topic Monitoring Group, Environment, Sustainable Development, Territory Unit, Swiss Federal Statistical Office, Neuchâtel, Switzerland

Dr. Giuseppe Feola
Copernicus Institute of Sustainable Development, Utrecht University, Utrecht, the Netherlands

Ms. Livia Fritz
Laboratory for Human-Environmental Relations in Urban Systems (HERUS), École Polytechnique Fédérale de Lausanne (EPFL), Lausanne, Switzerland

Prof. Björn Frostell
Former professor of Industrial Ecology, Royal Institute of Technology, Stockholm, Sweden
Ecoloop AB, Stockholm, Sweden

Mr. Baptiste Gex
Enoki Sàrl, Fribourg, Switzerland

Mr. Pekka Halla
Laboratory for Human-Environmental Relations in Urban Systems (HERUS), École Polytechnique Fédérale de Lausanne (EPFL), Lausanne, Switzerland

Mr. Michael Hutter
Faculty of Social and Political Sciences, University of Lausanne, Lausanne, Switzerland

Dr. Jürgen Kopfmüller
Institute for Technology Assessment and Systems Analysis (ITAS), Karlsruhe Institute of Technology (KIT), Karlsruhe, Germany

Prof. Klaus Krumme
Centre for Logistics & Traffic (ZLV), University of Duisburg-Essen (UDE), Duisburg, Germany

Dr. Rafael Laurenti
Laboratory for Human-Environmental Relations in Urban Systems (HERUS), École Polytechnique Fédérale de Lausanne (EPFL), Lausanne, Switzerland

Unit of Integrated Product Development, Royal Institute of Technology (KTH), Stockholm, Sweden

Prof. François Maréchal
Laboratory of Industrial Process and Energy Systems Engineering (IPESE), École Polytechnique Fédérale de Lausanne (EPFL), Lausanne, Switzerland

Dr. Emanuele Massaro
Laboratory for Human-Environmental Relations in Urban Systems (HERUS), École Polytechnique Fédérale de Lausanne (EPFL), Lausanne, Switzerland

Ms. Franziska Meinherz
Laboratory for Human-Environmental Relations in Urban Systems (HERUS), École Polytechnique Fédérale de Lausanne (EPFL), Lausanne, Switzerland

Mr. João Vitor Meirelles (or João Meirelles)
Laboratory for Human-Environmental Relations in Urban Systems (HERUS), École Polytechnique Fédérale de Lausanne (EPFL), Lausanne, Switzerland

Dr. Albert Merino-Saum
Laboratory for Human-Environmental Relations in Urban Systems (HERUS), École Polytechnique Fédérale de Lausanne (EPFL), Lausanne, Switzerland

Dr. Susan Mühlemeier
Laboratory for Human-Environmental Relations in Urban Systems (HERUS), École Polytechnique Fédérale de Lausanne (EPFL), Lausanne, Switzerland

Prof. Vinicius M. Netto
School of Architecture and Urbanism EAU, Universidade Federal Fluminense (UFF), Rio de Janeiro, Brazil

Ms. Anna Pagani
Laboratory for Human-Environmental Relations in Urban Systems (HERUS), École Polytechnique Fédérale de Lausanne (EPFL), Lausanne, Switzerland

Ms. Melissa Pang
Laboratory for Human-Environmental Relations in Urban Systems (HERUS), École Polytechnique Fédérale de Lausanne (EPFL), Lausanne, Switzerland

Dr. Damiano Pasetto
Laboratory of Ecohydrology (ECHO), École Polytechnique Fédérale de Lausanne (EPFL), Lausanne, Switzerland

Dr. Achilleas Psyllidis
Spatial Data Science, Delft University of Technology (TU Delft), Delft, the Netherlands

Prof. Ulf Ranhagen
Visiting Professor at Dalarna University, Falun, Sweden
Chief Architect, SWECO
Professor Emeritus, KTH Royal Institute of Technology, Stockholm, Sweden

Prof. Fabiano L. Ribeiro
Department of Physics, Federal University of Lavras (UFLA), Lavras, Minas Gerais, Brazil

Prof. Andrea Rinaldo
Laboratory of Ecohydrology (ECHO), École Polytechnique Fédérale de Lausanne (EPFL), Lausanne, Switzerland

Prof. Marlyne Sahakian
Institute of Sociological Research (IRS), University of Geneva, Geneva, Switzerland

Dr. Thorsten Schilling
Laboratory for Human-Environmental Relations in Urban Systems (HERUS), École Polytechnique Fédérale de Lausanne (EPFL), Lausanne, Switzerland

Dr. Flurina Schneider
Centre for Development and Environment, University of Bern, Bern, Switzerland

Dr. Volker Stelzer
Institute for Technology Assessment and Systems Analysis (ITAS), Karlsruhe Institute of Technology (KIT), Karlsruhe, Germany

Dr. François Vuille
Director of the energy department of the Canton of Vaud, Lausanne, Switzerland

Prof. Robert Webb
Fenner School of Environment and Society, Australian National University (ANU), Canberra, Australia

Dr. Romano Wyss
Laboratory for Human-Environmental Relations in Urban Systems (HERUS), École Polytechnique Fédérale de Lausanne (EPFL), Lausanne, Switzerland

General Introduction

Claudia R. Binder, Romano Wyss, Emanuele Massaro

The sustainability of urban systems is a pressing topic now, and will be even more so in the future. Currently, more that 50 percent of the world's population (74 percent in the EU) lives in cities, and this share is expected to keep increasing, posing new challenges for sustainable development. Although cities only cover 3 percent of the earth's surface, they account for 75 percent of global CO_2 emissions, and consume about 75 percent of resources and produce 50 percent of the waste worldwide. However, cities also provide income (80 percent of global GDP) and education, and are hotspots for innovation (Acuto & Panel 2016; Wigginton, et al., 2016). The ambiguous role of cities poses large challenges and renders it necessary to develop tools to assess urban strategies and developments from a sustainability perspective.

Sustainability and sustainable development are complex concepts, running the range from "strong" or steady-state to "weak" or capital–nature substitution sustainability (Pezzey, 1992; Daly, 1997; Neumayer, 2003). Although there is almost universal agreement that sustainable development is a worthy goal, this agreement does not lead to a straightforward prescriptive agenda. Sustainable development was defined by the World Commission on Environment and Development's 1987 Brundtland Report (1987) thus: "[sustainable development] meets the needs of the present without compromising the ability of future generations to meet their own needs." The Brundtland Report outlined three diverse and potentially conflicting areas (environmental, social, and economic) related to sustainable development. However, the very broad scope of the definition allows for many interpretations based on academic disciplinary perspectives, ideological preferences, or even political expediencies (Binder et al., 2010).

At the policy level, the approach to operationalizing the concept of sustainable development has focused mainly on developing measurable indicators and parameters, which describe important features of the environmental, economic, and social aspects of a society (Parris and Kates, 2003). Such sets of indicators, however, vary greatly depending on the scale of the assessment and the sectors being studied (Chapter 14). Additionally, there are important trade-offs between indicators which cannot be neglected if sustainability assessment is to be meaningful for policy-making (Wiek and Binder, 2005; Binder et al., 2010; Chapter 8 and Chapter 9).

It has been claimed that sustainability assessments are an essential tool to support the transition toward sustainability (Pope et al. 2004). They can play an important role in helping decision-makers and policy-makers decide which of all the actions available to them they should or should not take when attempting to help move society toward sustainability (Pope et al. 2004). Sustainability assessments, when done correctly, should ensure that "plans and activities make an optimal contribution to sustainable development" (Pope et al. 2004). And although sustainability assessments are a good first step, several issues are yet unresolved:

1. How can we decide upon what is sustainable, specifically in the context of urban systems?
2. What role do normative and systemic aspects play in assessing sustainability?
3. Which stakeholders should be included in the assessment process and how can they best be involved?
4. How can we identify and deal with trade-offs in sustainability indicator sets?

In light of the issues, this book provides guidelines for successful sustainability assessment of urban systems, to be used by experts and policy-makers alike. It integrates tools and knowledge from sustainability assessments with concepts from systems science, to enable well-conceived sustainability assessments for cities around the world, taking into account the concepts of sustainability assessment already in use and offering new ways of conceptualizing these issues in the urban setting.

Structure and Use of the Book

The book is structured into four parts. Each of the parts can be studied or used independently from the others and is preceded by a short introduction. The first part, "Background to Sustainability Assessment," discusses the underlying theoretical and conceptual aspects of sustainability assessment. It (1) sets out the basis for understanding sustainability and the different facets of sustainability assessment (Chapter 1); (2) provides insights into key systems-science concepts and how they relate to sustainability assessment (Chapter 2), (3) deepens and further explores the role of normativity within the discussion of sustainability and sustainability assessment (Chapter 3); (4) analyzes the role of power within participatory processes in sustainability assessments (Chapter 4); and (5) explores pathways for dynamic sustainability assessment by considering resilience and transition perspectives (Chapter 5).

This part can be used by scholars, students, and practitioners who want to get an overview of key theoretical background concepts in sustainability assessment. We purposefully treat the systemic, normative, participatory, and resilience perspectives separately so that the reader can easily focus on a particular topic of interest.

The second part of the book, "Integrative Approaches for Sustainability Assessment," presents and discusses a number of selected integrative sustainability assessment approaches. The presented approaches share several criteria that we consider indispensable for sustainability assessment in urban systems: all approaches include normative and systemic perspectives, have a broad scope, and are applicable to different cases, and at different scales and aggregation levels. The four approaches were chosen to represent (1) qualitative approaches – in situations where we are confronted with low data availability and a variety of actors, and there is a need to integrate and develop a consistent sustainability assessment with which all parties agree (Chapter 6); (2) integrative conceptual approaches – aiming at integrating top-down normative views with contextual requirements (Chapter 7); (3) semi-quantitative approaches – providing a way to analyze trade-offs between the indicators, in cases where conflict between stakeholders and over options might be envisioned (Chapter 8); and (4) participatory multi-criteria approaches, which are flexible quantitative and semi-quantitative approaches and can be used in combination with the other three approaches (Chapter 9).

This part allows scholars to choose between different methods depending on the requirements of the assessment. The methods are described so that they are easy to understand and exemplified with simple case studies. References to the chapters in Part I support readers who are interested in obtaining a more in-depth perspective of the underlying conceptual backgrounds.

The third part of the book, "Perspectives on Urban Sustainability," sets the stage for urban sustainability assessment. Its main goal is to provide different overarching perspectives on how to study urban systems in relation to sustainability. Thereby, this part (1) analyzes how different metaphors for conceptualizing urban systems are related to urban sustainability assessment (Chapter 10); (2) develops a framework for understanding the effect of urban systems and their development on sustainability issues more broadly (Chapter 11); (3) provides a framework for evaluating urban supply systems (Chapter 12); (4) looks at two distinct indicators sets for assessing the sustainability of urban systems (Chapter 13); and (5) develops an ontology for structuring and qualifying indicator sets (Chapter 14).

The chapters within Part III allow the reader to look into specific perspectives on the sustainability assessment of urban systems. They provide an overview of the issues to be considered in the sustainability assessment of urban systems. The chapters can be read and used independently from each other and from the chapters in Parts I and Part II, depending on the interest of the reader and the research problem and question at hand.

The fourth part of the book, "Focal Points of Urban Sustainability," provides some deep dives into urban sustainability issues. Thereby, the first three chapters address key problems of urban sustainability in a conceptual and holistic way. Specifically, they look into (1) energy challenges of urban systems (Chapter 15); (2) how to conceptualize and assess the sustainability of the housing system (Chapter 16); and (3) how to assess urban agriculture as part of the food system (Chapter 17). The last four chapters in Part IV present case studies analyzing very specific urban sustainability issues. They include (1) simulating the effect of proximity on interaction patterns (Chapter 18); (2) assessing ecological impacts within urban systems, focusing on the particular case of Stockholm (Chapter 19); (3) analyzing the sustainability of ride sharing in Santiago de Chile (Chapter 20); and (4) providing a new framework to study the sustainability aspects of mosquito-borne diseases (Chapter 21).

This part provides the reader with very specific case studies where sectoral aspects of sustainability have been addressed within an urban system. As with the rest of the book, the reader is able to use the chapters independently from each other. If a more in-depth explanation of theoretical aspects and/or methods is needed, the reader will be referred to specific chapters in the other parts of the book.

These four parts with their very distinct purposes seek to provide a holistic perspective on the sustainability assessment of urban systems. Confronted with having to perform a sustainability assessment, scholars will have to reflect upon the sustainability concept they want to base the assessment on, whom they want to include, what the sustainability targets are likely to be, and which method they would like to use to assess the system at hand. This book aims at making these key aspects of sustainability assessment explicit, thus contributing to a more conscious performance of a sustainability assessment. The practical examples are intended to show the complexity of an urban system and the different ways in which it can be approached. Thus, they provide illustrations of the methods presented, use modeling approaches to analyze very specific aspects of sustainability, or conceptualize specific functions of the urban system itself. It is evident that we do not aim to prescribe a specific method, normative view, or way of performing a sustainability assessment of an urban system. Rather we aim to inspire scholars to think beyond their own perspective and dive into new methods and new normative perspectives, and use these as decision-support tools in the transition toward more sustainable urban systems.

We hope that the readers will enjoy and use the book in the diverse ways in which we envision it could provide benefit to them.

References

Acuto, M., & Parnell, S. (2016). Leave no city behind. *Science*, 352(6288), 873. DOI:10.1126/science.aag1385.

Binder, C. R., Feola, G., & Steinberger, J. K. (2010). Considering the normative, systemic and procedural dimensions in indicator-based sustainability assessments in agriculture. *Environmental Impact Assessment Review*, 30(2), 71–81. https://doi.org/10.1016/j.eiar.2009.06.002.

Brundtland, G. H. (1987). *Report of the World Commission on Environment and Development: "Our Common Future."* United Nations.

Daly, H. E. (1997). *Beyond Growth: The Economics of Sustainable Development*. Beacon Press.

Parris, T.M., & Kates, R. W. (2003). Characterizing and measuring sustainable development. *Annual Review of Environment and Resources*, 28, 559–86.

Pezzey, J. (1992). *Sustainable Development Concept: An Economic Analysis*. The World Bank.

Pope, J., Annandale, D, & Morrison-Saunders, A. (2004). Conceptualising sustainable development. *Environmental Impact Assessment Review*, 24, 595–616.

Wiek, A., & Binder, C. (2005). Solution spaces for decision-making: A sustainability assessment tool for city-regions. *Environmental Impact Assessment Review*, 25(6), 589–608. https://doi.org/10.1016/j.eiar.2004.09.009.

Wigginton, N. S., Fahrenkamp-Uppenbrink, J., Wible, B., & Malakoff, D. (2016). Cities are the future. *Science*, 352(6288), 904–905. DOI:10.1126/science.352.6288.904.

Part I

Theoretical Background

With more than 50 percent of the Earth's population already living in urban areas, according to the United Nations, and with this percentage rapidly increasing, especially in Africa and Asia, questions of how to deal with urban sustainable development are becoming more and more pressing.

In the first part of the edited volume, we focus on the fundamentals that underpin approaches to sustainability assessment, both from a historical as well as from an epistemological and methodological point of view.

The history of sustainability assessment goes back more than 20 years, with the first scientific articles devoted to the matter appearing in the mid-1990s, as laid out in Chapter 1. Starting off with approaches strongly influenced by the older tradition of environmental impact assessments, the authors of Chapter 1 show how the sustainability assessment community has slowly but steadily transcended these origins to include more and more social and economic aspects of sustainability over the years, thereby considerably broadening the conceptual basis of sustainability assessment practices.

One promising way of doing this was to take on a system-based perspective of sustainability, informed by cybernetics and the emerging research field of sustainability science. This is what Chapter 2 is devoted to. By rejecting linear reasoning and emphasizing the systemic interaction between social, economic, and environmental subsystems, a system-based perspective makes it possible to assess all three spheres of sustainability – the economic, social, and environmental – on equal terms, while taking into account their mutual interdependence.

The way we look at a system, the political convictions we have, or the concepts of justice and efficiency that are dominant in a certain social setting are all issues that have an effect on the design of a sustainability assessment, and on the following (policy) evaluations. Chapter 3 deals with these normative issues, highlighting the importance of the underlying power issues and societal values that are at play when it comes to defining seemingly objective indicator sets while showing how a higher level of critical reflectiveness can lead to more pertinent assessment approaches.

Chapter 4 takes up the power dimension of sustainability assessments and pursues the question of how power and public participation are interlinked. Dealing with the contexts and specific settings of sustainability assessments, the importance of public opinion and public engagement in specific assessment contexts is problematized. The chapter also shows to what extent, and how, the participation of nonacademic actors in assessment processes can lead to better and more realistic assessment results, and ultimately enhance the transformative power of participatory sustainability assessments.

Chapter 5, lastly, highlights how to integrate transition dynamics into sustainability assessment by falling back on resilience thinking in order to overcome this problem. The authors propose the concept of resilient sustainability transitions (RST) and propose a set of theoretically derived measures to operationalize the concept in the sustainability assessment context.

1

Sustainability Assessment: Introduction and Framework

Pekka Halla and Claudia R. Binder

1.1 Introduction

The concept of sustainability has been steadily increasing in salience and urgency in general societal discourses, as well as in the strategies of various public- and private-sector actors. Despite the prominence of this concept, however, understanding the meaning and requirements of sustainability continues to be a formidable task. This is not only due to possible technical difficulties involved in measuring sustainability, but even more fundamentally because the concept itself has proven to be highly contestable and elusive to precise definition. In response, a myriad of approaches has emerged for facilitating the creation of sustainability-relevant knowledge, and for assisting decision-making by translating the abstract concept of sustainability into more concrete goals and strategies. These approaches draw from the insights, concepts, and tools of a wide spectrum of scientific disciplines. In this context, the concept of sustainability assessment (hereafter SA) has been receiving increasing scientific attention (see Figure 1.1).

However, literature on SA does not display a uniform understanding of its meaning and characteristics. Therefore, it is essential to begin by clarifying what SA is taken to mean in the context of this volume. Specifically, it is argued here that SA is best thought of as an umbrella term characterized by a set of aims and principles, and as such includes many possible methods and measurement tools that can be applied depending on the specific problems at hand. Despite this variety in the actual applications of SA, it is possible to detect a number of pertinent dimensions of SA, representing topics and questions that can be used in the design and analysis of SA processes.

The chapter proceeds as follows: Section 1.2 gives a brief introduction to the concept of sustainability and some of the debates surrounding it. Section 1.3 then engages with sustainability assessment, including its scientific background, definitions, and characteristics. Section 1.4 presents a framework capturing the dimensions of SA based on a review of the related topics, concepts, and questions. Finally, Section 1.5 concludes with condensed key messages drawn from the chapter.

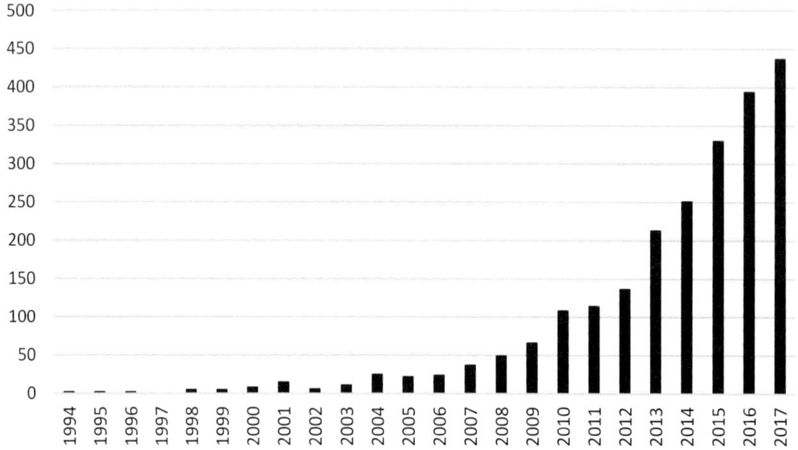

Figure 1.1 Articles per year found on Web of Science with the keyword "sustainability assessment". Source: own illustration

1.2 Sustainability

1.2.1 The Contemporary Challenge of Sustainability

Today, sustainability is an ubiquitous concept. At the same time, sustainability is not a new challenge for humanity. In fact, the concept can be traced back as far as 1713, when the German mining administrator Hanns Carl von Carlowitz used it in his handbook on forestry (Grober, 2007). Moreover, sustainability as considered more broadly in the sense of survival and reproduction has been a central preoccupation for humans throughout history, provoking human curiosity and fostering the evolution of new technologies and forms of social organization. Yet, despite the concept's deep historical roots, there are both material and philosophical particularities that render the contemporary sustainability challenge historically distinct.

Materially speaking, these particularities relate to the unprecedented scientific and technological advances of the last few centuries, which have been accompanied by explosive growth in human population and in the scale of human economic activity (Hashemian et al., 2017). As a consequence, the challenge of sustainability is no longer limited to local settings, but now exists at a truly global scale. Moreover, as Ulrich Beck has argued (1992), many of the existential risks facing humanity today are manufactured – that is, produced by humans themselves – and not stemming from external factors. Philosophically, the contemporary sustainability challenge exists in tension with the ideals of progress and growth, ideals distinct to the modernist worldview. This means that demands for sustainability today compete not only with the urgent need for global poverty reduction, but also with the widely ingrained idea of perpetual economic growth (Gibson et al., 2005; Norgaard, 1994).

Explicit awareness of the sustainability challenge in its contemporary form began to gain ground during the latter half of the twentieth century. During this period, an increasing number of critical voices challenged the modernist narrative of inexorable progress. These voices included such pioneers as Carson (1962) and Boulding (1966) who pointed to serious environmental and social problems emerging despite – or because of – the strong post-war economic development of the Western world. Meanwhile, the post-colonial movement (Fanon, 1965; Said, 1979) highlighted the issue of persisting cultural and economic inequalities between different regions of the world. Furthermore, in 1972, the existence of global biophysical limits was brought to wider public attention by the release of the Club of Rome's Limits to Growth report (Meadows et al., 1972).

In the political sphere, the year 1972 also saw the United Nations Conference on the Human Environment take place in Stockholm. It was the first global conference on the environment, thus paving the way for later multilateral treaties (Jabbour et al., 2012). The Stockholm conference was remarkable in that it forcefully revealed a rift between the needs of developing and developed countries, particularly concerning the issue of how to balance environmental protection against the urgent need for poverty reduction. Acknowledging the difficulty of such questions spurred the United Nations a decade later to set up an independent commission to investigate how to reconcile these competing demands. The output of the commission's work was Our Common Future (Brundtland, 1987), commonly known as the Brundtland Report, which defined sustainable development as "development that meets the needs of the present without compromising the ability of future generations to meet their own needs" (p. 43). Arguably, the main achievement of the report was the mainstreaming of sustainable development as a concept that recognizes the systemic interconnections between the needs of environmental protection and of development, making these two problems unsolvable in isolation.

The Brundtland Report has since been followed by a flurry of sustainability-related initiatives in both the public and private spheres. International landmarks include Agenda 21, adopted in 1992 at the United Nations Conference on Environment and Development in Rio; the Kyoto and Paris agreements dealing with the looming threat of climate change; and the United Nations Sustainable Development Goals adopted in 2015. However, while certainly promising, the prominence of the sustainability agenda has yet to be translated into measures that are effective in limiting human activities to sustainable levels. In fact, by many measures, human activities today are even further from sustainable levels than they were when sustainable development first found its way onto the public agenda (Millennium Ecosystem Assessment, 2005; Steffen et al., 2015).

It is notable that while the Brundtland Report and organizations like the UN mainly use the term "sustainable development," the subject matter of this volume is "sustainability" assessment. Indeed, there has been a longstanding definitional debate about the relationship between "sustainable development" and "sustainability" (Waas et al., 2011). For example, a distinction is often made between the former as a process and the latter as a state to be reached. However, differences in connotation between these terms are reduced by the insight that, in a dynamic world, sustainability is not a static state but involves continuous development. Therefore, the decision taken here is to follow the increasingly common practice of using the terms interchangeably (Gibson, 2016a; Waas et al., 2011).

1.2.2 Interpreting Sustainability

As the discussion in Section 1.2.1 showed, the contemporary sustainability challenge is generally understood as a challenge that contains important tensions between dynamic developmental demands and the simultaneous need to secure the integrity of the Earth's environmental systems for the future. However, this general understanding of sustainability also leaves many questions open at the more detailed and practical levels. Indeed, several approaches exist for further elaborating the concept of sustainability, each loaded with particular descriptive and normative views of the subject, and therefore leading to vastly different conceptualizations of what sustainability entails and how it is to be achieved (Redclift, 2005). For example, approaches departing from particular academic disciplines highlight different aspects of the concept in ways that reflect the tools, concepts, and emphases of each discipline. Patterson et al. (2017) distinguish between four such disciplinary interpretations of sustainability, as shown in Box 1.1.

Across the different conceptualizations of sustainability, an overall rough distinction can be made between approaches that conceptualize sustainability as consisting of distinct domains and those that reject such a separation in favor of a more strongly integrated perspective. The former type of sustainability is often expressed through the idea of the three pillars of sustainability (Figure 1.2a), which has been translated into the popular managerial principle of triple bottom-line accounting ("people, planet, and profit" – Slaper & Hall, 2011). This conceptualization tends toward "weak" forms of sustainability (Pearce & Turner, 1990), which allow for sacrifices to be made in one domain in order to achieve gains in another one. In practice, this often leads to the prioritization of economic development at the expense of other aspects of sustainability (Scerri & James, 2010).

In contrast, approaches based on an integrated and interconnected perspective tend to adopt ecocentric and "strong" forms of sustainability, whereby human activity occurs nested within the wider biophysical environment (Figure 1.2b). This perspective also challenges substitutability between different domains (e.g., compensating for environmental damage with economic gains) by attributing a unique inherent value to each domain. An

Box 1.1 **Disciplinary interpretations of sustainability (paraphrased from Patterson et al., 2017)**

(1) **Ecological interpretations**: emphasize the ideas of thresholds, the steady state, carrying capacity, interdependence, and the embeddedness of socioeconomic subsystem within the biophysical system
(2) **Economic interpretations**: emphasize the idea of social welfare and the external environmental costs associated with economic activity
(3) **Thermodynamic and ecological–economic interpretations**: situate ecological sustainability in the context of the entropic nature of economic–environmental interactions
(4) **Public policy and planning theory**: emphasize the social, institutional, economic, and environmental aspects of sustainability in an integrative framework

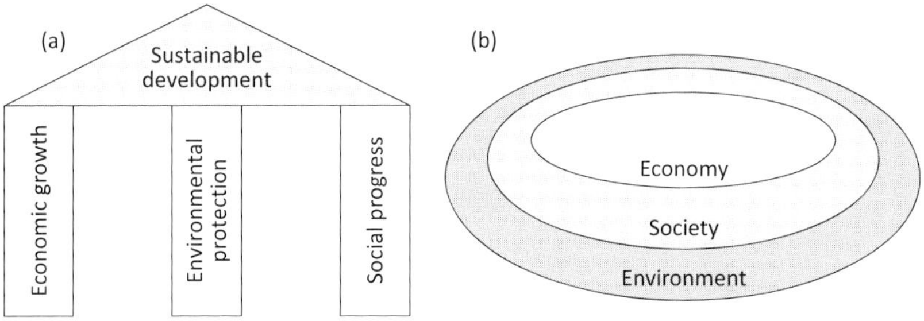

Figure 1.2 The three pillars model (a) and the concentric model (b) of sustainability. Source: own illustration

example of this type of approach is the "doughnut model" introduced by Raworth (2012). In this perspective, the doughnut represents a space of human activity that lies between, on the one hand, a ceiling set by planetary ecological boundaries (Rockström et al., 2009), and on the other hand, a foundation set by fundamental human and social needs. It thereby acknowledges the tension between environmental and developmental needs which lies at the heart of the contemporary sustainability challenge.

Our discussion illustrates a dilemma in defining sustainability. On the one hand, the comprehensiveness of the issue lends itself to generic, all-encompassing definitions (like the one from the Brundtland Report), which lack utility for practical applications. On the other hand, trying to pin down narrower, more workable definitions can easily lead to disagreements that demonstrate the difficulty of catering to everyone's vision of sustainability. There is, however, a possible middle ground, enabled by 30 years of research since the Brundtland Report, research that has produced progress and convergence in our understanding of the fundamental building blocks of sustainability (Lélé, 1991; Waas et al., 2014; White, 2013). Instead of trying to capture the essence of sustainability in precise prescriptions, these building blocks typically define sustainability in terms of abstract features that provide a basis for more pragmatic definitions to be made on a case-by-case basis. Common building blocks discussed in the literature relate both to normative principles (e.g., equity, inclusiveness, and precaution) underpinning sustainability, as well as to its typical characteristics, such as dynamism, systemic integratedness, complexity, and value-ladenness (Christen & Schmidt, 2012; Cilliers, 2008; Gibson et al., 2005; Gibson, 2016a; Waas et al., 2011).

Whether or not one ascribes to such general principles of sustainability, it is clear that when addressing specific sustainability challenges, there is a need to translate the concept of sustainability into instructions and criteria that are actionable and contextually appropriate, as each specific problem setting is bound to emphasize certain aspects and criteria of sustainability over others. For example, when addressing the sustainability of urban systems – the topic of this volume – the operationalization of sustainability is bound to reflect the specific characteristics of urban areas (see Chapter 11 (Meirelles et al., 2020)). Hence, there is a need to use tools that can operationalize sustainability and support decision-making toward it in specific contexts and problem situations. One such tool is

SA, which has the potential to serve the important purpose of providing tangible solutions for the multiple concrete sustainability challenges we are currently facing and will continue to face.

1.3 Sustainability Assessment

1.3.1 Background

When considering the scientific background of SA, two fields of science and practice in particular can be mentioned: sustainability science and the impact assessment tradition. To begin with the former, sustainability science has emerged as a distinct field over the past two decades (Kates et al., 2001) and has the goal of establishing a coherent and rigorous research program around the problem of sustainability. Kates (2011) has distilled the problematics of sustainability science into seven key questions, presented in Box 1.2.

The necessity for a dedicated field of sustainability science derives from the inherently integrated and value-laden character of sustainability, which poses a challenge both to science and to practice founded on traditional scientific disciplines. In contrast to these, transdisciplinarity is a built-in feature of sustainability science. Furthermore, sustainability science exists "in constructive tension between a descriptive-analytical and a transformational mode" (Wiek et al., 2012, p. 5). In other words, sustainability science ventures outside the traditional role of science as a purely objective and detached endeavor to one that more directly assumes responsibility for informing societal decision-making. Epistemologically, sustainability science shares much with what is known as post-normal science (Funtowicz & Ravetz, 1993; Osorio et al., 2009), which promotes knowledge creation as a cooperation not only between different scientific disciplines, but also between scientists and other social actors. SA, the principal theme of this volume, can be thought of

Box 1.2 **Key questions in sustainability science (Kates, 2011)**

(1) What shapes the long-term trends and transitions that provide the major directions for this century?
(2) What determines the adaptability, vulnerability, and resilience of human-environment systems?
(3) How can theory and models be formulated that better account for the variation in human–environment interactions?
(4) What are the principal trade-offs between human well-being and the natural environment?
(5) Can scientifically meaningful "limits" be defined that would provide effective warning for human–environment systems?
(6) How can society most effectively guide or manage human–environment systems toward a sustainability transition?
(7) How can the "sustainability" of alternative pathways of environment and development be evaluated?

as one approach in the toolbox of sustainability science, helping operationalize the concept of sustainability in concrete evaluations and practical decision-making situations, and thus also helping answer some of the important questions posed in Box 1.2.

As mentioned, in addition to being part of the field of sustainability science, SA is also associated with the tradition of impact assessment (IA). The International Association for Impact Assessment (IAIA) defines IA as "the process of identifying the future consequences of a current or proposed action" (International Association for Impact Assessment, 2012). The history of the IA tradition stretches back to the 1960s, when it emerged with an explicit focus on environmental concerns (Gibson et al., 2005; Glasson et al., 2013). Environmental impact assessment (EIA) was formally established in the United States in 1969 by the National Environmental Policy Act (NEPA), which made EIA a mandatory part of decision-making by federal agencies. NEPA has since then acted as a blueprint for both national and international legal instruments that are in use today across most of the world (Morgan, 2012). The IA field has spawned numerous more specific types of impact assessment (Morrison-Saunders et al., 2014) which are used by both public and private actors, and which cover topics from health to tourism.

The development of new forms of assessment has not, however, been limited to broadening the range of topics to which they are applied. Gibson et al. (2005) identify several major trends that have strongly shaped and changed EIA since its inception. These include the adoption of perspectives that are more comprehensive (considering both socioeconomic as well as environmental effects), integrative (considering systemic interconnections), and pluralistic (accepting different kinds of knowledge and open to participation). Assessments are also applied more widely and earlier in planning processes, as well as monitored more closely. Regarding their aims, assessments have become simultaneously more ambitious (in terms of their goals) and humbler (in terms of claims for the certainty of their results). Furthermore, impact assessment has been increasingly enshrined in formal legal structures.

In the course of these developments, the original EIA was first distinguished from a newer form of impact assessment called strategic environmental assessment (SEA). This separation has also been coded into a number of legal instruments, such as the European Union's SEA Directive. The two approaches are distinguished by the fact that the EIA is associated with the assessment of particular projects while SEA refers to the assessment of longer-term plans, programs, and policies (Bond et al., 2015). The latter is thereby ideally undertaken at an earlier stage and at higher, more strategic levels of decision-making. After the distinction between EIA and SEA, a second major development in the IA tradition came through the introduction of the concept of sustainability, leading to the concept of sustainability assessment (SA). In the genealogy of the IA tradition, SA thus represents the third generation, following EIA and SEA (Bond et al., 2012).

As Pope et al. (2017) put it, "the defining feature of sustainability assessment compared with other forms of impact assessment is that some attempt is made to engage with the concept of sustainability in all its complexity" (p. 206). Consequently, it should be considered as a distinct concept with ontological, epistemological, and methodological differences from other forms of integrated or impact assessment (Sala et al., 2015). In principle, then, to realize this distinction and to fully appreciate the complexities involved in sustainability, SA should explicitly incorporate insights and approaches developed in the field of sustainability science (Audouin et al., 2015).

1.3.2 Definitions and Characteristics

As we have discussed, the distinct nature of SA is derived from its position at the confluence of sustainability science and the impact assessment tradition. Accordingly, textbooks define SA in ways that reflect the characteristics of sustainability, especially with regard to the quest for sustainability as an open and deliberative process (Bond et al., 2012; Gibson 2016a). Box 1.3 presents three examples of definitions from recent SA literature. Collectively, these definitions describe SA essentially as a process that operationalizes sustainability and integrates it into decision-making processes. This open definition means that SA can, in principle, take a wide variety of possible forms and cover many possible decision-making situations, expanding SA well beyond the more limited original domain of IA. Furthermore, due to the breadth of scope covered by SA, it is increasingly considered in the literature (e.g., Ness et al., 2007) to be an umbrella term with a toolkit that contains a wide variety of methods and processes, including, but not limited to, those developed within the IA tradition.

To understand in more detail the framework that SA establishes in its function as an umbrella term, it is necessary to identify its distinguishing characteristics from the related literature. In fact, as illustrated in Figure 1.1, academic interest in SA has been rapidly increasing in recent years, and by now the multitude of publications presents somewhat of a management problem. In response, a number of articles have sought a meta-perspective on the existing literature in order to synthesize general frameworks or sets of characteristics for SA (Gibson et al., 2005; Bond et al., 2012; Pintér et al., 2012; Waas et al., 2014; Sala et al., 2015; Pope et al., 2017). These frameworks can be either prescriptive (what SA should be) or descriptive (what SA currently is).

Box 1.3 **Definitions of sustainability assessment**

Bond et al. (2015, p. 3): "Sustainability assessment can be simply defined as any process that directs decision-making towards sustainability."

Gibson (2016b, p. 16): "Sustainability assessment is essentially an organized approach to deliberation and decision making ... [which] overlaps with, and plays a role in, governance for sustainability."

Waas et al. (2014, p. 5516): "Sustainability assessment is any process that aims to:

- Contribute to a better understanding of the meaning of sustainability and its contextual interpretation (interpretation challenge);
- Integrate sustainability issues into decision-making by identifying and assessing (past and/or future) sustainability impacts (information-structuring challenge);
- Foster sustainability objectives (influence challenge)."

A number of characteristics of SA can be established from the work of the above authors. As a starting point, similar to the concept of sustainability itself, prescriptive literature (e.g., Pintér et al., 2012; see Box 1.4) on SA operates largely at the level of abstract principles, leaving the concrete ends and means of each SA application to be defined contextually and on a case-by-case basis. Consequently, SA processes vary considerably in practice depending on the legal and governance structures in place, and on local interpretations of sustainability (Bond et al., 2012). When defining goals, SA aims for a positive contribution toward sustainability in decision-making, rather than for a mere limitation of negative impacts (Bond et al., 2012). To address the challenge of sustainability in an adequate manner, a standard in SA literature is to underline the need for a comprehensive, system-based approach to the definition of the objects and questions being assessed (Wiek & Binder, 2005). Furthermore, in the literature, the procedural requirements of SA receive extensive attention. These requirements include transparency and inclusion in decision-making, openness to transdisciplinarity and pluralism, as well as an emphasis on social learning and political impact (Bond et al., 2012). Finally, like sustainability science in general, SA balances an objective scientific stance with a more goal-driven attitude, the goal being to support and encourage decision-making toward sustainability.

Box 1.4 **Bellagio STAMP principles to guide SA processes, paraphrased from Pintér et al. (2012)**

(1) **Guiding vision:** SA criteria should be based on the principles of sustainability.
(2) **Essential considerations:** The system as a whole should be taken into account, as well as its internal interactions; this includes issues of governance, dynamics, drivers, risks and uncertainties, and cross-boundary effects.
(3) **Adequate scope:** SA should consider both short- and long-term effects of current policy decisions and human activities, and capture both their local and global effects.
(4) **Framework and indicators:** SA should have a conceptual framework as a basis for identifying core indicators and models; use the most recent data and standardized measurement methods wherever possible; use targets and benchmarks where possible.
(5) **Transparency:** In SA, transparency and accessibility of results are crucial; choices, assumptions, and uncertainties have to be clearly reported; sources of funding and potential conflicts of interest have to be disclosed.
(6) **Effective communications:** SA should use clear language to ensure effective communication and to attract the broadest possible audience; information should be presented in a fair and objective way.
(7) **Continuity and capacity:** SA requires a continuous monitoring phase with repeated measurement and responsiveness; develop and maintain adequate capacity for continuous learning and improvement.
(8) **Broad participation:** SA should strengthen legitimacy and relevance, engaging early on with users of the assessment, reflecting the views of the public while providing active leadership.

Within the framework established by these (ideal) definitions and characteristics, SA covers a broad collection of possible assessment tools. The choice to deploy a particular tool depends on the specificities of the problem setting of each SA. The tools available for SA can be categorized according to different typologies (e.g., Ness et al., 2007; Gasparatos & Scolobig, 2012; Singh et al., 2012). For example, Ness et al. (2007) demarcate three categories of SA tools – namely (i) indicators/indices; (ii) product-related assessment tools; (iii) integrated assessment tools – which are also distinguished by their temporal focus (ex ante vs. ex post). Interestingly for the subject matter of this volume, there exists an increasingly rich reservoir of SA literature particularly aimed at urban contexts (James, 2014; Mori & Christodoulou, 2012; Phillis et al., 2017; Shen et al., 2011; Turcu, 2013; Wiek & Binder, 2005). Furthermore, different governmental and transgovernmental actors, such as the United Nations (UN, 2017) and the European Union (Science for Environment Policy, 2018), have published their own preferred approaches for the assessment of urban sustainability.

However, as indicated by Box 1.3, instead of being defined by any specific tool, SA should be considered first as a forum for engaging with the value-laden and complex topic of sustainability. The technical toolkit of SA adds to its scientific rigor, but the role of the tools is to support the qualitative and deliberative aspects of the process, not the other way around (Bond et al., 2012; Scerri & James, 2010). As Jasanoff states, "environmental knowledge achieves robustness through continual interaction, or conversation, between fact-finding and meaning-making" (2010, p. 248). The potential of SA lies precisely in the facilitation of such a connection between expert-defined sustainability facts and the contextual everyday reality of people. The connection is essential for ensuring the effectiveness and social legitimacy of sustainability initiatives in practice.

Based on these ideas, the following definition of SA is proposed:

Sustainability assessment is a purposeful process that aims to facilitate engagement with the concept of sustainability and to advance sustainability-based objectives in decision-making. The process itself is framed by selected goals and principles of sustainability, and requires a toolkit of methods at its disposal for their contextually appropriate interpretation, operationalization, and evaluation.

1.3.3 Limitations in Theory and Practice

While there may be increasing convergence and clarity in the literature regarding the aims and characteristics of SA, several limitations persist both in theory and in practice. First, existing methodologies in use are often lacking in their appreciation of the systemic complexities involved in sustainability (Wiek & Binder, 2005; Grace & Pope, 2015). Attempts to consider different aspects of sustainability most commonly use indicators divided into a triple bottom-line framework (Pope et al., 2017), which, however, represents a simplistic understanding of sustainability that neglects feedbacks and interconnections between these areas of sustainability. It also masks the need to base the assessment on a systematic, as well as systemic, conceptualization of the assessment situation. These shortcomings weaken the quality of the sustainability knowledge produced by SA. Second, the influence of the IA tradition in SA can be seen in an overemphasis on environmental indicators at the expense of a more balanced socioecological conceptualization of sustainability (Sala et al., 2015; Sharifi & Murayama, 2013). This deficiency is arguably particularly pertinent for urban SA, due to the high social density and complexity present in cities. Third, SA continues to be often framed as a matter of technical and scientific management, understating its sociopolitical and ethical aspects. This undermines the effectiveness of SA in informing policy-making and in promoting solutions with local social legitimacy and relevance (Turcu, 2013; Waas et al., 2014). Fourth, important procedural limitations remain. In particular, current SA practice is limited in its systematic integration with governance processes, as well as in processes for knowledge sharing and participation. This leads to a lack of influence, benchmarking, and social learning (Shen et al., 2011; Bond et al., 2012).

To some extent, these shortcomings derive simply from understandable practical difficulties in the application of SA. Most notably, pursuing the full extent of what in theory is required of SA would demand significant investments of time and resources (Bond et al., 2012). This entails a delicate balance between parsimony and sufficiency (Wiek & Binder, 2005). That is, SA in practice needs to operationalize the complex topic of sustainability into workable packages that are simple enough to be dealt with within given time and budget constraints, but which still capture the systemic complexity of sustainability to a sufficient degree. Moreover, the transdisciplinarity required by SA can mean that it does not easily fit into decision-making processes shaped by entrenched power relationships and institutional divisions of responsibility (Audouin & de Wet, 2012; Waas et al., 2014). Despite being understandable to an extent from a practical point of view, the existing limitations in SA practice carry a risk of resulting in decisions that do not lead to improvements in long-term sustainability.

1.4 Framework for Dimensions of Sustainability Assessment

As presented in the previous discussion, SA is an umbrella term covering many forms of assessment. Moreover, in the literature, it is defined by a number of aims, characteristics, and principles that set a more or less loose framework within which concrete applications are to operate. While there is good reason to keep the definitions of SA at such an open and abstract level (i.e., being able to tailor SA to the needs of each specific context), as recipes for the design and analysis of SA processes they may be inadequate and confusing. To offer one possible way forward, this section purports to present a framework for the relevant dimensions of SA in a comprehensive manner. The framework is offered as a pragmatic heuristic tool for organizing and spelling out clearly the topics, concepts, and questions related to SA. As such, it also serves as a basis for placing the contributions of the different authors in this volume into the bigger picture of SA.

The framework is developed based on a review of recent SA literature, especially articles that have identified constitutive elements of SA from a meta-level perspective (Bond et al., 2012; Gibson et al., 2005; Gibson, 2016a; Pintér et al., 2012; Pope et al., 2017; Sala et al., 2015; Waas et al., 2014; Wiek & Binder, 2005). The structure of the framework is a synthesis of this meta-level literature, developed with the explicit goal of making a distinction between the dimensions of the SA process itself and the broader contextual factors that influence the design of individual applications of SA.

The distinction between the context of sustainability assessment and the assessment process itself is illustrated in Figure 1.3. This distinction makes explicit that applications of SA always occur in the context of wider sociopolitical settings and considerations, with which they necessarily have a two-way relationship. As the diagram indicates, in practical terms the entry point to SA most often is a concrete problem situation that requires assessment, such as a new technology or a government policy. This problem situation is then interpreted within the contextual dimensions, and the design of an SA process

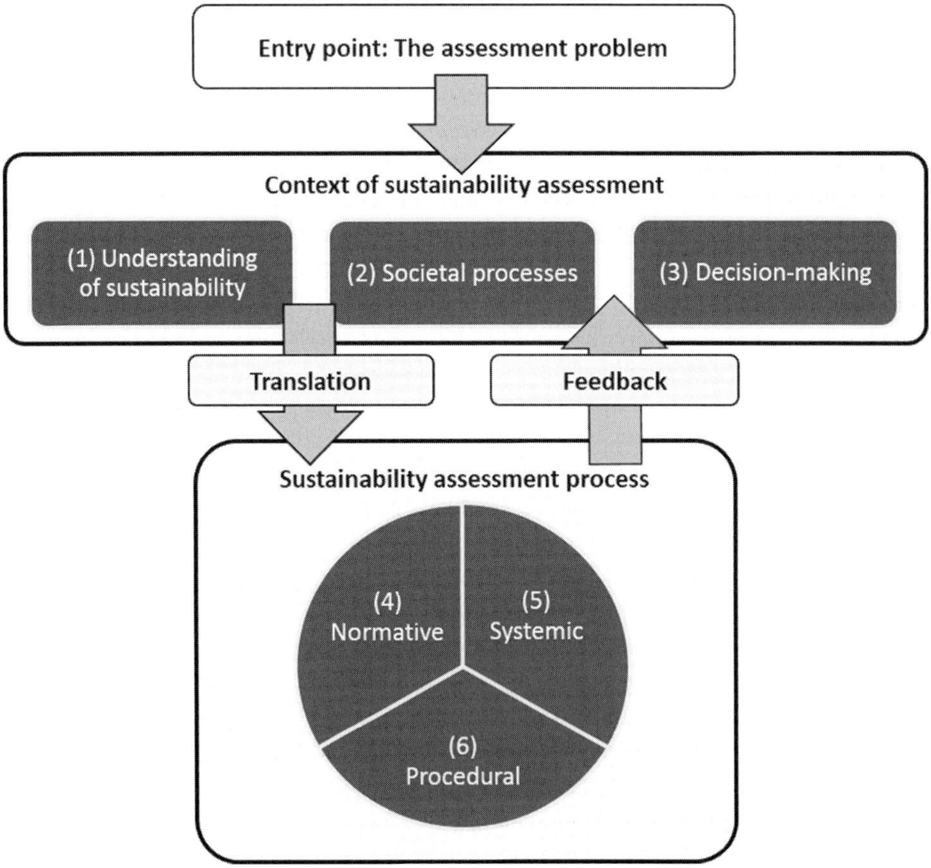

Figure 1.3 A diagram of sustainability assessment. Source: own illustration

represents a translation of the contextually framed problem into operational terms. In addition, any SA process should ideally feed back into societal processes of governance and learning, and influence decision-making as well as broader conceptions of sustainability.

Table 1.1 defines the six dimensions of the framework in more detail. Each dimension is further divided into three topics, making it possible to scrutinize and reflect on the different aspects of sustainability assessment. Examples for each topic of the framework are shown in Table A in the appendix of this chapter. The three dimensions that embed SA into wider sociopolitical contexts are (i) understanding of sustainability, (ii) societal processes, and (iii) decision-making (Table 1.1a). The first dimension, understanding of sustainability, concerns the interpretation of the complex concept of sustainability. As the three topics within this dimension demonstrate, three different layers can be detected in ideas of sustainability. Being aware of which layer is being addressed can help avoid misunderstandings when discussing questions around sustainability. The most abstract layer (1.1) deals with general discourses of sustainability. The next layer (1.2) describes the guiding principles that are considered essential when formulating sustainability goals and procedures. The third layer (1.3) then describes conceptual end-goals like "resilience" (for elaboration on this concept, see Chapter 5 (Schilling et al., 2020)). The second contextual dimension describes the coupling of SA to societal processes and institutions of governance, learning, and innovation (2.2–2.3). This dimension also contains the definition of the purposes of SA and the evaluation of its effectiveness (2.1). The topics of this dimension underline that any design of SA should include, as an integral component, considerations of its impact on potential stakeholders and their activities. The third contextual dimension concerns the what, who, and how of decision-making. This dimension highlights the need to clearly define the decision-making situation, which includes the subject and boundaries of the assessment (3.1; see Wiek & Binder, 2005), responsible parties (3.2), and decision-making rules (3.3). This dimension is of particular relevance to practitioners, whose starting point to SA is often a particular problem to be assessed (see Figure 1.3), and for whom the topic of defining and delimiting the subject of the assessment is among the first issues to be addressed. As such, this dimension can be considered as a passageway from the practical problem situations to the consideration of the different dimensions and topics of SA listed in Table 1.1.

Table 1.1b follows the idea from Wiek and Binder (2005) and Binder et al. (2010) of dividing the assessment process into normative, systemic, and procedural dimensions, and proceeds by itemizing the relevant topics within each of the three dimensions. The normative dimension includes translating the discourses and conceptualizations of sustainability found in the respective contextual dimension (1.1–1.3) into concrete goals (4.1) that are meaningful for the assessment process. For these concrete goals, it is also necessary refer to the "what" of the assessment (3.1). More precisely, different actors and actor groups will have to find consensus on a common goal and a common definition of sustainability. For analyzing the trade-offs and synergies (4.2), as well as for the final formulation of normative evaluations of the results (4.3), it is necessary to refer to the underlying rules for

Table 1.1 a *The contextual dimensions of sustainability assessment*

Dimension	Topic	Description
(1) Understanding of sustainability	(1.1) Underlying discourses	*The general, often implicit ideas underlying sustainability efforts*
	(1.2) Principles and values	*The characteristics and guiding principles pertaining to sustainability*
	(1.3) Conceptual goals	*The concepts and frameworks used to express sustainability in terms of goals and criteria*
(2) Societal processes	(2.1) Purposes and effectiveness	*The aims of SA and the criteria by which its impact can be evaluated*
	(2.2) Political and learning processes	*The integration of SA processes into wider processes and institutions of policy-making and societal learning*
	(2.3) Experiments and innovation	*The integration of SA into processes of experimentation and innovation*
(3) Decision-making	(3.1) Subject of assessment	*The definition of the subject and scope of the sustainability assessment process*
	(3.2) Stakeholders and responsibilities	*Identifying the party responsible for undertaking the assessment and performing stakeholder analysis*
	(3.3) Rules for evaluation and decision-making	*The question to be answered, the possible approaches for evaluation, and the rules of participation*

evaluation and decision-making (3.3). The systemic dimension, in turn, concerns the conceptualization of the subject of the assessment and its systemic context (5.1), as well as the selection of appropriate measurement tools and indicators (5.2). Here again choices made within the contextual dimensions play an essential role (see Chapter 8 (Binder et al., 2020a)), especially when it comes to the definition of the subject and boundaries of the assessment (3.1) and the underlying framing of sustainability (1.1–1.3). Dealing with measurement tools and indicators also involves considering their quality criteria as well as the technical management of the obtained results (5.3), which connects back to the decision-making rules agreed upon within the contextual dimensions (3.3).

Table 1.1 b *The dimensions of the sustainability assessment process*

Dimension	Topic	Description	Input
(4) Normative	(4.1) Concrete goals	*Translating sustainability discourses, principles, and concepts into concrete, contextually relevant goals*	1.1–1.3; 3.1
	(4.2) Trade-offs and synergies	*Identifying conflicts among goals, applying chosen rules for trade-offs, and/or adjusting the goals*	3.3
	(4.3) Assessment of results	*Making normative judgments about the results*	3.3
(5) Systemic	(5.1) Conceptualization	*The conceptualization of the subject and its systemic context*	1.1–1.3; 3.1
	(5.2) Choice of tools and/or indicators	*The expression of the system and its sustainability through the use of specific tools and tool frameworks*	1.1–1.3; 3.1; 3.3; 5.1
	(5.3) Technical management of tools/indicators	*The technical treatment of results and quality criteria for the evaluation of SA tools and indicators*	3.3; 5.1
(6) Procedural	(6.1) Steps of the process	*Planning the necessary steps of the assessment process and their succession*	2.1–2.3; 3.1
	(6.2) Stakeholder participation	*Engaging with stakeholders and constructing the methods of their involvement*	1.2; 2.1–2.3; 3.2–3.3
	(6.3) Feedback and learning	*Planning the dissemination and discussion of the results to inform decision-makers and facilitate social learning*	2.1–2.3; 3.2; 4.3

Finally, the procedural dimension covers the step-by-step design of the assessment process (6.1), including any stakeholder participation (6.2) and knowledge sharing (6.3). This dimension is affected by various considerations within the contextual dimensions. The design of the necessary steps of the assessment process (6.1) needs to take into account the purpose (2.1) and scope (3.1) of the exercise, as well as its intended connection to decision-making processes (2.2–2.3). Here, it is important to be clear what the purpose of each step is, who needs to be involved, and how the process can be designed to be as effective as possible (see Webb et al., 2018). A central aspect of the procedural dimension concerns the concrete measures for engagement with stakeholders (6.2). This is supported by considerations with regard to the purpose of the process (2.1–2.3), as well as the underlying stakeholder analysis (3.2). Finally, we consider that feedback and learning processes (6.3) have to be explicitly incorporated in the procedural dimension. The question to be tackled here refers to how and when the results of the assessment can be integrated into the relevant decision-making and societal learning processes (2.2–2.3, 3.2).

As is evident, there are significant interconnections and overlaps between the dimensions of the framework. This implies that design choices made regarding one dimension influence the decisions to be made with regard to other dimensions. We propose that when designing an SA process, the questions related to the contextual dimensions of SA should be addressed as explicitly as possible early in, or even before, the SA process. This helps in ensuring the consistency and comprehensiveness of the SA process design, and in preventing irreconcilable differences from arising later during the execution of the assessment process. It also makes sure that stakeholders are identified early enough that they can adequately participate in the design of the dimensions of the assessment process. This will, on the one hand, allow for the inclusion of different perspectives on the problem, and on the other hand, support the implementation of the results in practice later on, as acceptance of the results and any decisions derived from them is likely to be higher if the relevant stakeholders were involved in the process of obtaining the results (see Chapter 4 (Fritz & Meinherz, 2020)).

The framework presented identifies in a comprehensive manner the dimensions relevant for SA, and can thus act as a checklist of the different topics and choices that a thorough design of SA needs to consider. As such, it can serve as an excellent foundation for a better systematization of SA process designs, as well as for the consolidation of relevant tools. In addition, making explicit the dimensions of SA offers a basis for greater comparability of SA process designs, and, ultimately, for a deeper understanding of the meaning and significance of the results obtained from different assessments. A problem, however, that one might encounter today is that tools and processes that facilitate connections between the contextual dimensions and the assessment process itself are undeveloped and scarce. Finally, it should be noted that since the framework presented here is primarily descriptive, it can be combined with other, explicitly prescriptive frameworks (see Box 1.4; Section 1.3.2). The latter provide principles for guiding the many interpretations and choices that need to be made with regard to the dimensions identified in Table 1.1 when designing and conducting an SA process.

1.5 Summary

Sustainability is a concept wrapped in complex socio–economic–ecological interconnections, uncertainties, and values. While scientific work on the concept has distilled a number of possible framings and characteristics that form the basic building blocks of sustainability, it simultaneously always entails elements defined by contextual interpretations, depending on one's values, the specific problem at hand, and the cognitive and material tools available (for further discussion of this topic, see Chapter 3 (Meinherz et al., 2020)).

Sustainability assessment is a distinct form of assessment, whose defining characteristic is the attempt to engage with sustainability in all its complexity. Accordingly, SA is an integrated process which reflects selected principles of sustainability, and which can draw from a toolkit of methods for their contextually appropriate interpretation, operationalization, and evaluation. Rather than a mere technical (measurement) exercise, SA should be considered as a vehicle for deliberation that achieves its goals best through an integrated approach that connects the SA process with wider sociopolitical processes and visions of sustainability. Therefore, as in the framework set out in Table 1.1, it is useful to explicitly consider contextual aspects of SA in addition to the different dimensions of the assessment process itself.

Incorporating sustainability in all its complexity into assessment is not a trivial matter, and it entails balancing a number of dichotomies (e.g., contextual relevance vs. comparability; scientific objectivity vs. normative goals; qualitative vs. quantitative indicators; expert vs. user-created knowledge) and dealing with practical challenges (e.g., sufficient scope within given resources; integration of pluralism). At the level of practical applications, SA is not yet fully developed to meet all the important requirements identified in theoretical literature. This situation can partly be attributed to SA's relatively recent emergence as an independent concept. Nevertheless, the increasing urgency of the sustainability problem requires that workable solutions be found soon to the many challenges facing SA practice. Only then can SA fully realize its potential as a bridge connecting scientific facts, ethics, social meanings, and political decision-making.

Appendix

Table A *The dimensions of the sustainability assessment process*

Dimension	Topic	Examples
(1) Understanding of sustainability	(1.1) Underlying discourses	Discourses in SA: (i) pragmatic integration of development and environment; (ii) the idea of limitations on human activities; (iii) process of directed change (Hugé et al., 2013)
	(1.2) Principles and values	Principles of sustainability, according to Waas et al. (2014): (i) equity; (ii) dynamics; (iii) integration; (iv) normativity
	(1.3) Conceptual goals	Possible conceptual goal frameworks: (i) optimization of the three pillars of sustainability; (ii) socioecological system

Table A (*cont.*)

Dimension	Topic	Examples
		integrity, resilience, and adaptive capacity (Gibson, 2016a; Pope et al., 2017)
(2) Societal processes	(2.1) Purposes and effectiveness	The aim of SA is to answer the sustainability challenges of: (i) information structuring; (ii) interpretation; (iii) influence (Waas et al., 2014). Criteria for evaluation of SA: (i) procedural effectiveness; (ii) substantive effectiveness; (iii) transactive effectiveness; (iv) normative effectiveness; (v) pluralism; (vi) knowledge and learning (Bond et al., 2012)
	(2.2) Political and learning processes	SA can induce learning at different levels (individual, organizational, social, and policy learning) through public engagement and follow-up mechanisms embedded in the SA process (Bond et al., 2012)
	(2.3) Experiments and innovation	Types of experiments: (i) niche experiment; (ii) bounded socio-technical experiment; (iii) grassroots experiment; (iv) transition experiment; (v) sustainability experiment (Sengers et al., 2016)
(3) Decision-making	(3.1) Subject of assessment	Possible subjects of assessment: (i) technologies, products, projects and processes; (ii) strategic policies, plans, and programs; (iii) persistent/wicked problems; (iv) entire systems (a city, an ecosystem, etc.); (v) national/global goals and limits (Gibson, 2016b; Pope et al., 2017)
	(3.2) Stakeholders and responsibilities	Possible responsible parties: (i) regulators; (ii) proponents; (iii) third parties (Pope et al., 2017). Stakeholder analysis contains three steps (identifying and categorizing stakeholders, and investigating their relationships), with Reed et al. (2009) discussing each step
	(3.3) Rules for evaluation and decision-making	Decision questions may involve thresholds (Is this good enough?), choices (Best alternative?) or absolutes (Does this make a contribution to sustainability?) (Pope et al., 2017); Stagl (2012) discusses different techniques of evaluation (e.g., social multi-criteria evaluation, etc.) and Gibson et al. (2005) propose rules for trade-offs

Table B *The dimensions of the sustainability assessment process*

Dimension	Topic	Examples	Input
(4) Normative	(4.1) Concrete goals	Moving from generic criteria to specific goals (or goal ranges) is discussed by Wiek and Binder (2005) and Gibson (2016b)	1.1–1.3; 3.1
	(4.2) Trade-offs and synergies	Applying the chosen rules for trade-offs (Gibson et al., 2005); Conflicting goals can also be harmonized by prioritization, adjustment of targets, or adaptation of the system model (Wiek and Binder, 2005)	3.3
	(4.3) Assessment of results	Here, the chosen evaluation methods and decision-making rules are applied to produce normative statements of the results vis-à-vis the set goals (including trade-offs)	3.3
(5) Systemic	(5.1) Conceptualization	General approaches for conceptualization include disaggregated triple bottom line, aggregated, and systems-perspective frameworks (Pope et al., 2017)	1.1–1.3; 3.1
	(5.2) Choice of tools and/or indicators	Ness et al. (2007) categorize SA tools into indicators/indices, product-related tools, integrated tools, and monetary valuation tools; also, important elements of SA tools include integration of nature and society, and the inclusion of spatial and temporal aspects	1.1–1.3; 3.1; 3.3; 5.1
	(5.3) Technical management of tools/indicators	Quality criteria for indicators (Waas et al., 2014): robustness, democracy, longevity, relevance; Singh et al. (2012) discuss the weighting, normalization, aggregation, and uncertainty management of the chosen tools.	3.3; 5.1
(6) Procedural	(6.1) Steps of the process	Generic steps (Waas et al., 2014): (i) establish the system's socioenvironmental context; (ii) set objectives and strategies; (iii) select indicators; (iv) application and follow-up	2.1–2.3; 3.1
	(6.2) Stakeholder participation	Citizen involvement in three main stages (Sharifi & Murayama, 2013): (i) defining targets, core criteria, and indicators; (ii) weighing different criteria; (iii) providing feedback that helps planners update the system	1.2; 2.1–2.3; 3.2–3.3

Table B (*cont.*)

Dimension	Topic	Examples	Input
	(6.3) Feedback and learning	Ensuring opportunities for learning, following Thabrew et al. (2009): (i) stakeholder interaction at all stages; (ii) promote consensus-building; (iii) transparent access to information allowing the examination of the assumptions and projected outcomes of decisions; (iv) communication of results and impacts to the stakeholders in a clear way	2.1–2.3; 3.2; 4.3

References

Audouin, M., & de Wet, B. (2012). Sustainability thinking in environmental assessment. *Impact Assessment and Project Appraisal*, 30(4), 264–274. https://doi.org/10.1080/14615517.2012.742695.

Audouin, M., Burns, M., Weaver, A., et al. (2015). An introduction to sustainability science and its links to sustainability assessment. In A. Morrison-Saunders, J. Pope, & A. Bond (eds.), *Handbook of Sustainability Assessment*. Cheltenham, UK: Edward Elgar Publishing, pp. 321–348.

Beck, U. (1992). *Risk Society: Towards a New Modernity*. London: Sage Publications.

Binder, C. R., Feola, G., & Steinberger, J. K. (2010). Considering the normative systemic and procedural dimensions in indicator-based sustainability assessments in agriculture. *Environmental Impact Assessment Review*, 30(2), 71–81. https://doi.org/10.1016/j.eiar.2009.06.002.

Binder, C.R, Hutter, M., Pang, M., & Webb, R. (2020). System science and sustainability assessment. In C. R. Binder, E. Massaro, & R. Wyss (eds.), *Sustainability Assessment in Urban Systems*. Cambridge University Press, pp. 30–64.

Bond, A., Morrison-Saunders, A., & Pope, J. (2012). Sustainability assessment: The state of the art. *Impact Assessment and Project Appraisal*, 30(1), 53–62.

Bond, A., Pope, J., & Morrison-Saunders, A. (2015). Introducing the roots, evolution and effectiveness of sustainability assessment. In A. Morrison-Saunders, J. Pope, & A. Bond (eds.), *Handbook of Sustainability Assessment*. Cheltenham, UK: Edward Elgar Publishing, pp. 3–19.

Boulding, K. E. (1966). The economics of the coming spaceship earth. In H. Jarrett (ed.), *Environmental Quality in a Growing Economy*. Baltimore, MD: Johns Hopkins University Press, pp. 3–14.

Brundtland, G. H. (1987). *Our Common Future: Brundtland Report*. Oxford: Oxford University Press.

Carson, R. (1962). *Silent Spring*. Boston: Houghton Mifflin.

Christen, M., & Schmidt, S. (2012). A formal framework for conceptions of sustainability: A theoretical contribution to the discourse in sustainable development. *Sustainable Development*, 20(6), 400–410. https://doi.org/10.1002/sd.518.

Cilliers, P. (2008). Complexity theory as a general framework for sustainability science. In M. Burns & A. Weaver (eds.), *Exploring Sustainability Science: A Southern African Perspective*. Stellenbosch, South Africa: African Sun Media, pp. 9–26.

Fanon, F. (1965). *The Wretched of the Earth*. New York: Grove Press.

Fritz, L., & Meinherz, F. (2020). The politics of participatory sustainability assessment: an analysis of power. In C. R. Binder, E. Massaro, & R. Wyss (eds.), *Sustainability Assessment in Urban Systems*. Cambridge University Press, pp. 87–122.

Funtowicz, S. O., & Ravetz, J. R. (1993). For the post-normal age. *Futures*, 25(7), 739–755.

Gasparatos, A., & Scolobig, A. (2012). Choosing the most appropriate sustainability assessment tool. *Ecological Economics*, 80, 1–7. https://doi.org/10.1016/j.ecolecon.2012.05.005.

Gibson, R. B. (2016a). Foundations: Sustainability and the requirements for getting there. In R. B. Gibson (ed.), *Sustainability Assessment: Applications and Opportunities*. New York: Routledge, pp. 1–15.

Gibson, R. B. (2016b). Applications: From generic criteria to assessments in particular places and cases. In R. B. Gibson (ed.), *Sustainability Assessment: Applications and Opportunities*. New York: Routledge, pp. 16–43.

Gibson, R. B., Hassan, S., Holtz, S., Tansey, J., & Whitelaw, G. (2005). *Sustainability Assessment: Criteria and Processes*. London: Earthscan.

Glasson, J., Therivel, R., & Chadwick, A. (2013). *Introduction to Environmental Impact Assessment*. London: Routledge.

Grace, W., & Pope, J. (2015). A systems approach to sustainability assessment. In A. Morrison-Saunders, J. Pope, & A. Bond (eds.), *Handbook of Sustainability Assessment*. Cheltenham, UK: Edward Elgar Publishing, pp. 285–320.

Grober, U. (2007). Deep roots: A conceptual history of 'sustainable development' (Nachhaltigkeit) (Discussion Papers / Wissenschaftszentrum Berlin für Sozialforschung, 2007-002). Berlin: Wissenschaftszentrum Berlin für Sozialforschung gGmbH.

Hashemian, B., Massaro, E., Bojic, I., Arias, J. M., Sobolevsky, S., & Ratti, C. (2017). Socioeconomic characterization of regions through the lens of individual financial transactions. *PloS one*, 12(11), e0187031.

Hugé, J., Waas, T., Dahdouh-Guebas, F., Koedam, N., & Block, T. (2013). A discourse-analytical perspective on sustainability assessment: Interpreting sustainable development in practice. *Sustainability Science*, 8(2), 187–198.

International Association for Impact Assessment (2012). *Impact Assessment*. www.iaia.org/news-details.php?ID=30 (accessed 2.5.18).

Jabbour, J., Keita-Ouane, F., Hunsberger, C., et al. (2012). Internationally agreed environmental goals: A critical evaluation of progress. *Environmental Development*, 3, 5–24. https://doi.org/10.1016/j.envdev.2012.05.002.

James, P. (2014). *Urban Sustainability in Theory and Practice: Circles of Sustainability*. London: Routledge.

Jasanoff, S. (2010). A new climate for society. *Theory, Culture & Society*, 27(2–3), 233–253. https://doi.org/10.1177/0263276409361497.

Kates, R. W. (2011). What kind of a science is sustainability science? *Proceedings of the National Academy of Sciences*, 108(49), 19449–19450. https://doi.org/10.1073/pnas.1116097108.

Kates, R. W., Clark, W. C., Corell, R., et al. (2001). Sustainability science. *Science*, 292(5517), 641–642. https://doi.org/10.1126/science.1059386.

Lélé, S. M. (1991). Sustainable development: A critical review. *World Development*, 19(6), 607–621. https://doi.org/10.1016/0305-750X(91)90197-P.

Meadows D. H., Meadows D. L., Randers J., & Behrens W. (1972). *The Limits to Growth*. London: Earth Island.

Meinherz, F., Fritz, L., & Schneider, F. (2020). How Values Play into Sustainability Assessments: Challenges and a Possible Way Forward. In C. R. Binder, E. Massaro, & R. Wyss (eds.), *Sustainability Assessment in Urban Systems*. Cambridge University Press, pp. 65–86.

Meirelles, J., Pagani, A., Athanassiadis, A., & Binder, C.R. (2020). Sustainability issues in urban systems from a metabolic perspective. In C. R. Binder, E. Massaro, & R. Wyss (eds.), *Sustainability Assessment in Urban Systems*. Cambridge University Press, pp. 261–289.

Millennium Ecosystem Assessment. (2005). *Ecosystems and Human Well-Being: Synthesis*. Washington, DC: Island Press.

Morgan, R. K. (2012). Environmental impact assessment: The state of the art. *Impact Assessment and Project Appraisal*, 30(1), 5–14. https://doi.org/10.1080/14615517.2012.661557.

Mori, K., & Christodoulou, A. (2012). Review of sustainability indices and indicators: Towards a new City Sustainability Index (CSI). *Environmental Impact Assessment Review*, 32(1), 94–106. https://doi.org/10.1016/j.eiar.2011.06.001.

Morrison-Saunders, A., Pope, J., Gunn, J. A. E., Bond, A., & Retief, F. (2014). Strengthening impact assessment: A call for integration and focus. *Impact Assessment and Project Appraisal*, 32(1), 2–8. https://doi.org/10.1080/14615517.2013.872841.

Ness, B., Urbel-Piirsalu, E., Anderberg, S., & Olsson, L. (2007). Categorising tools for sustainability assessment. *Ecological Economics*, 60, 498–508. https://doi.org/10.1016/j.ecolecon.2006.07.023.

Norgaard, R. B. (1994). *Development Betrayed: The End of Progress and a Coevolutionary Revisioning of the Future*. London: Routledge.

Osorio, L. A. R., Lobato, M. O., & Del Castillo, X. Á. (2009). An epistemology for sustainability science: A proposal for the study of the health/disease phenomenon. *International Journal of Sustainable Development & World Ecology*, 16(1), 48–60. https://doi.org/10.1080/13504500902760571.[1]

Patterson, M., McDonald, G., & Hardy, D. (2017). Is there more in common than we think? Convergence of ecological footprinting, energy analysis, life cycle assessment and other methods of environmental accounting. *Ecological Modelling*, 362, 19–36. https://doi.org/10.1016/j.ecolmodel.2017.07.022.

Pearce, D. W., & Turner, R. K. (1990). *Economics of Natural Resources and the Environment*. London: Harvester Wheatsheaf.

Phillis, Y. A., Kouikoglou, V. S., & Verdugo, C. (2017). Urban sustainability assessment and ranking of cities. *Computers, Environment and Urban Systems*, 64, 254–265. https://doi.org/10.1016/j.compenvurbsys.2017.03.002.

Pintér, L., Hardi, P., Martinuzzi, A., & Hall, J. (2012). Bellagio STAMP: Principles for sustainability assessment and measurement. *Ecological Indicators*, 17, 20–28. https://doi.org/10.1016/j.ecolind.2011.07.001.

Pope, J., Bond, A., Hugé, J., & Morrison-Saunders, A. (2017). Reconceptualising sustainability assessment. *Environmental Impact Assessment Review*, 62, 205–215. https://doi.org/10.1016/j.eiar.2016.11.002.

Raworth, K. (2012). A safe and just space for humanity: Can we live within the doughnut? *Oxfam Policy and Practice: Climate Change and Resilience*, 8(1), 1–26.

Redclift, M. (2005). Sustainable development (1987–2005): An oxymoron comes of age. *Sustainable Development*, 13(4), 212–227.

Reed, M. S., Graves, A., Dandy, N., et al. (2009). Who's in and why? A typology of stakeholder analysis methods for natural resource management. *Journal of Environmental Management*, 90(5), 1933–1949. https://doi.org/10.1016/j.jenvman.2009.01.001.

Rockström, J., Steffen, W., Noone, et al. (2009). Planetary Boundaries: Exploring the Safe Operating Space for Humanity. *Ecology and Society*, 14(2). https://doi.org/10.5751/ES-03180-140232.

Said, E. W. (1979). *Orientalism*. New York: Vintage Books.

Sala, S., Ciuffo, B., & Nijkamp, P. (2015). A systemic framework for sustainability assessment. *Ecological Economics*, 119, 314–325. https://doi.org/10.1016/j.ecolecon.2015.09.015.

Scerri, A., & James, P. (2010). Accounting for sustainability: Combining qualitative and quantitative research in developing "indicators" of sustainability. *International Journal of Social Research Methodology*, 13(1), 41–53. https://doi.org/10.1080/13645570902864145.

Schilling, T., Mühlemeier, S., Wyss, R., & Binder, C. R. (2020). A Concept for Sustainability Transition Assessment (STA): A Dynamic Systems Perspective Informed by Resilience Thinking. In C. R. Binder, E. Massaro, & R. Wyss (eds.), *Sustainability Assessment in Urban Systems*. Cambridge University Press, pp. 123–138.

Science for Environment Policy. (2018). *Indicators for Sustainable Cities*. In-depth Report 12. Produced for the European Commission DG Environment by the Science Communication Unit, UWE, Bristol.

Sengers, F., Wieczorek, A. J., & Raven, R. (2016). Experimenting for sustainability transitions: A systematic literature review. *Technological Forecasting and Social Change* (2016). https://doi.org/10.1016/j.techfore.2016.08.031.
Sharifi, A., & Murayama, A. (2013). A critical review of seven selected neighborhood sustainability assessment tools. *Environmental Impact Assessment Review*, 38, 73–87. https://doi.org/10.1016/j.eiar.2012.06.006.
Shen, L. Y., Jorge Ochoa, J., Shah, M. N., & Zhang, X. (2011). The application of urban sustainability indicators: A comparison between various practices. *Habitat International*, 35(1), 17–29. https://doi.org/10.1016/j.habitatint.2010.03.006.
Singh, R. K., Murty, H. R., Gupta, S. K., & Dikshit, A. K. (2012). An overview of sustainability assessment methodologies. *Ecological Indicators*, 15(1), 281–299.
Slaper, T., & Hall, T. (2011). The triple bottom line: What is it and how does it work? *Indiana Business Review*, 86, 4–8.
Stagl, S. (2012). Value articulating institutions and changing social preferences. In E. Brousseau, T. Dedeurwaerdere, & B. Siebenhüner, eds., *Reflexive Governance for Global Public Goods*. Cambridge: MIT Press, pp. 225–240. https://doi.org/10.7551/mitpress/9780262017244.003.0237.
Steffen, W., Richardson, K., Rockström, J., et al. (2015). Planetary boundaries: Guiding human development on a changing planet. *Science*, 347(6223), 1259855. https://doi.org/10.1126/science.1259855.
Thabrew, L., Wiek, A., & Ries, R. (2009). Environmental decision making in multi-stakeholder contexts: Applicability of life cycle thinking in development planning and implementation. *Journal of Cleaner Production*, 17(1), 67–76. https://doi.org/10.1016/j.jclepro.2008.03.008.
Turcu, C. (2013). Re-thinking sustainability indicators: Local perspectives of urban sustainability. *Journal of Environmental Planning and Management*, 56(5), 695–719. https://doi.org/10.1080/09640568.2012.698984.
UN. (2017). *Sustainable Development Goal 11. Make Cities and Human Settlements Inclusive, Safe, Resilient and Sustainable*. https://sustainabledevelopment.un.org/sdg11 (accessed 2.5.18).
Waas, T., Hugé, J., Block, T., Wright, T., Benitez-Capistros, F., & Verbruggen, A. (2014). Sustainability assessment and indicators: Tools in a decision-making strategy for sustainable development. *Sustainability*, 6(9), 5512–5534. https://doi.org/10.3390/su6095512.
Waas, T., Hugé, J., Verbruggen, A., & Wright, T. (2011). Sustainable development: A bird's eye view. *Sustainability*, 3(12), 1637–1661. https://doi.org/10.3390/su3101637.
Webb, R., Rissik, D., Petheram, L., Beh, J. L., & Stafford Smith, M. (2018). Co-designing adaptation decision support: Meeting common and differentiated needs. *Climatic Change*, 2018, 1–17. https://doi.org/10.1007/s10584-018-2165-7.
White, M. A. (2013). Sustainability: I know it when I see it. *Ecological Economics*, 86, 213–217. https://doi.org/10.1016/j.ecolecon.2012.12.020.
Wiek, A., & Binder, C. (2005). Solution spaces for decision-making: A sustainability assessment tool for city-regions. *Environmental Impact Assessment Review*, 25(6), 589–608. https://doi.org/10.1016/j.eiar.2004.09.009.
Wiek, A., Ness, B., Schweizer-Ries, P., Brand, F. S., & Farioli, F. (2012). From complex systems analysis to transformational change: A comparative appraisal of sustainability science projects. *Sustainability Science*, 7 (S1), 5–24. https://doi.org/10.1007/s11625-011-0148-y.

2

Systems Science and Sustainability Assessment

Claudia R. Binder, Michael Hutter, Melissa Pang, and Robert Webb

> *Since the fundamental character of the living thing is its organisation, the customary investigation of the single parts and processes cannot provide a complete explanation of the vital phenomena. This investigation gives us no information about the coordination of parts and processes. Thus, the chief task . . . must be to discover the laws of . . . systems (at all levels of organisation). . . . The view is considered as a method of investigation, we shall call . . . "the system theory."*
>
> *(Bertalanffy 1962, pp. 64ff, 190, 46, shortened and adapted by the authors)*

2.1 Introduction

In recent centuries, governments and industries across the globe have exhibited strong, growing interest in sustainable development, as evidenced by the widespread incorporation of sustainability concepts in urban and industrial development plans (Fiksel, 2006; Linton et al., 2007; Ukidwe & Bakshi, 2008; Wedding & Crawford-Brown, 2007). Consequently, sustainability assessment has become increasingly prevalent – as a decision-making tool and a key component of performance evaluation – in both the public and private sector areas (see Chapter 1 (Halla & Binder, 2020)).

To measure sustainability, the very concept itself must first be simplified, given the infeasibility of designing complex models that represent every last detail (see Chapter 1 (Halla & Binder, 2020)). Despite the fuzziness that surrounds its definition, there is no question that the notion of sustainability minimally encompasses three aspects: (i) the economy, (ii) the environment, and (iii) society (Grace & Pope, 2015; Singh et al., 2009; World Commission on Environment and Development, 1987). Conventional sustainability assessment methodologies typically employ (composite) indicators, pertaining to one specific aspect, that simplify the system representation while allowing the system to be monitored (Wiek & Binder, 2005). An example of a sustainability indicator with an obvious economic focus is the green net national product (or environmentally adjusted net domestic product), while the Ecological Footprint and the Human Development Index are widely used examples of environmental and social sustainability indicators respectively. The appeal of using such sustainability indicators is clear: they are easy to implement, to communicate, and to understand. They can be combined and modified to form composite indicator sets, or lists, that consider the multiple aspects of sustainable development. In practice, many efforts to measure and evaluate sustainability have only one area of focus. Nevertheless, even the integrated, holistic approaches that do take into account all three perspectives – environmental, social, and economic – often merely consider each of them as separate compartments that supplement one another and can eventually be aggregated.

However, there are drawbacks to the use of indicator-based tools for sustainability assessment. Sustainability indices are typically reductionist in nature, and many have argued that this conventional scientific reductionist methodology cannot adequately address complex concepts such as sustainability (Adetunji et al., 2003; Gasparatos et al., 2009; Hester & Adams, 2017; Sala et al., 2015). The reductionist approach fails to account for emergent properties – of which sustainability is an example – that arise from relationships among the various interacting components, and therefore cannot be attributed to any singular component or subsystem (Audouin & de Wet, 2012; Cilliers, 2005, 2008; Hester & Adams, 2017). The use of indicator sets might not accurately – i.e., parsimoniously and sufficiently – represent the system being assessed and its associated problems. They do not appropriately account for the multiple dimensions of sustainability, nor the complex relationships among indicators within the system, nor the interdependency with other systems (Scholz & Tietje, 2002; Vester, 1988; Wiek & Binder, 2005). Moreover, the initial compartmentalization creates significant problems when it comes to re-integrating the different components for sustainability assessment and making them functional for decision-making (Audouin & de Wet, 2012; Grace & Pope, 2015; Wilber, 2011).

It is evident, therefore, that a different approach to sustainability assessment is necessary. The shortcomings of the conventional "indicator lists" methodology just discussed highlight the systemic nature of issues pertaining to sustainability, and consequently the need for integrated systems-based strategies (Adetunji et al., 2003; Hester & Adams, 2017; Wiek & Binder, 2005). In contrast to the reductionist approach, a systems approach allows the system and its subsystems to be studied as an integral whole of their subsidiary parts, and never as "the mechanistic aggregate of parts in isolable causal relations" (Adetunji et al., 2003; Laszlo, 1975). The focus is hence on "thinking in terms of connectedness, relationships, and context" (Gallopín, 2003). This facilitates the abstraction from the complex notion of sustainability – of the important, fundamental elements – thus reducing confusion and ambiguity in sustainability assessment and research (Gallopín, 2003).

This chapter aims to show how systems science can be used to frame and support a sustainability assessment. It first provides a short overview of systems science and its key theoretical foundations, presenting the utility of these concepts in the area of sustainability assessment. We then propose a methodological procedure for applying systems science in a sustainability context. Thereafter, we present empirical case studies in the area of assessing the sustainability of energy and urban systems and reflect upon how the case studies and system characteristics are related to each other. Finally, we draw some conclusions from the theoretical and empirical analysis.

2.2 Systems Science and System Theory

2.2.1 What is a System?

The concept of systems (from late Latin *systema* "arrangement," and from Greek *systema* "organized whole") can be traced back to the philosophers of ancient Greece. Aristotle explained the holon ("the whole") as being characterized by its parts, on the one hand, and the interrelations among the parts, on the other (Ropohl, 1999). Even though he did not use the term "system," he described two core properties of systems, namely elements and structure. Lambert (1782) is said to be the first one to define a system as "a whole composed by parts in a purposeful way" (Ropohl, 1999, p. 3). Thus, Lambert stresses that function is essential to systems. In addition, system integrity can be seen as another core property (Bossel, 1999). This means that the inside and outside of a system can often be defined, although its boundaries might not always be clear. Systems are also often hierarchical (i.e., they consist of subsystems), complex, and thus emergent (i.e., they feature new properties or structures which cannot only be explained by their components). Bossel (1999, p. 20) summarizes these system characteristics in the following definition, also depicted in Figure 2.1:

> "A system is anything that is composed of system elements connected in a characteristic system structure. This configuration of system elements allows it to perform specific system functions in its system environment. These functions can be interpreted as serving a distinct system purpose. The system boundary is permeable for inputs from and outputs to the environment. It defines the system's identity and autonomy."

2.2.2 Systems Science

As with the definition of a system, the origins of systems science are as old as European philosophy. Aristotle (384–322 BC) stated: "The whole is more than the

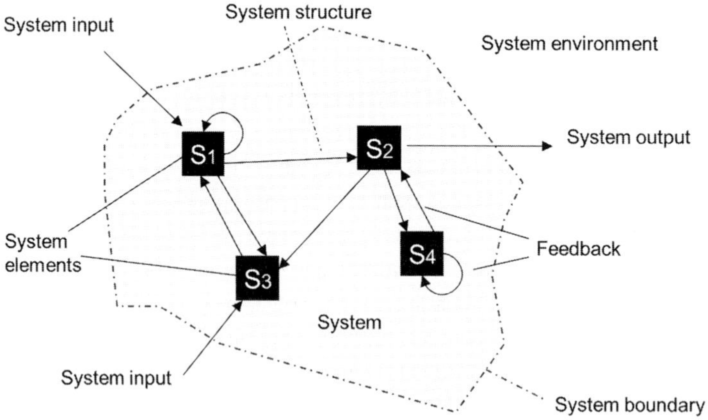

Figure 2.1 Graphical systems representation. An open system interacts with its environment through system inputs and outputs (after Bossel, 1999; Ossimitz and Lapp, 2006)

sum of its parts" (Bertalanffy, 1962). Since then, systems science has been applied in formal sciences, phenomenological sciences, and normative sciences, as well as across disciplines (e.g., theology, mathematics, physics, biology). Within the different disciplinary fields, the main goal of systems science has been to integrate knowledge across disciplines and between science and practice related to a certain domain or problem area, allowing for a holistic perspective on the issue at hand (Hieronymi 2013). Thus, systems science focuses on interrelations and feedbacks within systems and aims at understanding the dynamics of systems, gaining insights into future developments, and developing management approaches to deal with mostly complex problems. As M'Pherson (1974) puts it: "[Systems science] does not aim to find the one true representation for a given type of system, but to formulate general principles about how different representations of different systems can be constructed so as to be effective in problem-solving" (p. 229).

2.2.3 Systems Science and Sustainability

In the field of sustainability, some of the most prominent scientists who have advocated the application of systems science are Kay, Meadows, and Holling (Hieronymi 2013). They recognized its role in tackling complex, higher-order notions like the sustainability and resilience of systems, as the limitations of classical reductionist methodologies became more evident. Beginning in the 1970s, Odum (1977) called attention to the importance of holism and an integrated systems approach to ecological studies, and thus paved the way for a new paradigm in the field of ecology. He argues that science should be "synthetic and holistic in the sense of seeking to understand large components as functional wholes" (Odum, 1977, p. 1289). Similarly, Meadows (2008) promoted the systems model as the new paradigm according to which global problems and challenges should be addressed. For example, when trying to assess sustainability, the indicators used should be "dynamic" and need to be developed using a systems perspective because it can shed light on the "critical linkages, dynamic tendencies, and leverage points for action" (Meadows, 1998, p. 27).

More importantly, these pioneering systems thinkers conceptualized important systems-based frameworks and methods to guide sustainable development and sustainability assessment. Kay et al. (1999) proposed that human and ecological systems be portrayed as self-organizing holarchic open systems (SOHO), where the principles of non-equilibrium thermodynamics are used to understand system relationships and behaviors. The result of extensive international collaboration, the adaptive methodology for ecosystem sustainability and health (AMESH) was developed as Kay and other scientists worked to incorporate complex system theories into sustainable development projects (Waltner-Toews & Kay, 2005). In the 1980s, Max-Neef developed the Human-Scale Development approach (HSD) to evaluate economic and sustainable development processes using a systemic approach (Cruz et al., 2009; Max-Neef et al., 1991). The HSD approach redefined the existing reductionist, market-centered approach that was dominant at that time. In the same vein, Vester (1988) proposed a bio-cybernetic approach to systems planning that has both concrete and didactic applications. One concrete application would be the possibility of using this bio-cybernetic approach as a basis for tackling environmental issues: it provides a conceptual framework – a "cybernetic sensitivity model," that reinvents classic systems modeling and simulation techniques – that allows for "ecologically sound systems design" (Vester, 1988, p. 399). As mentioned, Meadows (1998) highlighted the importance of integrating systems insights into the design of sustainability indicators and recommended the Daly Triangle framework for indicator development. Similarly, Bossel also strongly advocated the systems science approach and proposed structural frameworks (e.g., basic orientors of system viability) to define sustainable development indicators (Bossel, 1999, 2003). Finally, in several publications, Ison acknowledged the importance of, and recommended the application of, systems thinking and system-based methods in higher education programs that focus on environmental sustainability and sustainable development (Blackmore et al., 2015; Ison, 1999; Maiteny & Ison, 1997).

2.2.4 System Theory

In the 1950s, Bertalanffy, Gerard, Rapoport, Boulding, and Miller (see Hammond, 2002, 2003) founded the Society of General System Theory (later named the International Society of Systems Science). They aimed at consolidating systems approaches and overcome the boundaries both within disciplines in academia and between academia and practice by creating a general systems theory that would be valid across disciplines and scales (Straussfogel & Von Schilling, 2009). However, given the different disciplinary uses and application of systems science, over time, six different streams of thought emerged, each with its specific characteristics (see Hester and Adams, 2017 for a review): (1) general systems theory (Bertalanffy, 1949, 1950, 1968; Boulding, 1956); (2) living systems theory (Miller, 1978); (3) mathematical systems theory (Klir, 1968; Mesarovic, 1967; Wymore, 1967; Wymore, 1993); (4) cybernetics (Ashby, 1947; Forrester, 1961, 1969, 1971; Rosenblueth et al., 1943); (5) social systems theory (Buckley, 1967; Luhmann, 1995; Parsons, 1970); and (6) philosophical systems theory Bunge, 1997, 2004; (Laszlo, 1972).

None of these six streams of systems theory provides one general accepted perspective for any type of system (Hester & Adams, 2017). However, each of them offers concepts and notions which can be generalized and are relevant for different types of systems independent of their disciplinary background. Adams et al. (2014), based on an analysis of 42 scientific fields, developed seven interconnected axioms of systems theory (Table 2.1), which may serve as principles with which to analyze real-world systems.

These axioms are relevant for how to define a system, how to understand and interpret system dynamics, how to assess a system, and how to steer a system. Some of the elements of these axioms relevant for sustainability assessment are referred to in the rest of this chapter as well as in Chapter 5 (Schilling et al., 2020).

Table 2.1 *Axioms derived from systems theory (for details, see Adams et al., 2014; Hester & Adams, 2017)*

No.	Axiom	Definition (Adams et al., 2014)	Examples and references
1	Centrality Axiom	*Central to all systems are two pairs of propositions: emergence and hierarchy, and communication and control.*	Emergence (Aristotle, 2002) / Hierarchy (Pattee, 1973) / Communication (Shannon, 1948a, 1948b) / Control (Checkland, 1993)
2	Contextual Axiom	*System meaning is informed by the circumstances and factors that surround the system.*	Holism (Smuts, 1926) / Darkness (Cilliers, 1998) / Complementarity (Bohr, 1928)
3	Goal Axiom	*Systems achieve specific goals through purposeful behavior using pathways and means.*	Equifinality (Bertalanffy, 1950) / Multifinality (Buckley, 1967) / Purposive behavior (Rosenblueth et al., 1943) / Satisficing (Simon, 1955, 1956)
4	Operational Axiom	*Systems must be addressed in situ, where the system is exhibiting purposeful behavior.*	Dynamic equilibrium (d'Alembert, 1743) / Relaxation time (Holling, 1996) / Basin of stability (Kauffman, 1990) / Homeostasis & homeorhesis (Cannon, 1929) / Self-organization (Ashby, 1947) / Suboptimization (Hitch, 1953) / Redundancy (Pahl et al., 2011)
5	Viability Axiom	*Key parameters in a system must be controlled to ensure continued existence.*	Viability (Beer, 1979) / Requisite variety (Ashby, 1956) / Requisite hierarchy (Aulin-Ahmavaara, 1979) / Feedback (Wiener, 1948) / Circular causality (Korzybski, 1994) / Recursion (Beer, 1979)
6	Design Axiom	*System design is a purposeful imbalance of resources and relationships.*	Requisite parsimony (Miller, 1956) / Requisite saliency (Boulding, 1966) / Minimum critical specification (Cherns, 1976, 1987) / Pareto (Pareto, 1896) / Power laws (Newman, 2005)
7	Information Axiom	*Systems create, possess, transfer, and modify information.*	Information redundancy (Shannon & Weaver, 1949) / Information entropy (Shannon and Weaver, 1949) / Information inaccessibility (Hunt, 1975) / Redundancy of potential command (McCulloch et al., 1959)

2.2.4.1 Axiom 1: Centrality

The centrality axiom brings together two key aspects of systems. The first is a structural aspect and relates to two interlinked concepts, emergence, and hierarchy (Adams et al., 2014). Emergence is the phenomenon that states that higher system levels are characterized by new qualities not prevalent at lower levels. This also implies that the system cannot be described completely on just one level of hierarchy (principle of excluded reductionism; Adams et al., 2014). For example, each cell has its own quality, but the combination of the cells leads to an organ which has a new quality by itself.

The second aspect relates to the management of the system itself. It includes concepts mainly related to communication and control (Adams et al., 2014). Thereby, communication can be defined as the way in which information is transported within a system, considering its hierarchies. The way in which a system establishes its communication structure is essential for regulating (controlling) the system itself.

Relevance for Sustainability Assessment: The centrality axiom is relevant in two ways for sustainability assessment. On the one hand, hierarchies within the system have to be considered when designing the system and its subsystems, e.g., functions that urban systems have to fulfill or the social, ecological, and infrastructural subsystems therein. Hierarchies within the social system are, for example, individuals, groups, organizations, and institutions. When performing a sustainability assessment, we might be assessing a system at one specific point in time and within a specific space or hierarchical level (snapshot). However, it is important to appreciate that the system structure determines the dynamics of the system (see Chapter 5 (Schilling et al., 2020)). On the other hand, each sustainability assessment should be aware that the implementation of its results requires the knowledge of how the communication structures and regulating institutions are linked to each other and where the assessment results can feed the decision-making process (see Chapter 1 (Halla & Binder, 2020)).

2.2.4.2 Axiom 2: Context

The contextual axiom relates to the fact that the meaning of the system is linked to the circumstances and factors that are outside the system border. According to Hester and Adams (2017), three principles describe the contextual axiom: (i) holism, (ii) darkness, and (iii) complementarity.

The principle of holism is one of the central aspects of systems science identified by Aristotle. It states that the whole is more than the sum of its parts. Thus, to understand a system, it is not sufficient to study its parts, or its subsystems; rather, the system has to be viewed as a whole (which is also necessary to be able to understand emergence patterns). The principle of system darkness tells us that we will never be able to completely understand or know a system (Hester & Adams, 2017), as all of us have limited access to information. Finally, complementarity allows us to take different perspectives with respect to the same system. Each of these different views provides a valuable insight into the system and its dynamics.

Relevance for Sustainability Assessment: The contextual axiom is critical for structuring the system to be assessed (e.g., the system boundary, subsystems to be included, system elements) and for the interpretation of the results. As shown in Chapter 1 (Halla & Binder, 2020), sustainability assessment requires a specific focus on what is it that will be assessed. This might be an urban system to be compared to others, a project within an urban system, or function of an urban system. In any of these cases, we have to be aware that each of these perspectives is only a part of the larger system. In particular, following the holistic principle, the analysis of trade-offs between subsystems or elements might become relevant. Furthermore, the complementarity principle suggests that having different expert and/or stakeholder groups validate the system and perform the assessment separately might be a critical step to take. The latter will reveal preferences and disagreements regarding views or perspectives on sustainability (see Chapter 1 (Halla & Binder, 2020)).

2.2.4.3 Axiom 3: Goal

The goal axiom postulates that each system aims at achieving a specific goal; i.e., it performs purposeful behavior (Hester & Adams, 2017). Four principles are related to this axiom: equifinality, multifinality, purposive behavior, and satisficing. The principle of equifinality asserts that a specific final or end state can be reached even if the point of departure (initial state) differs. The principle of multifinality affirms that systems which start from the same initial state may end up in different end states. Furthermore, each human-made system displays purposeful behavior, which is to say that the system behaves so as to reach or obtain a specific goal (Hester & Adams, 2017). However, given the trade-offs between goals, and given that humans do not have complete information for decision-making, the best result of their behavior might not be the optimal one, but rather a satisfactory one, i.e., "satisficing."

Relevance for sustainability assessment: In our view, the goal axiom is one of the key axioms for sustainability assessment. Knowing that human-made systems pursue purposeful behavior, and that the principles of equifinality and multifinality apply, the role of sustainability assessment in providing decision-making support for obtaining, as far as is possible, the optimal end state becomes clear. Sustainability assessment can be used from this point of view as a monitoring tool, to analyze to what extent or in which direction the system is developing in relation to the envisioned end state (see Chapter 5 (Schilling et al., 2020)).

2.2.4.4 Axiom 4: Operational

The operational axiom states that the system should be looked at in situ (rather than from a theoretical perspective) – that is, in the place where it aims to reach its goal (Hester & Adams, 2017). This axiom involves seven principles: dynamic equilibrium, relaxation time, basins of stability, homeostasis and homeorhesis, self-organization, suboptimization, and redundancy. All these principles relate to the behavior of the system over time. The first three principles relate to the system and its equilibrium. The key issue they look into is whether the system is attracted to a specific stable basin, whether that is true for all the subsystems, and how long it takes the system to bounce back after a specific challenge. The fourth and fifth principles relate to the system organizing itself and achieving specific states. Finally, the last two principles refer to the satisficing principle presented in Section 2.2.4.3. For a detailed description, please see Hester and Adams, 2017.

Relevance for Sustainability Assessment: The operational axiom is relevant because it puts the system dynamics (stability, equilibrium) in relation to the system's direct environment. It is essential for interpreting the actual relevance of the assessment and the management strategies that might result therefrom. Taking the example of urban infrastructure, one might ask how much redundancy has to be built into a system in order for it to be stable in the face of external influences such as earthquakes, migration, etc.

2.2.4.5 Axiom 5: Viability

The viability axiom highlights another aspect of the system, namely its continued existence over time. This principle focuses on how long the system can continue to exist with the same identity (viability principle); how the external forces the system is exposed to can be structured (orientation theory); how diverse system components have to be to sustain the system's existence (requisite variety); what type of hierarchy is required in order to steer the system best (requisite hierarchy); what type of feedback loops are present within the system; and to what extent do they lead to vicious or virtuous cycles (feedback and circular causality). See Hester and Adams (2017) for more detail.

Relevance for Sustainability Assessment: The viability axiom provides an input into (i) what the drivers and barriers toward a more sustainable system state might be; (ii) what the inherent system pathways and possible lock-ins of the system are (see Chapter 5 (Schilling et al., 2020)); and (iii) what might be needed for pursuing the long-term existence of a more sustainable system.

2.2.4.6 Axiom 6: Design

The design axiom provides guidance for how the system should be designed and how its development can be steered. It first suggests that there should be between five and nine different elements such as goals, objectives, and hierarchies (requisite parsimony). The second aspect to be considered is that an optimal design is determined by the design target or goal and the current situation. The different design parameters should be ranked by the designers themselves (requisite saliency). Furthermore, in designing the system one should be aware of what the minimum specifications required are (need-to-have and nice-to-have).

Relevance for Sustainability Assessment: The design principles should be considered when setting up the system for performing a sustainability assessment. It should be considered to what extent the design principles have been met and, if not, what the consequences are for the sustainability of the system (e.g., an urban system) and its assessment. In particular, the minimum specifications for a sustainable development of the system can be included as an additional element when analyzing the sustainability of the system itself (see Chapter 1 (Halla & Binder, 2020)).

2.2.4.7 Axiom 7: Information

The information axiom provides insight into how information and system development are interlinked. Aspects such as information entropy, information accessibility, information capacity, and the redundancy of these various forms have to be considered here. The point to be noted is that only a share of the information delivered might reach its target. This might be because information is lost, not understood, or not accessible. Since not all of the information reaches its final destination, commands might have to be designed in a redundant way.

Relevance for Sustainability Assessment: The information axiom relates to the period following a typical sustainability assessment. It is relevant when designing policies based on the assessment performed. In terms of the assessment itself, it implies that information is grouped and channeled in such a way that the relevant issues are understood and designed so that different target stakeholders are reached.

2.2.5 Defining a System for Sustainability Assessment

The combination of essential system characteristics and the seven axioms provide the basis for designing a system in a way that facilitates sustainability assessment. We derived four systems characteristics, drawing on Bossel's (1999) definition quoted in Section 2.2.1, and mapped the axioms onto each characteristic (see Table 2.2). The first characteristic focuses on delineating the system boundaries and context and is informed by the contextual axiom (Axiom 2). The second characteristic includes defining the purpose and goals of the system, the function it has to fulfill, and the decision-making that expresses purposive behavior in human systems. It is informed by Axiom 3 (goal) and parts of Axiom 6 (design) and Axiom 1 (centrality – control and communication). The third characteristic focuses on the design of the system, its structure, and its emerging dynamics. Thereby, questions of hierarchy, emergence, and systems operation, viability, and design have to be considered (Axioms 1 [part thereof], 4, 5, 6). Finally, within the fourth characteristic, we need to consider system information and monitoring that is integral to the ability to effectively design and influence systems over time in Axioms 1 (part thereof), and 7.

2.2.5.1 System Boundary, Context, and Environment

The system boundary defines what is inside the system to be analyzed and what belongs to the system context. Furthermore, the system boundary defines the inputs and outputs of the system. When studying or assessing complex systems, we are mostly confronted with nested systems, that is, we might encounter a hierarchy of systems. For example, depending on the system perspective, a systems element might become a subsystem. Elements of a system boundary typically include space and time.

The interpretation of a sustainability assessment strongly depends on the system context. The latter has to be considered when designing the system to be assessed because (1) the

Table 2.2 *System characteristics and axioms*

System characteristics	Description	Axioms
1. System boundary, context, and environment	Delimits the system in space and time, and defines inputs and outputs. Situates the system in relation to its surroundings by including: circumstances, factors, conditions, values, and patterns.	**Contextual Axiom (2)**
2. System purpose, goals, and decision-making	Goal and function of the system (e.g., self-preservation, conservation of a stable state, transformation to a new state). Includes design and decision-making processes and criteria across multiple goals.	**Goal Axiom (3)** **Centrality Axiom (1)** (*Communication, Control principles*) **Design Axiom (6)** (*Requisite parsimony, Requisite saliency principles*)
3. System structure and dynamics	Refers to elements, processes, and their interrelations: e.g., hierarchy and subsystems, system elements (types, diversity, parsimony, sufficiency), interrelation between system elements (connectivity, feedbacks), emergence, adaptability of a system	**Centrality Axiom (1)** (*Hierarchy, Emergence principles*) **Operational Axiom (4)** **Viability Axiom (5)** **Design Axiom (6)**
4. System information, monitoring, and learning	Refers to how a system can be monitored, and which variables and parameters have to be measured to assure progress toward sustainability, including indicators. These inform both ex ante and ex post sustainability assessments.	**Centrality Axiom (1)** (*Communication, Control principles*) **Information Axiom (7)**

system at hand is an open system and cannot be studied in isolation from its environment; and (2) every improvement in one system, in terms of its sustainability, has an effect on its surrounding systems (see also first- and second-order cybernetics, and resilience; Keppie, 2006). Hester and Adams (2017) propose that five elements should be considered when analyzing a system's context: circumstances, factors, conditions, values, and patterns.

2.2.5.2 System Purpose, Goals, and Decision-Making

Each system has a purpose, a goal, or a function it has to fulfill. The definition of the purpose is relevant as it shapes the system elements which define the system as well as the system interactions studied (see Section 2.2.3.4). For the sustainability assessment of urban systems, thus, the functions have to be characterized and it is necessary to define when a system no longer fulfills its function properly or which function has priority over the other (see also normative perspective in Chapter 3 (Meinherz et al., 2020)). This characteristic explicitly includes decision-making, as this is integral to purposive behavior and is also the focus of ex ante sustainability assessment.

2.2.5.3 System Structure and Dynamics

The system structure relates to the elements the system is composed of and how they are related to each other. A systems structure is defined by (i) subsystems and their hierarchy; (ii) specific system elements and their characteristics (types, diversity, parsimony, sufficiency); and (iii) the relation or interaction between the system elements (connectivity, feedbacks).

There are several ways to define subsystems. Typically, their definition depends on the function of the system and the purpose of the analysis or assessment. The definition of subsystems should (i) support the analysis and understanding of the system to be assessed or problem to be solved, and (ii) divide the problem into researchable units, without losing the holistic view.

The elements of the system or subsystems themselves can be viewed as processes, which mathematically defined are functions that transform inputs into outputs within a certain period of time and in a certain space (Baccini & Bader, 1996). Typically, processes can be production (e.g., production of goods), decision-making (e.g., investment decisions), transport, and service provision processes (e.g., health, shelter, occupation).

The links between processes are represented by flows. Flows can be (i) physical flows, such as elements, materials or goods; (ii) flows of people; or (iii) information flows generated through a process or created by monitoring a process. Thereby, the flows can be just the connection between processes, as in a production chain; e.g., "farming" produces "food" as a flow, which enters the process "food processing," with the output "processed food." Alternatively, the flows can feed into a feedback process. This is a process by which information concerning the adequacy of a system in its operation is fed back to the system itself or its governance body. A feedback can, in its simplest form, be a flow that goes back to a process (see Figure 2.1).

In defining a system, the criteria of diversity, parsimony, and sufficiency should be considered. To account for the diversity of the system's components, we have to make sure that we represent the variety of elements prevalent in the system, that the elements are distinctly different from each other (disparity; Stirling, 2007), and that they are sufficiently balanced so as to represent the sustainability issues to be tackled Binder et al., 2017; (Stirling, 2007). The parsimony principle states that a system should be defined as simply as possible to fit the purpose of the sustainability assessment. Finally, to comply with the sufficiency principle, the system should be designed to be as complex as necessary and as simple as possible.

We have to keep in mind that the structure of the system determines its behavior and its dynamics. That is, given the relationships and feedbacks between the system elements and processes, we observe linear, exponential, oscillating, or sigmoidal growth, or overshoot-and-collapse behavior (Ossimitz & Lapp, 2006). Special attention could also be given to emergent processes.

2.2.5.4 System Information, Monitoring, and Learning

In designing our system, we have to consider where and how we would like to monitor its progress toward sustainability. This means we have to consider which system properties are necessary for reaching a system's goal, stabilizing the system, or making the system resilient and transformable (see Chapter 5 (Schilling et al., 2020)). A solid system analysis and understanding will support the derivation and use of indicators to measure the progress of the system (see Chapters 8 (Binder et al., 2020) and 13 (Boesch & de Montmollin, 2020)). Such information supports both ex ante and ex post sustainability assessments, and the ex post assessment is itself an information feedback that can inform or prompt next-stage decision-making.

2.3 Illustrations

In the following, we present two case studies to illustrate the key system characteristics we have presented and how they support and facilitate the assessment of sustainability. The first illustrates the relationship between system context, environment, system goal, system structure, and the sustainability assessment of the energy system in the case of the energy systems program at the International Institute for Applied Systems Analysis (IIASA). The second case study illustrates how a system perspective is used to analyze and assess urban development in Australia. We then discuss the lessons learned of both case studies for sustainability assessment of urban systems.

2.3.1 Case Study 1: The Energy Systems Program at the IIASA and the Development of Systems Analysis (1973–1981)

2.3.1.1 Outline: IIASA and the Energy Systems Project (ESP)

This case study retraces the practices and development of systems analysis at the International Institute for Applied Systems Analysis. It is not just that systems models and systems thinking intrinsically extended their scope of analysis due to the rise of computer power. System characteristics and the delimitation of what belonged to a system were continuously widened through the influence of a broader scientific and social context. In this respect, the analysis of the technical and logical feasibility of cheap energy production was only one aspect of a wider interest in assessing energy production and the related social and environmental constraints. This case study of energy systems and energy futures reinvestigates how systems analysis developed and consolidated as an integrated method, given the contextual impetus of the 1970s. Due to external constraints (changes in the system context and environment), energy systems analysis evolved from a technical energy analysis to an analysis that included several elements of what constitutes sustainability assessment.

In the early 1970s, systems analysis was interpreted as policy analysis: the political spectrum and societal fields surrounding a systems analysis were key elements for innovation. The IIASA example demonstrates how systems analysis as a toolset developed within an international and interdisciplinary institution. Systems knowledge was being actively debated by international researchers in Austria, at a time when large-scale predictions by experts were usually considered as delivering clear, objective, and final scientific arguments that could resolve or even prevent contentious debates during policy-making processes. IIASA imagined to encompass knowledge that originated from different needs, different cultures, and different ideologies. Energy dilemmas such as oil scarcity called for the implementation of a unified systems approach. An integrated systems framework was proposed to guide management decisions in regard to the global environmental and societal problems (Rindzevičiūtė, 2016). The methodological debate was determined by a changing context, however. Its outcome was the production and dispersion of integrated, more nuanced forms of systems science.

The making of the energy systems analysis is closely linked to IIASA's institutional existence. IIASA was founded by national research organizations and academies of sciences from the USSR, the USA, the GDR, and France, among others – that is, from countries in both the Eastern and Western blocs. Given the rise of environmental debates, foremost due to the 1972 United Nations Conference on the Human Environment in Stockholm that had reunited the scientific and governmental elite to face environmental issues, but also due to the widespread public response to the end-of-the world systems models that appeared in the Limits to Growth report by the Club of Rome (Meadows et al., 1972), several national governments paid new attention to solving the common problems of industrialized societies by the application of systems thinking. In this vein, IIASA was established to apply systems analysis in global environmental and resource-related research programs. About 80–100 researchers started to predict the future behavior and shapes of global, local, or regional systems. Among them, the energy systems project (ESP) explored a coherent planning and implementation strategy for energy transitions due to the modeling of interdependencies between environmental impact and different forms of energy production (Häfele, 1974).

The characteristics and development of the ESP had three phases, and focusing on these provides insights into how systems approaches at IIASA during the 1970s approximated toward current discourses of systems sciences and goals of sustainability assessment, which are scrutinized in this volume. Each of these phases at IIASA developed due to a specific system context, system goal, system boundary, or the experience of systems analysis outcome.

2.3.1.2 Phase 1: Nuclear Energy as a Solution to Energy Scarcity (1973–1975)

The assumption of abundant energy supply was challenged in autumn 1973, when the majority of OPEC states halted their cheap oil exports. This "oil embargo" aggravated the risk that industrialized countries would not be able to maintain stable energy supply levels during a period of increasing energy demand.[1] The effects of the oil embargo led to political and governmental tensions over energy policymaking and provided the context that shaped systems analysis and IIASA's interest in participating in a study of the transition of energy supply. IIASA's supporting national member states were largely dependent on cheap oil imports (Graf, 2014). As a consequence, in 1973, the time horizon of the analysis was mainly focused on short-term perspectives, which is linked to the fact that there was a specific need to overcome the lack of energy resources in Western states. Long-term analyses were primarily related to the question of necessary future investments or to general political support for nuclear energy as a way to secure the abundant supply of energy sources; a minor project at IIASA extended the scope of analysis by projecting the structural problems of renewable solar power in comparison to nuclear energy. The key goal was to guarantee and to stabilize the energy supply by using nuclear fission as a replacement technology for conventional energy sources, such as coal.

The first structure of the energy system was influenced by researchers and methodologies from the US think tank RAND Corporation, whose staff had been working with systems analysis in the policymaking area outside the military realm since 1947 (Levien, 2000). Moreover, the input from nuclear physicists, who participated in the development and implementation of novel nuclear technologies in the FRG, the USSR, or the USA shaped the decisions of what became a component IIASA ESP. Following the first criticism against the mechanized appearance of systems analysis from the 1960s, where human affairs did not appear as a key component of the system (Seefried, 2015), the founders of IIASA and the first supporters of ESP took up this critique during the negation period for the new institute at the end of the 1960s and propagated methods that "stress[ed] the systems approach to social problems (in the widest sense)" (Helmer, 1967). Systems analyses were broadened in their structure even though the objective was the transition to nuclear energy technology. Systems analysis was conceived as a specific vantage point that provides novel information for decision-making. Researchers should therefore not explore and study solely "the sum of the components but the structure of the entire problem" (IIASA, 1973). Regarding energy problems in particular, energy systems analysts at IIASA were directed to first develop a general system model of the energy transition problem. This pre-analysis should inform, in a second step, the discipline-oriented scientific view of each researcher. Only thereafter should the larger systems problem be structured into disciplinary sub-questions for the exploration of each factor (IIASA, 1974). Systems analysis in itself, therefore, became inherently a joint exercise between participating researchers with different disciplinary backgrounds.

IIASA advocated the adoption of nuclear technology to solve energy problems for the future (IIASA, 1974). The main outcomes were assessments of different nuclear reactor technologies, the organization of sufficient safeguard systems for nuclear energy and radiation control, and calculations of the most efficient siting criteria for building nuclear plants to respond to rising energy demand. The IIASA focused on the tracing of systems behaviors, projecting these simulations for the assessment of future behavior of the system. For example, the ESP projected the development of energy resources, energy demand, as well as energy systems impacts up to the year 2050. As early as 1973, however, ESP researchers were critical toward the idea that technology-centered projections would be best to highlight the benefits of nuclear energy in comparison to other form of energy production, notably in respect to the environmental impact of each.

Reflection Regarding Sustainability Assessment: Given the strong social demand for energy (system context), the system analysis and sustainability assessment was mostly focused on how to ensure the flexibility of energy supply. The need for an energy transition from fossil fuels toward nuclear energy was propagated by nuclear physicists and systems analysts with ties to the nuclear industry and safeguard systems research. Thus, nuclear energy was and remained the ESP's figurehead, visible in the consideration and modeling of new nuclear energy technologies, notably the widespread technological implementation of fast breeder reactors that were expected to increase efficiency and reduce waste heat. At that time, environmental issues, perceived as systems problems, primarily concerned the regional or local effects of nuclear reactor siting, plant construction, and plant operation.

2.3.1.3 Phase 2: The Politics of ESP Modeling (1974–1977)

In the mid-1970s, a series of antinuclear movements gained new momentum in the public realm and in scientific research. The negative effects of the emerging nuclear fuel industry were robustly discussed within committees composed of prominent experts, such as at the widely known Pugwash Conferences, where renowned nuclear physicists advocated the abolition of nuclear material (Kaplan, 1976; Levai, 1977). In IIASA's ESP, participants worried that these discussions could misleadingly contribute to an irrational perception on the part of the public and help spread "very strongly [the] widespread but erroneous impression that most of the scientists in the United States are against nuclear power" (IAEA Archives, 1975). The ESP members considered this discussion as an unnecessary obstruction to their objectives of securing a cheap and environmentally benevolent energy supply. Nevertheless, these debates – in which nuclear fission, in particular, was at stake as the main option for securing a common energy future – reshaped the elements of IIASA researchers' energy systems analyses. The boundaries of the energy system were enlarged to design robust energy systems that could be easily communicated and applied to the policy arena. IIASA moved away from nuclear safeguard systems analysis and tackled the combination and comparison of various risk spectra for the implementation of energy supply technologies. Societal issues, such as how much a society would be willing to pay for safety with respect to their desire to continue to consume energy abundantly, were included: ESP systems analyses were referring to methodological premises of risk-benefit analyses.

The ESP's goal was to develop a systems model that highlighted each of the risks and benefits of contemporary practised energy technology. The key was to thereby show the miniscule risk level of nuclear energy compared to other sources of energy supply, and communicate therefore convincing models so as to respond to scientific as well as public opposition.

The ESP systems analysis research moved from technological premises and debates about siting criteria toward systems structures that exposed the benefits and risks of nuclear energy in relation to conventional energy sources and other alternative forms of energy supply, i.e., of nuclear power plant siting and the limits and risks of centralized solar energy plants. The new systems structure included two important dimensions: (1) a social dimension, where societal opinion and perceptions of nuclear energy were defined in systems as concrete values by studies of anthropologists, social scientists, and economists from different countries (IIASA, 1975); and (2) a managerial dimension, where, similarly to a transdisciplinary approach, systems analysis included experiences from industry and policy.

The inclusion of social factors resulted in what Sheila Jasanoff and Sang-Hyun Kim called one of "several landmark policy actions from the 1950s to the 1980s" (Jasanoff & Kim, 2009). The new dimensions of system analysis included risk assessment methods and a managerial dimension which strengthened links to regulatory entities wishing to address public anxieties about nuclear energy. At that time, it seemed as if IIASA did not foresee the complex effects of this system boundary expansion. The ESP mainly kept formalizing psychological determinants of public risk perception (IIASA, 1976). They were asked to monitor and clarify "the basic forces and the mechanisms determining the very regular and secular behavior of society in adopting new technologies and products, in particular new primary energy resources" (IIASA 1976). However, including social aspects led to new grounds for critique that again reshaped the original premises of ESP's systems analysis from 1973. Questions emerged, such as whether and how social and public interest had been influenced, and how experts reflected upon their own background and premises. This, in turn, led to developing more normative approaches for drawing systems analysis goals (Wynne 1984).

Reflection Regarding Sustainability Assessment: In this phase, we can observe a paradigm shift in energy systems analysis. Each form of energy supply was attributed an absolute value of its risk. Furthermore, public and scientific opinion were calculated into units of risk (Otway & Fishbein, 1977). It became evident that guaranteeing and stabilizing energy supply and securing the implementation of nuclear policy had to be better embedded in the environmental discourse, mainly by comparing the risk of nuclear fission to the negative influence on the environment and society of conventional energy production. Thus, energy sustainability did not only refer to securing energy supply but required the inclusion of large-scale economic perspectives, as financial stakes were considerable, as well as of social values, in order to frame and stabilize policies in ways that would secure favorable public opinion.

2.3.1.4 Phase 3: Holistic Modeling through Technological and Methodological Consolidation (1975–1981)

After 1975, nuclear fission was still stridently contested. At the same time, the rising internal institutional influence of the Resources and Environment project (REN) influenced methods in the ESP. C. S. Holling consolidated the methodology of a global environmental systems analysis within IIASA's environmental modeling. REN developed global simulation models of ecosystems problems, focusing on the robustness of systems management and adaptation due to perturbation or resilience (IIASA 1979). Likewise, Holling's perspective on resilience and the increasing body of knowledge about atmospheric and greenhouse gas emissions provided a new impetus for ESP's analysis and its coupling of global models within ESP's risk-comparison models (Williams, 2013).

These developments led to another enlargement of the system boundary. The ESP systems analysis extended geographical visions to encompass a global scale and focused more specifically on the tracing of the long-term dynamics of a system, i.e., developing plausible macroeconomic scenarios up to the year 2030. In so doing, the IIASA ESP still maintained the social and environmental indicators for simulating the resilience of a system. Furthermore, when computer facilities doubled their calculation capacity (IIASA, 1978), the ESP "began the work of synthesising its research results" (IIASA, 1977).

In this phase, the goal of the ESP was to include the macroeconomic interconnectedness between energy demand and supply, while also evaluating the global ecological and social constraints over time. As such, the ESP was seeking to fulfill the needs of policymakers that combined nuclear energy policies with a development paradigm, stating that energy, and nuclear energy in particular, would sustain a rising world population, including food supply, pure air, shelter, and transportation. Key questions addressed within ESP were: How do resources and constraints on global energy demand codevelop? How can one accelerate nuclear energy innovation and yet respond to the criticism against nuclear energy as the most efficient and least risky energy technology?

To respond to these objectives, the ESP elaborated a procedural methodology of systems analysis that would assist policymakers in comparing the risks and benefits of different energy resources, particularly with the rising awareness of CO_2 emissions. IIASA ESP coined this new process WELMM, as it combined fine-grained sub-systems analyses of each energy source with analysis of its effect on water, energy, land, materials, and manpower. The WELMM approach fostered research about sustainable energy production, and also integrated decision-makers to participate in shaping a system's management aspects. The ESP relied on WELMM analyses to determine effective policy options. At first, energy chains, built upon activities that were performed by concurrent processes, were conceived within a system (IIASA, 1975). IIASA primarily focused on the testing of a system analysis chain for a nuclear reactor technology that amounted to the entire calculation of its technological composition (mining, milling, uranium enrichment, fuel manufacture, reactor construction, reactor operation, reprocessing, waste storage). After analyzing the interdependency of these indicators, the energy production chain was incorporated within a larger system of water, land, and material usage (IIASA, 1975). Thereupon, IIASA calculated an energy chain model for each energy option. Starting in 1977, WELMM data from computers were combined, which should in "its final form . . . become an integral part of the interlinked strategy model chain" (IIASA, 1977). These chain models were juxtaposed with large-scale world models which continued shaping systems analysis at IIASA until at least the beginning of the 1980s.

The complexity of energy systems within computerized simulations of world energy models and world environment models from WELMM made them unstable, particularly with the influences of what they called "social fabric" (Otway, 1975). Political movements opposed, in the opinion of the researchers, the researchers' own rationally elaborated models of risk estimations. The ESP interpreted its role as an apolitical and objective outside expert that would attempt to integrate the understanding of these "second (and higher) order consequences of a decision and the subsequent estimation" (Otway, 1975). To demarcate the efficiency of the IIASA in 1978, the WELMM approach resulted in a showroom – a fair to display ESP's scientific capacities, demonstrating, for example, ESP's computerized model of the environmental impact of coal-fired electric power plants that were hypothetically placed near an endangered river system (IIASA, 1978). The significance of ESP and the dispersion of their systems knowledge and monitoring capacity became international: the IIASA convened WELMM conferences with more than 135 outside participants from 22 countries (IIASA 1978). Energy systems analysis as a knowledge-based and problem-driven methodology was meant to provide a stable spectrum of energy in its environment, but without a political aim (IIASA 1978).

Reflection Regarding Sustainability Assessment: The WELMM approach provided the underlying structure for the ranking and provisions of long-term societal behavior. It prompted IIASA to reconsider and enlarge the social and environmental aspect of energy systems analyses. Public perception and environmental resource depletion represented important factors that would harm the stability of any energy chain when tested within the WELMM approach. The ESP was severely concerned by the influence of society on the planning of energy transitions. The inclusion of societal matters as a study of "resilience of a trajectory" remained crucial in ESP's "topological representation of macroeconomic-societal models" (Häfele, 1976). Thus, in the sustainability assessment of the different energy transition options, it meant that researchers as well as politicians had to deal with more holistic and less certain model outputs, which, while claimed by different groups, also decreased the credibility of the models themselves.

2.3.1.5 Lessons Learned and the Pitfalls of ESP's Systems Approach

When analyzing the development of ESP's system approach from 1970 to 1981, we observe a coevolution between the integration of contextual factors on the one hand and the related turn to sustainability assessment of energy transition options on the other. This manifested itself first in the analysis of systems and the models themselves through changes in the system boundaries chosen, the widening of the goals of the model, and the processes

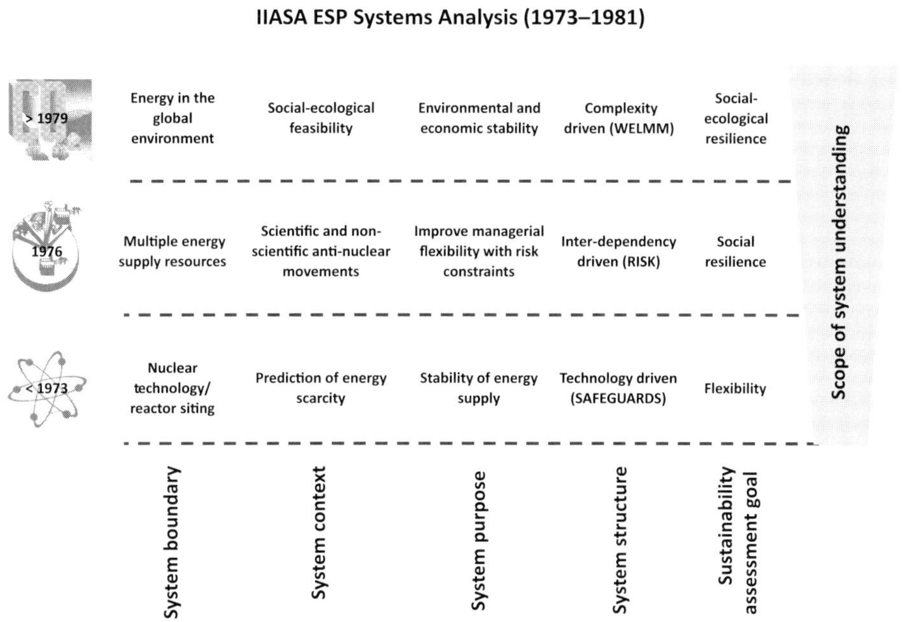

Figure 2.2 Development of systems elements and the evolving scope of system understanding during three phases of the ESP (1973–1981). Source: own illustration

included within the model. We can observe that the definition of systems concepts developed from technology-centered to resilience-centered approaches within systems analysis. Concomitantly, ESP models evolved during the 1970s from technological analyses to large-scale projects that included social, economic, and environmental factors as constraints. Thus, it became possible to assess different scenarios, and their sustainability, from a technological, environmental, economic, and social point of view.

Second, when IIASA first started including social values and the society in its research portfolio, these were mainly aggregated parameters that influenced the analysis. At the end of the 1970s, however, a shift in the (epistemological) understanding of the role of scientific research in itself had occurred: systems analysis in the energy sector required a more elaborated inclusion of social factors and became a setting where support for the involvement of different actors during several stages of a systems analysis became state-of-the-art (Clark et al., 1979). Thus, actors may play different roles in the definition of the system for sustainability assessment. On the one hand, they represent the focus of the study (parameters); on the other hand, if they are included in developing the analysis themselves, their values and perspectives enter into the system definition and later on the assessment (see Chapter 4 (Fritz & Meinherz, 2020)).

Third, ESP research highlighted a certain path dependency in system development and the assessment process itself. In the case of IIASA, one can observe that some of the basic assumptions and objectives IIASA had with respect to energy policymaking work were challenged in the 1980s. Nevertheless, certain factors and relationships were favored, while others, depending on IIASA's institutional priorities, were ignored (Wynne, 1984). Even though ESP researchers noted the limited extent of any modeling project (Basile et al., 1980), the ESP considered their model scenarios as being of objective scientific value (Wynne, 1984). IIASA continuously promoted the image of systems analysis as a general methodology that could be used for different settings, but already a change of very basic systems premises demonstrated that the ESP systems were strongly linked to nuclear energy and originated in IIASA's premises for the making of energy systems analyses (Wynne 1984).

In this respect, the ESP case once again reflects how the historical development and contextual struggles out of which certain models have emerged, when aiming to recycle sustainability models approaches, influenced current methods of systems thinking. It is therefore crucial to understand the changes in the definition of research problems, and the context that shaped the reasoning and pre-analysis of its objectives, when applying previously used systems methods. This case study urges us to historicize our own methodological practices: in this case, a widely spread methodological toolset at the ESP at IIASA represented a complex pathway of systems analysis that became de-contextualized from the primary objectives of its creators.

2.3.2 Case Study 2: Australian Urban Systems Transformation (AUST) Initiative

Australian cities are facing major sustainable development challenges. These include:

- managing significant future population growth (e.g., Melbourne and Sydney are both projected to double in size to eight million people by 2061) while reducing resource footprints and decarbonizing the cities' processes;
- increasing resilience to externally driven change, including climate, technological, and economic change;
- fostering innovation and economic productivity; and
- addressing growing inequity in citizens' access to affordable housing, infrastructure, services, and jobs.

Australia already has a very high level of urbanization, and there is increasing recognition that cities will largely determine success or failure in overall sustainability. Between 2015 and 2017, an interdisciplinary network of Australia-based researchers initiated a codesign exercise with urban stakeholders (policy- and decision-makers) from national, state, regional, and local levels, which became the Australian Urban Systems Transformation (AUST) initiative (Webb et al., 2018a). The objective was to see how the urban challenges could be collaboratively framed and addressed in a more holistic way, bringing about transformational change toward sustainability. It also aimed to inform the agenda for Future Earth Australia (FEA) which was established in 2016 as the local link to Future Earth (Future Earth, 2014).

The initiative identified existing barriers to sustainable urban development in Australian cities, and priority urban issues that provide high leverage for transformational change. This included the need for a "whole-of-system" approach to address multiple goals and related synergies and trade-offs, as well as the development of an "urban systems framework" (Webb et al., 2018a, figure 2) to assist urban knowledge development, mapping, and sharing.

To relate the case study experience to systems science concepts, the system characteristics and axioms summarized in Section 2.2.3 of this chapter have been mapped onto the components of the urban systems framework (see Figure 2.3).

The choice of decision-making domain (which corresponds to the "subject of sustainability assessment" – see Chapter 1 (Halla & Binder, 2020) was "integrated metropolitan-regional scale urban strategies for individual cities," which, in relation to the four subject levels identified in Chapter 1 (Halla & Binder, 2020), corresponds to "Level 3: persistent or wicked problems/issues."

With this context, we summarize how systems science concepts relate to the case study under each component of the urban systems framework and how they relate to the sustainability assessment of Australian cities.

2.3.2.1 System Boundary, Context, and Environment

The choice of decision-making domain established the initial scope (boundary) as being a high-level understanding of the key sustainable development issues facing each of Australia's federal and state capital cities and their associated regions, with no limitation on sectors (holism principle). The time horizon was around 30 years to encourage transformative thinking.

Pitching the boundary at this relatively high level provides significant leverage for urban sustainability and decision-making. Looking within the boundary, it forces the analysis of key interdependencies between subsystems that make up the city. Beyond the boundary, it highlights the federal and state government policies and programs and other key external drivers, and impacts on the surrounding region, and beyond (e.g., resource use, GHG emissions).

Such broad framing raises the degree of difficulty in analyzing the system – one reason why many sustainability assessments start at lower levels and progressively extend upwards as more systemic issues become apparent. However, starting at the higher level can better challenge current personal/institutional mental models, values, and practices, while still encouraging lower-level niche activities. It was also recognized that knowledge and complexity limitations require taking several partial and complementary views of the city to build understanding of the whole system (darkness and complementarity principles).

2.3.2.2 System Goals and Decision-Making

The boundary-setting determines which stakeholders need to be involved initially, and this in turn facilitates the codetermination of goals and related design and decision making principles and opportunities.

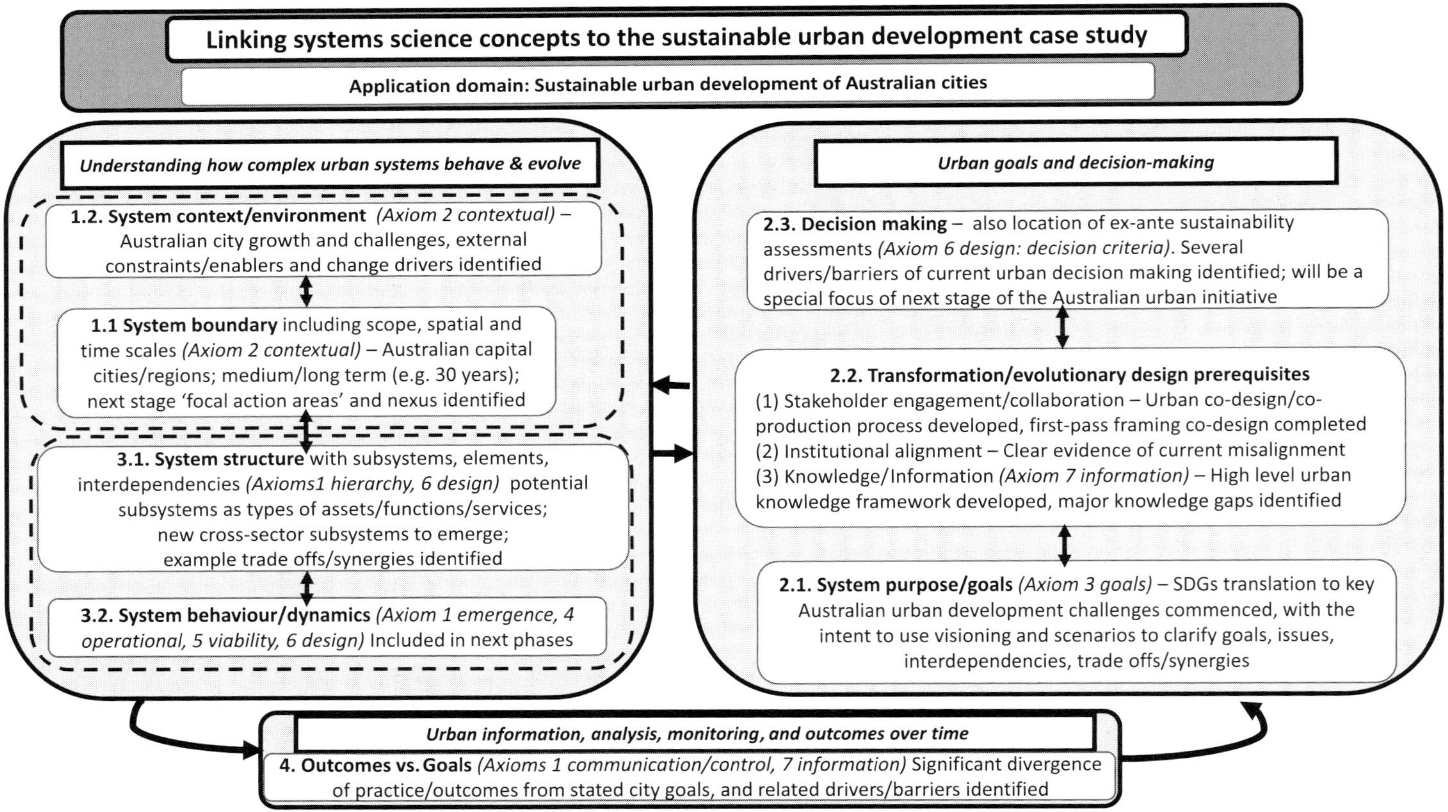

Figure 2.3 Conceptual systems characteristics (bold type) and axioms (italics) (see Table 2.1) mapped onto the urban systems framework (based on Webb et al. (2018a, figure 2))

Setting Goals. It was considered that future city planning would benefit from a translation of the UN Sustainable Development Goals (United Nations, 2015) into the Australian cities context, noting that all 17 goals are relevant to urban development (United Cities and Local Governments, 2015). Some work has commenced on this, identifying a smaller number of Australian-specific urban goals (the requisite parsimony principle) and developing an improved understanding of key interdependencies. These goals will aim for the city-region systems to be healthy and develop in their environment (viability axiom), and through transformation move beyond self-preservation toward local and global sustainability.

Meeting multiple goals and interdependencies invoked a number of systems science perspectives:

- Urban sustainability assessment requires a complex social-ecological-technical systems (SETS) understanding (McPhearson et al., 2016), and this needs to be reflected in any sustainability indicators selected.
- Typical urban trade-offs and synergies were identified, and it was recognized that resolving these will require stakeholder-informed decision-making rules (requisite saliency); and that some trade-offs (e.g., where infrastructure redundancy is less efficient but provides greater resilience) will mean that not all goals can be optimized (satisficing principle).
- Dynamic, emergent, and uncertain system outcomes will require iterative systems analysis and progressive boundary and goal modifications (e.g., extending or contracting the scope) either during an ex ante assessment process or following an ex post assessment.

As a foundational step to address these issues, the AUST initiative has prioritized collaborative urban visioning and scenario development for Australian cities, to better understand alternative, feasible, and preferred urban systems outcomes and pathways (equifinality and multifinality principles) and to identify key system interdependencies.

Decision-Making Support for urban decision-making at all levels is a central objective of the AUST initiative, with a focus on priority areas identified in the framing stage and identifying key decision entry points in organizations' business processes (Webb et al., 2018b). This is also the location of ex ante sustainability assessment processes. The preceding boundary- and goal-setting provide a basis for designing an assessment process that meets leading practice effectiveness criteria and uses the most appropriate systems analysis methods and tools (see Chapter 1 (Halla & Binder, 2020)).

The AUST analysis concluded that addressing increasing Australian city pressures will require intentional evolutionary design and planning (Costanza, 2014), working on key systems leverage points (Abson et al., 2017), complemented by local innovations and recognition of the self-organizing nature of cities (Portugali et al., 2012). Given the complexities, timescales, and uncertainties involved, there will also be an emphasis on adaptive pathways and learning approaches (Wise et al., 2014).

Support for evolutionary systems change requires standing in the shoes of the decision-makers and stakeholders who need to take ownership of the key design objectives (urban goals, design principles, and decision criteria). However, it was also apparent from the outset that, in the urban case, no one "owns" the overall system. A key challenge therefore is to assist decision-makers and stakeholders to see themselves as being within the overall system (components 1 and 3 in Figure 2.3), and thus subject to other system influences, and not merely outside and operating on the system (components 2 and 4 in Figure 2.3).

The AUST framework also confirmed the significance of three prerequisites for transformational decision-making to take effect (Gorddard et al., 2016):

(a) **Aligned Stakeholder Values and Goals:** The systems view requires engagement with a very broad range of stakeholders. The initial codesign process (Webb et al., 2018a, figure 1) focused on researchers working with decision-makers from national, state, regional, and local government agencies who are most likely to take a systemic view. The next stage, moving to collective visioning and specific strategies, is involving the private and community sectors, as well as a more extensive coverage of Australian government and research institutions, and will require a variety of engagement techniques to expose and address alignment issues (e.g., network analysis, workshopping, participatory modeling, experimental and demonstration pilots, narratives and storytelling).

(b) **Aligned Institutional Arrangements:** It became clear that many of the current barriers to urban sustainability are institutional: e.g., a lack of shared vision and values; a lack of coherence of policy and practice across and within governance levels; and narrowly framed and shorter-term decision-making. This confirmed the need to engage with the government and coordinating agencies most likely to influence future institutional arrangements.

(c) **Relevant and Accessible Knowledge about the System:** A review of Australian urban research concluded that while several programs focus on sectoral issues (e.g., energy, water, housing, planning), there is little research on systemic multiple-goal, cross-sector, and cross-scale issues, especially at the broader spatial scale (from the precinct to the city and beyond). There is also fragmentation of the knowledge base and issues of accessibility and usability of both existing and new solutions-oriented knowledge. To address these gaps, an FEA/AUST national symposium of researchers has agreed to codevelop with stakeholders a National Strategic Plan for urban knowledge.

2.3.2.3 System Structure and Dynamics

The overall urban system, as the ultimate in social-ecological-technical systems (McPhearson et al., 2016), combines elements of all of the systems types identified in Figure 2.1, and may be broken down into subsystems in several ways. A key judgement is how to segment the system into subsystems (hierarchy principle) that keep analysis and action manageable (again, the parsimony principle applies), but still provide major transformational leverage on the multiple goals.

This has only been explored at a broad level to date, drawing on concepts such as urban patterns, processes, and metabolisms; urban functions and services; and multiple feedbacks (Batty, 2009; Bettencourt, 2013; Grimm et al., 2015; Pickett et al., 2016); and the need to take both the spatial and process views to analyze urban sustainability. However new subsystem concepts and boundaries are likely to evolve as the issues at the next level down are framed, which will provide useful windows into the urban system (complementarity principle).

For example, the AUST process identified a small number of high-leverage "focal action areas" for future stages to capture the most significant system issues, processes, and interdependencies (e.g., the "land use-transport-productivity-health nexus" and associated processes mostly in this case of service delivery; also the "decarbonization-resilience-productivity-health nexus," the "food-energy-water nexus," and "sustainable consumption and production" analysis, all with substantial goods- and service-delivery process components). In each case, analysis also needs to reflect information and decision-making processes, and to be assessed across multiple urban spatial scales and in the context of current issues in specific cities. Analyzing such major urban subsystems and the connection between them would give a more holistic understanding of the urban system.

The initiative also summarized commonly stated "sustainable urban development planning and design principles" (Webb et al., 2018a) but it was acknowledged that the evidence base behind many of these is weak, especially for application in a complex systems context. Also, integrated modeing capability was found to be good at the building and precinct levels, but much less developed at the broader spatial scales (see also The Ecological Sequestration Trust, 2013).

Therefore, next-level analyses will need to better reflect the other aspects of systems structure and dynamics (e.g., emergence, feedback cycles, dynamic equilibrium, tipping points, self-organization) with identification of leverage points to design and implement strategic policy and practice interventions. Occasional examples of such features were raised in the AUST process and discussions, but the challenge ahead is to address urban analysis and understanding, especially at the broader spatial scales, in a far more systematic way.

2.3.2.4 System Information, Monitoring, and Learning: Outcomes against Goals

This is the natural location for ex post sustainability assessments, and ideally leads to learning and follow-up action, adaptive management being especially important for complex systems. Indeed, the AUST initiative carried out a synthesis of goals and design principles from current long-term planning documents for each capital city and concluded that while they were generally consistent with sustainability aspirations, actual decisions on the ground are, in many critical areas, making such goals unachievable. A set of key drivers of such decisions and related barriers/enablers to achieving the goals were identified, both internal and external to the city. These included the lack of a shared urban vision across multiple stakeholders; inconsistent and fragmented policy- and decision-making between and across the three levels of government in Australia; conflicting incentives and values across state and local government, developers, and the community; and a genuine lack of and/or fragmentation of knowledge and support for more complex and holistic decision-making. These insights have underpinned the need to develop a transformative urban initiative going forward.

2.3.2.5 Lessons Learned

More specific lessons learned from the codesign project to date have been incorporated into the Discussion, Section 2.4. However, an overarching finding was that the level of urban systems transformation required for sustainable development will only be achieved with major changes to current institutional arrangements at national, state, and metropolitan levels, challenging many existing norms and practices. Bringing about such change will require long-term collaborative effort, transcending normal political and business cycles. Building on the framing stage, Future Earth Australia, supported by the Australian Academy of Science, is now working with all stakeholders to codevelop such an approach, initially focussing on enhanced national urban knowledge development and use, this being crucial in its own right, but also as a lever into broader stakeholder and institutional support, understanding, and change.

2.4 Discussion and Concluding Remarks

This chapter provides an insight into the role of systems sciences for sustainability assessment. Based on the seven axioms and next-level-down principles developed by Adams et al. (2014) and Hester and Adams (2017), we propose a way to structure and analyze systems following four system characteristics:

1. System boundary, and interactions with the external environment
2. Purpose, goals, and associated decision-making drivers and criteria for the system
3. System structure (subsystems, elements, and their interactions), dynamics, and emerging behavior
4. System information, outcomes monitoring, and learning

These four characteristics provide an excellent guideline for developing a system analysis within these broader systems perspectives that supports sustainability assessment. Two case studies provided examples of approaches to sustainability and related issues.

In the first case study, the energy systems analysis at IIASA demonstrated that the criteria upon which the "sustainability" of the energy system was assessed evolved from securing energy supply, to reducing risks, to including societal desirability and acceptability of energy production. It became clear that the four system characteristics are interconnected and that the way in which the sustainability of the energy system was defined and interpreted was shaped through changes in the entire system environment. In fact, feedback through societal and technological interventions, scientific opposition, and international cooperation fueled the changes in the system definition and subsequent systems modeing.

Thus, we have to be aware that defining goals and finding solutions to large-scale problems of systems were and are likely to be highly influenced by political and social debates. As shown for the case of energy, societal and political worldviews constantly reshaped the systems analysis approach and methodology, from its origins that assumed depoliticized, objective criteria (Rindzevičiūtė, 2016). This dilemma also informs current approaches in sustainability assessment in respect to how paradigms of researchers and a primarily technological framing can unduly shape the outcome of any analysis.

The second case study, of Australian cities, represents the early stages of an ambition to analyze and assess urban sustainability from a broader whole-of-system perspective across sectors, across scales (spatial and temporal), and across institutional boundaries and levels. While framed initially at the whole-of-city/whole-of-region level, it also recognizes the importance of complementing this with various subsystem analyses and local niche activities, any of which could be the subject of sustainability assessments. The urban systems framework, developed as part of this AUST case study, maps well onto the systems concepts introduced earlier in this chapter. However, in the real-world collaborative process, they emerged in a much messier way than implied by the framework. Insights developed on multiple components at once, initially without clear interconnections. This reflected the different initial framing of issues by diverse participants, and at least at the outset, the lack of a shared or agreed upon systems framework to work with.

While the diverse participants in the AUST codesign process reached consensus on findings relatively quickly, it was acknowledged that a key issue in collaborative system-change projects is the difficulty participants have in influencing their own institutions to look outside their traditional roles (Polk, 2015). This applies not only to deciding and bringing about the change itself but also to gaining collective agreement on the associated ex ante and ex post sustainability assessments that reflect a necessary systems understanding. Future AUST stages involving a broader range of government as well as private- and community-sector stakeholders will undoubtedly find this more challenging. It will require long-term collaborative effort that transcends normal political and business cycles. In this context, we become aware – from the AUST case study – that stakeholder engagement to understand diverse normative values, issues in gaining institutional and governance alignment, and the way information or system knowledge is available and shared, will add additional perspectives to be considered when designing a sustainability assessment procedure for urban systems (see also Chapter 3 (Meinherz et al., 2020) and Chapter 4 (Fritz & Meinherz, 2020)), especially when transformational change is sought. Coproduced knowledge can help change and enhance underlying systems understanding and the development of more holistic urban systems sustainability assessments, and so better support individual decisions. This is therefore the focus of the next stage of this national AUST initiative.

Drawing on the theory and the case studies, we can summarize the implications from systems science for sustainability assessment of urban systems as follows:

- Cities (and indeed smaller urban settlements) are among the most complex social-ecological-technical systems, such that sustainability assessment needs to start from a systems

perspective to identify interdependencies, trade-offs and synergies, and emergent properties at various levels. This requires definition and understanding of the relevant system, as well as its subsystems and processes, and a systemic approach to decision-making.
- The systems analysis framework presented here, comprising the four generic system characteristics, informed by seven systems-science axioms and their associated design principles, provide a good basis for putting the elements of a system analysis into its broader context, and designing purposeful interventions. Especially for more transformational change, alignment of stakeholder values, institutional arrangements, and available knowledge become key leverage points.
- We have to be aware that the definition of the system as well as the assessment of the sustainability of urban systems might, as it was for the energy system, be highly contested and determined by political processes and normative developments in the society. As such, we have to consider the effect of the context of the system on system definition and the interpretation of the assessment results.
- In a systems approach to sustainability assessment there are always choices as to how to frame the issue, and these will help determine the "subject of assessment" (see Chapter 1 (Halla & Binder, 2020)). In the urban context, there is value in assessments at multiple levels which can support practical decision-making while also progressively leading to whole-of-city (and beyond) sustainable development.
- Developing key indicators is still important for sustainability assessments, developed and agreed in ex ante assessments and monitored in ex post assessments. However, targets and associated indicators need to reflect interdependent goals, key leverage points, and proxy indicators that demonstrate the health of system development. It may or may not be possible to map these as triple bottom line (social, economic, environmental) indicators, but this is less important than the fact that they should derive from a true systems understanding.
- Complex urban systems are emergent with uncertain outcomes, such that decision-making for sustainability needs to be seen as a process and not an endpoint. Therefore, sustainability assessment indicators should focus not only on system performance at a particular point in time, or projected into the future, but also on the extent and quality of systemic understanding, analysis, and adaptive management processes in place.

Systems-based sustainability assessments can be challenging but are necessary if consistent progress is to be made on sustainable urban development. The frameworks presented in Chapter 1 (Halla & Binder, 2020) and this chapter, supported by systems-based case studies and growing experience, provide a robust conceptual platform for such assessments.

Acknowledgments

The authors thank Kevin Adams, Livia Fritz, Pekka Halla, and Susan Mühlemeier for their excellent comments and review, Hannah Robertson for language editing, and Charlène-Aurore Ruppli and Marta G. Baldi for organizational support.

Note

1. The decision of the OPEC states led to a fourfold increase in oil prices (Graf, 2014).

References

Abson, D. J., Fischer, J., Leventon, J., et al. (2017). Leverage points for sustainability transformation. *Ambio*, 46(1), 30–39.

Adams, K., Hester, P., Bradley, J., Meyers. T. J., & Keating, C. (2014). Systems theory as the foundation for understanding systems. *Systems Engineering*, 17(1). DOI:http://10.1002/sys.21255.

Adetunji, I. O., Price, A. D. F., Fleming, P. R., & Kemp, P. (2003). The application of systems thinking to the concept of sustainability. https://dspace.lboro.ac.uk/dspace-jspui/handle/2134/19873.

Aristotle. (2002). *Metaphysics, Book H: Form and being at work*, J. Sachs, Trans., 2nd edition. Santa Fe: Green Lion Press.

Ashby, W. R. (1947). Principles of the self-organizing dynamic system. *The Journal of General Psychology*, 37(2), 125–128. DOI:http://10.1080/00221309.1947.9918144.

Ashby, W. R. (1956). *An Introduction to Cybernetics*. New York: J. Wiley.

Audouin, M., & de Wet, B. (2012). Sustainability thinking in environmental assessment. *Impact Assessment and Project Appraisal*, 30(4), 264–274. DOI:http://10.1080/14615517.2012.742695.

Aulin-Ahmavaara, A. (1979). The law of requisite hierarchy. *Kybernetes*, 8(4), 259–266.

Baccini, P., & Bader, H.-P. (1996). Regionaler Stoffhaushalt. Heidelberg7 Spektrum Akademischer Verlag. www.ulb.tu-darmstadt.de/tocs/48751952.pdf.

Basile, P. S., Agnew, M., Hölzl, A., et al. (1980). *The IIASA set of energy models: Its design and application*. Laxenburg, Austria: International Institute for Applied Systems Analysis. http://pure.iiasa.ac.at/12459/.

Batty, M. (2009). Cities as complex systems: Scaling, interaction, networks, dynamics and urban morphologies. In R. A. Meyers (ed.), *Encyclopaedia of Complexity and Systems Science*. New York: Springer, pp. 1041–1071. DOI:https://doi.org/10.1007/978-0-387-30440-3_69.

Beer, S. (1979). *The Heart of Enterprise*. New York: John Wiley & Sons.

Bertalanffy, L. von. (1949). General systems theory. *Biologia Generalis*, 19(1), 114–129.

Bertalanffy, L. von. (1950). An outline of general system theory. *The British Journal for the Philosophy of Science*, 1(2), 134–165.

Bertalanffy, L. von. (1962). *Modern Theories of Development: An Introduction to Theoretical Biology*, J. H. Woodger, Trans. New York: Harper.

Bertalanffy, L. von. (1968). *General System Theory: Foundations, Development, Applications*, revised ed. New York: George Braziller.

Bettencourt, L. (2013). *The kind of problem a city is* (Working Paper 2013–03-008). Santa Fe, USA: Santa Fe Institute. www.santafe.edu/research/results/working-papers/the-kind-of-problem-a-city-is.

Binder, C. R., Baldi, M. G., Gex, B., & Massaro, E. (2020b). The sustainability solution space. In C. R. Binder, E. Massaro, & R. Wyss (eds.), *Sustainability Assessment in Urban Systems*. Cambridge University Press, pp. 181–208.

Binder, C. R., Mühlemeier, S., & Wyss, R. (2017). An indicator-based approach for analyzing the resilience of transitions for energy regions. Part I: Theoretical and conceptual considerations. *Energies*, 10(1), 36. DOI:http://10.3390/en10010036.

Blackmore, C., Reynolds, M., Ison, R., & Lane, A. (2015). Embedding sustainability through systems thinking in practice: some experiences from the Open University. In L. Wyness (ed.), *Education for Sustainable Development Pedagogy: Criticality, Creativity, and Collaboration*. Pedrio Occasional Paper 8, pp. 32–35.

Boesch, A., & de Montmollin, A. (2020). Indicators for assessing the sustainability of cities. In C. R. Binder, E. Massaro, & R. Wyss (eds.), *Sustainability Assessment in Urban Systems*. Cambridge University Press, pp. 311–331.

Bohr, N. (1928). The quantum postulate and the recent development of atomic theory. *Nature*, 121 (3050), 580–590.

Bossel, H. (1999). Indicators for sustainable development: Theory, method, applications. A report to the Balaton Group, International Institute for Sustainable Development. www.ulb.ac.be/ceese/STAFF/Tom/bossel.pdf.
Bossel, H. (2003). Assessing viability and sustainability: A systems-based approach for deriving comprehensive indicator sets. *Conservation Ecology*, 5(2). DOI:http://10.5751/ES-00332-050212.
Boulding, K. E. (1956). General systems theory: The skeleton of science. *Management Science*, 2(3) 197–208. DOI:http://10.1287/mnsc.2.3.197.
Boulding, K. E. (1966). *The Impact of the Social Sciences*. Bombay: Vakils, Feffer and Simons Private.
Buckley, W. (1967). *Sociology and Modern Systems Theory*. Oxford, UK: Prentice-Hall.
Bunge, M. (1997). Mechanism and explanation. *Philosophy of the Social Sciences*, 27(4), 410–465.
Bunge, M. (2004). How does it work?: The search for explanatory mechanisms. *Philosophy of the Social Sciences*, 34(2), 182–210. DOI:http://10.1177/0048393119702700402.
Cannon, W. B. (1929). Organisation for physiological homeostasis. *Physiological Reviews*, 9(3), 399–431. DOI:http://10.1152/physrev.1929.9.3.399.
Checkland, P. B. (1993). *Systems Thinking, Systems Practice*. New York: Wiley.
Cherns, A. (1976). The principles of sociotechnical design. *Human Relations*, 29(8), 783–792. DOI: http://10.1177/001872677602900806.
Cherns, A. (1987). Principles of sociotechnical design revisited. *Human Relations*, 40(3), 153–161. DOI:http://10.1177/001872678704000303.
Cilliers, P. (1998). *Complexity and Postmodernism: Understanding Complex Systems*. London: Routledge.
Cilliers, P. (2005). Complexity, deconstruction and relativism. *Theory, Culture & Society*, 22(5), 255–267. DOI:http://10.1177/0263276405058052.
Cilliers, P. (2008). Complexity theory as a general framework for sustainability science. *Exploring Sustainable Science: A South African Perspective*, 39–57.
Clark, W. C., Jones, D. D., & Holling, C. (1979). Lessons for ecological policy design: a case study of ecosystem management. *Ecological Modelling*, 7(1), 1–53.
Costanza, R. (2014). A theory of socio-ecological system change. *Journal of Bioeconomics*, 16(1), 39–44.
Cruz, I., Stahel, A., & Max-Neef, M. (2009). Towards a systemic development approach: Building on the Human-Scale Development paradigm. *Ecological Economics*, 68(7), 2021–2030.
d'Alembert, J. le R. (1743). *Traité de l'équilibre et du mouvement des fluids*. Librarie David, l'aîné: Paris.
Fiksel, J. (2006). Sustainability and resilience: toward a systems approach. *Sustainability: Science, Practice, & Policy*, 2(2), 14–21.
Fritz, L., & Meinherz, F. (2020). The politics of participatory sustainability assessments: an analysis of power. In C. R. Binder, E. Massaro, & R. Wyss (eds.), *Sustainability Assessment in Urban Systems*. Cambridge University Press, pp. 87–122.
Forrester, J. W. (1961). *Industrial Dynamics*. Cambridge, MA: MIT Press.
Forrester, J. W. (1969). *Urban Dynamics*. Cambridge, MA: MIT Press.
Forrester, J. W. (1971). *World Dynamics*. Cambridge, MA: MIT Press.
Future Earth. (2014). Future Earth Strategic Research Agenda 2014: Priorities for a global sustainability research agenda. Science Committee and Interim Engagement Committee. www.futureearth.org/sites/default/files/strategic_research_agenda_2014.pdf.
Gallopín, G. (2003). *A Systems Approach to Sustainability and Sustainable Development*. United Nations Publications.
Gasparatos, A., El-Haram, M., & Horner, M. (2009). The argument against a reductionist approach for measuring sustainable development performance and the need for methodological pluralism. *Accounting Forum*, 33(3), 245–256.
Gorddard, R., Colloff, M. J., Wise, R. M., Ware, D., & Dunlop, M. (2016). Values, rules and knowledge: Adaptation as change in the decision context. *Environmental Science & Policy*, 57, 60–69.

Grace, W., & Pope, J. (2015). A systems approach to sustainability assessment. In A., Morrison-Saunders, J. Pope, & A. Bond (eds.), *Handbook of Sustainability Assessment*. Northampton, MA: Edward Elgar, pp. 285–320. DOI:http://10.4337/9781783471379.

Graf, R. (2014). *Öl und Souveränität: Petroknowledge und Energiepolitik in den USA und Westeuropa in den 1970er Jahren*. Walter de Gruyter.

Grimm, N. B., Cook, E. M., Hale, R. L., & Iwaniec, D. M. (2015). *A Broader Framing of Ecosystem Services in Cities*. Routledge Handbooks Online. DOI:10.4324/9781315849256.ch14.

Häfele, W. (1974). *Future Energy Resources*. Laxenburg, Austria: International Institute of Applied Systems Analysis. http://pure.iiasa.ac.at/id/eprint/74/1/RR-74-020.pdf.

Häfele, W. (1976). *Second Status Report of the IIASA Project on Energy Systems*. Laxenburg, Austria: International Institute of Applied Systems Analysis. http://pure.iiasa.ac.at/542/.

Halla, P., & Binder, C.R. (2020). Sustainability Assessment: Introduction and Framework. In C. R. Binder, E. Massaro, & R. Wyss (eds.), *Sustainability Assessment in Urban Systems*. Cambridge University Press, pp. 7–29.

Hammond, D. (2002). Exploring the genealogy of systems thinking. *Systems Research and Behavioral Science*, 19(5), 429–439. DOI:http://10.1002/sres.499.

Hammond, D. (2003). *The Science of Synthesis: Exploring the Social Implications of General Systems Theory*. Boulder: University Press of Colorado.

Helmer, O. (1967). Memorandum M-2027 15 March 1967. Sent to Tom Brown, Herbert Coldhamer, Oleg Hoeffding, Arnold Horelick, Roger Levien, Richard Nelson, Ed Quade, Harry Rowen, Sid Winter, Albert Wholstetter, and Charles Wolf, "Addendum to my previous Memo M-1929, On the East-West Center." Ford Foundation Archive.

Hester, P. T., & Adams, K. M. (2017). *Systemic Decision Making:Fundamentals for Understanding Problems and Messes*, 2nd ed. Cham: Springer International Publishing.

Hieronymi, A. (2013). Understanding Systems Science: A Visual and Integrative Approach. *Systems Research and Behavioral Science*, 30(5), 580–595.

Hitch, C. (1953). Sub-optimization in operations problems. *Journal of the Operations Research Society of America*, 1(3), 87–99. DOI:http://10.1287/opre.1.3.87.

Holling, C. S. (1996). Engineering resilience versus ecological resilience. In Schulze P., ed., *Engineering within Ecological Constraints*. Washington DC: National Academies Press, pp. 31–43.

Hunt, P. (1975). Funds position: Keystone in financial planning. *Harvard Business Review*, 53(3), 106–115.

IAEA Archives. (1975). Letter from Jan M. Døderlein, Director Safety Dept., Institut for Atomeneri, Kjeller, Norway to Otway. 16.12.1975, IAEA/IIASA Joint Cooperation.

IIASA. (1973). *IIASA Annual Report 1973*. Laxenburg, Austria: International Institute for Applied Systems Analysis.

IIASA. (1974). *IIASA Annual Report 1974*. Laxenburg, Austria: International Institute for Applied Systems Analysis.

IIASA. (1975). *IIASA Annual Report 1975*. Laxenburg, Austria: International Institute for Applied Systems Analysis.

IIASA. (1976). *IIASA Annual Report 1976*. Laxenburg, Austria: International Institute for Applied Systems Analysis.

IIASA. (1977). *IIASA Annual Report 1977*. Laxenburg, Austria: International Institute for Applied Systems Analysis.

IIASA. (1978). *IIASA Annual Report 1978*. Laxenburg, Austria: International Institute for Applied Systems Analysis.

IIASA. (1979). *IIASA Annual Report 1979*. Laxenburg, Austria: International Institute for Applied Systems Analysis.

Ison, R. (1999). Applying systems thinking to higher education. *Systems Research & Behavioral Science*, 16(2), 107–112. DOI:http://10.1002/(SICI)1099-1743(199903/04)16:2<07::aid-sres278>3.0.CO;2-E.

Jasanoff, S., & Kim, S.-H. (2009). Containing the atom: Sociotechnical imaginaries and nuclear power in the United States and South Korea. *Minerva*, 47(2), 119.

Kaplan, M. M. (1976). 26th Pugwash Conference Mühlhausen, Report of the Director-General. In Leo Szilard Papers, California Digital Library. https://library.ucsd.edu/dc/object/bb7578448 h.

Kauffman, S. A. (1990). The Sciences of Complexity and "Origins of Order." In *PSA: Proceedings of the Biennial Meeting of the Philosophy of Science Association*. Chicago: Philosophy of Science Association, pp. 299–322.

Kay, J. J., Regier, H. A., Boyle, M., & Francis, G. (1999). An ecosystem approach for sustainability: Addressing the challenge of complexity. *Futures*, 31(7), 721–742.

Keppie, D. M. (2006). Context, emergence, and research design. *Wildlife Society Bulletin*, 34(1), 242–246.

Klir, G. J. (1968). *An Approach to General Systems Theory*. Princeton, NJ: Nostrand.

Korzybski, A. (1994). *Science and Sanity: an Introduction to Non-Aristotelian Systems and General Semantics*, 5th edition. Englewood, NJ: Institute of General Semantics.

Lambert, J. H. (1782). *Logische und philosophische Abhandlungen*, vol. 1. Berlin/Dessau/Leipzig.

Laszlo, E. (1972). *Introduction to Systems Philosophy: Towards a New Paradigm of Contemporary Thought*. New York: Gordon and Breach, Science Publishers.

Laszlo, E. (1975). *The Systems View of the World: The Natural Philosophy of the New Developments in the Sciences*. Creskill, NJ: Hampton Press.

Levai, A. (1977). 27th Pugwash Conference Munich, FRG- – Where lies the real danger of nuclear power? In Leo Szilard Papers, California Digital Library. https://library.ucsd.edu/dc/object/bb0138107 n.

Levien, R. E. (2000). RAND, IIASA, and the conduct of systems analysis. In A. C. Hughes & T. P. Hughes (eds.), *Systems, Experts, and Computers: The Systems Approach in Management and Engineering, World War II and After*. Cambridge, MA: MIT Press.

Linton, J. D., Klassen, R., & Jayaraman, V. (2007). Sustainable supply chains: An introduction. *Journal of Operations Management*, 25(6), 1075–1082.

Luhmann, N. (1995). *Social Systems* (Bednarz, J. trans., Baecker D. ed.). Stanford University Press.

Maiteny, P., & Ison, R. (1997)."Learner-Centred Evaluation of Systems, Systems Courses, and Future Needs in Systems Learning. In Frank A. Stowell, Ray L. Ison, Rosalind Armson, Jacky Holloway, Sue Jackson, & Steve McRobb (eds.), *Systems for Sustainability*. Boston: Springer, pp. 257–262.

Meinherz, F., Fritz, L., & Schneider, F. (2020). How Values Play into Sustainability Assessments: Challenges and a Possible Way Forward. In C. R. Binder, E. Massaro, & R. Wyss (eds.), *Sustainability Assessment in Urban Systems*. Cambridge University Press, (pp. 65–86).

Max-Neef, M. A., Elizalde, A., & Hopenhayn, M. (1991). *Human Scale Development: Conception, Application and Further Reflections*. New York: Apex Press.

McCulloch, W. S., Arbib, M. A., Lettvin, J. Y., & Papert, S. A. (1959). *Embodiments of Mind*. Cambridge, MA: MIT Press.

McPhearson, T., Pickett, S. T. A., Grimm, N. B., et al. (2016). Advancing urban ecology toward a science of cities. *BioScience*, 66(3), 198–212.

Meadows, D. H., Meadows, D. L., Randers, J., & Behrens, W.W. (1972). *The Limits to Growth: A Report for the Club of Rome's Project on the Predicament of Mankind*. New York: Universe Books.

Meadows, D. H. (1998). *Indicators and Information Systems for Sustainable Development: A Report to the Balaton Group*. Hartland Four Corners, VT: The Sustainability Institute.

Meadows, D. H. (2008). *Thinking in Systems: A Primer*. White River Junction, VT: Chelsea Green Publishing.

Mesarovic, M. D. (1967). General systems theory and its mathematical foundation. In *Record of the IEEE Systems Science and Cybernetics Conference*, vol. 3. New York: Institute of Electrical and Electronic Engineers, pp.1–22.

Miller, G. A. (1956). The magical number seven plus or minus two: Some limits on our capacity for processing information. *Psychological Review*, 63(2), 81–97. DOI:http://10.1037/h0043158.

Miller, J. G. (1978). *Living systems*. New York: McGraw Hill.

M'Pherson, P. K. (1974). A perspective on systems science and systems philosophy. *Futures*, 6(3), 219–239.
Newman, M. E. (2005). Power laws, Pareto distributions and Zipf's law. *Contemporary Physics*, 46 (5), 323–351. DOI:http://10.1080/00107510500052444.
Odum, E. P. (1977). The emergence of ecology as a new integrative discipline. *Science*, 195(4284), 1289–1293.
Ossimitz, G., & Lapp, C. (2006). *Das Metanoia-Prinzip: eine Einführung in systemisches Denken und Handeln*. Hildesheim: Franzbecker.
Otway, H. J. (1975). *Risk Assessment and Societal Choices* (IIASA Research Memorandum). Laxenburg, Austria: International Institute of Applied Systems Analysis. http://pure.iiasa.ac.at /514/.
Otway, H. J., & Fishbein, M. (1977). *Public Attitudes and Decision Making*. Laxenburg, Austria: International Institute of Applied Systems Analysis. http://pure.iiasa.ac.at/id/eprint/761/.
Pahl, G., Beitz, W., Feldhusen, J., & Grote, K.-H. (2011). *Engineering Design: A Systematic Approach*, 3rd edition. Darmstadt: Springer.
Pareto, V. (1896). *Cours d'économie politique*. Lausanne: Rouge.
Parsons, T. (1970). On building social system theory: A personal history. *Daedalus*, 99(4), 826–881. DOI:http://10.2307/20023975.
Pattee, H. H. (1973). *Hierarchy Theory: The Challenge of Complex Systems*. New York: George Braziller.
Pickett, S. T. A., Cadenasso, M. L., Childers, D. L., McDonnell, M. J., & Zhou, W. (2016). Evolution and future of urban ecological science: Ecology in, of, and for the city. *Ecosystem Health and Sustainability*, 2(7), e01229.
Polk, M. (2015). Transdisciplinary co-production: Designing and testing a transdisciplinary research framework for societal problem solving. *Futures*, 65, 110–122.
Portugali, J., Meyer, H., Stolk, E., & Tan, E. (Eds.). (2012). *Complexity Theories of Cities Have Come of Age: An Overview with Implications to Urban Planning and Design*. Berlin/Heidelberg: Springer-Verlag. www.springer.com/gp/book/9783642245435.
Rindzevičiūtė, E. (2016). *The Power of Systems: How Policy Sciences Opened up the Cold War World*. Ithaca, NY: Cornell University Press.
Ropohl, G. (1999). Philosophy of Socio-Technical Systems. *Techné: Research in Philosophy and Technology*, 4(3), 186–194. DOI:http://10.5840/techne19994311.
Rosenblueth, A., Wiener, N., & Bigelow, J. (1943). Behavior, purpose and teleology. *Philosophy of Science*, 10(1), 18–24.
Sala, S., Ciuffo, B., & Nijkamp, P. (2015). A systemic framework for sustainability assessment. *Ecological Economics*, 119, 314–325.
Schilling, T., Mühlemeier, S., Wyss, R., & Binder, C.R. (2020). A Concept for Sustainability Transition Assessment (STA): A Dynamic Systems Perspective Informed by Resilience Thinking. In C. R. Binder, E. Massaro, & R. Wyss (eds.), *Sustainability Assessment in Urban Systems*. Cambridge University Press, pp. 123–138.
Scholz, R., & Tietje, O. (2002). *Embedded Case Study Methods*. Thousand Oaks, CA: SAGE Publications. DOI:http://10.4135/9781412984027.
Seefried, E. (2015). *Zukünfte: Aufstieg und Krise der Zukunftsforschung 1945–1980*, vol. 106. Walter de Gruyter.
Shannon, C. E. (1948a). A Mathematical Theory of Communication, Part 1. *The Bell System Technical Journal*, 27, 379–423.
Shannon, C. E. (1948b). A Mathematical Theory of Communication, Part 2. *The Bell System Technical Journal*, 27, 623–656.
Shannon, C. E., & Weaver, W. (1949). *The Mathematical Theory of Communication*. Champaign: University of Illinois Press.
Simon, H. A. (1955). A behavioral model of rational choice. *The Quarterly Journal of Economics*, 69 (1), 99–118. DOI:http://10.2307/1884852.
Simon, H. A. (1956). Rational choice and the structure of the environment. *Psychological Review*, 63 (2), 129–138. DOI:http://10.1037/h0042769.

Singh, R. K., Murty, H. R., Gupta, S. K., & Dikshit, A. K. (2009). An overview of sustainability assessment methodologies. *Ecological Indicators*, 9(2), 189–212.
Smuts, J. C. (1926). *Holism and Evolution*. New York: Viking Press.
Stirling, A. (2007). A general framework for analysing diversity in science, technology and society. *Journal of the Royal Society Interface*, 4(15), 707–719.
Straussfogel, D., & Von Schilling, C. (2009). Systems theory. In R. Kitchin & N. Thrift. (eds.), *International Encyclopaedia of Human Geography*. Oxford: Elsevier, pp.151–158.
The Ecological Sequestration Trust. (2013). Review of Current Advanced Integrated Models for City-Regions, Presented at the Technology Strategy Board's Future Cities Catapult, London, UK. https://ecosequestrust.org/latest/publications/review-of-current-advanced-integrated-models-for-city-regions/.
Ukidwe, N. U., & Bakshi, B. R. (2008). Resource intensities of chemical industry sectors in the United States via input–output network models. *Computers & Chemical Engineering*, 32(9), 2050–2064.
United Cities and Local Governments. (2015). *The Sustainable Development Goals: What Local Governments Need to Know*. Barcelona: United Cities and Local Governments.
United Nations. (2015). Transforming our world: the 2030 Agenda for Sustainable Development. New York, USA. https://sustainabledevelopment.un.org/post2015/transformingourworld.
Vester, F. (1988). The bio cybernetic approach as a basis for planning our environment. *Systems Practice*, 1(4), 399–413.
Waltner-Toews, D., & Kay, J. (2005). The evolution of an ecosystem approach: The diamond schematic and an adaptive methodology for ecosystem sustainability and health. *Ecology and Society*, 10(1). DOI:http://10.5751/ES-01214-100138.
Webb, R., Bai, X., Smith, M. S., & Thomson, G. (2018a). Sustainable urban systems: Co-design and framing for transformation. *Ambio*, 47(1), 57–77.
Webb, R., Rissik, D., Petheram, L., Beh, J.-L., & Smith, M. S. (2018b). Co-designing adaptation decision support: meeting common and differentiated needs. *Climatic Change*, 1–17. DOI:https://doi.org/10.1007/s10584-018-2165-7.
Wedding, G. C., & Crawford-Brown, D. (2007). Measuring site-level success in brownfield redevelopments: A focus on sustainability and green building. *Journal of Environmental Management*, 85 (2), 483–495.
Wiek, A., & Binder, C. (2005). Solution spaces for decision-making: A sustainability assessment tool for city-regions. *Environmental Impact Assessment Review*, 25(6), 589–608.
Wiener, N. (1948). Cybernetics. *Scientific American*, 179(5), 14–19.
Wilber, K. (2011). *The Marriage of Sense and Soul: Integrating Science and Religion*. New York: Random House Publishing Group.
Williams, J. (2013). Carbon Dioxide, Climate and Society: Proceedings of a IIASA Workshop cosponsored by WMO, UNEP, and SCOPE, February 21–24, 1978. Elsevier.
Wise, R. M., Fazey, I., Stafford Smith, M., & Campbell, B. (2014). Reconceptualising adaptation to climate change as part of pathways of change and response. *Global Environmental Change*, 28, 325–336.
World Commission on Environment and Development. (1987). *Our Common Future*. Oxford/New York: Oxford University Press.
Wymore, W. (1967). *A Mathematical Theory of Systems Engineering: The Elements*. New York: John Wiley & Sons.
Wymore, W. (1993). *Model-Based Systems Engineering*. Boca Raton, FL: CRC Press.
Wynne, B. (1984). The institutional context of science, models, and policy: The IIASA Energy Study. *Policy Sciences*, 17(3), 277–320.

3

How Values Play into Sustainability Assessments: Challenges and a Possible Way Forward

Franziska Meinherz, Livia Fritz, and Flurina Schneider

No knowledge is "pure" knowledge, and so there are good political reasons why certain kinds of research trends develop rather than others.

(Mumby and Clair, 1997, p. 185)

3.1 Introduction

A sustainability assessment has as its objective fostering progress toward sustainability. Empirical observations and scenarios are classified as more or less sustainable (Grunwald, 2004). A sustainability assessment is therefore centered around some notion of sustainability, which serves as the reference (Frame & Brown, 2008). Sustainability is, however, not a concept with one universally agreed-upon definition. There exists a plethora of conceptions of what sustainability means (Kates et al., 2005; Kemp & Martens, 2007; Martens, 2006). Essentially, the notion of sustainability makes reference to a desirable state of the world – it embodies a vision for society and its relationship with its environment. And different definitions of sustainability can be traced back to different such visions (Frame & Brown, 2008; Funtowicz & Ravetz, 1993; McCool & Stankey, 2004). By making reference to sustainability, a sustainability assessment is tied to the values which play into the visions for society and its relationship with the world that are captured in the notion of sustainability. As such, a sustainability assessment is fundamentally normative[1] (Frame & Brown, 2008; Grunwald, 2004; Kates et al., 2005; Kemp & Martens, 2007; Waas et al., 2014; Ziegler & Ott, 2011).

This raises questions with regard to the knowledge that is produced in a sustainability assessment. If a sustainability assessment is, indeed, tied to values, this means that its results or even the very process by which these results are obtained are unlikely to find much support outside the social context in which these values are considered legitimate. No sustainability assessment could then ever be definitive or universally acknowledged (Hirsch Hadorn et al., 2006; Kates et al., 2005; Kemp & Martens, 2007). The core purpose of a sustainability assessment is, however, to provide sound information, based on which decisions regarding sustainability issues can be taken (Kemp & Martens, 2007; Waas et al., 2014). How to produce such information in a context of strong normative positions is a question that remains unanswered, but various authors are working on clarifying it. On a conceptual level, approaches are being developed that distinguish different forms of knowledge and discuss the role these should play in the assessment process (cf. Hirsch Hadorn et al., 2006; Schneidewind 2013, 2015). Other authors focus more on the operational level and are developing approaches by which they hope to bridge the need to produce sound knowledge and the presence of strong normative positions (cf. Ravetz & Funtowicz, 2015; Videira et al., 2010; Waas et al., 2014; and Chapters 6 (Schneider), 7 (Stelzer & Kopfmüller), 8 (Binder et al.), and 9 (Merino-Saum), in this volume).

With this chapter, we aim to contribute to these efforts by looking in more detail at how values actually shape notions of sustainability, how they come into being, and their implications on a knowledge-production process such as a sustainability assessment. Indeed, as van der Hel (2018) noted, while the normative dimension of sustainability is increasingly acknowledged by researchers in the field, a thorough investigation of how different values shape knowledge production for sustainability is still missing. In Section 3.2, we draw on literature from economic philosophy and political ecology to explore how values play into notions of sustainability. With this, we aim to better understand where this normativity of sustainability is located and how it plays out, and the challenges this presents for conducting sustainability assessments. In Section 3.3, we reflect on the implications of the necessity to refer to sustainability values for knowledge-production processes such as sustainability assessments and point to different positions regarding how science should engage with values. We illustrate that these different positions are ultimately expressions of different epistemic values. In Section 3.4, we look at how different values are interrelated with social and material dynamics and how knowledge-production processes are embedded in these interrelations. This allows us to identify further challenges that need to be addressed when conducting a sustainability assessment. Lastly, in Section 3.5, we develop suggestions for how the identified challenges could be addressed. With the discussion which we launch in this chapter, we aim to facilitate a critical reflection on the implications of different configurations of values on knowledge production for sustainability – a reflection which we hope will play into the application of the different approaches for conducting sustainability assessments that are presented in this volume.

3.2 The Value-Loadedness of Sustainability: An Analysis Based on Approaches to Ethics and Ecology

In this section, we flesh out the often-made assertion that different conceptions of sustainability are motivated by different values (cf. Kates et al., 2005) – that sustainability, per se, is a fundamentally normative concept (Frame & Brown, 2008; Grunwald, 2004; Kemp & Martens, 2007; Waas et al., 2014; Ziegler & Ott, 2011). We look at how different definitions of sustainability can be traced back to different underlying values; to ways of seeing the world and one's position in it. For this, we look at what sustainability, as a concept, actually seeks to define.

On the one hand, the concept of sustainability marks a commitment to satisfying the "unmet needs of society" (Hirsch Hadorn et al., 2006, p. 120), to ensuring that "the needs of the present [are met] without compromising the ability of future generations to meet their own needs" (World Commission on Environment and Development, 1987, p. 8), and to providing "for the fundamental needs of humankind in an equitable way without doing violence to the natural systems of life on earth" (Kemp & Martens, 2007, p. 5). On the other hand, as can already be seen from these quotes, the concept of sustainability describes a vision for the relationship between society and its environment (cf. Rametsteiner et al., 2011).

To illustrate how reflections both on human needs and on the relationship between humankind and its environment tie the sustainability concept to underlying values, we look at how human-made CO_2 emissions are conceptualized in different sustainability discourses. As Hayward (2007) notes, human-made CO_2 emissions can be thought of (1) as something that industries, people or countries have a right to, or (2) as something that industries, people or countries should be held accountable for. Proponents of either position tend to agree that the current level of human-made CO_2 emissions risks fundamentally altering the planetary climate balance, with consequences that are difficult to anticipate. They disagree, however, on the conclusions that should be derived from this. In Section 3.2.1, we show how their disagreement can be traced back to different perspectives on ethics, and in Section 3.2.2 how it reflects differences in how the relationship of society with its environment is conceived. We also touch upon how this affects the domain of sustainability assessments (Section 3.2.3).

3.2.1 CO_2 Emissions as a Means to an End or as Morally Unjust: Consequentialist and Deontological Ethics

Conceiving of human-made CO_2 emissions as something that industries, people, or countries have a right to boils down to seeing them as a means to the end of socioeconomic development. Such a perspective can be traced back to a consequentialist and utilitarian approach to ethics – meaning that an action is judged by the ends it makes it possible to achieve (cf. O'Neill, 2008). In our example, this means that whether any amount of CO_2 emissions is deemed acceptable depends on what they make it possible to achieve in terms of socioeconomic development. Defining sustainability then corresponds to finding the optimal balance between the potential suffering induced by the impact of human-made CO_2 emissions on the planetary climate balance and the socioeconomic benefits they make possible. In this approach to sustainability, well-being is understood as the experience of pleasure in the absence of suffering. Consequently, the best course of action is the one that maximizes pleasure and minimizes suffering over all sentient entities concerned by it (cf. O'Neill, 2008).

The Brundtland Report, which coined one of the most widely used conceptions of sustainability, forms part of this tradition. Its call to manage the current human-made environmental impact in such a way that future generations can still access the same socioeconomic benefits as their predecessors (cf. World Commission on Environment and Development, 1987) represents a guideline for thinking about the negative consequences of human-made environmental impacts alongside the positive outcomes they enable.

In such an approach, a key task for any sustainability assessment is assessing the positive and negative impacts of any course of action for all concerned parties. This is no trivial exercise: well-being is generally thought of as a multidimensional concept, with a plethora of elements playing into it. There is, however, no agreement on what these elements entail – on what the conditions are that need to be met for human well-being to be ensured (Max-Neef, 1991; O'Neill & Uebel, 2015; Rao & Min, 2017). A sustainability assessment based on a consequentialist and utilitarian approach thus needs to answer the difficult question of which elements play into human well-being and how they should be prioritized. Additional complexity arises from the frequent trade-offs between these elements. It might well be that contributions in one domain of well-being entail losses in another domain of well-being (Max-Neef, 1991; O'Neill & Uebel, 2015).

If, on the other hand, human-made CO_2 emissions are to be condemned irrespective of the ends they make it possible to achieve, the difficulty is located elsewhere. If we assume that this condemnation of human-made CO_2 emissions derives from some underlying moral principle – such as, for instance, to refrain from "doing violence to the natural systems of life on earth" (Kemp & Martens, 2007, p. 5) – we are in a deontological approach to ethics. From such a perspective, human well-being is more than the experience of pleasure in the absence of pain. To experience well-being, people must also be able to live in accordance with the fundamental moral principles which define their existence. From a deontological perspective, life has a moral purpose, and to experience well-being, one must be able to fulfill this moral purpose (cf. O'Neill, 2008). For instance, people with the moral belief that natural life systems should not be harmed cannot experience well-being if they are obliged to live in a way that forces them to go against this belief.

Consequently, if this moral purpose involves refraining from harming natural life systems, no amount of human-made CO_2 emissions would ever be justified, regardless of the ends they make it possible to achieve. This greatly limits the potential for trade-offs: violations of such a fundamental principle cannot simply be compensated for by gains in some other domain. In a sustainability assessment, a core task, then, is to determine whether any course of action violates such a moral principle. This, however, presumes that there is agreement on the moral principles that are to be upheld. As Okereke (2010) notes, this is not necessarily the case. Humankind cannot be looked at as one society that shares a common value system – or, in other words, the same fundamental moral principles.[2] And given that fundamental moral principles are the object of disagreement, finding an agreement on how to resolve contradictions between them might not be trivial.

In fact, the very contrast between consequentialist and deontological ethics can be understood as such a disagreement between different underlying moral principles. That the ends justify the means – the basic underlying premise of consequentialism – stands opposed to the premise that the means are to be judged irrespective of the ends they make possible. Agreement between people arguing from either one of these perspectives might thus be difficult to reach. A person who fundamentally disagrees with the premise that CO_2

emissions can be justified in some cases might well refuse to enter in negotiations on how to balance their positive and negative impacts.

3.2.2 *Nature as a Resource, Spiritual Entity, or Metabolism: Different Ecologies*

After having illustrated how different conceptions of sustainability can be traced back to fundamentally different ethical principles, in this subsection, we make the point that different conceptions of sustainability are furthermore rooted in fundamentally different conceptions of the relationship of society with its environment. To designate these perspectives, we use the terminology used by scholars from political ecology; other fields use different names for the perspectives that we mention in this text.[3]

Approaches to sustainability that conceive of human-made environmental impacts as a means to an end are often rooted in what can be called an anthropocentric worldview. In this view, the planetary system is considered as a resource or input to a production process geared toward the satisfaction of human needs (Imran et al., 2014; Leff, 2002). From an anthropocentric perspective, the planetary system is valuable insofar as it can be exploited by humans for their own purposes. Sustainability, in this view, boils down to managing what are termed "natural resources" in such a way that their current use by humans does not compromise the well-being of future generations of humans. Specifically, this means that society needs to shift from a dependency on non-renewable to renewable natural resources and to a mode of production and consumption that takes into account their capacity for renewal (cf. Costanza & Daly 1992; Daily et al., 2000, 2009). In the case of CO_2 emissions, this would mean that the planetary capacity for absorbing CO_2 is a resource at the disposal of humankind, but that it is limited, and that consequently, in order to be sustainable, societal CO_2 emissions need to be within this capacity. The task of a sustainability assessment, in this perspective, is to assess the degree to which any given course of action allows us to ensure the resource needs of humankind in the long term.

Another perspective, which builds on an anthropocentric perspective, is the view that sustainability can be achieved through the development of technology (cf. O'Neill & Uebel, 2015). In the case of CO_2 emissions, this would involve developing technology that emits less CO_2 or developing technology that increases the global capacity for CO_2 absorption. Some people argue that through technological progress, society can become completely independent of the limits set by ecosystem processes – meaning that there are no natural limits to socioeconomic growth. Others take a precautionary approach, based on the premise that it is uncertain whether such a decoupling of socioeconomic growth from planetary limits can be achieved, especially within the needed time frame (cf. Costanza & Daly, 1992; Martinez-Alier & Muradian, 2015).

This conception of technology as the means by which the planetary system can be exploited for the satisfaction of human needs is rooted in a technocentric perspective. From a technocentric perspective, a nature that follows mechanistic laws stands opposed to intention-driven humans. Humans, gifted with reason, can understand natural processes by making use of the scientific method and design technologies to utilize them for the satisfaction of their needs. Or, put another way, humans are gifted with the capacity to engineer nature to fit their needs (cf. Brown, 1995; Capra, 1997; Imran et al., 2014; Merchant, 1990). The recent focus on the development of carbon capture and sequestration technology can be read in this sense. Rather than adjusting the mode of production to the planetary limits for CO_2 absorption, those planetary limits are extended to match societal CO_2 emissions. In such a perspective, the task of a sustainability assessment becomes to assess to which degree a given technology is suitable for ensuring that societal resource needs[4] can be met in the long term.

Approaches to sustainability that condemn actions that harm natural life systems on principle are rooted in what is called an ecocentric worldview. From an ecocentric perspective, humankind is just one of the many interconnected and interdependent parts of which the planetary system consists. And all parts of that system have an intrinsic value. Humans, their needs, and their creative potential are not considered any more important or valuable than other parts of the planetary system (cf. Imran et al., 2014; Leff, 2002; Robinson, 2004). Sustainability, in this view, involves humans gaining awareness of their interconnectedness with the planetary system. "What is needed . . . is a new ethic; a new set of values; and a new way of relating to the natural world" (Robinson, 2004, p. 376). There are, however, divergences between different currents of ecocentric thought about what this means.

Some ecocentric perspectives start from the premise that it is not just humans, but all parts of the planetary system that are sentient. In this view, the road to sustainability lies in developing a deep respect for the integrity of this sentient nature and minimizing all human interference in ecosystem processes, since it corresponds to a violation of this integrity (Brown, 1995; Capra, 1997; Imran et al., 2014; Merchant, 1990; Robinson, 2004). Such approaches build on the moral principle that nature's integrity should be protected at all costs. In this view, engineering solutions around planetary limits would constitute a violation of nature's integrity just as much as fundamentally changing the global climate balance through human-made CO_2 emissions that exceed the planetary capacity for CO_2 absorption would. In such a view, the task of a sustainability assessment would be to identify all instances in which humankind interferes with natural processes.[5]

Political ecology offers an ecocentric perspective that looks both at the relationship of humankind with its environment and at humankind itself, i.e., at social organization (cf. Bryant 2015). The planetary system is thought of as one metabolism, with human labor being one of the many processes through which matter and energy are transformed (Foster, 2009; Marx, 1968; Saito, 2016). Human labor, in this sense, is not any different or more valuable or problematical than the transformation processes induced by ecosystem processes (Foster, 2009; Marx, 1968). However, from a political-ecological perspective, these transformation processes need to be analyzed with regard to the power dynamics inherent to them. Political ecology is built on the moral principle that forms of exploitation and oppression are to be condemned and abolished (cf. Marx, 1983; Saito, 2016). From this perspective, in a sustainable future, "that some individuals have a right of ownership over the globe will seem just as absurd as the idea that one human can have a right of ownership over another human [*translation from German by the authors*]" (Marx, 1983, p. 784). The social order and the relationship of society with its environment are thought of together, and one cannot be in equilibrium without the other. The task of a sustainability assessment would then be to assess to which degree the planetary metabolism is equilibrated and free of oppressive and exploitative power relations.

3.2.3 One Planet, Many Worldviews

In the previous sections, we showed that our underlying values and worldviews radically change not only the goals we want to pursue, but also how we conceive of the road toward them. This has consequences for sustainability assessments: Being able to make reference to shared values has been identified as a conditio sine qua non for agreeing on a frame of evaluation for an argument (Okereke, 2010). Hence, if the parties involved in or concerned by a sustainability assessment[6] cannot refer to shared values, both the validity of the assessment process and its results might be rejected by those parties whose values are not reflected in the process or are violated by it (Frame & Brown, 2008; Grunwald, 2004; McCool & Stankey, 2004). For instance, a sustainability assessment process that aims at finding an optimal trade-off between different aspects will hardly be acknowledged as valid by people whose moral positions make trade-offs between these respective aspects a priori impossible. Disagreements in sustainability assessments can thus persist on different levels: on the one hand, within one set of values and worldviews, and on the other hand, across different sets of values and worldviews. In Table 3.1, we summarize the values and worldviews presented in this section, and highlight how, depending on the underlying values that shape understandings of sustainability, the kind of solutions that are taken into consideration for addressing sustainability issues can change fundamentally.

The presentation of ideal-typical values and worldviews in Table 3.1 points to the kind of disagreements that exist between different approaches to sustainability. For instance, agreement between approaches that are rooted in an anthropocentric and consequentialist perspective and approaches that are rooted in a deontological and political-ecological perspective might be hard to reach. Whereas proponents of anthropocentric and consequentialist approaches to sustainability have concluded that one way of preventing the unsustainable use of planetary resources is to integrate them into the market economy by ascribing a monetary value to their contribution to human well-being (cf. Costanza & Daly, 1992; Daily et al., 2000, 2009), proponents of political-ecological approaches claim that the economization of nature further advances exploitative and oppressive power relations, in that ecosystem processes are marketed as services owned by some humans from whom other humans have to purchase them (cf. Leff, 2002). In this sense, the economization of an increasing number of aspects of the planetary system would correspond to the construction of a "universe in which the domination of nature has remained linked to the domination of man" (Marcuse, 1968, p. 135) – which, in the political-ecological perspective, is a fundamentally unsustainable course of development. What is identified as a promising path toward sustainability based on one perspective thus fundamentally contradicts what is identified as sustainable based on another perspective.

Table 3.1 *A non-exhaustive overview of different ideal-typical worldviews and values and the conceptions of sustainability they imply*

Perspective	Implied worldview	Implied understanding of sustainability	Examples for solution spaces
Technocentric anthropocentrism	"Engineering nature to fit humankind's needs"	Substitutability of ecosystem services; substitutability of technology and ecosystem services; environmental protection/destruction as a means to an end (consequentialist)	Ecological modernization (integration of environmental conservation into the market economy); rent-seeking mechanisms as steering elements
Technosceptic anthropocentrism	"In the face of uncertainty, precaution is better and society should not gamble on future technological progress"	Maximally partial substitutability of ecosystem services; maximally partial substitutability of technology and ecosystem services; environmental protection/destruction as a means to an end (consequentialist)	Ecological modernization (integration of environmental conservation into the market economy); stabilization or reduction of resource and energy demand with unclear consequences for rent-seeking
Essentialist ecocentrism	"Respecting the integrity of Mother Nature"	All human interference in earth system processes is oppressive and to be condemned (deontological)	Rejection of private (corporate) ownership; rejection of rent-seeking; rejection of urbanization; rejection of industrialization
Political ecology	"Equilibrating the planetary metabolism"	Embedding society in the flows of the planetary metabolism and freeing the planetary metabolism of forms of exploitation (deontological)	Rejection of private (corporate) ownership; rejection of rent-seeking; rejection of alienating and exploitative forms of labor; rejection of forms of oppression

It is, however, important to note that the different conceptions of the relationship of society with its environment as we have portrayed them in this section and in Table 3.1 correspond to ideal types, and that positions on sustainability can incorporate elements of different perspectives. For instance, the Intergovernmental Science-Policy Platform on Biodiversity and Ecosystem Services (IPBES) has recently suggested replacing the notion of ecosystem services with the concept of "nature's contribution to people" (Díaz et al., 2018). This step has been motivated by the desire to demonetize the relationship of society with its environment. The idea is also that, depending on the cultural context, these contributions of nature to people can be perceived differently – that there is not a universal value to a specific aspect of the ecosystem. Although the approach is still people-centered and could thus be deemed an anthropocentric perspective, it explicitly recognizes that both anthropocentric and ecocentric perspectives on the world exist and aims to create reporting categories that account for both perspectives and all the positions that lie in between (cf. Díaz et al., 2018).

3.3 How to Deal with Values in Knowledge Production: Different Epistemologies

Accepting that sustainability is a fundamentally normative concept raises important challenges for conducting sustainability assessments. To select relevant research topics and questions, identify meaningful indicators and thresholds, and interpret the results, sustainability assessments must refer to sustainability values. The intensity and controversy that have characterized the historical debate on the appropriate relationship between science and values illustrates that engaging with values is no trivial task for researchers (e.g., Churchman, 1979; Davydova & Sharrock, 2003; Fleck, 2012; Putnam et al., 2002; Ravetz & Funtowicz, 2015; Ziegler & Ott, 2011). In this section, we explore three ideal-typical positions regarding how science can and should relate to values and show how these positions relate to different ontologies and epistemologies – that is, values regarding what good science is and should be.

The first position is the so-called fact-value split. It argues that researchers should maintain a distance from normative issues (Winckelmann, 1968) and focus on the production of neutral facts. In research, explicit normative statements should be avoided. In this view, politics is the realm within which competing values are negotiated (Pielke & Roger, 2007), whereas science is thought to be free of values. This position is rooted in the ideas of the sociologist Max Weber and represents one of the most dominant epistemological ideals of modern science (Potthast, 2015). Today, this position is held by many natural and social scientists who consider scientific knowledge production to be objective and value-free. Disagreement between different proponents of this perspective persists, however, regarding how science should deal with sustainability values. While some authors argue that sustainability, as a field, is too normative for scientists to engage with, others refrain from acknowledging the values inherent to notions of sustainability and treat sustainability as if it were a purely factual concept. A middle position is taken by those who approach the issue through "what if" clauses.

This first position is underpinned by several ontological and epistemological assumptions: facts and values are thought to be two ontologically different things, which can be separated. Proponents of this position suggest a clear separation of the respective roles of science and society/politics, as well as quality criteria for good scientific work. To justify the fact-value split, its proponents often refer to Hume (2003), who concluded in the eighteenth century that the normative or "what ought to be" cannot be derived directly from "what currently is." What ought to be is defined by personal and societal values, preferences, and worldviews. For instance, whether society should strive for a sustainability vision based on consequentialist or deontological ethics cannot be derived from an empirical or philosophical analysis of the current earth system; it depends on people's values. This claim is supported by most philosophers. However, it is important to understand that the choice to exclude science from value negotiations is in itself a normative claim (Ziegler & Ott, 2011): it draws on epistemological values regarding what good science and the respective roles of science and society should be.

The second position considers facts and values as inseparable and highlights that science cannot and should not be regarded as value-free. This position was brought up by scholars of science studies and philosophy who demonstrated that scientific findings are not neutral facts but reflect the cultures and value systems of their time (e.g., Berger & Luckmann, 2005; Fleck, 2012; Kuhn, 2012). They state that, in practice, the separation between facts and values is very difficult to achieve and that alleged facts often contain a plethora of normative weightings (Kaiser, 2015). This is particularly true in the field of sustainability, where many issues are contested and different perspectives exist on what can be regarded as problematic or desirable developments. In this context, even the selection of the research questions represents a strong normative position, as it defines what comes into the focus of research.

Scholars who consider facts and values as inseparable on an ontological level generally also criticize the epistemological ideal of science as a value-free endeavor, since they claim that this does not reflect the reality of scientific practice. Moreover, they argue that a strict separation of science from values bears the risk of science becoming irrelevant for societal questions such as sustainability. Consequently, they suggest alternative approaches to science or novel forms of collaboration between science and society. The suggested approaches embrace post-normal science (Ravetz & Funtowicz, 2015), Mode2 knowledge production (Nowotny et al., 2001), action research (Bradbury, 2015), and transdisciplinary research (Hirsch Hadorn et al., 2006). What these approaches have in common is that they eschew the separation between science and society and integrate societal actors in the process of knowledge production. From this perspective, doing good science means acknowledging the value dimensions involved in any form of knowledge production, and dealing with it through extending the peer communities and applying rigorous self-reflective approaches.

The third position takes a middle ground between the previous two: it follows the first position in concluding that facts and values belong to two different realms and the second position in acknowledging the impossibility of fully separating the two from each other. A proponent of this position is the philosopher Potthast (2015) who stresses that although facts and values are often merged (particularly in contested situations), analytically they nevertheless belong to two different realms and should be distinguished. He argues neither for pretending that facts and values should be clearly separated, nor for believing that they are always blurred, which would make all knowledge arbitrary. Rather, he stresses that the presence of moral issues within facts should be acknowledged and unraveled retrospectively in order to make them communicable and open for deliberation. Many proponents of the approaches to knowledge production introduced with the second position might also subscribe to this third one.

These three ideal-typical positions illustrate that the decision on how to deal with sustainability values in sustainability assessments depends to a large degree on the epistemological values – i.e., values that define what is understood by good science – that are held by individual scientists or which prevail in a given discipline. While such epistemological values are generally acknowledged by scientists on a theoretical level, in scientific practice they are often overlooked.

3.4 The Embeddedness of Ways of Knowing and Thinking about the World in Social and Material Orders

In this section, we show that different (epistemological) values and worldviews are historically constructed. They are tied to the socioeconomic, sociotechnological, and socioecological order and one's position in it. We flesh out the point made by Jasanoff: "[S]ociotechnical formations loop back to change the very terms in which we human beings think about ourselves and our positions in the world . . . the ways in which we know and represent the world (both nature and society) are inseparable from the ways in which we choose to live in it" (2004, p. 2).

We begin this section with a short historical illustration of this claim, by showing how the anthropocentric worldview and the notion of an objective scientific method have historically emerged in conjunction with industrialization. We show that industrialization marks not only the beginning of a new socioeconomic and sociotechnological order, but that it also changed the ways in which humankind conceives of the planetary system and its own position in it. We then identify two challenges which result from this co-constructedness of socioeconomic, sociotechnological, and socioecological orders and worldviews and values: The first concerns the tendency of this configuration to facilitate the reproduction of hegemonic values and worldviews, and the second concerns the difficulties that arise from the impossibility of disentangling worldviews and values from the socioeconomic, sociotechnological, and socioecological order.

3.4.1 On the Historical Co-constructedness of Values and Worldviews and Social and Material Orders

Merchant (1990) highlights the historical coincidence of socioeconomic, sociotechnological, and socioecological arrangements with worldviews and values which are coherent with them. She shows how with the technological developments that marked the beginning of industrialization emerged the idea of a mechanistic nature which can be controlled through human ingenuity. Such a vision of the world was much more coherent with how humans experienced the world than the previously prevailing idea of nature as a powerful and uncontrollable force to which humans are subjugated and have to adjust to (Merchant, 1990, 2006).[7] Scientific thought is part of this continuously emerging coherence of how people experience the socioeconomic, sociotechnological, and socioecological order and the worldviews and values they uphold. The idea of an objective scientific method implies a worldview based on the idea of a mechanistic nature which can be understood and controlled by ingenious, reasonable, and creative humans (Merchant, 1990).[8] Correspondingly, in the present day, ecocentric perspectives can be identified as characteristic of non-industrialized societies (Leff, 2002; Merchant, 1990).

To further illustrate how the socioeconomic, sociotechnological, and socioecological order shapes values and worldviews, we again use the example of human-made CO_2 emissions. As we have shown in Section 3.2.1, human-made CO_2 emissions can be thought of either as a means that to some degree can be justified by the ends it makes it possible to achieve, or as something that is to be judged per se, irrespective of the ends it makes it possible to achieve. Hayward (2007) notes, however, that in a carbon-dependent society, human-made CO_2 emissions are, in fact, a necessary means to an end. They are the condition for a number of sociotechnological and socioeconomic activities which are crucial for society. Hence, to reject human-made CO_2 emissions without jeopardizing society as a whole, a different socioeconomic, socioecological, and sociotechnological order – one that is not carbon dependent – is a conditio sine qua non. This illustrates that questions of which moral position can be pursued, which values can be upheld, depend on the socioeconomic, sociotechnological, and socioecological order of society. And at the same time, values, worldviews, and ways of knowing shape this order. By producing categories such as "ecosystem services," knowledge production for sustainability frames how we understand the world and interact with it (Healy et al., 2015; van der Hel, 2018). By shaping how humankind acts on its environment, values, worldviews, and forms of knowledge production contribute to creating a socioeconomic, sociotechnological, and socioecological order with which they are coherent. In short, the socioeconomic, sociotechnological, and socioecological order and worldviews, values, and ways of knowing about the world mutually constitute and reproduce each other (Fletcher et al., 2015; Jasanoff, 2004).

3.4.2 All Values Are Equal, but Some Values Are More Equal than Others: Hegemony

This mutual reproduction of socioeconomic, sociotechnological, and socioecological orders and worldviews and values facilitates the emergence of hegemonic values and worldviews. This can be illustrated by the example of recent trends in sustainability research and debates. There we can see how approaches to sustainability that originate from specific worldviews and values contribute to reproducing a socioeconomic, sociotechnological, and socioecological order that is coherent with these values.

Scholars from political ecology and ecological economics have noted an increasing emphasis in sustainability discourses on ecological modernization; a concept that is rooted in anthropocentric and technocentric values (cf. Blythe et al., 2018; Fletcher et al., 2015; Healy et al., 2015; Salleh, 2015; van der Hel, 2018). An approach to sustainability that is based on the concept of ecological modernization is based on the premise that the solution to the impending ecological crisis lies in the internalization of nature into the market economy. This has given rise to a conception of nature as a service provider. This trend is notably evident in the emergence of the concept of "ecosystem services." Examples of the commodification of these services include carbon trading schemes and mitigation banking, both concepts that have inspired major international initiatives (Blythe et al., 2018; Fletcher et al., 2015; Salleh, 2015).[9] And such an approach to sustainability reproduces a socioeconomic, sociotechnological, and socioecological order that is coherent with its underlying worldview and values. Ecosystem services – just like other goods, services, and labor – are commodified in monetary terms and traded on the market (cf. Fletcher et al., 2015; O'Neill & Uebel 2015). The purpose of scientific research and technological development increasingly becomes to "objectify, 'design and control' living human and external nature as a resource base for entrepreneurs" (Salleh, 2015, p. 436). Nature is subjugated to the needs of humankind (Salleh, 2015). Consequently, "there is less space for 'nature' to function as its own actant: it is needed for its 'services'" (Fletcher et al., 2015, pp. 365–366). And the growing prevalence of such approaches in science, policy, and civil society increasingly excludes other ways of seeing the world: people or groups whose values, worldviews, and ways of knowing are incoherent with the ones that derive from ecological modernization either are not heard – because they defy the commonly agreed-upon logic and as such might appear irrational or illogical – or exclude themselves from discussion spaces in which they do not feel represented. And this, in turn, leads to a further narrowing of the way in which sustainability is thought of – in science, policy, and civil society (cf. Díaz et al., 2018; Healy et al., 2015; Shove, 2010). For instance, a dominant approach that conceives of human interactions – with other humans and with the non-human environment – entirely in terms of market mechanisms, forecloses approaches that go beyond this logic and which would entail a reflection on how we as a community conceive of our existence and of how we live in interaction with our environment (cf. Fletcher et al., 2015; O'Neill & Uebel, 2015). Thinking of nature as a resource base at the disposal of humankind means that nature is treated as a foreign object. This forecloses the idea of an integrated planetary system of which humankind is one part (cf. Latour, 1997).

This example illustrates how powerful the mechanisms of mutual reproduction of worldviews and values and the socioeconomic, sociotechnological, and socioecological order can be. It also shows how the increasing hegemony of a given set of worldviews and values excludes perspectives that differ from it (Healy et al., 2015).

The argumentation that led the IPBES to abandon the notion of ecosystem services and to replace it with that of nature's contribution to people recognizes the power of the mechanisms by which hegemony is created and can be read as an attempt to break with them. The IPBES states that the framework that comes with thinking of the world in terms of ecosystem services and market relations has complicated and delayed the analysis and valuation of important aspects of the ecosystem – aspects which could not easily be phrased in these terms. Thinking the world in terms of ecosystem services resulted in a socioeconomic, sociotechnological, and socioecological order from which people whose experience of the world is not reflected in the values that underlie this concept were excluded. These people's increasing opposition to notions such as ecosystem services has led the IPBES to promote the adoption of a more inclusive concept – the notion of nature's contribution to people (cf. Díaz et al., 2018).

3.4.3 The Challenge of Achieving Change

An increasing number of actors from different academic disciplines, civil society, and politics agree that the current way in which society interacts with the world is unsustainable and that fundamental change is needed to avoid an impending ecological crisis (cf. EEA, 2015; Fischer-Kowalski, 1998; Haberl et al., 2011; IPCC, 2018; Latour 1991; Merchant, 2006; OECD, 2012; Robinson 2004; Rockström et al., 2009; Spaargaren 2011; WWF, 2016). But as we illustrated in Sections 3.4.1 and 3.4.2, the mutual co-constitution of worldviews, values, and ways of knowing with the socioeconomic, socioecological, and sociotechnological order, and the tendency for hegemony, pose challenges for achieving change. The embeddedness of worldviews and values in socioeconomic, sociotechnological, and socioecological orders and the mutual reproduction of these means that it is difficult to induce changes in one of them without, at the same time, challenging others. Indeed, if we act on worldviews and values that are coherent with the socioeconomic, sociotechnological, and socioecological order in which they are embedded, we might end up reproducing this order.

And there are voices that claim that this is what can currently be observed in the domain of sustainability. Authors from political ecology and also some from science and technology studies claim that the impending ecological crisis is partly the result of the very policies that aim to prevent it – that the increasing hegemony of anthropocentric and neoliberal values in the domain of sustainability gives rise to policies that further aggravate the problems which they aim to solve (cf. Blythe et al., 2018; Brown, 1995; Büscher 2012; Fletcher et al., 2015; Foster, 2009; Healy et al., 2015; Latour, 1997; Leff, 2002; Merchant, 1990; Robinson, 2004; Salleh, 2015); and that these policies stem from the "paradoxical idea that capitalist markets are the answer to their own ecological contradictions" (Büscher, 2012, p. 30). They base this claim notably on the point that current sustainability policies reproduce an unsustainable mode of production and consumption.

Currently, most goods in the market society are positional, meaning that it is not the absolute amount one possesses of them that matters for well-being, but rather how much of them one possesses as compared to other people. This results in a pattern of ever-increasing consumption which violates the limits set by the finite planetary system, resulting in ecological problems (O'Neill, 2008). And shifting toward finding well-being in non-positional goods while remaining in the current socioeconomic order would be difficult, if not impossible: the capitalist socioeconomic order depends on a productivist logic to maintain itself. It depends on a sustained accumulation of capital for the sake of increasing private profits. Consumerism is a fundamental condition to this productivist logic (cf. Fletcher et al., 2015; Kallis, 2011; O'Neill, 2008; Salleh, 2015; Tanuro, 2012).

Instead of challenging this logic, current sustainability policies tend to embrace this very same logic: the conclusions of an increasing number of policy documents and research proposals "have to do with encouraging certain styles of purchasing (in which 'green' is the brand of choice)" (Shove, 2010, p. 1277). Such approaches to sustainability follow a consumerist logic and are in line with the prevailing socioeconomic order (Shove, 2010). Sustainability policies based on this logic thus reflect and reproduce the very problems they aim to solve, and highlight the pertinence of the claim that the solutions to current sustainability issues cannot come from the same structures that have caused them (cf. Farrell, 2011; Funtowicz & Ravetz, 1990; Robinson, 2004). The question of how we can achieve change in a context in which our fundamental worldviews and values are shaped by our experience of the socioeconomic, sociotechnological, and socioecological order and at the same time shape how we interact with the world and thus tend to reproduce this very order is, indeed, not a trivial one.

3.5 Lessons for Sustainability Assessments

In this chapter, we first looked at what makes a sustainability assessment a fundamentally normative exercise. In Section 3.2, we illustrated that different notions of sustainability can be traced back to fundamentally different understandings of ethics and the relationship of humankind with its environment – to different beliefs on how actions should be evaluated and on how we conceive of and value the planetary system. Sustainability – the reference that should guide a sustainability assessment – is thus normative. In Section 3.3, we further showed that not only the reference but also the method of a sustainability assessment is normative – that there are different perspectives on what a good scientific method is that can be traced back to different epistemological values. Second, in Section 3.4, we looked at how different values regarding ethics, the relationship of humankind with its environment, and epistemology are shaped by the socioeconomic, sociotechnological, and socioecological order and at how they simultaneously reproduce this order by shaping how people interact with the world.

From these reflections, we have identified several challenges involved in conducting a sustainability assessment. First, it has been noted that a sustainability assessment might be rejected by people whose values are not reflected in or are violated by the process or its underlying conception of sustainability. At the same time, given the fundamental differences that can exist between different values, it is difficult to include and respect them all. Second, the fact that values and the socioeconomic, sociotechnological, and socioecological order mutually constitute each other facilitates the emergence of hegemonic values and worldviews. This affects the values and worldviews that are considered in a sustainability assessment, since values that stand in conflict with the hegemonic ones might not be considered legitimate. Third, this mutual reproduction of values and the socioeconomic, sociotechnological, and socioecological order means that knowledge-production processes and policy interventions that are coherent with the prevailing order risk reproducing it. This presents a challenge for sustainability assessments that aim to inform a transition to a different and more sustainable order. In this section, we present some possible options for addressing these challenges.

First, we suggest that the normativity of sustainability assessments should be recognized and that the values that shape the assessment process should be clarified. This requires that both the values that shape the underlying conception of sustainability, as well as the epistemological values that shape the assessment process, need to be rendered explicit. It needs to be clarified how these values shape the different aspects of the sustainability assessment – the research questions and problem definitions, the applied methods, and the interpretation of the results. It is then possible to identify which values and understandings are reproduced in and by the assessment, and consequently also which values and understandings are not considered in the process. We insist that such a process of reflecting on and spelling out the values that guide a sustainability assessment must always take place, regardless of the scope and method of the sustainability assessment, including when the sustainability assessment follows a standardized and seemingly uncontested procedure and when the underlying definition of sustainability is widely accepted. Indeed, that a procedure or definition is uncontested does not mean that it is not normative – it is only a sign that the values that shape this procedure or definition are largely uncontested and have developed a certain hegemony.

Spelling out and reflecting on the values that guide the assessment makes it possible to situate it – to identify which sociocultural understandings or societal discourses it is embedded in, and consequently, how it relates to specific configurations of the socioeconomic, sociotechnological, and socioecological order. Acknowledging and reflecting on the situatedness of the sustainability assessment makes it possible to get a grasp of its underlying assumptions, and hence of the limitations of the assessment. Any sustainability assessment is based on a very specific idea regarding ethics, the relationship of humankind with its environment, and good science, and excludes other conceptions thereof.

Second, we suggest that acknowledging that any sustainability assessment is normative and includes some values at the expense of others is also primordial when it comes to reflecting on the process by which any specific sustainability assessment should be conducted. In some cases, it can be important that the assessment finds support with specific people or groups. In these cases, it is essential that the people or parties whose support for the assessment is needed can acknowledge the legitimacy or validity of its underlying values. The sustainability assessment process thus needs to be designed in such a way that this can be achieved. This requires an understanding of these people's or parties' values, as well as a process which brings their different values into dialogue and which facilitates finding a consensus between them. This involves not only an openness to other conceptions of sustainability, but also to forms of expertise or knowledge that are not typically considered in scientific knowledge production.

If this is achieved by means of a participatory and deliberative process, it is essential that the deliberation respects the principles of ideal speech laid out by Habermas (1981) – meaning that speech is not strategic or shaped by unequal power relations, and that, consequently, deliberation can take place based on the pertinence of the voiced arguments. Only then is it possible for the different parties involved to reasonably assume that the positions that are being voiced and the narratives of experiences of the socioeconomic, sociotechnological, and socioecological order are genuine – that what is being said is being said to enable a dialogue among equals, rather than to advance one party's interests. The principles of ideal speech are, however, particularly difficult to uphold where power imbalances between different narratives are very strong. Salleh (2015), for instance, noted that in the face of the hegemony of anthropocentric, technocentric, and neoliberal values, these values tend to also frame deliberative exchanges and that this is all the more likely if deliberative processes are formalized under the guidance of institutions that act as cornerstones of the established socioeconomic order (cf. Salleh 2015). Such considerations need to be taken into account when reflecting on how a sustainability assessment process should be designed.[10]

Third, we suggest that the acknowledgment of and reflection on the normativity of sustainability assessments are coupled with a reflection on the implications of the assessment on the socioeconomic, sociotechnological, and socioecological order. This implies two things. First, in the case of a specific assessment, the aftermath of the assessment process must be monitored – information must be gathered on how the produced knowledge is translated into specific ways of interacting with the socioeconomic, sociotechnological, and socioecological order, and on whether the observed developments go in the direction of the goals set during the assessment process. We understand this suggestion as a necessary consequence of the complexity of the issues that sustainability assessments should help clarify. Given the complexity of sustainability issues, we suggest following Frame and Brown (2008) in conceiving of the interaction between knowledge production for sustainability, the design and implementation of political actions, and reflections on values as a complex experimental process with a high learning potential. Second, more research must be conducted on how knowledge production for sustainability is embedded in specific socioeconomic, sociotechnological, and socioecological orders and on how such knowledge production acts as a tool to reinforce or counteract existing dynamics. This means that the values that play into both conceptions of sustainability and of the scientific method, and their embeddedness in the socioeconomic, socioecological, and sociotechnological order must become an object of research.

This chapter provided some first indications on how values shape sustainability assessments and on how values are intertwined with the socioeconomic, sociotechnological, and socioecological order. We hope that if more research is conducted on how these processes play out in specific cases, we will be better equipped to study sustainability issues by "characterising and analysing the emergent qualities and characteristics of different types of sociotechnical configurations" (Shove, 2010, p. 1278). In this way, not only does our analysis of sustainability issues become more complete, but our responses to them can take into account their complexity more holistically. We express the hope that this would allow us to work toward "radical innovations . . . which redefine the rules of the game; which render previously important forms of competence redundant; and which reconfigure interpretations of value and significance" (Shove, 2010, p. 1278) – that is, working toward the radical change which is so desperately needed in order to not jeopardize the planetary balance.

Notes

1. Normativity designates the "value loadedness of human reality" (Rutgers, 2012, p. 11). It makes reference to the subjectivity of the human experience of the world. Values connote something positively or negatively (Kates et al., 2005; Rutgers, 2012). They are essential in the coordination of our actions and provide orientation as to what we should think, do, or say. They provide direction and guide us in the question of who or what we ought to be (Kates et al., 2005; Korsgaard, 1996; Reynaud & Richeb´e, 2009; Rutgers, 2012). Put another way, values refer to how we see the world and our position in it, and guide how we interact with it.
2. Different strands of literature use different words to refer to concepts that we consider synonymous in the context of the discussion in this chapter. A moral principle, like values, shapes how we see the world and our position in it, and guides how we interact with it.
3. The distinction of different approaches to the relationship of humankind with its environment is made in various fields; scholars from different fields, however, use, different terminologies to denominate them. In political ecology, the term "anthropocentrism" is used to refer to a worldview that revolves around the needs of humans, and the term "ecocentrism" is used to refer to a worldview based on an integrated planetary system of which humans are one part (cf. Imran et al., 2014). Coming from economic philosophy, O'Neill and Uebel (2015) distinguish two bodies of literature, one which they call "science-based" and which studies the material and ecological conditions for human well-being, and one which they call "science-sceptical," and which looks at the ecological crisis as being an intrinsic part of the dominant socioeconomic, sociotechnological, and socioecological order. Capra (1997), coming from physics, distinguishes between "shallow ecology," which sees "humans as above or outside of nature, as the source of all value, and ascribes only instrumental, or 'use,' value to nature" (Capra, 1997, p. 7), and "deep ecology," which describes the world "as a network of phenomena that are fundamentally interconnected and interdependent [and] recognizes the intrinsic value of all living beings." (Capra, 1997, p. 7). Merchant (1990), a historian of science, uses the terms "mechanistic" and "organic" to distinguish between a perspective in which nature becomes a kind of "inert, lifeless matter, [that is] passively obeying mechanical laws" (Brown, 1995, p. 191), and one in which nature is seen as an interconnected whole, of which humans are but one part (Merchant, 1990; Brown, 1995).
4. In this context, we understand the planetary capacity for CO_2 absorption as a resource on which humankind depends.
5. Such ecocentric approaches have been criticized on the grounds that they contain an internal contradiction. While they call for nature to be respected as a sentient entity on equal terms with humans, they in fact dehumanize nature completely. It is indeed to humans that the power is given

to define what nature's integrity means, and it is to humans that the responsibility is given to respect it. Humans are thus to speak on nature's behalf and are to take a paternalistic attitude toward it. The internal contradiction inherent to this perspective also emerges from the premise that humans should not interfere in natural processes – this draws a clear boundary between humans and nature and thus goes against the idea that humankind is one part of an integrated system (Brown, 1995; Latour, 1991).

6. For a more extensive discussion of different conceptions of what a "party concerned by a sustainability assessment" is, and of what motivates the involvement of different parties in a sustainability assessment, refer to Chapter 4 (Fritz & Meinherz).
7. Merchant (1990) notes that although, according to Christian dogma, humans were to be the masters of the Creation, this did not correspond to the lived experience of pre-industrial Europeans.
8. As Kaiser (2015) notes, this trend toward an objective scientific method can further be understood as the result of the perceived necessity to de-ideologize knowledge and to clearly distinguish it from value-laden and absolutist ideologies.
9. Carbon trading schemes translate into trading rights to the planetary capacity to absorb CO_2 as a market good. The term "mitigation banking" describes the ambition to compensate for damage done to habitats that fulfill a certain function by creating functionally equivalent habitats elsewhere.
10. For a more extensive discussion of the different forms of power – including discursive power – that can occur in a sustainability assessment and their implications on the assessment process, refer to Chapter 4 (Fritz & Meinherz).

References

Berger, P. L., & Luckmann, T. (2005). *Die gesellschaftliche Konstruktion der Wirklichkeit*. Berlin: Fischer.

Blythe, J., Silver, J., Evans, L., et al. (2018). The dark side of transformation: Latent risks in contemporary sustainability discourse. *Antipode*, 50(5), 1206–1223.

Bradbury, H. (2015). *The Sage Handbook of Action Research*. New York: Sage.

Brown, C. S. (1995). Anthropocentrism and ecocentrism: The quest for a new worldview. *The Midwest Quarterly*, 36(2), 191.

Bryant, R. L. (2015). *The International Handbook of Political Ecology*. Cheltenham: Edgar Elgar.

Büscher, B. (2012). Payments for ecosystem services as neoliberal conservation: (Reinterpreting) evidence from the Maloti-Drakensberg, South Africa. *Conservation and Society*, 10(1), 29–41.

Capra, F. (1997). *The Web of Life: A New Scientific Understanding of Living Systems*. New York: Anchor.

Churchman, C. W. (1979). *The Systems Approach and Its Enemies*. New York: Basic Books.

Costanza R., & Daly, H. E. (1992). Natural capital and sustainable development. *Conservation biology*, 6(1), 37–46.

Daily, G. C., Söderqvist, T., Aniyar, S., et al. (2000). The value of nature and the nature of value. *Science*, 289(5478), 395–396.

Daily, G. C., Polasky, S., Goldstein, J., et al. (2009). Ecosystem services in decision making: time to deliver. *Frontiers in Ecology and the Environment*, 7(1), 21–28.

Davydova I., & Sharrock, W. (2003). The rise and fall of the fact/value distinction. *The Sociological Review*, 51(3), 357–375.

Díaz, S., Pascual, U., Stenseke, M., et al. (2018). Assessing nature's contributions to people. *Science*, 359 (6373), 270–272. DOI:10.1126/science.aap8826.http://science.sciencemag.org/content/359/6373/270.

EEA. (2015). *The European Environment: State and Outlook 2015: Synthesis Report*. Copenhagen: European Environment Agency.

Farrell, K. N. (2011). Snow White and the wicked problems of the west: A look at the lines between empirical description and normative prescription. *Science, Technology, & Human Values*, 36(3), 334–361.

Fischer-Kowalski, M. (1998). Society's metabolism. *Journal of industrial ecology*, 2(1), 61–78.

Fleck, L. (2012). *Genesis and Development of a Scientific Fact*. Chicago: University of Chicago Press.

Fletcher, R., Dressler, W., & Büscher, B. (2015). Nature^{TM} Inc.: Nature as a neoliberal capitalist imaginary. In R. L. Bryant (ed.), *The International Handbook of Political Ecology*. Cheltenham: Edgar Elgar, pp. 359–372.

Foster, J. B. (2009). *The Ecological Revolution: Making Peace with the Planet*. New York: Monthly Review Press.

Frame, B., & Brown, J. (2008). Developing post-normal technologies for sustainability. *Ecological Economics*, 65(2), 225–241.

Funtowicz, S. O., & Ravetz, J. R. (1990). *Uncertainty and Quality in Science for Policy*, vol. 15. New York: Springer Science & Business Media.

Funtowicz, S. O., & Ravetz, J. R. (1993). Science for the post-normal age. *Futures*, 25 (7), 739–755.

Grunwald, A. (2004). Strategic knowledge for sustainable development: the need for reflexivity and learning at the interface between science and society. *International Journal of Foresight and Innovation Policy*, 1(1–2), 150–167.

Haberl, H., Fischer-Kowalski, M., Krausmann, F., Martinez-Alier, J., & Winiwarter, V. (2011). A socio-metabolic transition towards sustainability? Challenges for another great transformation. *Sustainable Development*, 19(1), 1–14.

Habermas, J. (1981). *Theorie des kommunikativen Handelns*., Frankfurt: Suhrkamp.

Hayward, T. (2007). Human rights versus emissions rights: Climate justice and the equitable distribution of ecological space. *Ethics & International Affairs*, 21(4), 431–450.

Healy, H., Martinez-Alier, J., & Kallis, G. (2015). From ecological modernization to socially sustainable economic degrowth: Lessons from ecological economics. In R. L. Bryant (ed.), *The International Handbook of Political Ecology*. Cheltenham: Edgar Elgar, pp. 577–590.

Hirsch Hadorn, G., Bradley, D., Pohl, C., Rist, S., & Wiesmann. U. (2006). Implications of transdisciplinarity for sustainability research. *Ecological economics*, 60(1), 119–128.

Hume, D. (2003). *A Treatise of Human Nature*. North Chelmsforth:Courier Corporation.

Imran, S., Alam, K., & Beaumont, N. (2014). Reinterpreting the definition of sustainable development for a more ecocentric reorientation. *Sustainable Development*, 22 (2), 134–144.

IPCC. (2018). *Global Warming of 1.5 C: An IPCC Special Report on the Impacts of Global Warming of 1.5 C above Pre-industrial Levels and Related Global Greenhouse Gas Emission Pathways, in the Context of Strengthening the Global Response to the Threat of Climate Change, Sustainable Development, and Efforts to Eradicate Poverty*. Incheon: Intergovernmental Panel on Climate Change.

Jasanoff, S. (2004). The idiom of co-production. In S. Jasanoff (ed.), *States of Knowledge: The Co-production of Science and Social Order*. Abingdon: Routledge.

Kaiser, M. (2015). Ethics of science and a new social contract for knowledge. In S. Meisch, J. Lundershausen, L. Bossert, & M. Rockoff (eds.), *Ethics of Science in the Research for Sustainable Development*. Baden-Baden: Nomos Verlagsgesellschaft, pp. 153–178.

Kallis, G. (2011). In defence of degrowth. *Ecological Economics*, 70(5), 873–880.

Kates, R. W., Parris, T. M., & Leiserowitz, A. A. (2005). What is sustainable development? *Environment*, 47(3), 8.

Kemp, R., & Martens, P. (2007). Sustainable development: How to manage something that is subjective and never can be achieved? *Sustainability: Science, Practice, & Policy*, 3(2).

Korsgaard, C. M. (1996). *The Sources of Normativity*. Cambridge: Cambridge University Press.

Kuhn, T. S. (2012). *The Structure of Scientific Revolutions*. Chicago: University of Chicago press.

Latour, B. (1991). *Nous n'avons jamais été modernes*. Paris: La Découverte.

Latour, B. (1997). *Politiques de la nature: Comment faire entrer les sciences en démocratie*. Paris: La Découverte.

Leff, E. (2002). Die Geopolitik nachhaltiger Entwicklung: Ökonomisierung des Klimas, Rationalisierung der Umwelt und die gesellschaftliche Wiederaneignung der Natur. In C. Görg

and U. Brand (eds.), *Mythen globalen Umweltmanagements: Rio + 10*. Munster: Verlag Westfälisches Dampfboot, pp. 92–117.
Marcuse, H. (2013). *One Dimensional Man: Studies in Ideology of Advanced Industrial Society*. Abingdon: Routledge.
Martens, P. (2006). Sustainability: Science or fiction? *Sustainability: Science, Practice, & Policy*, 2(1).
Martinez-Alier, J., & Muradian, R. (2015). *Handbook of Ecological Economics*. Cheltenham: Edward Elgar Publishing.
Marx, K. (1968). *Das Kapital. Kritik der politischen Ökonomie. Band 1: Der Produktionsprozess des Kapitals*. Berlin: Dietz Verlag.
Marx, K. (1983). *Das Kapital. Kritik der politischen Ökonomie. Band 3: Der Gesamtprozess der kapitalistischen Produktion*. Berlin: Dietz Verlag.
Max-Neef, M. A. (1991). *Human scale development: Conception, application and further reflections*. New York and London: The Apex Press.
McCool, S. F., & Stankey, G. H. (2004). *Environmental management*, 33(3), 294–305.
Merchant, C. (1990). *The Death of Nature: Women, Ecology, and the Scientific Revolution*. New York: Harper Collins.
Merchant, C. (2006). The scientific revolution and *The Death of Nature*. *Isis*, 97(3), 513–533.
Mumby, D. K., & Clair, R. P. (1997). Organizational discourse. In T. A. Van Dijk (ed.), *Discourse as Social Interaction*, vol. 2. Thousand Oaks: Sage, pp. 181–205.
Nowotny, H., Scott, P., Gibbons, M., and Scott, P. B. (2001). *Re-thinking Science: Knowledge and the Public in an Age of Uncertainty*. Cambridge: Polity.
OECD. (2012). *OECD Environmental Outlook to 2050: The Consequences of Inaction*. Paris: Organisation for Economic Co-operation and Development.
Okereke, C. (2010). Climate justice and the international regime. *Wiley Interdisciplinary Reviews: Climate Change*, 1(3), 462–474.
O'Neill, J. (2008). Happiness and the good life. *Environmental Values*, 17(2), 125–144.
O'Neill, J., and Uebel, T. (2015). Analytical philosophy and ecological economics. In *Handbook of Ecological Economics*. Cheltenham: Edward Elgar Publishing. pp. 48–78.
Pielke, J., and Roger, A. (2007). *The Honest Broker: Making Sense of Science in Policy and Politics*. Cambridge: Cambridge University Press.
Potthast, T. (2015). Ethics in the sciences beyond Hume, Moore and Weber: Taking epistemic-moral hybrids seriously. In S. Meisch, J. Lundershausen, L. Bossert, and M. Rockoff (eds.), *Ethics of Science in the Research for Sustainable Development*. Baden-Baden: Nomos Verlagsgesellschaft, pp. 129–152.
Putnam, H., et al. (2002). *The Collapse of the Fact/Value Dichotomy and Other Essays*. Cambridge, MA: Harvard University Press.
Rametsteiner, E., Pülzl, H., Alkan-Olsson, J., and Frederiksen, P. (2011). Sustainability indicator development: Science or political negotiation? *Ecological Indicators*, 11(1), 61–70.
Rao, N. D., and Min, J. (2017). Decent living standards: Material prerequisites for human wellbeing. *Social Indicators Research*, 138(1), 225–244.
Ravetz, J., and Funtowicz, S. (2015). Post-normal science. In S. Meisch, J. Lundershausen, L. Bossert, and M. Rockoff (eds.), *Ethics of Science in the Research for Sustainable Development*. Baden-Baden: Nomos, pp. 101–112.
Reynaud, J.-D., and Richebé, N. (2009). Rules, conventions and values: A plea in favor of ordinary normativity. *Revue Française de Sociologie*, 50(5), 3–35.
Robinson, J. (2004). Squaring the circle? Some thoughts on the idea of sustainable development. *Ecological Economics*, 48(4), 369–384.
Rockström, J., Steffen, W., Noone, K., et al. (2009). Planetary boundaries: Exploring the safe operating space for humanity. *Ecology and Society*, 14(2).
Rutgers, M. R. (2012). A pantheon of public values: A historical and conceptual approach to the normativity of facts and values. *A paper presented at The Public Values Consortium Biennial Workshop, Chicago, IL*. www.narcis.nl/publication/RecordID/oai: uva. nl, volume 376695.

Saito, K. (2016). *Natur gegen Kapital: Marx' Ökologie in seiner unvollendeten Kritik des Kapitalismus*. Frankfurt: Campus Verlag.
Salleh, A. (2015). Neoliberalism, scientism and earth system governance. In R. L. Bryant (ed.), *The International Handbook of Political Ecology*. Cheltenham: Edgar Elgar, pp. 432–446.
Schneidewind, U. (2013). Transformative literacy: Gesellschaftliche ver¨anderungsprozesse verstehen und gestalten. *GAIA-Ecological Perspectives for Science and Society*, 22(2), 82–86.
Schneidewind, U. (2015). Transformative Wissenschaft-Motor fu¨r gute Wissenschaft und lebendige Demokratie. *GAIA-Ecological Perspectives for Science and Society*, 24(2), 88–91.
Shove, E. (2010). Beyond the ABC: Climate change policy and theories of social change. *Environment and Planning A*, 42(6), 1273–1285.
Spaargaren, G. (2011). Theories of practices: Agency, technology, and culture: Exploring the relevance of practice theories for the governance of sustainable consumption practices in the new world-order. *Global Environmental Change*, 21(3), 813–822.
Tanuro, D. (2012). *L'impossible capitalisme vert*. Paris: La Découverte.
van der Hel, S. (2018). Science for change: A survey on the normative and political dimensions of global sustainability research. *Global Environmental Change*, 52: 248–258.
Videira, N., Antunes, P., Santos, R., and Lopes, R. (2010). A participatory modelling approach to support integrated sustainability assessment processes. *Systems Research and Behavioral Science*, 27(4), 446–460.
Waas, T., Hugé, J., Block, T., et al. (2014). Sustainability assessment and indicators: Tools in a decision-making strategy for sustainable development. *Sustainability*, 6(9), 5512–5534.
Winckelmann, J. (1968). *Gesammelte Aufsätze zur Wissenschaftslehre*. Heidelberg: Mohr.
World Commission on Environment and Development. (1987). *Our Common Future*. Oxford: Oxford University Press.
WWF. (2016). *Living Planet Report 2016. Risk and Resilience in a New Era*. Gland, Switzerland: WWF International.
Ziegler, R., and Ott, K. (2011). The quality of sustainability science: A philosophical perspective. *Sustainability: Science, Practice and Policy*, 7(1), 31–44.

4

The Politics of Participatory Sustainability Assessments: An Analysis of Power

Livia Fritz and Franziska Meinherz

> We should admit . . . that power produces knowledge (and not simply by encouraging it because it serves power or by applying it because it is useful); that power and knowledge directly imply one another; that there is no power relation without the correlative constitution of a field of knowledge, nor any knowledge that does not presuppose and constitute at the same time power relations.
>
> *(Foucault, 1977, p. 27)*

4.1 Introduction

Sustainability assessments are part of policy assessments – a family of techniques to assess the impact of a policy ex ante or to ensure that policy design is well informed and accounts for possible side effects. Since the 1990s, these instruments have rapidly spread across OECD member states and have become a mandatory part of policy planning in some countries (Adelle & Weiland, 2015; Sala et al., 2015). Together with other policy assessment tools, sustainability assessments are becoming normalized as part of the governance process. More generally, the act of assessing and auditing has come to be considered a key organizing principle of contemporary societies (Power, 1997).

Unlike in other policy fields, with regard to sustainability, the benchmark for the assessment is contested and surrounded by fundamental uncertainties (Holmes & Scoones, 2000). As Meinherz et al. have illustrated (see Chapter 3) with regard to sustainability, an "objective" and purely scientific assessment procedure is challenged by diverse normative claims attached to the notion of sustainability, the need to make trade-offs between different targets, and the need to take decisions in the face of uncertainty. To respond to these challenges, the involvement of societal actors has been advanced as gold standard of sustainability assessment procedures (Frame & Brown, 2008; Gibson et al., 2013; Santos et al., 2006; Sharifi & Murayama, 2013; Videira et al., 2012). The call for rethinking ways of researching and governing sustainability problems has become a priority on the international policy agenda (e.g., the United Nations' Agenda 21 or the Aarhus Convention). With regard to these developments in the field of policymaking for sustainability, and also similar trends in science policy and practice, some scholars speak of a "participatory turn" (Bäckstrand, 2003; Jasanoff, 2003), a "participatory return" (Wynne,

2007) and a "deliberative turn" (Dryzek, 2000). Concomitantly, new approaches to knowledge production have emerged, such as "post-normal science," which posits that when "facts are uncertain, values in dispute, stakes high and decisions urgent," expanded forms of knowledge production are needed (Funtowicz & Ravetz, 1993, p. 744). Similarly, "Mode 2 knowledge production" states that non-academic rationales are increasingly framing the production and validation of knowledge (Gibbons et al., 1994).

In the case of sustainability assessments, this means that designated experts in the field of sustainability assessments – or in the scientific disciplines that are relevant for the sustainability issue at hand – are joined by other societal actors. These actors can be those concerned, those having access to practical and contextual knowledge, and/or those having a stake (Frame & Brown, 2008; Santos et al., 2006; Videira et al., 2012). While forms and methods of involvement vary, many authors attach high expectations to participation in sustainability assessments and herald the power of discursive, participatory processes in facilitating societal learning, holding that these foster participants' trust in the results and their commitment to the derived policies. Indeed, participatory approaches are seen as key for achieving transformative change and innovation (Glass et al., 2013). However, some authors have noted that a participatory process per se does not guarantee these positive outcomes (Kropp, 2013). The way in which the process is laid out and the context within which it is embedded affect how participants relate to the process, and which stakes, values, and expertise are taken into account in it (Beierle, 1999; Muro & Jeffrey, 2008; Videira et al., 2006).

In the vast literature on participatory approaches to sustainability assessment, critical reflections on the layout of the participatory process in the respective contexts and its implications for the assessment process have been called for (Cashmore & Richardson, 2013). Particularly the importance of power in shaping processes of participation is acknowledged (Kristiansen & Bloch-Poulsen, 2013; Lawrence, 2013; Muro & Jeffrey, 2008; Raik et al., 2008; Sinclair et al., 2015), pointing toward the need for comprehensive enquiries into the multiple dimensions of power that pervade such processes. Participatory processes are deeply embedded in wider societal relations and inherently political (Cornwall, 2008), and an analysis of diverse forms of power is inevitable when addressing questions of societal transformations (Avelino, 2017; Brand, 2016). Considering that assessments, audits, and measurements of projects, programs, and policies have emerged as powerful elements of policymaking and are expected to provide an evidence base for informed decisions (Power, 1997), addressing questions of power in the construction of participatory assessment processes seems all the more essential. Yet, there are numerous challenges for grounding the practice of and research on sustainability assessments in social and political theories of power. The conceptualization of power that underlies considerations of participatory processes is often unidimensional (Cook et al., 2013) and poorly equipped to take into account the complex entanglements of knowledge, power, and politics in participatory sustainability assessments.[1]

4.1.1 Goals and Structure of the Chapter

In this chapter, we put the spotlight on the politics of participatory sustainability assessments and argue that an analysis of power in and stemming from participatory sustainability assessments contributes to leveraging the transformative capacities of these tools. Guided by social theories of power, we explore how power relations shape participatory sustainability assessments and how such assessments act on power relations. In doing so, we take into account the potentially repressive side of power (domination, manipulation) as much as its productive side (making do, empowerment). We develop a framework for analyzing different forms of power at different points in the process of assessing sustainability: (i) in defining and framing the problem to be assessed, (ii) in the knowledge-production and assessment process, and (iii) in the learning and governance processes in which the results of the assessment are acted upon. A multidimensional conceptualization of power allows us to prepare the ground for discussions on fundamental questions, such as which form of power leads to which kind of change, or which form of power prevents change. Such questions illustrate that an analysis of power is not only of theoretical interest, but also of practical relevance. Overall, we aim to launch a broader debate on the phenomenon of power in sustainability assessments.

The following questions guide our reflections:

- What does participation in sustainability assessments mean and how can we conceive of it?
- How can we analytically and empirically grasp the dimensions of power that exist in and shape participatory sustainability assessments?
- What can a multidimensional analysis of power teach us in regard to enhancing the transformative power of participatory sustainability assessments for sustainability transitions?

In Section 4.2, we look at conceptualizations of participation and illustrate that participation is a contested concept that goes beyond methodological questions. To equip ourselves for a discussion of the politics of participatory sustainability assessments, in Section 4.3, we propose a multidimensional conceptualization of power, based on theories from the social and political sciences. This allows us to move beyond one-dimensional accounts of power and to look, in Section 4.4, for diverse traces of power throughout the assessment process. We conclude that those in charge of a participatory sustainability assessment have to be aware of the constructed nature of and the power dynamics at play in participatory processes, as well as of their own crucial role as (co-)designers and facilitators. (Self-) Reflexivity is an essential process within collaborative approaches to sustainability assessment (Dryzek & Pickering, 2017; Popa et al., 2015; Stirling, 2008).

4.2 Meanings of Participation in Sustainability Assessments

The choice of methods for selecting and involving diverse actors in a sustainability assessment is tied to the underlying conceptualization of participation. Participation is a polyvalent term, occurs in different forms, and is associated with multiple ends, without one universally accepted definition. In this section, we elaborate on different meanings and conceptualizations of participation. We discuss conceptualizations of participation according to the underlying motivations and goals, as well as typologies based on the degree of involvement, thus illustrating how understandings of participation implicitly or explicitly influence forms and intensities of involvement.

4.2.1 Conceptualizations of Participation According to Motivation

Conceptualizations of participation according to motivation revolve around the question of whether participation is/should be implemented primarily for functional reasons (i.e., to help make better decisions, to produce better knowledge) or because the democratization of all societal fields is critical for sustainable development (van den Hove, 2006).

This question can also be found in Fiorino's (1989) conceptualization of three imperatives underwriting participatory practices: the normative imperative, in which participation is an end in and of itself; the substantial imperative, in which participation has the goal of achieving better ends; and the instrumental imperative, in which participation is aimed at securing particular interests. While the first is process-oriented, the latter two focus on outcomes (Stirling, 2008). The goal of outcome-oriented approaches to participation can be to improve the decision-making quality by including diverse forms of knowledge; to include diverse values and priorities about what the future should look like; and to build trust, foster ownership, and encourage learning among participants (Whitmarsh et al., 2009). Another, similar, categorization is that of Blok (2007), who distinguishes three virtues of public deliberation: civic virtue (more informed and involved citizens), governance virtue (enhancing the legitimacy of decisions), and cognitive virtue (fostering learning). The latter, cognitive virtue, is critical in situations of uncertainty, as is the case for most sustainability issues (Whitmarsh et al., 2009). Van Asselt Marjolein and Rijkens-Klomp's (2002) typology of participation in impact assessments follows a similar logic. They map participatory methods on a spectrum of goals ranging from "process as a goal" to process as a means and on a spectrum of outputs ranging from "mapping out diversity" to "reaching consensus."

A fine-grained differentiation of approaches to participation on which scholars from sustainability science draw[2] is developed by Renn und Schweizer (2009) in the context of risk governance. They present six ideal–typical ways of structuring public input into policymaking: functionalist, neoliberal, deliberative, anthropological, emancipatory, and post-modern. Distinct worldviews and understandings of democracy underpin each of these categories. As with Fiorino's distinction, in this typology, forms of participation, and instruments used to structure the participation process, vary in accordance with deeper-rooted rationales (Renn & Schweizer, 2009). In the functionalist approach, participation appears as a necessity for addressing complex societal functions that require the input of knowledge and values from different constituencies. The aim is to improve the quality of the decision output. Methods such as the Delphi method, workshops, hearings, or citizen advisory committees are particularly suited to fulfill these expectations toward participation. In the neoliberal approach, participation is aimed at representing values and preferences proportionally to their share in the affected population, in order to arrive at informed consent and win-win solutions. In this rationale, referenda, focus groups, or digital participation are appropriate instruments. The deliberative approach strives for the inclusion of all relevant arguments in order to achieve consensus through debate. In this approach, discourse-oriented models, consensus conferences, and citizen juries are frequently used. In contrast, participation in the post-modern approach aims to demonstrate plurality as well as the legitimacy of dissent. It is rooted in the acknowledgment of plural rationalities and considers mutually acceptable arrangements, and not necessarily consensus, as a successful result. Instruments such as open forums or open-space conferences are well suited to organizing participation for this purpose (Renn & Schweizer, 2009, pp. 177–180).

4.2.2 Conceptualizations of Participation According to Degree of Involvement

Linked to these categorizations according to motivations and goals, participation is furthermore described with regard to the degree of involvement of societal actors (Fritz, 2018). Ideals regarding the appropriate and desirable degree of involvement are tied to the motivations underlying a participation process. Representing what we have described above as a normative rationale, in the field of sustainability research participation is frequently conceptualized in reference to the "Ladder of Participation" by Arnstein (1969). She categorizes eight uses of the term "participation" and arranges them in a ladder pattern according to the degree to which societal actors are involved. Adaptions of the ladder for the context of sustainability research are numerous (e.g., Schneider & Buser, 2018; Stauffacher et al., 2008).

Arnstein's conceptualization of participation assumes a logic of "the more participation, the better." Climbing up the ladder goes hand in hand with the redistribution of power from the power-holding actors to the to-be-empowered citizens (Chilvers & Kearnes, 2015). In this sense, participation claims to challenge the power relations that stabilize the societal status quo (Gaventa & Cornwall, 2001). In Arnstein's conceptualization, power is seen as a commodity that is held by some actors and wielded over others (Hayward, 2000). Although in such conceptualizations participation is inherently linked to power and is seen as a means to redistribute power, many advocates of participation echo ideals of deliberative democracy (Cornwall & Coelho, 2007), based on Habermas' (1981) principles of ideal speech. Such ideal deliberative procedures involve "free debate and dispute in which the only legitimate force is a good argument" (Dryzek, 1993, p. 229). This communicative rationality results from interactions that are "competent and free from delusion, deception, power and strategy" (Holmes & Scoones, 2000, p. 9). Accordingly, participatory processes within sustainability assessments are thought to counterbalance and manage power relations, but are not analyzed as being formed by power relations themselves

(Hartz-Karp et al., 2015). Following these theoretical premises, analyses that build on communicative rationality tend to focus on consensus and pay little attention to the negotiation processes or the potential conflicts among participants (Leeuwis, 2000; van den Hove, 2006). In the face of fundamental differences in perspectives and values, as in the case of sustainability issues, the pertinence of consensus as a meaningful goal has been called into question (Spash, 2007).

Conceptualizations of participation according to degree of involvement have their origin in the field of planning and participatory governance. They are not based on experiences with participation in knowledge production or the inclusion of different epistemic cultures in research processes (Fritz & Binder, 2018). This needs to be considered when addressing participatory sustainability assessments that at least to some degree involve joint knowledge production by diverse actors. Epistemologically, participatory approaches to knowledge production and assessments blur the boundaries and division of labor between research and policymaking (Jasanoff, 2004). Drawing on knowledge of diverse provenances in a participatory sustainability assessment requires understanding the underlying premises of different knowledge systems, as well as paying attention to the different degrees of credibility, trustworthiness, and authority ascribed to them.

4.2.3 Toward Critical Participation Studies

Increasingly, scholars have called for paying attention to the ways in which participation is constructed and co-produced with societal order. Critical perspectives on the participation of heterogeneous actors in knowledge production and research processes have gained ground (Chilvers & Kearnes, 2015; Hegger & Dieperink, 2015; Klenk et al., 2013). Concomitantly, interest in the interrelations of power, participation, and knowledge in sustainability research has grown. Following this emerging scholarship, in this chapter we conceptualize participation as a space in between research and policy. Inspired by metaphors of space, such as "epistemic living spaces" (Felt, 2009), "spaces for transformation" (Cornwall, 2004), and "closed, invited and claimed space" (Gaventa, 2006), we look at participation as a relational space embedded in wider science–society relations. This perspective implies that participation is not merely the result of the motivation and intention of those setting up the process, but shaped through an interplay of actions and structures (Fritz & Binder, 2018). Conceptualizing participation as a dynamic and complex process is a prerequisite for better understanding when it contributes to transformation and when it reproduces an unsustainable status quo (Kropp, 2013). Accordingly, we understand participation as being "in the making" and are interested in the diverse factors that constitute and continuously shape participation processes in sustainability assessment. These include the degree of coherence with the institutional and systemic contexts, the availability and distribution of resources, the worldviews or expectations of actors, and power relations (Fritz & Binder, 2018).

Conceiving of participation as a space compels us to ask a series of analytical questions with regard to how power, entangled with knowledge, shapes the forms and outcomes of participation in sustainability assessments. It requires us to look at the individual actors and their ways of interacting as much as at the societal and material context within which participation takes place, including discursive elements such as negotiation and political cultures and the dominant models of expertise and sustainability discourses. In the remaining sections, we focus on power as a key crosscutting issue that is entangled with numerous other factors shaping participation in sustainability assessments. The transversal nature of the power concept allows us to shed light on critical aspects in the making of participation spaces throughout the sustainability assessment process.

4.3 Toward a Multidimensional Conceptualization of Power

With this plurality of meanings of participation in our mind, we turn to the second key notion of this chapter: power. Here we introduce different theoretical ways of grasping the notion of power before we embark on an illustration of how participation and power can be interwoven in sustainability assessment practices. Power is a highly contested concept with multiple meanings. Some theorists describe power as being held by actors, some of whom are powerful and others of whom are comparatively powerless. Power in this perception is a "zero sum game," in which the gain of power by some actors happens at the expense of others. Other theorists see power as embodied in complex relations and discourses and, while it affects everyone, it cannot be held by any single actor. Such approaches understand power as potentially accumulative. Here power is not a finite resource, but can be shared or created by actors and their networks in various ways. Means of social organization can increase the overall power of a group of people, so that the group's potential to take action increases, without any single member of the group losing power in this process. While some perceive power as a generally negative attribute that is exercised in order to control others, others attach positive attributes to it, such as the capacity to act (Gaventa, 2006).

Instead of opting for any one of these partly contrasting interpretations of power, we rely on a multidimensional understanding of power. As suggested by Partzsch (2015) in her work on power in sustainability research, we base our analytical grid on the conceptualization of power by Allen (1998). In the context of feminist studies, she offers a comprehensive conceptualization of power and merges theories of "power over," "power to," and "power with" in order to explain the complexity and diversity of women's experiences with power. Where needed, we complement her conceptualization with elements of particular relevance regarding participation in knowledge-production processes. This adaptation ensures that we can operationalize power in our study context (sustainability assessment).

4.3.1 Power Over (Coercion and Manipulation)

"Power over" addresses power that is exerted over actors, structures, and discourses. Weber (1972) established the understanding of power, widely known today, as the realization of one's own will in asymmetrical relations. In the meantime, "power over" has been expanded and is often theorized along four dimensions or so-called faces of power (Partzsch, 2015, p. 51).

1st Face: Power as the Capacity of Powerful Actors to Directly Influence the Action of Less Powerful Actors

This refers to the classical understanding of power by Dahl (1957), who understands power as the ability of A to get B to do what B might not otherwise do. In this face, the capacity of actors to access and mobilize resources in order to influence a debate is crucial. Research and knowledge might be conceived as resources that are mobilized to influence debates. In this view, approaches to influence policy, knowledge, and action come down to countering expertise with other expertise (Gaventa & Cornwall, 2008, p. 173). This form of power is considered visible and observable in decision-making.

2nd Face: Power Means Being Able to Set the Agenda

With their work on "the two faces of power," Bachrach and Baratz (1962) redefine much of the debate over power in political science. They argue that Dahl's conceptualization of power reflected only one face of power relationships and stipulate that the scope of power is wider (Digeser, 1992). In their more expansive understanding, power encompasses more than conflicts over who wins and who loses. The powerful can prevent conflict from taking place in the first place by limiting the scope of decision-making to "safe issues" that do not threaten the status quo (Hayward, 2000, p. 15). Limiting power to the understanding contained in the first face would mean that the absence of certain voices from a debate is due to their own apathy or inefficacy. In the second face, this very mechanism becomes a process of exclusion from the political process, hence an exercise of power (Gaventa & Cornwall, 2001; Hayward, 2000). This form of power is referred to as hidden, in that certain groups of actors control who can come to the table and what is put on the agenda. These dynamics work through different mechanisms that delegitimize the concerns of other groups (Gaventa, 2006, p. 29). For example, established rules of the game can facilitate access to the process for some groups while hampering meaningful participation on the part of others. As a result, even when formally excluded actors are given access to the process, they may be required to mimic the language and knowledge of the powerful (Gaventa & Cornwall, 2008, p. 174).

3rd Face: Power Is Exerted through Influencing and Shaping the Formation of Ideas, Norms, and Intentions

Lukes (1974) adds a third, "radical" view on power that stipulates that power can also be exerted if B consciously wants to do what A desires. In this face, power is exercized through the manipulation of the very desires of B (Digeser, 1992, p. 979). The first two faces of power describe how power can be used by A to overtly get B to do what A wants, even if it goes against B's own will. In this third face, power is invisible and subtle. It describes how power can covertly manipulate others to do something by altering what they think they want. "Invisible power" is exerted through norms and ideas, and shapes the "psychological and ideological boundaries" of participation (Gaventa, 2006, p. 29). Knowledge and the control of knowledge are seen as key elements for influencing people's consciousness. In that sense, power in this dimension resembles Gramscian notions of "hegemony" or Freirean ideas on a "culture of silence" that is produced via the internalization of knowledge by the oppressed (Gaventa & Cornwall, 2008, p. 174).

4th Face: Power Means that Subjectivity is Socially Constructed and Embedded in Historical Processes

Largely relying on Foucault's writing, interrelations between knowledge, power, and politics are understood as a fourth dimension of power (Digeser, 1992). While in the first three faces As and Bs are taken for granted, the fourth face goes one step further in that subjects are not expected to exist in a natural state. Power in this dimension means that subjectivity and individuality respectively are social constructs, the formation of which is historically contingent (Partzsch, 2015). Foucault uses the notion of power to describe parts of this construction process. According to him, power works through discourses, institutions, and practices that are productive of power effects, framing the boundaries of possible action (Digeser, 1992; Gaventa & Cornwall, 2008). To understand power, the roots and effects of norms and values need to be addressed. In this view, knowledge and power mutually constitute each other (Foucault, 1977). While in the three prior forms of power there is a possibility for relationships to not be mediated by power and to be "power-free," in this dimension power is omnipresent and cannot be erased.

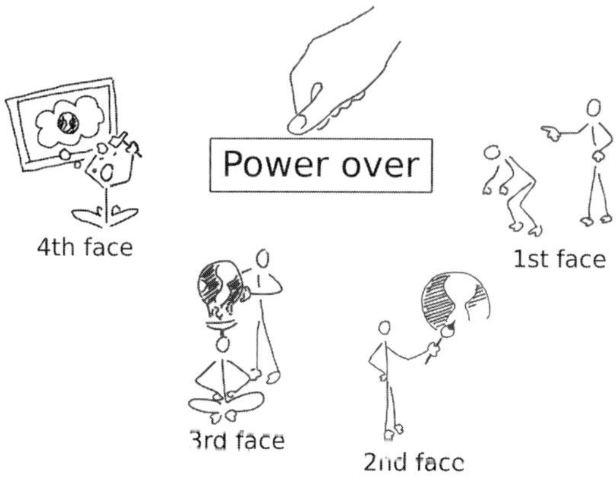

Figure 4.1 The four faces of "power over" (own illustration)

4.3.2 Power To (Resistance and Empowerment)

In this conceptualization, power is understood as the capacity of individual actors to form and shape processes despite resistance (Haugaard, 2002). The term "power to" is roughly synonymous with "empowerment" (Partzsch, 2015). Following Allen (1998, pp. 34–35) "power to" is "the ability of an individual actor to attain an end or series of ends." On the example of feminism, she argues that just as one can assert power to act "in response to a system of domination," one can also assert "power to act by dominating others, not simply by resisting." Thus, she concludes that resistance is one possible form of "power to," just as domination is one particular form of "power over" (Allen, 1998). Her example shows how different forms of power are not exclusive, but deeply entangled, and might be mutually reinforcing or weakening. The emphasis in this conceptualization lies on the agency of individuals and their individual capacity to act.

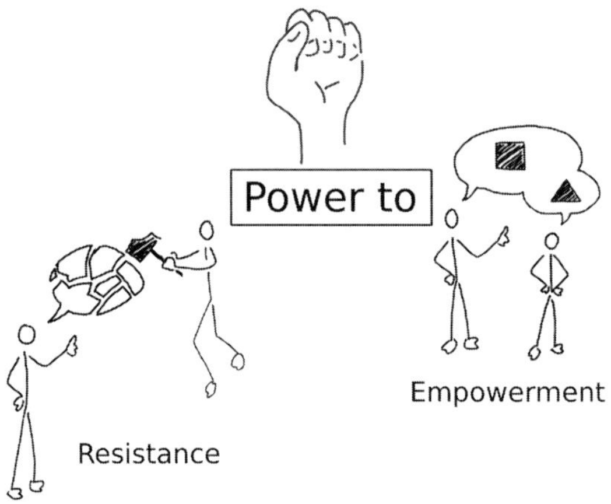

Figure 4.2 Resistance and empowerment as forms of "power to" (own illustration)

4.3.3 Power With (Cooperation and Learning)

In "power with," power refers to the capacity to collectively learn and act. The term has been coined to refer to "the building of a common ground between different interests" (Eyben et al., 2006, p. 8). Processes of finding commonalities and of developing collective strengths are placed at the center of analyses of "power with." In this regard, the notion refers to learning processes and to the development of a new consciousness on the part of a group or a community of individuals (Partzsch, 2015). "Power with" is often associated with Arendt's (1970, p. 44) view that power is "the human ability not just to act but to act in concert." Upon that basis, Allen (1998, p. 35) describes "power with" as "the ability of a collectivity to act together for the attainment of a common or shared end or a series of ends." "Power with" emphasizes the productive forces of power (Partzsch, 2015).

Box 4.1 **Power and the question of legitimacy**

Questions of power are closely linked to the normative question of whether the particular dynamics of power found in a specific situation are legitimate (Haugaard, 2003). We briefly illustrate this interrelatedness for the example of "power to." Hardy and Clegg (2006) link the discussion of power to the question of legitimacy, by stating that strategic agency ("power to", in the words of Allen) potentially challenges legitimized structures of domination. In a system in which the hierarchical organization of society is considered normal, such strategic agency is considered an illegitimate form of power, while the power embedded in the hierarchical structure (a form of "power over") is considered legitimate. This implies a differentiation between formally prescribed or normalized organizations of power and actual power relations (Hardy & Clegg, 2006). Whether "power to" is seen as empowerment or as resistance thus depends on the normalized or legitimized vision of how power is organized in a society. Hardy and Clegg (2006) emphasize that legitimizing forms of power or the outcomes of a mobilization of power (independent of the form of power that was used) are a means of avoiding opposition and achieving stability. Consequently, in the view of those mobilizing power, it is attractive to normalize their form of power. In so doing, they mobilize power not only to achieve physical outcomes, but also to legitimize these outcomes, or even the form of power that is being held.

Figure 4.3 "Power with" as cooperation and learning (own illustration)

4.3.4 Studying "Power Over," "Power To," and "Power With" in Participatory Processes

The multifaceted conceptualization of power presented here, which we adapted from Allen (1998), differs from the definitions of those social and political theorists who understand power in just one of these dimensions (Haugaard, 2012). In the subsequent analysis, we illustrate that such a multidimensional approach, which explicitly highlights the interrelatedness of "power over," "power to," and "power with," is crucial with regard to the complexity of participation in the context of sustainability assessments. The three dimensions allow for different analytical foci and call attention to different aspects and mechanisms of power. "Power over" urges us to pay attention to the ways in which actors, structures, or discourses exert power over others and hints toward the conflictual nature of power. "Power to" directs our analytical focus to the capacity of individual actors to act and achieve their respective goals. "Power with" suggests we look for moments in which collectives emerge that act jointly to achieve common goals. Here consensual facets of power are highlighted.

The different dimensions of power must be understood as analytical, rather than ontological, categories – they might occur simultaneously in any given situation (Allen, 1998, p. 37). They provide us with the necessary tools for analyzing the complexity of power relations in different phases of participatory sustainability assessments, as well as the diverse experiences with power. For instance, a multidimensional approach helps us to see that consensual forms of power or empowerment can be pervaded by "power over" mechanisms, which determine the capacities of individual actors to articulate their concerns and result in the marginalization of weak groups within a community. Or the other way round, a multidimensional approach pushes us to ask how "power with" leads to changes in discourses or structures that reproduce "power over" (Partzsch, 2015). Thus, a multidimensional approach allows us to take into account the productive aspects of power without losing sight of potentially unproductive and negative facets in our analysis.

Based on this theoretical framework, in Table 4.1. we present analytical questions that can be used to systematically explore the role of power throughout participatory sustainability assessments.

Table 4.1 *Dimensions of power and guiding questions derived for analyzing power in participatory sustainability assessments*

Dimension	Definition	Guiding questions for analyzing participation in sustainability assessments
Power over	Power that is exerted over actors, structures, and discourses, including: (1) power as the capacity of powerful actors to directly influence the action of less powerful actors (2) power as the capacity to set the agenda (3) power as the capacity to influence and shape the formation of ideas, norms, and intentions (4) power as the social constructedness and embeddedness of subjectivity in social and historical processes	• Which actors are able/entitled to define the problem to be assessed, the concept of sustainability to be adopted, or the options to be assessed in the participatory sustainability assessment? • Which actors decide who is (not) invited to the table and set the terms of how participants in the sustainability assessment interact? • How are the resources required to take part in the sustainability assessment distributed among actors? • In which ways does the process setup influence the capacity of actors to articulate their concerns and expertise?

Table 4.1 (*cont.*)

Dimension	Definition	Guiding questions for analyzing participation in sustainability assessments
		• In which ways do norms regarding what defines valid knowledge set the boundaries of participation in the sustainability assessment? • Whose knowledge and whose values enter and shape the participatory sustainability assessment? • How far does the participatory sustainability assessment challenge established institutions and practices? • On which forms of social and material organization is the participatory sustainability assessment contingent?
Power to	Power as the individual capacity to act; empowerment and resistance	• Which individual actors involved in the participatory sustainability assessment achieve their goals? • Which individual actors face resistance, and which of them nonetheless have the capacity to shape the participatory sustainability assessment? • In which ways does the participatory process increase the capacities of actors to achieve their goals?
Power with	Power as the capacity to collectively learn and act	• How do actors cooperate in and learn from the participatory sustainability assessment? • To what extent do new goals, understandings, and/or collectives emerge in the course of the participatory sustainability assessment? • Are bridges built between different interests in the participatory sustainability assessment?

4.4 Dimensions of Power in Participatory Sustainability Assessments: An Illustrative Analysis

With this theoretical backing, we now turn to spaces of participation in sustainability assessments and apply the multifaceted framework to an illustrative analysis of power in (1) defining and framing the problem to be assessed, (2) the knowledge-production and assessment process, and (3) governance processes in which results of the assessment are acted upon. We assume a generic sustainability assessment process in which participatory elements can occur at all stages of the assessment (see Figure 4.4).

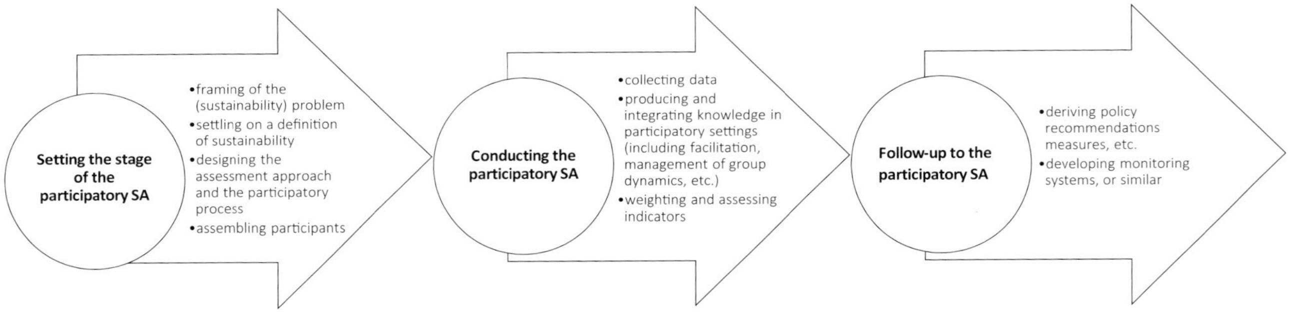

Figure 4.4 Selected elements of a generic participatory sustainability assessment. Source: own illustration; based on process elements mentioned in Binder et al. (2010); Morrison-Saunders et al. (2014); Sala et al. (2015)

Guided by the questions formulated in Table 4.1, we illustrate how, depending on the context and on the ways in which the participatory sustainability assessment is laid out, different forms of power can be present at these different stages (for an overview see Table 4.2). We acknowledge that in the reality of sustainability assessment practice this linearity is oversimplifying and the process might equally be an iterative one.

4.4.1 Setting the Stage for the Participatory Sustainability Assessment

Setting the stage for a sustainability assessment involves defining the problem that is to be assessed. This implies finding a definition of sustainability that serves as the reference in the assessment process (see Chapter 3 (Meinherz et al., 2020)) as well as framing the problem and the system of interest (see Chapter 8 (Binder et al., 2020b)). Setting the stage further includes deciding which approach is to be used, who is participating in the process at which stage and in which role, and how the outcomes of the process will play into governance processes. These decisions influence the remainder of the sustainability assessment.

4.4.1.1 Framing the Problem and the System of Interest

As Bloomfield et al. (1998, p. 11) argue "power lies substantially with those who decide where the boundaries are drawn." The drawing of boundaries with regard to the system of interest is of particular importance when conducting an assessment based on multifaceted and fuzzy concepts such as sustainability. If the problem at the core of the sustainability assessment is decided upon by one person or organization irrespective of the will of other people or organizations, we are typically in an instance of "power over." Some authors show that if the objectives are predefined and cannot be adapted by participants, this negatively impacts on the process and ultimately lowers the chances of reaching these objectives (Kallis et al., 2006, p. 231). Button and Mattson (1999, p. 623) describe this in the case of a deliberative inclusionary process (DIP) where "the perspective of land as something to be cherished and not as something to be used was clearly marginalized within the context of this highly technocratic discussion of 'resource management'." In reaction, a representative of a Native American group "expressed anger at being excluded from the planning of the event where there would have been a chance to move the forum away from a purely technical discourse." Similarly, Tewdwr-Jones and Thomas (1998) argue that the participation process in their case study was critically constrained by the fact that key elements of the policy discourse – e.g., the status of a national park and the question of what a local development plan should (not) include – were non-negotiable. These issues were outside the boundaries set by the responsible agency. This starting assumption and the political context shaped the process and its results (Stirling & Mayer, 1999). Both cases exemplify that those framing the problem and setting the system boundaries (intentionally or not) exert significant "power over" the participatory process.

Such observations point to tensions and dilemmas inherent to participation in the field of sustainability: aiming at an inclusive framing of the problem and the reference system on the one hand, and institutionally framed objectives that impose a pre-existing framing not necessarily shared by all participants on the other (Kallis et al., 2009, p. 985). Participatory methods rest on the idea that those involved are entitled to shape the process and set its goals and outputs (Kallis et al., 2006, p. 231). Reflecting on a deliberative visioning process, Kallis et al. (2009) show that the institutionally defined emphasis on ecological objectives did not receive support from the participants, who feared an externally imposed environmental agenda. The researchers took the decision to put the goals of the process up for debate. This entailed a focus in the problem framing on "quantitative" water management issues, of which the participants were aware. In this case, the aim of ensuring the internal coherence of the participatory approach implied that various combinations of economic, social, and environmental goals led to a watering down of legislation-set ecological objectives (Kallis et al., 2006, p. 261). If people or groups claim space in the sense that they get their stances to be represented in the problem definition, as exemplified with the water management case mentioned, we are in a context of "power to." In such an instance, actors who are not by default in charge develop the capacity to act in their interest.

If, however, in the course of the process, goals, knowledge, and understandings are newly developed and come to shape the problem definition and system understanding, this stage of the assessment process is characterized by "power with." In the water-management case study, this would have required that instead of a process in which the institutional ecological norms and the quantitative water-management norms of the participants remained intact and mutually exclusive, a process would have taken place in which new norms emerged – a new shared understanding of the problem. "Power with" can also take place if the problem is defined collectively by a group of people on the basis of a long-term collaboration process.

4.4.1.2 Settling on a Definition of Sustainability

Similar reflections apply to the definition of sustainability that underpins the assessment. Settling on a conceptualization of sustainability implies a decision regarding the worldviews and values that are considered in the assessment, and is accompanied by an exclusion of alternative conceptualizations (Kemp & Martens, 2007; Robinson, 2004). Operationalizing sustainability in a given context can hence be interpreted as a form of social or political control, implying power relations (Frame & Brown, 2008). If an established definition of sustainability is taken as the benchmark, or if one organization or person decides upon a definition of sustainability regardless of other stances, we are in a context of "power over." Discursive forms of "power over" (fourth face) manifest if the underpinning nature–society conceptualizations or definitions of "development" and "well-being" are unquestioned while others are discredited as utopian (see Chapter 3 (Meinherz et al., 2020)). Pointing toward "power over," science and technology studies scholars address the authority of scientific expertise when it comes to defining sustainability problems and show that in participatory settings experts often dominate by framing environmental issues as primarily technological issues (Berg & Lidskog, 2018). Seemingly paradoxically, societal actors tend to attribute the key role in describing the "true" nature of the issue at stake to science. This way, those participating "take a technical framing for granted, which limits their capacity to discover, understand and internalize challenges that arise outside a particular frame" (Berg & Lidskog, 2018, p. 12). Such participatory sustainability assessments echo and risk reproducing technocentric and anthropocentric worldviews.[3] Just like the problem framing, settling on a definition of sustainability can be marked by instances of "power to" or "power with."

4.4.1.3 Designing the Assessment Approach and the Participatory Process

In this step, the cornerstones of participation spaces are set. This step is most commonly shaped by instances of "power over." In most cases, the assessment is initiated by one party, who lays out the process, i.e., defines which method is to be applied, which steps are to be conducted in which way, and where and in which form participation comes in (Kallis et al., 2006). In research-oriented processes, it is mostly researchers who initiate the sustainability assessment and its participatory elements (Rosendahl et al., 2015). With regard to policy-oriented processes, Cook et al. (2013) note that participation is often initiated by the traditional decision-makers to either empower specific publics, or to legitimize their own decisions.[4]

Although rare, it is conceivable that the design of the participatory sustainability assessment is embedded in a context of "power with," such as when grassroots movements culminate in a formal assessment of a specific sustainability problem. The initiation of a sustainability assessment also takes place in a context of "power with" when it emerges from prior collaborative processes, e.g., when actors jointly launch a follow-up project.

4.4.1.4 Assembling Participants

The question of who enters spaces of participation, and in which role, reflects power relations. It is linked to decisions regarding which worldviews and forms of knowledge are considered valuable and valid in the context of the assessment, and/or who is considered a legitimate representative of a claim, as well as who feels entitled to participate. The question of who is to represent the claims of large groups that are not necessarily organized or clearly defined, such as consumers or residents, or the claims of non-human species, earth processes, or future generations is particularly challenging (Latour, 2005; Lövbrand & Stripple, 2013; Spash, 2007).

The decision of who is to participate can be marked by instances of "power over," "power to," or "power with." A spontaneously self-organized movement, of which anybody can be part, can be seen as an example of "claimed spaces" (Gaventa, 2006) and an emergence of participation in a context of "power with." Such spaces also emerge when actors make their way into different stages of a sustainability assessment, because they mobilize forms of "power to," either in the form of resistance or empowerment. In sustainability assessments applied by administrative bodies, we most likely find "invited spaces" (Gaventa, 2006). If

Box 4.2 **"When": The timing of participation**

The point in time at which one or several participatory methods are applied in a sustainability assessment varies and participatory elements can alternate with more scientific expert-based assessment steps. Moreover, the degree to which the outcomes of participatory elements influence the consequent steps in the assessment process varies. In the context of "neighbourhood sustainability assessment" tools, Sharifi et al. (2013) identify three moments where participatory elements can feed into the process: (i) when defining sustainability, targets, and indicators; (ii) when weighting criteria and indicators; and (iii) when developing an intervention based on the assessment. The "sustainability solution space" approach proposes an iterative and transdisciplinary process to elicit the normative sustainability goals of all participants and to contribute to the development and weighting of indicators (Wiek & Binder, 2005). Likewise, the "sustainability wheel approach" combines a comprehensive system analysis with the consideration of normative aspects as represented in stakeholders' experiences and perspectives. Both expert and stakeholder knowledge are gathered. The involvement of the latter is here particularly central in visioning processes as well as in the development of principles and indicators for the local context in which the assessment is embedded (see Chapter 8 (Binder et al., 2020b)); Chapter 6 (Schneider, 2020); Schneider et al., 2015). The moment at which participation is best built into a sustainability assessment also depends on the larger process within which the assessment is embedded. Whether it is part of a research- or policy-oriented process (e.g., decision-making at the end of the participatory sustainability assessment) marks an important difference. The wider process which the participatory sustainability assessment feeds into implicates different power dynamics (Kallis et al., 2006).

the administrative body decides who to invite to participate in the process, we observe an instance of "power over." This is also the case if specific actors are convoked in the process, either because this enhances the legitimacy of the process or because they hold a specific kind of knowledge. Situations of "power over" can thus be marked by different motivations: participants can be involved in the process either to render it more inclusive and to pursue social justice, or for utilitarian reasons that serve the interest of those designing the process (Reed et al., 2009). In the case of "invited spaces," those asked to take part have the possibility of refusing to participate or of dropping out of an ongoing process. Ensuring lasting commitment on the part of participants is described as a major challenge in participatory sustainability research (Siew et al., 2016) – pointing toward the complexity of power relations and mutual dependencies between actors.

Power dynamics also underpin actor understandings. Frequently, participants in sustainability assessments are conceptualized as "stakeholders." The term "stakeholder involvement" implies that the issues "at stake" are already agreed upon (Wynne & Felt, 2007). Seeing and labelling participants as stakeholders ascribes them specific roles. Relying on stakeholder involvement as opposed to wider conceptualizations of citizenship is likely to be marked by "power over" (second face) as it closes an open debate by starting from an already set problem definition (Reed et al., 2009). By inviting actors whose positions are

Box 4.3 "Who": Selection of participants

Regardless of the approach to and timing of participation, those initiating the participatory process need to decide who to involve. The criteria that inform this choice are tied to the purpose of the participatory process. Participants can be selected based on their (perceived) political influence, their expertise, the envisaged plurality of perspectives to be present in the process, the degree to which participants are affected by or can affect the outcome of the assessment process, the perceived legitimacy of their claims regarding the issue at hand, or their integrity or enthusiasm (Hage et al., 2010; Reed et al., 2009). Although frequently used, the approach of seeing participants through the filter of stakeholders is one approach among others, ascribes a specific role to participants, and impacts on power dynamics. An unsolved conundrum in stakeholder approaches is whether a clear delineation of the problem indicates those who have a "stake," or whether the definition of the problem should be guided by the concerns of heterogeneous actors in the first place (Reed et al., 2009). Ultimately, the decision of who is involved and who is omitted in an assessment determines "whose reality counts" (Chambers, 1997) and shapes the evolution and results of the participatory process.

known, those in charge of the sustainability assessment can select stakeholders with "fitting" positions and prevent controversy and conflict from the outset (Schikowitz, 2016).

4.4.2 Conducting the Participatory Sustainability Assessment

After having illustrated how different dimensions of power can shape the stage of defining the problem, the assessment process, and the notion of sustainability, we look at instances of power at the stage of conducting the actual assessment. This stage typically involves producing and/or integrating different forms of knowledge in a larger process of establishing and measuring indicators, as well assessing them against some sustainability criteria.

4.4.2.1 Knowledge Production and Integration

Participatory processes aimed at bringing together different forms of knowledge for a sustainability assessment do not per se cancel out existing knowledge hierarchies. Interpreted in the context of "power over" (second face), knowledge and its production, "contribute very strongly to the mobilization of bias" (Gaventa & Cornwall, 2001, p. 75). Scientific criteria and rules can be used (intentionally or not) to declare the knowledge of some groups more valid than others, e.g., of "certified experts" over "non-certified experts" (Collins & Evans, 2002). In participation spaces that are tailored to fit the most normalized forms of knowledge (e.g., scientific knowledge) less normalized forms of knowledge (e.g., local knowledge) struggle to have the same weight in the process (Klenk & Meehan, 2015).[5] Particularly when alternative framings of an issue lead to incommensurable visions, the dominance of some forms of knowledge over others becomes apparent (Holmes & Scoones, 2000).

Forms of knowledge that are difficult to integrate into the frames of reasoning of the more normalized forms of knowledge risk being excluded. Such mechanisms of "power over" have been discussed with regard to simulation and computer models that act as integration tools across epistemic boundaries. On the example of transdisciplinary sustainability research, it has been demonstrated how models "include but also exclude certain kinds of knowledge . . . and how they (re)produce orders, roles, and identities within the relation between science and society" (Igelsböck, 2016, p. 133). Similarly to the example of models, indicators can act as boundary objects in sustainability assessments (Turnhout, 2009), giving comparatively more power to those forms of knowledge which transfer well into measurable indicators.

Forms of "power over" (third and fourth faces) also pervade participatory events aimed at joint knowledge production. With regard to environmental policymaking, Holmes and Scoones (2000) illustrate that the authority of actors in participatory processes is tied to having privileged access to "objective factual knowledge" (Sanderson, 1999). In an analysis of seven DIPs, citizens were found to be locked into a referential and passive role. Their exchanges with scientific experts who relied on technical language reflected pre-existing power relations and hampered a deliberative process (Button & Mattson, 1999). In another case study, participants demanded more scientific data and quantified knowledge was particularly used in order to tackle the uncertainty and complexity of water governance. Simultaneously, privileging scientific knowledge undermined the collaborative spirit of the group and some participants perceived the scientific assessment as concealing a political program (Kallis et al., 2009).

Inscribed in "power over" (fourth face), knowledge can reflect established institutional dynamics, or alternatively, perpetuate dominant structures and ideas. Knowledge and social order appear as co-produced (Jasanoff, 2004). This embeddedness of knowledge production can inhibit innovation and societal change by preventing new ideas and creative solutions from gaining traction in the sustainability assessment process. This interdependency of knowledge and social order means that different contexts (e.g., democratic cultures) influence how actors perceive their capacity to participate, as well as the meaningfulness of their participation (Cook et al., 2013). The latter implicates that participants' motivation is predicated on trust that the process will be effective and improve a given situation. If the process proves to be protracted or participants do not see discernible results from the participation process, they are unlikely to stay committed (Holmes & Scoones, 2000; Kallis et al., 2009).

In addition to discursive power in knowledge production, "power over" in its first face forms the participation of diverse actors. Asymmetries in the distribution of financial resources among participants determine their respective capacities to invest time in and shape knowledge production processes (Fritz & Binder, 2018).

4.4.2.2 Managing Spaces of Participation: Facilitation and Group Dynamics

Some scholars ascribe considerable "power over" to facilitators and moderators in shaping the evolution of a participatory event, be it a group discussion, a participatory scenario workshop, or a group modeling workshop (see Box 4.4.). While they might not have a stake in the sustainability issue under debate, they might have an interest in promoting specific methods or hold particular values with regard to collaboration, participation, or the need for democratizing sustainability science. In reflecting on their own roles as facilitators of participatory workshops, scholars share concerns that they might have pushed too much for a compromise in cases in which one might not have emerged spontaneously. In dealing with power relations, facilitators face the dilemma of remaining neutral while at the same time encouraging those who are reluctant to speak: "Intervention raises the question who to privilege and why, i.e. according to what criteria should the levelling be done? . . . From a different perspective, non-intervention is still an indirect act in favour of the status quo" (Kallis et al., 2009, p. 985). Additionally, macro-societal structures, such as gender relations, imply power relations. This is observed in participatory rural appraisal projects where women were not at ease sharing their experience in workshop settings (Holmes, 2001). Linked to the reproduction of macro-societal power relations, group dynamics embody another manifestation of power in participatory processes (Bell et al., 2012). Hidden power dynamics take place when, for example, self-censoring occurs or participants act tactically so as to extract benefits in other settings. With regard to who dominates in workshop settings, differences of personality as well as the capacity to articulate arguments and convince others are decisive (Kallis et al., 2009).[6] Findings from a community-based food-security planning process show how the viewpoints of less influential participants were gradually aligned with those of more powerful actors (McCullum et al., 2004). The results mirrored the "power over" dynamics within the group, even though the "result was deemed a consensus and the process itself considered fair, energizing and satisfying by the internal participants and external observers" (Muro & Jeffrey, 2008, p. 337).

4.4.2.3 Weighting and Assessing Indicators: Trade-offs and Incommensurability of Values

An important challenge at this stage of the sustainability assessment concerns the weighting of indicators and deciding which value or range represents the threshold of what is (un) sustainable (see Chapter 8 (Binder et al., 2020b)). Here, power struggles surrounding trade-offs between different indicators and dimensions of sustainability start to manifest. An example is the decision of how much environmental degradation we consider bearable in exchange for increased production capacities, employment rates, and economic growth.[7] Inevitably, these decisions are normative and mirror the worldviews of those participating, not all of which might be equally heard, i.e., if some have "power over" others.

Those conducting the assessment are confronted with tensions between valuing diversity and plurality of perspectives on the one hand, and the quest for consensus built into many participatory endeavors on the other. Perspectives might not only be contradictory but incommensurable (Martinez-Alier et al., 1998; Pellizzoni, 2003). In this case, the absence of a shared language or common reference system renders any attempt to compare different options impossible. Such a situation is diametrically opposed to the Habermasian ideal-speech situation held up in various conceptualizations of participation, most notably those inspired by Arnstein's (1969) ladder of participation. Pellizzoni (2003, p. 12) argues that equalizing resources might maintain incommensurability by "translating discordant knowledge, concepts and expressions into dominant ones." Rather than acknowledging differences, they are camouflaged ("power over"). Participatory or social multi-criteria assessments are considered particularly apt for tackling situations in which perspectives starkly diverge (Martinez-Alier et al., 1998; Spash, 2007) and the roots of conflicts need to be disclosed (Kallis et al., 2006).[8] Conversely, an assessment relying on cost-benefit analysis encourages participants to focus on monetizing an environmental entity and puts aside incommensurable values (Spash & Vatn, 2006). This look at methods illustrates the power of the value-articulating institutions that are referred to in a process (Vatn, 2005).[9]

Even when values are commensurable, the quest for consensus tends to silence the voices of marginalized groups through hidden mechanisms of "power over." This is particularly pronounced when the values of some actors are subordinated to those of more articulate or persuasive actors in the participatory process. Often win-win outcomes are prevented by historically embedded institutions, reflected in power relations (Spash, 2007). In such a context, striving for consensus "does not provide the most just system for handling differences of opinion, but produces an outcome that does not rise above a low common denominator" (Holmes & Scoones, 2000, p. 33). Failure to address particular interests leaves room for the strategic and hidden manipulation of participatory processes. Such forms of "power over" occur when actors pretend to seek consensus, while covertly pursuing an individual agenda (Pellow, 1999; van den Hove, 2006).[10] Negotiation does inevitably take place in participatory processes. It is, hence, critical to ensure that "negotiation is framed in as fair as possible procedures in order to avoid the perverse effect of reinforcing the power of the strongest actor" (van den Hove, 2006, p. 13). Some scholars suggest that participatory processes need to be designed such that conflict becomes a driving force in the development of solutions and learning processes rather than a hindrance (Mouffe, 2000; Spash, 2007; van den Hove, 2006).[11]

The role of "power over" in dealing with the plurality of values and trade-offs in participatory sustainability assessments points to the importance of early phases of the assessment in which the cornerstones of a common ground are set. Manipulative forces can manifest if participants in the knowledge-production process end up contributing to the achievement of a goal that is not their own. Such a situation can occur if the actors involved in outlining the problem or the working definition of sustainability are not the same as those involved in the knowledge-production process. That there is a sense of purpose to sustainability, a form of vision (Hirsch Hadorn et al., 2006), means that to some extent the knowledge-production process of a sustainability assessment subscribes to this purpose or vision (Farrell, 2011). If we think of a multi-criteria assessment, "power over" occurs when development options or assessment criteria have been defined prior to the consultation. By predefining which options are up for debate, those in charge exert the power to keep other options off the table and restrict the space of what is "negotiable." In the context of technology appraisal, Stirling (2008) observes that incumbent interests tend to instrumentally frame an appraisal so as to limit the range of commitments that it might entail.

Box 4.4 "How": Participatory methods

Diverse methods exist to involve societal actors in sustainability assessments. For participation in research addressing complex problems, the following methods are frequently used: focus groups, participatory scenario analysis, participatory or mediated modeling, citizen juries, consensus conferences, participatory planning, and science–stakeholder workshops. The following publications provide comprehensive overviews of participatory methods used in the field of sustainability: Hartz-Karp et al. (2015), Kasemir (2003), Rauschmeyer et al. (2009), van Asselt Marjolein and Rijekens-Klomp (2002). The choice of methods to involve participants is not a merely technical one, but is tied to the underlying rationale and approach to participation (see Section 4.4.2.). For example, participatory multi-criteria assessment has been found useful for taking into account the high plurality of values regarding controversial sustainability issues and for dealing with their possible incommensurability (Martinez-Alier et al., 1998; Munda, 2006; Polatidis et al., 2006). Participatory modeling of complex sustainability issues has proven powerful in facilitating compromise and actionable conclusions (Stave, 2002; Videira et al., 2010). Depending on whether procedural goals (e.g., the development of policy recommendations) or social goals (e.g., social learning) are at the center, participation can be more appropriate at different stages of the modeling process (Videira et al., 2006). The entire modeling process can be participatory, e.g., in group model building (Vennix, 1996), or a model developed by a group of researchers can be used in a group discussion to facilitate dialogue about different perceptions regarding the system under discussion (Stave, 2002). Yet another method applied in sustainability assessments is that of participatory scenario and visioning processes. In participatory scenario analyses, the focus is on assessing available choices and on finding agreement on a desirable course of action in the face of trade-offs. In participatory visioning processes, the emphasis lies on developing a shared vision of a desirable future and only later on the pathways for its realization. Participatory visioning processes help identify common ideals and are particularly useful at early stages of a sustainability assessment process. Participatory scenario analyses are useful at later stages, when decisions need to be made based on the knowledge that was produced during the assessment (O'Brien & Meadows, 2001; Zurek & Henrichs, 2007). For participatory multi-criteria assessment and participatory visioning, see Chapter 6 (Schneider, 2020), Chapter 8 (Binder et al., 2020), and Chapter 9 (Merino-Saum, 2020).

4.4.3 Learning and Governance Processes as the Follow-Up to a Sustainability Assessment

Understanding the politics of participation requires us to extend our exploration to the stage at which the results of a sustainability assessment are eventually acted upon. Sustainability assessments are generally conducted with a specific action in mind, be it the implementation of a new policy, the construction of an industrial site, or the development of a company's corporate strategy (McCool & Stankey, 2004; Rametsteiner et al., 2011; Waas et al., 2014). Although the implementation phase is strictly speaking not part of the sustainability assessment (Morrison-Saunders et al., 2014), considering power dynamics at this follow-up stage is important when thinking about the transformative power of these processes.

It is with regard to the follow-up that the powerful role of the wider context within which the assessment and its participatory elements are located becomes particularly tangible. The importance of methodological advances notwithstanding, a reflection on the example of a deliberative visioning process affirms that the contribution to society of such a process depends heavily on the context of its implementation and its integration with broader social or policy change (Kallis et al., 2006). An unfavorable institutional and environmental context, in which spontaneously emerging collectives are not valued, has been found to shut down the possibilities for follow-up actions based on a deliberative visioning process (Kallis et al., 2009).

At this stage, normative questions arise, such as who the process results benefit and whether they stabilize or disrupt power relations that perpetuate an unsustainable status quo (Kropp, 2013). Participatory processes can result in the promotion of incumbent actors' interests, unless due attention is paid to how their outputs are invoked in the policy process (Kothari & Cooke, 2001). For instance, a traditional decision-maker might be inclined toward participatory elements in a sustainability assessment in order to legitimize the resulting decisions, and to facilitate their implementation. This points to an intersection of a knowledge-production process characterized by "power with" with forms of "power over," in that the outcomes are instrumentalized with a goal in mind that was not jointly framed in the participatory process.

If the assessment is conducted in a way that novel or previously unheard bodies of knowledge emerge, it may mobilize forms of "power to" or "power with" in follow-up steps. By informing policies, expertise that is not traditionally part of the decision-making process comes to play a role in governance and claims that are not typically influential in the political arena are empowered.[12] In their landmark publication on sustainability science, Kates et al. (2001, p. 641) refer to such productive forms of power, stating that "[c]ombining different ways of knowing and learning will permit different social actors to work in concert, even with much uncertainty and limited information." By unfolding productive power, participatory knowledge-production processes can foster social learning, institutional trust, and cooperation in governing sustainability problems (Garmendia & Stagl, 2010; Hage et al., 2010; Reed et al., 2009; Santos et al., 2006; Videira et al., 2006). Following Hirsch-Hadorn et al. (2006), practice changes toward sustainability are most likely if the actors concerned are aware of the available bodies of knowledge, monitoring, and implementation strategies. Decision-making on complex problems in this reading becomes a process in which actors engage in continuous learning (Garmendia & Stagl, 2010), thus mobilizing "power with." Inscribing the implementation stage in a context of "power with" can contribute to the proactive and adaptive management of the issue at hand.[13]

Zooming out of an individual participatory process, sustainability assessments at large can be understood as a historically constructed social practice. This practice has gained importance to the point where it has become an integral part of how we conceive of governance and knowledge production for governance. This institutionalization of sustainability assessments echoes "power over" (fourth face). By inscribing sustainability values in the governance process, the institutionalization of sustainability assessments in policy processes enforces sustainability as a guiding principle for action. These reflections illustrate that, since it is a form of policy assessment, a sustainability assessment is not neutral in terms of the power dynamics at play in society at large. Assessments and the actors implementing them become constitutive of an attempt to alter power relations by shaping the very values and practices of governance (Cashmore & Richardson, 2013).

Table 4.2 *Matrix of possible forms of power throughout participatory sustainability assessments*

Dimension phase	Setting the stage of the participatory SA	Conducting the participatory SA	Follow-up to the participatory SA
Power over	• One actor (group) has and makes use of the capacity to lay out the sustainability assessment and decide who is to be involved in the process (process design) • One actor (group) has and makes use of the capacity to set the priorities and values of the sustainability assessment (problem framing, sustainability definition, system boundaries)	• Knowledge production exists in the framework of one actor group and impedes the meaningful participation of other knowledge forms • Integration tools privilege the inclusion of some forms of knowledge over others • Facilitators shape group dynamics in participatory workshops • Downplaying plurality of values and perspectives to reach consensus • Uneven distribution of resources to engage in and influence the process	• Derived (policy) measures strongly favor one actor (group); instrumentalization of results by some actors • Inscribing sustainability values in governance processes • The institutionalization of sustainability assessments as a policy assessment tool enforces specific values as guiding principles of governance
Power to	• Different actor groups can make their views count in the definition of the problem • The proposition of an established authority is	• Diverse ways of knowing or producing knowledge enter the process either through invitation or by actors claiming space	• Results of the participatory assessment enable actors to achieve their policy aims by informing policies • Expertise that is not traditionally part of

Table 4.2 (*cont.*)

Dimension phase	Setting the stage of the participatory SA	Conducting the participatory SA	Follow-up to the participatory SA
	questioned and modified as a result of debate on the issue	• (Self-)empowerment	decision-making plays a role in governance • Values that are not typically influential in the political arena are empowered
Power with	• Emergence of a group that collectively initiates the assessment process, e.g., on an issue that was, at least in its final form, on none of the single actors' agendas • Collaborative design of the sustainability assessment as follow-up to previous collaboration and learning	• Social learning processes • Knowledge coproduction and collaborative development of new ideas, solutions	• Collective action on the basis of the sustainability assessment • Social learning process • Contribution to adaptive management

4.5 Concluding Discussion

Participation has been heralded as a key instrument in sustainability assessments. The involvement of diverse actors is thought essential to deal with the plurality of normative claims surrounding the definition of sustainability and the need to take decisions in a context of trade-offs and uncertainty. Despite the fact that participatory sustainability assessments are linked to ideas of action and societal change, critical reflections on the workings of power within, as well as resulting from, participatory assessments have been rare. We presented a conceptualization of power inspired by feminist studies that combines three forms of power: "power over," "power to," and "power with" (see Table 4.1). In a generic analysis we showed how, depending on the layout of the process and the configuration of the social context in which it takes place, different forms of power emerge (see Table 4.2). This suggests that in a participatory sustainability assessment, power works in multiple ways, and is as such neither good nor bad, but can be productive as well as undesirable. Judging the latter is intrinsically normative and depends on the context as well as the observer's standpoint. In this concluding section, we explore possible implications of power for the achievement of specific goals as regards participation and argue that, depending on the desired outcomes of the sustainability assessment, different power dynamics are productive when it comes to the goal of participation. Consequently, awareness of and reflexivity with regard to the power dynamics at play, and their conscious management, are crucial for participation to reach its goals.

4.5.1 From Spaces of Participation to Spaces of Transformation?

With regard to sustainability transformations, participation is often advocated based on the normative assumption that more participation is better – because participation is a goal per se, because participation is thought to foster civic learning and involvement and reinforce democratic processes, or because participation enhances the legitimacy of the process and commitment to its outcomes. As this analysis, guided by a multidimensional approach to power, has illustrated, mechanisms of "power over" or "power to" can restrict spaces of participation, undermine social learning, and limit the transformative potential of the process. More involvement does not necessarily overcome these challenges. If, for instance, the process fails to disrupt dominant discourses, remains subscribed to an established normative position, or in some other way gives over-proportional weight to one set of claims, "power over" and "power to" can also occur in processes characterized by a high intensity of involvement. In such cases, the participatory process runs the risk of concealing the reproduction of an unsustainable status quo. Such dynamics are aggravated if existing power relations and knowledge hierarchies in the social context of the assessment are neglected. For instance, in a context of rigid knowledge hierarchies and unbalanced power relations, new knowledge, civic learning, or social involvement might only unfold if marginalized claims or ways of knowing are deliberately empowered, or if the process is managed in a top-down fashion. This way it might be possible to steer and counterbalance the existing power relations. Such a process, however, compromises deliberative ideals that underlie the normative position that participation is an end in itself. Thus, depending on the context, trade-offs between different motivations for and goals of participation can be unavoidable.

Similarly, a participatory process that is embedded in a dominant discourse might have limited transformative potential, regardless of when and how participation takes place in the sustainability assessment. Examples of discourses that might be tacitly reproduced in a participation process include dominant economic paradigms or the weak conceptualization of sustainability on which technocratic discourses around solving sustainability issues rest (see Chapter 1 (Halla & Binder, 2020) and Chapter 3 (Meinherz et al., 2020)). The pervasiveness of these discourses and the long-standing authority on which they rely reduce the likelihood that actors whose worldviews differ substantially can make themselves heard. If a discourse is, however, only locally dominant, it might be possible to trigger a much greater transformative potential if "power over" is mobilized to introduce new discourses. Again, this interferes with the deliberative ideals ascribed to participation.

Even if the prevailing power dynamics complicate or render unlikely the emergence of truly novel conceptualizations of the problem domain, a participatory sustainability assessment has the potential to produce innovative solutions within a set problem domain or discourse. This is the case if the knowledge-production phase takes place in a context of inclusivity and dynamics of "power with." Similarly, approaches can be developed in which the implementation of the results of an assessment is shaped by instances of "power with." This might favor an adaptive management strategy and foster social learning processes. The chances of this potential being unleashed might be higher if the process embraces plurality and differences in perspectives and ways of knowing, and confronts conflict instead of concealing it.

In a context in which some claims remain unheard because they do not resonate with the dominant discourse, or in which some forms of knowledge are marginalized because they do not integrate easily into the normalized knowledge system, it might be more productive to the goal of finding a promising governance strategy to consciously manage the process by mobilizing forms of "power over," and by empowering specific claims ("power to").

In contrast to these situations embedded in a context of "power over," the configuration of knowledge hierarchies and power relations can be such that throughout the assessment a participatory process characterized by "power with" is possible. In this a case, the transformative potential of the sustainability assessment might be greater if such power dynamics are fostered at the earlier phase of setting the stage. Processes of social learning and deliberation might point to problems or value claims that would not have emerged otherwise. Such an approach might also give more legitimacy to the process of defining the problem space and the reference definition of sustainability.

To conclude, regardless of the motivation behind making a sustainability assessment participatory, power dynamics pervade all stages of the process. While some might be minimized by careful design and the choice of the most appropriate method(s), others might be more elusive. All of them, however, need to be taken into account to ensure that the process results in the desired outcomes.

4.5.2 The Need for Reflexivity and Transparency

Our discussion suggests that more participation does not always lead to the outcomes commonly associated with it. Depending on the prevailing power dynamics, hierarchical processes might unleash a higher transformative potential than inclusive ones. Silver bullets do not exist and different contexts require different approaches. What is needed is reflexivity and critical reflection on existing knowledge hierarchies, discourses, and organizations of power, as well as on how the participatory sustainability assessment process interacts with them. On this basis, the process can be designed in such a way that it is most likely to reach its objectives. Our illustrative analysis has shown that trade-offs between the different goals associated with a participatory sustainability assessment might be necessary. The proposed conceptualization of power makes it possible to identify these trade-offs ex ante, and facilitates the taking of informed decisions on how to design the sustainability assessment process. Our analysis has demonstrated that the participation of diverse actors in an assessment exercise is both a question of methods and techniques and a deeply political endeavor. Hence, a participatory sustainability assessment cannot be looked at in isolation from its surrounding sociopolitical context. The various negotiation processes that form participation spaces throughout a sustainability assessment, the multiple purposes for which they can be mobilized, as well as their role in the wider governance landscape, show the need to pay greater attention to the politics of participatory sustainability assessments.

Despite their relevance in shaping results, detailed information on the participatory processes is lacking in many publications on participatory sustainability assessments and in sustainability research more generally. Further research is required to extend the generic analyses of the dimensions of power provided in this chapter through enquiries into real-world participatory sustainability assessments. More detailed and transparent accounts of participation processes would facilitate learning and the development of best practices. The analytical framework presented in this chapter can guide such critical reflections on power dynamics and how they are influenced by the sustainability assessment approach, as well as how they subsequently influence the outcomes of the latter. By stressing the diverse dimensions of power, we hope to encourage sustainability researchers to acknowledge and study both the productive and the restricting forms of power, as well as the unintended side effects they might produce in participatory processes.

Acknowledgments

We would like to thank Anne von Streit and Albert Merino-Saum for their valuable and constructive comments on earlier versions of this chapter.

Notes

1. Reflecting work on the "politics of knowledge" (Rubio & Baert, 2012), we use the notion of politics to refer to the deep entanglements of knowledge and values that are particularly visible in participatory knowledge-production processes, such as participatory sustainability assessments. In this view, and unlike in "liberal views" of knowledge (Merton, 1973), in participatory knowledge production, knowledge and societal order are not separate, but mutually constitute one another. Consequently, studying these relations, and the power struggles they entail, is crucial.
2. In the field of sustainability, Mielke et al. (2016) build on this approach to develop a typology of scientific perspectives on stakeholder involvement in sustainability science, including a technocratic type, a neoliberal-rational type, a functionalist type, and a democratic type.
3. See Chapter 3 (Meinherz et al., 2020) for a detailed account of the role of different worldviews and values with regard what sustainability is and should be. The authors also critically discuss the role of hegemonic discourses and their repercussions for pluralist approaches.
4. They further note that participation is often promoted by those who it empowers. This shows how a situation of "power over" – for instance, a traditional decision-maker considers that participation is opportune – can intersect with "power to" – a group is empowered to partake in participatory processes. However, it is possible that such a process, although empowering on paper, does not live up to the ambition because the traditional decision-makers fall back on their established modes of governing, regardless of the process (Cook et al., 2013) – or because strong dynamics related to the third and fourth face of "power over" are at play.
5. Those invited to take part may be required to imitate the language of those framing the process in order to be heard (Gaventa & Cornwall, 2008). If the knowledge-production practices of one group dominate, those familiar with these practices have a comparative advantage over those who are not.
6. In a case study on water governance, these characteristics however did not necessarily correlate with political or economic power outside the participatory space (Kallis et al., 2009).
7. For a case study example on trade-offs with regard to hydropower production in a Swiss Alpine region, see Chapter 6 (Schneider, 2020).

8. For a discussion of multi-criteria assessments, see Chapter 9 (Merino-Saum (2020)).
9. The concept of value-articulating institutions was initially proposed by Jacobs (1997) and developed further by Vatn (2005). The concept suggests that the kind of institutions that are "invoked in the process of expressing values, influences both the values that come forward and the conclusions that can be drawn on the basis of them" (Vatn, 2005, p. 210).
10. With regard to stakeholder involvement in strategies for corporate social responsibility, numerous examples are reported, for instance, for the tobacco industry (Burton & Rowell, 2002).
11. Thereby negotiation is understood as "a dynamic process in which preferences are endogenously constructed during the process itself, and where power relations are susceptible to change" (van den Hove, 2006).
12. In this sense, the participation of heterogeneous actors in knowledge production – in our case, in the sustainability assessment process – challenges the well-established role of science as the exclusive source of truth for political decision-making (Hoppe, 1999).
13. For suggestions on how sustainability assessments can incorporate the wider transition processes toward sustainability in which they are embedded, see Chapter 5 (Schilling et al., 2020). Furthermore, in Chapter 3, Meinherz, Fritz, and Schneider (2020) point to the need for experimental approaches.

References

Adelle, C., & Weiland, S. (2015). Sustainability assessment at the policy level. In *Handbook of Sustainability Assessment*. Cheltenham & Northhampton, MA: Edward Elgar Publishing, pp. 103–124.

Allen, A. (1998). Rethinking power. *Hypatia*, 13(1), 21–40. https://doi.org/10.1111/j.1527-2001.1998.tb01350.x.

Arendt, H. (1970). *On Violence*. San Diego, New York, London: Harcourt Brace jovanovich.

Arnstein, S. R. (1969). A ladder of citizen participation. *Journal of the American Institute of Planners*, 35(4), 216–224.

Avelino, F. (2017). Power in sustainability transitions: Analysing power and (dis)empowerment in transformative change towards sustainability. *Environmental Policy and Governance*, 27(6), 505–20. https://doi.org/10.1002/eet.1777.

Bachrach, P., & Baratz, M. (1962). Two faces of power. *American Political Science Review*, 56, 947–995.

Bäckstrand, K. (2003). Civic science for sustainability: Reframing the role of experts, policy-makers and citizens in environmental governance. *Global Environmental Politics*, 3(4), 24–41.

Beierle, T. C. (1999). Using social goals to evaluate public participation in environmental decisions. *Review of Policy Research*, 16(3–4), 75–103.

Bell, S., Morse, S., & Shah, R. A. (2012). Understanding stakeholder participation in research as part of sustainable development. *Journal of Environmental Management*, 101, 13–22. https://doi.org/10.1016/j.jenvman.2012.02.004.

Berg, M., & Lidskog, R. (2018). Deliberative democracy meets democratised science: A deliberative systems approach to global environmental governance. *Environmental Politics*, 27(1), 1–20. https://doi.org/10.1080/09644016.2017.1371919.

Binder, C. R., Baldi, M. G., Gex, B., & Massaro, E. (2020b). The sustainability solution space. In C. R. Binder, E. Massaro, & R. Wyss (eds.), *Sustainability Assessment in Urban Systems*. Cambridge University Press, (pp. 181–208).

Binder, C. R., Feola, G., & Steinberger, J. K. (2010). Considering the normative, systemic and procedural dimensions in indicator-based sustainability assessments in agriculture. *Environmental Impact Assessment Review*, 30(2), 71–81.

Blok, A. (2007). Experts on public trial: On democratizing expertise through a Danish consensus conference. *Public Understanding of Science*, 16(2), 163–182.

Bloomfield, D., Collins, K., Fry, C., & Munton, R. (1998). Deliberative and inclusionary processes: Their contributions to environmental governance. *ESRC DIPs in Environmental Decision-Making*, 17.

Brand, U. (2016). "Transformation" as a new critical orthodoxy: The strategic use of the term "transformation" does not prevent multiple crises. *GAIA-Ecological Perspectives for Science and Society*, 25(1), 23–27.
Burton, B., & Rowell, A. (2002). British American tobacco's socially responsible smoke screen. *PR Watch*, 9(4), 6–12.
Button, M., & Mattson, K. (1999). Deliberative democracy in practice: Challenges and prospects for civic deliberation. *Polity*, 31(4), 609–637.
Cashmore, M., & Richardson, T. (2013). Power and environmental assessment: Introduction to the special issue. *Environmental Impact Assessment Review*, 39, 1–4. https://doi.org/10.1016/j.eiar.2012.08.002.
Chambers, R. (1997). *Whose Reality Counts? Putting the First Last*. London: Intermediate Technology Publications Ltd (ITP).
Chilvers, J., & Kearnes, M. (2015). *Remaking Participation: Science, Environment and Emergent Publics*. Abington and New York: Routledge.
Claudel, M., Massaro, E., Santi, P., Murray, F., & Ratti, C. (2017). An exploration of collaborative scientific production at MIT through spatial organization and institutional affiliation. *PloS one*, 12(6), e0179334.
Collins, H. M., & Evans, R. (2002). The third wave of science studies: Studies of expertise and experience. *Social Studies of Science*, 32(2), 235–296. https://doi.org/10.1177/0306312702032002003.
Cook, B. R., Kesby, M., Fazey, I., & Spray, C. (2013). The persistence of "normal" catchment management despite the participatory turn: Exploring the power effects of competing frames of reference. *Social Studies of Science*, 43(5), 754–779. https://doi.org/10.1177/0306312713478670.
Cornwall, A. (2004). Spaces for transformation? Reflections on issues of power and difference in participation in development. In S. Hickey & G. Mohan (eds.), *Participation: From Tyranny to Transformation*. London and New York: Zed Books, pp. 75–91.
Cornwall, A. (2008). Unpacking 'participation': Models, meanings and practices. *Community Development Journal*, 43(3), 269–283. https://doi.org/10.1093/cdj/bsn010.
Cornwall, A., & Coelho, V. S. (2007). *Spaces for Change? The Politics of Citizen Participation in New Democratic Arenas*, vol. 4. Zed Books.
Dahl, R. A. (1957). The concept of power. *Systems Research and Behavioral Science*, 2(3), 201–215.
Digeser, P. (1992). The fourth face of power. *The Journal of Politics*, 54(4), 977–1007.
Dryzek, J. (1993). Policy analysis and planning: From science to argument. In F. Fischer & J. Forester (eds.), *The Argumentative Turn in Policy Analysis and Planning*. Durham, NC: Duke University Press.
Dryzek, J. (2000). *Deliberative Democracy and Beyond: Liberals, Critics, Contestations*. Oxford: Oxford University Press.
Dryzek, J., & Pickering, J. (2017). Deliberation as a catalyst for reflexive environmental governance. *Ecological Economics*, 131, 353–360.
Eyben, R., Harris, C., & Pettit, J. (2006). Introduction: exploring power for change. *IDS Bulletin*, 37(6), 1–10.
Farrell, K. N. (2011). Snow White and the wicked problems of the west: A look at the lines between empirical description and normative prescription. *Science, Technology, & Human Values*, 36(3), 334–361.
Felt, U. (2009). *Knowing and living in academic research: Convergences and heterogeneity in research cultures in the European context*. Prague: Institute of Sociology of the Academy of Sciences of the Czech Republic.
Fiorino, D. J. (1989). Environmental risk and democratic process: A critical review. *Columbia Journal of Environmental Law*, 14, 501.
Foucault, M. (1977). *Discipline and Punish: The Birth of the Prison*. New York: Vintage Books.
Frame, B., & Brown, J. (2008). Developing post-normal technologies for sustainability. *Ecological Economics*, 65(2), 225–241.
Fritz, L. (2018). (De-)constructing participation in transdisciplinary sustainability research: A critical review of key concepts. In J. Engelschalt, A. Maibaum, F. Engels, & J. Odenwald (eds.), *Schafft*

Wissen–Gemeinsames und geteiltes Wissen in Wissenschaft und Technik (SSOAR). München: SSOAR, pp. 106–124.
Fritz, L., & Binder, C. R. (2018). Participation as relational space: A critical approach to analysing participation in sustainability research. *Sustainability*, 10(8), 2853. https://doi.org/10.3390/su10082853.
Funtowicz, S. O., & Ravetz, J. R. (1993). The emergence of post-normal science. In R. Von Schomberg (ed.), *Science, Politics and Morality*. Dordrecht: Springer, pp. 85–123.
Garmendia, E., & Stagl, S. (2010). Public participation for sustainability and social learning: Concepts and lessons from three case studies in Europe. *Ecological Economics*, 69(8), 1712–1722. https://doi.org/10.1016/j.ecolecon.2010.03.027.
Gaventa, J. (2006). Finding the spaces for change: A power analysis. *IDS Bulletin*, 37(6), 23–33.
Gaventa, J., & Cornwall, A. (2001). Power and knowledge. In P. Reason & H. Bradbury (eds.), *Handbook of Action Research*, Concise Paperback Edition. London, Thousand Oaks, New Delhi: Sage, pp. 72–81.
Gaventa, J., & Cornwall, A. (2008). Power and knowledge. In P. Reason & H. Bradbury (eds.), *The Sage Handbook of Action Research: Participative Inquiry and Practice*, 2nd edition. London, Thousand Oaks, New Delhi: Sage, pp. 172–189.
Gibbons, M., Limoges, C., Nowotny, H., Schwartzman, S., Scott, P., & Trow, M. (1994). *The New Production of Knowledge: The Dynamics of Science and Research in Contemporary Societies*. Los Angeles: Sage.
Gibson, B., Hassan, S., & Tansey, J. (2013). *Sustainability Assessment: Criteria and Processes*. London: Routledge.
Glass, J. H., Scott, A. J., & Price, M. F. (2013). The power of the process: Co-producing a sustainability assessment toolkit for upland estate management in Scotland. *Land Use Policy*, 30(1), 254–265. https://doi.org/10.1016/j.landusepol.2012.03.024.
Habermas, J. H. (1981). *Theorie des kommunikativen Handelns*. Frankfurt: Suhrkamp.
Hage, M., Leroy, P., & Petersen, A. C. (2010). Stakeholder participation in environmental knowledge production. *Futures*, 42(3), 254–264.
Halla, P. & Binder, C. R. (2020). Sustainability Assessment: Introduction and Framework. In C.R. Binder, E. Massaro, & R. Wyss (eds.), *Sustainability Assessment in Urban Systems*. Cambridge University Press, (pp. 7–29).
Hardy, C., & Clegg, S. R. (2006). Some dare call it power. In S. R. Clegg, C. Hardy, T. B. Lawrence & W. R. Nord (eds.), *The SAGE Handbook of Organization Studies*. London: Sage Publications, pp. 754–775.
Hartz-Karp, J., Pope, J., & Petrova, S. (2015). A deliberative collaborative governance approach to sustainability assessment. In A. Morrison-Saunders, J. Pope, & A. Bond (eds.), *Handbook of Sustainability Assessment*, Cheltenham and Northhampton, MA: Edward Elgar, pp. 375–402.
Haugaard, M. (2002). *Power: A Reader*. Manchester Manchester University Press.
Haugaard, M. (2003). Reflections on seven ways of creating power. *European Journal of Social Theory*, 6(1), 87–113.
Haugaard, M. (2012). Rethinking the four dimensions of power: Domination and empowerment. *Journal of Political Power*, 5(1), 33–54.
Hayward, C. R. (2000). *De-facing Power*. New York: Cambridge University Press.
Hegger, D., & Dieperink, C. (2015). Joint knowledge production for climate change adaptation: What is in it for science? *Ecology and Society*, 20(4). www.ecologyandsociety.org/vol20/iss4/art1/.
Hirsch Hadorn, G., Bradley, D., Pohl, C., Rist, S., & Wiesmann, U. (2006). Implications of transdisciplinarity for sustainability research. *Ecological Economics*, 60(1), 119–128. https://doi.org/10.1016/j.ecolecon.2005.12.002.
Holmes, T. (2001). A participatory approach in practice: Understanding fieldworkers' use of participatory rural appraisal in ActionAid The Gambia. *IDS Working Papers*, 123.
Holmes, T., & Scoones, I. (2000). Participatory environmental policy processes: Experiences from North and South. IDS Working Paper, Institute of Development Studies, University of Sussex. Brighton.

Hoppe, R. (1999). Policy analysis, science and politics: From "speaking truth to power" to "making sense together." *Science and Public Policy*, 26(3), 201–210. https://doi.org/10.3152/147154399781782482.
Igelsböck, J. (2016). Designing "integration machines." In B-J. Krings, H. Rodríguez, & A. Schleisiek (eds.), *Scientific Knowledge and the Transgression of Boundaries*. Wiesbaden: Springer, pp.133–160.
Jacobs, M. (1997). Environmental valuation, deliberative democracy and public decision-making institutions. *Valuing Nature*, 211–231.
Jasanoff, S. (2003). Technologies of humility: Citizen participation in governing science. *Minerva*, 41 (3), 223–244.
Jasanoff, S. (2004). *States of Knowledge: The Co-production of Science and the Social Order*. London and New York: Routledge.
Kallis, G., Hatzilacou, D., Mexa, A., Coccossis, H., & Svoronou, E. (2009). Beyond the manual: Practicing deliberative visioning in a Greek island. *Ecological Economics*, 68(4), 979–989.
Kallis, G., Videira, N., Antunes, P., et al. (2006). Participatory methods for water resources planning. *Environment and Planning C: Government and Policy*, 24(2), 215–234.
Kasemir, B. (2003). *Public Participation in Sustainability Science: A Handbook*. Cambridge University Press.
Kates, R. W., Clark, W. C., Corell, R., et al. (2001). Sustainability science. *Science*, 292(5517), 641–642.
Kemp, R., & Martens, P. (2007). Sustainable development: How to manage something that is subjective and never can be achieved? *Sustainability: Science, Practice and Policy*, 3(2), 5–14.
Klenk, N., & Meehan, K. (2015). Climate change and transdisciplinary science: Problematizing the integration imperative. *Environmental Science & Policy*, 54(Supplement C), 160–167. https://doi.org/10.1016/j.envsci.2015.05.017.
Klenk, N., Reed, M. G., Lidestav, G., & Carlsson, J. (2013). Models of representation and participation in model forests: Dilemmas and implications for networked forms of environmental governance involving indigenous people. *Environmental Policy and Governance*, 23(3), 161–176.
Kothari, U., & Cooke, B. (Eds.) (2001). Participatory development: Power, knowledge and social control. In *Participation: The New Tyranny?* London: Zed Books, pp. 139–152.
Kristiansen, M., & Bloch-Poulsen, J. (2013). Participatory knowledge production and power. In L. Phillips, M. Kristiansen, M. Vehviläinen, & E. Gunnarsson (eds.), *Knowledge and Power in Collaborative Research: A Reflexive Approach*. Taylor & Francis, pp. 193–212.
Kropp, C. (2013). Demokratische Planung der Klimaanpassung? Über die Fallstricke partizipativer Verfahren im expertokratischen Staat. In A. Knierim, S. Baasch, & M. Gottschick (eds.), *Partizipation und Klimawandel–Ansprüche, Konzepte und Umsetzung* München: Oekonom, pp. 55–74.
Latour, B. (2005). *Reassembling the Social: An Introduction to Actor-Network-Theory*, vol. 1. Oxford: Oxford University Press.
Lawrence, D. P. (2013). *Impact Assessment: Practical Solutions to Recurrent Problems and Contemporary Challenges*. Wiley Online Library. DOI 10.1002/9781118678381.
Leeuwis, C. (2000). Reconceptualizing participation for sustainable rural development: Towards a negotiation approach. *Development and Change*, 31(5), 931–959.
Lövbrand, E., & Stripple, J. (2013). Bringing governmentality to the study of global climate governance. In J. Stripple & H. Bulkeley (eds.), *Governing the Climate: New Approaches to Rationality, Power and Politics*. Cambridge University Press, pp. 27–41.
Lukes, S. (1974). Power: A *Radical View*. London and New York: Macmillan.
Martinez-Alier, J., Munda, G., & O'Neill, J. (1998). Weak comparability of values as a foundation for ecological economics. *Ecological Economics*, 26(3), 277–286.
McCool, S. F., & Stankey, G. H. (2004). Indicators of sustainability: Challenges and opportunities at the interface of science and policy. *Environmental Management*, 33(3), 294–305.
McCullum, C., Pelletier, D., Barr, D., Wilkins, J., & Habicht, J.-P. (2004). Mechanisms of power within a community-based food security planning process. *Health Education & Behavior*, 31(2), 206–222.

Meinherz, F., Fritz, L., & Schneider, F. (2020). How Values Play into Sustainability Assessments: Challenges and a Possible Way Forward. In C. R. Binder, E. Massaro, & R. Wyss (eds.), *Sustainability Assessment in Urban Systems*. Cambridge University Press, (pp. 65–86).

Merino-Saum, A. (2020). Assessing sustainability through participatory multi-criteria approaches (PMCAs): An updated comparative analysis. In C. R. Binder, E. Massaro, & R. Wyss (eds.), *Sustainability Assessment in Urban Systems*. Cambridge University Press, (pp. X–X).

Merton, R. K. (1973). *The Sociology of Science: Theoretical and Empirical Investigations*. University of Chicago Press.

Mielke, J., Vermassen, H., Ellenbeck, S., Milan, B. F., & Jaeger, C. (2016). Stakeholder involvement in sustainability science: A critical view. *Energy Research & Social Science*, 17, 71–81.

Morrison-Saunders, A., Pope, J., Bond, A., & Retief, F. (2014). Towards sustainability assessment follow-up. *Environmental Impact Assessment Review*, 45, 38–45.

Mouffe, C. (2000). *Deliberative Democracy or Agonistic Pluralism*. Vienna: Institute for Advanced Studies.

Munda, G. (2006). Social multi-criteria evaluation for urban sustainability policies. *Land Use Policy*, 23(1), 86–94. https://doi.org/10.1016/j.landusepol.2004.08.012.

Muro, M., & Jeffrey, P. (2008). A critical review of the theory and application of social learning in participatory natural resource management processes. *Journal of Environmental Planning and Management*, 51(3), 325–344.

O'Brien, F., & Meadows, M. (2001). How to develop visions: A literature review, and a revised CHOICES approach for an uncertain world. *Systemic Practice and Action Research*, 14(4), 495–515.

Partzsch, L. (2015). Kein Wandel ohne Macht: Nachhaltigkeitsforschung braucht ein mehrdimensionales Machtverständnis. *GAIA-Ecological Perspectives for Science and Society*, 24(1), 48–56.

Pellizzoni, L. (2003). Uncertainty and participatory democracy. *Environmental Values*, 12(2), 195–224. https://doi.org/0.3197/096327103129341298.

Pellow, D. N. (1999). Negotiation and confrontation: Environmental policymaking through consensus. *Society & Natural Resources*, 12(3), 189–203.

Polatidis, H., Haralambopoulos, D. A., Munda, G., & Vreeker, R. (2006). Selecting an appropriate multi-criteria decision analysis technique for renewable energy planning. *Energy Sources*, Part B, 1(2), 181–193.

Popa, F., Guillermin, M., & Dedeurwaerdere, T. (2015). A pragmatist approach to transdisciplinarity in sustainability research: From complex systems theory to reflexive science. *Futures*, 65, 45–56.

Power, M. (1997). *The Audit Society: Rituals of Verification*. Oxford, New York: Oxford University Press.

Raik, D. B., Wilson, A. L., & Decker, D. J. (2008). Power in natural resources management: An application of theory. *Society and Natural Resources*, 21(8), 729–739.

Rametsteiner, E., Pülzl, H., Alkan-Olsson, J., & Frederiksen, P. (2011). Sustainability indicator development: Science or political negotiation? *Ecological Indicators*, 11(1), 61–70.

Rauschmayer, F., van den Hove, S., & Koetz, T. (2009). Participation in EU biodiversity governance: How far beyond rhetoric? *Environment and Planning C: Government and Policy*, 27(1), 42–58.

Reed, M. S., Graves, A., Dandy, N., et al. (2009). Who's in and why? A typology of stakeholder analysis methods for natural resource management. *Journal of Environmental Management*, 90(5), 1933–1949.

Renn, O., & Schweizer, P.-J. (2009). Inclusive risk governance: concepts and application to environmental policy making. *Environmental Policy and Governance*, 19(3), 174–185. https://doi.org/10.1002/eet.507.

Robinson, J. (2004). Squaring the circle? Some thoughts on the idea of sustainable development. *Ecological Economics*, 48(4), 369–384.

Rosendahl, J., Zanella, M. A., Rist, S., & Weigelt, J. (2015). Scientists' situated knowledge: Strong objectivity in transdisciplinarity. *Futures*, 65, 17–27. https://doi.org/10.1016/j.futures.2014.10.011.

Rubio, F. D., & Baert, P. (2012). The politics of knowledge: An introduction. In F.D. Rubio & P. Baert (eds.), *The Politics of Knowledge*. Oxon: Routledge, pp. 1–10.

Sala, S., Ciuffo, B., & Nijkamp, P. (2015). A systemic framework for sustainability assessment. *Ecological Economics*, 119, 314–325. https://doi.org/10.1016/j.ecolecon.2015.09.015.

Sanderson, I. (1999). Participation and democratic renewal: from 'instrumental' to 'communicative rationality'? *Policy & Politics*, 27(3), 325–341.

Santos, R., Antunes, P., Baptista, G., Mateus, P., & Madruga, L. (2006). Stakeholder participation in the design of environmental policy mixes. *Ecological Economics*, 60(1), 100–110.

Schikowitz, A. (2016). Choreographies of togetherness: Re-ordering collectivity and individuality in transdisciplinary sustainability research in Austria (Doctoral thesis). Wien.

Schilling, T., Mühlemeier, S., Wyss, R., & Binder, C.R. (2020). A Concept for Sustainability Transition Assessment (STA): A Dynamic Systems Perspective Informed by Resilience Thinking. In C. R. Binder, E. Massaro, & R. Wyss (eds.), *Sustainability Assessment in Urban Systems*. Cambridge University Press, pp. 123–138.

Schneider, F. (2020). A mixed-method, dialogue based approach to sustainability assessments: Fostering learning towards sustainable development. In C. R. Binder, E. Massaro, & R. Wyss (eds.), *Sustainability Assessment in Urban Systems*. Cambridge University Press, pp. 141–160.

Schneider, F., Bonriposi, M., Graefe, O., et al. (2015). Assessing the sustainability of water governance systems: The sustainability wheel. *Journal of Environmental Planning and Management*, 58(9), 1577–1600.

Schneider, F., & Buser, T. (2018). Promising degrees of stakeholder interaction in research for sustainable development. *Sustainability Science*, 13(1), 129–142. https://doi.org/10.1007/s11625-017-0507-4.

Sharifi, A., & Murayama, A. (2013). A critical review of seven selected neighborhood sustainability assessment tools. *Environmental Impact Assessment Review*, 38, 73–87.

Siew, T. F., Aenis, T., Spangenberg, J. H., et al. (2016). Transdisciplinary research in support of land and water management in China and Southeast Asia: Evaluation of four research projects. *Sustainability Science*, 813–829. https://doi.org/10.1007/s11625-016-0378-0.

Sinclair, A. J., Diduck, A. P., Vespa, M., Morrison-Saunders, A., Pope, J., & Bond, A. (2015). Public participation in sustainability assessment: Essential elements, practical challenges and emerging directions. In A. Morrison-Saunders, J. Pope, & A. Bond (eds.), *Handbook of Sustainability Assessment*. Camberley: Edward Elgar, pp. 349–375.

Spash, C. L. (2007). *Deliberative Monetary Valuation (DMV) in Theory*. CSIRO Sustainable Ecosystems Working Paper Series.

Spash, C. L., & Vatn, A. (2006). Transferring environmental value estimates: Issues and alternatives. *Ecological Economics*, 60(2), 379–388.

Stauffacher, M., Flüeler, T., Krütli, P., & Scholz, R. W. (2008). Analytic and dynamic approach to collaboration: A transdisciplinary case study on sustainable landscape development in a Swiss prealpine region. *Systemic Practice and Action Research*, 21(6), 409–422.

Stave, K. A. (2002). Using system dynamics to improve public participation in environmental decisions. *System Dynamics Review*, 18(2), 139–167.

Stirling, A. (2008). "Opening up" and "closing down" power, participation, and pluralism in the social appraisal of technology. *Science, Technology & Human Values*, 33(2), 262–294.

Stirling, A., & Mayer, S. (1999). *Rethinking Risk: A Pilot Multicriteria Mapping of a Genetically Modified Crop in Agricultural Systems in the UK*. Brighton: Science Policy Research Unit, University of Sussex.

Tewdwr-Jones, M., & Thomas, H. (1998). Collaborative action in local plan-making: Planners' perceptions of "planning through debate." *Environment and Planning B: Planning and Design*, 25(1), 127–144.

Turnhout, E. (2009). The effectiveness of boundary objects: The case of ecological indicators. *Science and Public Policy*, 36(5), 403–412.

van Asselt Marjolein, B. A., & Rijkens-Klomp, N. (2002). A look in the mirror: Reflection on participation in Integrated Assessment from a methodological perspective. *Global Environmental Change*, 12(3), 167–184.

van den Hove, S. (2006). Between consensus and compromise: Acknowledging the negotiation dimension in participatory approaches. *Land Use Policy*, 23(1), 10–17. https://doi.org/10.1016/j.landusepol.2004.09.001.

Vatn, A. (2005). Rationality, institutions and environmental policy. *Ecological Economics*, 55(2), 203–217.

Vennix, J. A. (1996). *Group Model Building: Facilitating Team Learning Using System Dynamics*. Chichester and New York: John Wiley and Sons.

Videira, N., Antunes, P., Santos, R., & Lobo, G. (2006). Public and stakeholder participation in European water policy: A critical review of project evaluation processes. *Environmental Policy and Governance*, 16(1), 19–31.

Videira, N., Antunes, P., Santos, R., & Lopes, R. (2010). A participatory modelling approach to support integrated sustainability assessment processes. *Systems Research and Behavioral Science*, 27(4), 446–460.

Videira, N., Lopes, R., Antunes, P., Santos, R., & Casanova, J. L. (2012). Mapping maritime sustainability issues with stakeholder groups. *Systems Research and Behavioral Science*, 29(6), 596–619.

Waas, T., Hugé, J., Block, T., Wright, T., Benitez-Capistros, F., & Verbruggen, A. (2014). Sustainability assessment and indicators: Tools in a decision-making strategy for sustainable development. *Sustainability*, 6(9), 5512–5534.

Weber, M. (1972). *Wirtschaft und Gesellschaft*. 5. rev. edition. Tübingen: Mohr.

Whitmarsh, L., Swartling, A. G., & Jäger, J. (2009). Participation of experts and non-experts in a sustainability assessment of mobility. *Environmental Policy and Governance*, 19(4), 232–250.

Wiek, A., & Binder, C. (2005). Solution spaces for decision-making: A sustainability assessment tool for city-regions. *Environmental Impact Assessment Review*, 25(6), 589–608.

Wynne, B. (2007). Public participation in science and technology: Performing and obscuring a political–conceptual category mistake. *East Asian Science, Technology and Society*, 1(1), 99–110.

Wynne, B., & Felt, U. (2007). *Taking European Knowledge Society Seriously: Report of the Expert Group on Science and Governance to the Science, Economy and Society Directorate, Directorate-General for Research, European Commission*. Luxembourg: Office for Official Publications of the European Communities.

Zurek, M. B., & Henrichs, T. (2007). Linking scenarios across geographical scales in international environmental assessments. *Technological Forecasting and Social Change*, 74(8), 1282–1295.

5

A Concept for Sustainability Transition Assessment (STA): A Dynamic Systems Perspective Informed by Resilience Thinking

Thorsten Schilling, Susan Mühlemeier, Romano Wyss, and Claudia R. Binder

5.1 Introduction

Sustainability has become a key guiding principle for societal development in recent decades (Gallopín, 2003; Kates et al., 2001; Westley et al., 2011). In the face of major societal challenges such as climate change, increasing inequality of capital distribution, or biodiversity loss, scholars and politicians are looking for ways to guide our society toward more sustainable ways of living, doing business, and organizing leisure (Grin et al., 2010; Markard et al., 2016; O'Neill et al., 2018). In this context, methods and tools to assess sustainability based on specific indicator sets have increased enormously in popularity, in both the academic and applied spheres (Gibson, 2016; Pope et al., 2017). A broad canon of literature around sustainability assessment practices has emerged over the past 20 years (see Chapter 1 (Halla & Binder, 2020)).

Sustainability assessment generally encompasses an integrated perspective on all dimensions of sustainability (i.e., social, ecological, economic; Halla & Binder, 2020). Typically, the system is assessed at a specific point in time and using a selected set of indicators. A systemic understanding of sustainability thereby goes beyond a separate conception of the three dimensions of sustainability – namely the economic, ecological, and social – and considers trade-offs, feedbacks, and cause–effect relations (see Chapter 8 (Binder et al., 2020a)).

Systemic sustainability assessments usually start off by establishing a general understanding of the functioning of the system of interest: for example, in the form of a system model covering system elements and their relations (Sala et al., 2015). Subsequently, indicators are derived, which capture the sustainability of the system, respecting the rules of parsimony and sufficiency (see Chapter 8 (Binder et al., 2020a)).

Based on these indicators, it is possible to derive information on the sustainability of a system on a system-wide level (Singh et al., 2009). The assessment aims to reveal any discrepancy between the current system state and what system actors define as a sustainable system state. Furthermore, the effect of interventions can be estimated and qualitatively evaluated with regard to their potential to reduce the discrepancy between the current situation and what is perceived as being a sustainable future system state (Pope et al., 2017). However, a number of authors have identified the need to apply a more dynamic systems perspective in sustainability assessment practices (Gibson, 2016; Pintér et al., 2012; Wiek & Binder, 2005).

In current societal transitions, a sustainability assessment is often embedded in a complex context within which systems aim at becoming more sustainable: e.g., by means of deliberate policy choices (Luthe & Wyss, 2015). Yet, existing sustainability assessment approaches still largely fall short when it comes to considering the time dimension and the systemic context within which the system actors are embedded (see, e.g., Loorbach et al., 2017). While a number of authors have pointed to the importance of the time dimension when designing sustainability assessment approaches and implementing sustainability assessment indicators, in practice, most approaches remain static in the way they conceptualize and measure sustainability (Hugé et al., 2013; Pope et al., 2017).

If sustainability assessment is to provide the knowledge base for decision-making in a sustainability transition context, it needs to take into account the history and potential path dependencies of the system to be assessed. Considering previous system developments makes it possible to put the results of an assessment into a temporal context, learn from past developments, and derive more effective measures to facilitate sustainable development in the future. This requires a sound understanding of the system's transition toward sustainability and goes beyond assessing the sustainability of a system state. Moreover, it puts the overall transition process into focus: "sustainability assessment" becomes "sustainability transition assessment" (STA).

In this context, the following questions arise: How can the dynamics of a transition process be taken into account in sustainability assessment practices? Which specific measures and strategies have to be considered in order to assess whether a system is capable of transitioning toward higher levels of sustainability? Which steps can broaden the scope of current assessment practices as they move toward an STA?

This chapter proposes a concept that allows for the embedding of sustainability assessment within a sustainability transition perspective. We start by showing the relevance of considering system development over time. Based on this dynamic understanding, we present the cornerstones of an STA framework, namely the progress, stability, and adaptability of a transition, as three analytical perspectives (Schilling et al., 2018). These provide the basis for developing a concept for assessing sustainability transitions. To support the application of the concept, we operationalize the three STA perspectives in a set of guiding questions, considering the history of a system's development, its current state, and its potential future states. We then propose three steps for applying the STA concept in the actual assessment process: description, interpretation, and evaluation. We finish with a reflection on how our ideas can complement current sustainability assessment practices and what further steps are required for a full operationalization of STA.

5.2 Conceptualizing Sustainability Transition Assessment (STA)

In STA, the focus is on the development of a system toward sustainability. An ideal-typical STA approach thereby goes beyond asking whether or not a system state is sustainable. At the center of interest lies the question of whether the system is capable of successfully *transitioning* to higher levels of sustainability. To address this question, it is necessary to consider the time axis (historical development, current state, future development) while working with a multi-scalar perspective that takes into account the broader system context along with sub-systemic dynamics (see Gibson, 2006 for an exemplification of multi-level dynamics in sustainability assessments).

5.2.1 Understanding the History, Current State, and Future Development of the Transition Process toward a Higher State of Sustainability

To understand the sustainability of a sociotechnical or socioecological system and make reasonable assumptions about its future, it is essential to start off with an understanding of the dynamics of its past development (Avelino et al., 2016). Path dependency is a key concept in this context, and has been widely applied in innovation studies and institutional economics (Foxon, 2011; Hall & Taylor, 1996; Hassink, 2005). It is essential for understanding which drivers and resistances shaped the development of the system and how the current path of a transition emerged (North, 2012). Understanding path dependencies allows us to learn from past developments and past experiences of actors, adjust regulatory and institutional frames, and plan future actions. In doing so, future intervention options can be assessed by studying the impact of similar interventions in the past. Thus, this process allows decision-makers to learn from past system dynamics (Farla et al., 2012).

A historical perspective can also help us to understand why certain systems and/or subsystems are locked into unsustainable system states. If central actors block novel approaches and the application of more sustainable technologies, or if large parts of society are not willing or able to adapt their behavior, potential transition pathways toward sustainability can be blocked, at least temporarily (Foxon, 2002; Geels, 2011). Such situations call for specific transition-management approaches that open up new development pathways (Westley et al., 2011).

Looking into the future, the plans, visions, and goals of future system states play an important role in driving and stabilizing transition processes, since they have the potential to generate motivation and engagement and guide the overall transition process. They can facilitate consensus-building and commitment among system actors and create a sense of planning security during the transition process. Consequently, ideas of the future can affect both the progress and the stability of the sustainability transition process (Meadowcroft, 2011; Wiek et al., 2006).

Based on these reflections, we propose the following temporally embedded view for a sustainability transition assessment that takes into account historic, current, and potential future states of a complex system that is embedded in a dynamically evolving context (see Figure 5.1). The assessment is performed for the time t 0, but concurrently considers the historic development of the system (t -1), the current situation (t 0), and envisioned future system states (t 1).

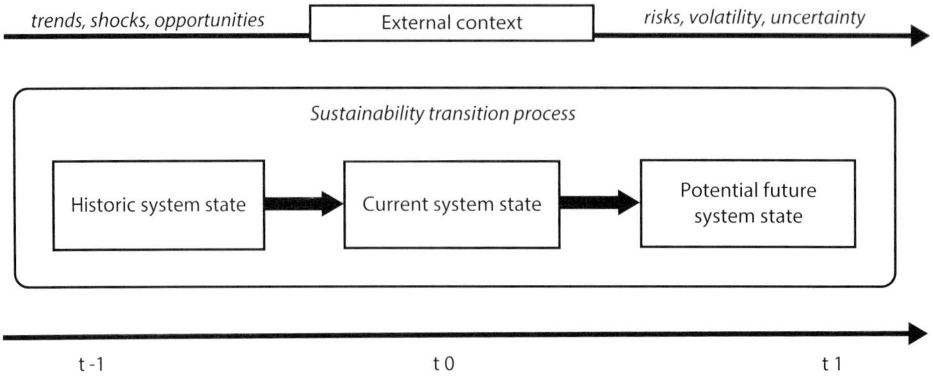

Figure 5.1 Conceptual frame for sustainability transition assessment (STA). Source: own illustration

5.2.2 Sustainability Transition Assessment Perspectives Based on Resilience Thinking

Resilience thinking (Sinclair et al., 2017) can help in further working out and operationalizing temporally dependent factors that affect transition processes. Based on the definition of resilience by (Walker et al., 2004), we propose to understand the resilience of a sustainability transition as "the capacity of a system to absorb disturbance and adapt the sustainability transition process so as to still essentially retain its progress, goals, and pathway" (p. 5). In other words, the resilience of a sustainability transition determines whether the system is capable to successfully go through a sustainability transition process and eventually reach a higher state of sustainability (Schilling et al., 2018). To grasp the complexity of central transition characteristics and their development over time, we propose three distinct perspectives. These assessment perspectives build on key insights from previous work (Binder et al., 2017; Mühlemeier, Binder, & Wyss, 2017; Mühlemeier, Wyss, & Binder, 2018; Schilling et al., 2018; Wyss et al., 2018) and take up notions and ideas from the resilience and sustainability transitions literature. They include the (1) progress, (2) stability, and (3) adaptability of the sustainability transition process. In line with the requirements mentioned above, they consider system-external context conditions that support or hinder the sustainability transition of the system of interest and take into account subsystem dynamics, i.e., the appearance of innovations or interventions that can scale up and become driving or hindering forces for the sustainability transition (Aalbers & Sehested, 2018; Luederitz et al., 2017).

5.2.2.1 Progress of the Sustainability Transition

In this first perspective, we address all aspects related to transition progress, such as drivers, resistances, and the envisioning of future, more sustainable system states. At any point during a transition process, progress is determined by the relation between drivers for and resistances against change (Schilling et al., 2018).

Transition drivers (i.e., social innovations, such as the breakthrough of a technical artifact, economic investments, or political interventions) can change a system's structure and the way it works (functionality). Drivers can have different characteristics that are relevant in classifying their contribution to the transition process: (1) scale of impact on the system (Kemp et al., 2007; Loorbach & Rotmans, 2010), as some drivers can trigger fundamental changes to the overall system, while others cause only small, incremental changes on a sub-systemic scale; and (2) direction of change (Loorbach et al., 2017), as drivers can direct the system in different directions of change, i.e., supporting different pathways toward sustainable development.

The counterpart of drivers for transition are *resistances* against transition (Geels et al., 2014; Luthe & Wyss, 2016). Resistances might neutralize or hinder initiatives to drive the transition in a specific direction and are, thus, of crucial importance to understanding the progress of sustainability transitions. Resistances against changes can emerge for various reasons, such as economic interests (Hashemian et al., 2017), cultural conservatism, or protectionist policy agendas. Identifying path dependencies is crucial in an STA perspective, in order to reveal resistances and understand why some transition goals and pathways might be easier to implement than others.

Furthermore, formal and informal sustainability goals, as well as the power of actors supporting these goals, are of critical importance for the progress of a transition process, since they can have a strong influence on the relation between drivers and resistances (see Chapter 3 (Meinherz et al., 2020) for a discussion of normative goals in sustainability). Many powerful system actors agreeing upon a specific set of sustainability goals can help support the progress of a sustainability transition, especially if the expectations regarding the envisioned future system state are more attractive than those of the current or even previous system states for a majority of affected people. Powerful actors can, however, also significantly hinder the transition progress. An integrative, participative visioning process is thus essential to ensure the commitment of the involved actors and, furthermore, to align the direction of change of transition activities (Sala et al., 2015). A widely shared vision of a potential future state can help maximize the impact of single drivers on the transition progress (see Chapter 4 (Fritz & Meinherz, 2020) for further reflection on the role of participation in sustainability assessment processes).

Sustainability transition assessments should be directed at both drivers for and resistances against sustainability transitions, taking into account the social context, the history of the system, and the normative values that form the basis of the sustainability transition goals expressed in the specific context within which the assessment takes place. The analysis of formal and informal transition goals is therefore an important part of sustainability transition assessments.

5.2.2.2 Stability of the Sustainability Transition

In this second perspective, we address the stability of the transition process and thus the related risks, uncertainties, shocks, and disturbances that could negatively affect it. In this perspective, system resilience helps to maintain basic system structures and functions, whereas the resilience of the transition pathway "protects" the current transition process against spontaneous reorientation and the deliberate counteracting of sustainability goals (Massaro et al., 2018).

In every transition process, a varying amount of uncertainty regarding system, goal, and transformation knowledge exists (CASS, 1997). Future developments of the system remain difficult to predict most of the time, even if a transition process is highly managed and monitored. An even higher uncertainty usually exists regarding the dynamics in the external context of the system of interest (Nair & Howlett, 2016; Sala et al., 2015). Rapid market fluctuations, changing discourses, or political elections can exert pressures on the system and disturb its transition process toward sustainability. If the sustainability transition is stable enough, the system is able to cope with shocks and disturbances, as well as to recover and eventually return to the original transition pathway without losing its previous orientation toward higher levels of sustainability.

In many cases, a continuous struggle between advocates of the old system state and supporters of innovation and change exists in sustainability transition processes and can cause conflicts (Avelino & Wittmayer, 2016). Especially in times of disruptive changes or crisis, previous system states can become attractive again as familiar and time-tested alternatives to the sustainability transition pathway, which might be perceived as uncertain and insecure. Thus, supporters of the old system gain momentum (e.g., Cowell, 2013; Cretney & Bond, 2014). This can slow down the transition process and even cause a reversal of the transition direction, i.e., a regression or bouncing back to previous system states. To reduce the risk of a regression or bouncing back process, a phasing out of the old system is required, ensuring a continuous and smooth change process that is not disruptive and incrementally reduces the stakes connected to old system states (Loorbach, 2014).

Sustainability transition assessments should, thus, look for ways to assess a system's capacity to deal with uncertainty and cope with disturbances and shocks from inside and outside the system. Thereby, the assessment perspective should provide insights about the resilience of the system in transition by assessing how basic identity, functions, structure, and feedbacks are either maintained or altered (Folke, 2016; Walker et al., 2004), while maintaining the direction, drivers, goals, and pathway of the sustainability transition.

5.2.2.3 Adaptability of the Sustainability Transition

As a third major analytical perspective, we address the system's capacity to adapt the sustainability transition process, including its pathway and goals, to changing external and internal conditions. Both in the case of continuously changing boundary conditions and in the case of more sudden, disruptive events – such as the breakthrough of a revolutionary technology, e.g., nuclear fusion for energy production – previous ideas about sustainability goals and transition pathways might become suboptimal or obsolete and adaptations necessary (Nair & Howlett, 2016). In such a case, a very rigid transition process can prevent desirable reorientations. Extreme forms of stability (see Section

5.2.2.2) can obstruct necessary adaptations and cause pathway lock-ins, leading to undesirable transition outcomes.

In practice, there is a fine line between perceiving a new or changing situation as a threat or perceiving it as an opportunity. Some system actors might see a change as an opportunity to further propel the transition toward sustainability, therefore supporting adaptations of the sustainability goals and/or transition pathway, while others might interpret the situation as a threat to their original ideas or ideals and object to adaptation measures in order to protect their ideas. Ideally, actors in a system with a high level of adaptability are capable of constantly reassessing their situation and effectively renegotiating the implementation of adaptation measures with regard to the sustainability transition process (Wiese, 2016). A reliable assessment of threats and opportunities, however, is only possible if monitoring of system and context dynamics takes place, allowing decision-makers to take informed decisions with respect to the planning and implementation of specific adaptation measures (Hester & Adams, 2017).

Sustainability transition assessments should consider the capacity of the system to adapt the sustainability transition process to changing system configurations, external pressures, and dynamic goal-system states. Specific attention should be given to rigidities in the system, which can lead to lock-ins, where desirable transition pathways are no longer pursued due to nested interests of influential actors in the system, despite the knowledge that these would lead to better outcomes.

5.2.3 Toward a Framework for Assessing Sustainability Transitions

Broadening the current static, mono-temporal approaches to sustainability assessment with a more dynamic understanding of sustainability transitions will help enlarge the scope and support the reliability of assessment endeavors on different scales and in different contexts. The ideas brought forward here – building on key characteristics of sustainability transitions, namely progress, stability, and adaptability – allow us to develop assessment procedures that are better informed both temporally and contextually (see Figure 5.2 for a graphical representation). STA can serve as a basis for developing tools in order to assess a sustainability transition process, while also figuring as an information source for decision-making to support initiatives and measures that strengthen future progress, stability, and adaptability.

5.3 Steps toward Assessing Sustainability Transitions

Based on the conceptual reflections and the STA perspectives we have introduced, we propose a set of guiding questions as a first step toward the operationalization of STA (Table 5.1).

We structure the set of questions along the temporal dimensions of an ideal-typical STA: (i) the historic system state, (ii) the current system state, and (iii) potential future system states.

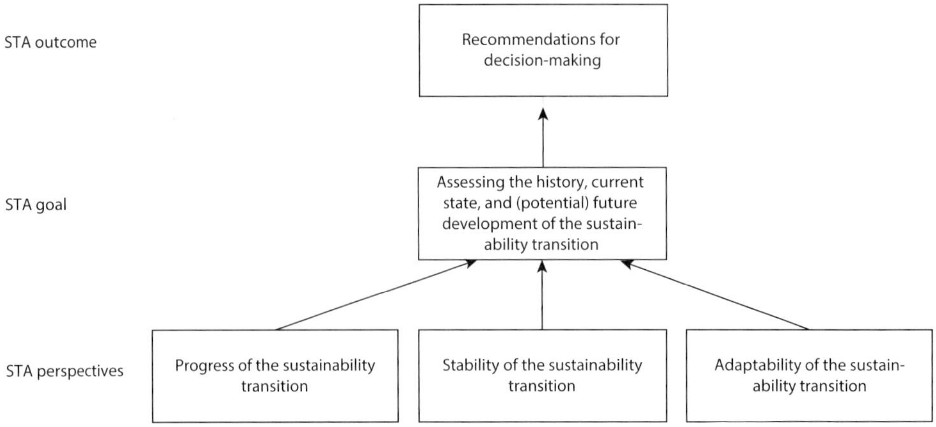

Figure 5.2 Outcome, goal, and perspectives of a sustainability transition assessment (STA). Source: own illustration

The questions enable an understanding of how the transition process has taken place, where we stand today, and what potential future developments might unfold. They build the foundation for a context-sensitive description of the sustainability transition process up to the point of the assessment and make it possible to reflect on implications for future developments.

Regarding the progress of the transition, we investigate what factors were and are key in driving the transition and what factors led to resistances against the transition process in the past and in the current state. Finally, we investigate whether visions of a future development exist, whether stakeholders agree on these visions, and whether there is a shared sense of urgency among actors.

Analogously, we look at the stability of the transition process along the temporal axis (see Table 5.1). How resilient was the system in the past, and how resilient is it today? Has the transition pathway been stable in the face of external shocks and disturbances up until now? Is there potential to further improve system and transition stability?

With regard to adaptability, we address whether it is possible to identify path dependencies and lock-ins that affect the current and future transition or to what extent this system transition was and is currently monitored and managed.

For the actual application of the STA, we propose the following three assessment steps:

- Description of primary data based on the guiding questions (data collection)
- Interpretation of primary data (data analysis) and integration of findings along the temporal dimension
- Evaluation of findings in the light of the resilience of transition perspective (integration of three STA perspectives)

Table 5.1 *Guiding questions for sustainability transition assessment (STA)*

	Progress of the sustainability transition	Stability of the sustainability transition	Adaptability of the sustainability transition
Historic system state	• What were the key factors that drove the system transition in the past? • What were the key factors that led to resistances within the system against transition processes in the past?	• What were the shocks and disturbances that affected the system in the past? • Was the system able to recover from these shocks and disturbances and, if so, how? • Did shocks or disturbances alter the transition pathway in the past?	• How effective were previous management activities (interventions and decision-making) with regard to the transition process? • Who were the key actors who influenced the historic development of the system? • Are there path dependencies or lock-ins that could affect adaptations in the sustainability transition process?
Current system state	• What are the current key drivers of the progress toward sustainability transition? • What is the current status of the sustainability transition? (e.g., stuck in predevelopment) • Do specific resistances against the sustainability transition exist and, if yes, against which aspects specifically?	• What are risks for the system and its transition toward sustainability? • Do institutionalized procedures exist for dealing with uncertainty and recovering from unexpected developments, shocks, or disturbances? • How resilient is the system in general? • How stable is the current transition process toward sustainability (goals and pathway)? • Is there a risk of bouncing back to previous system states?	• How is the sustainability transition of the system monitored? • Is the sustainability transition process managed effectively in terms of consensually adapting, if necessary, development goals/visions and transition pathways toward sustainability? • Do management structures exist and are there entities in place that are responsible for steering the transition process? • Who are the key actors who have decision-making rights and how are they empowered/legitimized to act in the transition context?
Potential future system states	• Do visions exist that are, in the long term, economically, socially, and environmentally more attractive than the current system state? • To what extent do system actors agree on a common vision and corresponding goals for sustainability? • Is there a shared sense of urgency among system actors, increasing the speed of transition?	• How volatile and uncertain are influencing factors external to the system context as well as within the subsystems? • How flexible are system structures when it comes to reacting to changing external circumstances? • Are there any system aspects, entities, or context conditions that could cause a high risk for bouncing back in the future?	• Are there ways to improve adaptability and transition management in the future development of the system? • Is there a risk of the development of path dependencies or lock-ins that might hinder necessary adaptations in the future?

5.3.1 Description of the System in Transition

As a first step, we collect data (reports, measurements, interviews, etc.) in order to answer the questions stated in Table 5.1. Answering these questions allows us to attain an in-depth understanding of the transition process and fill the progress, stability, and adaptability perspectives with information in the form of a sound case description for the transition process. This gives insights into the extent to which the system development has led, and could lead in the future, to a successful transition of the system at stake.

5.3.2 Interpretation

In order to come to an interpretation of the transition process as a whole, the case description for the transition process that was built in the "description" step around the questions in Table 5.1 has to be reduced through aggregation and interpretation. Taking into account the social, geographical, economic, and technical context in which the assessment takes place, the interpretation aims to extract the essence of the description and reflect the results along the time axis to come up with an aggregated and distinct conclusion for each STA perspective (a possible illustration for the progress dimension could be that due to many and influential drivers and few resistances, the transition process facilitates fast and effective interventions for sustainability). These aggregated conclusions build the foundation for the following evaluation.

5.3.3 Evaluation

In the last step, the conclusions drawn from the description and interpretation of the sustainability transition process need to be evaluated against a suitable reference frame. Therefore, it is necessary to define the "ideal" state of the transition, which serves as a benchmark to compare the current state with in order to evaluate the discrepancy between the two to give the final results of the assessment. For "traditional" sustainability assessments, this reference frame is "sustainability." Consequently, the current state of the system is evaluated against what is perceived as a sustainable state of the system, with the discrepancy being the final result of the assessment. Analogously, the current state of the sustainability transition process needs to be evaluated against a reference frame that defines the "ideal" state of the process in an STA. In the context of sustainability transitions, this ideal state of a transition process maximizes the chances of the system reaching a higher state of sustainability successfully. Therefore, the transition process needs to be as resilient as possible.

According to Schilling et al. (2018) the resilience of sustainability transitions (RST) depends on the balance between progress, stability, and adaptability. Since the three dimensions are interrelated, trade-offs between individual dimensions can unfold. Extreme stability, for example, can cause lock-ins and hinder necessary adaptations. Similarly, radical drivers that have a large effect on the system state in a short amount of time can negatively affect system resilience by destabilizing essential system structures. To what extent such trade-offs unfold, and whether or not they critically affect the resilience of the transition process, depends on the context of each specific application. Therefore, the balance between the three dimensions that represents a resilient transition process varies across different contexts. Similar to the context-dependent definition of sustainability, which is an integral part of a sustainability assessment, a sustainability transition assessment requires a context-dependent definition of a resilient transition process as a reference frame for the evaluation of the current state.

Consequently, the evaluation of a sustainability transition assessment requires a case-by-case definition of the balance between progress, stability, and adaptability that maximizes the chances of the sustainability transition process being successful and thus resilient. Subsequently, this ideal state needs to be compared to the current state of the sustainability transition process that results from the description and interpretation steps of the assessment. The discrepancy between the two serves as the final result of the sustainability transition assessment.

5.4 Discussion and Concluding Remarks

In this chapter, we proposed three perspectives – progress, stability, and adaptability – for a sustainability transition assessment. These enable the past, present, and potential future states of the system of interest to be included in the assessment, while being sensitive to external, systemic, and sub-systemic conditions and developments. A sustainability transition assessment that is sensitive to the dimension of time, as proposed here, makes it possible to assess not only the current state of the system, but also the state of the overall sustainability transition process with respect to the sustainability goals. Consequently, it facilitates a deeper understanding of the system's potential to successfully go through a sustainability transition process and eventually reach a higher state of sustainability.

We have provided a set of guiding questions and proposed three steps (description, interpretation, and evaluation) through which the STA perspectives can be applied in a sustainability assessment process. Thereby, we showed how the additional analytical layers of the STA contribute to a deeper understanding of the overall system development by answering the question of whether the system under scrutiny is suited to successfully transitioning toward higher states of sustainability.

STA is meant to be an extension of, rather than a substitute for, existing sustainability assessment approaches. Whether or not an STA perspective is suitable depends not only on the interests of an assessment, but also on the time and financial resources at hand. The implementation of a full-scale STA goes along with an increased resource demand for the collection of data and its interpretation. Therefore, the application of an STA makes most sense if the sustainability transition process of the system of interest and its dynamics are of importance for informing decision-makers: for example, in the case of major infrastructure investments or specific policy initiatives.

A further critical aspect that has to be taken into account when designing and conducting an STA is the normativity of the sustainability concept as such, which holds true for all sustainability assessment approaches (see Chapter 3 (Meinherz et al., 2020)). Applying an STA requires normative issues to be included right from the start, as part of the system analysis. Only by knowing about existing perceptions of sustainability goals and principles can we identify resistances to and drivers of sustainability transitions. The normative understanding of sustainability can vary between different cases or between different points in time, which is why we need a critical and reflective perspective on the meaning of sustainability in STA processes. Perceptions of sustainability are to be seen as an integral part of the analysis and are important to understanding system dynamics.

Future research on sustainability transition assessments should engage in further operationalization of the three analytical perspectives, as well as the real-world testing of indicators, based on case studies from various fields. Potential applications of STA might be particularly interesting and important for empirical research looking at critical infrastructure, such as water, energy, or food supply chains. In these sectors, which provide fundamental services and goods for society, the success of sustainability transitions is of critical importance for the functionality of the system and these services must be provided in a reliable way. Once fully developed, STA will be able to provide additional insights that can complement traditional sustainability assessment schemes in this context.

References

Aalbers, C. B. E. M., & Sehested, K. (2018). Critical upscaling: How citizens' initiatives can contribute to a transition in governance and quality of urban greenspace. *Urban Forestry & Urban Greening*, *29*, 261–275. https://doi.org/10.1016/j.ufug.2017.12.005.

Avelino, F., Grin, J., Pel, B., & Jhagroe, S. (2016). The politics of sustainability transitions. *Journal of Environmental Policy & Planning*, 18(5), 557–567. https://doi.org/10.1080/1523908X.2016.1216782.

Avelino, F., & Wittmayer, J. M. (2016). Shifting power relations in sustainability transitions: A multi-actor perspective. *Journal of Environmental Policy & Planning*, 18(5), 628–649. https://doi.org/10.1080/1523908X.2015.1112259.

Binder, C. R, Hutter, M., Pang, M., & Webb, R. (2020a). "System science and sustainability assessment. In C. R. Binder, E. Massaro, & R. Wyss (eds.), *Sustainability Assessment in Urban Systems*. Cambridge University Press, pp. 30–64.

Binder, C. R., Mühlemeier, S., & Wyss, R. (2017). An indicator-based approach for analyzing the resilience of transitions for energy regions. Part I: Theoretical and conceptual considerations. *Energies*, 10(1), 36. https://doi.org/10.3390/en10010036.

CASS, P. (1997). Research on sustainability and global change: Visions in science policy by Swiss researchers. *ProClim: Forum for Climate and Global Change and Swiss Academy of Sciences, Bern.*

Cowell, M. M. (2013). Bounce back or move on: Regional resilience and economic development planning. *Cities*, 30, 212–222. https://doi.org/10.1016/j.cities.2012.04.001.

Cretney, R., & Bond, S. (2014). "Bouncing back" to capitalism? Grass-roots autonomous activism in shaping discourses of resilience and transformation following disaster. *Resilience*, 2(1), 18–31. https://doi.org/10.1080/21693293.2013.872449.

Farla, J., Markard, J., Raven, R., & Coenen, L. (2012). Sustainability transitions in the making: A closer look at actors, strategies and resources. *Technological Forecasting and Social Change*, 79(6), 991–998.

Folke, C. (2016). Resilience (Republished). *Ecology and Society*, 21(4). https://doi.org/10.5751/ES-09088-210444.

Foxon, T. J. (2002). Technological and institutional 'lock-in' as a barrier to sustainable innovation. *Imperial College Centre for Policy and Technology Working Paper.*
Foxon, T. J. (2011). A coevolutionary framework for analysing a transition to a sustainable low carbon economy. *Ecological Economics*, 70(12), 2258–2267.
Fritz, L., & Meinherz, F. (2020). The politics of participatory sustainability assessments: An analysis of power. In C. R. Binder, E. Massaro, & R. Wyss (eds.), *Sustainability Assessment in Urban Systems*. Cambridge University Press, pp. 87–122.
Gallopín, G. (2003). *A Systems Approach to Sustainability and Sustainable Development*. United Nations Publications.
Geels, F. W. (2011). The multi-level perspective on sustainability transitions: Responses to seven criticisms. *Environmental Innovation and Societal Transitions*, 1(1), 24–40. https://doi.org/10.1016/j.eist.2011.02.002.
Geels, F. W., Tyfield, D., & Urry, J. (2014). Regime resistance against low-carbon transitions: Introducing politics and power into the multi-level perspective. *Theory, Culture & Society*, 31(5), 21–40. https://doi.org/10.1177/0263276414531627.
Gibson, R. (2016). *Sustainability Assessment: Applications and Opportunities*. Oxon and New York: Routledge.
Gibson, R. B. (2006). Sustainability assessment: basic components of a practical approach. *Impact Assessment and Project Appraisal*, 24(3), 170–182.
Grin, J., Rotmans, J., & Schot, J. (2010). *Transitions to Sustainable Development: New Directions in the Study of Long Term Transformative Change*. New York: Routledge.
Hall, P. A., & Taylor, R. C. (1996). Political science and the three new institutionalisms. *Political Studies*, 44(5), 936–957.
Halla, P., & Binder, C.R. (2020). Sustainability Assessment: Introduction and Framework. In C. R. Binder, E. Massaro, & R. Wyss (eds.), *Sustainability Assessment in Urban Systems*. Cambridge University Press, pp. 7–29.
Hashemian, B., Massaro, E., Bojic, I., Arias, J. M., Sobolevsky, S., & Ratti, C. (2017). Socioeconomic characterization of regions through the lens of individual financial transactions. *PloS one*, 12(11), e0187031.
Hassink, R. (2005). How to unlock regional economies from path dependency? From learning region to learning cluster. *European Planning Studies*, 13(4), 521–535. https://doi.org/10.1080/09654310500107134.
Hester, P. T., & Adams, K. M. (2017). *Systemic Decision Making: Fundamentals for Understanding Problems and Messes* (2nd ed.). Cham: Springer International Publishing.
Hugé, J., Waas, T., Dahdouh-Guebas, F., Koedam, N., & Block, T. (2013). A discourse-analytical perspective on sustainability assessment:interpreting sustainable development in practice. *Sustainability Science*, 8(2), 187–198.
Kates, R. W., Clark, W. C., Corell, R., et al. (2001). Sustainability Science. *Science*, 292(5517), 641–642. https://doi.org/10.1126/science.1059386.
Kemp, R., Loorbach, D., & Rotmans, J. (2007). Transition management as a model for managing processes of co-evolution towards sustainable development. *International Journal of Sustainable Development & World Ecology*, 14(1), 78–91. https://doi.org/10.1080/13504500709469709.
Loorbach, D. (2014). *To transition! Governance panarchy in the new transformation*. https://drift.eur.nl/wp-content/uploads/2016/12/To_Transition-Loorbach-2014.pdf.
Loorbach, D., Frantzeskaki, N., & Avelino, F. (2017). Sustainability transitions research: Transforming science and practice for societal change. *Annual Review of Environment and Resources*, 42(1), 599–626. https://doi.org/10.1146/annurev-environ-102014-021340.
Loorbach, D., & Rotmans, J. (2010). The practice of transition management: Examples and lessons from four distinct cases. *Futures*, 42(3), 237–246. https://doi.org/10.1016/j.futures.2009.11.009.
Luederitz, C., Abson, D. J., Audet, R., & Lang, D. J. (2017). Many pathways toward sustainability: Not conflict but co-learning between transition narratives. *Sustainability Science*, 12(3), 393–407. https://doi.org/10.1007/s11625-016-0414-0.

Luthe, T., & Wyss, R. (2015). Introducing adaptive waves as a concept to inform mental models of resilience. *Sustainability Science*, 10(4), 673–685. https://doi.org/10.1007/s11625-015-0316-6.
Luthe, T., & Wyss, R. (2016). Resilience to climate change in a cross-scale tourism governance context: a combined quantitative-qualitative network analysis. *Ecology and Society*, 21(1). https://doi.org/10.5751/ES-08234-210127.
Markard, J., Suter, M., & Ingold, K. (2016). Socio-technical transitions and policy change: Advocacy coalitions in Swiss energy policy. *Environmental Innovation and Societal Transitions*, 18, 215–237. https://doi.org/10.1016/j.eist.2015.05.003.
Massaro, E., Ganin, A., Perra, N., Linkov, I., & Vespignani, A. (2018). Resilience management during large-scale epidemic outbreaks. *Scientific Reports*, 8(1), 1859.
Meadowcroft, J. (2011). Engaging with the politics of sustainability transitions. *Environmental Innovation and Societal Transitions*, 1(1), 70–75. https://doi.org/10.1016/j.eist.2011.02.003.
Meinherz, F., Fritz, L., & Schneider, F. (2020). How Values Play into Sustainability Assessments: Challenges and a Possible Way Forward. In C. R. Binder, E. Massaro, & R. Wyss (eds.), *Sustainability Assessment in Urban Systems*.Cambridge University Press, pp. 65–86.
Mühlemeier, S., Binder, C. R., & Wyss, R. (2017). 'It's an endurance race': An indicator-based resilience analysis of the energy transition in the Allgäu Region, Bavaria. *GAIA – Ecological Perspectives for Science and Society*, 26(S1), 199–206.
Mühlemeier, S., Wyss, R., & Binder, C. R. (2018). Ein indikatorengestützter Ansatz zur Resilienzanalyse von Energiesystemen in Transition. In M. Karidi, M. Schneider, & R. Gutwald, *Resilienz*. Wiesbaden: Springer, pp. 293–326. https://doi.org/10.1007/978-3-658-19222-8_15.
Nair, S., & Howlett, M. (2016). From robustness to resilience: Avoiding policy traps in the long term. *Sustainability Science*, 11(6), 909–917. https://doi.org/10.1007/s11625-016-0387-z.
North, D. C. (2005, November 12). *Understanding the Process of Economic Change*. Princeton and New York: Princeton University Press. https://doi.org/10.4324/9780203023846-11.
O'Neill, D. W., Fanning, A. L., Lamb, W. F., & Steinberger, J. K. (2018). A good life for all within planetary boundaries. *Nature Sustainability*, 1(2), 88. https://doi.org/10.1038/s41893-018-0021-4.
Pintér, L., Hardi, P., Martinuzzi, A., & Hall, J. (2012). Bellagio STAMP: Principles for sustainability assessment and measurement. *Ecological Indicators*, 17, 20–28. https://doi.org/10.1016/j.ecolind.2011.07.001.
Pope, J., Bond, A., Hugé, J., & Morrison-Saunders, A. (2017). Reconceptualising sustainability assessment. *Environmental Impact Assessment Review*, 62(Supplement C), 205–215. https://doi.org/10.1016/j.eiar.2016.11.002.
Sala, S., Ciuffo, B., & Nijkamp, P. (2015). A systemic framework for sustainability assessment. *Ecological Economics*, 119, 314–325. https://doi.org/10.1016/j.ecolecon.2015.09.015.
Schilling, T., Wyss, R., & Binder, C. R. (2018). The resilience of sustainability transitions. *Sustainability*, 10(12), 4593. https://doi.org/10.3390/su10124593.
Sinclair, K., Rawluk, A., Kumar, S., & Curtis, A. (2017). Ways forward for resilience thinking: Lessons from the field for those exploring social-ecological systems in agriculture and natural resource management. *Ecology and Society*, 22(4). https://doi.org/10.5751/ES-09705-220421.
Singh, R. K., Murty, H. R., Gupta, S. K., & Dikshit, A. K. (2009). An overview of sustainability assessment methodologies. *Ecological Indicators*, 9(2), 189–212. https://doi.org/10.1016/j.ecolind.2008.05.011.
Walker, B., Holling, C. S., Carpenter, S., & Kinzig, A. (2004). Resilience, adaptability and transformability in social–ecological systems. *Ecology and Society*, 9(2). www.ecologyandsociety.org/vol9/iss2/art5/inline.html.
Westley, F., Olsson, P., Folke, C., et al. (2011). Tipping toward sustainability: Emerging pathways of transformation. *AMBIO: A Journal of the Human Environment*, 40(7), 762–780. https://doi.org/10.1007/s13280-011-0186-9.
Wiek, A., & Binder, C. (2005). Solution spaces for decision-making: A sustainability assessment tool for city-regions. *Environmental Impact Assessment Review*, 25(6), 589–608. https://doi.org/10.1016/j.eiar.2004.09.009.
Wiek, A., Binder, C., & Scholz, R. W. (2006). Functions of scenarios in transition processes. *Futures*, 38(7), 740–766. https://doi.org/10.1016/j.futures.2005.12.003.

Wiese, F. (2016). Resilience thinking as an interdisciplinary guiding principle for energy system transitions. *Resources*, 5(4), 30. https://doi.org/10.3390/resources5040030.

Wyss, R., Mühlemeier, S., & Binder, C. R. (2018). An indicator-based approach for analysing the resilience of transitions for energy regions. Part II: Empirical application to the case of Weiz-Gleisdorf, Austria. *Energies*, 11(9), 2263. https://doi.org/10.3390/en11092263.

Part II

Integrative Approaches for Sustainability Assessment

With the increasing popularity of the term sustainability, a high variety of sustainability assessment tools has emerged. These tools are either specific to one area or sector, focus solely on one specific area – i.e., environmental, economic, or social – or develop aggregate indices for specific purposes. To assess sustainability issues within urban systems, approaches are needed which are applicable to a variety of cases and sectors. The second part of our book, "Integrative Approaches for Sustainability Assessment," presents and discusses four selected integrative sustainability assessment approaches. The approaches presented share several criteria that we consider indispensable for sustainability assessment in urban systems: all approaches include normative and systemic perspectives, have a broad scope, and are applicable to different cases, and at different scales and aggregation levels. The four approaches were chosen to represent the following: (1) qualitative approaches – in situations where we are confronted with low data availability and a variety of actors, and where there is a need to integrate and develop a consistent sustainability assessment with which all parties agree; (2) integrative conceptual approaches – in situations where there might be too many indicators and a sound way of reducing the indicators is needed, as these approaches provide a set of rules for selecting and reducing the indicators; (3) semi-quantitative approaches that provide a way to analyze trade-offs between the indicators, in cases where conflict between stakeholders and over options might be envisioned; and (4) multi-criteria approaches that are quantitative and semi-quantitative and offer very flexible approaches that can be used in combination with the other three approaches.

Chapter 6, "A Mixed-Method, Dialogue-Based Approach to Sustainability Assessments: Fostering Learning toward Sustainable Development," presents a qualitative, dialogue-based approach to sustainability assessments. This approach can be very fruitful for gaining a holistic and comprehensive perspective on contested sustainability situations when complex and heterogeneous knowledge (e.g., research from natural and social sciences, qualitative and quantitative knowledge) needs to be structured. It can enhance the creation of a shared understanding of sustainability problems and solutions, and facilitate communication with stakeholders. In this chapter, the author presents a conceptual and methodological approach for qualitative sustainability assessments, based on what we call the sustainability wheel. It is an approach that combines transparent identification of sustainability principles, their regional contextualization through sub-principles (indicators), and the scoring of these indicators through deliberative dialogue within an interdisciplinary team of experts, taking into account their different qualitative and quantitative knowledge.

Chapter 7, "Sustainability Assessment: Integrative Concept, Methodology, and Examples," provides an integrative concept of sustainable development (ICoS). The approach combines top-down and bottom-up perspectives on sustainability development. By providing three general sustainability goals and deriving 25 sustainability rules, ICoS provides a way for deriving, for each specific case, a set of indicators that on the one hand consider the normative sustainability perspective being adopted and on the other hand emerge from the specific context. The indicators are part of a stepwise, systematic, and consistent construction that links theoretical abstraction to deliberative action: the political and societal practice of sustainable development.

In Chapter 8, "Sustainability Solution Spaces" – (SSP) are presented as an integrative method for assessing sustainability. An SSP represents the room to maneuver (or wiggle room) in the system at hand so that it can develop sustainably. The SSP method can be pursued in a participatory (qualitative) and an expert (quantitative) way. The expert approach requires large amounts of data, preferably over time or for a large number of cities, and is thus well suited to comparing large sets of cities with each other, clustering and providing benchmarks for specific city types, and delivering general indications of which areas policy development is required in. The participatory approach can be applied in a qualitative way and might be particularly useful for assessing the impact of a specific project or analyzing in depth a specific sector, such as mobility or housing.

Finally, Chapter 9, "Participatory Multi-Criteria Approaches (PMCAs)," presents a comparative analysis of four PMCAs usually applied in sustainability assessments (SMCE, MCM, 3-SPM, and INTEGRAAL). The approaches are presented in detail and subsequently compared to each other according to three elementary yet crucial questions: who assesses?; what is assessed?; and how is it assessed? Results outline potential synergies and theoretical incompatibilities among the four approaches. The analysis also supports future applications of PMCAs when choosing one particular approach according to key meta-principles (i.e., epistemological stance, methodological emphasis); logistical constraints (e.g., time, budget); local idiosyncrasies (e.g., pertinent geographical scales, power asymmetries); and organizational factors.

6

A Mixed-Method, Dialogue-Based Approach to Sustainability Assessments: Fostering Learning for Sustainable Development

Flurina Schneider

6.1 Introduction

Considering the long-lasting challenges of unsustainable governance of natural resources, there is a need for comprehensive sustainability assessments (Reed & Kasprzyk, 2009; Wiek & Larson, 2012) that allow us to understand the current and possible future development situations from a holistic perspective, while at the same time fostering learning among multiple actors involved in order to induce necessary actions. However, this endeavor is quite challenging for several reasons:

First, sustainability is a multidimensional concept involving biophysical, sociocultural, and economic aspects and their complex interrelationships (see Chapter 8 (Binder et al., 2020a)); Reed & Kasprzyk, 2009; Wiek & Larson, 2012). Hence, to assess the sustainability of a situation, systemic, interdisciplinary, and integrative approaches are needed. This means that knowledge about very different phenomenon (e.g., material water availability or quality, concerns of different water users, and possible immaterial meanings they attribute to water), which are usually generated under the different theoretical assumptions of distinct disciplines (e.g., qualitative vs. quantitative research paradigms), must be brought together and evaluated in a coherent way.

Second, sustainability is a normative concept, involving values and goals of how a more desirable future would look (see Chapter 3 (Meinherz et al., 2020) and Schneider & Rist, 2014). In other words, sustainability values and visions are the normative compass of sustainability assessments. Recently, an overall global sustainability vision has been endorsed by the General Assembly of the United Nations (UN): the 2030 Agenda and its 17 Sustainable Development Goals (SDGs). However, there are alternative sustainability visions such as the Brundtland Report, national sustainability strategies or suggestions by scientists (e.g., Wiek & Larson, 2012). Hence, to assess the sustainability of a situation, researchers are challenged to incorporate normative questions in a coherent and reflexive way (Schneider et al., 2020; Ziegler & Ott, 2011).

Third, while these sustainability visions can be regarded as an overall compass, what sustainability means in certain contexts is usually very contested among multiple societal actors (Pahl-Wostl, 2009; Schneider & Rist, 2014), for example, if a new hydropower plant contributes to sustainability or not. Some actors might argue that this is positive for the production of clean energy, while others might highlight the loss of aquatic ecosystems. Hence, for sustainability assessments, general principles as outlined in the above-mentioned reports must be translated to the specific situations under consideration (e.g., a regional water governance system).

Fourth, considering the complexity and contested nature of sustainability, communicability of insights gained in sustainability assessments merits particular consideration.

However, there are rather few holistic approaches that tackle these challenges in a systematic way – particularly in the field of sustainable governance of water and land resources (Wiek & Larson, 2012). Most existing approaches emphasize singular aspects such as quality and supply of resources (Kondratyev et al., 2002), infrastructure, adaptive capacity (Hill, 2013), or social learning (Pahl-Wostl et al., 2009). Moreover, studies that investigate the sustainability of resource governance systems from holistic perspectives (e.g., Larson et al., 2013) often focus on the present situation without in-depth assessments of possible future developments.

Against this background, we argue that a mixed-method, dialogue-based approach to sustainability assessments can be very fruitful. Mixed-method approaches attempt to consider multiple viewpoints and perspectives, including the standpoints of qualitative and quantitative research (Creswell & Clark, 2017; Johnson et al., 2007). They have the advantage that they can well represent the complexity and dynamic nature of resource governance systems. Purely quantitative approaches often require (over) simplifying complex issues such as resource governance arrangements (Ioris et al., 2008), and purely qualitative approaches disregard the potential of quantifying phenomena such as resource availability and use. With mixed-method approaches, heterogeneous knowledge sources can be integrated (data triangulation), and aspects that are hard to measure or hard to quantify, such as informal governance practices, can be considered (e.g., Lachavanne & Juge, 2009).

Dialogue methods are one way these different types of knowledge can be integrated. Dialogue methods help structure group conversation processes that aim to "jointly create meaning and shared understanding about real-world problems by bringing together knowledge from relevant disciplines and stakeholders" (McDonald et al., 2009, p. 5). They consider that sustainability assessments involve more than bringing together knowledge in terms of "facts," but also include appreciating different epistemologies, values, interests, and wordviews. Dialogue methods emphasize conversation criteria such as equal participation, active listening, and mutual probing of assumptions (Franco, 2006; McDonald et al., 2009). They can be used to organize stakeholder participation processes as outlined in Chapter 4 (Fritz & Meinherz, 2020), but they can also be used to structure interdisciplinary knowledge integration among researchers.

In this chapter, we present a mixed-method, dialogue-based approach called the sustainability wheel. In the following, we shortly present the overall conceptual approach. Then, we apply it to a specific resource governance system: sustainable water governance. By doing so, we outline the specific methods used and report on key results. Finally, we conclude with some reflections about the relevance of the developed methodological approach.

6.2 Overall Conceptual Approach

Our conceptual approach follows four main steps:

1 **Interdisciplinary, systemic analysis of the resource governance system:** a systemic understanding that relates ecological, social, economic, technical, legal, and cultural aspects is the fundamental basis of a sustainability appraisal (Reed & Kasprzyk, 2009; Wiek & Larson, 2012). This appraisal must encompass reflections on the boundaries of the resource governance system, the areas of focus, the systemic cause–effect structures, and possible future developments (Wiek & Larson, 2012). It involves issues of resource availability and use, decision-making and governance, as well as societal actors' perspectives on the issues under study. Taking the normative and contested nature of sustainability into account, integration of societal actors' different perceptions, priorities, and future visions is particularly important. This, in turn, requires developing and synthesizing empirical knowledge originating from different scientific disciplines and practice in a transdisciplinary process.

2 **Development of sustainability principles**: while many studies and reports of resource governance refer to the concept of sustainability, few of them systematically reflect on the value base of sustainability (Schneider & Rist, 2014). Consequently, only few authors specify transparent and value-laden sustainability principles (Wiek & Larson, 2012). In-depth reflection on the underlying values of a more sustainable future and its contextualization for specific resource governance systems, however, is fundamental for assessing sustainability and finally defining actions for more sustainable governance and recasting policy discourse. Therefore, our second step involves the identification of basic sustainability principles to be considered.

3 **Contextualization and indicator development:** in order to make the rather abstract principles (step 2) for resource sustainability operational, they need to be further broken down into more concrete sub-principles that spell out what it means to make specific governance arrangements in specific contexts (step 1) more sustainable (Schneider & Rist, 2014). In other words, a contextualized understanding of the sustainability principles is needed to achieve a certain fit with the local circumstances (Hartmuth et al., 2008). In our approach, we therefore develop specific indicators for each sustainability principle that are relevant for the local context. Considering affected societal actors' sustainability values and norms is indispensable for this step.

4 **Assessment of the sustainability of the resource governance system: the sustainability wheel:** the sustainability wheel allows us to bring together the systemic and the normative approaches of the previous steps in order to achieve a comprehensive assessment of the sustainability of the resource governance system under question. Its design and structure are inspired by the work of Gupta et al. (2010) on adaptive capacity ("the adaptive capacity wheel"). This step involves assessment of the sustainability indicators defined in step 3, taking into consideration the totality of knowledge generated in step 1. The assessment is done through a systematic rating exercise. To jointly create meaning

and shared understanding about the sustainability situation, we suggest using dialogue methods for accomplishing this final assessment.

6.3 Application of the Sustainability Wheel to Water Governance

In this section, we provide an example of how the sustainability wheel can be applied to the assessment of a specific resource system. We use the case of sustainable water governance as in this case the complex and dynamic interrelationships between different aspects such as hydrology, economy, and regional development are most evident, as well as the multiple societal actors' different perspectives on how the resource should be used and managed. For example, there are usually many different water users (households, farmers, industry, tourism, hydropower, nature, etc.) with different ideas and priorities regarding sustainable water governance. Details can be found in the original article (Schneider et al., 2015).

6.3.1 The Case Study Area

The case study area, Crans-Montana-Sierre region, is located on a southern slope in the canton Valais, one of the driest areas of Switzerland. It contains considerable variation in elevation and a strong hydrological gradient; the difference between precipitation and evapotranspiration averages about 150 mm/y at the valley bottom and more than 2,200 mm/y at high elevations. The region encompasses eleven communes and four main watersheds and is drained by several small streams flowing toward the Rhône River. The discharge of meltwater from the Plaine Morte Glacier is an important water resource for the region. The organization of the study area in terms of land and water use is characterized by a stratified altitudinal structure: a regional center (Sierre, with a population of 15,000) in the Rhône River valley bottom; several villages with residential and agricultural (viticulture, livestock) activities in the lower parts of the mountainside; and the tourist resort of Crans-Montana (skiing, golf, hiking) at more than 1,500 masl. With more than 37,000 tourist beds, Crans-Montana is one of the largest mountain tourist resorts in Switzerland. Moreover, the largest amount of water by far is used for hydropower production and stored in an artificial reservoir (Tseuzier Lake).

6.3.2 Interdisciplinary, Systemic Analysis of the Resource Governance System

We aimed to gain a holistic, systemic understanding of the water governance system by focusing on four interrelated areas, taking into consideration present and future (2050) conditions:

- Water availability: how much water is available?
- Water use: how much water is used?
- Decision-making: how are decisions made over water distribution and use?
- Stakeholders' perspectives: what meaning do stakeholders give to water?

Research on the status of the current system was based on hydro-meteorological and land use measurements and modeling, participatory observation, qualitative interviews, analysis of existing reports and statistical data, and regular stakeholder workshops (group RegiEau). Research on possible future situations was based on visioning techniques, modeling, and calculations. Taking the normative and contested nature of sustainability into account, in a participatory process with the group RegiEau, we developed four future visions that encompass stakeholders' different priorities of how their region should develop (regional development, infrastructure, and institutional reforms); the fourth vision (Vision RegiEau) represents a consensus of the participating stakeholders. Important aspects of the four visions are displayed in Table 6.1 (for more details see Schneider & Rist, 2014, Reynard et al., 2014). These visions were then translated to water use scenarios as a basis for simulating future water demands. For modeling future water use, as well as resource availability, we used IPCC A1B climate change scenarios (CH2011, 2011).

6.3.3 Development of Sustainability Principles for Water Governance

For specifying sustainability for water governance, we referred to the Brundland Report, which states that, "sustainability implies a concern for social equity between generations, a concern that must logically be extended to equity within each generation" (WCED, 1987). This means that sustainable water governance systems should allow the current generation to meet their societal goals in an equitable way without compromising the water options of future generations (ASCE & UNESCO, 1998). Based on these general ideas, and considering other literature on water sustainability or governance (e.g., Gibson, 2006; Gleick, 1998; Hill, 2013; Pahl-Wostl, 2009; Wiek & Larson, 2012), we derived four main principles for sustainable water governance systems:

1. **Contribution to societal goals of regional development:** this first principle states that people living today, and in the future, should be able to meet their development goals. Water availability should allow them to satisfy diverse needs ranging from household consumption and recreation to economic activities such as production of food, energy, or other goods and services.
2. **Maintenance of ecological and hydrological integrity:** maintaining the ecological and hydrological integrity of water resource systems is crucial for meeting development goals of not only the current population, but especially of future generations. This second principle is about the quality and quantity of surface and groundwater as well as about the benefits and harms to the ecosystem resulting from diverse water uses (Kondratyev et al., 2002).
3. **Contribution to social justice:** as stated in the Brundtland definition of sustainability (WCED, 1987), justice concerns should not only be considered between generations, but also within the current generation. Consequently, social justice has to be regarded as basic element of water sustainability.
4. **Adaptive capacity:** in times of increasing uncertainty due to socioeconomic and climate changes, the ability to flexibly respond and adapt to changing supply and demand is an

Table 6.1 *Overview on the four future visions (adapted from Schneider & Rist, 2014)*

Topics	Vision1: Growth strategy	Vision 2: Stabilization strategy	Vision 3: Moderation strategy	Vision of the RegiEau group
Overall strategy	Growth is at the heart of the region's development. Mass tourism, lucrative activities, and second homes are the main focus. Water resources and landscape are important, but not top priorities. Indeed, the inhabitants of Crans-Montana-Sierre feel that there is enough water for the future thanks to engineering measures (supply management).	Water and landscape are among the region's most important resources. They are indispensable both for tourism and for the local population's well-being. For this reason, regional development in Crans-Montana-Sierre follows alternative approaches aimed at more efficient resource use. Water management focuses in particular on optimizing water consumption (demand management).	Development in the Crans-Montana-Sierre region is oriented primarily toward improving quality of life for residents and visitors. Creating jobs is just as important as maintaining an adequate drinking water supply and conserving a healthy cultural landscape. Water and landscape use are in line with the needs of the local economy.	Consensus based on stakeholders' discussions of the other three visions. It represents a mixture of Visions 2 and 3.
		Regional development		
Demography	Strong population growth	Slight population growth	Population decrease	Slight population growth
Water consumption	No water-saving efforts Drinking water is at times used for irrigation	Water supply has become more efficient Separate drinking water and irrigation water networks	Water supply has become more efficient Separate drinking water and irrigation water networks Great efforts to save water	Water supply has become more efficient Separate drinking water and irrigation water networks, including in residential areas

Spatial planning	Unrestrained building activities (under current legislation)	Densification Construction of second homes is restricted Construction of small apartment buildings is encouraged	Building industry has developed into reconstruction and energy-efficient renovation industry Some previous building areas have been rezoned as non-developable areas	Densification Construction of second homes is restricted Construction of small apartment buildings is encouraged
Tourism	Mass tourism based mainly on skiing and golf (new snow cannons and golf greens)	Tourism has become more attractive all year round Skiing area has been reduced	Tourism industry focuses on "soft" tourism based on gastronomic and outdoor activities linked with a broad range of cultural and educational offers	Tourism has become more attractive all year round Skiing area has been reduced
Agriculture	Agriculture is not a priority Farming has become increasingly extensive	Agriculture plays important role in food production (especially meat)	Agriculture is highly important to the region and primarily serves tourism, nature conservation, and landscape maintenance	Agriculture is highly important to the region and serves tourism, nature conservation, and landscape maintenance
Viticulture	Viticulture has been intensified (increased profitability) Sprinkler irrigation	Viticulture is continued at same level of intensity (high-quality wine) Drip irrigation	Viticulture has become increasingly extensive (high-quality wine, biodiversity) Drip irrigation	Viticulture is continued at same level of intensity (high-quality wine) Drip irrigation
Hydropower	Hydropower production is of utmost importance The hydropower potential of all rivers is fully tapped	Hydropower production has high priority, but other water needs are considered equally important (irrigation, drinking water, etc.)	Hydropower production is important, but the goal is to reduce energy consumption and diversify energy sources	Hydropower production is important, but the goal is to reduce energy consumption and diversify energy sources

Table 6.1 (*cont.*)

Topics	Vision1: Growth strategy	Vision 2: Stabilization strategy	Vision 3: Moderation strategy	Vision of the RegiEau group
		Infrastructure development		
Pipelines	New storage, transport, and pumping infrastructures are built	Interlinked drinking water network, separation of drinking water and irrigation water, perfect maintenance	Interlinked drinking water network, separation of drinking water and irrigation water, perfect maintenance	Interlinked drinking water network, separation of drinking water and irrigation water, perfect maintenance New storage, transport, and pumping infrastructures are built
Storage capacities	New storage lake	No additional storage capacities	Dispersed storage of rainwater by households	Dispersed storage of rainwater
		Institutional reforms		
Collaboration	No new forms of collaboration Putting one's own needs first	Centralized water management, however, decision-making power stays with the communes	United water management for the well-being of all inhabitants of the region	United water management for the well-being of all inhabitants of the region
Water rights	No water rights reform	Water rights reform	Water rights reform (from private to public rights)	No waters right reform
Residual water	No water withdrawals when discharge is less than 25 l/s	No water withdrawals when discharge is less than 50 l/s	No water withdrawals when discharge is less than 100 l/s	No water withdrawals when discharge is less than 50 l/s

essential requirement for the sustainability of water governance systems (Pahl-Wostl, 2009). Adaptive capacity is therefore considered a fourth main principle of a sustainable water governance system (ASCE & UNESCO, 1998). It refers to the capacity of actors to create and respond to variability and change, as well as the impacts on the state of the system in both proactive and reactive ways (Adger et al., 2005; Hill, 2013).

6.3.4 Contextualization and Indicator Development for the Case Study Region

Subsequently, through iterative discussions, the team broke down the four main principles into three to five indicators each, considering the scientific literature (Babel et al., 2011; Ioris et al., 2008; Sullivan & Meigh, 2007; Valenzuela Montes & Matarán Ruiz, 2008; Wiek & Larson, 2012), the meanings local societal actors give to water and sustainability, as well as the specific characteristics of the case study region (identified in step 1). In a first step, the researcher responsible for knowledge integration developed a draft set of indicators. For doing so, she reviewed the indicators proposed in the scientific literature, analyzed interviews/workshops to capture the stakeholders' perspectives, and assessed them against the background of her overall regional context knowledge based on the research of step 1. Then, the draft indicators and their descriptions were discussed and refined by the interdisciplinary research team, and later by the stakeholders of the group RegiEau.

Concretization of the first principle – contribution to societal goals of regional development – was based on the participatory visioning process and a set of stakeholder interviews. These brought four major dimensions to the forefront: water for basic needs, recreation and enjoyment, agriculture, and hydropower production. For specifying the other three principles, we mainly drew on existing literature and context knowledge within the team of researchers.

For the principle of ecological integrity, we found that quality and quantity of surface and groundwater resources are among the most widespread indicators that are relevant for our region (e.g., Ioris et al., 2008; Sullivan & Meigh, 2007; Wiek & Larson 2012). Moreover, we defined a forth indicator on benefits and harms of water use, as in our region ecosystems benefit from, or are harmed by, specific water uses such as irrigation of species-rich dry meadows or artificial snow production (Rixen et al., 2003).

For the principle of justice we referred to recent literature (Fraser, 2009; Schlosberg, 2007) that stipulates that justice assessments should not only focus on just outcomes of resource distribution processes (distributive justice), but also on the fairness of governance processes themselves (procedural justice), as well as on the context, "which incorporates the pre-existing conditions that limit or facilitate people's access to decision-making procedures, resources and, thereby, benefits" (contextual justice) (McDermott et al., 2013). We choose these three justice indicators, as our research showed that all three dimensions are relevant in our region.

For the principle of adaptive capacity, the indicators are derived from a study of members of our team (Schneider & Homewood, 2013) that found that the adaptive capacity of the water governance system in the case study region is influenced by the actors' access to financial, material, and social resources including collaborative capacity and entitlements (Babel et al., 2011; Olsson et al., 2006), as well as effective demand management mechanisms (resource efficiency) and a high learning capacity, which allows anticipating potential problems and developing farsighted solutions (Folke et al., 2005; Olsson et al., 2006; Pahl-Wostl et al., 2009; Tompkins & Adger, 2004). See Table 6.2 for an overview of the indicators we have defined for the study region.

Table 6.2 *Description of indicators for the four sustainability principles for the Crans-Montana-Sierre region*

Principles	Indicators	Description
Regional development	*Basic needs*	Water governance should allow the people to meet their basic needs concerning household water uses such as drinking, cooking, and sanitation.
	Recreation and enjoyment	Water governance should enable the people to pursue recreation and enjoyment, specifically by benefiting from water in the landscape (historical water channels, lakes, rivers, wetlands, cultural irrigated landscapes, glaciers), and tourism-related activities.
	Agriculture	Water governance should enable the people to practice agriculture and viticulture to produce local food and forage, and to maintain the cultural landscape.
	Hydropower production	Water governance should allow benefit from the region's high potential for hydropower production.
Ecological integrity	*Groundwater quantity*	Aquifers should not be overexploited beyond the long-term regeneration and recharge rates.
	Surface water quantity	Minimum flows in surface water (rivers, lakes, water channels) should be guaranteed for fish, wildlife, and ecosystems, as well as for recreation and enjoyment.
	Water quality	The quality of water resources for ecosystems and humans should be ensured by eliminating, reducing, or mitigating pollution.
	Benefits (and harms) of water use	Water uses in the landscape, such as artificial snow production and irrigation, should not harm the ecosystem.
Justice	*Distributive justice*	Benefits, costs, and risks are equitably distributed among all actors involved in water use and governance.
	Procedural justice	Decision-making processes related to water use and governance are based on normative frameworks (rule of law), disclosure of relevant information (transparency), and principles of impartiality (non-discrimination). There are institutions that facilitate negotiation and collective decision-making between all actors concerned.
	Contextual justice	Different water user groups and communes have comparable capabilities to access and benefit from water.

Table 6.2 (*cont.*)

Principles	Indicators	Description
Adaptive capacity	*Material and financial capital*	Available financial capital and infrastructure should allow exploiting the available water resource, flexibly diverting it, and buying water from others.
	Collaborative capacity	Actors involved are able to respond to water problems through formal and informal means of coordination and cooperation based on trust, joint visions, and power sharing (e.g., functional water markets, effective cooperation platforms and networks, joint planning).
	Institutions and entitlements	Institutions and entitlements (e.g., property rights, concessions, formal and informal rules) of water governance arrangements provide predictability and certainty, as well as flexibility, in order to respond to water shortage crises.
	Resource efficiency	Water demand can be reduced through effective water demand management including more efficient irrigation techniques, separation of drinking water and irrigation water, repairing leaky infrastructure.
	Learning capacity	Actors are involved in continuous learning processes, allowing them to anticipate potential problems and to find adequate answers. There are opportunities for learning by doing, knowledge exchange, transparency of information, monitoring and assessments, as well as participatory strategy development.

6.3.5 Assessing the Sustainability of the Resource Governance System: The Sustainability Wheel

After setting the framework, we assessed the defined sustainability indicators, taking into consideration the totality of knowledge available through the previous literature and novel research results of the participating researchers, including interviews with stakeholders. The sustainability wheel enabled us to structure this comprehensive information and increase the ease with which it is communicated to further societal actors. The inner circle shows the four main principles of sustainable water governance (step 2); the outer circle presents the indicators that specify each principle (step 3) (see Figure 6.1).

In order to consider the multifaceted and complex interrelationships characterizing the collected knowledge about the water governance system in place, we did not conduct a quantitative assessment, but a qualitative one. Thus, the assessment of the indicators was based on a deliberative dialogue and scoring process within our team of 13 interdisciplinary researchers (hydrologists, sociologists, glaciologists, human and physical

Figure 6.1 The sustainability wheel of the water governance system Crans-Montana-Sierre

geographers, specialists in water and land use, and management). It took place in a two-day workshop following the scoring protocol proposed by Gupta et al. (2010). In a first step, knowledge and research results that were relevant for assessing certain indicators were presented. Based on this information, each researcher rated each indicator on a five-point scale (very good, good, moderate, poor, very poor). To visualize the results and ease their interpretation, the traffic light color system was applied, where dark red means very poor sustainability, yellow moderate, and dark green very good sustainability. Subsequently, we discussed the ratings in order to find common ground and agree on a single rating per indicator. This procedure was repeated for each indicator for the present as well as for four different future visions. Finally, all indicators were jointly reassessed in order to harmonize the ratings and to get a coherent overall picture. After this, we translated the collected information to a storyline in order to give meaning to the individual indicator scores.

A qualitative, dialogue-based assessment of sustainability indicators is at risk for being judged as subjective, since it requires that the researchers interpret and score research results. To address this risk, we organized the scoring process as transparently as possible and required that the scoring was justified by evidence (if this was not possible, the indicator was not rated). Furthermore, a moderator oversaw that the knowledge bases and arguments of the participating researchers were considered equally and that the final scoring was based on an agreement of the best argument.

The resulting sustainability wheels, their scoring, and related storylines are presented in Sections 6.3.6 and 6.3.7.

6.3.6 Sustainability Assessment of the Present

The sustainability wheel of the present (Figure 6.2) clearly shows that the present water governance system of Crans-Montana-Sierre region can principally allocate sufficient water to achieve society's goals of regional development (scored as good); however, its performance regarding ecological integrity, adaptive capacity (both scored as moderate), and especially regarding justice (scored as poor) are more limited.

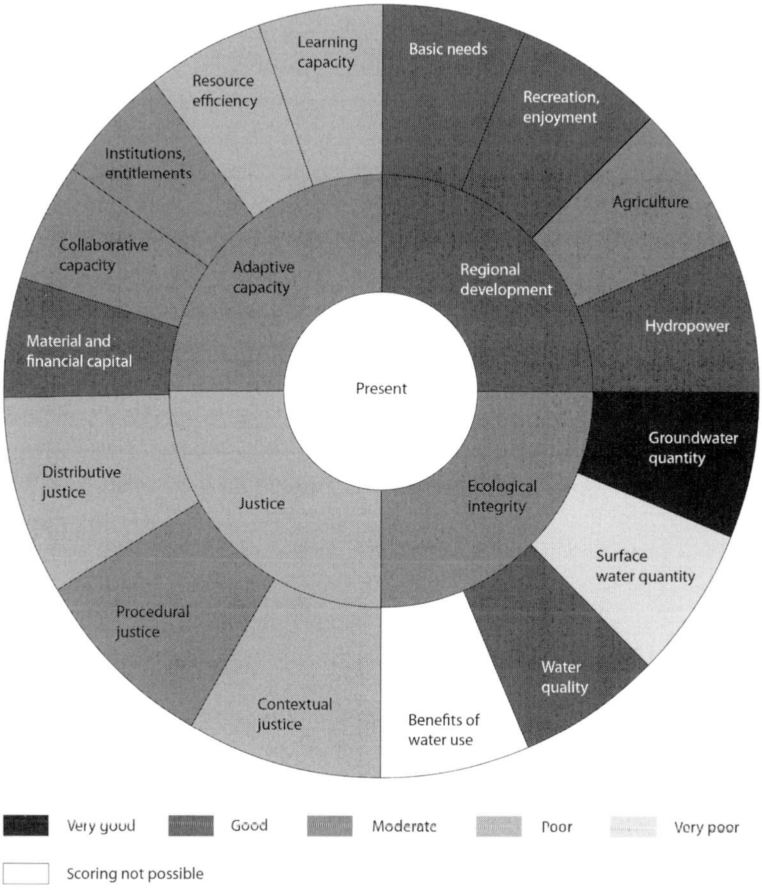

Figure 6.2 The sustainability wheel of the present for the Crans-Montana-Sierre region

The good evaluation of this first principle was the product of the good rating of three indicators; only agriculture is scored as moderate. Overall, water supply of all the inhabitants and visitors is guaranteed throughout the year, but during some periods (winter low discharge months, dry periods in summer) there is always the risk for the dependent communes without water rights to face shortages. Regarding recreation and enjoyment, there are only minor constraints, mostly in dry years when the lakefronts become unattractive due to reduced water levels or no water flows in the rivers and water channels. In the last 20 years, hydropower production has been considered to have been fully profitable from an economic point of view, but even more water resources could be included. Agriculture/grassland production is the economic activity currently most affected by water shortages. In dry years, use of irrigation water can be restricted causing income losses for farmers.

The ratings of the various ecological integrity indicators are very diverse. Groundwater quantity is rated very good as there are few real aquifers on the steep slopes of the study region and springs cannot be overused as they are recharged during snow melt season and after rain events. *Water quality* is not a significant problem in the region, but occasionally it can occur because of livestock husbandry. However, *surface water quantity* is rated very poor as in many smaller streams and brooks little water flow is observed. This is due to the fact that, in the existing concessions for water withdrawals for hydraulic power production and for irrigation, no residual flow rules were imposed. Due to insufficient knowledge, no rating was possible for the *benefits of water use*.

The justice principle indicator ratings show that water justice as a whole is currently rather poor in the region, whether in terms of resource allocation and costs or at a legislative level. Costs, risks, and benefits of water are very unequally distributed in the region. For instance, the water-richest commune, with just a few hundred inhabitants, can use more than 50 percent of the water resources available. Also, the capabilities of the communes and other water users to access water are very unequal for various reasons. For example, communes that have historically held water rights for sources outside their communes have more opportunity to obtain sufficient water. Procedural justice is rated slightly better as access to water and the organization of public management bodies are basically regulated, but most problematic is the aspect of inclusiveness: No institution exists that embraces all relevant water users on a regional level and can mediate the diverse interests of the water users.

The appraisal of the adaptive capacity indicators provides very heterogeneous results. While the adaptive capacity based on *material and financial capital* is rated as good (extensive, though fragmented, supply and distribution infrastructure, and high financial capital to buy water from others), adaptive capacity based on *collaboration* and *entitlements* are both rated as moderate (e.g., many case-by-case agreements, but limited integral planning between up- and downstream users and legal obscurity). *Resource efficiency* and *social learning* are even rated as poor (e.g., weak water demand management and opportunities for reflecting holistic regional water visions and underlying values).

6.3.7 Sustainability Assessment of the Future

By comparing the sustainability wheels of the four different future visions (Figure 6.3), it is apparent that sustainability will decline with Vision 1, while it will improve with Visions 2, 3, and RegiEau. The reasons for these results, however, are complex and come from different combinations of regional development, infrastructure projects, and institutional reforms.

For example, in Visions 2 and 3, sustainability of most indicators is predicted to improve to good status, but the reasons are different. In Vision 2, this is despite the fact that the

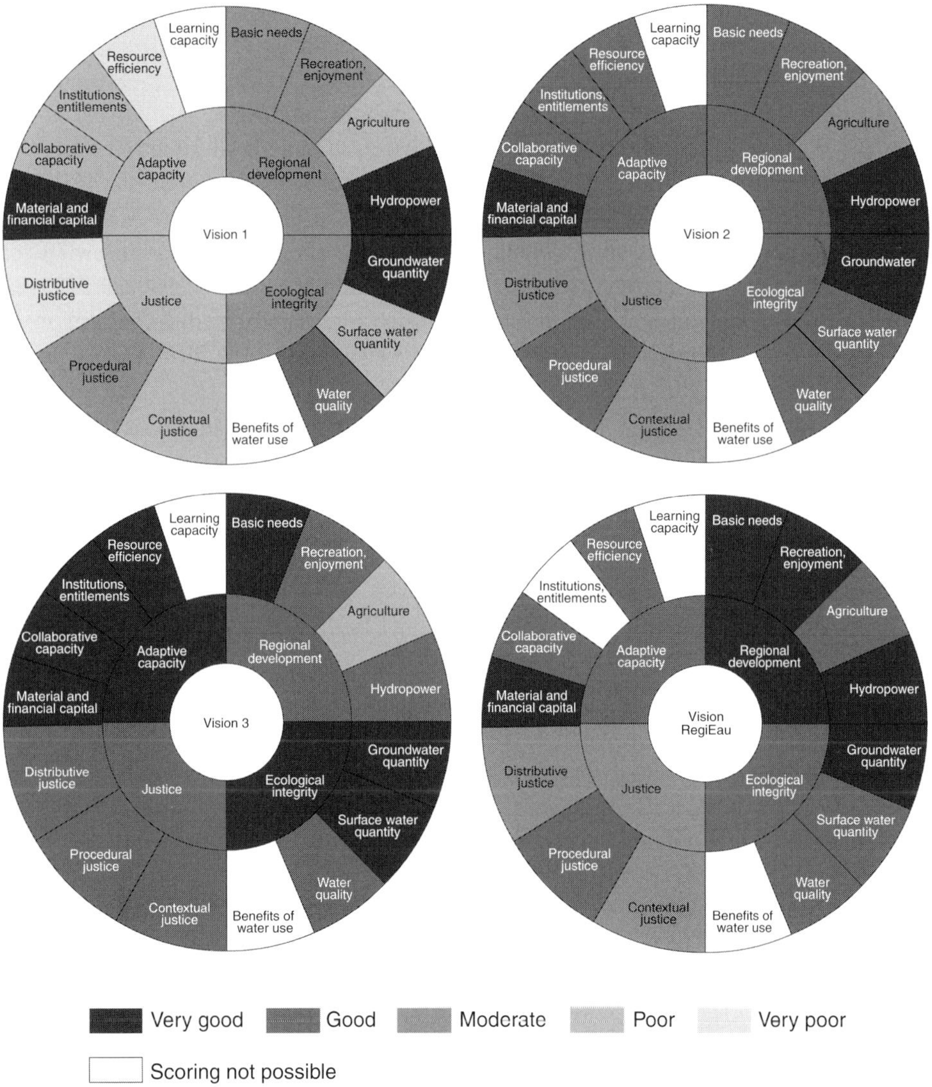

Figure 6.3 The sustainability wheels of four different future visions for 2050

overall water demand is assumed to increase due to the increasing importance of agricultural production and the related use of irrigation water. This vision does not only foresee infrastructure developments (diverse water storage and diverting projects), but is also guided by an optimization philosophy where all water uses are optimized and important institutional reforms, such as centralized water management and water rights reforms are implemented. Thus, the assessment determined that these combined management efforts are able to deal with the increased water demands in most cases and even contribute to higher justice. However, the assumed intensification of agriculture, the most significant water user in the region, will also make the sector more vulnerable to drought conditions, which are considered to become more frequent in the future (see hydrological modeling). Moreover, the justice situation is still set as only moderate, as decisions must be made unanimously and therefore water-rich communes can hinder negotiation processes toward the well-being of all.

In Vision 3, sustainability is determined to increase even more to the good and very good ranks. This is the result of decreasing water demands due to adapted economic activities (e.g., no artificial snow production), reduced population, and extensive water saving practices, combined with an optimized management system that is oriented toward the well-being of all people of the region. This is particularly beneficial for the justice scores. However, the satisfaction of the water demand for agriculture will clearly decrease. It is the requirement to leave greater residual water flow in rivers that will decrease the water availability for irrigation, especially in the latter part of summer when river flows are naturally quite low and the water needs for irrigation and evapotranspiration higher.

6.4 Conclusions

We have presented a mixed-method, dialogue-based approach for assessing the sustainability of resource governance systems. The application of the sustainability wheel used an approach that combined transparent identification of sustainability principles, their regional contextualization through sub-principles (indicators), and the scoring of these indicators through deliberative dialogue within an interdisciplinary team considering their joint knowledge and understandings.

We applied the sustainability wheel to the case of sustainable water governance and the study area Crans-Montana-Sierre region, demonstrating the following advantages:

1 It allowed very different sources of knowledge (research from natural and social sciences, qualitative and quantitative knowledge, empirical and interpretative approaches) to be combined and brought to fruition. Consequently, it facilitated in-depth interactions, knowledge exchange, and learning among the interdisciplinary team.

2 It allowed the consideration of complex relationships between issues of resource availability, use, and management. In doing so, it was evident that certain measures might improve one indicator but affect others. Furthermore, it could clearly be shown that

sustainable futures can be reached (and also impeded) through different means. For example, Vision 3 envisioned reduced resource demands, while Vision RegiEau foresees extensive infrastructure developments. However, it also became clear that technical solutions alone will not solve the existing access and distribution. These solutions need to be embedded in fundamental institutional reforms.

3 It allowed us to easily discern which sustainability dimensions are most critical, both for today and for the different future visions, facilitating communication with societal actors considerably. For example, they could easily see that sustainable futures are possible, although this highly depends on the social, economic, technical, and institutional reforms they are willing to take. Discussions about the reasons for certain scoring made the societal actors aware of possible trade-offs between the indicators (e.g., strongly increased residual flows improve the indicator of surface water quantity but downgraded the indicator of agriculture). The sustainability wheel can thus be considered an excellent communication instrument. However, the following challenges should be carefully considered in future applications of the sustainability wheel:

3.1 The heterogeneity of the principles and indicators, and the complexity of the interrelationships, made a consistent assessment very demanding. For example, better collaborations through novel governance organizations can have an effect on different indicators such as collaborative capacity, learning capacity, procedural justice, but also on resource security as a whole. Therefore, these possible relationships should be clearly outlined in the beginning of the scoring process and a facilitator should be assigned to make sure that they are thoroughly considered.

3.2 The sustainability wheels, with their ample color scoring systems, are very strong messengers and they suggest priorities of action. Therefore, it is of crucial importance to carefully consider in which cases an indicator is assessed as good, or bad, keeping the overall picture and the related message in mind. For example, what is a moderate level of justice compared to a moderate level of ecological integrity?

3.3 To jointly assess the multitude of interdisciplinary knowledge, the participating researchers need a high level of communication skills, willingness to listen the arguments of other researchers and basic understanding of the topics of other researchers. In our study, this was achieved through an intense collaboration and learning process that began at the start of the research project. Thus, if a deliberative sustainability assessment is planned, emphasis should be placed on social learning processes during and in preparation of the event.

3.4. We have often been asked if step 4 (assessing the sustainability of the resource governance system through the sustainability wheel) should not better be done by the local population to give justice to their local knowledge and enable a truly participatory process. Indeed, conducting this step with local stakeholders could have many advantages such as the creation of an opportunity for social learning and building of ownership. But in our case, local stakeholders and researchers alike favored a science-based assessment. Stakeholders preferred a "neutral"

> assessment of "external" actors, and several researchers liked the idea to use the sustainability wheel as a tool for a scientific synthesis. However, as the assessment was integrated in an overall participatory process with our stakeholder group, perspectives, knowledge, and values of local stakeholders could also be considered this way. We assume that this embeddedment in a participatory process was key for the high acceptance of the assessment results.

By considering the aforementioned points, the presented methodological approach can be applied to a variety of sustainability topics in urban areas. Urban systems are usually shaped by high complexity, and multiple stakeholders' perspectives (see Chapter 9 (Merino-Saum, 2020)). They are interlinked with their environment through various different flows of natural resources such as water, energy, and food, which are crossing the boundaries of the urban areas. Due to the high intensity of economic and social activities taking place, urban areas are usually net consumers of these resources, and they are often degraders of the environment. Moreover, what urban sustainability means and what system boundaries should be considered can be very contested among different stakeholder groups (Turcu, 2013).

Hence, while the four main steps proposed for a mixed-methods, dialogue-based sustainability assessment will be suitable for most urban situations, their specific organization should be adapted according to specific local characteristics, and resources under consideration. For example, when focusing on urban food sustainability, in step 1, researchers must identify and investigate key processes and structures involved in urban food governance systems. The four general principles suggested in step 2 might be relevant for most issues, but, for contextualization and indicator development in step 3, researchers need to carefully reflect on what indicators might best represent the food system. For example, the indicator on ecological integrity must represent key ecological dimensions related to food production and consumption. For doing so, they can draw on sustainability indicators that have recently been identified for different urban issues (e.g., Mori & Christodoulou, 2012; Shen et al., 2011; Turcu, 2013). Finally, in step 4, researchers can follow again the procedure as suggested in the article.

As mentioned, we further think that the approach presented here can also successfully be applied by groups of societal actors (local population), professional experts, or mixed teams of researchers and other actors. Each of these options has advantages and disadvantages. In all cases, however, it is important that the process is accompanied by a facilitator who oversees sound planning; equal involvement of all participants and knowledge bases; and coherency of the rating process and the developed storylines.

References

Adger, W. N., Arnell, N. W., & Tompkins, E.L. (2005). Successful adaptation to climate change across scales. *Global Environmental Change*, 15, 77–86.

ASCE, UNESCO (1998). Sustainability criteria for water resource systems. ASCE, Reston.

Babel, M., Pandey, V., Rivas, A., & Wahid, S. (2011). Indicator-based approach for assessing the vulnerability of freshwater resources in the Bagmati River Basin, Nepal. *Environmental Management* 48, 1044–1059.

Binder, C. R, Hutter, M., Pang, M., & Webb, R. (2020). System science and sustainability assessment. In C. R. Binder, E. Massaro, & R. Wyss (eds.), *Sustainability Assessment in Urban Systems*. Cambridge University Press, pp. 30–64.

Bonriposi, M. (2013). *Les usages de l'eau dans la région de Crans-Montana-Sierre: description, quantification et prévisions* (Doctoral thesis). University of Lausanne, Switzerland.

CH2011 (2011). *Les scénarios du changement climatique en Suisse CH2011.* www.ch2011.ch (accessed 08.05.2012).

Creswell, J. W., & Clark, V. L. P. (2017). *Designing and Conducting Mixed Methods Research*. Los Angeles, London, New Delhi, Singapore, Washington, DC: Sage Publications.

Folke, C., Hahn, T., Olsson, P., & Norberg, J. (2005). Adaptive governance of social-ecological systems. *Annual Review of Environment and Resources*, 30, 441–473.

Franco, L. (2006). Forms of conversation and problem structuring methods: A conceptual development. *Journal of the Operational Research Society*, 57(7), 813–821.

Fraser, N. (2009). *Scales of Justice: Re-imagining Political Space in a Globalizing World*. New York: Columbia University Press.

Fritz, L., & Meinherz, F. (2020). How Values Play into Sustainability Assessments: Challenges and a Possible Way Forward. In C. R. Binder, E. Massaro, & R. Wyss (eds.), *Sustainability Assessment in Urban Systems*. Cambridge University Press, pp. 87–122.

Gibson, R. B. (2006). Sustainability assessment: Basic components of a practical approach. *Impact Assessment and Project Appraisal*, 24, 170–182.

Gleick, P. H. (1998). Water in crisis: Paths to sustainable water use. *Ecological Applications*, 8, 571–579.

Gupta, J., Termeer, C., Klostermann, J., et al. (2010). The adaptive capacity wheel: A method to assess the inherent characteristics of institutions to enable the adaptive capacity of society. *Environmental Science & Policy*, 13, 459–471.

Hartmuth, G., Huber, K., & Rink, D. (2008). Operationalization and contextualization of sustainability at the local level. *Sustainable Development*, 16, 261–270.

Hill, M. (2013). *Climate Change and Water Governance: Adaptive Capacity in Chile and Switzerland*. Dordrecht: Springer.

Ioris, A. A. R., Hunter, C., & Walker, S. (2008). The development and application of water management sustainability indicators in Brazil and Scotland. *Journal of Environmental Management*, 88, 1190–1201.

Johnson, R. B., Onwuegbuzie, A. J., & Turner, L. A. (2007). Toward a definition of mixed methods research. *Journal of Mixed Methods Research*, 1(2), 112–133. DOI:http://10.1177/1558689806298224.

Kondratyev, S., Gronskaya, T., Ignatieva, N., Blinova, I., Telesh, I., & Yefremova, L. (2002). Assessment of present state of water resources of Lake Ladoga and its drainage basin using sustainable development indicators. *Ecological Indicators*, 2, 79–92.

Lachavanne, B., & Juge, R. (2009). LEMANO. Pour une gestion durable de l'eau. *Lémaniques*, 72, 1–16.

Larson, K. L., Wiek, A., & Withycombe Keeler, L. (2013). A comprehensive sustainability appraisal of water governance in Phoenix, AZ. *Journal of Environmental Management*, 116, 58–71.

McDermott, M., Mahanty, S., & Schreckenberg, K. (2013). Examining equity: A multidimensional framework for assessing equity in payments for ecosystem services. *Environmental Science & Policy*, 33, 416–427.

McDonald, D., Bammer, G., & Deane, P. (2009). *Research Integration Using Dialogue Methods*. Canberra: ANU E Press.

Meinherz, F., Fritz, L., & Schneider, F. (2020). The value-loadedness of sustainability: Implications for the transformative potential of sustainability assessments. In C. R. Binder, E. Massaro, & R. Wyss (eds.), *Sustainability Assessment in Urban Systems*. Cambridge University Press, pp. 65–86.

Merino-Saum, A. (2020). Assessing sustainability through participatory multi-criteria approaches (PMCAs): An updated comparative analysis. In C. R. Binder, E. Massaro, & R. Wyss (eds.), *Sustainability Assessment in Urban Systems*. Cambridge University Press, pp. 209–238.
Mori, K., & Christodoulou, A. (2012). Review of sustainability indices and indicators: Towards a new City Sustainability Index (CSI). *Environmental Impact Assessment Review*, 32, 94–106.
Olsson, P., Gunderson, L. H., Carpenter, S. R., et al. (2006). Shooting the rapids: Navigating transitions to adaptive governance of social-ecological systems. *Ecology and Society*, 11, 18. www.ecologyandsociety.org/vol11/iss11/art18/.
Pahl-Wostl, C. (2009). A conceptual framework for analysing adaptive capacity and multi-level learning processes in resource governance regimes. *Global Environmental Change*, 19, 354–365.
Reed, P. M., & Kasprzyk, J. (2009). Water resources management: The myth, the wicked, and the future. *Journal of Water Resources Planning and Management*, 135, 411–413.
Reynard, E., Bonriposi, M., Graefe, O., et al. (2014.) Interdisciplinary assessment of complex regional water systems and their future evolution: How socio-economic drivers can matter more than climate. *WIREs Water*, 1, 413–426.
Rixen, C., Stoeckli, V., & Ammann, W. (2003). Does artificial snow production affect soil and vegetation of ski pistes? A review. *Perspectives in Plant Ecology, Evolution and Systematics*, 5, 219–230.
Schlosberg, D. (2007). *Defining Environmental Justice: Theories, Movements, and Nature*, New York: Oxford University Press.
Schneider, F., & Homewood, C. (2013). Exploring water governance arrangements in the Swiss Alps from the perspective of adaptive capacity. *Mountain Research and Development*, 33, 225–233.
Schneider, F., & Rist, S. (2014). Envisioning sustainable water futures in a transdisciplinary learning process: combining normative, explorative, and participatory scenario approaches. *Sustainability Science* 9, 1–19.
Schneider, F., Bonriposi, M., Graefe, O., et al. (2015). Assessing the sustainability of water governance systems: The sustainability wheel. *Journal of Environmental Planning and Management*, 58, 1577–1600.
Schneider, F., Kläy, A., Zimmermann, A., Buser, T., Ingalls, M., & Messerli, P. How Can Science Support the 2030 Agenda for Sustainable Development? Four Tasks to Deal with the Normative Dimension of Sustainability. *Sustainability Science*, 1–12.
Shen, L.-Y., Jorge Ochoa, J., Shah, M. N., & Zhang, X. (2011). The application of urban sustainability indicators: A comparison between various practices. *Habitat International*, 35, 17–29.
Sullivan, C., & Meigh, J. (2007). Integration of the biophysical and social sciences using an indicator approach: Addressing water problems at different scales. *Water Resources Management*, 21, 111–128.
Tompkins, E. L., & Adger, W. (2004). Does adaptive management of natural resources enhance resilience to climate change? *Ecology and Society*, 9, 10. www.ecologyandsociety.org/vol19/iss12/art10.
Turcu, C. (2013). Re-thinking sustainability indicators: Local perspectives of urban sustainability. *Journal of Environmental Planning and Management*, 56, 695–719.
Valenzuela Montes, L. M., & Matarán Ruiz, A. (2008). Environmental indicators to evaluate spatial and water planning in the coast of Granada (Spain). *Land Use Policy*, 25, 95–105.
WCED. (1987). *Our Common Future ("The Brundtland Report")*. Oxford: Oxford University Press.
Wiek, A., & Larson, K. (2012). Water, People, and Sustainability: A systems framework for analyzing and assessing water governance regimes. *Water Resources Management*, 26, 3153–3171.
Ziegler, R., & Ott, K. (2011). The quality of sustainability science: A philosophical perspective. *Sustainability: Science, Practice and Policy*, 7, 31–44.

7

Sustainability Assessment: Integrative Concept, Methodology, and Examples

Volker Stelzer and Jürgen Kopfmüller

7.1 The Integrative Concept of Sustainable Development (ICoS)

Since the Earth Summit conference in Rio de Janeiro in 1992, debates have arisen internationally about how the concept of sustainable development could be made more concrete and ready for operationalization. This is of particular interest in relation to assessment contexts and decision-making processes.

Kopfmüller (2006) describes how these debates formed the background against which the German federal government mandated the Institute of Technology Assessment and System Analysis (ITAS) to engage with an interdisciplinary team from various research institutes to develop a concept for the operationalization of sustainable development. As a result, between 1999 and 2002, a theoretically substantiated, well-founded, and consistent sustainability concept was systematically developed: the Integrative Concept of Sustainable Development (ICoS).

The practicability of this concept was first demonstrated in the study "Global Sustainable Development – Perspectives for Germany" (Grunwald et al., 2001; Kopfmüller et al., 2001). The sustainability performance of different societal fields of activity in the Federal Republic of Germany was analyzed, such as "mobility and transport", "housing and construction", and "nutrition and agriculture" (Grunwald et al., 2001). Since this first project, ICoS has been applied in different contexts, such as city planning (Hartmuth et al., 2012); urban development (Barton & Kopfmüller, 2012); housing and construction (Jörissen et al., 2005); energy supply (Rösch et al., 2009; Rösch et al., 2017; Simon et al., 2012; Stelzer et al., 2017); water (Lehn et al., 2012; Nayono et al., 2016; Parodi, 2008); waste (Bräutigam et al., 2012; Hartlieb et al., 2012); mobility (Justen et al., 2012); economy (Paulesich, 2012; Schäfer, 2012; Schumacher et al., 2012); technologies (Schidler, 2012); and education (Emmrich & Melzer, 2012).

The core characteristic of ICoS is the scientifically based combination of a normative top-down process and a problem-related bottom-up process (see Figure 7.1 and Kopfmüller et al. (2001)).

In 2015, the UN set out 17 sustainability goals, including 169 sub-goals, that should be achieved by 2030 (UN, 2015). At first glance, this set of goals seems similar to ICoS with its 15 sustainability rules. Yet a comparison of these two systems shows three main differences:

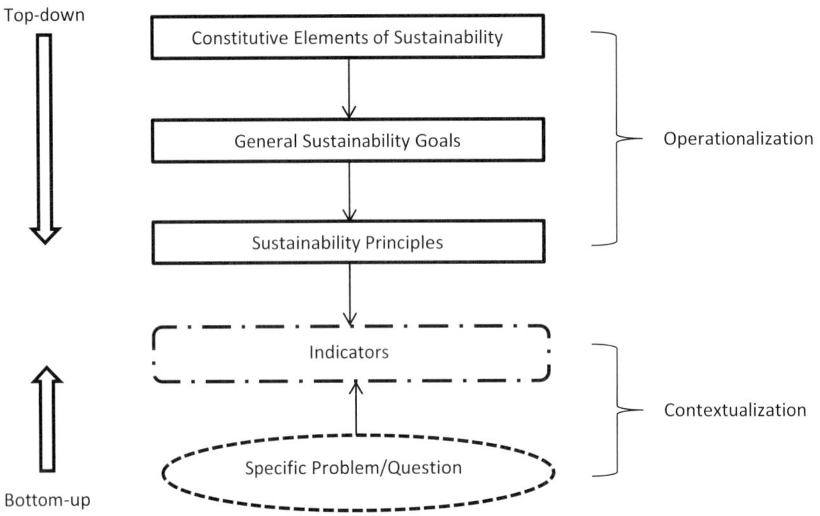

Figure 7.1 ICoS assessment schema, (based on Kopfmüller et al. (2001))

1 Whereas in ICoS minimum requirements for sustainable development are defined, the SDGs are more problem-oriented, addressing thematic fields such as cities, water, energy, etc., and also particular actors, such as industry.
2 ICoS consists of defined rules that can be used, by means of contextualized indicators, for sustainability assessments of various topics and at various scales (as we have discussed). The SDGs mainly address nations, and perhaps regions.
3 Whereas the SDGs include clearly determined targets to be reached by nations in 2030, the targets for ICoS-based indicators are to be defined specifically in each assessment context.

Depending on the particular topic of an assessment, it is possible that some goals or indicators from the SDGs may be used for assessments based on ICoS.

The following explanations about the science-based, normative, top-down process within ICoS are mainly based on Kopfmüller (2006). The top-down process consists of determining the "constitutive elements of sustainability" and, based on this, defining "general sustainability goals" and "sustainability rules".

The starting point for the definition of sustainable development in ICoS – in contrast to other existing approaches – is not what are known as the pillars of sustainable development (economy, ecology, social issues), but three constitutive elements derived from the Brundtland Report (WCED, 1987), Agenda 21 (UN, 1992a), and the Rio Declaration (UN, 1992b):

7.1.2 The Three Constitutive Elements of Sustainability:

- **The postulate of inter- and intragenerational justice:** It is crucial here that responsibility toward human beings living today and responsibility toward future generations are regarded as equally weighted. Distribution issues and problems related to income, assets, natural resources, and social positions, as well as rights and obligations of all kinds, are relevant for the course of social development, as well as the emergence of numerous problems and conflicts at the national and international level.

- **A global perspective:** With reference to the objectives of the Rio Conference and the follow-up process to develop a long-term strategy for the well-being of global society, this perspective is justifiable on an ethical basis, since the moral right of all people to satisfy at least their basic needs is accepted worldwide (WCED, 1987). Action-oriented considerations are to be used, as the increasingly global nature of social development, as well as of many sustainability problems (climate change, water scarcity, poverty, etc.) and their spatial distribution and interdependence, require appropriate global analyses and solution strategies. In the sense of "think globally, act locally", this general rule is interpreted as a "primary global perspective"; i.e., fundamental sustainability goals or guidelines must first be formulated at a global level, but then have to be broken down and implemented predominantly at the local level.
- **An anthropocentric approach:** In contrast to bio-based or pathocentric approaches, this states that the guiding rule of sustainability is primarily geared toward human needs (WCED, 1987). In the "enlightened" version, on which ICoS is based, this includes the careful use of natural resources and functions, but also aesthetic and cultural aspects, based on the properly understood self-interest of humankind.

From these three constitutive elements, it is necessary to derive a holistic, integrative understanding of sustainable development in which economic, ecological, social, institutional, and cultural issues are adequately considered and a priori equally weighted.

In order to further concretize these three constitutive elements in ICoS, the theory of a "planetary trust", developed by Edith Brown-Weiss (1989), was used, which commits all people to solidarity and responsible action in space and time. The basic idea of the planetary trust is that each generation is entitled to use the natural, economic, social, and cultural heritage inherited from previous generations. At the same time, however, generations are obliged to hold this heritage in trust for subsequent generations. Following Rawls's theory of justice (1971), the authors of ICoS assumed that every human being has a right to access to certain basic goods, such as income, development opportunities, or freedoms, which are indispensable for a self-determined, dignified life (Acker-Widmaier, 1999). On this basis, the constitutive elements of sustainability were "translated" into three general overarching sustainable development goals:

- **Securing human existence:** This is the very basic requirement that those people currently alive should not endanger the foundations of their own existence and/or that of future generations.
- **Maintaining society's productive potential:** This objective calls for the preservation of the material prerequisites for social development and productive power. This potential is comprised of natural capital, tangible capital (buildings, plants, etc.), human and knowledge capital, as well as social capital (social structures, norms, traditions, etc.), and should be passed on to future generations in as undiminished form as possible.

- **Preserving society's options for development and action:** This is to formulate the predominantly immaterial preconditions of sustainable development that are necessary for the permanent safeguarding of a humane existence for all human beings, which are just as essential as the material preconditions.

In the next step, these general sustainability objectives were substantiated in the form of **25 sustainability rules**. These rules build the core of ICoS. They reflect the fundamental ideas of the before mentioned international sustainability documents, as well as the main debates about aspects of sustainability, such as justice, basic needs, and participation. A distinction was made between substantial rules describing the minimum requirements for sustainable development to be guaranteed for every human being, and instrumental rules describing essential political or societal instruments that are necessary to meet the substantial requirements (Table 7.1).

The rules incorporate some essential functions and characteristics which underpin the basic idea of ICoS and the conduct of analyses, highlighting some key differences between ICoS and other sustainability concepts (based on Kopfmüller (2006, p. 28ff)).

7.1.3 Characteristics of ICoS:

- On the basis of the constitutive elements, the rules develop the **normative content of the sustainability model** by providing a concrete positive definition of what sustainable development should be. On the one hand, they describe the rules that should guide future societal development. On the other, they serve as criteria for sustainability assessments, and thus operate as a compass in answering the question of what is more or less sustainable, or which strategies and measures are suitable for solving particular problems. The rules thus provide a "reference line" that makes it possible to, for example, make statements about which sustainability problems exist in a society.
- The rules are interpreted as being **universally valid** to a first approximation, i.e., contextually independent of different societal systems and cultures. They are therefore formulated in a relatively abstract manner. For analyses based on specific spatial or thematic fields of application, they form a baseline that subsequently has to be contextualized in light of the particular conditions and concretized by using appropriate indicators. Quantitative context-related targets should be defined for these indicators whenever possible. These are necessary in order to classify certain phenomena as problems and be able to assess them, to allow social actors a level of certainty for planning, and to ensure that it is possible to determine the necessary type and depth of any intervention using problem-solving instruments.
- The rules describe the **minimum requirements** that each human being in each generation has a moral claim to have fulfilled. Thus, the rules do not cover all conceivable political or economic, individual or social goals, but merely a "welfare base" (Birnbacher, 1999) of basic needs. Beyond that, many legitimate goals are both thinkable and desirable

Table 7.1 *The 25 rules of ICoS (Rösch etal. (2017), modified, based on Kopfmüller etal. (2001, p. 172ff)*

Substantial Rules		
Securing human existence	Maintaining society's productive potential	Preserving society's options for development and action
S1. Protection of human health S2. Satisfaction of basic needs S3. Autonomous subsistence based on income from own work S4. Just distribution of opportunities to use natural resources S5. Reduction of extreme income and wealth inequality	S6. Sustainable use of renewable resources S7. Sustainable use of non-renewable resources S8. Sustainable use of the environment as a sink for waste and emissions S9. Avoidance of technical risks with potentially catastrophic impacts S10. Sustainable development of man-made, human, and knowledge capital	S11. Equal access for all to information, education, and occupation S12. Participation in societal decision-making processes S13. Conservation of cultural heritage and cultural diversity S14. Conservation of the cultural function of nature S15. Conservation of social resources

Instrumental Rules	
I1. Internalization of external social and ecological costs	I6. Society's ability to respond
I2. Adequate discounting	I7. Society's ability of reflexivity
I3. Limitation of public debt	I8. Society's capability of government
I4. Fair international economic framework conditions	I9. Society's ability of self-organization
I5. Promotion of international co-operation	I10. Balance of power between societal actors

(growth, wealth, etc.), but they are not considered to be constitutive of sustainable development. They are therefore "permissible" only to the extent that they do not lead to violations of the sustainability rules.

- The rules reflect the two central components of the sustainability mission statement, which some critics refer to as contradictory: the **postulate of conservation** (e.g., of important natural or societal system functions or resources) and the **postulate of development** (i.e., the ability of a society to change or adapt in ways that it considers necessary).
- **All rules** are to be considered as **equally weighted**; that is to say, each rule can be valid only within the limits of all the other rules, and the fulfillment of a rule at the expense of non-fulfillment of other rules is therefore not allowed. In addition, in the sense of a working hypothesis, it is assumed that all **minimum requirements** can be **fulfilled at the same time**. In fact, this ideal conception is challenged by the trade-offs that often arise when searching for suitable action strategies. Such conflicts can be handled differently. Two approaches should be emphasized here. The first is searching primarily for

those strategies or combinations of instruments that make it possible to simultaneously achieve conflicting goals (win-win solutions). A second approach was outlined when ICoS was first published, but has not been systematically implemented so far. The idea here is to distinguish between a core and a peripheral area for each rule, which could be defined by different corridors of targets for certain indicators. The core area of a rule has always to be fulfilled, while within the peripheral area weightings and negotiations are allowed in order to determine the extent to which a rule can be violated.
- Due to changes in societal values, distributional or other conflicts that may arise, or changing understandings of the role of the state, ICoS must be open to the **possibility of historical relativization**. Its key philosophy, as well as certain rules or definitions of rules, may therefore be subject to according changes over time, while nevertheless retaining a key function as a compass on the way to a more sustainable development.

All in all, ICoS, with a rule-based system at its core, provides a well-founded and consistent basis for **sustainability analyses of all kinds** (Schulz et al., 2008). Such analyses are an important element of the necessary social dialogue about what sustainable development should look like for a society, and which strategies and control processes it is appropriate to design and implement.

The integrative nature of ICoS has three main facets (Kopfmüller, 2006):

- First, the rules and their contents are conceived as **trans-dimensional**. The departure from the search for criteria for an "economic, ecological or social sustainability" (Spangenberg, 2005) and the alternative orientation toward a comprehensively understood postulate of justice, as well as the global and anthropocentric perspectives, are intended to overcome problems and prevent conflicts (for example, the classical conflict between economy and ecology).
- A second element of its integrative nature consists of the consideration of the **whole analytical chain and the interactions between its individual elements**: formulating a basic orientation to action, concretizing it by means of suitable indicators, setting target values for these indicators, identifying and analyzing the most urgent problems, as well as developing and analyzing action strategies to achieve targets or solve existing problems. This requires a corresponding integrative approach on the part of the analysis. It requires an interdisciplinary and transdisciplinary approach in which the various scientific disciplines and non-scientific actors work together to determine goals, problems, and strategies.
- Third, integration is understood **spatially**, in the sense that the diverse interactions and interdependencies between different regions, or between the local, national, and international levels, are identified and considered.

Due to limited space, it is not possible here to discuss in detail the derivation, justification, and considerations that led to the selection and formulation of the 25 rules. These can be found in Kopfmüller et al. (2001). The rules are divided into 15 substantial and 10 instrumental rules (Boxes 7.1, 7.2).

Box 7.1 **The 15 substantial sustainability rules of ICoS (Stelzer et al. (2017) modified, based on Kopfmüller et al. (2001))**

I Main goal: Securing human existence

S1 Protection of human health: Nobody may damage the environment through substances or other influences to an extent that will, or may, harm humans.

S2 Satisfaction of basic needs: A minimum level of basic services, as well as protection against the key risks of life, must be guaranteed for all members of society.

S3 Autonomous subsistence based on income from own work: Every person must be able to secure their livelihood through their own work, undertaken voluntarily. This also includes raising children, caring for dependents, or engaging in community work.

S4 Just distribution of opportunities to use natural resources: All humans living today, as well as future generations, have the right to use nature for themselves within appropriate limits. Resources shall be distributed fairly. Nobody may be excluded from using them.

S5 Reduction of extreme income and wealth inequality: Extreme differences in income and wealth distribution need to be reduced.

II Main goal: Maintaining society's ability to manufacture products or provide services

S6 Sustainable use of renewable resources: Humankind shall not use more from nature than nature is able, of its own accord, to provide or restore. Any ecosystem important to humankind must have the chance to survive.

S7 Sustainable use of non-renewable resources: Non-renewable resources may only be consumed to a limited degree, to ensure that future generations will still be able to use them.

S8 Sustainable use of the environment as a sink for waste and emissions: Humankind may not release more harmful residues and waste into the environment than it is able to absorb.

S9 Avoidance of technical risks with potentially catastrophic impacts: Technical processes with potentially disastrous consequences for humankind and the environment must be avoided.

S10 Sustainable development of man-made, human, and knowledge capital: We must leave our descendants an inheritance made up not only of goods but also of skills, competencies, knowledge, and know-how.

III Main goal: Preserving options for development and action

S11 Equal access for all to information, education, and occupation: All members of a society must enjoy equal opportunities when it comes to access to education, information, employment, social standing, and political office.

S12 Participation in societal decision making processes: All members of a society must be empowered to take part in decision-making processes of societal importance.

S13 Conservation of cultural heritage and cultural diversity: The cultural heritage of mankind and its cultural diversity must be preserved.

S14 Conservation of the cultural function of nature: Especially unique landscapes which have either been created by man or left untouched must be conserved.

S15 Conservation of social resources: Social cohesion must be maintained and strengthened.

Box 7.2 **The 10 instrumental sustainability rules of ICoS (based on Rösch et al. (2018) and Kopfmüller et al. (2001, p. 273ff))**

IV Instrumental Rules

I1 Internalization of external social and ecological costs: Implementing the "polluter pays" principle, energy prices and regulations must reflect external environmental and social costs. To evaluate the degree of internalization, information is needed about the amount of these costs and mechanisms of internalization (e.g., via taxes).

I2 Adequate discounting: When discounting is used, neither current nor future generations should be discriminated against.

I3 Limitation of public debt: In order not to restrict the future scope of action of the state, the state's current expenditures must, in principle, be financed from current income.

I4 Fair international economic framework conditions: The global economic framework conditions must be designed in such a way that economic actors from all states can participate fairly in the economic process.

I5 Promotion of international co-operation: To overcome global imbalances in opportunities and burdens, different actors (governments, companies, NGOs) need to work together in a spirit of global partnership, including the creation of necessary political, legal, and factual framework conditions. This also addresses the question of how to define and implement globally differentiated responsibilities to cope with global challenges such as greenhouse gas emissions, poverty, water scarcity, etc.

I6 Society's ability to respond: The ability of societies to identify and react appropriately to problems in environmental and social systems has to be maintained or improved. This requires answering questions regarding, in particular, which developments or events society should be prepared for, and establishing suitable information, communication, institutional, and organizational structures.

I7 Society's ability of reflexivity: This principle demands that measures and framework conditions should be developed in a way that goes beyond addressing mere particularistic challenges or the interests of actors. This requires suitable consideration of the consequences of actions in particular thematic fields or social subsystems on others. Setting up tools for information-sharing and communication should be one component of realizing this principle.

I8 Society's capability of government: This means that measures have to support the capability of the government in order that it can help society to develop in a more sustainable way. Based on the knowledge that in today's highly complex world governing a society cannot be done in a direct way, the art of government is in helping a society to activate their own resources and find their own solutions.

I9 Society's ability of self-organization: Potential opportunities for the autonomous organization of societal actors have to be promoted to complement top-down regulatory structures. It is crucial that these forms of civil society can be developed by using network structures and participatory decision-making, and that they can also be integrated into pluralistic and democratic planning processes.

I10 Balance of power between societal actors: Opinion-making, negotiation, and decision-making processes must be open to societal actors to articulate their thoughts and exert influence; procedures have to be transparent and allow for broad participation. This requires, for instance, avoiding or reducing a high concentration of power, asymmetric communication, and limited access to information and consultation.

The substantial rules form the substantive core of the assessment of sustainability. While in principle ignoring certain rules in particular assessment situations has to be justified, practical experiences in different contexts show that not all rules are equally relevant to every question. For example, if analyses are about whether the further development of a specific energy technology influences the sustainability of a particular region, the instrumental rules are likely to be unaffected.

7.2 ICoS as an Assessment Tool

The overall sustainability rules developed from the constitutive elements of sustainability and the general sustainability goals cannot be used directly for assessment. Rather, it is necessary to operationalize them. This is done in ICoS by **contextualizing the set of rules** by combining the more science-based, **top-down element** with a problem-oriented, **bottom-up element** that often involves stakeholders (Figure 7.1).

As the first step of operationalization, a **scoping process** is established in which it is decided which of the sustainability rules are likely to be important for the particular question at hand (Figure 7.2). The result of this process is a **problem-specific set of sustainability rules** (examples are Rösch et al. (2007) and Stelzer (2017)), selected based on the information available at that time. It is important that the set of problem-specific rules defined in scoping remains open to future changes. If there are indications during the assessment process that a rule is not relevant any more, or another rule turns out to be relevant, these may be removed or included as deemed necessary.

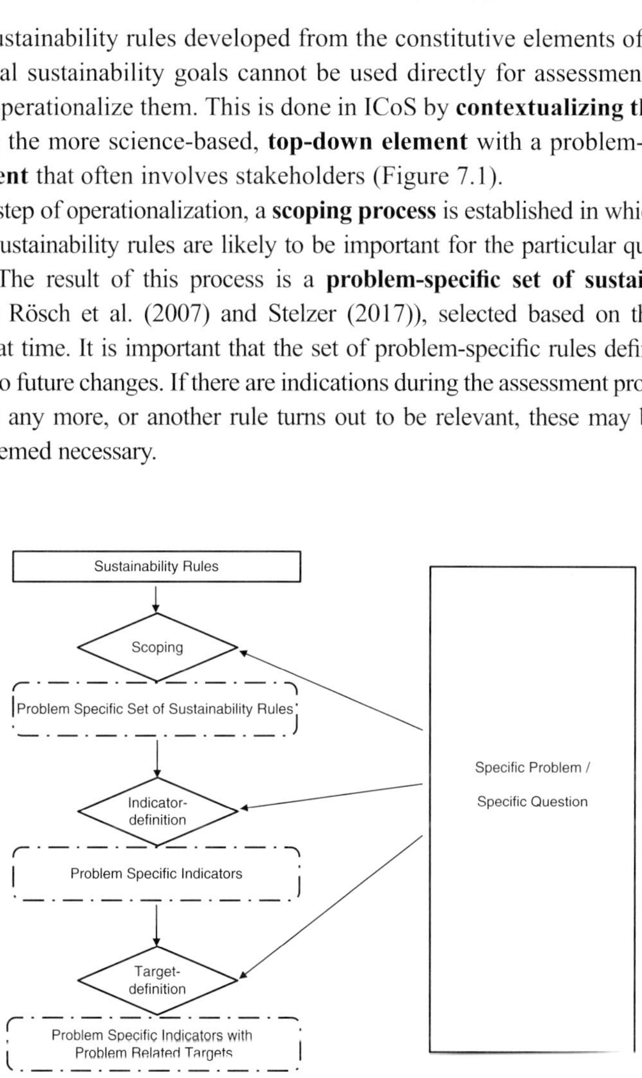

Figure 7.2 Procedure to develop sustainability indicatores with ICoS, (based on Kopfmüller et al. (2001)), expanded

In a second step, for the rules selected, **indicators are determined based on the following criteria:**

- **Unambiguity:** The indicator should not be formulated such that it can be interpreted in different ways.
- **Representativeness:** The indicator must represent the rule that is to be chosen, as well as the problem situation that is addressed in the research question.
- **Transparency:** it should be clear which topic is addressed by an indicator and why it was selected. This is one of the reasons why indices, as values resulting from the mathematical combination of values representing different contents, should not be used in isolation, but should be complemented at least by information about the indicators that are aggregated in the index.
- **Data availability:** For this purpose, the data necessary to analyze the indicator should already be available, or should be made available at an acceptable time and at a reasonable cost.
- **Data validity:** The data collection methods and conditions must be made transparent and must meet minimum requirements.
- **Directional certainty:** An indicator should make it clear which expression is considered to be more sustainable and which is less sustainable.

For ICoS assessments, the result is typically a set of indicators, potentially providing information about current sustainability performances, historic developments (if possible), or even future performances, if combined with the scenario method (an example for the future-related perspective is the Risk Habitat Megacity project presented in Section 7.3).

7.2.1 The ratings can be designed differently:

- Distance to defined targets
- Relation to the starting situation

On the one hand, in determining the indicators to be used for assessment, it has to be considered that the indicators represent the rule as comprehensively as possible in relation to the question to be assessed. On the other hand, if the results of the assessment are to be used in practice for decision-making, it is necessary that the type and number of indicators are appropriate for the decision-makers. Indicators have to be understandable by the decision-makers, who are usually not experts on particular issues. It should also be noted that in practice decision-makers have only limited time available to prepare the decision, which is often insufficient to deal with several hundred aspects of an issue, for example. Therefore, they often prefer being confronted with only a few indicators. For this reason, indicator sets should represent a balance between the goal of representing sustainable development in a particular context as completely as possible, which would imply a higher number of indicators, and the goal of being operable in practice, which would imply a lower number. The ultimate **number of indicators is often a pragmatic and context-dependent solution** to this dilemma.

Current activities in which ICoS is used include the assessment of the "socio-technical interface" of energy transitions in the EnergyTrans project (Rösch et al., 2017; Rösch et al., 2018), a navigation system for evaluating energy policy packages in the Kopernikus Project ENAVI (Quitzow et al., 2018), energy futures of different energy technologies in the project ES 2050 (ES 2050, 2018), and transforming urban quarters in Real World Lab 131 and Energy Dialogue (District Future – Urban Lab, 2018). At the international level, ICoS has been applied, for example, in the context of sustainable waste management in Belo Horizonte (Fuss et al., 2018), sustainable water management in Indonesia (Nayono et al., 2016), and the sustainable energy–water nexus in Latin America.

7.3 Sustainability Performance of the Energy System of Santiago de Chile

The project Risk Habitat Megacity was carried out from 2007 to 2010 by a research consortium of more than 60 scientists from different German and Chilean institutions (Heinrichs et al., 2012). One of the goals was to assess the sustainability situation in the Metropolitan Region of Santiago de Chile. For this purpose, sustainability assessments were carried out at the level of the special topics of energy, water, transport, and waste, but also at a general level (Heinrichs et al., 2012). In the following, results from the field of energy are presented, which are mainly based on Simon et al. (2012) and Stelzer et al. (2014).

7.3.1 The Current and Future Energy Situation in Santiago de Chile

Chile's energy system is characterized by strong growth in energy consumption, as well as a high degree of privatization and the economic concentration of energy service providers, which are controlled by the National Energy Commission (Comisión Nacional de Energía, or CNE) and the Energy Ministry. Total energy use in Chile (primary consumption) increased from 789 PJ (petajoules) in 1999 to 1,593 PJ in 2012 (Energy Ministry, 2013), an annual average growth of 5.6 percent. This results mainly from population growth, highly dynamic economic development, and deficiencies in energy efficiency. Approximately three-quarters of primary energy consumption are based on fossil resources, almost all of which are imported.

The energy consumption of the Santiago Metropolitan Region (SMR) is dominated by the transport sector, which accounts for 38 percent of final energy consumption, followed by industry (27 percent), households (22 percent), and trade and services (13 percent) (data based on calculation in Simon et al. (2010)). By taking a closer look at the resource mix of the energy consumed for different end uses, it can be seen that – due especially to the transport sector – oil derivatives account for almost half of final energy consumption. The other half is more or less equally distributed between gas and electricity.

The SMR can only produce enough electricity to meet 25 percent of demand; therefore, three-quarters of the electricity used has to be imported. In the SMR, 50 percent of power is generated by fossil-fired thermal power plants, and 50 percent from hydroelectricity.

Industry consumes the largest share of electricity in the SMR (30 percent), followed by households (26 percent), and trade and services (22 percent). Mining accounts for 7 percent, agriculture for 2 percent, and other sectors for 13 percent (National Institute of Statistics, 2011). The power consumption per capita in the category "households" varies considerably between the different districts of Santiago. While people in Vitacura – one of the municipalities with the highest average household income – use around 1,200 kWh of electricity per capita each year, people in the poorer municipalities of Alhué and El Monte consume less than 360 kWh (Ministry of Planning, 2006).

In order to generate results for different possible scenarios, it was particularly important to show systematically how the framework conditions of the energy supply might develop in the coming years. This involved a detailed review of the risks and opportunities of different energy paths for the region. This was based on different data – for example, from Barton et al. (2007) and Quevedo (2010), as well as interviews with stakeholders.

As a first step, based on data analysis and expert knowledge, three explorative framework scenarios for the year 2030 were developed, including assumptions regarding key demographic, economic, social, or political factors. With the help of energy experts, the interrelations between the framework scenarios and the energy sector were analyzed (Simon, 2010). This was the starting point for the development of the three explorative energy scenarios "Business as Usual" (BAU), "Collective Responsibility" (CR), and "Market Individualism" (MI) (unpublished data; Simon, 2012).

Some of the main characteristics of the **BAU scenario** are outlined as follows. Population growth of 1.1 million people, from 6.9 million in 2008 to 8.0 million in 2030, is projected in the SMR; energy consumption is projected to grow accordingly. This trend will be reinforced by the projected decrease in the number of people per household, shrinking from 3.5 to 3.0, which will lead to a larger number of private apartments, thus raising energy consumption for heating, ventilation, cooling, and lighting. This, together with the increasing consumption of resources and new technologies, will lead to a growing residential energy demand. This trend will probably be reduced due to the policy plans of MINVU (2006), but could also accelerate due to growing demand from industry and increasing mobility.

As a result of these trends, it is assumed that the total primary energy demand will rise 77 percent by 2030, and that the growth of energy demand in the residential and transport sector will be higher than that in the total economy. In terms of final energy consumption, fuel demand will rise rapidly while the demand for electricity and gas will experience a much slighter increase. The growing demand for energy for heating will mainly be satisfied by fossil fuels. But on the other hand, the use of solar panels for hot water and heating will also increase. As a result, the power generated from renewable energies in the SMR will increase, starting from the current low level of 55 percent in 2007, to 66 percent in 2030.

The main trends of the **CR scenario** are as follows. As a result of the development of newly emerging economic sectors, such as tourism, in regions outside the SMR, and the state pursuing a continued decentralization strategy, the population in the SMR will only grow to 7.6 million by 2030 in the CR scenario. In contrast to BAU, the number of people per household will only shrink from 3.5 to 3.2. In addition, the government will fund housing projects with the aim of improving the quality of life of those people most in need. This entails a significant increase in space for private use, similar to the BAU scenario. Social groups with low incomes will also increase their earnings, which will lead to the purchase of more electrical appliances. As a result, it is assumed that the total primary energy demand will also grow by 2030, but less than is expected in the BAU scenario, and that the rise in energy demand in the transport sector will be higher than in private households, trade, services, and industry. Regarding final energy consumption, fuel demand will go up by a certain degree, while electricity and gas demands will show a controlled rise with a tendency to abate in the following years. To increase the efficiency of producing heat for buildings, combined heat and electricity plants will be established and the heat from industrial processes will be used to heat offices and homes. The increase in the total heat demand will mainly be covered by fossil fuels. But over time, more biomass plants will be instaled, particularly for solids and sludge. In communities adjacent to agricultural regions, the use of agricultural residues is also considered as a possibility in this scenario. In general, the use of biomass will grow more slowly than the rest of non-conventional renewable energy (NCRE). Almost all the potential of roofs to produce electricity and heat will be realized. As a result, the use of NCRE in the SMR will increase to 75 percent in 2030.

The **MI scenario** was characterized as follows. As a result of the attractiveness of the SMR compared to other regions of Chile, an additional 1.3 million people will live there by 2030 – the highest population growth of the three scenarios. This will cause energy consumption to increase accordingly. This trend will be reinforced by a decrease in the number of people per household from 3.5 to 2.8, which will lead to a higher number of private homes. Together with an increase in the consumption of raw materials, this will lead to higher energy demand. As a result, it is assumed that the total primary energy demand will rise 66 percent by 2030 and that the increase in energy demand in the residential and transport sectors will be much higher than in the production sector. Regarding final energy consumption, the demand for gasoline, electricity, and gas will rapidly rise. But on the other hand, the use of renewable energies will also increase dramatically so that by 2030, NCRE will account for 76 percent of the energy supply.

7.3.2 Sustainability Analysis of Santiago's Energy Sector

In a **scoping process** for this analysis, conducted together with local and international experts, it was decided that the following rules would be used for the assessment: "satisfaction of basic needs", "sustainable use of renewable resources", "sustainable use of non-renewable resources", "sustainable use of the environment as a sink for waste and emissions", "limitation of public debt", and "balance of power between societal actors".

A comprehensive set of 44 **indicators** was compiled based on a systematic review of international literature (Stelzer et al., 2010). Then 16 core sustainability indicators were

Table 7.2 *Rules and indicators for the sustainability assessment of the energy sector of SMR (based on Stelzer et al., (2014))*

Nr.	Sustainability rule	Indicator	Unit
S2	Satisfaction of basic needs	Share of rural households in the SMR with no access to electricity	%
S2	Satisfaction of basic needs	Duration of electricity supply interruptions in the SMR	h
S2	Satisfaction of basic needs	Percentage of primary energy use based on imported energy	%
S6	Sustainable use of renewable resources	Share of electricity production from renewable energies	%
S7	Sustainable use of non-renewable resources	Total primary energy consumption	PJ
S8	Sustainable use of the environment as a sink for waste and emissions	Energy-related CO_2 emissions per capita	t
I3	Limitation of public debt	Energy per GDP	GJ/ Bil CHP*
I10	Balance of power between societal actors	Degree of economic concentration in the energy sector	%

*= gigajoule per billion Chilean pesos

chosen from the list, in particular regarding the appropriate representation of the selected rules. Finally, eight indicators for the assessment of scenario results were chosen, primarily based on the following criteria: (a) possibility of determining target values and (b) availability of SMR-related data (Table 7.2).

In cases where insufficient data was available for the SMR, national or regional values were collected for the respective indicators. Target values were identified for all indicators based on existing local, regional, or national values. If this was not possible, scientific expertise was taken as a basis. The future development of the indicators was estimated and assessed in the framework of the three energy scenarios (Simon et al., 2012). The sustainability analyses of the current performance against the indicators, and of how performance will develop under each scenario, show a heterogeneous picture for the different scenarios (Table 7.3 and Stelzer et al. (2014)). Numerous positive developments will occur, but so will cases where there are large discrepancies from the target values.

As an example, a closer look at the indicator "**percentage of primary energy use based on imported energy**" is presented here.

The main sustainability deficit for Chile (and the SMR) consists in the high dependency on fossil-fuel imports, as this increases vulnerability to supply shortages and price increases. For many years, Chile has been importing more than two-thirds of the country's required energy resources. The share of primary energy that is imported increased from 50 percent in 1990 to more than 70 percent in 2007. Reasons for this include the growing energy demand and the scarce reserves of conventional energy carriers in Chile.

Table 7.3 *Scenario results for the energy sector of the SMR (Stelzer et al.,2014)*

Indicator	Unit	Current value	Target value 2030	BAU 2030		CR 2030		MI 2030	
Share of rural households in the SMR with no access to electricity	%	0.4 (2008)	0.0	0.0	☺	0.0	☺	0.0	☺
Duration of electricity supply interruptions in the SMR	h	2.8 (2008)	0.0	0.6	☹	0.2	☹	0.4	☹
Percentage of primary energy use based on imported energy	%	77 (2007)	≤ 50	69	☹	52	☹	67	☹
Share of electricity production from renewable sources	%	55 (2007)	≥ 70	66	☹	75	☺	76	☺
Total primary energy consumption	PJ	497 (2007)	as low as possible	880	☹	680	☺	824	☹
Energy-related CO_2 emissions per capita	t	4.8 (2007)	2.5	5.3	☹	3.1	☹	4.6	☹
Energy per GDP	GJ/ Bil CHP	85 (2008)	≤ 40	65	☹	50	☹	60	☹
Degree of economic concentration in the energy sector	%	90 (2003)	≤ 70	90	☹	86	☹	95	☹

☺ = target reached, ☹ = more to do

The results of the three scenarios show that different development pathways are possible. The dependency on imports is reduced in both the BAU and MI scenarios. But in these scenarios the growing energy demand raises the absolute amount of imported energy resources. An absolute as well as a relative decrease would only be possible in the CR scenario, resulting from both the significantly smaller increase in energy demand and the increased use of domestic renewable energies. In this scenario, the dependency on imports could be reduced to around 55 percent.

The process and results of this assessment in the Risk Habitat Megacity project can give an insight into the process of applying ICoS in practice. More details are given in Simon et al. (2012) and Stelzer et al. (2014). The respective approaches and results for the case of transport in the SMR can be found in Justen et al. (2012), water in Lehn et al. (2012), waste in Bräutigam et al. (2012), and the overall situation in Kopfmüller et al. (2012).

7.4 Sustainable Energy Balance in Cities

A project to apply ICoS in order to develop an indicator to support city governments in decision-making regarding energy investments recently started. The availability of energy or at least energy services is essential for all modern economies. As part of the global energy transition, each city must realign its energy supply. Since the old energy supply paradigm, based on large-scale power plants fired by fossil fuels or nuclear energy and often owned by the state or large companies, differs significantly from the future of energy systems in many cities of the world, it is important for decision-makers to be able to orient themselves in this rapidly changing field. Determining the potential of renewable energies to supply cities will provide important information for the upcoming transformations. Such a parameter could provide orientation for decision-makers in restructuring the current energy supply. To this end, the sustainable energy performance indicator "**Sustainable Energy Balance**" (**SEB**) is proposed, using ICoS for a sustainability assessment that provides the basis for this indicator.

As a first step, the **potential of all technically and economically usable renewable energy resources of a city** are determined (**TEEnPo**). However, it usually does not make sense to develop all the potential resources that it is technically possible to exploit, since the use of renewable energies can also have negative effects. Examples of this are the use of geothermal energy in areas in which anhydrite is present, which causes the risk of ground elevation; the presence of wind farms in bird sanctuaries; or the cultivation of maize monoculture for biogas production, which can lead to high erosion or the pollution of groundwater by nitrates. For this reason, as a next step, a sustainability assessment of the existing renewable energy potential will be carried out. In order to be relatively sure that no important aspect is neglected in this evaluation, ICoS is used.

On the basis of ICoS, a **universal core indicator set (CIS)** for assessing the sustainability of energy sources provision will be set up by applying the delphi method with international experts. For the assessment of a particular city, the CIS can be supplemented by indicators defined by the local government or local civil society. The result is the **regional city indicator set (RIS)**. The RIS can vary from city to city.

By applying the RIS, it is possible to identify those areas within the city which are not suitable for sustainable energy production, such as bird reserves in the case of wind turbines, regions with anhydrite deposits at depth in the case of geothermal energy, or areas with a slope greater than 20 percent in the case of the cultivation of maize. The result of this sustainability assessment gives the "**Sustainable Energy Potential**" **(SEnPo)** of the city.

It is important for city energy planning to know how this potential relates to the amount of energy needed in the city. As a first step, total final energy consumption in TJ per year from the most recent statistically available year is considered. However, specific assumptions have to be made to deal with the fact that the current energy requirements of a city usually do not correspond to future energy requirements. For this reason, well-founded assumptions about the future development of the city are to be used to estimate future demand. This "Future **Energy Demand**" **(EnCo)** is compared to the SEnPo. To create the SEB, the SEnPo of a city area is divided by the EnCo of the city.

SEB = 1: The SEnPo is equal to the EnCo. If the potential is fully exploited, the city would be able to provide itself with sustainable energy more than one year on average.
SEB > 1: The SEnPo is greater than the EnCo. If the potential is fully exploited, the city could be fully supplied with energy on balance and still be able to export energy.
SEB < 1: The SEnPo is smaller than the EnCo. Even if the potential is fully exploited, the city could not completely supply itself with energy. Energy imports should be organized in the city.

From this SEB it is possible to determine whether the sustainably recoverable energy potential of a city is sufficient to cover the demand or not. This indicator can provide assistance in decision-making on matters such as the extent to which the potential of locally available renewable energies should be exploited, and whether provisions must be made to import energy from other regions if a city's own resources are insufficient.

7.5 Conclusions and Future Development

In conclusion, ICoS has proven to be a viable sustainability assessment tool in more than 15 years of applications to a wide range of subjects of investigation. Its main strengths are

- the science-based, theoretically well-founded development of its basic architecture, including the rules as a key element,
- its interdisciplinarity,
- its high flexibility due to the combination of globally defined minimum requirements with locally specific aspects of sustainability,
- the transparency of the method,
- the possibility of combining scientific knowledge with stakeholder and civil society experiences and values, and
- the possibility of using the methodology in citizen science contexts, as has already been done in the context of the real-world lab in Karlsruhe.

One field where ICoS is still difficult to implement is pure technology assessment, because nearly every technology has a wide range of applications and impacts that depend on social and individual factors. These "frameworks" for using the technology impede valid evaluations of single technologies, whereas comparative analyses of alternative technological options are a common approach.

Besides the ongoing application of ICoS and the potential new fields that will open up in future (see Section 7.2), the relationship between ICoS and the SDGs will be described in more detail, to reflect previous experiences with the use of ICoS in a systematic way to provide suitable lessons learned, and to analyze suitable approaches to systematically deal with trade-offs.

References

Acker-Widmaier, G. (1999). *Intertemporale Gerechtigkeit und nachhaltiges Wirtschaften. Zur normativen Begründung eines Leitbildes*. Marburg: Metropolis-Verlag.

Barton, J., Jordan, F. R., León, A. S. M., & Solis, M. O. (2007). *¿Cuán sustentable es la Región Metropolitana de Santiago? Metodologías de evaluación de la sustentabilidad*. Santiago de Chile: Comisión Económica para América Latina y el Caribe (CEPAL), pp. 65–70.

Barton, J., & Kopfmüller, J. (2012). Sustainable urban development in Santiago de Chile: Background – concept – challenges. In D. Heinrichs, K. Krellenberg, B. Hansjürgens, & F. Martinez (eds.), *Risk Habitat Megacity*. Heidelberg: Springer, pp. 65–86.

Birnbacher, D. (1999). Kommentargutachten, beauftragt im Rahmen des HGF-Projekts „Untersuchung zu einem integrativen Konzept nachhaltiger Entwicklung. Bestandsaufnahme, Problemanalyse, Weiterentwicklung." Düsseldorf Edition.

Brandl, V., Jörissen, J., Kopfmüller, J., & Paetau, M. (2001). Das integrative Konzept: Mindestbedingungen nachhaltiger Entwicklung. In A. Grunwald, R. Coenen, J. Nitsch, A. Sydow, & P. Wiedemann (eds.), *Forschungswerkstatt Nachhaltigkeit – Wege zur Diagnose und Therapie von Nachhaltigkeitsdefiziten*. Berlin: edition sigma, pp. 79–102.

Bräutigam, K.-R., Gonzalez, T., Szanto, M., Seifert, H., & Vogdt, J. (2012). Municipal solid waste management in Santiago de Chile: Challenges and perspectives towards sustainability. In D. Heinrichs, K. Krellenberg, B. Hansjürgens, & F. Martínez (eds.), *Risk Habitat Megacity*. Heidelberg: Springer, pp. 279–301.

Brown-Weiss, E. (1989). *In Fairness to Future Generations: International Law, Common Patrimony and Intergenerational Equity*. Dobbs Ferry, NY: The United Nations University and Transnational Publishers.

District Future – Urban Lab. (2018). www.itas.kit.edu/english/num_current_paro11_quazu.php (accessed 26.4.2018).

Emmrich, R., & Melzer, M. (2012). Das integrative Nachhaltigkeitskonzept der HGF als Baustein der Bildung für eine nachhaltige Entwicklung. In J. Kopfmüller (ed.), *Ein Konzept auf dem Prüfstand: Das integrative Nachhaltigkeitskonzept in der Forschungspraxis*. Berlin: edition sigma, pp. 171–188.

Energy Ministry. (2013). Balance National de Energía 2012. Santiago de Chile. www.minenergia.cl/documentos/balance-energetico.html (accessed 10.11.2018).

ES 2050. (2018). Energy System 2050: A Contribution of the Research Field Energy. www.helmholtz.de/en/research/energy/energy_system_2050/ (accessed 26.4.2018).

Fuss, M., Vasconcelos Barros, R. T., & Poganietz, W. R. (2018). Designing a framework for municipal solid waste management towards sustainability in emerging economy countries: An application to a case study in Belo Horizonte (Brazil). *Journal of Cleaner Production*, 178, pp. 655–664.

Grunwald, A., Coenen, R., Nitsch, J., Sydow, A., & Wiedemann, P. (2001). *Forschungswerkstatt Nachhaltigkeit: Wege zur Diagnose und Therapie von Nachhaltigkeitsdefiziten*. Berlin: edition sigma.

Hartlieb, N., Bräutigam, K.-R., Kopfmüller, J., Sardeman, G., Achternbosch, M., & Kupsch, C. (2012). Das Nachhaltigkeitskonzept im Kontext der Abfallwirtschaft. Anwendung auf das Beispiel der Cadmiumstoffströme. In J. Kopfmüller (ed.), *Ein Konzept auf dem Prüfstand: Das integrative Nachhaltigkeitskonzept in der Forschungspraxis*. Berlin: edition sigma, pp. 213–233.

Hartmuth, G., Huber, K., & Rink, D. (2012). Downscaling von Nachhaltigkeit: Das Integrative Nachhaltigkeitskonzept als Bauplan für kommunale Indikatorensysteme. In J. Kopfmüller (ed.), *Ein Konzept auf dem Prüfstand: Das integrative Nachhaltigkeitskonzept in der Forschungspraxis*. Berlin: edition sigma, pp. 99–114.

Heinrichs, D., Krellenberg, K., Hansjürgens, B., & Martínez, F. (2012). *Risk Habitat Megacity*. Heidelberg: Springer.

Jörissen, J., Coenen, R., & Stelzer, V. (2005). *Zukunftsfähiges Wohnen und Bauen. Herausforderungen, Defizite, Strategien*. Berlin: edition sigma.

Justen, A., Martinez, F., Lenz, B., & Cortés, C. (2012). Santiago 2030: Perspectives on the urban transport system. In D. Heinrichs, K. Krellenberg, B. Hansjürgens, & F. Martínez (eds.), *Risk Habitat Megacity*. Heidelberg: Springer, pp. 207–227.

Kopfmüller, J. (2006). Das integrative Konzept nachhaltiger Entwicklung: Motivation, Architektur, Perspektiven. In J. Kopfmüller (ed.), *Ein Konzept auf dem Prüfstand: Das integrative Nachhaltigkeitskonzept in der Forschungspraxis*. Berlin: edtion sigma, pp. 23–37.

Kopfmüller, J. (2011). The integrative sustainability concept of the Helmholtz Association. The "Risk Habitat Megacity" project as a case of application. In: G. Banse, G. L. Nelson, & O. Parodi (eds.), *Sustainable Development – The Cultural Perspective. Concepts – Aspects – Examples*. Berlin: edition sigma, pp. 137–149.

Kopfmüller, J., Brandl, V., Jörissen, J., et al. (2001). *Nachhaltige Entwicklung integrativ betrachtet. Konstitutive Elemente, Regeln, Indikatoren*. Berlin: edition sigma.

Kopfmüller, J., Barton, J., & Salas, A. (2012). How sustainable is Santiago? In D. Heinrichs, K. Krellenberg, B. Hansjürgens, & F. Martínez (eds.), *Risk Habitat Megacity*. Heidelberg: Springer, pp. 305–326.

Lehn, H., McPhee, J., Vogdt, J., et al. (2012). Risks and opportunities for sustainable management of water resources and services in Santiago de Chile. In D. Heinrichs, K. Krellenberg, B. Hansjürgens, & F. Martínez (eds.), *Risk Habitat Megacity*. Heidelberg: Springer, pp. 251–278.

Ministry of Planning. (2006). Final results of energy sector in metropolitan region, year 2006. Santiago de Chile.

MINVU – Ministerio de Vivienda y Urbanismo (2006). Manual de aplicación, Reglamentación térmica. MINVU e Instituto de la Contrucción. Santiago de Chile. www.sodal.cl/files/1_Manual %20A%20 R%20 T.pdf (accessed 10.11.2018).

National Institute of Statistics (2011). Electric generation and distribution. Historical series: Electric distribution by sector in GWh, years 1997–2010. Santiago de Chile. www.ine.cl/canales/chile_es tadistico/estadisticas_economicas/energia/series_estadisticas/series_estadisticas.php (accessed 10.11.2018).

Nayono, S., Lehmann, A., Kopfmüller, J., & Lehn, H. (2016). Improving sustainability by technology assessment and systems analysis: The case of IWRM Indonesia. *Applied Water Science*, 6(3), 279–292. DOI:http://0.1007/s13201-016-0427-y.

Parodi, O. (2008). *Technik am Fluss: Philosophische und kulturwissenschaftliche Betrachtungen zum Wasserbau als kulturelle Unternehmung*. Munich: oekom.

Paulesich, R. (2012). EaseyX. Der HGF-Ansatz in einem Modell zur Bewertung börsennotierter Unternehmen. In J. Kopfmüller (ed.), *Ein Konzept auf dem Prüfstand: Das integrative Nachhaltigkeitskonzept in der Forschungspraxis*. Berlin: edition sigma, pp. 189–212.

Quevedo, D.L. (Ed.) (2010). Escenarios Energéticos Chile 2030. Santiago de Chile.

Quitzow, R., Ollier, L., Bangert, A., et al. (2018). *Multikriterieller Bewertungsansatz für eine nachhaltige Energiewende: Von der Analyse zur Entscheidungsfindung mit ENavi*. Potsdam: IAAS.

Rawls, J. (1971). *A Theory of Justice*. Cambridge, MA: Harvard University Press.

Rösch, C., Raab, K., Skarka, J., & Stelzer, V. (2007). *Energie aus dem Grünland: Eine nachhaltige Entwicklung?* Karlsruhe: Karlsruhe Institute of Technology, Institute of Technology Assessment and Systems Analysis. www.itas.kit.edu/english/num_completed_roes03_gruen.php (accessed 12.10.2018).

Rösch, C., Skarka, J., Raab, K., & Stelzer, V. (2009). Energy production from grassland: Assessing the sustainability of different process chains under German conditions. *Biomass & Bioenergy*, 33(4), 689–700. DOI:10.1016/j.biombioe.2008.10.008.

Rösch, C., Bräutigam, K. -R., Kopfmüller, J., Stelzer, V., & Lichtner, P. (2017). Indicator system for the sustainability assessment of the German energy system and its transition. *Energy, Sustainability and Society*, 7(1), 1–13. DOI:10.1186/s13705-016-0103-y.

Rösch, C., Bräutigam, K. -R., Kopfmüller, J., Stelzer, V., Lichtner, P., & Fricke, A. (2018). *Indicator-based Sustainability Assessment of the German Energy System and its Transition*. Karlsruhe: Karlsruhe Institute of Technology.

Schäfer, M. (2012). Der Beitrag wirtschaftlicher Akteure zu nachhaltiger Entwicklung und Lebensqualität. In J. Kopfmüller (ed.), *Ein Konzept auf dem Prüfstand: Das integrative Nachhaltigkeitskonzept in der Forschungspraxis*. Berlin: edition sigma, pp. 115–137.

Schidler, S. (2012). Interdisziplinäre Bildung von Nachhaltigkeitskriterien. Fallbeispiel Nachwachsende Rohstoffe: Grüne Bioraffinerie. In J. Kopfmüller (ed.), *Ein Konzept auf dem Prüfstand: Das integrative Nachhaltigkeitskonzept in der Forschungspraxis*. Berlin: edition sigma, pp. 157–169.

Schultz, J., Brand, F., Kopfmüller, J., & Ott, K. (2008). Building a "theory of sustainable development": Two salient conceptions within the German discourse. *International Journal for Environment and Sustainable Development*, 7(4), 465–482. DOI:10.1504/IJESD.2008.022390.

Schumacher, U., Bonas, I., & Tisch, A. (2012): Gemeinschaftseinrichtungen zur nachhaltigen Entwicklung in Brandenburg. In J. Kopfmüller (ed.), *Ein Konzept auf dem Prüfstand: Das integrative Nachhaltigkeitskonzept in der Forschungspraxis*. Berlin: edition sigma, pp. 139–156.

Simon, S., Stelzer, V., Quintero, A., et al. (2010). Thematic field: Energy. In K. Krellenberg, J. Kopfmüller, & J. Barton (eds.), *How Sustainable is Santiago de Chile? Current Performance – Future Trends – Potential Measures: Synthesis Report of the Risk Habitat Megacity Research Initiative (2007–2011)*. Leipzig: UFZ.

Simon, S., Stelzer, V., Vargas, L., Gonzalo, P., Quintero-Márquez, A., & Kopfmüller, J. (2012). Energy systems. In D. Heinrichs, K. Krellenberg, B. Hansjürgens, & F. Martínez (eds.), *Risk Habitat Megacity*. Heidelberg: Springer, pp. 183–205.

Spangenberg, J. (2005). *Die ökonomische Nachhaltigkeit der Wirtschaft. Theorien, Kriterien und Indikatoren*. Berlin: edition sigma.

Stelzer, V., Kopfmüller, J., & Simon, S. (2010). Nachhaltige Energieversorgung in Megacities. Das Beispiel Santiago de Chile. *Technikfolgenabschätzung Theorie und Praxis*, 19(3), 30–38.

Stelzer, V., Knapp, M., Meyer, R., & Pehle, A. (2017). Integrative sustainability assessment to evaluate OUI biomass scenarios over URR. In K. Schumacher, K. W. Fichtner, and F. Schultmann (eds.), *Innovations for Sustainable Biomass Utilisation in the Upper Rhine Region*. Karlsruhe: KIT Scientific Publishing, pp. 218–226.

Stelzer, V., Quintero, A., Vargas, L., et al. (2014). Indicator based sustainability analysis of future energy situation of Santiago de Chile. In J. Awrejcewicz, M. Shitikova, V. Niola, T. Panagopoulos, W. Wenzel, F. Gorunescu, I. Horova, & A. Korobeinikov (eds.), *Energy, Environment, Biology and Biomedicine*. Prague: WSEAS – World Scientific and Engineering Academy and Society. ISBN: 978–1-61804–232-3, pp. 24–27.

UN – United Nations (1992a). *Agenda 21*. New York: United Nations. https://sustainabledevelopment.un.org/content/documents/Agenda21.pdf (accessed 12.10.2018).

UN – United Nations (1992b). Report of the United Nations conference on environment and development, Rio de Janeiro, 3–14 June 1992, Annex I, Rio declaration on environment and development. A/CONF.151/26(I). New York: United Nations.

UN – United Nations (2015). *Sustainable Development Goals*. New York: United Nations. www.un.org/sustainabledevelopment/sustainable-development-goals/ (accessed 12.10.2018).

WCED – World Commission on Environment and Development (1987). *Our Common Future*. Oxford: Oxford University Press.

8

Sustainability Solution Spaces

Claudia R. Binder, Marta G. Baldi, Baptiste Gex, and Emanuele Massaro

8.1 Introduction

Cities are becoming the center of all human activities, welfare, and environmental footprints. It has been anticipated that cities will be the places of the most important environmental, social, and economic challenges of the future (Bibri & Krogstie, 2017). Thus, their sound development is becoming one of the most pressing issues of our century. How can cities remain a place of innovation, economic growth, and social stability while preserving environmental quality (Hashemian et al., 2017)? How should we deal with limited resources of space that must be divided between living, transportation, and leisure? The key issues underlying these questions relate to how to assess sustainability in cities; how to benchmark cities and make them comparable to each other; how and when to include stakeholders; and how to identify and deal with trade-offs.

Starting from the original definition of sustainable development (SD) – development that meets the needs of the present without compromising the ability of future generations to meet their own needs (Brundtland, 1987) – authors have tried to theorize and to develop methods to include the human, economic, and environmental contexts. According to Bakshi et al. (2011), there are two main interrelated weaknesses of most efforts devoted to formulating definitions and establishing metrics for assessing sustainability. First, sustainability is often defined in only a somewhat qualitative manner across several disciplines, and second, as a consequence, too many, and too diverse, sets of proposed metrics have been introduced (Bakshi et al., 2011).

Most approaches to assessing the sustainability of urban systems rely on indicator sets (Klopp & Petretta, 2017). During the last two decades, several international institutions and companies, as well as many local-level initiatives, have been developing their own indicator sets (Boesch & de Montmollin, 2020). The advantage of indicators is that they can be used to disaggregate and simplify the system at hand. However, cities being complex systems, the assessment of the indicators – i.e., whether the system is becoming more or less sustainable – is difficult. There are three main issues that should be considered. First, it is not always clear what the target value for an indicator could be (Boesch & de Montmollin, 2020). Furthermore, stakeholders are more likely to agree on a range within which the indicator could be sustainable rather than a specific value (Binder et al., 2012). Second, indicators capture only one point in time and, thus, they cannot capture the system dynamics and have to be put into context (Schilling et al., 2020). Third, the interpretation of the indicator values (and their development) regarding sustainability is challenging, as the interaction between the indicators is usually not considered. Thus, the increase of one indicator might imply the reduction of another one, whereby it is not clear whether the final outcome is a more sustainable one. That is, there is a need to (1) define the sustainability ranges for the indicators; (2) include the context of the system when interpreting the indicator values; and (3) include the relation between the indicators and analyze potential trade-offs among them (Binder et al., 2010; Wiek & Binder, 2005).

In light of these discussions, some reaserchers (Nijkamp & Vreeker, 2000; Wiek & Binder, 2005) were among the first authors to propose sustainability assessment tools by differentiating between the normative, systemic, and procedural dimensions of sustainability assessment. From a **normative** perspective, the relevant questions are what is considered sustainable or which direction is desirable, and who decides on this. The answers to these questions depend on the scale of the analysis. Whereas when assessing specific cities or neighborhoods it might be key to derive consistent and flexible targets from the general concept of sustainability that also match the real problems of the city-region (see Chapter 1 (Halla & Binder, 2020) and Chapter 3 (Meinherz et al., 2020)), when looking at benchmarking across city-regions, general and mostly policy-derived indicators might be more desirable, e.g., Holden et al., (2014). Regarding the **systemic** perspective, the question is how to describe a system in such a way that it is easy to understand and captures the major features and key interrelations and feedbacks prevalent in the urban system (Wiek and Binder, 2005; see Chapter 8 (Binder et al., 2020a)). Finally, the **procedural** dimension looks into the question of who has to be included in the assessment process itself, and when and how (Nijkamp and Vreeker, 2000; Wiek and Binder, 2005; see Chapter 4 (Fritz & Meinherz, 2020)).

In this chapter, we present the method of sustainability solution spaces for decision-making (SSP) as an integrative method for assessing sustainability (Wiek and Binder, 2005). The approach fulfills the criteria discussed above, namely: (i) systemic criteria, i.e., providing sufficient representation of the system, including functional interaction among indicators; (ii) normative criteria, i.e., considering the different value perspectives of stakeholders by using targets or ranges; and (iii) procedural criteria, i.e., pursuing the assessment in an expert-led or participatory way.

The chapter is structured as follows: First, we situate the SSP in the context of other sustainability assessment methods applied to urban systems. Second, we present the general process for carrying out the SSP. We thereby highlight the key steps to be pursued and compare the two ways in which the SSP can be performed, the expert approach and the participatory approach. Third, we describe and present an example of the expert approach. Fourth, we present the participatory approach with an example. Finally, we discuss the implications of the SSP for the sustainability assessment of urban systems.

8.1.1 Putting the Sustainability Solution Space in Context: A Short Overview of Sustainability Assessment Methods for Urban Systems

To position the sustainability solution space tool for decision-making in a broader context, we need to look into sustainability assessment from an urban planning perspective (Ness et al., 2007). When looking at urban planning approaches at the community scale, we find that there are many sustainability standards, rating systems, labels, and other type of indicators that are used to try to define what is sustainable or not. According to our experience in the sustainability evaluation of urban systems, four types of assessment methods were identified: (1) mono-dimensional approaches, (2) multi-criteria approaches, (3) benchmarking indicator sets, and (4) ecology-driven assessments.

1 Single-dimensional or mono-metrical approaches are based on the evaluation of a single common unit, be it monetary, physical, or other, and assume that there is only one language of evaluation. Ecological footprinting, energy balances, or material flow analysis are examples of single-dimensional approaches to sustainability assessment (Singh et al., 2012). These approaches are typically applied at different levels and are not specifically developed for urban systems.

2 Approaches based on **multi-criteria analysis** (MCA), on the contrary, try to accommodate the plurality of values and perspectives regarding environmental issues, and to account separately for the different forms of "capital." MCAs are decision-making tools developed for complex problems (see Chapter 9 (Merino-Saum, 2020). Multi-criteria approaches are gaining increasing attention, as they are easily understood thanks to the high number of assumptions they include and because they allow a step implementation for each criterion (Berardi, 2012). However, one of the limitations of multi-criteria systems is their structure, basing the final and overall result of the assessment on the sum of different evaluations.

3 Many **benchmarking systems** use indicators for ranking cities, e.g., the European Commission's system (European Commission, Directorate-General for the Environment, Intrasoft International, University of the West of England (UWE), & Science Communication Unit, 2017). The United Nations (UN) developed a "City Prosperity Index" (CPI) that considers 17 indicators divided into 6 dimensions: environmental sustainability, infrastructure development, urban governance, quality of life, equity-social inclusion, and productivity and legislation.[1] The 77 indicators grouped in 10 dimensions are used to evaluate the "Cities in Motion index" (CiM) and 70 indicators are used to evaluate the "Global Power City Index" (GPCI).[2] These approaches consider the pillars of sustainability separately, and so fail to meet the increasingly popular request on the part of decision-makers for the links between these pillars to be better defined and quantified using linkage-based frameworks for sustainability assessment (Waheed et al., 2009).

4 **Environment-based assessments** can be seen as the predecessors of environmental sustainability assessment. Ecologists and physicists have developed and tested methods for monitoring, assessing, and managing ecological integrity through the use of indicators of

ecological change, referred to as Ecological Indicators (EIs); all are quantitative and based on environmental thermodynamics. Many authors, in order to achieve sustainability, use EIs, such as embodied energy, emergy (Kangas, 2002), ecological footprinting (Rees & Wackernagel, 1996), and exergy (Sciubba, 2008). The following can be considered a concise and unambiguous definition of an EI (Sciubba, 2008): an EI is an aggregate, quantitative measure of the impact of a community on its surroundings. EIs ought not to be used to establish value rankings or to provide guidance in ethical or social issues. They can only be used to assess an industrial process, a societal sector, or an economic strategy applied to one society or another, in a completely specified environment. Within these bounds, they may be used to compare alternative scenarios. EIs have to be defined in such a way that they may convey at the same time some quantitative and qualitative information. This is not an easy task, and several global EIs have been proposed that for one reason or another lack the necessary precision. Sciubba also presents a critical view of some of the main existing EIs (Sciubba, 2008). EIs can be useful for addressing communities' policies and urban planning, especially with regard to the management of a community's sustainability.

This short overview of sustainability assessment methods shows that currently we find a broad variety of approaches trying to address the complexity and uncertainness in a system. Our overview suggests that it is difficult to (1) define how sustainability is practicably evaluable; (2) develop a consistent framework that makes it possible to analyze the consequences of an action in terms of sustainability; (3) find a simple approach that makes it possible to identify the systemic elements and the underlying normative views, and (4) figure out who should be involved in the assessment itself and at what stage. These are, however, key elements for supporting sustainability decisions in communities.

8.2 The Sustainability Solution Space

In the following, we present the method of the sustainability solution space (SSP) for assessing the sustainability of urban systems. The SSP represents the room to maneuver (or wiggle room) of the system at hand so that it can develop sustainably. As mentioned in Section 8.1, the SSP considers the systemic, normative, and procedural perspectives of an assessment. We propose two approaches: an expert approach and a participatory approach, which can be selected depending on the goal of the assessment, data availability, and the user group envisaged (Table 8.1).

The expert approach is appropriate when the goal is (1) to assess urban systems where data is abundant; (2) to compare cities with each other, for which similar data is available; (3) to cluster and provide benchmarks for specific city types; and (4) based on the comparison, for example, to deliver general indications to policymakers on areas of intervention. The expert approach requires high quality of data, preferably either over time or for a large number of cities.

The participatory approach is recommended when the goal of the assessment is (1) to assess the impact of a specific project on the overall sustainability of the city; (2) to assess in depth a specific sector, such as mobility or housing (Pagani et al., 2020); or (3) to follow-up on the sustainability of an intervention within a city. For some research questions, we suggest first identifying the problem areas of the city using an expert approach and then following up this analysis using a participatory approach. The participatory approach is more flexible regarding data requirements and can also deal with qualitative or Likert scale data. Furthermore, systems can be analyzed in a semi-quantitative way in workshops or expert interviews.

8.2.1 General Procedure of the SSP

The construction of the sustainability solution space consists of four steps: (1) the preparatory phase, (2) system analysis and indicator selection, (3) data collection and data analysis, and (4) the assessment itself (Figure 8.1). Whereas the procedural dimension concerns how the different steps are carried out, the systemic and normative dimensions influence different parts of the assessment as we will discuss (see also Binder et al., 2012; Binder & Wiek, 2007; Wiek & Binder, 2005). Furthermore, Figure 8.1 also includes Step 5 and Step 6, which are carried out after the assessment has been performed. In the following, the main four steps are presented.

Step 1: Preparatory Phase

In the preparatory phase, the goal of the assessment is defined, as well as a function that it should fulfill. This includes the definition of the context (space, time, and scale; see Chapter 8 (Binder et al., 2020a)); the decision as to which sustainability concept will be used in the assessment, as in Chapter 1 (Halla & Binder, 2020); and the decision about whether to pursue an expert approach or a participatory approach. The definition of these aspects determines the stakeholders that should be involved.

Step 2: System Analysis and Indicator Selection

The second step is the analysis of the system and selection of the indicators. Hereby we refer to Chapter 2 (Binder et al., 2020) where four key system characteristics are defined: (i) system boundary, context, and environment; (ii) system purpose and goal; (iii) system structure and dynamics; and (iv) system information and learning. In the second step of the SSP, the system boundary and the system structure are important (system purpose and goal feed into Step 1, and system information and learning relate to the steps that follow the assessment itself).

Based on the definition of the context, the system boundaries for the assessment are set. This consists of the definition of the city to be assessed. The spatial boundaries relate to whether we are assessing the city itself or a neighborhood, and whether we are considering political or geographical boundaries (i.e., of a watershed). The time-related boundaries refer to the time span we are including in our assessment. When we aim to compare cities, a yearly assessment is needed; if we aim at assessing a project within the city, one could assess the point before and after the intervention. Finally, another issue to be defined is whether to include the interactions of the studied urban system with its neighboring systems, as shown in Chapter 2 (Binder et al., 2020).

When the system boundaries have been defined, there are several ways to select the indicators. The indicators selected should fulfill the following criteria: First, they should fulfill the principles of parsimony and sufficiency (systems criteria). The *parsimony* principle states that a system should be defined to be as simple as possible to fit the purpose of the sustainability assessment. To comply with the *sufficiency* principle the system should be designed to be as complex as necessary and as simple as possible – see Chapter 2 (Binder et al., 2020). Second, indicator selection should be based on the underlying concept of sustainability. One way to do this is to select indicators that address the ecological, economic, and social dimensions of sustainability (see Section 8.2.2 on the expert approach). Third, indicators can be selected depending on their function in the system – i.e., are they useful for monitoring the progress of an urban system or are they drivers of the system? These indicators will support Steps 5 and 6 (Figure 8.1). Finally, data for these indicators should be available or they should be easy to measure. Alternative ways for selecting the indicators are presented in Chapter 7 (Stelzer & Kopfmüller, 2020).

One might consider initially selecting a large set of indicators that can be reduced at a later stage. The principles of sufficiency and parsimony can be also applied in this case. Additionally, if two indicators measure the same item, the indicator with the better data availability should be selected. For reducing the indicator set and still complying with the underlying concept of sustainability, different rules can be applied as suggested in Chapter 7 (Stelzer & Kopfmüller, 2020), or by Bossel (1999).

After selecting the indicators, the relationships among the indicators is determined either through an expert (correlations) or a participatory (influence matrix) approach. For the latter, the key processes and interactions depicting the feedbacks within the system are determined. A causal loop diagram (CLD) might be useful for doing so (Williams & Hummelbrunner, 2011).[3] The CLD is the basis for developing a dynamic system model.

Step 3: Data/Data Analysis

The third step deals with data collection, data measurement, and data processing. A key aspect to be considered in this step, is that the different indicators should be made comparable to each other.

The interaction and trade-offs between the indicators can be analyzed in several ways: (i) if longitudinal data are available, the relationship between the indicators can be calculated using regression models; (ii) if the indicators were derived from a quantitative dynamic system model, the trade-offs can be analyzed by running the model and testing the effect of different types of strategies on the selected indicators; (iii) if such a quantitative model does not exist, an impact analysis can be performed (see participatory approach, Section 8.2.3; Wiek and Binder, 2005).

Step 4: Assessment

Definition of the sustainability ranges or thresholds. In order to assess the sustainability of an urban system, we need to first define the sustainability thresholds or sustainability ranges within which the system is sustainable (normative dimension). According to Wiek

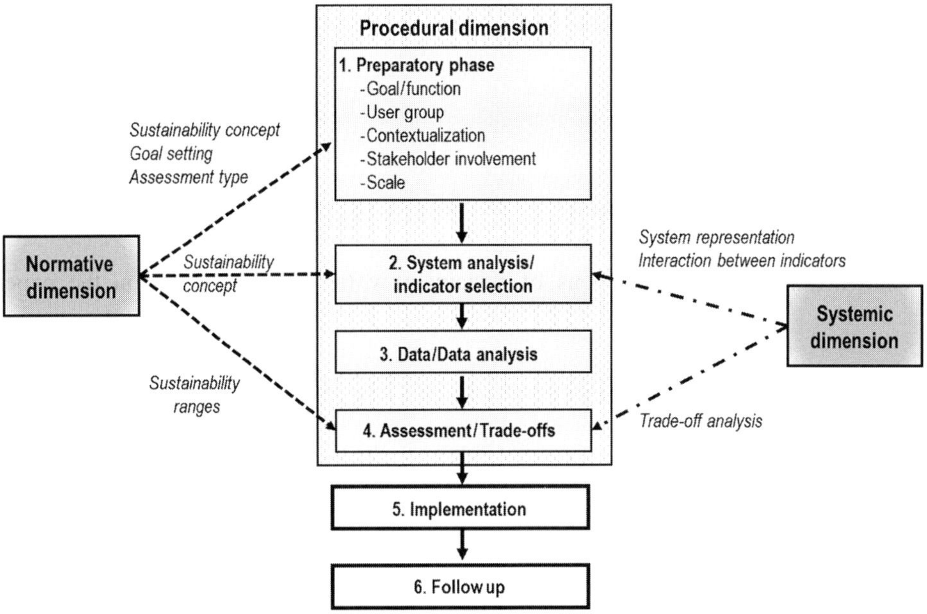

Figure 8.1 The SSP process (after Binder et al., 2010)

and Binder (2005) a sustainability range is "the largest range within which the sustainable development of an indicator is possible" (p. 598). The lower and upper value of each indicator, which constitute the sustainability range, are either (i) determined based on a legal value (e.g., threshold values in ecology); (ii) derived from goals that have been set at the national or international level (e.g., EU goals on energy transition); or (iii) determined by the actors, who are involved in the process itself. One has to consider that the sustainability ranges might, first, be context-dependent and, second, change over time, as they depend on the boundary conditions of the systems and on societal values and goal-setting processes (see Chapter 8 (Binder et al., 2020a) and Chapter 5 (Schilling et al., 2020)).

Second, the relative weights of the different indicators (or their relevance in relation to the overall goal) have to be set (see also Chapter 9 (Merino-Saum, 2020)). And finally, the interaction between the indicators, supporting the analysis of trade-offs, has to be determined. Based on these components, the SSP can be developed and measures for improving the sustainability of the system selected – e.g., city, neighborhood, building – can be set and their impact analyzed.

Differences between the expert and participatory approaches. The expert and the participatory approaches differ from each other with respect to Steps 2, 3, and 4 – i.e., system analysis, data measurement and analysis, and the way the final assessment is performed – as well as in the role of participation, the stakeholders involved, and the methods used (see Table 8.1).

Table 8.1 *Comparison between the expert and the participatory approaches to urban sustainability assessment*

	Expert Approach	Participatory Approach
1 Preparatory phase		
Goal	Assessing the sustainability of a city and identifying points of action	Assessing the sustainability of a city and identifying points of action
User group	Policymakers and city planners	Policymakers and city planners
Function	Benchmarking, evaluating, monitoring, steering	Evaluating, steering, monitoring
Participation	Informative, consultative	Codevelopment of indicators, sustainability ranges, and actions possible
Actors	Experts	Experts and stakeholders
2 System analysis		
System boundaries	Data-dependent: political boundaries, one year	Problem-dependent: for example, city, neighborhood, sector
Indicator selection	Sustainability concept	Sustainability concept and system-based
System representation	Clustering and scoring of urban systems	Causal loop diagrams
3 Data measurement and analysis		
Data	Data on urban indicators from official statistics, longitudinal or panel data	No specific requirements – also qualitative data for one year possible
Method	Data Analysis	Interviews, workshops, system analysis, crowd-sourcing
4 Assessment		
Thresholds	Scientific, international goal setting	Contextualized goal representation
Trade-offs	Correlations	Influence matrix, workshops
Weighting	Stakeholder involvement	Stakeholder involvement

8.2.2 The Expert Approach

In the following section, we present the expert approach, illustrated with the example of city statistics. The conceptual considerations are intertwined with the application of the approach in the example.

(1) Preparatory Phase

The goal of the expert approach is to assess the sustainability of a city and identify points of action. Thus, the assessment aims at providing a benchmark, evaluating the current state of the city, and supporting the design of a monitoring system. Key recipients of the assessment are policymakers and city planners with the goal of obtaining a more sustainable urban system.

In the following, we focus on Steps 2–4 of the SSP:

Step 2 System analysis and indicator selection
Step 3 Data and data analysis
Step 4 Assessment and defining points of action

(2) System Analysis and Indicator Selection

System boundaries: We selected the political boundaries of cities, as defined in city statistics, as the system boundaries for this analysis. To select the relevant indicators for assessing the sustainability of the urban system, Brundtland's concept of sustainability was chosen (Holden et al., 2014). This definition of sustainability consists of three pillars: economic, ecological, and social. Based on the goals presented, and the data requirements for the expert approach (Table 8.1), the indicators chosen to assess the sustainability of the urban system have to fulfill the following requirements:

- They should represent the concept of sustainability chosen, i.e., consider the three pillars as stated.
- They should allow for comparison among different cities and different countries.
- Data should be available for several cities, so that a comparative analysis can be performed.

(3) Data and Data Analysis

The data was collected for 30 cities across the globe from different available sources, as reported in Table 8.2. Most of the data was collected from World Council Data web portal.[4] The other two most representative database are the UN SDG Data Portal[5] and from the US Central Intelligence Agency (CIA).[6] The other points were collected from 23 other databases, as described in the legend below Table 8.2.

(4) Assessment and defining points of action

Definition of sustainability ranges or thresholds: In the expert approach, the experts determine the thresholds or ranges of sustainability for each indicator. These values rely on extensive literature research and may refer to legal thresholds, goals set by the international community (e.g., climate-change-related goals), or national goals.

General procedure to determining the SSP: In general, we select N indicators, $X = [x_1, x_2, \dots, x_N]$, and V cities, $Y = [y^1, y^2, \dots, y^V]$. Each indicator is then defined as *positive* or *negative* (see the column *Sign* in Table 8.3): for instance, if x_i is a positive indicator, the city y^j is defined as sustainable for that indicator if $x_i^j > x_i^T$ where x_i^T is the sustainable threshold. For the purposes of determining the sustainability ranges, each indicator is expressed as a function of the all the other indicators. So, given a pair of indicators x_i and x_{i+1}, the city y^j is defined as sustainable if:

Table 8.2 *Value of the selected indicators for each city of this study*

City	Country/Region	UNSD	GDP per capita	Renewable energy produced (%)	GHG emissions	Gini Coefficient	Life expectancy	Population in poverty %
Amsterdam	Netherlands	Western Europe	187404.47	14.54	5.40	0.33	80.30	11.81
Athens	Greece	Southern Europe	140902.26	0.00 (2)	10.40 (4)	0.45 (24)	810 (5)	16.40 (1)
Auckland	NewZealand	Oceania	31528.66	72.70 (2)	10.90 (3)	0.33 (11)	82.30 (17)	15.00 (12)
Barcelona	Spain	Southern Europe	104288.38	4.45	2.36	0.35 (16)	83.00	18.28
Bogota	Colombia	South America	19787.16	72.70 (2)	10.90 (3)	0.33 (11)	82.30 (17)	15.00 (12)
Boston	UnitedStates	North America	617757.80	10.82	20.82	0.48	80.50	10.85
Brisbane	Australia	Oceania	61001.52	8.50	20.80	0.39	82.10	13.90
Buenos Aires	Argentina	South America	109270.15	0.00	4.40	0.38	77.20	29.07
Cape Town	SouthAfrica	Africa	15748.55	0.00	6.18	0.62	62.50	26.68
Chicago	UnitedStates	North America	240747.50	5.93	21.32	0.48	79.00	14.38
Detroit	UnitedStates	North America	374970.88	7.88	22.33	0.47	78.20	17.91
Dubai	UnitedArabEmirat	Western Asia	27162516.38	0.08	20.19	0.40	78.00	0.00
Guadalajara	Mexico	North America	53979.93	1.92	4.61	0.42 (13)	75.18	33.30
Lagos	Nigeria	Africa	7076.38	12.50 (2)	1.40 (9)	0.64 (13)	53.00	22.00 (18)
Lisbon	Portugal	Southern Europe	142042.09	0.10 (2)	16.70	0.33 (8)	81.14 (6)	25.00 (7)
London	UnitedKingdom	Northern Europe	108099.80	2.03	4.89	0.34 (16)	82.05	25.77
Los Angeles	UnitedStates	North America	251760.56	32.57	15.94	0.49	80.80	17.44
New Orleans	UnitedStates	North America	197123.85	3.68	17.19	0.50	75.70	20.62
New York	UnitedStates	North America	193899.98	24.15	19.28	0.51	80.50	14.61
Oslo	Norway	Northern Europe	116665.33	100.00 (2)	3.50 (4)	0.31 (10)	82.10 (19)	10.00 (21)
Paris	France	Western Europe	378787.88	10.00 (2)	5.20 (4)	0.38 (16)	83.35 (15)	14.00 (14)
Porto	Portugal	Southern Europe	144636.21	21.40	4.80	0.33 (8)	80.70	18.70
Pune	India	South Asia	44295.64	1.04	1.46	0.35	68.00	40.00 (23)
Riyadh	SaudiArabia	Western Asia	24424.86	0.00	9.10	0.55	74.20	12.00
San Francisco	UnitedStates	North America	540287.09	32.57	19.05	0.49	80.80	12.20
San Jose	UnitedStates	North America	246328.78	32.57	18.72	0.46	80.80	9.74
Taipei	Taiwan	East Asia	82757.49	8.71	4.48	0.31	83.43	1.76
Toronto	Canada	North America	107867.57	31.20	7.33	0.44 (16)	83.00	22.60
Valencia	Spain	Southern Europe	76056.60	4.74	3.55	0.35	82.69	26.20
Vancouver	Canada	North America	169564.81	31.00 (2)	4.90 (4)	0.41 (3)	81.4 (5)	13.20 (22)

1	https://www.dianeosis.org/en/2016/06/extreme-poverty-greece-survey/
2	data.cdp.net/Cities/Cities-Renewable-Energy-Targets/hztn-by6p
3	https://censusmapper.ca/maps/165#5/49.067/-121.135
4	http://siteresources.worldbank.org/INTUWM/Resources/340232-1205330656272/4768406-1291309208465/PartIII.pdf
5	http://www.worldlifeexpectancy.com/greece-life-expectancy (country data)
6	https://teleport.org/cities/lisbon/
7	https://www.irp.wisc.edu/dispatch/poverty-rate-portugal/ (country data)
8	http://theportugalnews.com/news/the-great-divide-lisbon-home-to-largest-income-gap/26279 (country data)
9	http://www.c40.org/cities/lagos
10	https://www.ssb.no/en/inntekt-og-forbruk/statistikker/inntgeo/aar/2010-05-20
11	http://www.c40.org/cities/lagos (Counrtry data)
12	https://www.parliament.nz/en/pb/research-papers/document/00PlibCIP181/household-incomes-inequality-and-poverty (country data)
13	https://unhabitat.org/wp-content/uploads/2014/03/Table-3.1-Gini-Coefficient-for-Selected-Cities-and-Provinces.pdf
14	https://france3-regions.francetvinfo.fr/paris-ile-de-france/paris/plus-de-pauvres-paris-qu-ne-le-penserait-selon-la-gazette-des-communes-404757.html
15	https://france3-regions.francetvinfo.fr/paris-ile-de-france/esperance-vie-age-moyen-portrait-robot-du-francilien-1177681.html INSEE 2014
16	https://blog.euromonitor.com/2013/03/the-worlds-largest-cities-are-the-most-unequal.html
17	https://www.nzherald.co.nz/lifestyle/news/article.cfm?c_id=6&objectid=11488228
18	https://borgenproject.org/poverty-lagos-nigeria/
19	wordbank (country data)
20	http://www.geog.uvic.ca/wellness/wellness2011/Ch12_8.pdf
21	http://www.newsinenglish.no/2011/05/04/poverty-hits-10-percent-in-oslo/
22	https://www.vancouverobserver.com/news/bc-home-canada-s-second-highest-poverty-rate
23	https://borgenproject.org/poverty-in-pune-india/
24	http://www.athenssocialatlas.gr/en/article/income-groups/
	SDG
	https://www.cia.gov/library/publications/the-world-factbook/geos/aq.html
	ISO 37120

- **CASE 1:** x_i and x_{i+1} are positive

$$y_j \text{ is sustainable if } x_i^j \geq x_i^T \text{ and } x_{i+1}^j \geq x_{i+1}^T.$$

- **CASE 2:** x_i is negative and x_{i+1} is positive

$$y_j \text{ is sustainable if } x_i^j \leq x_i^T \text{ and } x_{i+1}^j \geq x_{i+1}^T.$$

- **CASE 3:** x_i is positive and x_{i+1} is negative

$$y_j \text{ is sustainable if } x_i^j \geq x_i^T \text{ and } x_{i+1}^j \leq x_{i+1}^T.$$

- **CASE 4:** x_i and x_{i+1} are negative

$$y_j \text{ is sustainable if } x_i^j \leq x_i^T \text{ and } x_{i+1}^j \leq x_{i+1}^T.$$

A normalization process is therefore necessary: the value of each indicator is normalized according to the following conditions:

$$\hat{x}_i = \frac{(x_i - x_i^T)}{x_i^T} \quad \text{if } x_i \text{ is positive} \tag{8.1}$$

$$\hat{x}_i = \frac{(x_i^T - x_i)}{x_i^T} \quad \text{if } x_i \text{ is negative}$$

This normalization allows us to create a 2D Cartesian plane of sustainability as shown in Figure 8.2.

Each city is represented by a point with coordinates $[k_1, k_2]$ and a relative score $s = k_1 + k_2$ that could be a positive or negative score depending on the quadrant and on the distance from the point of sustainability, $p_s = [0, 0]$. Because of the normalization process described in Equation 1, the point of sustainability corresponds to the threshold of sustainability for each indicator. In order to compute the final score for each city, we repeat this process for each pair of indicators $c = \frac{1}{2} \cdot N \cdot (N - 1)$, as described in the following algorithm.

Algorithm 8.1. Iterative procedure for computing the score of each city $\boldsymbol{s}[\boldsymbol{k}]$ given all the pairs of indicators $\boldsymbol{i}$ and $\boldsymbol{j}$.

```
for i = 1 : N-1 do
    for j = i+1: N do
        for k = 1:V do
            compute s[k]+ = k1 + k2;
        end
    end
end
```

8.2.3 Application of SSP: An Example

(1) Indicator Selection

For our example of the application of the SSP, we chose to use the European targets for the year 2030 to determine the thresholds for the six indicators presented above (Holden et al., 2014). Two indicators represent the ecological dimension: The first indicator denotes the percentage of energy produced that comes from a renewable source, which does not necessarily imply that the energy source is clean. The second indicator is greenhouse gas emissions (GHGs), defined as the total greenhouse gas emissions per inhabitant of the city per year, which is directly linked to global warming. The third and

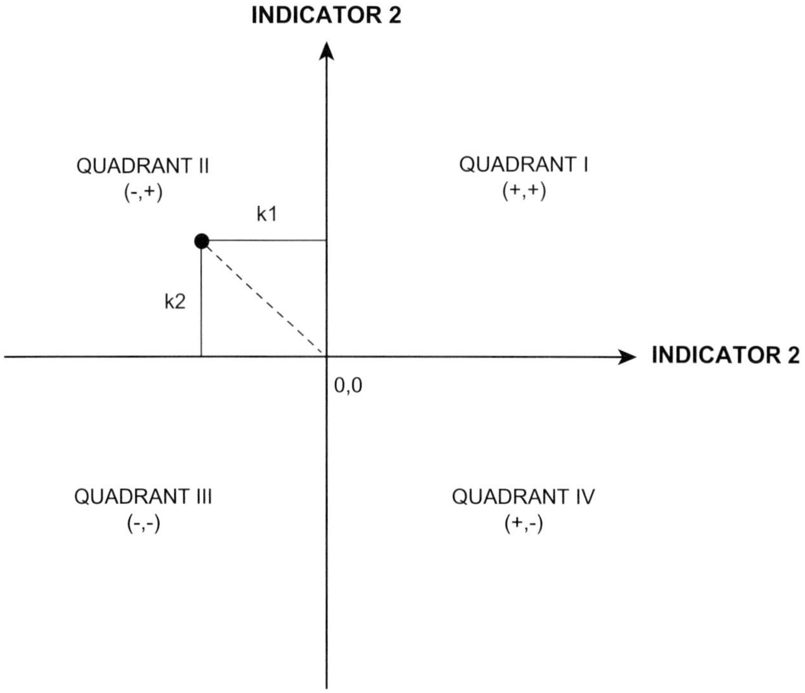

Figure 8.2 The SSP in the expert approach for a set of indicators: *INDICATOR 1* and *INDICATOR 2*. Due to the normalization, the point $p_s = [0, 0]$ corresponds to the threshold of sustainability. *QUADRANT 1* is the space of sustainability where both the indicators respect the conditions of sustainability. For each point with coordinates $[k_1, k_2]$, we give a score s that is the sum of the two coordinates, i.e., $s = k_1 + k_2$.

fourth indicators represent the social dimension. The third indicator (Gini coefficient) measures the disparities between the inhabitants of the same city. The Gini coefficient measures the inequality among values of a frequency distribution (for example, levels of income). A Gini coefficient of zero expresses perfect equality (for example, where everyone has the same income). A Gini coefficient of one (or 100 percent) expresses maximal inequality (e.g., for a large number of people, if only one person has all the income or consumption, and all the others have none, the Gini coefficient will be very close to one). Regarding the economic pillar, we choose indicators like the number of people living below the poverty line and GDP per capita. The first entry is concerned with extreme poverty. The World Bank is the main source for global information on extreme poverty today and it sets the International Poverty Line. The poverty line was revised in 2015 – a person is now considered to be in extreme poverty if they live on less than 1.90 international dollars (int.$) per day. This poverty measurement is based on the monetary value of a person's consumption. Income measures, on the other hand, are only used for countries for which reliable consumption measures are not available. This is the value of all final goods and services produced within a nation in a given year, converted at market exchange rates to current US dollars, divided by the average population for the same year.

(2) Definition of the Indicator Thresholds

Regarding the ecological indicators, for the first indicator, *renewable energy*, a satisfactory percentage of renewable energy production is 27 percent according to the European goals for 2030.[7] *GHG emissions* should be reduced by 40 percent by 2030 compared to 1990 levels.[8] Knowing that 5,716.4 million tons of CO_2-eq. were produced in 1990 by the EU28 countries,[9] a 40 percent cut would represent 3428.84 million tons of CO_2-eq. for those 28 states. By dividing that number by the population of the EU28 states in January 2017 (511.5 Million) the threshold of GHG emissions becomes 6.07 tons of CO_2-eq. per capita per year. Regarding the social indicators, for determining the threshold of the *Gini coefficient*, we relied on UN Habitat (UN-Habitat, 2012) and the paper "Our Common Future: Revisited" (Holden et al., 2014) and determined the Gini coefficient threshold value to be 0.4. For the *life expectancy* indicator, we choose the threshold of 80.8 years: the average life expectancy at birth of the global population in 2016.[10] Regarding the economic indicators, for *people living below the poverty line* we rely on the SDGs. The United Nations Sustainable Development Goals (SDGs) state that by 2030,[11] every country should reduce by at least half the proportion of men, women, and children of all ages living in poverty in all its dimensions, according to national definitions. Consequently, the threshold used in this study is half the average poverty level of the cities studied, which corresponds to 7.67 percent. Finally, for *GDP*, we assume that a city is sustainable if the GDP per capita is at least 10 percent of the GDP of the country the city is in (or the state for cities in the United States).

Assessment. For the case presented, similar to the work for countries by Holden et al. (2014), a city is considered sustainable if the value of each pair of indicators presented is above the thresholds of sustainability (i.e., Quadrant I in Figure 8.2). For each indicator (see Table 8.2 for the complete list of indicators and their respective values), it is therefore important to find a value to use as a threshold (see Table 8.3). Above this threshold, the city is considered to be performing sufficiently well. In this model, a city is considered sustainable if it exceeds the threshold for each of the indicators presented. In Figure 8.3 we show the results in the SSP for all 30 cities for each possible pair of indicators, i.e., $0.5.6.(6 - 1) = 15$ combinations while in Table 8.5 we show the top 10 sustainable cities according to our SSP tool. The results of the SSP expert approach are not trivial and need some explanation. Taipei and Oslo result as the most sustainable cities, achieving similar scores and appearing the same number of times in the SSP (Figure 8.3). Taipei City, the political, economic, and cultural center of Taiwan, is

Table 8.3 *The table shows the name of the indicator, the pillar of sustainability it relates to, its threshold of sustainability, and the sign*

Indicator	Pillar	Threshold	Sign
Renewable energy	Environment	27 %	+
GHG emissions	Environment	6.07 tons $C0_2$eq.	−
Gini coefficient	Social	0.6	−
Life expectancy	Social	80.8 years old	+
People living below the poverty line	Economy	7.7%	−
GDP per capita	Economy	10% of the Country	+

densely populated, with a population of more than 2,600,000. In 2010, its population density ranked seventh among world metropolitan areas. Today, Taipei City has become one of the most international, modern, and commercial cities in Asia; the existing built environments formed during these periods are intermingled with new construction. Taipei was included in Siemens' Asian Green City Index,[12] a report conducted by the Economist Intelligence Unit.[13] Overall, Taipei was placed in the "above average" category alongside five other cities.

The index evaluates 22 major Asian cities across 8 categories: energy and CO_2, land use and buildings, transport, waste, water, sanitation, air quality, and environmental governance. Taipei achieved above-average marks in seven out of eight categories, only falling to average status in its performance regarding water. Based on its quantitative score, Taipei achieved second place overall. Oslo, meanwhile, has recently been awarded the title of Europe's Green Capital of 2019 by the European Green City Award, an initiative of the European Commission.[14] Oslo, with its 660,000 inhabitants, is green not only due to its low carbon footprint of 1.9 tons per capita per year. It has introduced a range of integrated measures to cut emissions by 50 percent by 2020 (compared to 1990 levels) – for example, by promoting zero-emissions transport. In 2016, the city introduced a "Climate Budget," an initiative consisting of 42 separate measures across three sectors: energy and the built environment, transport, and resources. Carbon dioxide emissions are now being accounted for in the same way that funding would be accounted for in a financial budget. In third place in Table 8.4, we find the capital of Colombia, Bogotá, which appears only six times in the SSP but has a very high score if compared to Auckland (in fourth place). According to the Building Efficiency Accelerator (BEA) program released by WRI, the Colombian capital results prove it to be one of the most sustainable cities.[15] The aim of WRI is to provide a guide for leaders in the public and private sectors to follow in order to increase building efficiency and reach sustainability goals in their cities. On the other hand, our SSP expert approach ranks Cape Town in last place, a city that never appears in the SSP.

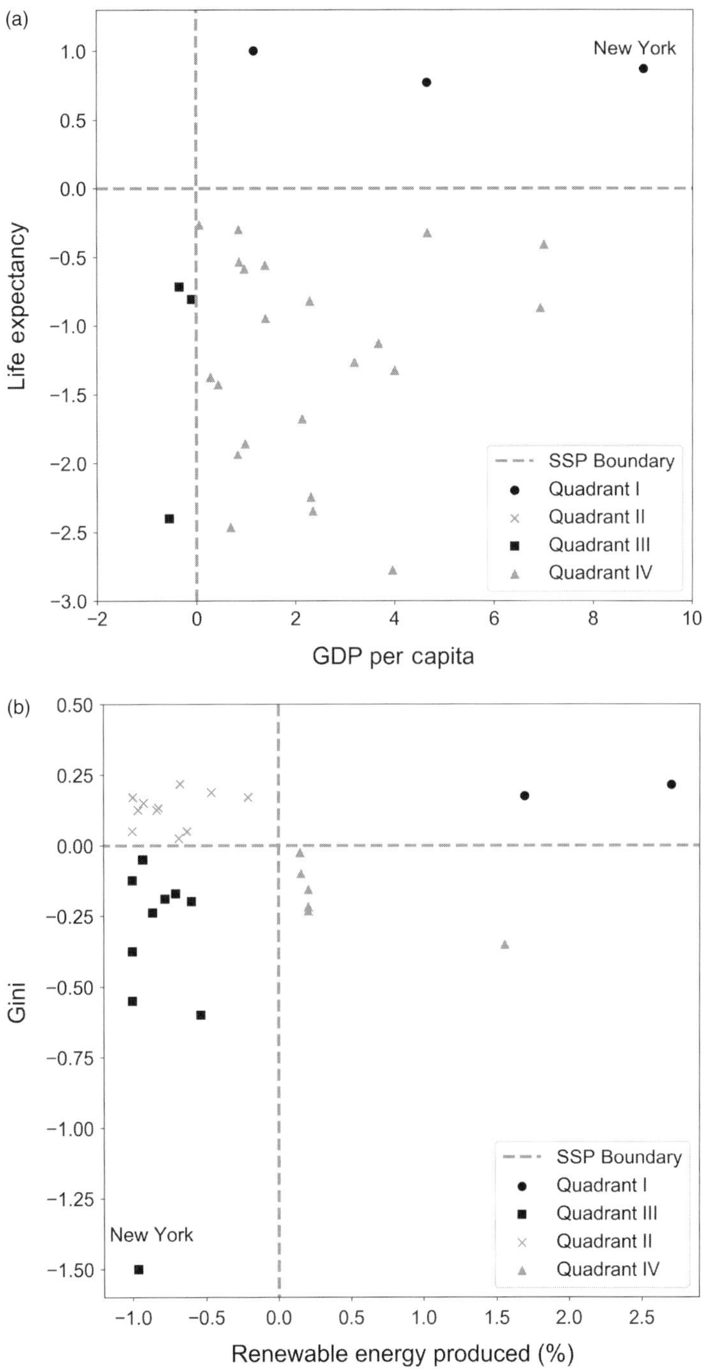

Figure 8.3 Cities in the sustainable solution space (SSP). The cities represented in black correspond to cities that are in quadrant I and quadrant IV respectively. The SSP can return different assessments for the same city in different cases. For instance, New York can be considered sustainable for the "life expectancy–GDP per capita" space but appears in the third quadrant for the "Gini-Renewable energy produced (%)" space. Source: own illustration

Table 8.4 *Top 10 cities ranked according to the SSP Expert Approach. The cities are sorted according to the number of times (Times) they are observed in the SSP (QUADRANT I) and their total score (Score)*

Rank	City	Score	Times in SSP
1	Taipei	26.9	10
2	Oslo	20.19	10
3	Bogotá	21.12	6
4	Auckland	8.35	6
5	Paris	5.97	6
6	Buenos Aires	2.88	6
7	Amsterdam	1.41	6
8	London	−2.16	6
9	Porto	−3.48	6
10	Barcelona	−5.2	6

8.2.4 The Participatory Approach

In the following, we present the participatory approach, illustrated with the example of the assessment of a sustainable buildings cooperative, Équilibre. The conceptual considerations are intertwined with the exemplary application of the approach.

(1) Preparatory Phase

The main research goal of the Équilibre case study was to understand the impacts on housing performance of a cooperative and participatory functioning, in terms of sustainable development. That is, the aim is to assess Équilibre's participatory approach to planning and providing housing. Thus, several aspects have to be considered: first, the environmental components of the building; second, the use of the building; and third, the sustainability of the way the buildings are used, including the satisfaction of the inhabitants. The recipient of the assessment is the cooperative's regulatory body, which aims to develop even more sustainable housing opportunities.

In the following, we focus on Steps 2–4 of the SSP:

Step 2 System analysis and indicator selection
Step 3 Data and data analysis
Step 4 Assessment and defining points of action

(2) System Analysis and Indicator Selection

Context: The case study presented here analyzes a housing cooperative, Équilibre, in Geneva, which owns several buildings and houses 115 households. These buildings share two common threads: on the one hand, they all have strict requirements regarding sustainable development (including from an environmental perspective) and, on the other hand, they are supportive of the active participation of future inhabitants of the flats. Thus, Équilibre indeed encourages its members to commit to their living environment, either by helping to design the building, taking part in the construction, or – very importantly – participating in ensuring the proper functioning of the building.

The **system boundary** are the buildings owned by Équilibre (rather than a neighborhood). However, as different spatial and temporal dimensions play a role, three perspectives were considered in developing the system model and selecting the indicators: *building*, *usage*, and *inhabitants*. The *building* itself is characterized, independently of the inhabitants, by, e.g., its location, the grey energy needed for its construction, and its investment costs. These correspond to the static properties of the system. The *usage of the building*, characterized by water, energy, and surface use, is partly influenced by the building itself and partly by the way inhabitants use it. That is, we refer here to the semi-dynamic system properties. Finally, the *inhabitants* themselves perform their own activities, habits, and lifestyles that might change over time, or the inhabitants themselves might change. We refer to these as dynamic properties.

Indicator selection: For the case of the Équilibre buildings presented above, 18 indicators were selected by the authors and validated with representatives of Équilibre and housing experts. They represent the three systemic perspectives (Figure 8.4) and consider two additional axes, one axis referring to the principles presented in Chapter 7 (Stelzer & Kopfmüller, 2020) – i.e., human capital, risks, resources – and one thematic axis, referring to water, energy, life conditions. Table 8.5 presents the indicators selected and their relation to the different axes.

System understanding: To understand how the indicators are related to each other and where the system can be influenced, a CLD was developed (Figure 8.4). This CLD only considers strong interrelationships. Local food production (on the terrain of the building itself) is, on the one hand, a key driver of environmental variables such as water consumption, permeable surface, and incinerated waste. On the other hand, the results suggest that the possibility to engage in local food production increases inhabitants' life satisfaction and their willingness to perform voluntary work. Another interesting aspect is that life satisfaction is increased through having, e.g., access to shared spaces and engaging in activities including voluntary work, and that effect tends to be weaker the greater the proximity to public transport.

(3) Data and Data Analysis

A mixed-method approach was pursued to gather the data. Data for the indicators related to the building (i.e., the way it was constructed) and some data on the use of the building (e.g., water consumption, waste related indicators) was available from Équilibre. Data related to the inhabitants was collected through interviews and surveys. Both interviews and surveys were developed in close collaboration with experts from Équilibre. About 64 percent of the households responded to the survey. For benchmarking purposes, the indicators were also

Table 8.5 *Indicators selected to characterize the three systemic perspectives*

Indicators	Label	Definition	Units	Boundaries	Topic
Building level					
Permeable surface	S1_a	Proportion of green surface or water surface where infiltration is easy, with respect to the total surface area of the parcel	%	75–90	Biodiversity
Waste water management	S1_b	Proportion of wastewater treated directly on site	%	35–100	Water
Grey energy	S1_c	Cumulative amount of nonrenewable energy used for building one square meter of permeable surface per year	[kWh/m^2 $_{SP}$/a]	26.5–0	Energy
Rental costs	S1_d	Monthly rental costs per square meter excluding electricity, heating, etc.	CHF/m^2	19.7–13	Living conditions
Shared spaces	S1_e	Sum of shared and polyvalent spaces with respect to the total number of rooms	m^2/rooms	0.3–1.5	Social cohesion
Proximity to public transportation	S1_f	Walking distance to the nearest public transport stop	m	400–0	Mobility
Use level					
Water consumption	S2_a	Water consumption per person per day	l/cap/day	20–55	Water
Energy consumption	S2_b	Final energy consumption for heating and ventilating one square meter of living area for one year	[kWh/m^2 SRE/an]	35–0	Energy
Renewable electricity	S2_c	Share of electricity consumption covered by renewable energy production on site	%	40–100	Energy
Local food production	S2_d	Available space per apartment for gardening	m^2/apartment	2–10	Food
Surface per person	S2_e	Net space for living per person	m^2/cap	35–17.5	Living conditions
Intergenerational mix	S2_f	Number of age classes represented in the building (one age class: 10 years)	Nr.	5–10	Social cohesion

Inhabitants					
Incinerated waste	S3_a	Amount of waste to be incinerated per person per year	Kg/cap/year	75–0	Waste
Recycling	S3_b	Proportion of waste that is sorted and recycled (e.g., PET, organic waste)	%	75–100	Waste
Share of work performed in the home	S3_c	Ratio between paid work and work performed in the home	%	1.9–0.1	Living conditions
Voluntary work	S3_d	Proportion of inhabitants who do at least one hour per week of voluntary work	%	50–100	Social cohesion
Life satisfaction	S3_e	Proportion of inhabitants satisfied with their life (>8 in scale of 1–10)	%	75–100	Satisfaction and comfort
Slow mobility	S3_f	Proportion of walking, biking, and public transport with respect to kilometers traveled per week	%	70–100	

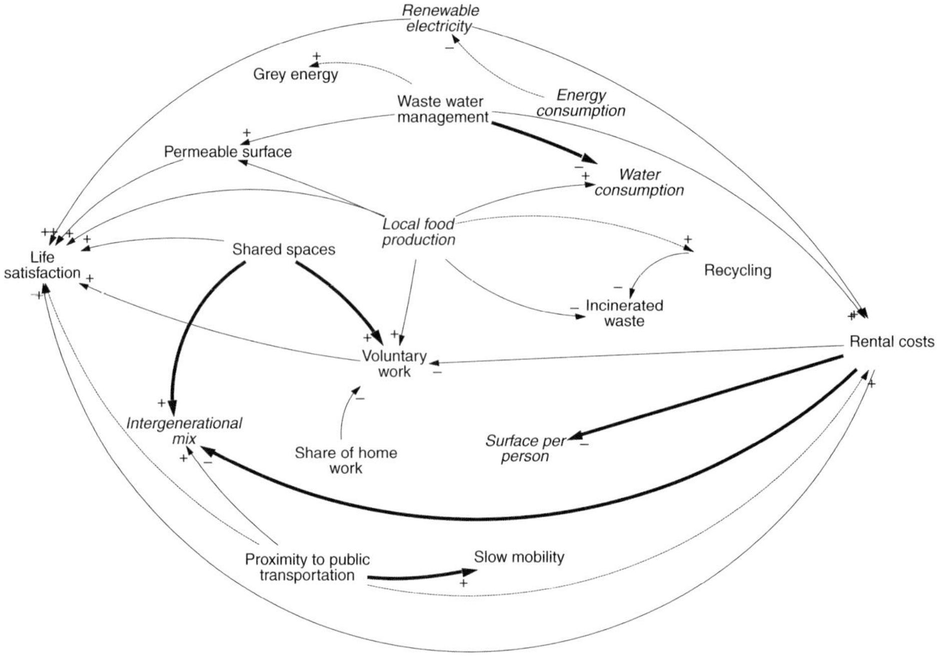

Figure 8.4 Causal loop diagram linking the selected indicators. Bold: building level; italics: usage level; underlined: inhabitants' level. Strong lines indicate strong relations (rated as 3), whereas dashed lines indicate weak relations (rated as 1). Source: own illustration

collected for average households at the city, regional, and national levels, depending on data availability, to determine the baseline conditions in the specific area.

To analyze the interrelation and trade-offs between the indicators, an influence matrix was developed in a participatory way. Thereby, for each pair of indicators, actors from Équilibre evaluated the strengths of the mono-directional influence (e.g., 0: no influence; 1: small influence; 2: large influence) among them. In special cases, the scale can also be enlarged (to include more steps). In addition, the type of influence was elicited (+: positive; –: negative). (See also Scholz & Tietje, 2002.)

Analysis of the influence matrix: The matrix was analyzed by summing the absolute values of the rows and the columns. The sum of the absolute values of the rows indicates the activity of the indicator, and the sum of the columns indicates its passivity. We distinguish four types of indicators:

- **Active indicators:** These influence the system strongly and are weakly influenced by other indicators in the system. They can be considered as steering or driving indicators.
- **Ambivalent indicators:** These influence the system strongly and are strongly influenced by other indicators in the system. They are key indicators for systemic understanding.

- **Passive indicators:** These are strongly influenced by other indicators and do not have a large influence on other indicators. They are important for monitoring the system.
- **Buffering indicators:** These are weakly influenced by other indicators and have little influence on other indicators. They have low systemic relevance.

Figure 8.5a shows the influence matrix for the Équilibre case study. We chose a scale from zero to three. On the right-hand side, the sum of the activity of the indicators is presented. Rental costs and local food production, as well as shared spaces, wastewater management, and proximity to public transportation, are important drivers of the system. This actually indicates that the way in which the buildings are constructed can shape other indicators, such as life satisfaction, intergenerational mix, and to some extent also the amount of voluntary work performed in the community.

Finally, the indicators can be positioned in the impact grid, showing their role in the system (Figure 8.5b). Ambivalent indicators – in this case, rental costs – play an important role for understanding the system as they influence several indicators, for example, surface per person, intergenerational mix, as well as the share of work performed in the home and the ability and motivation for voluntary work. At the same time, rental costs are also influenced by the way in which the buildings are designed, relating to environmental issues such as water and energy consumption and proximity to public transport (Figure 8.5b).

(4) Assessment and Defining Points of Action

Definition of the sustainability ranges: In the case of Équilibre, the sustainability ranges were (1) derived from the literature; (2) based on Swiss national goals (e.g., for the case of energy-related indicators); or (3) derived from discussions with experts in the field. Where no data was available, broad ranges were estimated.

Assessing the sustainability of a system: To assess the sustainability of the system, the values describing the system are compared to the sustainability ranges. In order to do this, the sustainability ranges are normalized either between one and zero, or as shown, between four and six. A possible representation of the sustainability solution space and the related current values is a spider diagram, which shows the areas where a system is sustainable, i.e., where values fall within sustainability ranges. The indicators for the values that are outside the sustainability range indicate the need for action. The results of the influence matrix and/or the system model can also be used to identify the potential effects of measures on other indicators, if measures are implemented to improve the identified area.

Figure 8.6 shows the sustainability solution space for Soubeyran, a project of the Équilibre cooperative. The project itself is one of Équilibre's newest buildings. Three key issues can be noted: first, in the dimensions relating to the building itself, it is slightly better than the benchmark. The main weak points lie in the amount of permeable surface. No data were available for grey energy. Slightly larger differences can be depicted when we look at the use of the building. There, the benchmark buildings are, except for intergenerational mix, outside the sustainability space, whereas in Soubeyran, use of the buildings tends to be

(a)

		S1						S2						S3						
		Permeable surface	Waste water management	Grey energy	Rental costs	Shared spaces	Proximity to public transportation	Water consumption	Energy consumption	Renewable electricity production	Local food production	Surface per person	Intergenerational mix	Incinerated waste	Recycled waste	Share of home-work	Voluntary work	Life satisfaction	Slow mobility	**Activity**
S1	Permeable surface		0	0	0	0	0	0	0	0	0	0	0	0	0	0	0	2	0	**2**
	Waste water management	2		1	2	0	0	-3	0	0	0	0	0	0	0	0	0	0	0	**8**
	Grey energy	0	0		0	0	0	0	0	0	0	0	0	0	0	0	0	0	0	**0**
	Rental costs	0	0	0		0	0	0	0	0	0	-3	-3	0	0	2	-2	-2	0	**12**
	Shared spaces	0	0	0	0		0	0	0	0	0	0	3	0	0	0	3	2	0	**8**
	Proximity to public transportation	0	0	0	1	0		0	0	0	0	0	2	0	0	0	0	1	3	**7**
S2	Water consumption	0	0	0	0	0	0		0	0	0	0	0	0	0	0	0	0	0	**0**
	Energy consumption	0	0	0	0	0	0	0		-2	0	0	0	0	0	0	0	0	0	**2**
	Renewable electricity production	0	0	0	2	0	0	0	0		0	0	0	0	0	0	0	2	0	**4**
	Local food production	2	0	0	0	0	0	2	0	0		0	0	-2	1	0	1	2	0	**10**
	Surface per person	0	0	0	0	0	0	0	0	0	0		0	0	0	2	0	0	0	**2**
	Intergenerational mix	0	0	0	0	0	0	0	0	0	0	0		0	0	0	0	0	0	**0**
S3	Incinerated waste	0	0	0	0	0	0	0	0	0	0	0	0		0	0	0	0	0	**0**
	Recycled waste	0	0	0	0	0	0	0	0	0	0	0	0	-2		0	0	0	0	**2**
	Share of home-work	0	0	0	0	0	0	0	0	0	0	0	0	0	0		-2	0	0	**2**
	Voluntary work	0	0	0	0	0	0	0	0	0	0	0	0	0	0	0		2	0	**2**
	Life satisfaction	0	0	0	0	0	0	0	0	0	0	0	0	0	0	0	0		0	**0**
	Slow mobility	0	0	0	0	0	0	0	0	0	0	0	0	0	0	0	0	0		**0**
	Passivity	**4**	**0**	**1**	**5**	**0**	**0**	**5**	**0**	**2**	**0**	**3**	**8**	**4**	**1**	**4**	**8**	**13**	**3**	

(b)

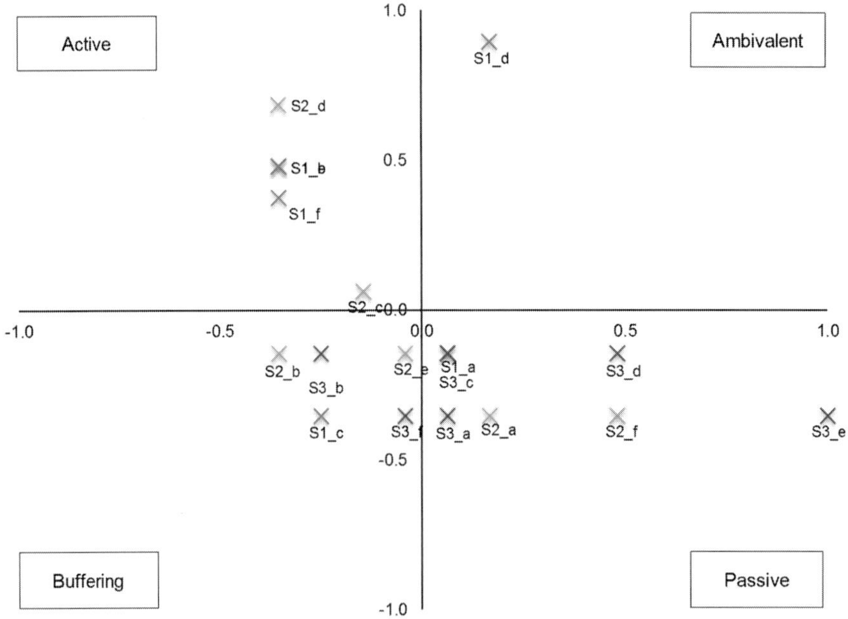

Figure 8.5 **(a)** Influence matrix of the Équilibre case study (right) and **(b)** impact grid for the Équilibre case study (left). The activity and passivity were normalized and plotted for each indicator. For the labeling, please see Table 8.5. Source: own illustration

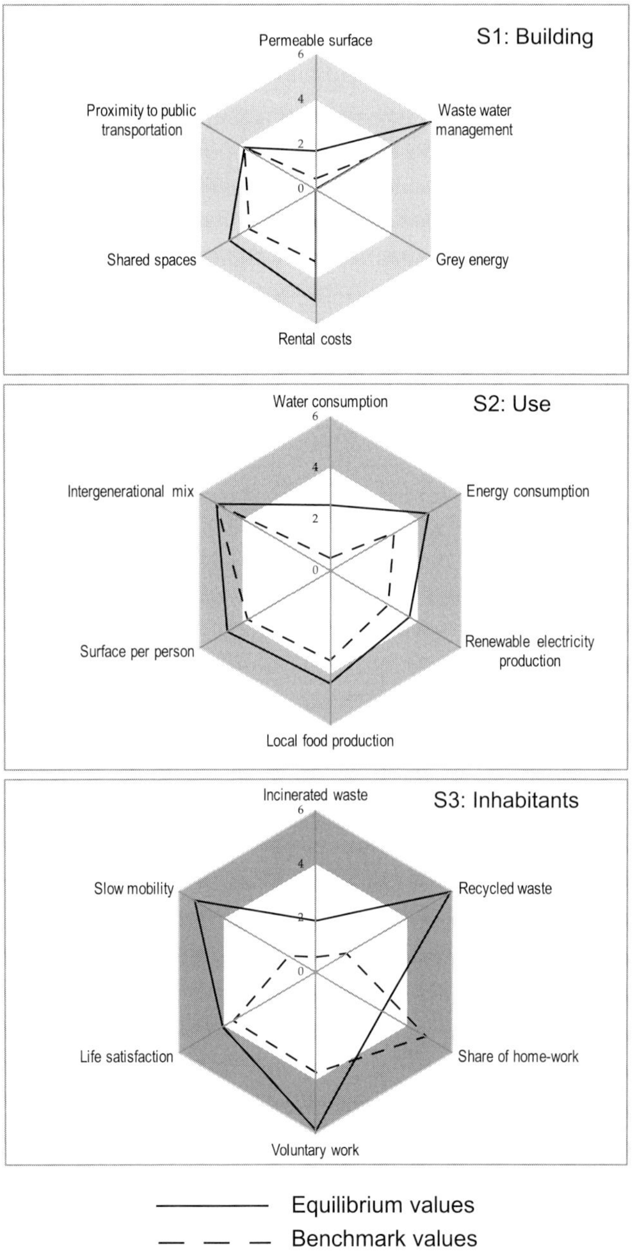

Figure 8.6 Sustainability solution space for the case of Soubeyran for the three systemic perspectives. The unbroken lines show the measured values at Soubeyran, the dashed lines display the average benchmark in the region. Source: own illustration

more sustainable, although still outside the sustainability range for water consumption and renewable energy production. The largest differences can be seen in the assessment of the inhabitants. By and large, except for the share of work performed in the home, the building performs better than the average. Interestingly, voluntary work and pro-environmental activities such as recycling and slow mobility performed very well in this case.

In order to move further toward sustainability, we might pose a question: how could life satisfaction and the share of work performed in the home be improved? When looking at the influence matrix, we can observe that life satisfaction is negatively influenced by rental costs and positively influenced by increasing permeable surfaces, increasing shared spaces, improving proximity to public transportation, and fostering local food production and renewable energy production. Whereas the current parcel size, as well as proximity to public transport, might not be very easy to change, one could think of innovative ways of increasing shared spaces and potentially pursuing local food production. This, however, might entail an increase in water consumption and in the time that needs to be spent at home. That is, with these tools, we are able to analyze the potential trade-offs involved in improving sustainability related to a specific indicator. It has to be noted that the two other Équilibre buildings analyzed perform even better with respect to the benchmark than Soubeyran. One additional aspect regarding the case study has to be mentioned. The results obtained suggest that the participatory and cooperative functioning of the housing cooperative Équilibre can be the basis for obtaining more sustainable dwellings, as the commitment of inhabitants helps create a habitat with high quality of life.

8.3 Discussion

This chapter presented the approach of using sustainability solution spaces to analyze the sustainability of urban systems, comparing different cities with each other and analyzing sectors or specific houses within an urban system.

SSP provides the following additional insights compared to other sustainability assessment approaches: (i) it makes the systemic and normative aspects of sustainability explicit; (ii) it is flexible and adaptable depending on the goal of the assessment and the context the city, or neighborhood, is located in; (iii) it provides two distinct approaches, an expert approach and a participatory approach, which can be adapted to the goal at hand; and (iv) it uses sustainability ranges and thresholds, rather than a specific sustainability value.

Whereas the expert approach requires a high quality of data, preferably either over time or over a large number of cities, the participatory approach is more flexible and can also deal with qualitative data. In addition, systems can be analyzed in a semi-quantitative way in participatory workshops or expert interviews. That is, the expert approach can be used to compare large sets of cities with each other, to cluster and provide benchmarks for specific city types, and to deliver general indications of which areas policy development is required in. The participatory approach might be particularly useful when dealing with cities, since it aims either to assess the impact of a specific project or to analyze in depth a specific sector, such as mobility or housing. For some research questions, it might even be a good idea to first screen for the problem areas in a city using an expert approach and then follow-up this analysis for the problematic areas analyzed with a participatory approach.

Indicators versus system models: There is one caveat that has to be considered when using indicators for assessing the sustainability of systems (see Chapter 5 (Schilling et al., 2020)). Indicators are, per se, static and can only represent parts of the system. They are usually used for describing key aspects of the system itself, assessing its sustainability and monitoring the progress of the system. However, even if we analyze the relationship between the indicators as shown both in the expert and in the participatory approach, this is a mere simplification and we have to be aware that this does not capture the complexity of the underlying system dynamics. To overcome this problem, the analysis of the relationship and trade-offs between the indicators provides a basis for deriving differentiated policy advice. The proposed qualitative system models based on causal loop diagrams make it possible to deepen the analysis by looking at the effect of a change in one indicator on the whole system (including feedbacks) rather than on one sole indicator. This makes it possible to position the indicators in the system itself and to qualitatively identify which parts of the system are affected by specific policies. This first ex ante analysis can then be complemented and monitored with indicators.

Selecting the indicators: The selection of the indicators by and large drives the sustainability assessment and has to be reflected from a normative point of view. This is clearly demonstrated in Chapter 14 (Massaro et al., 2020) where it became evident that current indicator sets for assessing the sustainability of cities were highly biased from one institution to the next. As reflected in Chapter 1 (Halla & Binder, 2020), the selection of indicators depends on the perspective taken on sustainability. Thus, an in-depth systems analysis of the urban problem at hand, considering the interaction between indicators and feedback loops through a solid systems analysis (e.g., causal loop diagrams), allows for the elucidation of normative biases and for reflecting on the selection of the indicators in relation to the system itself. Furthermore, this analysis supports the interpretation of the results in context and therewith the development of policy measures.

Dealing with normativity in the assessment: As mentioned in Chapter 1 (Halla & Binder, 2020) and Chapter 3 (Meinherz et al., 2020), normativity is already present in the assessment from the way we define the problem, the system, the selection of the indicators, the definition of sustainability, and the sustainability ranges. In the SSP, we propose making this normativity explicit, by making explicit the sustainability definition the assessment is based upon, and using sustainability ranges (derived from literature, policy goals, or expert opinions) rather than a specific sustainability value. The sustainability ranges also allow for a negotiation process between different interests and stakeholder groups.

Comparability across cities versus specificity: The examples presented in this chapter show that the expert approach, using data available in different countries for different cities, makes it possible to compare cities to each other. It is extremely valuable for monitoring progress made toward sustainability in different cities. Furthermore, it provides the basis for more in-depth analysis. However, as mentioned, it points to the areas to be focused on, but not to the mechanisms for improving their sustainability. The participatory approach, on the contrary, allows for and supports an in-depth understanding of the sustainability problem at hand and its potential trade-offs and dynamics. However, the insights gained for one city might not be valid for another one. Yet while the results themselves itself might not be valid across cities, the approach and maybe the general relationships might apply to similar types of urban systems (as could be identified with the expert approach). This implies that there is a trade-off and complementarity between comparability and generalizability. We consider that it would be desirable to use an expert approach for benchmarking and a participatory approach to focus on the specific aspects where an improvement is required.

Ontology. Finally, we consider that for assessing the sustainability of urban systems, an agreement on a minimum set of indicators would be desirable and should be adopted regardless of the approach chosen. In the long term, this would support the overall comparability and compatibility of the results gained with different approaches. As also shown in Chapter 14 (Massaro et al., 2020), the ontology can be a way to set up a database, which allows for more detailed data to be used for specific cases and very general data for the higher-level comparison.

8.4 Conclusions

In this chapter, we presented the sustainability solution space as one way to assess the sustainability of cities. The main contribution of the SSP is that it provides a space of action – or wiggle room – for developing policies that consider uncertainties in defining target values, diverse normative perspectives, and systemic relationships. The SSP can be carried out in two ways, using an expert or a participatory approach, both of which aim at providing policymakers and city planners or developers with a tool to assess and monitor the sustainability of their system. Next steps in the further development of the SSP are (i) to create a multidimensional optimization model; and (ii) to use the model as a serious game with which policymakers could assess their strategies and receive real-time, ex ante feedback on the sustainability impact of their decisions.

Notes

1. See the City Prosperity Initiative's 2015 Global City Report: http://cpi.unhabitat.org/publications UN-Habitat.
2. See the IESE Cities in Motion index from the IESE Business School: www.iese.edu/research/pdfs/ST-0396-E.pdf. See the 2016 Global Power City Index from the Mori Memorial Foundation: http://mori-foundation.or.jp/pdf/GPCI2016_en.pdf.
3. https://thesystemsthinker.com/guidelines-for-drawing-causal-loop-diagrams-2/.
4. www.dataforcities.org/.
5. https://sustainable-development-goals.iisd.org/country-data.
6. www.cia.gov/library/publications/the-world-factbook/.
7. https://ec.europa.eu/energy/en/topics/renewable-energy.

8. https://ec.europa.eu/clima/policies/strategies/2030_en.
9. https://ec.europa.eu/eurostat/tgm/refreshTableAction.do?tab=table&plugin=1&init=1&pcode=tec00001&language=en.
10. www.who.int/.
11. https://sustainabledevelopment.un.org/sdg1.
12. www.siemens.com/entry/cc/features/greencityindex_international/all/en/pdf/report_asia.pdf.
13. www.eiu.com/home.aspx.
14. http://ec.europa.eu/environment/europeangreencapital/index_en.htm.
15. http://wrirosscities.org/our-work/project-city/building-efficiency-accelerator.

References

Bakshi, B. R., Gutowski, T., & Sekulic, D. (Eds.). (2011). *Thermodynamics and the Destruction of Resources*. Cambridge: Cambridge University Press. https://doi.org/10.1017/CBO9780511976049.

Berardi, U. (2012). Sustainability assessment in the construction sector: Rating systems and rated buildings. *Sustainable Development*, 20(6), 411–424. https://doi.org/10.1002/sd.532.

Bibri, S. E., & Krogstie, J. (2017). Smart sustainable cities of the future: An extensive interdisciplinary literature review. *Sustainable Cities and Society*, 31, 183–212. https://doi.org/10.1016/j.scs.2017.02.016.

Binder, C. R., Feola, G., & Steinberger, J. K. (2010). Considering the normative, systemic and procedural dimensions in indicator-based sustainability assessments in agriculture. *Environmental Impact Assessment Review*, 30(2), 71–81. https://doi.org/10.1016/j.eiar.2009.06.002.

Binder, C. R., Hutter, M., Pang, M., & Webb, B. (2020a). System science and sustainability assessment. In C. R. Binder, E. Massaro, & R. Wyss (eds.), *Sustainability Assessment in Urban Systems*. Cambridge University Press, pp. 30–64.

Binder, C. R., Schmid, A., & Steinberger, J. K. (2012). Sustainability solution space of the Swiss milk value added chain. *Ecological Economics*, 83, 210–220. https://doi.org/10.1016/j.ecolecon.2012.06.022.

Binder, C. R., & Wiek, A. (2007). The role of transdisciplinary processes in sustainability assessment of agricultural systems. In C. R. Binder & A. Wiek, *From Common Principles to Common Practice: Proceedings and Outputs of the First Symposium of the International Forum on Assessing Sustainability in Agriculture (INFASA)*. Bern: International Institute of Sustainable Development and Swiss College of Agriculture, pp. 33–48.

Boesch, A., & de Montmollin, A. (2020). Indicators for assessing the sustainability of cities. In C. R. Binder, E. Massaro, & R. Wyss (eds.), *Sustainability Assessment in Urban Systems*. Cambridge University Press, pp. 311–331.

Bossel, H. (1999). *Indicators for Sustainable Development: Theory, Method, Applications: A Report to the Balaton group*. Winnipeg: IISD.

Brundtland, G. H. (1987). *Report of the World Commission on Environment and Development: "Our Common Future."* United Nations.

European Commission, Directorate-General for the Environment, Intrasoft International, University of the West of England (UWE), & Science Communication Unit. (2017). *Indicators for Sustainable Cities*.

Fritz, L. & Meinherz, F. (2020). The politics of participatory sustainability assessments: An analysis of power. In C. R. Binder, E. Massaro, & R. Wyss (eds.), *Sustainability Assessment in Urban Systems*. Cambridge University Press, pp. 87–122.

Halla, P., & Binder, C. R. (2020). Sustainability Assessment: Introduction and Framework. In C. R. Binder, E. Massaro, & R. Wyss (eds.), *Sustainability Assessment in Urban Systems*. Cambridge University Press, pp. 7–29.

Hashemian, B., Massaro, E., Bojic, I., Arias, J. M., Sobolevsky, S., & Ratti, C. (2017). Socioeconomic characterization of regions through the lens of individual financial transactions. *PloS one*, 12(11), e0187031.

Holden, E., Linnerud, K., & Banister, D. (2014). Sustainable development: *Our Common Future* revisited. *Global Environmental Change*, 26, 130–139. https://doi.org/10.1016/j.gloenvcha.2014.04.006.

Kangas, P. C. (2002). *Handbook of Emergy Evaluation*. Center for Environmental Policy.
Klopp, J. M., & Petretta, D. L. (2017). The urban sustainable development goal: Indicators, complexity and the politics of measuring cities. *Cities*, 63, 92–97. https://doi.org/10.1016/j.cities.2016.12.019.
Massaro, E., Athanassiadis, A., Psyllidis, A., & Binder, C. R. (2020). Ontology-based integration of urban sustainability indicators. In C. R. Binder, E. Massaro, & R. Wyss (eds.), *Sustainability Assessment in Urban Systems*. Cambridge University Press, pp. 332–350.
Meinherz, F., Fritz, L., & Schneider, F. (2020). The value-loadedness of sustainability: Implications for the transformative potential of sustainability assessments. In C. R. Binder, E. Massaro, & R. Wyss (eds.), *Sustainability Assessment in Urban Systems*. Cambridge University Press, pp. 65–86.
Merino-Saum, A. (2020). Assessing sustainability through participatory multi-criteria approaches (PMCAs): An updated comparative analysis. In C. R. Binder, E. Massaro, & R. Wyss (eds.), *Sustainability Assessment in Urban Systems*. Cambridge University Press, pp. 209–238.
Ness, B., Urbel-Piirsalu, E., Anderberg, S., & Olsson, L. (2007). Categorising tools for sustainability assessment. *Ecological Economics*, 60(3), 498–508. https://doi.org/10.1016/j.ecolecon.2006.07.023.
Nijkamp, P., & Vreeker, R. (2000). Sustainability assessment of development scenarios: Methodology and application to Thailand. *Ecological Economics*, 33(1), 7–27. https://doi.org/10.1016/S0921-8009(99)00135-4.
Pagani, A., Laurenti, R., & Binder, C. R. (2020). Sustainability assessment of the housing system: Exploring the interplay between the material system and the social structure. In C. R. Binder, E. Massaro, & R. Wyss (eds.), *Sustainability Assessment in Urban Systems*. Cambridge University Press, pp. 384–416.
Rees, W., & Wackernagel, M. (1996). Urban ecological footprints: Why cities cannot be sustainable – And why they are a key to sustainability. *Environmental Impact Assessment Review*, 16(4–6), 223–248. https://doi.org/10.1016/S0195-9255(96)00022-4.
Schilling, T., Mühlemeier, S., Wyss, R., & Binder, C. R. (2020). A Concept for Sustainability Transition Assessment (STA): A Dynamic Systems Perspective Informed by Resilience Thinking. In C. R. Binder, E. Massaro, & R. Wyss (eds.), *Sustainability Assessment in Urban Systems*. Cambridge University Press, pp. 123–138.
Scholz, R. W., & Tietje, O. (2002). *Embedded Case Study Methods: Integrating Quantitative and Qualitative Knowledge*. Thousand Oaks, CA: Sage Publications.
Sciubba, E. (2008). Exergy destruction as an ecological indicator. In *Encyclopedia of Ecology*. pp. 1510–1522. https://doi.org/10.1016/B978-008045405-4.00107-5.
Singh, R. K., Murty, H. R., Gupta, S. K., & Dikshit, A. K. (2012). An overview of sustainability assessment methodologies. *Ecological Indicators*, 15(1), 281–299. https://doi.org/10.1016/j.ecolind.2011.01.007.
Stelzer, V., & Kopfmüller, J. (2020). How Values Play into Sustainability Assessments: Challenges and a Possible Way Forward. In C. R. Binder, E. Massaro, & R. Wyss (eds.), *Sustainability Assessment in Urban Systems*. Cambridge University Press, pp. 161–180.
UN-Habitat. (2012). *The State of the World's Cities 2012/2013: Prosperity of Cities*. http://unhabitat.org/books/prosperity-of-cities-state-of-the-worlds-cities-20122013/.
Waheed, B., Khan, F., & Veitch, B. (2009). Linkage-based frameworks for sustainability assessment: Making a case for Driving Force-Pressure-State-Exposure-Effect-Action (DPSEEA) frameworks. *Sustainability*, 1(3), 441–463. https://doi.org/10.3390/su1030441.
Wiek, A., & Binder, C. (2005). Solution spaces for decision-making: A sustainability assessment tool for city-regions. *Environmental Impact Assessment Review*, 25(6), 589–608. https://doi.org/10.1016/j.eiar.2004.09.009.
Williams, B., & Hummelbrunner, R. (2011). *Systems Concepts In Action: A Practitioner's Toolkit*. Palo Alto, CA: Stanford Univesity Press. http://site.ebrary.com/id/10459535.

9

Assessing Urban Sustainability through Participatory Multi-Criteria Approaches (PMCAs): An Updated Comparative Analysis

Albert Merino-Saum

9.1 Introduction

Participatory multi-criteria approaches (PMCAs) have been increasingly applied over the last 30 years in sustainability assessments (SA) as an alternative approach to traditional monetary valuations and expert technical appraisals (Munda, 2004a; O'Connor, 2000; Proctor & Dreschler, 2006; Stagl, 2003; etc.). Like many other forms of sustainability appraisal (e.g., scenario-building, integrated assessment, mediated modeling), PMCAs have been created and methodologically formalized in parallel with the advent of the participatory paradigm at the end of the twentieth century. They are frequently presented as suitable approaches when dealing with challenges such as complexity, uncertainty, and ambiguity in sustainability matters (De Marchi et al., 2000; Martínez-Alier et al., 1998; O'Connor et al., 1996; etc.). Nowadays, PMCAs constitute a whole family of assessment approaches that share some core features, but are also differentiated from each other on several levels (conceptual, technical, procedural, etc.).

A comparative analysis like the one presented here seems scientifically pertinent for several reasons. First, it is by contrasting and exploring several PMCAs that we may better understand their theoretical roots, their distinctive technical characteristics, as well as their respective weaknesses and strengths. Second, comparative analyses may also shed light on potential synergies between PMCAs and thus support combined applications (which opens up new opportunities, since each PMCA focuses on one particular sustainability challenge). Finally, the present analysis may also pave the way for future research by specifying the most suitable approach taking epistemological standpoints, methodological concerns, and other contextual factors into account.

Previous comparative analyses may be found in either scientific or institutional literature (De Montis et al., 2000; Gerber et al., 2012; Omann, 2004; Proctor, 2009; Rauschmayer & Wittmer, 2006; Stagl, 2007; etc.). All these papers and reports deal with some of the approaches studied here (although none compares the four PMCAs considered in this book chapter) and compare them with other more or less similar evaluative frameworks across varied criteria. Our analysis adds several novel insights to the existing literature. First, it relies on a literature review that incorporates not only theoretical papers, but also a large sample of applications (26 case studies). This is a particularly important point, since PMCAs are essentially flexible and their implementation varies significantly from one case to another. Furthermore, by considering and contrasting several applications for each approach, we are able to identify the core features that are essential to each PMCA. In contrast to most previous analyses, the present study also pays attention to a small number of comparable approaches (only four). This allows for both in-depth investigation and thorough comparisons. As this chapter will demonstrate, although the four approaches were created by academics who have worked together and belong to very closely related, if not the same, scientific communities, in some cases there are very deep dissimilarities. Finally, the present study explicitly adopts an institutional perspective and methodically addresses how each PMCA influences potential decisions regarding sustainability issues.

The chapter is structured as follows. Section 9.2 provides a brief conceptual contextualization of participatory multi-criteria approaches, presented as a hybrid "value articulating institution" (VAI) combining elements from multi-criteria analysis (MCA) and participatory methods. The section also presents some shortfalls inherent to other VAIs, notably mono-criterion methods such as cost-benefit analysis (CBA), and highlights the main features of MCA. Section 9.3 presents in detail four PMCAs usually applied to sustainability issues: social multi-criteria evaluation (SMCE); multi-criteria mapping (MCM); the three-step participation model (3-SPM); and the INTEGRAAL approach. Section 9.4 provides a comparative analysis of these four approaches by considering three main questions: *who* assesses?; *what* is assessed?; and *how* is it assessed? Finally, in Section 9.5, we discuss our results and present our conclusions.

9.2 Contextualizing Participatory Multi-Criteria Approaches (PMCAs)

9.2.1 PMCAs as Value Articulating Institutions (VAIs)

PMCAs encompass a whole family of assessment frameworks whose core feature is that they combine one or several participatory methods (see Chapter 4 (Fritz & Meinherz, 2020)) with a multi-criteria structure (see Section 9.2.3 in this chapter). Originally applied in sustainability assessments (SA) as a way to overcome the limitations of both mono-criterion analyses (in particular, cost-benefit analysis, or CBA) and more traditional multi-criteria analysis, PMCAs have proven over the last 30 years to be particularly well suited to the challenges set by urban sustainability decision-making problems. PMCAs have been recently applied to urban water management (Cole et al., 2018), urban food system governance (Landert et al., 2017), and urban waste management (Lupo & Cusumano, 2018), to cite just a few examples. In the present chapter, we propose to look at PMCAs as an example of a value articulating institution (VAI) (Jacobs, 1997; pp. 207–221; Vatn,

2005a, p. 301; Vatn, 2005b, p. 211); i.e., as an institutional structure specifying a set of rules and procedures about the following:

who can participate in the assessment and with what specific role;

- PMCA may involve various types of participants, such as stakeholders, experts, or ordinary citizens randomly chosen from the population. The functions these participants are assigned may also vary significantly from one case to another (e.g., from simple consultation to prescriptive evaluation).

what counts as data and what form it should take (monetary units, narrative arguments, etc.);

- Several types of knowledge and measure (either quantitative or qualitative) are embedded in each PMCA. However, both the legitimacy and the evaluative role given to expert opinion (most often quantitative) and "lay" knowledge (generally qualitatively reported) vary considerably from one approach to another.

how these data are integrated into the evaluative process.

- Once again, significant differences exist across the approaches studied here: the algorithms on which PMCAs rely range from simple linear additive rules (e.g., MCM; 3-SPM) to relatively sophisticated formalizations such as the outranking method behind SMCE.

In general, three main types of VAI may be considered when evaluating alternative options in SA. These are: (1) mono-criterion analyses (such as CBA); (2) multi-criteria analyses (see Section 9.2.4); and (3) participatory methods (citizens' juries, focus groups, consensus conferences, etc.). As noted, PMCAs constitute a hybrid VAI, in the sense that they combine elements from (2) and (3) (see Figure 9.1). As will be explained in Sections 9.3 and 9.5, the

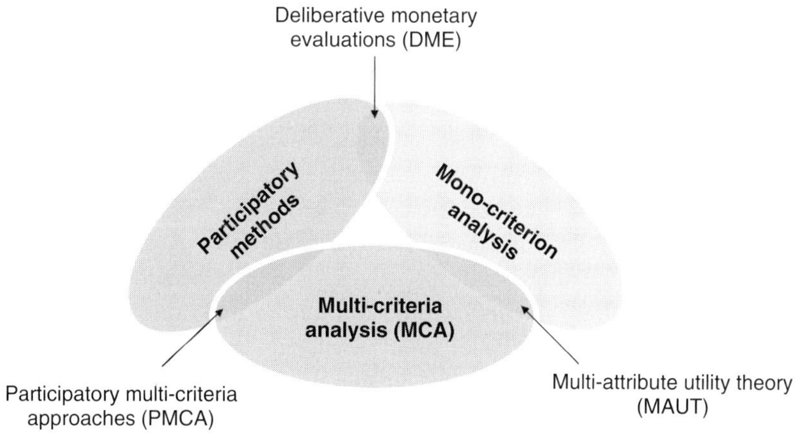

Figure 9.1 Value articulating institutions (VAIs) for sustainability assessments (own illustration; based on Vatn (2005a))

component on which the evaluative focus is placed (either on participation or on multi-criteria formalization) may vary significantly from one PMCA to another.

9.2.2 Why Non-inclusive Mono-criterion Analyses Are Not Suitable for Urban Sustainability Assessment (SA)

The choice of using the VAI concept here emphasizes the substantial influence that institutional structures have on the outcomes of SAs. As noted by Vatn (2005a, p. 300), such structures determine "which values may be expressed, how they can be expressed, and consequently which choices are found favourable." Therefore, the main interest of SAs cannot reside in the mere estimation of one concrete yet unavoidably artificial value, as mono-criterion analyses assume. The focus must rather be on the quality of information and justifications exchanged by the participants during the evaluation process (O'Neill, 1997; Spash, 2008). Since such justifications are most often incommensurable or weakly comparable (Martínez-Alier et al., 1998; O'Neill, 1993), they require inclusive and multi-dimensional evaluative frameworks where attention is no longer paid to compensation and optimization exercises, but rather to values elicitation and dialectical confrontation (Bromley, 2007; Jacobs, 1997; O'Connor, 1997; O'Connor et al., 2001).

In economic jargon, that corresponds to saying that the social preferences that traditional monetary valuation methods (e.g., contingent valuation, travel cost method, hedonic prices) pretend to reveal through objective and neutral techniques are not exogenous, as economic theory presupposes, but rather endogenous to the method applied (Lockwood, 1999, p. 396; Sagoff, 1998, p. 222). Therefore, the goal of SA cannot be to reveal hidden exogenous preferences, but rather to construct such preferences in the most pertinent and transparent way (Bromley & Paavola, 2002; Godard, 2004; Schkade & Payne, 1994;Vatn & Bromley, 1994). In terms of Gregory et al. (1993, p. 179), sustainability evaluators should not act as "archaeologists" looking for pre-existing values so much as "architects" building up contingent and controversial preferences. The thesis defended here is that such an architectural exercise requires VAIs that allow for inclusiveness and methodological pluralism.

This is not a mere theoretical debate. Analyses of urban sustainability have most often relied on command-and-control models reducing the *problématique* to a technical matter. Such models have thus systematically ignored sociopolitical struggles in defining what urban sustainability actually entails (Bulkeley & Betsill, 2005), as if sustainable cities were "ontologically pre-given objects" (Whitehead, 2003). These controversies – as well as the conflicts and incompatibilities they are based upon – constitute, however, the very core of urban sustainability, which is by definition a multidimensional process involving unavoidable trade-offs and sacrifices (Alberti & Susskind, 1996; Finco & Nijkamp, 2001; etc.). Their integration and subsequent articulation within SAs is thus a crucial prerequisite if an SA is to be socially acceptable and successfully implemented.

9.2.3 Multi-Criteria Analysis (MCA)

9.2.3.1 General Considerations and Historical Evolution

As the name suggests, the objective of multi-criteria analysis (MCA) is the study of decision-making "problems in which several points of view or criteria must be considered simultaneously" (Roy & Vincke, 1981, p. 207). In other words, MCA focuses on complex problems implying several non-equivalent descriptions (Giampietro, 2002; Janssen & Munda, 1999; Nijkamp et al., 1991; etc.) and incommensurable values (Martínez-Alier et al., 1998; Munda et al., 1995; etc.). MCA is thus perfectly suited to urban areas, which are frequently portrayed in the literature as dynamic complex systems (Ravetz, 2000; see also Chapter 10 (Halla et al., 2020)).

Originally developed as an algorithmic decision-making tool principally applied in the field of management studies, MCA has significantly evolved over the years in terms of both its conceptual premises and its methodological roots (Munda, 2004b; Proctor, 2009) (see Figure 9.2).

Nowadays, MCA involves a plethora of evaluative approaches, which share, however, a number of key elements: (i) the identification of a finite set of options; (ii) the determination of a limited number of evaluation criteria; (iii) the performance evaluation of each option according to each criterion; and (iv) the application of an aggregation procedure (Banville et al., 1998; Martel & Rousseau, 1993; etc.).

9.2.3.2 Basic Mathematical Formalization

From a formal point of view, a discrete multi-criteria problem can be described as follows (Banville et al., 1998, p. 24; Munda, 2003, p. 2; etc.):

A being a finite set of "potential actions," "options" or "alternatives" a_j $(j = 1,2, \ldots, n)$ and *G* the set of "points of view," "perspectives" or "evaluation criteria" considered relevant g_i $(i = 1,2, \ldots, m)$, option a_1 is considered better than option a_2 according to criterion *i*, only if the performance of a_1 for this criterion is better than the performance of a_2 for this same criterion, that is, when: $g_i(a_1) > g_i(a_2)$.

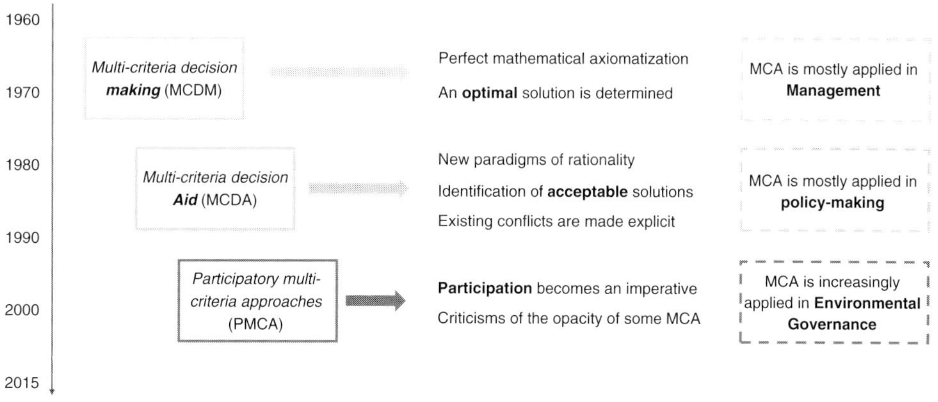

Figure 9.2 An historical perspective on MCA (based on Munda, 2004b, p. 137)

Table 9.1 *Illustration of a discrete multi-criteria problem (Source: Janssen and Munda 1999, p. 837)*

		Options			
Criteria	Units	$a_{j=1}$	$a_{j=2}$	(…)	$a_{j=n}$
$g_{i=1}$		$g_1(a_1)$	$g_1(a_2)$	…	$g_1(a_n)$
$g_{i=2}$		…	…	…	…
(…)		…	…	…	…
$g_{i=m}$		$g_m(a_1)$	$g_m(a_2)$	…	$g_m(a_n)$

This kind of decision problem can be represented in the form of a table or matrix (see Table 9.1). Given the sets *A* (feasible options) and *G* (evaluation criteria), and given the existence of *n* feasible options and *m* evaluation criteria, it is possible to build a matrix $(n \times m)$ whose elements $g_i(a_j)$ $(i = 1,2, \ldots, m; j=1,2, \ldots, n)$ indicate the performance of option *j* according to criterion *i*.

Table 9.1 also highlights one of the main characteristics of MCA, or at least of multi-criteria decision aid (MCDA): decision problems are "not well defined" from a mathematical point of view, in the sense that one option is not necessarily better than all the others according to all the criteria (Roy & Vincke, 1981, p. 207). There are often contradictions between the various points of view considered: option *a* can be better than option *b* according to one criterion, but worse according to a different criterion. Thus, adopting a multi-criteria prism implies admitting that the choice of one or another option is inevitably the result of a compromise between several conflicting perspectives (Roy & Bouyssou, 1993).

9.2.3.3 Main Aggregative Procedures Used in MCA

There exist dozens of possible aggregation methods for analyzing the information embedded in a multi-criteria evaluation framework. The choice needs to be made on a case-by-case basis, considering various factors, such as: the characteristics of the problem at hand; the type of decision to be taken; the amount and nature of available data; the profile and experience of the scientific team; etc. Hence, the choice of one particular aggregative method constitutes in itself a meta-problem requiring a multi-criteria framing (De Montis et al., 2000; Dodgson et al., 2009; Guitouni & Martel, 1998; Hwang & Yoon, 1981; Lahdelma et al., 2000; etc.).

The most frequent aggregative methods applied in SAs are: (i) linear additive methods such as the weighted sum, applied in MCM, 3-SPM, and INTEGRAAL; (ii) outranking methods as the one considered in SMCE; and (iii) analytical hierarchy processes (AHP), applied, for instance, by Proctor (2009) or De Montis and Lai (2008). Each of these methods has its own strengths and weaknesses (see De Montis et al., 2000; Dodgson et al., 2009; Munda & Nardo, 2003; etc.). Hence, to say that there is an ideal aggregative method that is universally applicable would be to fall into the same trap that mono-criterion analyses fall into (Martínez-Alier & Roca, [2000] 2001, p. 273).

9.3 Participatory Multi-Criteria Approaches (PMCAs)

In this section, we present four PMCAs usually applied in SA. Other PMCAs could have been considered in the present chapter, such as stakeholder multi-criteria decision aid (Banville et al., 1998), deliberative multi-criteria analysis (Liu et al., 2010; Proctor & Dreschler, 2006) or participatory multi-criteria analysis (Stagl, 2006). We decided, however, to focus the analysis on a limited number of approaches in order to be able to describe them and compare them thoroughly. The four PMCAs were selected according to different criteria, the most important being the availability of at least three documented applications for each approach. The analysis is based on a literature review that includes (i) theoretical papers and (ii) a sample of 26 empirical applications.[1] This Chapter also includes some excerpts from in-depth interviews with the creators of the four approaches.[2]

9.3.1 Social Multi-Criteria Evaluation (SMCE)

SMCE seeks to overcome the pitfalls of traditional technocratic evaluations by integrating different methods of sociological research into one MCA structure (Munda, 2004a). Ideally, SMCE is composed of seven steps that can be iteratively undertaken through continuous feedback loops. These steps are (1) isolation of relevant social actors; (2) isolation of actors' values, desires, and preferences; (3) generation of policy options and evaluation criteria; (4) construction of the "multi-criteria impact matrix"; (5) construction of the "equity matrix"; (6) application of a mathematical procedure; and (7) sensitivity and robustness analysis (Munda, 2008, p. 45). When time availability and/or financial resources are limited, simplified versions of SMCE may be also applied, while keeping the same philosophy.[3]

In SMCE, social actors are identified through institutional analysis; that is, the simultaneous study of relevant administrative, legislative, and historical documents. Such analysis is most often complemented with sociological research methods such as individual interviews (De Marchi et al., 2000), group meetings (Garmendia et al., 2010), or participant observation (Paneque Salgado et al., 2009).

SMCE may be used to evaluate different objects such as concrete management options or semi-qualitative scenarios. The approach requires only a finite number of alternatives (discrete problem) and a definitive and common characterization at the time of the evaluation. In other words, alternatives and evaluation criteria must be the same for all participants. The influence that analysts may have in identifying alternatives varies from case to case, but it is most often considerable: as a rule, the research team identifies the alternatives after considering inputs from both literature and fieldwork. The resulting set of options may be presented to key actors for consultation (see for instance: Garmendia et al., 2010).

With regard to the criteria, SMCE relies on the analyst (and not the participants) to define these according to very concrete methodological properties such as non-redundancy, legibility, etc. Indeed, in SMCE, criteria are perceived as "technical translations of social actors' needs, preferences and desires," the latter being used only as "rough" material or as a "source of inspiration" (Gamboa & Munda, 2007, p. 1570; Munda, 2004a, p. 670; Munda, 2008, p. 51).

Probably, the most characteristic feature of SMCE is that it relies on two distinct matrices: (1) what is known as the multi-criteria impact matrix (also known as the technical impact matrix), which is intended to reveal the performance of all compared alternatives; and (2) the equity matrix (or social impact matrix), which seeks to indicate the societal acceptability of these alternatives (Munda, 2009, p. 309).

As a rule, the technical impact matrix is completed by the research team, which evaluates all pertinent alternatives, considering the information obtained through fieldwork, consultation with experts, and/or any other analytical method(s). In practice, however, fulfilling this matrix often appears to be challenging. For instance, due to "time and resource constraints," De Marchi et al. (2000, p. 274) were only able to build a purely qualitative impact matrix made of linguistic variables. Similarly, Gamboa and Munda (2007, p. 1570) emphasize that "the expected effects of the alternatives are not always foreseeable" and also note that "many uncertainties" exist. In the same sense, Paneque Salgado et al. (2009, p. 999) highlight the difficulties encountered in completing their technical impact matrix, which ends up being "a matrix quite different from the researchers' expectations."

Regarding the social impact matrix, in which alternatives are evaluated across social actors, this may be completed either directly by the participants or by the research team. Social impact matrices have two main objectives. The first is to analyze antagonisms and potential coalitions between social actors, which generally leads to a "dendrogram of coalitions" (i.e., a tree diagram illustrating hierarchical clusters between actors). The second objective is to produce a ranking of alternatives for each potential coalition. Here, acceptability judgments are expressed through linguistic variables (e.g., "extremely good," "very good," "good," "moderate," "bad," etc.). It is worth noting that actors (or analysts) evaluate the acceptability of each alternative in a composite way, not criterion by criterion. Hence, strictly speaking, equity matrices do not rely on a multi-criteria reasoning.

With regard to the aggregative rules applied in SMCE, the approach is based upon an outranking method. As a rule, criteria are weighted by the research team and not by the participants, as is the case in other PMCAs studied here.[4] In practice, analysts usually give the same weight to each sustainability dimension. The influence of this weighting on results is generally studied through sensitivity analysis (step 7).

9.3.2 Multi-Criteria Mapping (MCM)

MCM was developed to address complex issues and to deal with uncertainty in the context of sustainable development (Stirling, 1997). Unlike most PMCAs, MCM is principally based on individual interviews (not on focus groups). Such interviews are generally structured in five steps, although it is possible to review, add, or remove elements at any stage. These steps are (1) choose options; (2) define criteria; (3) assess scores; (4) assign weights; and (5) calculate ranks: a concluding workshop is usually planned to close the evaluation process and "open wider discussions" (Stirling & Mayer, 2000, p. 44).

With regard to the first of these five steps (option selection), the interviewer prepares an initial list of options based on inputs from bibliographical study, previous individual interviews, or even one initial group meeting. Such a list is made up of a finite set of central (sometimes also called basic or core) options, which ensure a minimum "level of consistency across the perspectives of all participants" (Stirling, 2005, p. 14) and enable the comparison of all the evaluations. Interviewees may complete this initial list with options either chosen from an inventory of potential alternatives created by the analyst ("discretionary" options), or directly suggested by themselves ("additional" options).

The freedom participants are given is all the more important as the number of options under consideration may vary and no maximum number of options exists. Furthermore, new options can be incorporated at any point in the evaluation process. For illustration, participants in Stirling and Mayer (1999) and Hansen (2010) respectively add 18 and 22 "additional" options to the initial set of "basic" options.

Regarding evaluation criteria (second step), participants choose these as well. Once again, there is no constraint on the number of criteria. Participants may also add new criteria at any point in the evaluation process. Such freedom sometimes leads to a very high number of criteria. For instance, Stirling and Mayer (1999) count 117 criteria in their evaluation process. McDowall and Eames (2006) list 98 criteria and Hansen (2010) no fewer than 97.

In MCM, participants not only choose the criteria and select the alternatives, they also evaluate these options (third step) by assigning them "performance scores," criterion by criterion. The scores are numerically expressed according to a scale chosen by the participants (from zero to ten, from zero to 100, etc.). Another important (and unusual) feature of MCM is that participants are asked to assign two performance scores to each option under each criterion: one score under "pessimistic" assumptions, and another one under the "optimistic" assumptions. Hence, in MCM, evaluations are expressed as ranges of values (Stirling & Mayer, 2000, p. 49).

This scoring process requires considerable effort from participants: they must understand the logic and the purpose of the exercise and allocate a very large number of scores. It is therefore not surprising that participants in Millstone and Lobstein (2007, p. 36) criticize the evaluation process "for taking a long time (typically over 2 h of interview time)," for "requiring advance preparation (which some participants did not undertake adequately)," and because of "the complexity of the scoring process." Participants in Bellamy et al. (2013, p. 935) express similar criticisms. Also, in Hansen (2010, p. 1963), several participants find it "challenging" to assign so many scores (the number of numerical judgments requested from each participant was more than 70).

With regard to the weightings (fourth step), once again, participants weight the criteria they have previously selected.[5] MCM uses an extremely simple linear additive model in order to avoid a process that is excessively opaque for participants (fifth step).

Results are most often presented in a disaggregated way, in the form of a multitude of "judgment cards" or "charts" (either by participant or by category of actors). MCM does not end up with one single impact matrix (as is the case with SMCE), but rather with a plurality of matrices illustrating dissimilar rankings and levels of uncertainty. Such a feature may be seen as a strength, but also as a limitation for its applicability (Foster, 1997, p. 15).

9.3.3 Three-Step Participation Model (3-SPM)

The Three-Step Participation Model (3-SPM), formally set out by Renn and Webler (1992), is a multi-criteria approach that sequentially combines three different participatory methods; namely (i) value-tree analysis, (ii) the group Delphi method, and (iii) citizen panels. Each of these methods assigns a prominent role to one particular category of participants: (i) stakeholder groups, (ii) experts, and (iii) randomly selected citizens. This tripartite categorization relies on the idea that SA must integrate different kinds of knowledge. As Renn et al. (1996, p. 153) note, while stakeholders may bring "knowledge based on common sense and personal experience" and experts convey "knowledge based on technical expertise," randomly selected citizens are the best placed to deliver "knowledge derived from social interests and advocacy."

3-SPM has fewer and less-recent applications than the other PMCAs studied here. That is due to at least three factors: (i) the significant amount of time and resources the approach requires; (ii) the difficulties faced in practice when trying to separate values, scientific knowledge, and social preferences; and (iii) the almost impossibility of synchronizing participatory processes with real decision-making processes.[6]

During the first step of 3-SPM, stakeholders are invited to identify and select the evaluation criteria. This involves six sub-stages: (i) individual interviews with key stakeholders; (ii) hierarchical structuring of "values," "criteria," and "attributes" for each individual (conducted through value-tree analysis by the research team); (iii) presentation to stakeholders of this first structuring; (iv) iteration of the process until actors are satisfied; (v) combination of individual value-trees into a "mega-tree"; and (vi) validation by all stakeholders. The amount of information embedded in such an analysis may be quite important. As an illustration, the value-tree analysis developed by Renn (2003) is made up of 367 elements at its base.

As a rule, the research team subsequently transforms such criteria into operational indicators (similarly to in SMCE; see Section 9.3.1). In some cases, however, this transformation may also be "entrusted to a group of external experts" (Renn & Webler, 1992, p. 86). The indicators are then presented to stakeholders for validation.

The identification of pertinent options and the measurement of their respective impacts is structured through the group Delphi method; that is, a slightly adapted version of the original Delphi format, based on group interactions instead of written responses. The main idea consists of dividing experts from different academic fields into small working groups and then comparing the judgments of each group at a plenary meeting. The method seeks to overcome existing conflicts around "factual evidences" and to reach a "consensus via direct confrontation" among experts conveying heterogeneous knowledge (Renn, 2006, p. 37). As can be seen, 3-SPM aims at chronologically dissociating discussions on social values (first step) from controversies on scientific knowledge (second step). The approach thus relies on a dichotomy quite close to the one proposed by Munda (see Section 9.3.1).

At the plenary meeting, each group explains its performance scores. The more a group's rating deviates from the median score, the more time is allocated for this group to defend and explain its scores. The process is repeated in case of significant conflicts.

Once values (first step) and facts (second step) have been discussed, 3-SPM places its focus on social preferences (third step). The latter are integrated into the evaluation process through citizen panels, where randomly selected participants evaluate the alternatives, having considered both the criteria chosen by stakeholders and the performance profiles established by experts. The process is similar to a "US-American jury trial with experts and stakeholders as witnesses and advisers" (Renn, 2006, p. 38). Such panels may require a significant amount of resources and involve many participants. For instance, Renn (1986) conducts 24 panels with about 25 participants each. Similarly, in Schneider et al. (1998), more than 200 citizens are involved in this evaluative stage!

During the panels, citizens score all pertinent alternatives criterion by criterion. They also assign a relative weight to each criterion. An overall score for each option is then calculated using multi-attribute utility (MAU) analysis (the approach assumes full compensation between criteria and dimensions). The resulting evaluation is not intended to be an expression of the participants' final judgment, but rather as an element structuring an "intuitive" judgment (Renn et al., 1993, p. 197). In other words, the final recommendations made by citizens can qualify or contradict the numerical results obtained through the aggregation of mechanical scores (Renn, 2006, p. 38).

9.3.4 INTEGRAAL Approach

Developed in the 2000s by Martin O'Connor and colleagues (O'Connor, 2006; O'Connor, 2007; Reichel et al., 2010; etc.), INTEGRAAL is a "deliberative multi-criteria meta-method" structured in five main steps: (i) problem identification; (ii) problem framing; (iii) representation of the system; (iv) evaluation of options; and (v) communication of results. Although the chronological sequence of these five steps seems quite intuitive at first sight, the order in which they happen may be neither linear nor strictly sequential: INTEGRAAL allows backtracking, overlaps, or even inversions depending on the particularities and constraints of each case study.

The approach relies on two fundamental deliberative tools: (i) the "Deliberation Matrix" (DM), also referred to as the "Cube"; and (ii) the "KerBabel Indicator Kiosk" (KIK).[7] Both are simultaneously descriptive and normative. As a descriptive tool, DM provides a three-dimensional framing of any "social choice" problem comprising all potential combinations between (i) options, (ii) actors, and (iii) criteria. From a normative point of view, the Cube also provides an operational evaluative platform through which participants can make judgments about several options across several criteria or issues (such scoring is most often done through a software application available online, the so-called kerDST). What distinguishes DM compared to other PMCAs is that it explicitly and simultaneously combines these three components into a common framework, which can then be more or less disaggregated by adopting various alternative prisms. KIK is an interactive catalogue of candidate indicators allowing participants to (i) give a particular meaning to each criterion (through the choice of those indicators that, in their opinion, best define each criterion); and (ii) judge, indicator by indicator, the performance of each alternative according to each criterion.

During the first step of the approach (problem identification), the research team is expected to share basic information about the evaluation process (e.g., institutional partners, available budget, schedule, etc.) with (or deliver to) the participants. The idea is to avoid misunderstandings about the scope and objectives of the assessment (O'Connor et al., 2010, p. 9).

The identification of key actors, criteria, and options (i.e., problem framing) is generally based on a preliminary study of the existing documentation, individual interviews and/or group meetings (as SMCE does). The roles assigned to the research team and the participants vary from application to application, depending on both available resources (in terms of time, budget, and staff) and the goals of each case study. Most often, the research team leads this step, thereby influencing the way in which the problem is framed. Several rounds of consultation may be carried out to validate such framing (see, for instance, Merino-Saum, 2015).

It is important to note that all participants in INTEGRAAL evaluate the same options (or scenarios) across the same evaluation criteria (similar to what is proposed in SMCE or 3-SPM). However, when KIK is applied, participants are asked to choose those indicators they consider most appropriate for each criterion, independently from those selected by others. Thus, in such cases, INTEGRAAL involves a pluralistic framework that has very much in common with MCM.

During the third step (representation of the system), the research team is in charge of producing and/or bringing together various tools for representation, such as numerical or spatial modeling, official statistics, economic valuations, testimonials in narrative form, etc. All these inputs are expected to provide potential indicators and populate the KIK.

The evaluation itself (fourth step) is most often fulfilled by the participants themselves either online (via the kerDST system) or on paper, completing tables previously prepared by the research team. In some cases, the research team may also complete the evaluation by interpreting inputs from in-depth interviews (Da Cunha, 2010). One particularity of this approach is that performance scores assigned by participants are expressed through colors and linguistic variables (e.g., red = bad; yellow = not so bad; green = good; etc.). As already stated, when the KIK is applied, INTEGRAAL involves two different evaluative levels: options are evaluated first using a common set of criteria for all participants, and then using the particular indicators selected by each participant. In practice, some participants may negatively perceive the fact that actors evaluate options by themselves. In such cases, they may see the process as not "scientific enough" (Merino-Saum, 2015). Additionally, the dual system of evaluation (criteria/indicators) requires time and huge levels of abstraction.

Once the Cube is entirely filled in, results may be communicated in very different ways (fifth step). One possibility is to consider the exterior cells of the Cube, which aggregate the results of the respective rows in the format of color composites (the approach relies on a simple weighted sum method) (O'Connor, 2006). More often, however, the analyst presents the results in a disaggregated way, displaying instead the inner cells. Several options are then possible. Like a kaleidoscope, the DM allows the analyst to split the Cube into several bi-dimensional cross sections or segments, using as a prism each of the three evaluative dimensions considered (actors, criteria, options). Whichever prism is chosen, the evaluation process results in a plurality of matrices.

9.4 Comparing PMCAs

In this section, we propose a comparison of the four PMCAs previously presented by successively considering each of the three fundamental questions on which any VAI relies (see Section 9.2); that is, *who* assesses? (Section 9.4.1); *what* is assessed? (Section 9.4.2); and *how* is it assessed? (Section 9.4.3).

9.4.1 Who Assesses?

9.4.1.1 Stakeholders

In both MCM and INTEGRAAL, stakeholders play a leading role in the evaluation process. They not only influence (or even determine) the selection of both alternatives and evaluative criteria, but they also consider these criteria when judging the performance of different alternatives. Such a prominent role is almost hegemonic in the case of MCM, where stakeholders may further define any additional option they deem pertinent at any point in the process.

Stakeholders have more limited prerogatives in both SMCE and 3-SPM. Although they play a significant role, this is more informative or supportive than prescriptive. Moreover, while the stakeholders' influence is noteworthy at the beginning of the evaluation process (i.e., problem framing), it decreases progressively as the final decision gets closer (see Table 9.2). Actually, in these two approaches, the stakeholders' contribution is perceived as being inherently biased by their "own interests" and by "strategic behaviors" and as such, it can only carry imperfect information about social values, never accurate expertise about factual evidence. In that logic, replacing scientific proficiency with stakeholders' judgment in assessing the performance of different options could easily lead to unsustainable choices. Munda (2004a, p. 671) adds three reasons why stakeholders should not have a leading role in PMCA: (i) the most powerful stakeholders may influence the others; (ii) some stakeholders might not want to, or be able to, participate; and (iii) focus groups are never meant to be a representative sample of a population. For all these reasons, he repeatedly emphasizes that "participation is a necessary condition, but not a sufficient one"

Table 9.2 *Roles participants are given in the four PMCAs (by evaluative steps)*

		Citizens	Actors / Stakeholders	Experts	Research team / Analysts
Choosing OPTIONS	SMCE	May be consulted through surveys, questionnaires, etc.	Are most often consulted through focus groups or interviews (or both).	May be consulted by the research team when defining alternatives.	Choose options considering Institutional Analysis and fieldwork.
	MCM	May be consulted through surveys, questionnaires, etc.	Can define any additional issue they feel has been neglected by analysts.	May be consulted by the research team when defining "core" options.	Define a set of "core" options (based on document analysis and fieldwork).
	3-SPM	May make additions and modifications.	Can support the elucidation of options through interviews.	Are given the main role (they select pertinent options).	Can support the selection of options through internal brainstorming.
	DM-KIK	May be consulted through surveys, questionnaires, etc.	Are most often consulted by the research team when defining alternatives.	May be consulted by the research team when defining alternatives.	Define the most relevant options considering Institutional Analysis and fieldwork.
Defining CRITERIA	SMCE		Express "rough" inputs. These need to be translated by the research team.	May be consulted by the research team when defining criteria.	Define criteria by "technically translating" actors' values and arguments.
	MCM		Define the evaluation criteria. No constraint on the number.		
	3-SPM	May make additions and modifications.	Express concerns and objectives (value-trees). They also review the indicators.	May make additions and modifications.	Transform values into operational indicators.
	DM-KIK		They give particular meanings to the criteria (by using different indicators).		Identify criteria considering Institutional Analysis and fieldwork.
Assigning WEIGHTS	SMCE				Define "importance coef." Sustainability dimensions are most often equally weighted.
	MCM		Weight each criterion. Can also apply "principles" (compensability thresholds).		
	3-SPM	Weight the criteria previously chosen by stakeholders.			
	DM-KIK		Weight both criteria and indicators.		
Assessing SCORES	SMCE		Evaluate the acceptability of each alternative (linguistic variables; "equity matrix").	May support analysts when scoring the alternatives across each criterion.	Assign performance scores considering available data and scientific knowledge.
	MCM		Assign two performance scores (optim. and pessim.). They also choose the scale.		
	3-SPM	Evaluate options considering the performance profiles done by experts.	May make suggestions.	Construct performance profiles for each option (across selected indicators).	Verify experts' judgments (literature search and independent review)
	DM-KIK		Assign performance scores through color codes.	Inform the scoring process with all available data.	Inform the scoring process with all available data.
RANKING options	SMCE		Acceptability scores lead to equity matrix. Analysts create a "dendrogram of coalitions."		Outranking method (NAIADE). The approach leads to a final "impact matrix."
	MCM		Explore how rankings change with ≠ weights. Decide when the ranking is definitive.		Weighted sum. Rankings as ranges of values (several bar charts as final output).
	3-SPM	Make final recommendations. Act as members of a jury trial.	May intervene in citizen panels as witnesses. Provide arguments and evidence.	Participate in citizen panels as discussants or presenters.	
	DM-KIK		Actors can "play" with weights and explore how their scores evolve.		Options are ranked using the software application (weighted sum).

(Munda, 2004a, p. 674; 2004b, p. 151; 2006, p. 93; etc.). He also expressly names his approach "social" MCE, and not "participatory" or "deliberative" as other scholars do.

Both Stirling and O'Connor are aware of these limitations. For instance, O'Connor (2006, p. 17) explicitly reiterates the incomplete representability of deliberative instances and highlights the unavoidable influence of "parochial interests." He further underlines the problems that the "asymmetrical distribution of power" may cause in evaluation processes, and states that deliberation is not "necessarily reconciled with larger ecological, social, or long-term sustainability objectives" (p. 17). However, despite acknowledging all these limitations, O'Connor does not conceive of them as being critical. For him, SA is not about delivering one concrete final value or one best option, but rather about dialectical confrontation and social learning in the face of unavoidable value conflicts. Therefore, he still supports stakeholder-based assessments such as INTEGRAAL, where the goal is to provide participants with "an opportunity of collaborative learning" in face of an irreducible plurality of legitimate and most often antagonistic perspectives (O'Connor, 2006, p. 16–19).

To summarize, while in some PMCAs, stakeholders drive the assessment process and act as both "stakebuilders"[8] and performance evaluators, in others they are (only) passengers, certainly steered but not really at the wheel.[9]

9.4.1.2 Experts

When it comes to expert involvement, the analysis reveals almost the reverse of the observations presented above about stakeholder involvement. While both Stirling and O'Connor seem rather sceptical about experts' neutrality and their ability to solve sustainability issues, Renn and Munda seek to protect scientific enquiry from potential social biases (values).[10] As seen in Sections 9.3.1 and 9.3.3, both SMCE and 3-SPM procedurally formalize the conceptual distinction between ontological (or ecological) complexity and epistemological (or social) complexity.

Such a dichotomy does not make any sense in Stirling's eyes. According to him, facts and values are inextricably intertwined. Thus, if he pays particular attention to subjects it is not only because he is interested in them, but rather because he sees them as "the only way we can understand the object" (see Footnote 2). Similarly, for O'Connor, who defines himself as "ontologically agnostic," "complexity is more a way of addressing a problem, and less a property of the object under study" (Footnote 2). That is why INTEGRAAL aims at being an "anti-expert system" that allows people to participate as leading actors although they may have neither a theoretical competence nor a technical aptitude in a particular model (Footnote 2).

In contrast to this constructivist understanding, Munda conceives participatory methods as a way to better inform experts about social preferences and force them to explain why an option is better than the others, not "for giving people decisions" (Footnote 3). From this standpoint, experts are responsible as performance evaluators toward both policymakers and society, and in any case, public participation should question this role (Munda, 2004b, p. 151).

9.4.1.3 Randomly Selected Citizens

3-SPM is the only PMCA studied here that attributes an active, explicit, and distinctive role to citizens. In Renn's approach, citizens not only weight the criteria, they also evaluate alternatives and make explicit recommendations to policymakers (considering, of course, both expert judgments and stakeholder values). Such an involvement is not a trivial one: it clearly nuances the dichotomy between social claims and scientific evidence (see Section 9.4.1.2). In that sense, although both Renn and Munda perceive stakeholders' performance judgments as being inherently problematic, they do not address this issue in the same way. Whereas Munda sees all lay participants as potentially led by hidden agendas, Renn distinguishes stakeholders (driven by their own interests) from citizens (not directly concerned by the issue at hand). Thus, 3-SPM tackles the problem of strategic behaviors through an additional participatory technique, a sort of jury trial, where the participants involved have the last word. Of course, for this to make sense when assessing urban systems, such a technique requires either large scales of analysis (i.e., big cities or conurbations where the issue at hand might not directly concern selected participants) or juries from outside the area under analysis.

9.4.2 What is Assessed?

From a thematic point of view, the four approaches may be applied to assess quite diverse topics (see Table 9.3). That being said, whereas both MCM and 3-SPM have been more frequently applied to sociotechnological issues, applications of SMCE and INTEGRAAL predominantly relate to ecological conflicts, territorial planning, and "natural" risk management. Despite these empirical differences, which are largely due to the topics the creators of these approaches have been working on, it is important to outline that no theoretical or methodological limitation exists that prevents an individual approach from being applied to any issue.

Regarding the scales of analysis, local and regional levels are clearly predominant in all the approaches (see Table 9.3). Such an observation may be seen as an intuitive result since larger scales render participation much more complicated and, in most cases, clearly less impactful. Our comparative analysis does not reveal any clear distinction between the four PMCAs. From a theoretical point of view, INTEGRAAL is the most suitable approach for assessing global issues, since participants can participate in the assessment process remotely, through the kerDST online system.

At least five applications studied here explicitly focus on urban and/or suburban areas (see Table 9.3). The main topics covered by these studies are (i) air pollution and (ii) water management. Although we did not find any urban case studies for MCM and 3-SPM, this does not mean that these are not applicable at the urban scale.

Table 9.3 *Applications considered in the present study (by approach, year, topic, scale, related country, participatory methods, number of options, and number of criteria)*

PMCA	Author(s)	Year	Topic	Scale	Country	Participatory methods	n° options	n° criteria
3-SPM	Renn	1986	Energy policies	Nat.	Germany	Expert consultation, workshops, citizen panels, surveys	4	141
3-SPM	Renn et al.	1996	Locations for a landfill	Reg.	Switzerland	Expert consultation, workshops, citizen panels, surveys	9	?
3-SPM	Schneider et al.	1998	Waste management	Reg.	Germany	Expert consultation, workshops, citizen panels, surveys	?	?
MCM	Stirling & Mayer	1999	GMOs and farming systems	Nat.	UK	In-depth interviews, workshop	6+8=14	117
SMCE	De Marchi et al.	2000	Water management	Loc.	Italy	In-depth interviews, survey	8	9
SMCE	Quintana	2000	Atmospheric impacts	Loc.	Spain	In-depth interviews	5	15
MCM	McDowall & Eames	2006	Hydrogen as energy vector	Nat.	UK	Workshops, In-depth interviews	6	97
SMCE	Gamboa	2006	Aluminum smelter projects	Loc.	Chile	In-depth interviews, focus groups, workshop with young people	3	9
DM-KIK	Chamaret	2007	Uranium mining activities	Loc.	Niger	Focus groups	5	9 criter. 119 ind.
MCM	Millstone & Lobstein	2007	Policies against obesity	Int.	9 Eur. countries	In-depth interviews	7+13=20	107
SMCE	Gamboa & Munda	2007	Windfarm locations	Loc.	Spain	In-depth interviews, focus groups	7	9
DM-KIK	Maxim	2008	Impacts of insecticides on biodiv.	Reg.	France	In-depth interviews, focus groups	4	6
SMCE	Munda & Russi	2008	Rural electrification	Loc.	Spain	In-depth interviews	3	10
SMCE	Scolobig et al.	2008	Flood mitigation	Loc.	Italy	In-depth interviews, questionnaire, brainstorming sessions	6	11
SMCE	Paneque Salgado et al.	2009	Water governance	Loc.	Spain	Participant obs., questionnaires, in-depth interviews, focus groups	8	11
DM-KIK	Da Cunha	2010	Suburban agricultural syst.	Reg.	France	Interviews, focus groups	4	5 criter. n/a
DM-KIK	Reichel et al.	2010	Planning strategies	Loc.	France	Interviews, focus groups	3	7 criter. 128 ind.
DM-KIK	O'Connor et al.	2010	Planning and sustainable agriculture	Nat.	New Zealand	Focus group	2	6 criter. ?
DM-KIK	Remvikos et al.	2010	Air quality policies	Reg.	France	Interviews, focus groups	6	5 criter. 76 ind.
MCM	Hansen	2010	Nanotechnologies	Nat.	USA	Expert consultation, in-depth interviews	8+22=30	97
SMCE	Garmendia et al.	2010	Estuaries management	Loc.	Spain	In-depth interviews, open meeting, workshop, questionnaires	11	8
SMCE	Domenech et al.	2011	Urban water management	Loc.	Spain	Online survey	4	8
MCM	Bellamy et al.	2013	Geo-engineering and climate change	Int.	Global	In-depth interviews	7+7=14	61
DM-KIK	Merino-Saum	2015	Wildfire risk governance	Reg.	France	In-depth interviews	4	6 criter. 73 ind.
MCM	Royuela et al.	2016	Development scenarios on a small island	Loc.	Portugal	Focus groups, in-depth interviews, final workshop	7	25
SMCE	Walter et al.	2016	Mining activities	Loc.	Ecuador	Participant obs., in-depth interviews, workshops	2	7

With regard to the data that PMCAs may contain, the four approaches allow the integration of qualitative and quantitative indicators. What is clearly different from one case to another is the significance associated with these data and the function these data are given. In that sense, as already outlined, both 3-SPM and SMCE differentiate several kinds of knowledge and put strong emphasis on the formal delimitation between value-driven judgments and science-based conclusions. MCM and INTEGRAAL both adopt a more constructivist perspective and purposely merge these two dimensions into a common evaluative framework where facts and meanings are linked to each other.

Furthermore, while 3-SPM and SMCE tend to first open up the process and then progressively close it down, both MCM and INTEGRAAL imply in some way the inverse route, paying increasing attention over the process to the diversity of arguments, values, and justification principles that characterize the issue at hand. The concrete tools the four PMCAs rely on illustrate these contrasting features: whereas value-trees (3-SPM) and dendrograms (SMCE) involve per se an assembling and converging operation, both MCM and INTEGRAAL finish the evaluation process with an assortment of disaggregated bar charts (MCM) and cube segments (INTEGRAAL). In the same sense, as shown in Table 9.3, applications of MCM and INTEGRAAL systematically involve larger amounts of criteria/indicators. As Stirling explicitly points out, "from a technical point of view [in MCM] you can aggregate and optimize, but that is not the point. The point is to map all the possible optimizations that could be performed" (see Footnote 3). In other words, while some PMCAs put more emphasis on heuristics (i.e., exploring and meaningfully mapping all existing values, interests, and knowledge claims), others have a stronger prescriptive orientation and seek to support decision-making processes more directly.

9.4.3 How is it Assessed?

As far as the "how" question is concerned, the four approaches are quite flexible and allow for non-linear evaluative processes. This is particularly the case for MCM, SMCE, and INTEGRAAL. For 3-SPM, which implies a very developed (although heavy) procedure, it may be relatively more challenging to integrate particular constraints and allow adjusted applications (see Section 9.3.3).

Regarding the level of mathematical formalization, SMCE clearly embeds more advanced multi-criteria structuring. It is also the only approach that consistently avoids compensability between criteria. Munda is particularly clear on that point, insisting on the "importance of the algorithmic component" and "mathematical aggregation conventions" (Munda, 2004a, p. 674). That is the main reason why he considers MCM or INTEGRAAL to be "deliberative processes," rather than multi-criteria approaches *stricto sensu*. That being said, the use of mathematical algorithms may increase the opacity of the evaluation and thus make it less understandable by the participants (see Section 9.2.3.3). As Munda (2006, p. 93) states, "multi-criteria algorithms used in a social context should be as simple as possible." The understanding of what a simple multi-criteria axiomatization is, seems, however, rather ambiguous and relative to each PMCA developer. In practice, some

PMCAs may imply "a lack of accessibility and people cannot overcome the gap" (O'Connor) (see Footnote 2). In brief, inclusivity and robust multi-criteria structuring constitute two assessment goals that are not completely compatible with each other and, as such, they inevitably involve some concessions of one sort or another. PMCA being by definition a hybrid VAI, any concrete application thus entails hybridization trade-offs that need to be made clear.

The four PMCAs are also clearly differentiated from each other regarding weighting (i.e., how weights are theoretically conceived and how they are they concretely calculated, etc.). While in SMCE the research team decides the weights, citizens do so in 3-SPM and stakeholders choose them in both MCM and INTEGRAAL. For Munda, such an option is "technically difficult," "pragmatically not desirable" and "ethically unacceptable" (Munda, 2004a, p. 672). It can also involve "political de-responsibility" (p. 671). Therefore, he strongly recommends that analysts transparently decide the weights based on a particular ethical positioning (e.g., precautionary principle, sustainability paradigm). In contrast, neither Stirling nor O'Connor conceive of weightings as technical elements for a particular aggregative procedure. They both see them as informative pieces expressing a particular problem's representations and conflictual imperatives for action. Furthermore, given that the results of MCM and INTEGRAAL are most often presented in a disaggregated manner, their developers do not pay particular attention to technical discussions about weighting systems.

In terms of participatory methods, both SMCE and 3-SPM most often involve the sequential combination of several participatory methods (e.g., in-depth interviews, focus groups, surveys). In both cases, these inclusive methods are expected to be implemented in very concrete assessment steps depending on their respective features, so that the research team maximizes their potentials. Hence, methodologically speaking, SMCE and 3-SPM go further in the formal integration of participatory processes. It is important, however, to differentiate between the formal attention each approach pays to inclusive processes and the role(s) these processes are assigned. In that sense, although SMCE reserves a large amount of room for participation, this has limited impact on the final assessment. In contrast, MCM assigns key roles to participants, but it does not imply any concrete articulation between several inclusive processes.

On the other hand, given that MCM is largely based on individual interviews (see Section 9.3.2), it might be especially suitable in cases where collective discussions are not possible due to logistical issues (very large scale of analysis, absence of trained mediators, etc.), when adverse social conditions exist (particularly strong conflicts between actors), or when focus groups seem not pertinent because of strong power asymmetries.

Finally, in terms of deliberative philosophy, PMCAs also show different orientations: while some approaches are more consensus-driven and aim at solving conflicts (e.g., 3-SPM, SMCE), some others have a clear agonistic flavor and rather try to make use of conflicts through more pluralistic methods (e.g., INTEGRAAL, MCM). These different orientations are illustrated by, among other things, the contrast that exists between the common problem framing on which SMCE relies (see Section 9.3.1) and the eclectic object that both MCM and INTEGRAAL involve (see Sections 9.3.2 and 9.3.4).

9.5 Discussion and Concluding Remarks

All four PMCAs studied in this chapter combine multi-criteria framing with one or more participatory method(s) as a way to overcome traditional top-down and technocratic assessment methods. They all have been applied to assess sustainability issues and they all were developed by researchers belonging to the same scientific community. That being said, these approaches may significantly differ from each other at several points and on different levels (see Section 9.4). Using the VAI concept as the main theoretical background, the present chapter elucidates the key factors that practitioners and researchers must consider when selecting the most suitable approach prior to any possible application.

At the conceptual level, we bring out two key factors that may orientate the selection of one PMCA over the others:

1 the *epistemological position* the research team seeks to hold, which may be constructivist (as is generally the case in both MCM and INTEGRAAL applications) or positivist (e.g., SMCE);
2 the kind of *hybridization trade-off* the team envisions; that is, whether it prioritizes accessibility through algorithmic simplicity (e.g., MCM; INTEGRAAL; 3-SPM) or rather technical consistency with potentially limited intelligibility (SMCE).

At a more practical level, PMCAs may be more or less suitable depending on the following contextual factors (see also Table 9.4):

1 **logistical aspects** (e.g., time availability, budgetary constraints, technical/operational means);
2 **case-specific features** (e.g., most pertinent governance scales, breadth of the problem at hand, level of conflicts, kind of urban system to be assessed);
3 **organizational drivers** (e.g., pressures from professional supervisors, institutional partnerships).

Such contextual factors underline some obvious (in)compatibilities in real practice. Hence, for instance, 3-SPM should not be applied when the available budget is very low or when the assessment is expected to support a policymaking process already underway. Similarly, if the assessment is ordered by decision-makers expecting concrete and directly implementable results (because the process is already advanced), then neither MCM nor INTEGRAAL may be the best option.

Although these contextual factors are crucial, the selection of the most suitable PMCA should not be carried out without considering conceptual meta-factors. Indeed, given that each approach has its own philosophy, the exclusive consideration of

Table 9.4 *PMCAs considered in real practice (lessons from the 26 case studies)*

		SMCE	MCM	3-SPM	INTEGRAAL
LOGISTICAL ASPECTS	Budget constraints	Both are quite flexible and may be implemented very differently. Budget requirements must be estimated on a case-by-case basis and may vary significantly from one case to another.		Involves several participatory techniques and is probably more budget-consuming than other PMCAs.	Is also quite flexible. Case-by-case estimations are needed.
	Time availability	All PMCAs require several months to be correctly implemented (from 2 to 12, according to Stagl, 2007). Given its procedural complexity, 3-SPM possibly requires more time than others do.			
	Technical means	Although flexible, SMCE generally requires several persons leading/facilitating the assessment process.	Being largely based on individual interviews, MCM may be applied by one single researcher.	Does not seem conceivable to apply it without the support of several researchers and/or practitioners.	Is flexible and has been applied several times by one single researcher. As a rule, a team is needed.
CASE-SPECIFIC FEATURES	Level of conflicts	It explicitly investigates potential coalitions (*dendrogram*).	Individual interviews may give less powerful actors the chance to freely express their concerns and values.		The online system on which it relies may be useful when conflicts are particularly strong and group sessions are not feasible.
	Power issues	The influence that most powerful actors may have on the evaluation is rather limited (technical/social matrix).		The involvement of citizens in the evaluation process is a guarantee when lobbying groups are particularly strong.	
	Governance scale(s)	Although SMCE, MCM, and 3-SPM are particularly well adapted to local assessments, they have also been successfully applied at the national scale.			Since it allows interactive participation (online system), INTEGRAAL may be especially suitable for assessing global issues.

Table 9.4 (*cont.*)

		SMCE	MCM	3-SPM	INTEGRAAL
	Barriers to actors' involvement	The algorithms behind SMCE may discourage participants or even involve mistrust toward the assessment process.	Participants find it challenging to score the options as MCM expects. Participation rates may be low.		The evaluative system is time-consuming and might be difficult to understand.
	Adjustability in real processes		Being essentially heuristic, MCM is a better fit at the initial stages of an assessment process.	3-SPM's procedural heaviness is hardly compatible with real decision-making processes.	Some participants may not accept involving actors as "performance evaluators" (they may quit the process).
ORGANISAIZ-ATIONAL DRIVERS	Pressures from supervisors	Practitioners and researchers may be required by their hierarchical supervisor(s) to apply one particular approach. Although such a factor is similarly pertinent for all PMCAs (i.e., it does not differentiate between approaches), it is important enough to be outlined.			
	Problems with academic silos	It is typically difficult to produce an impact matrix with quantitative data (assessments results are often semi-qualitative).	Due to its philosophical roots, MCM may involve academic scepticism (in particular in technical faculties).		Due to its philosophical roots, INTEGRAAL may involve academic scepticism (in particular in technical faculties).

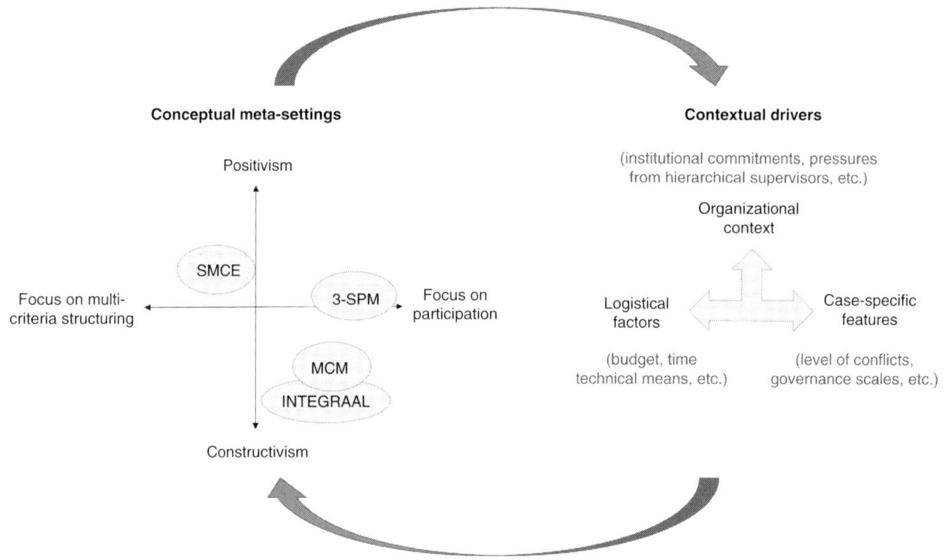

Figure 9.3 Articulating conceptual and contextual factors in the selection of the most suitable PMCA (own illustration)

contextual drivers may easily lead to logical impasses, intellectual frustration, and/or low acceptability on the part of local actors (when the conceptual narrative is not shared with participants from the beginning of the assessment process).

In fact, the selection should rather rely on a back-and-forth process between conceptual and contextual factors (see Figure 9.3). This implies a process through which the research team (i) first identifies the conceptual quadrant where the assessment must be anchored (depending on its own philosophical positioning and the research question(s) at hand); (ii) then checks all pertinent contextual factors; and (iii) subsequently fine-tunes the selection, eventually adapting the approach initially identified, or combining elements from different PMCAs with comparable conceptual narratives.

Given the plethora of alternative PMCAs that have been (and are being) applied to assess sustainability problems, a comparative framework, such as the one suggested here, may significantly improve both their scientific pertinence and their political usability. As explained above, depending both on the questions that researchers/practitioners want to address and on the context where the assessment takes place, some approaches might be a better fit than others. Any new PMCA application requires careful reflection about the assessment's goals and may need novel solutions (e.g., hybrid approaches, innovative adaptations). Automatic replications should be avoided. This chapter does not seek to bring comparable approaches into opposition, but rather to put them together within a common VAI family (PMCAs), which inevitably asks for critical thinking and creativity.

Acknowledgments

I gratefully acknowledge Professors Giuseppe Munda, Andy Stirling, Ortwin Renn, and Martin O'Connor for their availability and their participation in a series of in-depth interviews completed in 2009–2010. Anna Scolobig, Mariana Walter, and Alexandros Gasparatos actively participated in this interviewing process. I also sincerely thank Anna Scolobig and Sandra Veuthey for their valuable comments on earlier versions of this chapter. Their suggestions helped improve and clarify the paper. I also would like to thank Jessica Clément, Ian Gunderson, and Valeria Superti for proofreading.

Notes

1. The list of case studies here studied is neither exhaustive nor statistically representative. However, it can be seen as a fairly representative sample providing several contrasting illustrations for each approach. Additional applications could be added and thus complement the present analysis.
2. The interviews were recorded and transcribed in 2009–2010 as part of an unpublished paper involving the author of the present chapter, as well as Anna Scolobig, Mariana Walter, and Alexandros Gasparatos.
3. This "flexibility" (Munda, 2009, p. 309) is particularly well illustrated by the study conducted by Martí (2005), who applied a rudimentary version of SMCE working with indigenous communities in Ecuador.
4. Weights in SMCE are meaningful only as importance coefficients, not as trade-offs.
5. Participants may also consider some criteria as being principles that cannot be compensated. In such cases, options are evaluated as "acceptable" or "unacceptable."
6. These three points were raised by Renn himself during the interview (see Footnote 2).
7. DM was originally designed by O'Connor as part of the GOUVERNE project (2000–2003). It was subsequently formalized by O'Connor (2006). See also O'Connor and Spangenberg (2007).
8. We borrow this expression from Giacomo d'Alisa (4th THEMES Summer School on integrated analysis of complex adaptive systems; Brighton 2009).
9. The role stakeholders are given may significantly vary from one application to another within the same approach. The differences here outlined between the four PMCAs may thus become blurred.
10. In 3-SPM, however, the research team is expected to verify experts' judgments, taking into account both literature search and independent review (Renn & Webler, 1992, p. 89) (see also Table 9.2).

References

Alberti, M., & Susskind, L. (1996). Managing urban sustainability: An introduction to the Special Issue. *Environmental Impact Assessment Review*, 16, 213–221.

Banville, C., Landry, M., Martel, J. M., & Boulaire, C. (1998). A stakeholder approach to MCDA. *Systems Research and Behavioral Science*, 15, 15–32.

Bellamy, R., Chilvers, J., Vaughan, N. E., & Lenton, T. M. (2013). Opening up geoengineering appraisal: Multi-criteria mapping of options for tackling climate change. *Global Environmental Change*, 23, 926–937.

Bromley, D. W. (2007). Environmental regulations and the problem of sustainability: Moving beyond "market failure." *Ecological Economics*, 63, 676–683.

Bromley, D. W., & Paavola, J. (2002). Economics, Ethics, and Environmental Policy. In D. W. Bromley & J. Paavola, (eds.), *Economics, Ethics, and Environmental Policy: Contested Choices*. Oxford: Blackwell Publishing, pp. 261–276.

Bulkeley, H., & Betsill, M. (2005). Rethinking sustainable cities: Multilevel governance and the "urban" politics of climate change. *Environmental Politics*, 14(1), 42–63.

Chamaret, A. (2007). Une démarche top-down / bottom-up pour l''évaluation en termes multicritères et multiacteurs des projets miniers dans l''optique du développement durable. Application sur les mines d''Uranium d''Arlit (Niger). PhD Dissertation. University of Versailles Saint-Quentin-en-Yvelines, Guyancourt.

Cole, J., Sharvelle, S., Grigg, N., Pivo, G., & Haukaas, J. (2018). Collaborative, risk-informed, triple bottom line, multi-criteria decision analysis planning framework for integrated urban water management. *Water*, 10(12), 1722.

De Marchi, B., Funtowicz, S. O., Lo Cascio, S., & Munda, G. (2000). Combining participative and institutional approaches with multicriteria evaluation: An empirical study for water issues in Troina, Sicily. *Ecological Economics*, 34, 267–282.

De Montis, A., De Toro, P., Droste-Franke, B., Omann, I., & Stagl, S. (2000). Criteria for quality assessment of MCDA methods. Paper presented at the 3rd Conference of the ESEE, May 3–6, Vienna.

De Montis, A., & Lai, S. (2008). Multi-criteria evaluation and planning support choosing among alternative scenarios for an urban natural park in Sardinia, Italy. In R., Vreeker, M., Deakin, & S. Curwell (eds.), *Sustainable Urban Development, Volume 3: The Toolkit for Assessment*, London: Routledge, pp. 62–82.

Da Cunha, C. (2010). Quelle prise en compte de la diversité dans les enjeux de performances de l'activité agricole en Ile de France? : expérimentation d'une démarche d'évaluation participative multicritère. PhD Dissertation. University of Versailles Saint-Quentin-en- Yvelines, Guyancourt.

Dodgson, J., Spackman, M., Pearman, A., & Phillips, L. (2009). *Multi-criteria analysis: A manual*. London: Department for Communities and Local Government.

Domenèch, L., March, H., & Saurí, D. (2011). Degrowth initiatives in the urban water sector? A social multi-criteria evaluation of non-conventional water alternatives in Metropolitan Barcelona. *Journal of Cleaner Production*, 38, 44–55.

Finco, A., & Nijkamp, P. (2001). Pathways to urban sustainability. *Journal of Environmental Policy & Planning*, 3, 289–302.

Foster, J. (Ed.). (1997). *Valuing Nature? Economics, Ethics and Environment*, Routledge, London.

Gamboa, G. (2006). Social multi-criteria evaluation of different development scenarios of the Aysén region, Chile. *Ecological Economics*, 59, 157–170.

Fritz, L., & Meinherz, F. (2020). The politics of participatory sustainability assessments: an analysis of power. In C. R. Binder, E. Massaro, & R. Wyss (eds.), *Sustainability Assessment in Urban Systems*. Cambridge University Press, pp. 87–122.

Gamboa, G., & Munda, G. (2007). The problem of windfarm location: A social multi-criteria evaluation framework. *Energy Policy*, 35, 1564–1583.

Garmendia, E., Gamboa, G., Franco, J., Garmendia, J. M., Liria, P., & Olazabal, M. (2010). Social multi-criteria evaluation as a decision support tool for integrated coastal zone management. *Ocean & Coastal Management*, 53(7), 385–403.

Gerber, J. -F., Rodríguez-Labajos, B., Yánez, I., et al. (2012). *Guide to Multicriteria Evaluation for Environmental Justice Organisations*. EJOLT Report No. 8, 45 p.

Giampietro, M. (2002). Complexity and Scales: The Challenge for Integrated Assessment. *Integrated Assessment*, 3(2–3), 247–265.

Godard, O. (2004). La pensée économique face à la question de l''environnement. Cahiers du Laboratoire d''Econométrie de l''Ecole Polytechnique, Cahier n° 2004–013, Ecole Polytechnique, Palaiseau.

Gregory, R., Lichtenstein, S., & Slovic, P. (1993). Valuing Environmental Resources: A Constructive Approach. *Journal of Risk and Uncertainty*, 7, 177–197.

Guitouni, A., & Martel, J. M. (1998). Tentative guidelines to help choosing an appropriate MCDA method. *European Journal of Operational Research*. 109, 501–521.

Halla, P., Wyss, R., & Binder, C. R. (2020). Conceptualising Urban Systems for Sustainability Assessment: Four Powerful Metaphors. In C. R. Binder, E. Massaro, & R. Wyss (eds.), *Sustainability Assessment in Urban Systems*. Cambridge University Press, pp. 241–260.
Hansen, S. F. (2010). Multicriteria mapping of stakeholder preferences in regulating nanotechnology. *Journal of Nanoparticle Research*, 12, 1959–1970.
Hwang, C. L., & Yoon, K. (1981). *Multiple Attributes Decision Making Methods and Applications*. Berlin: Springer.
Jacobs, M. ([1991] 1997). *La Economía Verde. Medio Ambiente, Desarrollo Sostenible y la Política del Futuro*. Barcelona: Icaria.
Janssen, R., & Munda, G. (1999). Multi-criteria methods for quantitative, qualitative and fuzzy evaluation problem. In J. van den Bergh (ed.), *Handbook of Environmental and Resource Economics*. Cheltenham: Edward Elgar, pp. 837–852.
Lahdelma, R., Salminen, P., & Hokkanen, J. (2000). Using multicriteria methods in environmental planning and management. *Environmental Management*, 26(6), 595–605.
Landert, J., Schader, C., Moschitz, H., & Stolze, M. (2017). A holistic sustainability assessment method for urban food system governance. *Sustainability*, 9, 490.
Liu, S., Proctor, W., & Cook, D. (2010). Using an integrated fuzzy set and deliberative multi-criteria evaluation approach to facilitate decision-making in invasive species management. *Ecological Economics*, 69(12), 2374–2382.
Lockwood, M. (1999). Humans valuing nature: synthesising insights from philosophy, psychology and economics, *Environmental Values*, 8, 381–401.
Lupo, T., & Cusumano, M. (2018). Towards more equity concerning quality of Urban Waste Management services in the context of cities. *Journal of Cleaner Production*, 171, 1324–1341.
Martel, J. M., & Rousseau, A. (1993). *Cadre de référence d'une démarche multicritère de gestion intégrée des ressources en milieu forestier*. Rapport préparé pour le Gouvernement du Québec, Ministère du loisir, de la chasse et de la pêche, Ministère des Forêts et Ministère de l'Environnement, document technique 93/11, 49 pages.
Martí, N. (2005). *La multidimensionalidad de los sistemas locales de alimentación en los Andes peruanos: los chalayplasa del Valle de Lares (Cusco)*. PhD Dissertation. Universitat Autónoma de Barcelona.
Martínez-Alier, J., Munda, G., & O'Neill, J. (1998). Weak comparability of values as a foundation for ecological Economics. *Ecological Economics*, 26, 277–286.
Martínez-Alier, J., & Roca, J. ([2000] 2001). *Economía Ecológica y Política Ambiental*, México D.F.: Fondo de Cultura Económica.
Maxim, L. (2008). Mobilisation d'un outil multimédia d'aide à la délibération pour l'analyse socio-économique des changements de la biodiversité. Réflexions autour de trois études de cas, à l'échelle régionale (Île-de-France), nationale (France) et continentale (Europe). PhD Dissertation. University of Versailles Saint-Quentin-en- Yvelines, Guyancourt.
Merino-Saum, A. (2015). Vivre avec le feu en région méditerranéenne. Une approche participative multicritère et multi-scénarios appliquée au cas du massif des Maures (Var, France). PhD Dissertation. University of Versailles Saint-Quentin-en- Yvelines, Guyancourt.
McDowall, W., & Eames, M. (2006). *Towards a sustainable hydrogen economy: A multi-criteria mapping of the UKSHEC hydrogen futures*. London: Policy Studies Institute.
Millstone, E., & Lobstein, T. (2007). The PorGrow project: Overall cross-national results, comparisons and implications. *Obesity Reviews*, 8, 29–36.
Munda, G. (2003). Multicriteria assessment. In *Internet Encyclopedia of Ecological Economics*. International Society for Ecological Economics.
Munda, G. (2004a). Social multi-criteria evaluation: Methodological foundations and operational consequences. *European Journal of Operational Research*, 158, 662–677.
Munda, G. (2004b). Multi-criteria evaluation. In J. Proops & P. Safonov (eds.), *Modelling in Ecological Economics*. Cheltenham: Edward Elgar, pp. 130–154.
Munda, G. (2006). Social multi-criteria evaluation for urban sustainability policies. *Land Use Policy*, 23, 86–94.

Munda, G. (2008). *Social Multi-Criteria Evaluation for a Sustainable Economy*. Berlin Heidelberg: Springer-Verlag.

Munda, G. (2009). A conflict analysis approach for illuminating distributional issues in sustainability policy. *European Journal of Operational Research*, 194, 307–322.

Munda, G., & Nardo, M. (2003). Mathematical modelling of composite indicators for ranking countries, Proceedings of the First OECD/JRC Workshop on Composite Indicators of Country Performance, JRC, Ispra.

Munda, G., Nijkamp, P., & Rietveld, P. (1995). Qualitative multicriteria methods for fuzzy evaluation problems: An illustration of economic-ecological evaluation. *European Journal of Operational Research*, 82, 79–97.

Munda, G., & Russi, D. (2008). Social multicriteria evaluation of conflict over rural electrification and solar energy in Spain. *Environment and Planning C: Government and Policy*, 26, 712–727.

Nijkamp, P., Rietveld, P., Voogd, H. (1991). *Multicriteria Analysis for Physical Planning*. Amsterdam: Elsevier.

O'Connor, M. (1997). Environmental valuation: From the point of view of sustainability. In A. K. Dragun & M. J. Jakobsson (eds.), *Sustainability and Global Environmental Policy: New Perspectives*. Cheltenham: Edward Elgar, pp.149–178.

O'Connor, M. (2000). Pathways for environmental evaluation: A walk in the (Hanging) Gardens of Babylon. *Ecological Economics*, 34, 175–193.

O'Connor, M. (2006). Deliberative Sustainability Assessment: Multiple Scales, Multiple Stakeholders, Multidisciplinarity and Multiple Bottom Lines. Rapport de Recherche du C3ED, University of Versailles St-Quentin-en-Yvelines, Guyancourt.

O'Connor, M. (2007). *Deliberative Sustainability Assessment with the on line KerDST Deliberation Support Tool*. Cahiers du C3ED, n°07–03, University of Versailles St-Quentin-en-Yvelines, Guyancourt.

O'Connor, M., Faucheux, S., Froger, G., Funtowicz, S., & Munda, G. (1996). Emergent complexity and procedural rationality: Post-normal science for sustainability. In R. Constanza, O. Segura, & J. Martínez-Alier (eds.), *Getting down to Earth*, Island Press, Washington DC: International Society of Ecological Economics, pp. 223–247.

O'Connor, M., van den Hove, S. O'Neill, J., & Hue, C. (2001). Le Modèle Politique de la Démocratie Délibérative, Documentation interne du C3ED.

O'Connor, M., & Spangenberg, J. H. (2007). A methodology for CSR reporting: Assuring a representative diversity of indicators across stakeholders, scales, sites and performance issues. *Journal of Cleaner Production*, 16(13), 1399–1415.

O'Connor, M., Small, B., & Wedderburn, M. E. (2010). Sustainable Agriculture in Aotearoa: Social Learning through Piecewise Deliberation. *REEDS Working Papers series* 2010–10, Université de Versailles St-Quentin-en-Yvelines, Rambouillet.

Omann, I. (2004). Multi-criteria decision aid as an approach for sustainable development analysis and implementation. PhD Dissertation, University of Graz.

O'Neill, J. (1993). *Ecology, Policy and Politics*. London: Routledge.

O'Neill, J. (1997). Value pluralism, incommensurability and institutions. In J. Foster (ed.), *Valuing Nature? Economics, Ethics and Environment*. London: Routledge, pp. 75–88.

Paneque Salgado, P., Quintana, S. C., Guimaraes Pereira, A., Del Moral Ituarte, L., & Pedregal Mateos, B. (2009). Participative multi-criteria analysis for the evaluation of water governance alternatives: A case in the Costa del Sol (Málaga). *Ecological Economics*, 68, 990–1005.

Proctor, W. (2009). *Environmental Decision Making: An application of Multi-criteria Analysis to a Case Study of Australia's Forests*. Saarbrücken: Lambert Academic Publishing.

Proctor, W., & Dreschler, M. (2006). Deliberative multicriteria evaluation. *Environment and Planning C: Government and Policy*, 24, 169–190.

Quintana, S. C. (2001). *Una Metodología integrada de exploración y compensión de los procesos de elaboración de políticas públicas*. PhD Dissertation. University of La Laguna.

Rauschmayer, F., & Wittmer, H. (2006). Evaluating deliberative and analytical methods for the resolution of environmental conflicts. *Land Use Policy*, 23, 108–122.

Ravetz, J. (2000). Integrated assessment for sustainability appraisal in cities and regions. *Environmental Impact Assessment Review*, 20, 31–64.
Reichel, V., Chamaret, A., & O'Connor, M. (2010). *Les Avenirs de la Boucle de Moisson : un projet de réflexion participative pour un développement territorial soutenable*. Rapport de Recherche REEDS n° 2010-06, University of Versailles St-Quentin-en-Yvelines, Rambouillet.
Remvikos, Y., Mahamat, A., & Reichel, V. (2010). *L'interface science/décision au travers d'une évaluation multicritères et multi-acteurs du plan régional pour la qualité de l'air en Ile-de-France,* Cahiers du Centre REEDS n° 2010–12, University of Versailles St-Quentin-en-Yvelines, Rambouillet.
Renn, O. (1986). Decision analytic tools for resolving uncertainty in the energy debate. *Nuclear Engineering and Design*, 93(2–3), 167–180.
Renn, O. (2003). Social assessment of waste energy utilization scenarios. *Energy*, 28, 1345–1357.
Renn, O. (2006). Participatory processes for designing environmental policies. *Land Use Policy*, 23, 34–43.
Renn, O., & Webler, T. (1992). Anticipating Conflicts: Public Participation in Managing the Solid Waste Crisis. *GAIA*, 2, 84–94.
Renn, O., Webler, T., Horst, R., Dienel, P., & Johnson, B. (1993). Public participation in decision-making: A three-step procedure. *Policy Science*, 26, 189–214.
Renn, O., Webler, T., & Kastenholz, H. (1996). Procedural and substantive fairness in landfill siting: A Swiss Case Study. *RISK: Health, Safety & Environment*, 7(2), 145–168.
Roy, B., & Bouyssou, D. (1993). *Aide multicritère à la décision: méthodes et cas*. Paris: Economica.
Roy, B., & Vincke, P. (1981). Multicriteria analysis: Survey and new directions. *European Journal of Operational Research*, 8, 207–218.
Royuela, J. B., Eames, M., & Buckingham, S. (2016). "Participative foresight scenario mapping": Adapting an MCM method to appraise foresight scenarios for the long-term sustainable development of a small island. *International Journal of Multicriteria Decision Making*, 6(2), 118–137.
Sagoff, M. (1998). Aggregation and deliberation in valuing environmental public goods: A look beyond contingent pricing. *Ecological Economics*, 24, 213–230.
Schkade, D. A., & Payne, J. W. (1994). How people respond to contingent valuation questions: A verbal protocol analysis of willingness to pay for an environmental regulation. *Journal of Environmental Economics and Management*, 26, 88–109.
Schneider, E., Oppermann, B., Renn, O. (1998). Implementing structured participation for regional level waste management planning. *Risk: Health, Safety and Environment*, 9, 379–395.
Scolobig, A., Castán Broto, V., & Zabala, A. (2008). Integrating multiple perspectives in social multicriteria evaluation of flood-mitigation alternatives: The case of Malborghetto-Valbruna. *Environment and Planning C: Government and Policy*, 26, 1143–1161.
Spash, C. (2008). Contingent valuation design and data treatment: If you can't shoot the messenger, change the message. *Environment and Planning C: Government and Policy*, 26, 34–53.
Stagl, S. (2003). Multicriteria Evaluation and Public Participation: In Search for Theoretical Foundations. Paper presented at the ESEE Conference (European Society for Ecological Economics), Tenerife, Spain, 12–15 February.
Stagl, S. (2006). Multicriteria evaluation and public participation: the case of UK energy policy. *Land Use Policy*, 23, 53–62.
Stagl, S. (2007). Emerging Methods for Sustainability Valuation and Appraisal. *Rapid Research and Evidence Reviews*, The Sustainable Development Research Network.
Stirling, A. (1997). Multi-criteria mapping: Mitigating the problems of environmental valuation? In J. Foster (ed.), *Valuing Nature? Economics, Ethics and Environment*. London: Routledge, pp. 186–210.
Stirling, A. (2005). *Multi-Criteria Mapping: A Detailed Interview Protocol*. Unpublished technical report.
Stirling, A., & Mayer, S. (1999). *Rethinking Risk: A Pilot Multi-criteria Mapping of a Genetically Modified Crop in Agricultural Systems in the UK*. University of Sussex, Science Policy Research Unit.

Stirling, A., & Mayer, S. (2000). A precautionary approach to technology appraisal? A multi-criteria mapping of genetic modification in UK agriculture. *SCHWERPUNKTHEMA*, 3(9), 39–51.

Vatn, A. (2005a). *Institutions and the Environment*. Cheltenham: Edward Elgar.

Vatn, A. (2005b). Rationality, institutions and environmental policy. *Ecological Economics*, 55, 203–217.

Vatn, A., & Bromley, D. W. (1994). Choices without prices without apologies. *Journal of Environmental Economics and Management*, 26, 129–148.

Walter, M., Latorre Tomás, S., Munda, G., & Larrea, C. (2016). A social multi-criteria evaluation approach to assess extractive and non-extractive scenarios in Ecuador: Intag case study. *Land Use Policy*, 57, 444–458.

Whitehead, M. (2003). (Re)Analysing the sustainable city: Nature, urbanisation and the regulation of socio-environmental relations in the UK. *Urban Studies*, 40(7), 1183–1206.

Part III
Perspectives on Urban Sustainability

Urban systems assume an increasingly central significance in the global sustainability challenge. As hubs of social, scientific and economic activities, cities possess the potential for facilitating transitions toward sustainable ways of living. Therefore, tools like sustainability assessment are needed to help decision-makers unleash this positive potential of cities, while also limiting the negative impacts on their residents and environments. A major challenge with implications across different aspects of sustainability assessment concerns the conceptualization of the objects relevant for the assessment. This part of the book introduces concepts and methods to define urban systems and urban sustainability assessment.

Chapter 10 elaborates on the challenge of conceptualizing urban systems and introduces the idea of different metaphors of cities. The chapter then, proceeds to characterize the metaphors across different system theory concepts with the purpose of making explicit the distinct meanings of each metaphor. It finally consolidates the analysis of the metaphors into a discussion of their implications for sustainability assessment.

Chapter 11 briefly presents key research fields that have been looking into the question of urban sustainability from an urban metabolism lens. The authors derive a list of city characteristics from urban studies and explore their global sustainability implications. The chapter also considers more specifically the sustainability implications of the urban characteristics and tests the derived sustainability implications of the urban features against empirical evidences by collecting a list of indicators and studying their evolution over time in parallel to the global urbanization process. Finally, it discusses the importance of a new, more integrated and multidisciplinary approach of urban sustainability still required to develop a common language, consolidate research efforts, and eventually enable cross-pollination among existing research streams.

Chapter 12 addresses the issue that so far global urban networks and their related impact levels miss clear links to a proactive sustainability strategy. It develops a better understanding of the interrelationship between global sustainability and urban sustainability by (i) putting urban sustainability first in relation to the knowledge base of globalized urban network organization. It uses the predominant interpretive approach of global urban systems against the backdrop of material, financial and information flows to (ii) focus on networked urban supply systems.

Finally, in Chapter 13 the authors focus on urban indicators and with the goal to illustrate the diversity of sustainability assessment tools that were developed at the local level and their different and complementary uses by presenting two instruments in use throughout Switzerland: the Cercle Indicators, which is an all-encompassing tool for sustainability monitoring and benchmarking at the level of cantons and cities; and the Swiss implementation of the Europe-wide City Statistics (formerly Urban Audit), with specific developments for ensuring compatibility with the concept of quality of life as defined by the OECD for its "How's Life" initiative.

10

Conceptualizing Urban Systems for Sustainability Assessment: Four Powerful Metaphors

Pekka Halla, Romano Wyss, and Claudia R. Binder

10.1 Introduction

Urban systems are assuming an increasingly central significance in the global sustainability challenge. As hubs of social, scientific, and economic activities, cities possess the potential for facilitating transitions toward sustainable ways of living. Therefore, tools like sustainability assessment are needed to help decision-makers unleash this positive potential of cities, while also limiting the negative impacts on their residents and environments. A major challenge, with implications across different aspects of sustainability assessment, concerns the conceptualization of the objects relevant for the assessment. Specifically, in the case of assessing the sustainability of urban systems, the problem of conceptualization involves identifying the constituent parts of the urban system and the necessary aspects of its sustainability. Conceptualization constitutes a crucial step in the assessment process, since it is directly related to the selection of appropriate measurement tools and indicators, and to the definition of the goals and criteria for the evaluation. Conceptualization also influences procedural choices by implying who should be involved in the assessment process.

Grounding sustainability assessments in explicit and structured conceptual frameworks or models is an important requirement for these to be comprehensive and transparent. Given the multitude of possible conceptualizations of urban systems, however, it also becomes necessary to develop procedures for analyzing and comparing different approaches in terms of their relative emphases, strengths, and weaknesses. The idea put forward in this chapter is to base such analysis on a number of descriptive metaphors for cities (machine, organism, network, and melting pot), each conjuring up an intuitive mental image, and each accentuating different aspects of the urban system. The purpose of this exercise is to enhance reflexivity with regard to the underlying implicit visions of what an urban system is (or what it is supposed to be), and, thereby, to cast light on the fundamental contrasts and contradictions present in conceptualizing, measuring, and assessing cities.

The chapter is structured as follows. First, Section 10.2 elaborates on the challenge of conceptualizing urban systems and introduces the idea of different metaphors for cities. Section 10.3 then proceeds to characterize the metaphors across different system-theory concepts with the purpose of making explicit the distinct meanings of each metaphor.

Section 10.4 consolidates the analysis of the metaphors into a discussion of their implications for sustainability assessment. Section 10.5 finishes the chapter with condensed conclusions.

10.2 Conceptualizing Urban Systems

10.2.1 Conceptualization Frameworks

The use of conceptual frameworks is a central principle of sustainability assessment (Pintér et al., 2012). Perhaps the most famous conceptual framework used in sustainability assessments builds on the idea of the three pillars of sustainability (Pope et al., 2017) – economy, society, environment – sometimes augmented by a fourth domain of sustainability covering institutional and governance aspects (James, 2015; Shen et al., 2011; Turcu, 2013). Despite the ostensible ubiquity of the three-pillars thinking, a great number of frameworks exist that itemize in different – and often more refined – manners the different objects, structures, and dimensions of sustainability to be considered in assessments. Examples of such frameworks can be found in both academic literature (e.g., Bossel, 1999; Meadows, 1998) and in the stated approaches of different institutional actors (e.g., ISO, 2014; World Bank, 2018). Maclaren's (1996) typology of frameworks, illustrated in Figure 10.1, captures the variety of frameworks used in the assessment of urban systems. In the typology, domain-based frameworks (e.g., the three-pillars model) are joined by four other types of frameworks that each deconstruct urban systems along different categorizations (sectors, issues, goals, or causally related categories). In practice, few frameworks in use fall strictly within any of the first five types. Rather, most frameworks are of the sixth, combined type.

Proceeding from an explicit conceptualization of the assessment problem helps to enhance comprehensiveness with regard to covering the necessary aspects of sustainability when selecting the pertinent assessment tools and indicators (Griggs et al., 2013; Hák et al., 2016). If this conceptual framing is absent, there is a danger that important choices in the sustainability assessment process will end up being made in an arbitrary fashion, or will be biased by the simple availability of measurement tools or data. Indeed, one of the benefits of the conscious development of a framework is that it can point to areas and aspects of

Domain-based	Sectoral	Issue-based	Goal-based	Causal	Combined
• Environment • Economy • Society • Governance • etc.	• Housing • Welfare • Transport • Economy • etc.	• Urban sprawl • Waste management • Crime and safety • Job creation • etc.	• Carrying capacity • Basic human needs • Social well-being • Economic prosperity • etc.	• Drivers • Pressures • States • Impacts • Responses • etc.	Combination of one or more of the other types

Figure 10.1 A typology of frameworks for sustainability assessment, adapted from Maclaren (1996)

sustainability that have been hitherto under-appreciated, and thereby reveal the need for the development of new indicators or other measurement tools. In terms of participation, the use of a conceptual framework assists in the identification of stakeholders whose input to the assessment should be considered. The benefits of using a clear framework also extend beyond the assessment itself by better enabling the clear communication and interpretation of the assessment results.

10.2.2 The Requirement for Reflexivity and Transparency

As illustrated by the typology in Figure 10.1, when it comes to conceptualizing urban systems, several potentially legitimate descriptions of the system exist in parallel, with each description dissecting the system along a different set of axes and categories (Cilliers, 2008; Wells, 2012). At the same time, each of these descriptions unavoidably also represents a simplification of the true extent of the complexity involved. Here, it is important to acknowledge that the simplification, by virtue of emphasizing different aspects of the system as more or less important, also establishes a normative position that privileges certain values and interests over others (Gasparatos, 2010). To paraphrase Meadows (1998), these choices are a reflection of what we care about the most, but also, inversely, what is included in our conceptual descriptions (and what is *not* included) ends up shaping our sense of what is important. These normative implications bring forth the requirement for reflexivity and transparency with regard to the relative emphases, strengths, and weaknesses of different conceptualizations of cities, as well as the ensuing implications for different aspects of sustainability assessment.

The use of a structured conceptual framework, like those proposed in the typology in Figure 10.1, is a necessary first step for addressing this requirement. It allows for the comparison of different approaches in terms of their relative emphases across different aspects and categories of the urban system. However, conceptualization entails more than merely selecting a type of conceptual framework (such as one of the types described in Figure10.1) and then populating the framework with a list of categories. Rather, it extends to deeper visions about the nature of urban systems and their sustainability. Therefore, to more fully address the challenge of reflexivity and transparency in assessing urban systems, it is necessary to develop analytical tools that can render visible and make comparable these deeper visions. Essentially, the relevant question is: *What is it that we think cities are when we assess them?*

Our proposal for an analytical tool that can answer the above question is based on the idea of cities as quintessential complex systems (Bettencourt, 2015; de Roo et al., 2012; Portugali, 2016). As de Roo et al. argue, when it comes to complex systems, the traditional "analysis–synthesis" approach to creating knowledge needs to be complemented with a mechanism of "association–creativity." This mechanism refers to looking beyond the individual elements of a complex system to its interconnections and processes, and, thereby, to the purposes and meanings of the system as a whole. In this task, the use of associative metaphors provides an indispensable source of creativity and inspiration for recognizing themes and patterns in complex systems (Hodgson, 1997; Pickett et al.,

2004). Indeed, the creative use of metaphors also permeates our language of cities, and various metaphorical images of cities with contrasting connotations have attained prominence at different points in history (Bettencourt, 2015; Lynch, 1984). Today, as Nientied's (2016) review shows, the number of city metaphors has proliferated, each drawing attention to specific aspects of the city. As Bettencourt puts it, "the city is all of these things, of course, but none of them in particular" (2015, p. 219).

The idea of contrasting metaphorical images of cities presents an interesting access point into how the challenge of reflexivity and transparency in conceptualizing and assessing urban systems can be addressed. In particular, considering and comparing common metaphors of cities can clarify different points of view with regard to what it is that we assume cities fundamentally are – as well as what they should be. Following this line of reasoning, the goal of the rest of this chapter is to single out a number of parallel metaphors of cities and to systematically clarify what each of them suggests about the nature of urban systems, their sustainability, and the processes by which they should be assessed.

10.2.3 Scientific Perspectives on Cities: The Three Cultures

In order to identify an adequately broad and representative selection of metaphors of cities for our analysis, it is necessary to create an overview of different scientific perspectives to cities. The idea is that underlying these perspectives are different metaphorical images that inspire their particular foci and methods for researching and making sense of the complexity of cities. The history of studying cities reaches back at least to Georg Simmel's *The Metropolis and Mental Life* from 1903, where he discussed the effects of urban life on social organization and human psychology. During the twentieth century, several scientific disciplines developed an interest in cities, some treating them as special settings of social life and others as intriguing objects of analysis in their own right. To map this varied body of research, Portugali (2011) evokes C. P. Snow's (1964) famous observation of the two opposing cultures in science, and correspondingly divides perspectives on cities into two contrasting cultures. Albeit fairly rough, this dual distinction is a good point of departure for creating an overview of the existing scholarship on cities to date.

The "first culture of cities," according to Portugali, is inspired by the hard sciences, thus tending toward positivist and quantitative research. This culture was particularly dominant in urban research in the 1950s and 1960s. Famous early theories within this general approach include location theory, whose roots go all the way back to von Thünen's 1826 work *The Isolated State* (1826/1966), Auerbach's (1913) rank-size distribution theory of cities, and Christaller's (1933/1966) and Lösch's (1954) central place theories. Furthermore, Portugali assigns the Chicago school of urban sociology (e.g., Park et al., 1925) to the first culture of cities. Scholars associated with the Chicago school adopted the idea of cities as ecological systems comparable to natural systems, and although they originally approached the subject matter from a different perspective from that of the other scholars mentioned above, they also ended up describing cities by means of morphological models with specialized sectors or concentric zones. Overall, then, the conceptualization of cities advanced by the first culture implies that "the number of their parts is relatively small, they are connected (or rather assumed to be connected) by well-defined rules and causal relations and as such these cities are assumed to be fully predictable" (Portugali, 2011, p. 38).

The "second culture of cities," as Portugali defines it, consists of approaches inspired by social theory and philosophy. This culture became particularly prominent in the 1970s and directly criticized the earlier positivistic and quantitative approaches to cities as simplistic and socially problematic. Early examples based on structuralist and Marxist theories include works such as Lefebvre's *Right to the City* (1968), Castells' *The Urban Question* (1972), and Harvey's *Social Justice and the City* (1973). As the titles of these works suggest, a central theme of the second culture of cities has always been an ideological critique of the modern capitalist mode of social organization. Heading into the 1980s, a strand of the second culture of cities became influenced by postmodern social theory, and began to emphasize the ever-evolving, relational, and contingent nature of cities, as in Soja's *Postmodern Geographies* (1989) and Castells' *The Rise of the Network Society* (1996).

In addition to these two paradigmatic cultures, Portugali argues, a possible third culture of cities has been brewing. Forerunners of this perspective, such as Jane Jacobs (1961) and Christopher Alexander (1965), echoed the second culture of cities in terms of the criticism of the relatively simple models and methods of the first culture. However, instead of social or ideological reasons, their criticism was rooted in a conceptualization of cities as fundamentally complex systems with emergent properties and dynamics of self-organization. Since then, a field of complexity science focusing on cities has emerged, applying formal complexity theories that originated in physics and biology, resulting in conceptualizations of cities as, for example, dissipative (Allen & Sanglier, 1981), fractal (Batty & Longley, 1994), and self-organizing (Portugali, 1997) systems. Parallel to these formalized approaches to complexity, social science theories of cities have also picked up the vocabulary of complexity science, but applied them in a qualitative sense. In this context, for example, theories of cities based on the concept of an "assemblage" have gained traction (Blok & Farias, 2016; de Roo et al., 2012).

As Portugali argues, these complexity-science-based approaches to cities have the potential to form a third culture of cities that acts as a bridge between the two earlier cultures. This is due to the nature of complexity as a paradigm that, on the one hand, lends itself to quantification and computational methods, but that also has an affinity with strands of the postmodernism-influenced social science theory in the second culture of cities (Cilliers, 1998). To act in this bridging function, however, the field would need to acknowledge the nature of cities as particular kinds of (socially) complex systems. Therefore, instead of merely transferring the theories and quantitative methods used for studying natural complex entities to the domain of urban studies, there is a need to explicitly engage with qualitative questions related to cities and complexity. Otherwise, the complexity science approach to cities risks being merely an updated version of the first culture of cities.

10.2.4 Four Selected Metaphors for Cities

As is obvious from this brief review, the city as an object of research can be approached from a broad variety of scientific perspectives that can be decidedly contrasting or even antagonistic toward each other. However, rather than being a problem, this is merely a reflection of the complex nature of cities. What is more, although the presentation in Section 10.2.3 of the three cultures of cities places them in chronological order, this should not be taken to mean that one culture has been supplanted or made obsolete by the appearance of another one. Instead, each culture adds depth to our understanding of cities and to the vocabulary we use to describe them. Indeed, all three cultures, as well as the metaphorical images influencing them, are very much alive today, both in science and in practice. Therefore, our selection of a set of metaphors for describing cities needs to be representative of the breadth of all the three cultures.

A challenge stemming from this breadth of scientific perspectives on cities is that the number of related metaphors is equally large (Nientied, 2016). For practical reasons, however, only a limited number of metaphors could be selected for our analysis. Therefore, instead of discussing every potential city metaphor, we decided to try to identify a small number of "proto-metaphors" that could represent to an adequate degree the variety of existing approaches to cities. In the selection of the most pertinent metaphors, three criteria in particular were employed. First, the metaphors had to be clearly distinguishable from each other. Second, the selected metaphors had to be complementary to each other in providing different vantage points on cities. Third, the selected metaphorical concepts had to be intuitively familiar and simple. This last criterion was followed in order to enable the analysis of the metaphors (see description of the analytical process in the Section 10.3) and in order to allow the reader to follow the logic of the discussion without a deeper knowledge of the origin of the related concepts.

These considerations led us to ultimately select four metaphors: *machine*, *organism*, *network*, and *melting pot*. To be clear, these four proto-metaphors are to be considered as "ideal types," in the sense introduced by Max Weber (Månson, 2000). Here, "ideal" does not imply any normative ranking (as in "better" or "worse"). Instead, it refers to the deliberately exaggerated accentuation of chosen aspects of complex phenomena in order to create prototypes against which real instances of the phenomena can be compared.

Definitions for the four terms, as found in the Oxford Dictionary (2019), are presented in Table 10.1. Two definitions are presented for each term, one representing a literal meaning and another representing a metaphorical meaning. In addition, the associations between the three cultures of cities and the four metaphorical perspectives are depicted in Figure 10.2. The four approaches to cities are introduced below in more detail.

It must be noted that, strictly speaking, a network, instead of being a *metaphor*, should be considered as a *metonymy* for the city.[1] Depending on the source, metonymy is considered to be either a type of metaphor, or an altogether different concept (Fass, 1988). While acknowledging the difference between the terms, for the sake of fluency in the following discussion, the term metaphor is also used to designate the network approach to cities.

Table 10.1 *Oxford Dictionary (2020) definitions of the metaphorical concepts*

Metaphor	Definition
Machine	An apparatus using mechanical power and having several parts, each with a definite function and together performing a particular task; An efficient and well-organized group of powerful people.
Organism	An individual animal, plant, or single-celled life form; A system or organization consisting of interdependent parts, compared to a living being.
Network	An arrangement of intersecting horizontal and vertical lines; A group or system of interconnected people or things.
Melting pot	A pot in which metals or other materials are melted and mixed; A place where different peoples, styles, theories, etc., are mixed together.

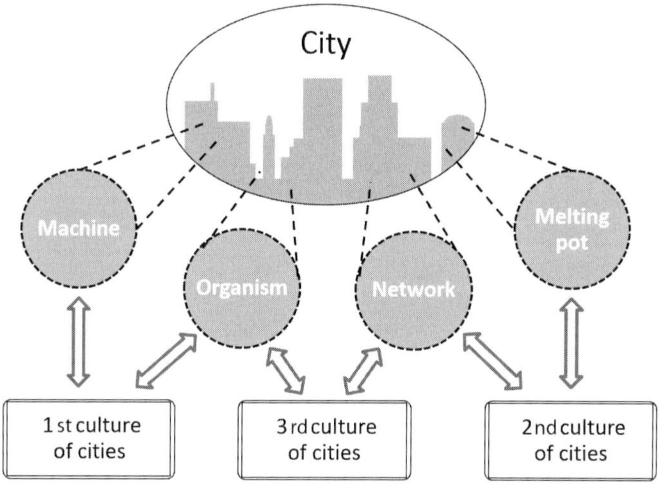

Figure 10.2 The three cultures of cities connected to the four metaphorical perspectives. Source: own illustration

The *machine* metaphor is associated with the first culture of cities. It represents the modernist ideal of solving the challenges associated with cities through rational and centralized urban planning (Lynch, 1984). A prominent example of this approach to cities is Le Corbusier's planned city *Ville Radieuse*, which sought to achieve optimization through strict functional zoning. In *Good City Form,* Kevin Lynch argues that "the machine model lies at the root of most of our current ways of dealing with cities: our practices of land subdivision, traffic engineering, utilities, health and building codes, zoning" (Lynch, 1984, p. 86). Lynch made his argument more than 30 years ago, and indeed, since then, the dominance of the machine view has been challenged by perspectives derived from the second and third cultures of cities. However, the image of cities as machines continues to wield influence both in science and in practice. For example, contemporary (perhaps more subtle) embodiments of the machine metaphor can be detected in the popular ideas of "smart" or "computable" cities (Angelidou, 2015; Batty, 1997).

Another metaphorical view with a long history is that of the city as an *organism*, which underlines the living character of cities (Lynch, 1984). This metaphor can be associated with both the first and third cultures of cities, because, on the one hand, it implies that cities can be studied with the methods of natural science, but on the other hand, also acknowledges that cities are more complex than mere machines. This perspective gained popularity originally as a reaction to the heavy industrialization of the nineteenth century. A classic example of the organic view of cities is the Garden City movement of Ebenezer Howard (1902). Today, the organic metaphor is prominent in, for example, initiatives for "greening" cities, as well as in several scientific fields studying cities, including industrial ecology (Lifset & Graedel, 2002), urban ecology (McDonnell, 2011), and parts of complexity science (Bettencourt et al., 2007).

The *network* view of cities has gained popularity more recently, and is associated with both the second and third cultures of cities. Alexander's (1965) thesis stating that a city is not a tree, but a semi-lattice structure, was a predecessor to this viewpoint. A couple of decades later, the network metaphor was forced into the center of public imagination by the advance of globalization and especially by the astonishing expansion of telecommunication networks in the 1980s and 1990s. Now, it is commonplace to conceptualize cities in terms of agglomerations of social, economic, and infrastructural connections that link places into networks that span both local and global scales. Scientific fields utilizing the network metaphor include complexity science (Batty, 2013; Bettencourt, 2015) and several strands of social science (Blok & Farias, 2016; Castells, 1996; Granovetter, 1973).

Finally, the metaphor of a city as a *melting pot* corresponds to the second culture of cities. The idea owes its origin to American cities that, especially in earlier times, were recipients of waves of immigration, and thereby hotbeds of multiculturalism. Although the metaphor is still commonly used, to some it is problematic as it connotes a more or less forced conformity with the dominant culture. Due to this, the melting pot metaphor is sometimes replaced with metaphors of the city as a kaleidoscope, a mosaic, or a salad bowl, which explicitly refer to a continuous coexistence of heterogeneous social groups and cultures (Fuchs, 1990; Hirschman, 1983; Kolb, 2009). Nevertheless, the issues that the melting pot metaphor raises, especially seeing the city as a site of intermingling and sometimes conflicting cultures and social groups, continue to be at the center of much of urban studies, including critical urban studies (Harvey, 2003) and urban political ecology (Heynen et al., 2006).

Table 10.2 presents a summary of the scientific fields, theories, and concepts that have been mentioned in the discussion, categorized under the umbrellas of the four metaphors. This list is by no means exhaustive, but represents an illustrative sample. In addition, as the four metaphorical perspectives represent ideal types, the categorization of the scientific fields and theories under a single metaphor is a simplification of their real nature. Nevertheless, the examples listed in the table are chosen because they are the ones that we perceive as being the closest representatives of the corresponding metaphorical perspectives.

Table 10.2 *Illustrative examples of scientific fields and theories for the four metaphors*

Metaphor	Machine	Organism	Network	Melting pot
Related culture of cities	1st	1st + 3rd	2nd + 3rd	2nd
Related scientific fields	• Physics • Economics	• Urban ecology • Industrial ecology	• Complex systems science • Economic sociology • Postmodern social science	• Critical social science • Urban political ecology
Related theories and concepts	• Location theory • Scaling laws	• Socioecological systems • Sociotechnical systems • Urban metabolism	• (Social) network theory • Complexity theory • Assemblage theory	• Marxist theory • Feminist theory

10.3 Analyzing the Selected Metaphors

10.3.1 Analytical Procedure

To facilitate a deeper understanding of the four approaches to cities, we devised an analytical framework consisting of system theory concepts that describe different aspects of a system (Bossel, 1999; Hester & Adams, 2017; see also Chapter 2 (Binder et al., 2020)). Table 10.3 lists these aspects and presents their definitions as they were understood within the context of this chapter. Eleven system aspects grouped under four themes were considered in total. Then, we characterized each metaphor across these eleven aspects. The analysis was performed through a collective discussion among the authors, with the ambition of capturing the characteristics of each metaphorical system in as few words as possible, and as clearly distinct from the other metaphors as possible. The results of this analysis are presented in Table 10.4 and discussed separately for each metaphor below. After the characterization of the metaphorical systems, our analysis proceeded to derive the implications that each approach has for assessing the sustainability of urban systems. These implications cover four dimensions of sustainability assessment: (i) the purpose of sustainability assessment; (ii) participants and their roles; (iii) the underlying principles of sustainability; (iv) the conceptual system model guiding indicator selection.

To repeat a point already made, the purpose of this analytical strategy is to consider the four metaphorical perspectives as "ideal types" that facilitate the analysis and comparison of real-life cases. As such, these ideal types are not expected to have perfectly matching counterparts in real-life cases, and therefore, are not meant as a typology for a strict classification of these cases. Rather, the four ideal typical approaches to urban systems, and the corresponding four ideal-typical sustainability assessment designs that are discussed in the following sections, act

Table 10.3 *The system aspects and their definitions used in characterizing the metaphors*

System aspects	Definition	Theme
Boundary	Describes the delimiting of the system in space and time, thus marking what is inside and what is outside.	Delimiting the system
Environment	Describes the system's relationship to its surroundings.	
Inputs/outputs	Describes what enters and exits the system across the system boundary.	
Purposes	Describes the overarching goal(s) toward which the behavior of the system is oriented.	Understanding the system
Functions	Describes the activities performed by the system in serving its purpose.	
Elements	Describes the constitutive parts of the system.	Analyzing the system
Organization	Describes the patterns and interrelations of the system's constituent elements.	
Dynamics	Describes the typical modes of changes in and of the system.	
Monitoring	Describes the typical objects and variables to be monitored for the governance of the system.	Governing the system
Information	Describes the types of data to be collected and knowledge to be produced (epistemology) about the system.	
Decision-making	Describes the typical character and goals of the steering processes of the system.	

as an analytical framework for detecting tendencies, similarities, and differences in real-life cases of approaches to urban systems and their assessment.

10.3.2 The City as a Machine

Interpretation of the metaphor – Likening an urban system to a machine portrays it as a clearly delineated unit, discrete from its surroundings. The inputs fed into the system are transformed into outputs through internal processes that can be expressed in mathematical production functions. In fact, the very meaning of the system can be expressed in clear instrumental terms: it is the satisfaction of well-defined needs by the deliberate use of the aforementioned production functions. The machine metaphor also emphasizes the tangible and human-made elements of the system and expects that they are organized into relatively clear-cut, static, and hierarchical structures. This suggests that the system behaves in a

Table 10.4 *The proposed characteristics of the four metaphors*

System aspects	Machine	Organism	Network	Melting pot
Boundary	Administrative	Functional	Arbitrary	Spatial and cultural
Environment	Decoupled	Rooted	Inseparable	Receptive
Inputs/outputs	In: materials and energy; Out: products	In: materials and energy; Out: secondary resources	In and out: everything	In: people, ideas, cultures; Out: innovation
Purposes	Satisfaction of practical needs	Survival and reproduction	Creating and maintaining associations	Coalescence and creation
Functions	Production	Metabolism	Transmission and movement	Assembly and mixing
Elements	Artificial and tangible materials and components	Natural and artificial; tangible materials and organs	Connections and nodes – artificial and natural; tangible and intangible	Intangible and tangible human constructs and processes
Organization	Hierarchical, designed, static, and clear units	Hierarchical structures; spontaneously but slowly evolving units	Ad hoc hierarchies; emerging and dynamic units	Formal and informal hierarchies; dynamic units
Dynamics	Linear and predictable	Evolutionary and homeostatic	Non-linear and non-causal	Unpredictable and discontinuous
Monitoring	Objects: inputs and outputs; Criteria: efficiency	Objects: organ functions; Criteria: health and resilience	Objects: networks; Criteria: connectivity and distances	Objects: social interactions; Criteria: harmony, equity, and innovation
Information	Objective quantitative data; general laws	Objective quantitative and qualitative data; general principles	Statistics, big data; correlations, predictions	Qualitative and quantitative data; heuristics, theory
Decision-making	Mode: top-down control; Aim: process optimization	Mode: top-down influence; Aim: learning, adaptation, and remediation	Mode: modular and experimental governance; Aim: reactive self-organization	Mode: top-down rules and bottom-up norms; Aim: conflict resolution and harmonious self-organization

linear and predictable manner. Thus, taking this perspective represents the ambition to tame complexity into manageable problems to be tackled in a top-down manner and with the tools and theories of natural sciences and economics.

Strengths and weaknesses of the metaphor – The merit of this perspective is that it urges us to systematically search for regularities in the behavior of the system as well as for rational explanations for these behaviors. In this way, the knowledge that is produced is more palatable to decision-makers, as it translates complex information about the system into more actionable generalizations. The weakness of the perspective derives from its tendency to drastically simplify the system. In this simplification, elements of the system (including human beings) are placed in strict categories that may be inappropriate. Also, the focus is biased toward *currently* existing (or dominant) structures and functions at the expense of ones that are yet non-existing (or subordinate). Perhaps the most serious danger with the machine metaphor is that it implicitly places power over the system in the hands of an all-knowing expert, while understating the variety of values and preferences present in urban systems.

Archetypal design for sustainability assessment – Following the logic of the machine metaphor, the *purpose of sustainability assessment* is to facilitate the optimization of the production processes of the system. The knowledge produced by the assessment is translated directly into decisions, which are executed in a top-down fashion. *Participants* are selected and involved in the assessment process based on their utility in providing information or in implementing the decisions that are taken. The selection of participants is also limited to stakeholders within the system. The machine metaphor postulates that the predominant *principle of sustainability* is efficiency, and the goals and criteria for the assessment are interpreted accordingly in terms of the efficiency of the production processes and the satisfaction of existing practical needs. The *system model* guiding the selection of relevant indicators consists of internal production processes and the related input-output relationships. The focus is on tangible and objectively measurable elements and variables. The boundary for the system is drawn along administrative lines.

10.3.3 The City as an Organism

Interpretation of the metaphor – Contemplating the urban system through the metaphor of an organism frames it as a discrete unit, but, compared to the machine metaphor, one that is more connected to and influenced by its surroundings. The system consumes its inputs in metabolic functions and discharges leftover products into its surroundings. The metabolic functions serve the system's ultimate purpose: survival and reproduction. The organism metaphor focuses on both human-made and natural elements within the system. These elements are grouped into differentiated but interdependent organs, which in turn are organized hierarchically and following a functional rationality. The system evolves steadily along homeostatic, self-regulating pathways. Compared to the machine metaphor, the organism metaphor thus retains a higher level of complexity. In science, these ideas are translated into the analysis of cities' metabolic flows, and into theories of cities as integrated socio-ecological-technical systems.

Strengths and weaknesses of the metaphor – The strength of the organism metaphor is that it reminds us that cities are interlinked human and natural systems. Changing the emphasis from immediate efficiency (as in the machine metaphor) to survival expands the time horizon from short-term to long-term thinking, and also brings into focus the system's impacts on its surroundings. In terms of shortcomings, although the organism metaphor does convey a more variegated and nuanced image of the city than the machine metaphor, like the latter, it also assumes a relatively small number of essential, static functions and purposes for the system. Normatively, then, aspects of the urban system that do not instrumentally contribute to these predefined functions are (at least implicitly) considered as undesirable and redundant. Again, considering the diversity of people in urban systems, such a view may have problematic practical and ethical consequences.

Archetypal design for sustainability assessment – The organism metaphor suggests that the *purpose of sustainability assessment* is to learn about the functional health of the different organs of the system, and to use the information to understand the areas where adaptations and remediation are necessary. The resulting decisions are implemented with consideration of possible systemic interdependencies and feedbacks. *Participant* selection for the assessment is based on decision-making authority and substantive expertise. This also includes representatives of stakeholders affected by the external impacts of the system. The central *principles of sustainability* promoted by the organism perspective are health and resilience, which form the criteria for evaluating the metabolic socioecological processes of the urban system. The boundary of the *system model* is drawn along functional lines (containing sources and sinks), and the model consists of distinct but interrelated functions and organs. The focus is thus particularly on indicators that represent tangible elements and variables.

10.3.4 The City as a Network

Interpretation of the metaphor – The network perspective integrates the urban system into its surroundings to such an extent that delineating the boundary of the system becomes a matter of arbitrary, ad hoc choice. The system is fully open to receiving any inputs, and indeed, the creation and maintenance of connections both locally and globally forms the central purpose of the system. The functions of the system deal primarily with the transmission and transport of all types of things (people, information, materials, etc.). That is, the focus covers human-made and natural, and tangible and intangible elements of the system. In terms of structural units of the system, the network image depicts the system as consisting of connected nodes, where the connections between nodes sometimes take on a greater importance than the nodes themselves. In its default state, the system displays an extremely flat hierarchy, from which more organized units may emerge on an ad hoc basis. The dynamics of the system are therefore more driven by self-organization than top-down planning. Predicting the behavior of the system depends on statistical analyses, while attributing causality becomes nearly impossible due to the presence of many feedbacks. Scientific theories and methods proceeding from the network metaphor deliberately embrace the complexity of the system and resist the urge to present it in neatly organized static models.

Strengths and weaknesses of the metaphor – Of the four perspectives under comparison here, the network perspective has the most dynamic image of systems. Consequently, the strength of this perspective is that it pushes for the development of theories and methods that are sophisticated enough to take on the full extent of the complexity of real-world urban systems. The metaphor can also be seen as beneficial from a democratic point of view, as it promotes a non-hierarchical, self-organizing form of social organization over top-down command. At the same time, the image can be criticized as naive, as it turns a blind eye to the inevitable existence of structural power differences and hierarchies within societies. In this way, analyses based on the network perspective sometimes remain superficial in their focus on overt data and their neglect of the causes of the observed phenomena.

Archetypal design for sustainability assessment – Taking the network approach, the *purpose of sustainability assessment* is to provide information for the self-organizing processes of the system. Therefore, the results of the assessment are disseminated to the system without decisions being implemented in any centralized fashion. The process is open to *participants*, who are determined based on voluntary interest and social connections. The *principles of sustainability* that inform the goals and criteria of the assessment relate to the connectivity of the system and the quality of the connections. The *system model* consists of a wide range of interconnected processes. The indicator list that is drawn from this model is built up of statistical measures of connections and flows. Because of the characteristic ad hoc nature of the system's boundary, the system model has to be tailored for each assessment according to the particular needs and mandate of the assessment in question.

10.3.5 The City as a Melting Pot

Interpretation of the metaphor – The metaphor of the melting pot stresses the social complexity that is present in urban systems. In this case, the system boundary is determined by the reach of social interactions, which are confined culturally and spatially. The functions of the melting pot bring together and mix different people, ideas, and cultures, and they constantly receive fresh inputs from the outside. The purpose of the system is to facilitate the coexistence and cross-pollination of these varied elements, thereby also enabling the creation of innovations and transformations of varying degrees. The metaphor pays most attention to elements related to the human world, with these elements organized into formal and informal hierarchies that change with varying speeds. The dynamics implied by the melting pot metaphor are unpredictable and discontinuous, as competing tendencies toward homogeneity and heterogeneity, as well as toward harmony and disharmony, exist simultaneously. These aspects of the urban system are typically researched with the help of theories and methods belonging to the fields of social, economic, and political sciences.

Strengths and weaknesses of the metaphor – The strength of the melting pot metaphor over the previous metaphors derives from its close attention to phenomena that are distinct to the social world. These include processes of innovation and social renewal, but also cultural and economic conflict. This sensitivity toward social complexity causes the perspective to tend toward inclusiveness and openness to pluralistic viewpoints. A weakness of the perspective relates to its anthropocentrism, as, arguably, the pure focus on social issues and interactions within urban systems tends toward a disregard of the material realities beyond the social sphere, such as the environmental effects of urban lifestyles. Also, as discussed above, depending on the specific interpretation given to the metaphor, it may be taken in some cases to gloss over the potential difficulties faced by marginalized groups when "melted" together with more hegemonic cultures and social groups. Therefore, when deploying the melting pot metaphor, an awareness of issues related to power is essential.

Archetypal design for sustainability assessment – From the point of view of the melting pot metaphor, the *purpose of sustainability assessment* is facilitating the detection and resolution of social conflict, as well as the promotion of mutual understanding and interaction among the inhabitants of a city. Accordingly, the process aims for broad *participation*, with stakeholders engaged from both the local government and from various community groups. The implementation of the findings of the assessment consists simultaneously of policymaking and community-based action. The melting pot metaphor implies the need to maximize the positive effects and limit the negative effects of social interactions. In other words, the central *principles of sustainability* for the metaphor are social harmony, equity, and innovation. These principles are applied to the evaluation of different social and political processes, which constitute the *system model* underpinning the assessment, and which can be both negative (e.g., crime) and positive (e.g., mutual learning). As already mentioned, the boundary of the system model is defined by the reach of social interactions.

10.3.6 Summary of Implications for Sustainability Assessment

This analysis began from four intuitive metaphorical images of cities, each with a legitimate claim to describe important aspects of urban systems. By elucidating their implications in more depth, our subsequent analysis then demonstrated how dramatically divergent these images indeed are. Table 10.5 summarizes the contrasts between the four perspectives when it comes to the implications that they have for different dimensions of sustainability assessment. The table demonstrates where the power of the metaphors lies; it is in their ability to create normative expectations about what is important in urban systems, what are the desired directions of development, how they are to be assessed, and by whom.

The framework provided by Table 10.5 can serve at least two distinct functions. First, it can be used as a framework for the analysis and comparison of past and present applications

Table 10.5 *Dimensions of sustainability assessment interpreted for the four metaphors*

Metaphor	Purpose of assessment	Participation	Sustainability principles	Model of the system
Machine	Optimization	Based on utility	Efficiency	Practical functions within an administrative boundary
Organism	Learning and adaptation	Based on decision-making authority and substantive expertise	Health and resilience	Metabolic functions within a functional boundary
Network	Provision of information	Based on voluntary interest and social connections	Connectivity	Connections and flows within an ad hoc boundary
Melting pot	Conflict resolution	Broad participation of government and community representatives	Harmony, equity, innovation	Social and political processes within a boundary defined by social interactions

of sustainability assessment. Second, the framework can be taken as a guideline for designing future applications of sustainability assessment. In both cases, the framework can serve to enhance the reflexivity and transparency of sustainability assessment practice.

10.4 Discussion and Conclusion

The premise of this chapter is the insight that cities as complex systems can be conceptualized in different, equally legitimate ways. At the same time, different perspectives are not identical in their normative implications. Therefore, to appreciate these value-laden consequences, there is a need for reflexivity and transparency with regard to the emphases, strengths, and weaknesses of different conceptual approaches in analyzing and assessing the sustainability of urban systems. The argument made here is that this requirement can be addressed by identifying a typology of ideal-typical approaches derived from commonly used metaphors of cities. This typology can then be deployed to understand in more depth differences in conceptualizations of cities and in practical applications of sustainability assessment. To this end, our analysis teased out two frameworks, one for discussing differences and similarities between approaches to conceptualizing urban systems in general (Table 10.4), and one directed more specifically at analyzing approaches to the assessment of urban systems (Table 10.5).

In the assessment of urban systems, it is possible to envision at least three different strategies for using the different metaphorical perspectives. First, the different metaphors may all be applied concurrently with the aim of creating a conceptualization that is as comprehensive and balanced as possible. The second and third strategies take a more qualified approach. The second strategy makes a distinction between different parts of the urban system, and applies the most appropriate metaphor for each part (e.g., efficient economy, equitable society, resilient ecology). The third strategy suggests a temporal distinction. For example, it may be that during different phases in the historical trajectory of a city, different metaphors become more apt for guiding the development and assessment of the urban system.

The use of metaphors is not merely a literary exercise, but in fact an indispensable tool for dealing with complex reality. Whether employed explicitly or implicitly, such mental models can be detected as underpinning conceptualizations and assessments of urban systems. However, the use of descriptive metaphors entails juxtaposing things that are not perfectly identical. Hence, the obfuscated or one-sided use of metaphors can also have adverse consequences if the extent of their applicability is not understood properly. In particular, while several metaphors exist that can provide valuable additions to our library of mental models, no metaphor alone can capture the urban system completely. Therefore, frames of analysis like those provided by this chapter are required to provide the language that enables communication and collaboration across the boundaries of different approaches and scientific disciplines. In particular, parallel to advances in machine learning and big data analysis, there is a need for equal advances in interdisciplinary conceptual frameworks that can help give meaning to the vast amounts of information produced by these methods.

As our presentation shows, the city as a problem transcends disciplinary boundaries. Therefore, for a comprehensive conceptualization of urban systems that covers all four metaphorical perspectives, it is necessary to draw insights from several scientific fields. For example, the socioecological systems (Ostrom, 2009) and sociotechnical systems (Geels, 2004) approaches can provide insights into and concepts for the natural and technological aspects of urban systems respectively. However, in order to address the self-organizing and emerging characteristics of urban systems, one has to turn to approaches more aligned with the concept of complexity, whether in its "hard" (Batty, 2013) or "soft" form (Blok & Farias, 2016; Morin, 2007). The more functionalist approaches to systems also have to be complemented with approaches sensitive to questions of power and conflict (Smith & Stirling, 2010). Finally, it is worthwhile to heed the warnings of those critical of even using the term "system" to begin with, as it may portray cities as static and definitively definable wholes, in contrast to seeing them as ever-evolving and intrinsically contested (Gillard et al., 2016).

Some interesting directions of research can be mentioned that would build on the work presented in this chapter. First, a comparative analysis of existing applications of sustainability assessment can be carried out with the analytical framework of Table 10.5. Second, the dimensions of sustainability assessment described in Table 10.5 can be augmented by identifying a set of indicators considered as typical for each of the four metaphors. This will concretize the metaphorical perspectives further, and thus enhance the potential of the metaphor typology as a scheme for designing assessments of urban systems. Furthermore, to add to the depth of consideration of different aspects of urban systems, the typology of the four metaphors can be refined further. For example, in the case of geographical and cultural contexts beyond those represented by the authors, additional metaphors to those considered in this chapter can prove to be fruitful and appropriate.

To conclude, we consider that the different metaphors do not merely accentuate different aspects of the reality of cities, but when used as blueprints for guiding the analysis and assessment of urban systems, they also represent different aspirational images of what the city should be. In other words, then, what is at stake in the rivalry between different metaphorical perspectives is the negotiation of a mutually liveable city for both its residents and those affected by it.

Note

1. Metaphor is defined as a "figure of speech in which a word or phrase literally denoting one kind of object or idea is used in place of another to suggest a likeness or analogy between them" (Merriam-Webster, 2020). Metonymy is defined as a "figure of speech consisting of the use of the name of one thing for that of another of which it is an attribute or with which it is associated" (Merriam-Webster, 2020).

References

Alexander, C. (1965). A city is not a tree. *Archit Forum*, *1965*(April-May), 58–62.

Allen, P. M., & Sanglier, M. (1981). Urban evolution, self-organization, and decisionmaking. *Environment and Planning A*, 13(2), 167–183. https://doi.org/10.1068/a130167.

Angelidou, M. (2015). Smart cities: A conjuncture of four forces. *Cities*, *47*, 95–106. https://doi.org/10.1016/j.cities.2015.05.004.

Auerbach, F. (1913). Das Gesetz der Bevölkerungskonzentration. *Petermanns Geographische Mitteilungen*, 59, 74–76.

Batty, M. (1997). The computable city. *International Planning Studies*, 2(2), 155–173. https://doi.org/10.1080/13563479708721676.

Batty, M. (2013). *The New Science of Cities*. Cambridge, MA; London: MIT Press.

Batty, M., & Longley, P. A. (1994). *Fractal Cities: A Geometry of Form and Function*. London: Academic Press.

Bettencourt, L. M. A. (2015). Cities as complex systems. In A. F. Bernardo, P. A. M. Sakowski, & M. H. Tóvolli (eds.), *Modeling Complex Systems for Public Policies*. Brasilia: Institute for Applied Economic Research, pp. 217–238.

Bettencourt, L. M. A., Lobo, J., Helbing, D., Kühnert, C., & West, G. B. (2007). Growth, innovation, scaling, and the pace of life in cities. *Proceedings of the National Academy of Sciences*, 104(17), 7301. https://doi.org/10.1073/pnas.0610172104.

Binder, C. R, Hutter, M., Pang, M., & Webb, R. (2020). System science and sustainability assessment. In C. R. Binder, E. Massaro, & R. Wyss (eds.), *Sustainability Assessment in Urban Systems*. Cambridge University Press: pp. 30–64.

Blok, A., & Farias, I. (Eds.). (2016). *Urban Cosmopolitics: Agencements, Assemblies, Atmospheres*. New York: Routledge.

Bossel, H. (1999). *Indicators for Sustainable Development: Theory, Method, Applications; A Report to the Balaton Group*. Winnipeg: IISD.

Castells, M. (1972). *La question urbaine*. Paris: François Maspero.

Castells, M. (1996). *The Rise of the Network Society, The Information Age: Economy, Society and Culture*, vol. I. Malden: Blackwell.

Christaller, W. (1966). *Central Places in Southern Germany*. Englewood Cliffs: Prentice Hall.
Cilliers, P. (1998). *Complexity and Postmodernism: Understanding Complex Systems*. London; New York: Routledge.
Cilliers, P. (2008). Complexity theory as a general framework for sustainability science. In M. Burns & A. Weaver (eds.), *Exploring Sustainability Science – A Southern African Perspective*. Stellenbosch: African Sun Media, pp. 9–26.
de Roo, G., Hillier, J., & van Wezemael, J. (2012). *Complexity and Planning: Systems, Assemblages and Simulations*. Farnham: Ashgate.
Fass, D. (1988). Metonymy and metaphor: What's the difference? *Proceedings of the 12th Conference on Computational Linguistics*, 177–181. https://doi.org/10.3115/991635.991671.
Fuchs, L. H. (1990). *The American kaleidoscope: Race, ethnicity, and the civic culture*. Hanover; London: Wesleyan University Press.
Gasparatos, A. (2010). Embedded value systems in sustainability assessment tools and their implications. *Journal of Environmental Management*, 91(8), 1613–1622. https://doi.org/10.1016/j.jenvman.2010.03.014.
Geels, F. W. (2004). From sectoral systems of innovation to socio-technical systems. *Research Policy*, 33(6–7), 897–920. https://doi.org/10.1016/j.respol.2004.01.015.
Gillard, R., Gouldson, A., Paavola, J., & Van Alstine, J. (2016). Transformational responses to climate change: beyond a systems perspective of social change in mitigation and adaptation. *Wiley Interdisciplinary Reviews: Climate Change*, 7(2), 251–265. https://doi.org/10.1002/wcc.384.
Granovetter, M. S. (1973). The strength of weak ties. *American Journal of Sociology*, 5(1), 1360–1380. https://doi.org/10.1086/225469.
Griggs, D., Stafford-Smith, M., Gaffney, O., et al. (2013). Sustainable development goals for people and planet: Policy. *Nature*, 495(7441), 305–307. https://doi.org/10.1038/495305a.
Hák, T., Janoušková, S., & Moldan, B. (2016). Sustainable development goals: A need for relevant indicators. *Ecological Indicators*, 60, 565–573. https://doi.org/10.1016/j.ecolind.2015.08.003.
Harvey, D. (1973). *Social Justice and the City*. London: Arnold.
Harvey, D. (2003). The right to the city. *International Journal of Urban and Regional Research*, 27(4), 939–941. https://doi.org/10.1111/j.0309-1317.2003.00492.x.
Hester, P. T., & Adams, K. M. (2017). *Systemic Decision Making*, 2nd ed. Cham: Springer International Publishing.
Heynen, N., Kaika, M., & Swyngedouw, E. (Eds.). (2006). *In the Nature of Cities: Urban Political Ecology and the Politics of Urban Metabolism*. London; New York: Routledge.
Hirschman, C. (1983). America's melting pot reconsidered. *Annual Review of Sociology*, 9(1), 397–423. https://doi.org/10.1146/annurev.so.09.080183.002145.
Hodgson, G. M. (1997). Metaphor and pluralism in economics: Mechanics and biology. In A. Salanti & E. Screpanti (eds.), *Pluralism in Economics: New Perspectives in History and Methodology*. Cheltenham; Brookfield: Edward Elgar, pp. 131–154.
Howard, E. (1902). *Garden Cities of To-morrow*. London: Swan Sonnenschein & Company.
ISO. (2014). ISO 37120:2014 – Sustainable development of communities: Indicators for city services and quality of life. www.iso.org/standard/62436.html (accessed 7.8.19).
Jacobs, J. (1961). *The Death and Life of Great American Cities*. London: Penguin Books.
James, P. (2015). *Urban Sustainability in Theory and Practice: Circles of Sustainability*. London ; New York: Routledge.
Kolb, E. (2009). *The Evolution of New York City's Multiculturalism: Melting Pot or Salad Bowl*. BoD–Books on Demand.
Le Corbusier (1964). *La ville radieuse: éléments d'une doctrine d'urbanisme pour l'équipement de la civilisation machinist*. Paris: Editions Vincent Fréal et Cie.
Lefebvre, H. (1968). *Le droit à la ville*. Paris: Anthropos.
Lifset, R., & Graedel, T. E. (2002). Industrial ecology: goals and definitions. In R. Ayres & L. Ayres (eds.), *A Handbook of Industrial Ecology*. Cheltenham; Northampton, MA: Edward Elgar, pp. 3–15.
Lösch, A. (1954). *The Economics of Location*. New Haven: Yale University Press.
Lynch, K. (1984). *Good City Form*. Cambridge, MA: MIT press.

Maclaren, V. W. (1996). Urban Sustainability Reporting. *Journal of the American Planning Association*, 62(2), 184–202. https://doi.org/10.1080/01944369608975684.
Månson, P. (2000). Max Weber. In H. Andersen & L. B. Kaspersen (eds.), *Classical and Modern Social Theories*. Malden, MA: Blackwell, pp. 75–95.
McDonnell, M. J. (2011). The history of urban ecology. In J. Niemelä, J. H. Breuste, T. Elmqvist, G. Guntenspergen, P. James, & N. E. McIntyre (eds.), *Urban Ecology: Patterns, Processes, and Applications*. Oxford: Oxford University Press, pp. 5–13.
Meadows, D. H. (1998). *Indicators and Information Systems for Sustainable Development: A Report to the Balaton Group*. Hartland Four Corners, VT: The Sustainability Institute.
Merriam-Webster. (2020). Online dictionary. www.merriam-webster.com/ (accessed 11.3.19).
Morin, E. (2007). Restricted complexity, general complexity. In C. Gershenson, D. Aerts, & B. Edmonds (eds.), *Worldviews, Science and Us: Philosophy and Complexity*. Singapore: World Scientific, pp. 5–29.
Nientied, P. (2016). Metaphor and urban studies: A crossover, theory and a case study of SS Rotterdam. *City, Territory and Architecture*, 3(1). https://doi.org/10.1186/s40410-016-0051-z.
Ostrom, E. (2009). A general framework for analyzing sustainability of social-ecological systems. *Science*, 325(5939), 419. https://doi.org/10.1126/science.1172133.
Oxford Dictionaries. (2020). English Dictionary. https://en.oxforddictionaries.com/ (accessed 3.6.18).
Park, R. E., Burgess, E. W., & McKenzie, R. D. (1925). *The City*. Chicago and London: University of Chicago Press.
Pickett, S. T. A., Cadenasso, M. L., & Grove, J. M. (2004). Resilient cities: Meaning, models, and metaphor for integrating the ecological, socio-economic, and planning realms. *Landscape and Urban Planning*, 69(4), 369–384. https://doi.org/10.1016/j.landurbplan.2003.10.035.
Pintér, L., Hardi, P., Martinuzzi, A., & Hall, J. (2012). Bellagio STAMP: Principles for sustainability assessment and measurement. *Ecological Indicators*, 17, 20–28. https://doi.org/10.1016/j.ecolind.2011.07.001.
Pope, J., Bond, A., Hugé, J., & Morrison-Saunders, A. (2017). Reconceptualising sustainability assessment. *Environmental Impact Assessment Review*, 62, 205–215. https://doi.org/10.1016/j.eiar.2016.11.002.
Portugali, J. (1997). Self-organizing cities. *Futures*, 29(4–5), 353–380. https://doi.org/10.1016/S0016-3287(97)00022-0.
Portugali, J. (2011). *Complexity, Cognition and the City*. Heidelberg; New York: Springer.
Portugali, J. (2016). What makes cities complex? In J. Portugali & E. Stolk (eds.), *Complexity, Cognition, Urban Planning and Design*. Cham: Springer International Publishing, pp. 3–19.
Shen, L. -Y., Jorge Ochoa, J., Shah, M. N., & Zhang, X. (2011). The application of urban sustainability indicators – A comparison between various practices. *Habitat International*, *35*(1), 17–29. https://doi.org/10.1016/j.habitatint.2010.03.006.
Simmel, G. (1903). *Die Großstädte und das Geistesleben [The metropolis and mental life]*. Dresden: Petermann.
Smith, A., & Stirling, A. (2010). The politics of social-ecological resilience and sustainable socio-technical transitions. *Ecology and Society*, 15(1). https://doi.org/10.5751/ES-03218-150111.
Snow, C. P. (1964). *The Two Cultures and a Second Look: An Expanded Version of The Two Cultures and the Scientific Revolution*. Cambridge: Cambridge University Press.
Soja, E. W. (1989). *Postmodern Geographies: The Reassertion of Space in Critical Social Theory*. London; New York: Verso.
Turcu, C. (2013). Re-thinking sustainability indicators: Local perspectives of urban sustainability. *Journal of Environmental Planning and Management*, 56(5), 695–719. https://doi.org/10.1080/09640568.2012.698984.
Von Thünen, J. H. (1966). *Isolated State: An English Edition of Der isolierte Staat*. Oxford: Pergamon Press.
Wells, J. (2012). *Complexity and sustainability*. London; New York: Routledge.
World Bank. (2018). *Urban Sustainability Framework*, 1st edition. Washington, DC: World Bank.

11

Sustainability Issues in Urban Systems from a Metabolic Perspective

João Meirelles, Anna Pagani, Aristide Athanassiadis, and Claudia R. Binder

11.1 Introduction

Identifying and measuring sustainability issues in urban systems seems a daunting task. Indeed, measuring "development that meets the needs of the present without compromising the ability of future generation to meet their own needs" (Brundtland, 1987) can seem like a very abstract and non-quantitative exercise. Translated into an urban context, sustainability could be understood as a state where inhabitants' needs can be met without compromising the needs of future generations both locally and globally (Alberti, 1996). Numerous organizations have attempted to measure the sustainability of cities (see Chapter 14 (Massaro et al., 2020)) and numerous key indicators have been developed for this purpose, but no consensus on how to do so exists as yet due to diverging definitions of what the sustainable city might entail and what the key sustainability challenges are (Alberti, 1996; see also Chapter 10 (Halla et al., 2020)). The endeavor of defining the sustainability of cities and identifying the associated challenges is made even more difficult by the fact that cities are open systems that are heavily dependent on a global supply area for the resources they use and for waste treatment, and therefore they affect the environment, the economy, and societies in numerous ways and at multiples scales (Grimm et al., 2008). The interconnected nature of cities – to each other through a global production-consumption network, as well as to local and global ecological services – highlights the fact that sustainability measures require a systematic interdisciplinary analysis across different spatial and temporal scales (Cumming et al., 2006; Ramaswami et al., 2012).

Alberti (1996) argues that urban sustainability indicators will not enable us to tackle sustainability challenges until we better understand both how cities function and what the relationship is between social and economic gains on the one hand and environmental quality at different scales on the other. Research on this topic is ever expanding, exploring different aspects of the aforementioned relationship and functioning (Bai, 2016; Beloin-Saint-Pierre et al., 2017; Dijst et al., 2018). While there are numerous perspectives from which to approach urban sustainability, one of the most prominent is urban metabolism, which studies the city as a system that mobilizes flows (of energy, materials, water, capital, etc.) (Pincetl et al., 2012). This analogy enables a systems-wide perspective, which appears to hold potential for taking into account all the entangled challenges of cities. Yet, as will be presented in the next section, urban metabolism has been tackled from very different perspectives and is not (yet) a consolidated research field. Therefore, there is still no comprehensive understanding of the effect urbanization has on global sustainability, assumed here to be a global version of the Brundtland Commission's definition: "Sustainable development is development that meets the needs of the present without compromising the ability of future generations to meet their own needs" (Brundtland, 1987).

The current chapter aims to provide an integrative view of the sustainability challenges of urban systems at an aggregate level. In doing so, we aim to look into how urbanization has affected the long-term sustainability of our societies and economies. Thus, we depart from a historical perspective and combine different evidences into a general and systemic metabolic view on the effects of urbanization on social, environmental, and economical sustainability.

This chapter is structured as follows: We first briefly present the key research fields that have been looking into the question of urban sustainability from an urban metabolism lens. While urban metabolism manages to incorporate a range of features of urban sustainability, it still fails to provide a comprehensive understanding of the relation between cities and sustainability. To provide a more general understanding, in Section 11.3, we derive a list of characteristics of cities from urban studies and explore their implications for global sustainability. From this, we seek to clarify what, according to the literature, are the intrinsic characteristics of cities and what differentiates them from other ways of organizing society spatially. Section 11.4 considers more specifically the sustainability implications of these urban characteristics and tests the derived sustainability implications of the urban features against empirical evidence by collecting a list of indicators and studying their evolution over time, in parallel to the global process of urbanization. Based on this analysis, we conclude that a new, more integrated and multidisciplinary approach to urban sustainability is still required to develop a common language, consolidate research efforts, and eventually enable cross-pollination among existing research streams (Dijst et al., 2018).

11.2 Looking at Urban Sustainability through an Urban Metabolism Lens

Urban metabolism has been described as a concept, analogy, phenomenon, disciplinary framework, or even accounting method that focuses on the sustainability of cities. This perspective is gaining considerable momentum in the academic realm, and lately also in the policy and practice realms, and numerous research outputs have been emerging (Musango et al., 2017). At its core, urban metabolism reveals cities as living organisms, in that they mobilize and transform flows of, for example, materials, energy, and information in order to function. This reading enables us to adopt a systems-wide perspective when considering urban challenges, and especially in terms of sustainability. In order to better capture the complexity of a city, as well as include the three pillars of sustainability (Brundtland, 1987), urban metabolism studies investigate human-environment relationships at different

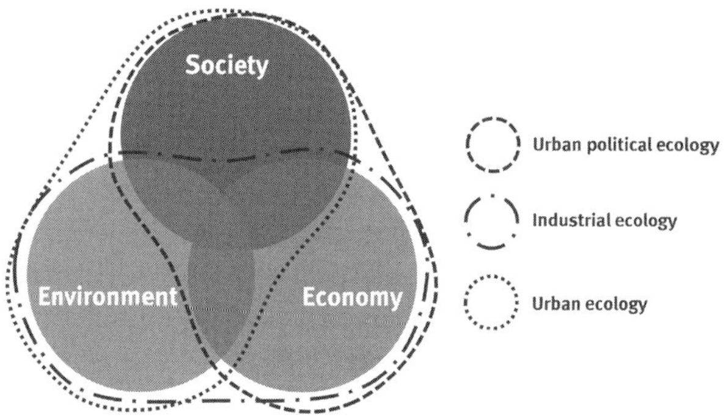

Figure 11.1 How the three ecologies of urban metabolism cover the pillars of (urban) sustainability. Source: own illustration

temporal and spatial scales and between different sub-systems. Yet, urban metabolism is not a consolidated field.

According to Wachsmuth (2012), the analogy of urban metabolism was used at different points in time and by different scholars to characterize the relationship between society and nature, especially during the twentieth century. Through his historical intellectual overview, he identified urban metabolism periods based on three different disciplines, namely human ecology, industrial ecology, and urban political ecology.

Newell and Cousins (2015) also identified three different "ecologies" that bring together a considerable share of the research carried out today in the urban metabolism field, namely, urban political ecology, urban ecology, and industrial ecology. In their study, human ecology was not included, as after the initial efforts of the Chicago School of Sociology, this discipline eventually tapered off. Nevertheless, while these communities use the same metaphor and analogy (although the use of some metaphors is criticized on linguistic grounds (Golubiewski, 2012)), they don't cover similar challenges and don't refer to similar intellectual references and backgrounds. In fact, their studies have created islands of knowledge with little interaction and cross-pollination (Bai, 2016; Newell and Cousins, 2015). The siloed approach of these communities results in them addressing neighboring urban sustainability challenges, failing to cover all three sustainability pillars simultaneously. Figure 11.1 presents, in a schematic and rather simplified manner, which aspects of urban sustainability each of these three research subdisciplines covers. To avoid any unnecessary confusion, this chapter will briefly describe these three ecologies separately and mention which aspects of urban sustainability they cover.

11.2.1 Urban Ecology

Urban ecology is perhaps the longest-lasting and most diverse research community of the three, due to the numerous theoretical and empirical disciplines encompassed (McPhearson et al., 2016). It is also the only one that truly originates from the science of ecology and therefore its name is semantically the most accurate. In reality, the metaphor "urban ecology" was also used during the human ecology period of urban metabolism previously mentioned, which emerged from the exchanges between ecologists, social scientists, and public-health advocates focusing on socio-spatial movements within cities (Park et al., 1925). While this movement (often described as the Chicago School of Sociology) eventually dissipated, urban ecology shifted its focus to "ecology in cities," or in other words, analyzing the species found in urban habitats and how they interact (Bai, 2016; Duvigneaud, 1974). The community continued to evolve, slowly transitioning toward the "ecology of cities," which focused on the interaction between social and ecological systems (Alberti, 2007; Duvigneaud & Denayer-De Smet, 1977; Liu et al., 2007). Today, urban ecology is described as a multidisciplinary field that studies the interrelationships, at different spatial and temporal scales, between local and global ecosystems on the one hand, and human activities on the other (see Figure 11.1).

The urban ecology community therefore offers significant tools with which to consider the patterns and feedback processes between these systems, which are essential when considering the present and future needs of urbanites, but it does not necessarily encompass the political, production, consumption, technological, and other facets of urban systems that have a considerable impact on urban sustainability. Finally, as will be presented in the final sections, urban ecology introduced two supplementary aspects that are now commonly integrated into urban sustainability, namely resilience (Massaro et al., 2018) and nature-based solutions.

11.2.2 Industrial Ecology

As illustrated in Figure 11.1, industrial ecology explores the materiality of our economies and, more specifically, the environmental consequences of our production and consumption activities (Adriaanse, 1997; Clift & Druckman, 2015; Matthews, 2000). The community originally started by making the analogy between industrial systems and natural systems, and how the former could be optimized in terms of resource use and waste disposal thanks to insights from the latter (Frosch & Gallopoulos, 1989). Since then, this community has developed or consolidated a number of methodological tools, such as material flow analysis, life cycle assessment (LCA), and input-output analysis (IOA), that enable the quantification of resource use and pollution flows entering and leaving industrial or other economic systems (Newell and Cousins, 2015). A smaller part of the industrial ecology community specifically focuses on cities. Following the seminal work of Wolman (1965), this growing community uses the abovementioned tools to quantify the flows entering and leaving urban systems in order to monitor their progress and propose optimized solutions thatcould lead toward a more resource-efficient state. Numerous case studies have been carried out, making it possible to emphasize the considerable impact cities have on the environment both locally and globally (Bai, 2007; Beloin-Saint-Pierre et al., 2017). Urban metabolism studies from an industrial-ecology perspective are now moving beyond the sole quantification of flows entering and leaving a city, considered as a homogeneous and static entity (Bai, 2016). In fact, studies now consider the heterogeneous aspect of cities, in order to identify resource use and pollution-emission flows by spatializing them (Athanassiadis et al., 2017; Pincetl et al., 2016). Indirect flows and the spatialization of global resource supply areas is also enabling urban administrations to develop more relevant (for instance, consumption-based) policies (Athanassiadis et al., 2018; Chen et al., 2016). Similar to the urban ecology subdiscipline, industrial ecology also fails to cover essential aspects of sustainability such the political, social, and even some ecological layers.

11.2.3 Political Ecology

The last "ecology" of urban metabolism presented here, is urban political ecology. Marx's metabolic rift (Marx, 2018) can be considered as one of the seminal works of political ecology. This relatively smaller community explores how urban and social activities physically transform natural elements (Gandy, 2004), but also how economic activities structure our cities and society (see Figure 11.1). It is a critical academic community that analyses the urban condition as a socioenvironmental process (Heynen et al., 2006). In fact, urban political ecology sees cities as physical habitats with very distinctive characteristics that come from the transformation of social and physical environments through the circulation of flows. Unlike the other communities, and as its name suggests, political ecology underlines the political and power relationships forged through the circulation of flows. Thus, urban political ecology questions who produces cities (or different and distinct socioecological configurations) and for whom (Heynen et al., 2006). In reality, the processes of urban production and the circulation of metabolic flows are not apolitical or neutral. Different social groups have access to or control over, or are excluded from, certain metabolic aspects of a city. Urban political ecology uses insights from history and geography to analyze the uneven power relations through which cities are formed and function, and ultimately proposes a more democratic and just use of cities (Hood & Gandy, 2003). While urban political ecology is the only one of the three subdisciplines discussed here to address social challenges in depth and link them with infrastructural, economic, and urban development, it still, like the other two subdisciplines, fails to address some essential elements of urban sustainability, namely the monitoring or modeling of the (bio)physical characteristics of urban systems and how they are linked with social challenges and political processes.

11.2.4 Shortcomings of the Urban Metabolism Lens for Addressing Urban Sustainability

The "ecologies" we have discussed greatly contribute to our understanding of specific aspects of the sustainability of urban systems. Nevertheless, as Newell and Cousins (2015) have pointed out, each of these subdisciplines has created its own isolated island of knowledge, with little cross-fertilization between the three. The lack of interaction between these disciplinary vantage points prevents them from creating bridges between them and covering potential gaps in urban sustainability knowledge, as well as from better grasping the mechanisms behind the relationship between social and economic environmental vectors within cities. In addition, there are a number of other disciplines that deal with urban sustainability challenges that are not covered by the urban metabolism lens, including policy analysis, transition theory, demographics, urban development, complexity theory, and many others.

Finally, it has to be noted that while the urban metabolism lens enables us to better understand the reciprocal relationship between urban areas and nature, it often makes abstractions of the specificities of urban settlements. At this stage, as most studies are interested in contemporary urban sustainability challenges, it is indeed still hard to distinguish which specific characteristics of cities are responsible for their (un)sustainability. Therefore, in this chapter, we argue that before speaking about and understanding the (un)sustainability of cities, it is essential to specify what makes and made a city. The next section dives deeper into the idiosyncratic features of cities after carrying out a brief overview of the history of cities. The subsequent section will attempt to understand how these intrinsic characteristics affect the (un)sustainability of cities over time. This chapter will conclude by advocating for the need to develop a more integrative and transdisciplinary urban (sustainability) science.

11.3 The Essence of Cities from a Metabolic Perspective

What are the specificities of cities? What is their essence? What, in their essence, is responsible for their (un)sustainability?

In order to provide an answer to these questions, it is essential to retrace a short history of cities: a history framed within a metabolic perspective, and whose goal is, in a very synthetic way, to highlight how – from the first settlements in Mesopotamia to present-day global cities, world cities, and megacities – specific elements have characterized cities. Understanding the characteristics of urban settlements in a temporal perspective means regarding them as the outcomes of specific historical factors, such as technological innovations, events, relationships, or responses to changing needs[1]; it means aligning our perspective with André Corboz's (1983) notion of "the land as a palimpsest," a land that accumulates traces, comprising heterogeneous dynamics – for example, material, social, cultural, biological.

Therefore, this section does not provide one univocal definition of cities, but rather describes them as the combination of characteristics, linked to a historical genealogy, whose outcomes are heterogeneous and asynchronous. It is by eliciting these characteristics that we try to unveil cities' "know-how" (Guallart, 2014).

After revealing the characteristics of cities that are embedded in history, these will be listed, providing the basis for a discussion on the sustainability implication of each one in the next section of this chapter.

It should become clear to the reader that these characteristics are deeply interlinked, and that the division proposed is no more than an artificial tool to bring some order to, and support our understanding of, the complexity of cities.

11.3.1 A Metabolic History of Cities

11.3.1.1 The Genesis of Cities: Shaping Urban Functions

The first settlements and fortified cities appeared from the ninth millennium BCE in the Fertile Crescent. From Mesopotamia to the Nile valley and the Mediterranean region, and in parallel to the Chinese and Indus cultures, cities like Uruk (3000 BCE) were founded (McIntosh, 2017). In their foundation, the importance of location was twofold: on the one hand, cities were generated in areas considered "strategic" (in relation to, e.g., topography, ecology, soil, water); on the other hand, they played a special and unique role within a regional system, which determined their emancipation from their regional context. This role was determined by the functions that urbanity covered.

To provide a deeper overview, in antiquity, areas of geographical (e.g., ports, rivers), religious, cultural, political, and military relevance were strategically used to establish settlements. As described by Cicero, humans recreated a "second nature" through the work of their hands (Geuze & Skjonsberg, n.d.). As people gathered around these territorial centers, so-called civil society was shaped, allowing, according to Aristotle, for the foundation of the concepts of citizenship, democracy, family, identity, creativity, and innovation (Soja, 2003). Contemporarily with societal functions, additional features were developed, such as political stability, control over resources, and the provision of security (related to the design of defence infrastructure). Supported by these characteristics, such as greater political stability, and their location on trade routes, cities became central locations for trading. In these nodes for exchange or marketplaces, new demands took shape, and the needs for specialized occupations arose[2] (Kraas et al., 2016).

When looking at cities in section, as proposed by Geddes (1925), the genesis of cities summarized here is clearly displayed. In the "valley section," the physical condition of the region (e.g., topography, soil, water) is linked to the basic human occupations that suit it (e.g., the miner, hunter, shepherd, or fisher) and the human settlements that arose from these. This "synoptic vision" (Skjonsberg, 2015) makes it possible to see the "rural" and the "urban" in the same context, both attempting to carry out a collective strategy for the survival of their communities: depending on the threat (e.g., environmental threats, war, famine), either the city or the countryside could provide shelter, each with a distinct function.

To summarize, in antiquity, the city became a method for the renewal and organization (Osterhammel, 2011) of space, society, and functions. Urban planning manifested in cultural development, political and military power, and the ability of a society to produce and trade, as well as to offer protection against environmental threats. While being shaped by society, cities also contributed to shaping it (Soja, 2003), providing access to extended rights and privileges, as opportunities for "self-cultivation." In this context, urbanity started fulfilling specific functions, some of which became revelatory of its emancipatory dimension (Kraas et al., 2016).

11.3.1.2 The Metabolic Rift

The active founding of cities that began in antiquity extended into the middle ages and the early-modern period, until new dynamics emerged that, in Europe in the eighteenth and nineteenth centuries, further shaped the prototype of civil society.

From 1750 up to WWII in Europe (and from 1950 in Africa and Asia), the demographic transition caused by the Industrial Revolution, as well as structural changes in agriculture, started the so-called third phase of urbanization. Cities started evolving in "diversified, polycentric and decentralised systems," increasing interurban trade, industrial production, and urban consumption (Kraas et al., 2016), including in the colonial territories. "Real systematic urban development" began, and the industrial economy flourished in places rich in raw material, energy sources, and human capital (Guallart, 2014). Job opportunities emerged in the increasingly dense and socially heterogeneous cities, together with poverty, exploitation, and class consciousness and struggle (Soja, 2003). New modes of transport created networks between cities, as well as between urban areas and their surrounding regions, and new settlements were strategically planned to further develop infrastructures. Cities' boundaries became broader thanks to the automobile, which allowed residents to escape from the industrial, overcrowded urban centers and led to the phenomena associated with suburbanization (e.g., the Garden City Movement). The urban zoning plans of the 1922 International Congress of Modern Architecture (CIAM), which involved geographically separating functions inside the city, emerged from the new possibility of reshaping space regardless of distance.

These new urban structures interrupted the traditional material cycle that had existed within cities. To shore up the urban economy, factories, raw materials, workers, and food were needed in large amounts, violating what were, in the past, the conditions of sustainability imposed by nature (Harvey, 1997). In fact, these conditions were broken by sending the nutrients from the soil to the cities (in the form of, e.g., food and agricultural products), without receiving them back (e.g., in the form of waste). This "metabolic rift" (Marx, 2018) therefore manifested through the robbery of the soil, with the goal of maintaining society's socioeconomic reproduction (Foster, 2000).

11.3.1.3 Following the Rift

In the fourth phase of urbanization, "postmodern globalization" has led to a progressive "homogenization" of the urban structure (Kraas et al., 2016). Different sociocultural models of urban development (e.g., the European, American, Latin American, and Oriental-Islamic city) have been, and are being, reshaped by new patterns of consumption, by the increasing global distribution of very similar products, and by the loss of spaces of encounter, facilitated by information and communication technology. Through a process of disanchoring, the urban world has emancipated itself from its regional resources, as well as from its identity. These factors are giving birth to "placeless cities" (Bourdin et al., 2014) or "non places" (Kraas et al., 2016; Rapport et al., 1996), where the city's geographical identity is endangered and its historical social practices tend to disappear.

Nevertheless, urban areas remain pioneers of social change today: they are places where individuals, groups, and movements with different socioeconomic background coexist, form networks, and shape a territorial identity and a political consciousness, while contributing to societal development (Soja, 2003). Density and heterogeneity support the accumulation of knowledge and creativity, leading to innovation. Proximity makes it possible to bring together specialized employees and service providers in the same place, to provide access to local markets, to facilitate access to suppliers, and to offer lower transaction and information costs (Marshall, 1982).

To summarize, cities can be seen as the accumulation of cultural constructions (Guallart, 2014; Marshall, 1982) having shaped and been shaped by the customs, traditions, and conflicts of a social sphere. Just like in ancient times, the drivers of urbanization remain location, resources, demographic structure, and economies, political systems, and infrastructure. And also just like in ancient times, the cultural, scientific, and political relevance of cities, together with their ability to trade, produce, and answer to functional demands, remain as core characteristics that are reflected in different urban forms, structures, and processes.

11.3.2 From History to Characteristics

As previously mentioned, there is no uniform definition that makes it possible to clearly distinguish urban areas from other types of human settlements: since administrative borders vary across different contexts, it becomes difficult to delineate, for example, inhabitants' thresholds. However, another approach can be adopted when seeking to define cities: when studying the history of their genesis, a set of characteristics emerges. These characteristics – i.e., recurring elements across different urban regions – do not serve to support definitions based on population size, density, or contiguity, but rather to identify a set of defining elements, a blueprint of urbanity, enabling discussion of the sustainability implications of inhabiting urban areas from a generic and more comprehensive perspective.

The list of characteristics identified is far from definitive and absolute. We derived a set of features from the historical evolution presented in Section 11.3.1. The selection is based on some of the fundamental urban characteristics presented in landmark urban studies publications (Batty, 2013; Fujita et al., 2001; Jacobs, 2016; Soja, 2003).

Table 11.1 relates the selected characteristics to the research field that proposed them. It has to be noted that the disciplinary fields go beyond the three "ecologies" we have presented. Indeed, several other research fields have contributed to analyzing cities, their development, and their sustainability.

In the rest of this chapter we describe the characteristics mentioned in Table 11.1 and show how they are relevant for urban areas. We focus on presenting emerging properties that derive from these main characteristics and have a clear definition. It has to be noted that

Table 11.1 *Urban characteristics and the research field where they originated*

Characteristics	Main research fields	Main authors
Population size, density, and hierarchy	Urban Economics, Complex Systems, Urban Anthropology	Batty, 2013; Soja, 2003; West, 2017
Social, cultural, and economic heterogeneity and disparities	Urban Geography, Urban Sociology, Urban Anthropology	Glaeser, 2011; Jacobs, 2016; Soja, 2003
Artificial and heterotrophic open system	Urban Ecology, Industrial Ecology	Alberti, 1996; Kennedy et al., 2007; Seto et al., 2015
Functional complexity	Urban Sociology, Complex Systems	Jacobs, 2016; West, 2017
Access to services and facilities	Urban Economics, Urban Anthropology, Urban Sociology	Glaeser, 2011; Jacobs, 2016; Soja, 2003
Economic growth, wealth creation	Complex Systems, Urban Economics	Fujita et al., 2001; Jacobs, 2016; West, 2017

similar properties can emerge from different characteristics. Thus, the following analyses do not claim to be mono-relational, but rather to facilitate a discussion about these relationships.

1 Population size, density, and hierarchy Statistical-administrative concepts define cities according to minimum population sizes and densities, which vary from country to country. But from a functional and more comprehensive perspective, the city only exists as a city "in relation to a form of life lower than its own" (Braudel, 1992). Empirical evidence suggests that systems of cities present universal patterns of population hierarchy (Gabaix, 1999) and density (Bettencourt et al., 2007). This makes it possible to expand the definition of cities to include different entities and hierarchies (e.g., number/types of firms, intellectual capabilities present on the territory).

Proximity, likelihood and organization of interactions, exchange of ideas, innovation The possibilities that cities, thanks to their density and proximity, create spaces for people to agglomerate has unique outcomes. Urban areas allow parallel cultures with few or no links to cohabit, to gather, to meet, and to frequently interact. This stimulates social synergies, while concentrating needs and challenges – creating the conditions from which innovations might arise (Soja, 2003). When agglomerating, individuals and firms with different "intellectual capabilities" are able to shape and disseminate new political or societal ideas, setting the stage for innovation, and job and wealth creation (Bettencourt, 2013; Fujita et al., 2001; Jacobs, 2016).

2 Social, cultural, and economic heterogeneity and disparities As discussed in Section 11.3.1.2, during the period of the Industrial Revolution, people moved to the growing cities, contributing to the sociocultural heterogeneity of these urban areas. Cities today are socially and culturally different between and among themselves. Depending on the conditions under which cities developed, they can host a broad range of social groups, generated reciprocally, as cities give form to new milieus.

Disparities However, aside from generating groups, cities also produce disparities at different scales. The goods and services (such as education, administration, or healthcare) offered by urban areas are allocated not only to their own population but also to the surrounding region. Nevertheless, an imbalance between urban areas and their surroundings emerges in terms of jobs, housing, and services.[3]

Disparity can also be found within the city, where inhabitants with different socioeconomic backgrounds live alongside each other. This heterogeneity is both the cause and the consequence of differences in rental prices or architectural design. The city displays the progressive individualization of lifestyles as well as the urgency of satisfying basic needs, which can manifest in slums as well as in gated communities (Kraas et al., 2016).

3 Artificial and heterotrophic open system It has been argued that by building cities, humanity has become independent from the "constraints of nature" (Brunotte, 2002). To survive, create shelter, and eventually satisfy their needs, humans have reshaped their natural landscapes. Since cities are subject to ecological strain, they depend on the resources of the surrounding region, thereby externalizing their ecological problems (Kraas et al., 2016).

Large-scale physical infrastructure Infrastructure plays an important role within individual cities as well as in the relationship between cities and their regional contexts. To overcome natural constraints and provide their inhabitants with basic services (e.g., drinking water, sewage, transportation, food), cities had to build up a complex physical and social (e.g., in the form of institutions) infrastructure to ensure the functioning of the system and the health of their inhabitants. The connection between cities and regions must be ensured for the functioning of the system (Alberti, 2007). This is clearly the case for infrastructural systems, as it is for ecological systems – when well correlated, these two systems form a mutually supportive dual network that can function as an armature for the open city.

4 Functional complexity From the first settlements to the functional zoning of CIAM, and today, cities fulfill multiple and varied functions. Cultural, political, economic, and social functions coexist and are spatially organized in different ways in different cities – central business districts, residential districts, open spaces, cultural centers, and industrial areas are distributed according to real estate and land markets – while also shaping cities in turn (Kraas et al., 2016).

Complexity of power and institutions To accompany these complexities, legal and governmental structures, both "protective and coercive," have been put in place. These different "forms of power" provide the stability necessary for social institutions to develop, for markets to operate (Braudel, 1992), and for security and to establish trust (Smith, 1776).

Division and specialization of labor Furthermore, as mentioned in Section 2.1.1, specialized occupations began to arise in antiquity, as a consequence of the process of agglomeration. "[W]here there is a town, there will be division of labor, and where there is any marked division of labor, there will be a town" (Braudel, 1992). In a globalizing world, the evolution of transportation as well as of information and communication has reinforced the trend toward the increasing division of labor and specialization of knowledge.

5 Access to facilities and markets Secondary schools, universities, hospitals, public services, health facilities, and administrative facilities are concentrated in urban centers. The availability of services attracts new residents, which generates increasing needs, in a self-reinforcing cycle: if dwellers in cities depend on central markets for obtaining basic goods (e.g., their food), it is their moving to the city that brings "prominence" to the market, commerce, and the institutions that support wealth accumulation and the rapid growth in standards of living (Jacobs, 2016; Seto et al., 2015).

6 Economic growth, wealth creation Various empirical evidence supports the claim that cities produce economic development and wealth. The mechanism behind this is known by economists as the "agglomeration effect." It describes the fact that clustered firms experience declining production costs due to the specialization/division of labor, competition between suppliers, and attraction of customers. Agglomeration economies are based on the savings in time and energy that derive from the phenomenon of clustering as opposed to spreading (Soja, 2003). Furthermore, with more people sharing the same area, new ideas are more likely to emerge due to the combination of a multiplicity of intellectual capabilities: it is indeed the heterogeneity and diversity of cities itself that becomes a source of economic growth (Jacobs, 2016; Quigley, 1998). From a spatial-microeconomic perspective, dense settlements provide better conditions for retail stores to survive due to the more frequent presence of pedestrians.

In this section, we presented a set of urban characteristics derived from these historical developments and selected landmark urban studies. In the following section, we evaluate the implications of these characteristics for the sustainability of society.

11.4 Sustainability Implications of Urban Characteristics

In this section, we debate the implications of the characteristics presented in Section 11.3, with respect to global sustainability. Organizing humans in cities provides advantages and difficulties for a society. The urban condition modulates interactions among a city's inhabitants and their relation to the surrounding region. The ways those interactions are regulated are far from simple: if the density of social interactions leads to material prosperity and the consumption of resources (Seto, 2015), it also might produce technological innovations and better waste/sewage/water treatment (although these effects are mostly time delayed). Similarly, if dense human settlements welcome a diversity of cultures and lifestyles providing multiple possible ways of living, they also produce inequalities that force undesired conditions on their inhabitants. From a sustainability perspective, it's hard to define one "resultant vector" out of these dynamics, since we are confronted with significant trade-offs, and innumerable, as yet unaccounted for, "externalizations of risk." Because of that, we focus on describing the impact of each of the indicated characteristics so as to qualify them in relation to the "three pillars of sustainability." Further in this part, we present indicators for the temporal dynamics of urbanization and of each sustainability category at a global scale.

11.4.1 A Compilation of Findings from a Metabolic Perspective

1 Population size, density, and hierarchy Empirical and theoretical evidence supports the idea that population size and density are the main drivers of the "Urban Condition" (Bettencourt et al., 2007; West, 2017). Both contribute to an increasing density and number of interactions that drive most urban characteristics, together with heterogeneity (Jacobs, 2016; Soja, 2003).

Social

Positive: The density of interactions in cities makes social organization easier. Engels, for example, proposes that during the first Industrial Revolution, dense agglomerations of workers in cities like Manchester stimulated both class consciousness and class struggle, securing the first set of workers' rights (Soja, 2003). This is a very important social feature of dense and heterogeneous settlements and, as in the Manchester example, has helped to guarantee valuable human rights over time. Minorities and the disenfranchized tend to find, in urban settlements, the critical mass necessary to organize themselves.

Negative: Population size and density could lead to dysfunctional social behavior (Schelling, 1971) and promotes, on average, more violent crimes (Alves et al., 2013) and increases segregation (Fossett & Dietrich, 2009).

Environmental

Positive: Due to increasing innovation and proximity, new technological developments occur, and production and transport efficiencies increase. Density also plays an important role in enabling mass transportation solutions to be implemented, reducing the average fuel consumption for transportation (Newman & Kenworthy, 1989). In the same vein, it tends to reduce surface-to-volume ratios, making buildings more energy-efficient in terms of heating (Seto et al., 2015).

Negative: We also observe important diseconomies in more densely populated areas such as air-quality deterioration, heat islands, and water contamination (Parikh, 1996). More importantly, rebound effects due to consumption of more efficient goods can be observed, i.e., consumption might increase as a consequence of reducing environmental costs (Greening et al., 2000).

Economic
Positive: According to Bettencourt et al. (2007) population size and density in urban areas can be seen as one of the main drivers of urban wealth. They suggest that this is because increased population densities reduce transportation cost and promote knowledge spillovers, fostering economic development and resilience (Jacobs, 2016; Quigley, 1998). Agglomerated industries tend to increase their productivity because of colocational advantages such as established networks supplying goods and trained workers, infrastructure built specifically for the industry, and higher accessibility due to transportation links.

Negative: Diseconomies of agglomeration also impact urban economies through processes such as inflation (land prices), traffic, and pollution (Richardson, 1995). Densely populated areas are also less resilient to and more impacted by natural hazards like flooding or hurricanes (Ovink & Boeijenga, 2018).

2 Social, cultural, and economic heterogeneity and disparities Together with population density, the sociocultural heterogeneity of cities is the primary trigger of urban innovation processes (Jacobs, 2016; Soja, 2003). But those are not the only heterogeneities we find in cities. Economic inequality tends to grow together with the "wealth production" process.

Social
Positive: In terms of social benefits, sociocultural plurality tends to support the emergence of different lifestyles and their endurance over time, giving urban dwellers a certain freedom over their lifestyle (Glaeser, 2011; Soja, 2003).

Negative: Conflicts can emerge from the interaction between different social groups (Pickett & Wilkinson, 2010). Economic inequality tends to increase social problems such as obesity, mental illness, homicides, incarceration, and drug use and to reduce social goods such as life expectancy, education, trust among strangers, and social mobility (Pickett & Wilkinson, 2015).

Environmental
Positive: Innovation processes heavily rely on a heterogeneous population and are one of the main processes reducing demand for resources and the environmental impacts of our activities (Jackson, 2011).

Negative: Economic inequality also tends to increase consumerism and conspicuous consumption, increasing resource consumption through low-social-value goods (Power et al., 2016).

Economic
Positive: Social heterogeneity is one of the main factors driving innovation in cities (Jacobs, 2016), which brings stability and adaptive capacity to urban economies.

Negative: Economic inequalities tend to generate several social, health, and environmental dysfunctions for an economy, such as mental illness or violence, jeopardizing well-being (Power et al., 2016).

3 Artificial and heterotrophic open system In the process of densification, urban land became completely dedicated to housing and services, drastically reducing food production. To be able to sustain themselves, cities have to import goods from other areas, heavily relying on their hinterlands.

Social
Positive: The dense and strong supply system provides access to goods and services for a majority of the population (Seto et al., 2015).

Negative: Natural landscapes have positive effects on human health and well-being (Annerstedt & Währborg, 2011; Seto et al., 2015). Artificial landscapes, on the contrary, can increase stress levels (e.g., through noise) and associated problems. Artificial landscapes reinforce the globalized economy because cities do not produce their products, which imposes serious geographic inequalities and explorations (Vercelli, 2002). This might change in the future for specific material flows. With the exhaustion of stocks of metals in nature, for example, and the accumulation of metals in urban landfills, we are starting to observe a new trend toward urban mining through recycling (Seto et al., 2015).

Environmental
Positive: Strong interaction between cities facilitates the exchange of products and knowledge, as well as the percolation of innovation, potentially leading to more efficient economies (Seto et al., 2015).

Negative: By turning their landscapes into artificial and sterile areas, urban settlements reduce primary production and become dependent on their hinterland (Marzluff, 2008). As a result, most of the natural resources consumed in a city come from elsewhere, producing further impacts associated with their transportation (Alberti, 2005). Urban heat islands are also a negative impact of high-albedo artificial regions (Seto et al., 2015).

Economic

Positive: The artificialization of urban landscapes has heavily influenced the process of globalization around the world, because it continued to generate demand for goods even after cities stopped producing and processing the goods they consumed (Batty, 2013; Seto et al., 2015). This guarantees access to goods and services.

Negative: The artificialization process also imposes global inequalities (Pickett & Wilkinson, 2015). The dependence on hinterlands puts cities in a vulnerable position vis-à-vis the supply of goods and services (Seto et al., 2015).

4 Functional complexity As mentioned, the functional complexity of cities triggers an iterative process of specialization, efficiency, and production. As workers specialize in more and more specific tasks, they tend to do it with more efficiency, increasing labor productivity. Functional complexity also leads to more complex political and police institutions.

Social

Positive: In the social dimension, high productivity and concomitantly lower prices render products more accessible to the general population. Another important social implication of this process is that it allows inhabitants to choose more precisely what they would like to work on (Durkheim & Halls, 1997). If in rural areas, basic needs force much of the population to work as farmers, the specialization of work in cities opens a broader range of possible activities. This freedom is evenly distributed across the urban population (Durkheim & Halls, 1997).

Negative: More complex political and police institutions are needed to ensure higher levels of security and resilience and to increase levels of surveillance and control, reducing privacy and freedom.

Environmental

Positive: Increasing labor productivity leads to innovation and environmental efficiency (Jacobs, 2016).

Negative: From an environmental point of view, specialization of labor reduces prices, making products cheaper (Smith, 1776), increasing sales, and consequently increasing the demand for resources needed to produce such products (Jackson, 2008). This is one of the main drivers of overconsumption in the world (Jackson, 2011).

Economic

Positive: From an economic perspective, functional complexity and division of labor and of processes guarantees efficiency, wealth generation, and resilience for industries and business (Jacobs, 2016; Smith, 1776).

Negative: Division of labor can lead to inequality and its associated economic problems (Power et al., 2016).

5 Access to services and facilities Urban areas facilitate access to facilities and services by means of colocational advantages.

Social
Positive: From a social perspective, access to facilities and services guarantees a broad access to basic needs as water treatment, sewage, and waste collection/treatment (World Health Organization, 2015).

Negative: At the same time, providing a service generates a demand for that service and it has been observed that, in cities, a proliferation of services with very low social value emerged (Jackson, 2008). Access to the market can also be a driving force toward increasing consumerism and its multiple social negative impacts, such as obesity and frustration (Jackson, 2008).

Environmental
Positive: Through technology and the development of facilities, some end- of-pipe environmental problems have been solved. As an example, access to sewage treatment services reduces the load of waste water discharged into water bodies. On the input side of environmental impacts, the adoption of new technologies can dematerialize the economy, reducing the demand for material extraction.

Negative: By institutionalizing the market, urban areas make access to products much easier. This is another factor driving consumerism in cities (Jackson, 2008). Consumerism and its material throughput (overconsumption) have negative consequences for global sustainability. Rebound effects tend to emerge when new technologies are introduced.

Economic
Positive: From an economic perspective, the institutionalization of facilities increases the demand for them, formalizing new markets and jobs. It also promotes microeconomies, generating wealth and economic resilience (Jacobs, 2016; Smith, 1776).

Negative: Access to facilities and the market can cause an increase in aggregate demand, promoting inflation in the long run (Samuelson, 1952).

6 Economic growth, wealth creation Economic growth in urban systems is an outcome of previously presented processes such as density, functional complexity, and the institutionalization of the market (Bettencourt et al., 2007; Seto et al., 2015).

Social
Positive: A richer society provides more and better services to its population, increasing well-being through access to services and facilities (Samuelson, 1952).

Negative: Economic growth can lead to overconsumption and all its associated problems like obesity or demerit goods (Jackson, 2008). It also generates inflation – in the form of rising land prices, for example – and making it hard for most of the population to make ends meet. It is common for economic growth to be accompanied by increasing wealth inequality (Sarkar et al., 2016).

Environmental

Positive: Economic growth can lead to the reduction of pollution through better regulations, improved technology, deindustrialization, and diminishing marginal utility of income. This phenomenon is known as the environmental Kuznets curve (Stern, 2004).

Negative: Economic growth and wealth are the main drivers of environmental impacts in cities. Economic growth increases consumption and demand for resources, producing a large number of externalities (Jackson, 2008; Parikh, 1996). It also increases waste production. From an environmental perspective, economic growth in a highly inefficient economy creates immense challenges for global environmental sustainability. Because of the buoyant economy, in a globalized economy, large amounts of resources from around the world are demanded (Ferrão & Fernández, 2013; Seto et al., 2015).

Economic

Positive: From an economic perspective, the wealth-creation process, in addition to boosting the economy, brings economic security and resilience to an urban settlement (Quigley, 1998; Smith, 1776). As this process is mainly driven by knowledge spillovers, it is much easier for dense and heterogeneous settlements to adapt their economic activities than it would be for other types of settlements (Jacobs, 2016).

Negative: Economic growth can promote negative externalities and, depending on the driver of the growth, it can also promote inflation (Samuelson, 1952).

In the following table, we summarize the main sustainability implications of the characteristics of cities.

This first analysis of the characteristics of cities and their implications for global sustainability shows, on the one hand, that there are significant trade-offs associated with urban development. Furthermore, we can observe that different characteristics might affect global sustainability in similar ways. This more in-depth understanding of the relationship between urbanity and sustainability also shows that there are ambiguities that cannot be resolved by looking at it from a disciplinary perspective.

In addition, the divide-and-conquer approach used here imposes a classic problem on science: it makes it hard to build a big picture, an overview (Raftopoulos, 2003). We still need to discuss the final interaction between the individual parts of the picture. What is the "resultant vector" of urban living to global sustainability? The next part of this chapter presents some empirical evidence in this regard.

Table 11.2 *Sustainability implications of urban characteristics (source: authors)*

Characteristics	Sustainability Pillar	Positive	Negative
Population size, density, and hierarchy	Social	Social organization, human rights	Violent crimes, segregation
	Environmental	Innovation, efficiency, mass transportation	Pollution, heat islands, rebound effects
	Economic	Wealth generation, productivity	Inflation, traffic, lower resilience
Social, cultural, and economic heterogeneity and disparities	Social	Plurality, freedom	Conflicts, inequality
	Environmental	Innovation, efficiency	Overconsumption
	Economic	Innovation, resilience	Inequality and accessibility
Artificial and heterotrophic open system	Social	Access to goods and services	Stress, geographic inequalities
	Environmental	Innovation, efficiency	Primary production dependency
	Economic	Access to goods and services	International inequality, vulnerability
Functional complexity	Social	Productivity, freedom	Security, resilience
	Environmental	Innovation	Overconsumption
	Economic	Efficiency, resilience	Inequality
Access to services and facilities	Social	Access to basic needs, sanitation	Proliferation of services with low social value, overconsumption
	Environmental	Pollution treatment, efficiency	Rebound effects, overconsumption
	Economic	Wealth generation	Inflation
Economic growth, wealth creation	Social	Access to goods and services	Overconsumption, inequality
	Environmental	Reduction of pollution	Increase in demand for resources
	Economic	Resilience	Negative externalities

11.4.2 Emerging Evidence

Our analysis suggests that, at an aggregate level, one should expect cities to produce wealth and guarantee the accessibility of goods and services to the general population. They do so by bringing together people from completely different backgrounds and triggering technological and social innovations. Unfortunately, these social and economic advantages

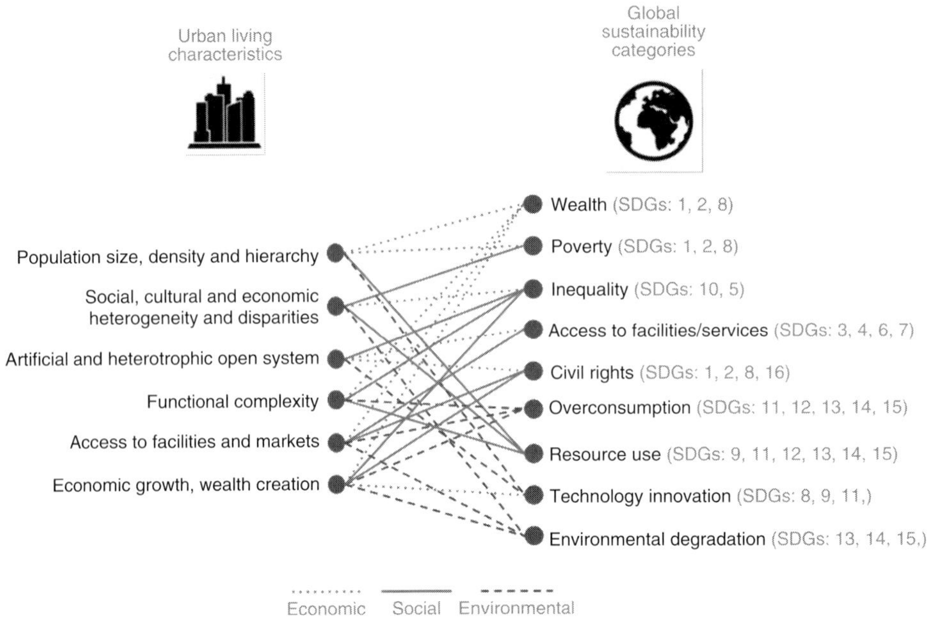

Figure 11.2 The effects of urban characteristics on global sustainability. The graph indicates a causal relationship between urban characteristics and global sustainability categories. The relations between categories and the UN's Sustainable Development Goals are indicated in parenthesis. Source: own illustration

are linked to increasing demand for resources and lead to environmental impacts, threatening the long-term sustainability of life on earth. Furthermore, inequalities and overconsumption seem to be other important drawbacks of urbanization.

In order to empirically test our theory-derived hypotheses, we look into the outcomes (of our urban characteristics) that are likely to have an impact on global sustainability. We first translate the urban characteristics into a set of global sustainability categories to be measured. The proposed global sustainability categories emerged from our urban living characteristics and were validated with the United Nations' Sustainable Development Goals (United Nations Publications, 2018). Figure 11.2 indicates the relations between urban characteristics and the global sustainability categories.

We translated the list of sustainability categories into a list of indicators that we found in the database *Our World in Data*,[4] comprising the total or average global figure. Several indicators were derived from specific aspects but we adopted the most adherent ones among the database, those that more clearly translated our sustainability categories. Figure 11.3 shows the global long-term dynamics for the selected indicators, represented by the global sustainability categories discussed above. The urban characteristics contribute to the categories in a complex way; the possible casualties were explained in the previous part. Although certainly important, the dynamics observed do not emerge only from the urban

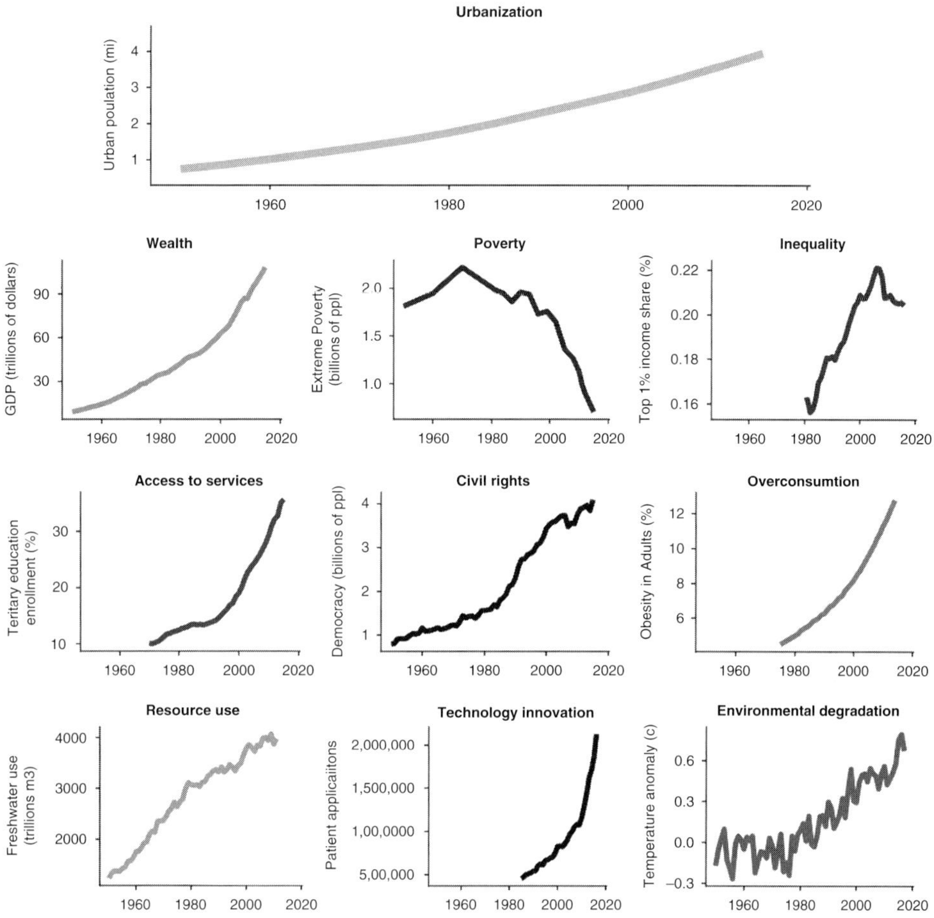

Figure 11.3 Temporal dynamics of urbanization and global sustainability categories. Source: own illustration, based on data for the global total or average from *Our World in Data*

characteristics presented or from urban growth, but also from other economic and social processes.

We can observe (Figure 11.3) that in very general terms, in parallel with the exponential growth of urban populations, wealth increases and poverty is reduced. However, as discussed in the previous section, these changes might not occur in the same place and at the same pace, leading to inequality and the relative growth of poverty. Concomitantly with urban population growth, access to facilities has been increasing, as has the presence of institutions ensuring civil rights. In terms of drawbacks, the impacts of overconsumption can be observed in different indicators, such as obesity rates and resource use, as well as in the related environmental consequences. Interestingly, technology innovation has to some extent balanced out overconsumption by increasing production efficiency. Once again, we are not arguing that urban development is the only driver behind those dynamics, but the mechanisms presented in this chapter could be helping to guide such developments.

The scale of impact categories can also be observed from our selection of indicators. While some variables reflect a very dynamic exponential development – e.g., urbanization, wealth, and civil rights – others show less precipitous but still substantial changes, such as overconsumption, resource use, environmental impacts, and poverty. Still, according to the chosen indicators, some categories have changed less than those mentioned above, such as access to facilities, inequality, and technological innovation.

Far from claiming to define a final relationship between urbanization and global sustainability, we have here presented an initial exploratory analysis of this relationship from a metabolic perspective. Our analysis took into consideration political and social dynamics, resource consumption, and the ecological implications of living in urban settlements. After describing the urban condition in a set of characteristics and discussing the social, environmental, and economic implications of these characteristics for global and local sustainability, we observe the complexity and the paradoxes they represent with respect to cities and sustainability. These different effects are representative of the complexity of urban systems and their impact on sustainability. It becomes apparent that within the assessment of sustainability we are likely to encounter significant trade-offs – within cities themselves, but also across regions. Whereas some general and rather surface-level conclusions can be derived from this initial analysis, further research should be performed if we want to better understand the relations involved. This requires also an integrative perspective on urban systems. The framework developed in this chapter is a first step in this direction and has proved to be useful in connecting the three pillars of sustainability.

11.5 Concluding Remarks: A Way Forward toward an Integrative Urban (Sustainability) Science

This chapter looked into sustainability issues with regard to urban systems. It thereby provided a new approach for identifying the sustainability problems that emerge out of urban characteristics. The latter were defined based on a historical analysis of urban development. It became clear that to identify, assess, and therefore address the sustainability issues that occur in urban systems, a disciplinary approach is not sufficient. Rather than aiming at providing a new approach, we propose to show the interfaces between the different disciplinary views and to make explicit what each disciplinary perspective can contribute and how they can be fruitfully combined. In doing so, we depart from the three ecology-based disciplines of the urban metabolism lens presented in the beginning, and expand on them by incorporating the perspectives that emerged through our historical analysis of urban characteristics and emerging patterns.

In doing so, our analysis contributes to providing an integrative perspective by taking a different approach. Having identified the key impact categories affected by the urban

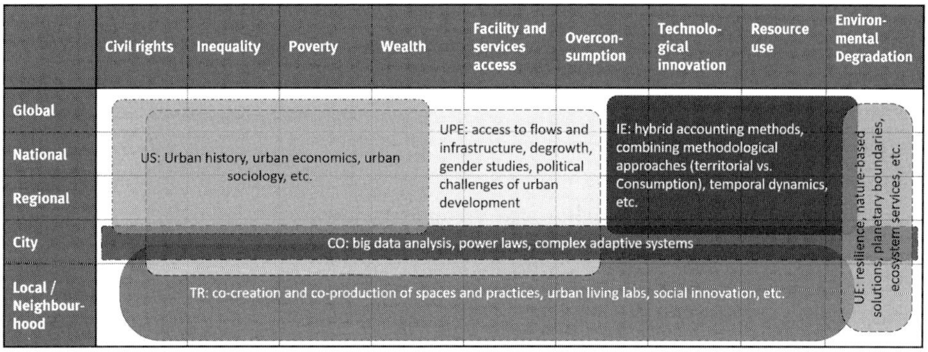

Figure 11.4 From three ecologies of urban metabolism to a patchwork of urban sustainability subdisciplines. Source: own illustration. US: urban studies; CO: complexity theory; TR: transition theory; UPE: urban political ecology; IE: industrial ecology; UE: urban ecology

characteristics, we conceive a matrix showing how each research field contributes to analyzing these impact categories, either with methodological approaches or with specific concepts related to the field. Figure 11.4 shows the core of the different research fields.

In addition, Figure 11.4 shows the scale at which the different disciplinary backgrounds work and the different sustainability challenges that they address. For instance, we can see the three disciplines mentioned earlier. Industrial ecology addresses key issues, such as overconsumption, resource use, and environmental impacts, and is able to allude to technological innovation at the city level, regional level, and national level. Thus, this disciplinary perspective contributes to understanding and assessing the environmental and economic component of urban sustainability. The rather robust accounting methods and models developed by industrial ecology make it possible to monitor the resource use and pollution emissions of (urban) systems and to propose policies and strategies for mitigation. Studies stemming from industrial ecology are generally heavily criticized due to their purely quantitative nature, which does not offer sufficient theoretical insights and does not take into account local urban characteristics and other societal challenges (Bai, 2016; Pincetl et al., 2012). This drawback can be overcome by including urban ecology approaches, which contribute to understanding patterns and feedback loops between human activities and natural ecosystems at local (local fauna and flora) and global (global biogeochemical cycles, biodiversity, etc.) scales. Yet, as Figure 11.4 suggests, urban ecology mainly focuses on the environmental aspect of cities. Finally, political ecology incorporates the ways that power relationships affect the shaping of cities and metabolic processes. It is the only community that is explicitly political and which reflects upon future democratic ways to reshape our habitats and how they work. Nevertheless, political ecology is criticized for only carrying out qualitative research that hinders the implementation of concrete action plans (Newell & Cousins, 2015).

As we can see in Figure 11.4, these three disciplinary perspectives somewhat complement each other and there is some overlap between them, which could lead to hybrid disciplines emerging, although at this stage they are still highly siloed (Bai, 2016; Newell & Cousins, 2015). Some authors (Newell et al., 2017) propose, for instance, to develop a political-industrial ecology of cities in order to combine the quantification methods of industrial ecology with the critical approaches of political ecology, in order to better characterize the extent to which some metabolic flows and urban processes create inequalities.

Nevertheless, as is evident, the three subdisciplines that adopt an urban metabolism lens do not paint the full picture of urban sustainability. There are still large gaps both on a spatial scale and from a disciplinary vantage point, resulting in only partial understandings of the complexity of urban sustainability, especially as regards taking into account the intrinsic characteristics of cities. As such, we conclude that new elements are needed both to consolidate existing research efforts, as well as to better include elements from urban studies and theory in order to cover all aspects of sustainability that are faced in cities.

Some authors call for a new urban science in order to understand the complex functioning of cities in a comprehensive and interdisciplinary way (Batty, 2013; McPhearson et al., 2016). This new urban science should not only bring together the most prominent elements of each subdiscipline, already developed in the introduction to this chapter, but also reach out to other communities, as well as developing integrated methods. For instance, these would include complexity theory (Batty, 2009; Bettencourt, 2013) and transition theory (Nevens et al., 2013). On top of adding new disciplinary vantage points that make it possible to comprehend the more complex aspects of urban phenomena, it is essential to integrate more traditional urban-studies disciplines, such as urban sociology, urban economy, urban history, urban planning, etc., in order to anchor sustainability in local contexts.

When including all of these disciplines, it is possible to observe some overlap across scales and impact categories. It is exactly at these overlapping points that bridges between different research fields can be built. In these crystallization points, the integration of concepts and methods becomes possible, such that we can create an urban science research field, allowing us to obtain a more comprehensive and systemic view of urban development and its link with sustainability, its positive impacts, and its trade-offs. Further research should be carried out in order to better understand those overlaps and trade-offs. This will provide the basis for the more sustainable development of urban systems and of society as a whole.

We consider that in order to address the potential problems and implications of urban characteristics for sustainability, we need to create interfaces between disciplinary approaches, following the ideas we have discussed. A transition away from a focus on urban ecosystems, urban metabolisms, and the social dimension of cities and toward understanding and assessing the link between social and biophysical systems is required. This new form of viewing urban systems by recognizing that urban characteristics do have an impact on social, ecological, and economic subsystems in both positive and the negative ways will support the creation of instruments, methods, and measures to guide policymakers in designing more sustainable urban systems.

Acknowledgments

We thank the reviewers whose comments/suggestions helped improve and clarify this manuscript.

Notes

1. For example, in the first half of the twentieth century, the automobile radically changed the shape of cities and the lifestyle they promoted, just as much as the diffusion of the elevator and the emergence of railroad infrastructures contributed to the design of high-rise buildings and the demolition of city walls (Guallart, 2014).
2. In the polis – later the cosmopolis – citizens gave up their extended knowledge of philosophy, diplomacy, and war, in exchange for specialized strategic expertise (Montanelli, 1959).
3. In ancient Greece citizens could access different types of privileges and rights from metics, today in China the household registration system allows only people with an urban *hukou* (or urban residence permit) to access to the services that the city provides (Bideau & Pagani, 2019; Chan & Zhang, 1999).
4. https://ourworldindata.org/.

References

Adriaanse, A. (1997). *Resource Flows: The Material Basis of Industrial Economies*. Washington, DC: World Resources Institute.

Alberti, M. (1996). Measuring urban sustainability. *Environmental Impact Assessment Review*, 16 (4–6), 381–424.

Alberti, M. (2005). The effects of urban patterns on ecosystem function. *International Regional Science Review*, 28(2), 168–192.

Alberti, M. (2007). *Advances in Urban Ecology: Integrating Humans and Ecological Processes in Urban Ecosystems*. New York: Springer Science & Business Media.

Alves, L. G. A., Ribeiro, H. V., & Mendes, R. S. (2013). Scaling laws in the dynamics of crime growth rate. *Physica A: Statistical Mechanics and Its Applications*, 392(11), 2672–2679.

Annerstedt, M., & Währborg, P. (2011). Nature-assisted therapy: Systematic review of controlled and observational studies. *Scandinavian Journal of Public Health*, 39(4), 371–388.

Athanassiadis, A., Christis, M., Bouillard, P., Vercalsteren, A., Crawford, R. H., & Khan, A. Z. (2018). Comparing a territorial-based and a consumption-based approach to assess the local and global environmental performance of cities. *Journal of Cleaner Production*, 173, 112–123.

Athanassiadis, A., Fernandez, G., Meirelles, J., Meinherz, F., Hoekman, P., & Cari, Y. B. (2017). Exploring the energy use drivers of 10 cities at microscale level. *Energy Procedia*, 122, 709–714.

Bai, X. (2007). Industrial ecology and the global impacts of cities. *Journal of Industrial Ecology*, 11 (2), 1–6.

Bai, X. (2016). Eight energy and material flow characteristics of urban ecosystems. *Ambio*, 45(7), 819–830.

Batty, M. (2009). Cities as complex systems: Scaling, interaction, networks, dynamics and urban morphologies. In R. A. Meyers (ed.), *Encyclopedia of Complexity and Systems Science*, New York: Springer, pp. 1041–1071.

Batty, M. (2013). *The New Science of Cities*. Cambridge, MA: MIT Press.

Beloin-Saint-Pierre, D., Rugani, B., Lasvaux, S., et al. (2017). A review of urban metabolism studies to identify key methodological choices for future harmonization and implementation. *Journal of Cleaner Production*, 163, S223–S240.

Bettencourt, L. M. A. (2013). The origins of scaling in cities. *Science*, *340*(6139), 1438–1441.
Bettencourt, L. M. A., Lobo, J., Helbing, D., Kühnert, C., & West, G. B. (2007). Growth, innovation, scaling, and the pace of life in cities. *Proceedings of the National Academy of Sciences of the United States of America*, 104(17), 7301–7306.
Bideau Graezer, F., Pagani, A. (2019). Shaping urbanity in Chinese New Towns: Politics and narratives. In M. Bonino, F. Governa, M. P. Repellino, & A. Sampieri (eds.), *The City after Chinese New Towns*. Birkhäuser. In publication, pp. 90–96.
Bourdin, A., Eckardt, F., & Wood, A. (2014). *Die ortlose Stadt: Über die Virtualisierung des Urbanen*. transcript Verlag.
Braudel, F. (1992). *Civilization and Capitalism, 15th–18th Century, Vol. III: The Perspective of the World*. Berkeley, CA: University of California Press.
Brundtland, G. H. (1987). *Our Common Future: Brundtland Report*. Oxford: Oxford University Press.
Brunotte, E. (2002). *Lexikon der Geographie: in vier Bänden*. Heidelberg/Berlin: Springer. pp. 29–31.
Chan, K. W., & Zhang, L. (1999). The Hukou system and rural-urban migration in China: Processes and changes. *The China Quarterly*, 160, 818.
Chen, G., Wiedmann, T., Hadjikakou, M., & Rowley, H. (2016). City carbon footprint networks. *Energies*, *9*(8), 602.
Clift, R., & Druckman, A. (2015). *Taking Stock of Industrial Ecology*. New York: Springer.
Corboz, A. (1983). The land as palimpsest. *Diogenes*, 31(121), 12–34.
Cumming, G. S., Cumming, D. H. M., & Redman, C. L. (2006). Scale mismatches in social-ecological systems: Causes, consequences, and solutions. *Ecology and Society*, 11(1). https://doi.org/10.5751/es-01569-110114.
Dijst, M., Worrell, E., Böcker, L., et al. (2018). Exploring urban metabolism: Towards an interdisciplinary perspective. *Resources, Conservation and Recycling*, 132, 190–203.
Durkheim, E., & Halls, W. D. (1997). *The Division of Labor in Society*. New York: Simon and Schuster.
Duvigneaud, P. (1974). *La synthèse écologique: populations, communautés, écosystèmes, biosphère, noosphère*. Paris: Doin.
Duvigneaud, P., & S. Denayer-De Smet. (1977). L'écosystème URBS: L'écosystème urbain bruxellois. In *Productivité biologique en Belgique*. Éditions Duculot. Paris, Gembloux.
Ferrão, P., & Fernández, J. E. (2013). *Sustainable Urban Metabolism*. Cambridge, MA: MIT Press.
Fossett, M., & Dietrich, D. R. (2009). Effects of city size, shape, and form, and neighborhood size and shape in agent-based models of residential segregation: Are Schelling-style preference effects robust? *Environment and Planning B: Planning & Design*, 36(1), 149–169.
Foster, J. B. (2000). *Marx's Ecology: Materialism and Nature*. New York: NYU Press.
Frosch, R. A., & Gallopoulos, N. E. (1989). Strategies for manufacturing. *Scientific American*, 261 (3), 144–152.
Fujita, M., Krugman, P. R., & Venables, A. (2001). *The Spatial Economy: Cities, Regions, and International Trade*. Cambridge, MA: MIT Press.
Gabaix, X. (1999). Zipf's law for cities: An explanation. *The Quarterly Journal of Economics*, 114(3), 739–767.
Gandy, M. (2004). Rethinking urban metabolism: water, space and the modern city. *Cityscape*, 8(3), 363–379.
Geddes, S. P. (1925). The Valley Plan of Civilization. *Survey*, LIV, 288–290, 322–325. www.unz.com/print/TheSurvey-1925jun01/.
Geuze, A., & Skjonsberg, M. (n.d.). Second nature: New territories for the exiled. In *Landscape*, Basel: Birkhäuser.
Glaeser, E. (2011). *Triumph of the City: How Urban Spaces Make Us Human*. London: Pan Macmillan.
Golubiewski, N. (2012). Is there a metabolism of an urban ecosystem? An ecological critique. *Ambio*, 41(7), 751–764.

Greening, L. A., Greene, D. L., & Difiglio, C. (2000). Energy efficiency and consumption – the rebound effect: A survey. *Energy Policy*, 28(6–7), 389–401.
Grimm, N. B., Faeth, S. H., Golubiewski, N. E., et al. (2008). Global change and the ecology of cities. *Science*, 319(5864), 756–760.
Guallart, V. (2014). *The Self-Sufficient City: Internet Has Changed Our Lives but It Hasn't Changed Our Cities, Yet*. Barcelona: Actar.
Halla, P., Wyss, R., & Binder, C. R. (2020). Conceptualising Urban Systems for Sustainability Assessment: Four Powerful Metaphors. In C. R. Binder, E. Massaro, & R. Wyss (eds.), *Sustainability Assessment in Urban Systems*. Cambridge: Cambridge University Press, pp. 241–260.
Harvey, D. (1997). *Justice, Nature and the Geography of Difference*. Hoboken, NJ: Wiley-Blackwell.
Heynen, N. C., Kaika, M., & Swyngedouw, E. (2006). *In the Nature of Cities: Urban Political Ecology and the Politics of Urban Metabolism*. London: Taylor & Francis.
Hood, C., & Gandy, M. (2003). Concrete and clay: Reworking nature in New York City. *Environmental History*, 8(2), 330.
Jackson, T. (2011). *Prosperity without Growth: Economics for a Finite Planet*. London: Routledge.
Jackson, T. (2008). Sustainable consumption and lifestyle change. In A. Lewis (ed.), *The Cambridge Handbook of Psychology and Economic Behaviour*, Cambridge: Cambridge University Press, pp. 335–362.
Jacobs, J. (2016). *The Economy of Cities*. New York: Vintage.
Kennedy, C., Cuddihy, J., & Engel-Yan, J. (2007). The Changing Metabolism of Cities. *Journal of Industrial Ecology*, 11(2), 43–59.
Kraas, F., Leggewie, C., Lemke, P., et al. (2016). *Humanity on the Move: Unlocking the Transformative Power of Cities: Flagship Report*. WBGU-German Advisory Council on Global Change.
Liu, J., Dietz, T., Carpenter, S. R., et al. (2007). Complexity of coupled human and natural systems. *Science*, 317(5844), 1513–1516.
Marshall, A. (1982). *Principles of Economics*, 8th edition. New York: Cosmino.
Massaro, E., Athanassiadis, A., Psyllidis, A., & Binder, C. R. (2020). Ontology- Based Integration of Urban Sustainability Indicators. In C. R. Binder, E. Massaro, & R. Wyss (eds.), *Sustainability Assessment in Urban Systems*. Cambridge: Cambridge University Press, pp. 332–350.
Massaro, E., Ganin, A., Perra, N., Linkov, I., & Vespignani, A. (2018). Resilience management during large-scale epidemic outbreaks. *Scientific reports*, 8(1), 1859.
Marx, K. (2018). *Capital, Vol. 3: A Critique of Political Economy; The Process of Capitalist Production as a Whole* (Classic Reprint). London: Forgotten Books.
Marzluff, J. (2008). *Urban Ecology: An International Perspective on the Interaction between Humans and Nature*. Berlin: Springer Science & Business Media.
Matthews, E. (2000). *The Weight of Nations: Material Outflows from Industrial Economies*. Washington, DC: World Resources Inst.
McIntosh, J. R. (2017). *Mesopotamia and the Rise of Civilization: History, Documents, and Key Questions*. Santa Barbara, CA: ABC-CLIO.
McPhearson, T., Pickett, S. T. A., Grimm, N. B., et al. (2016). Advancing urban ecology toward a science of cities. *BioScience* 66(3): 198–212.
Montanelli, I. (1959). *Storia dei Greci*. Milano: Rizzoli Editore.
Musango, J. K., Currie, P., & Robinson, B. (2017). *Urban Metabolism for Resource Efficient Cities: From Theory to Implementation*. Paris: UN Environment.
Nevens, F., Frantzeskaki, N., Gorissen, L., & Loorbach, D. (2013). Urban Transition Labs: Co-creating transformative action for sustainable cities. *Journal of Cleaner Production*, 50, 111–122.
Newell, J. P., & Cousins, J. J. (2015). The boundaries of urban metabolism: Towards a political–industrial ecology. *Progress in Human Geography*, 39(6): 702–728.
Newell, J. P., Cousins, J. J., & Baka, J. (2017). Political-industrial ecology: An introduction. *Geoforum; Journal of Physical, Human, and Regional Geosciences*, 85, 319–323.
Newman, P., & Kenworthy, J. R. (1989). *Cities and Automobile Dependence: A Sourcebook*. Farnham, UK: Gower Publishing Company.

Osterhammel, J. (2011). *Die Verwandlung der Welt: eine Geschichte des 19. Jahrhunderts*. Munich: C.H.Beck.
Ovink, H., & Boeijenga, J. (2018). *Rebuild by Design: New Approaches to Climate Change*. Rotterdam, NL: Nai010 Publishers.
Parikh, J., & Parikh, K. (1996). Consumption patterns: the driving force of environmental stress. *Pricing the Planet*, 39–48.
Park, R. E., Burgess, E. W., & McKenzie, R. D. (1925). *The City*. Chicago: University of Chicago Press.
Pickett, K. E., & Wilkinson, R. G. (2015). Income inequality and health: A causal review. *Social Science & Medicine*, 128, 316–326.
Pickett, K., & Wilkinson, R. (2010). *The Spirit Level: Why Equality is Better for Everyone*. London: Penguin, UK.
Pincetl, S., Bunje, P., & Holmes, T. (2012). An expanded urban metabolism method: Toward a systems approach for assessing urban energy processes and causes. *Landscape and Urban Planning*, 107(3), 193–202.
Pincetl, S., Graham, R., Murphy, S., & Sivaraman, D. (2016). Analysis of High-Resolution Utility Data for Understanding Energy Use in Urban Systems: The Case of Los Angeles, California. *Journal of Industrial Ecology*, 20(1), 166–178.
Power, M., Wilkinson, R., & Pickett, K. (2016). Inequality, economic democracy and sustainability. World social science report, 2016: Challenging inequalities; pathways to a just world, 160.
Quigley, J. M. (1998). Urban diversity and economic growth. *The Journal of Economic Perspectives: A Journal of the American Economic Association*, 12(2), 127–138.
Raftopoulos, A. (2003). Cartesian analysis and synthesis. *Studies in History and Philosophy of Science. Part B. Studies in History and Philosophy of Modern Physics*, 34(2), 265–308.
Ramaswami, A., Weible, C., Main, D., et al. (2012). A social-ecological-infrastructural systems framework for interdisciplinary study of sustainable city systems. *Journal of Industrial Ecology*, 16(6), 801–813.
Rapport, N., Auge, M., & Howe, J. (1996). Non-places: Introduction to an anthropology of supermodernity. *The Journal of the Royal Anthropological Institute*, 2(2), 359.
Richardson, H. W. (1995). Economies and Diseconomies of Agglomeration. In H. Giersch (ed.), *Urban Agglomeration and Economic Growth*, Berlin: Springer Science and Business Media, pp.123–155.
Samuelson, P. A. (1952). Economics: An introductory analysis. *Harvard Law Review*, 65(3), 542.
Sarkar, S., Phibbs, P., Simpson, R., & Wasnik, S. (2016). The scaling of income distribution in Australia: Possible relationships between urban allometry, city size, and economic inequality. *Environment and Planning B: Urban Analytics and City Science*, 45(4), 603–622.
Schelling, T. C. (1971). Dynamic models of segregation. *The Journal of Mathematical Sociology*, 1 (2), 143–186.
Seto, K. C., Solecki, W. D., & Griffith, C. A. (2015). *The Routledge Handbook of Urbanization and Global Environmental Change*. London: Routledge.
Smith, A. (1776). *The Wealth of Nations: An Inquiry into the Nature and Causes of the Wealth of Nations*. Petersfield, Reino Unido: Harriman House.
Soja, E. (2003). Writing the city spatially. *Cityscape*, 7(3), 269–280.
Skjonsberg, M. (2015). Metrics of Utopia: Optionality, Aesthetics and Patrick Geddes' Ideal of Synoptic Utopia. In Proceedings of the VIII International PhD Seminar "Urbanism & Urbanization"| Symposium Latsis EPFL 2015 (No. EPFL-CONF-217154, pp. 409–415). EPFL Press.
Stern, D. I. (2004). The rise and fall of the environmental Kuznets curve. *World Development*, 32(8), 1419–1439.
United Nations Publications. (2018). *The Sustainable Development Goals Report 2017*.
Vercelli, A. (2002). New Globalization and Sustainability. *SSRN Electronic Journal*. https://doi.org/10.2139/ssrn.304067.

Wachsmuth, D. (2012). Three ecologies: Urban metabolism and the society-nature opposition. *The Sociological Quarterly*, 53(4), 506–523.
West, G. (2017). *Scale: The Universal Laws of Life, Growth, Innovation, Sustainability, and the Pace Of Life in Organisms, Economies, and Companies*. London: Penguin.
Wolman, A. (1965). The metabolism of cities. *Scientific American*, 213(3), 178–190.
World Health Organization. (2015). *Progress on Sanitation and Drinking Water: 2015 Update and MDG Assessment*, World Health Organization.

12

Urban-Industrial Supply Systems

From Global Challenges to Strong Urban Sustainability

Klaus Krumme

12.1 The Urban System and Global (Un)Sustainability

In the twenty-first century, global urbanization has taken human progress into unknown, but most of all simultaneously risky and challenging, territories. Urbanization is not just an infrastructural process that changes patterns in the agglomeration of materials and people worldwide; it also represents increasingly ubiquitous urbanized network economies, societies, and lifestyles (Castells, 2002; Hashemian et al., 2017; Sassen, 2002; Taylor & Derudder, 2015). In this way, urbanization shapes the land use and structural appearance of super-artificial city systems and transforms natural ecosystems, interwoven with network flows of material resources, people, energy, and data in the changed source-sink relationships of globalized urban systems (Bai, 2007; Grimm et al., 2008; Rees, 1992).

The aim of this chapter is to develop a better understanding of the interrelationship between global sustainability and urban sustainability by (1) putting urban sustainability in relation to globalized urban network organization. The predominant interpretive approach of considering global urban systems against the backdrop of material, energy, financial, and information flows is used (2) to emphasize a focus on networked urban supply systems. To bring about a needed transformation, new concepts are developed, grounded in supply chain management (SCM) and extended by incorporating ideas of strong sustainability (Ekins et al., 2003; Neumayer, 2003; Pelenc & Ballet, 2015).

12.1.1 The Duality of Urban Power and the Root Causes of Global Un-Sustainability

Urbanization is linked with existential global processes of change in two central interrelated ways that have significantly shaped both the planet and human society, as parts of a global social-ecological system, in the recent past, continue to do so in the present, and will persist into the future as two sides of the same coin:

1 Cities are nuclei of global societal and demographic developments and of the globalized network economy as both business powerhouses and markets (Friedmann, 1986; Sassen, 1991; Sassen, 2015; Taylor, 1995).

The dominant global position of modern cities is in a way summarized by the term "global cities" (Sassen, 1991). The hereby indicated shift in the global economy and in global society toward a number of urban power hotspots in complex urban networks has opened a scientific discussion about how to generally analyze and describe the role of the world's urban centers in the patterns and trends of globalization (King, 2009).

Cities are key for the "widening, deepening and speeding up of worldwide interconnectedness in all aspects of social life" (Held et al., 2000). They enable corporate developments for transnational activities through infrastructure and expertise and by representing the major communication and supply network nodes. Thus, they are global hubs of incoming or outgoing activities and resulting innovation in business and society that control the overall developments of a "global village" (Sassen, 2010a; Taylor & Csomós, 2012). Dominance structures, functional hierarchies and nested organizational frames within emerging sets of cities and of connections between cities are underpinning this global impact and are determining a globalized pattern of economic relationships, social interdependencies as well as a still-emerging cultural development of global urbanism. These contexts have been subject to what has been described as "world city networks" (WCN: Taylor, 1997; Taylor, 2004; Taylor & Derudder, 2015).

The context of cities in networks of exchange described here has long been the subject of urban theory. Weber (1921) already saw the exchange of goods as a distinguishing feature of cities over other forms of settlement. Ullman (1953) considered the connections between settlement areas to be just as important as the characteristics of the areas themselves. In times when society and economics are part of globalized networks, Ullman's argument has rather yielded to the "dominance of the space of places by the space of flows" (Castells, 2002) and has further fueled the interplay between places and flows. Amin and Thrift (2002) finally replace the idea of the city as a territorial economic power spot with a definition of cities as places of and within spatially extended socioeconomic relations.

2 Urbanization and the emerging global urban system is closely linked to the fundamental drivers of the unsustainable forces threatening the planet's ecological capacity and integrity (Ahern, 2011; IPCC, 2015; Keivani, 2010; Rees, 1992; Seto et al., 2017).

With the increase of population, wealth production, and primary energy and material consumption concentrated in urban systems and directing most world resource stocks to urban areas, cities are the largest cause of global ecological impacts (Bai, 2007; Cajot et al., 2015; Wackernagel et al., 2006). While currently representing about 3 percent of the earth's surface, urban areas are home to slightly more than 50 percent of the earth's population, but consume approximately 75 percent of natural resources and almost 80 percent of the global greenhouse gas (GHG) emissions come from urban emitters (Girardet, 2000; Marchal et al., 2011; IPCC, 2015; Worldwatch Institute, 2016). The global overshoot is already causing acute or predictable scarcity of resources at regional or global scale, and is overstretching ecological capacities, for example, by destabilizing the global climate (Hoekstra & Wiedmann, 2014; Steffen et al., 2015). The impact of cities, measured as urban ecological footprints (Rees, 1992; Rees & Wackernagel, 1996; Wackernagel et al., 2006), is not just a result of cities' status as consumptive territories or "places," but an outcome of a "machinerie" of worldwide economic value-creation patterns driven by cities in terms of modern product life cycles/energy-supply systems and their correlated material flows and services (from resource extraction, design and production, and supply chains, to consumption and use).

Despite the progress made so far in technology for resource efficiency and substitution of harmful materials, the absolute global amount of resource consumption is still increasing; a decoupling from economic growth is not in sight and material efficiency has recently declined due to shifts in international economic production patterns (Schandl et al., 2018; Wiedmann et al., 2015).

The effects of climate change on production and supply capacities, and further increases in demand due to urbanization, will increase this problem nexus, since the proportion of urban dwellers in the world population is expected to be around 70 percent in 2050 (United Nations, 2017).

12.1.2 The Urban Turnaround: Toward Sustainable Urban Systems

As much as cities are currently a major force for un-sustainability, it is obvious that cities could equally be key to sustainability (Bugliarello, 2006; Rees & Wackernagel, 1996). Concepts to achieve urban sustainability have to be capable of reversing the contradictory relationship between urbanization and global sustainability, going beyond concepts of mitigation and adaptation, which, in the narrower focus on fighting climate change, have only been considered as a crucial but not sufficient aspect of sustainable urban development.

True sustainable urban development should be capable of integrating various fields of development at higher levels of understanding and with a view to identifying and executing comprehensive solutions. Thus, central to urban sustainability is a view of the city/cities as nested systems by exploring the root causes, feedbacks, and emergence of urban as well as global un-sustainability in their connectedness and in a comprehensive way.

There are still knowledge gaps and a necessity for new research priorities that need to be tackled before it is possible to view cities in this way (Seto et al., 2017). The need for more comprehensive concepts of the city has been articulated from different disciplinary perspectives. From the viewpoint of urban sociology and urban social theory, the demand for conceptually embedding cities in the context of ecosystems, as social systems and beyond their physical presence, has been reinforced by Harvey (1996). From a background of environmental geography and environmental studies, Seto et al. (2017) argue that a functioning planetary ecosystem needs a focus on urban systems; conversely, urban sustainability cannot succeed without a deep understanding of the ecological foundations of urban developments.

The resulting system to be transformed is complex because it involves multiple scales, dimensions, and transformation domains. On the one hand, the direct spatial scale of the city is affected. At this point, we know quite a lot about the emergence of so-called un-biological scaling behavior of cities and metropolitan regions due to internal network effects, which may partly explain, among other things, the disproportionate resource consumption of cities in relation to urban growth curves (Bettencourt & West, 2010). On the other hand, in socioeconomic terms, there are obvious network connections and interdependencies with respect to the bioregional hinterland in order to grasp system relationships of production and consumption in a more sustainable way (Jacobs, 1984; Newman, 1999; Newman, 2006; Newman & Jennings, 2012; Torreggiani et al., 2012; Zasada et al., 2013). This includes new relationships between local and regional/urban and rural producers, traders, and consumers on different regional scales.

To invert the un-biological scaling behavior of cities and metropolitan regions, Sassen and Dotan (2011) promote a mutual coping of the multi-scale ecological interconnectedness of cities with the biosphere. To establish sustainable cycles between cities and the biosphere, "third nature" capacities (mergences of boosted interplays between city and natural ecosystem functions), supported by groundbreaking technological and social innovations, will enable a productive interplay and a shift in the mode of consumption and production. This theoretical approach connects the urban socioeconomic system to ideas that are widely accepted in ecological economics (EE) (Costanza et al., 1992, Costanza & Patten, 1995) and puts technological innovation into dynamic relationships to social-ecological systems (SES) (Ostrom, 2009), as to the recent conceptualizations of social-ecological-technological systems (SETS) for urban sustainability (Grimm et al., 2017; Krumme, 2016; McPhearson et al., 2016).

However, still the majority of existing approaches either remain city-centered or relate the city to the direct functional spatial environment, for example, of the region. Multiple levels of globalized functional interaction, as demonstrated by WCN research, are largely not included. Given the level of global interconnectedness of production, supply, and consumption patterns with respect to urbanization, it seems that planetary teleconnections and resulting macroscale dynamics of cities are still under-recognized in the implementation of urban stewardship frameworks for planetary resources and ecosystemic relationships (Liu et al., 2013; Seitzinger et al., 2012; Seto et al., 2012). As Seto et al. (2017) point out: "[G]iven the magnitude of current urban transitions and the global reach of their production-consumption systems, there is a need to generate robust scientific knowledge on cross-scale interactions, tipping points, thresholds, and limits that are set off by urbanization to orient urban development towards more sustainable trajectories." Moser and Hart (2015) conceptualize eight categories of socioeconomic teleconnections in relation to global climate change without, however, emphasizing the magnitude of the global urban system. Liu et al. (2013) refer to teleconnections rather as physical interactions of natural (and already modified) systems and by definition separate globalization as the interaction of socioeconomic systems. Finally, they understand "telecoupling" as a framework that

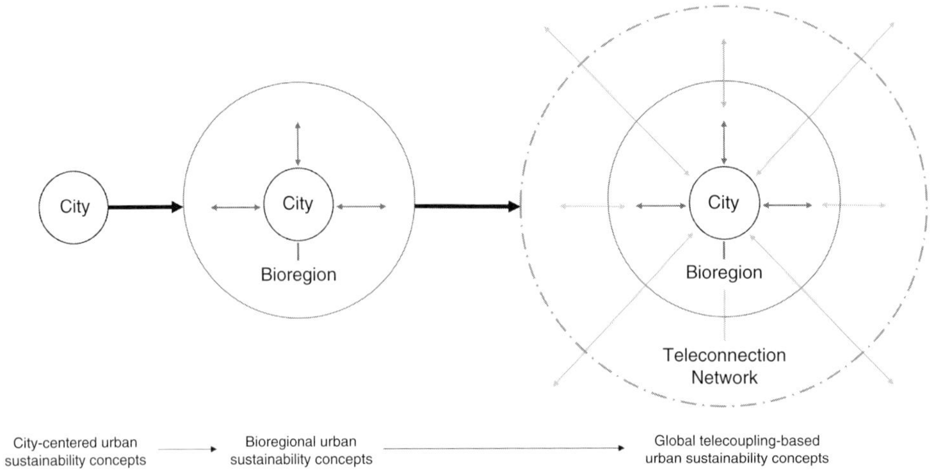

Figure 12.1 Scales of urban sustainability: City-centered, bioregional, telecouplings

combines the dynamics of both, as SES of not primarily territorial, but globally functional networked interactions via flows, agents, causes, and effects.

To take up again the basic idea of this chapter – Castells's notion of the dominance of flows over places – it is this globalized "space of flows," that determines the global urban ecological footprint through the nature of urban demand, supply needs, and practices, which has to be changed drastically (Grimm et al., 2008; McHale et al., 2015; Moore, 2015; Wackernagel et al., 2006). The required system integration for multilayered sustainability strategies (Liu et al., 2015) would rely on the power of cities to operationalize ecosystems, their services, (industrial) production, supply, consumption, and lifestyles both integratively and sustainably. Such an approach would affect both of the strategic integration levels identified by Liu et al. (2015): the interaction of (a) human-nature-nexuses and the integration of (b) telecoupling, understood as teleconnected socioeconomic and environmental interactions.

Figure 12.1 demonstrates scales of urban sustainability concepts from city-centered, via bioregional up to telecoupling-based (global) strategies.

However, the operationalizable system knowledge for this is missing in sustainability science and sustainability practice (Seto et al., 2017). Nevertheless, there are well elaborated, but still theoretically and practically disintegrated, approaches that can merge in a synergistic way to give alternative solutions. Those building blocks of a new concept are the subject of the next paragraph.

12.2 Sustainable Urban-Industrial Supply Systems

12.2.1 Conceptual Foundations: Challenges and Building Blocks

Based on the paradigm shift described by Castells (2002) as the "space of flows" and the causal relationship between these flows and the exceeding of the thresholds of planetary boundaries, WCN-compatible concepts are available, although they are primarily descriptive-analytically oriented and lack a stronger transformative sustainability-oriented component. It can hardly be doubted that the findings regarding the nested systems organization of global urban systems are not only relevant to the understanding of global un-sustainability (as explained earlier), but also provide several starting points for an inverted transformative theory. The aim must be to find the "safe operating space" for cities based on the planetary boundaries framework (Steffen et al., 2015) and to promote perspectives for sustainable development by means of modified qualities, quantities, and constellations of supply and demand in the global urban system.

As Friedmann (1986) postulates in his world city hypothesis, "the form and extent of a city's integration with the world economy and the functions assigned to the city in the new spatial division of labor will be decisive for any structural changes occurring within it." Following this, alternative constellations in the hierarchical functional order of urban systems would not have to reverse the globalization of cities in their networks, but would promote new orientations, especially for critical resource, information, and energy flows, that respect ecological capacities, as well as find opportunities within newly balanced multi-scale nested hierarchies of urban systems.

Although also not sustainability-oriented, an interesting concept that could be used originates from economic geography: the global commodity chain (GCC) framework (Gereffi & Korzeniewicz, 1994) is used to understand interrelated functions, operations, and transactions that produce, distribute, and globally consume commodities. Like WCN, GCC emerged as a "global network alternative" to city-centered or national small-scale analysis in urban and economic geography (Derudder & Witlox, 2010). In terms of a "world-system analysis," GCC analysis (as well as its derivatives, global value chains (GVC) and global production networks (GPN)) relates economic urban network centers to their role as financial, information, and trade nodes. It becomes clear that the upward trend of cities worldwide is a downstream result of urban functions in these networks (Derudder & Witlox, 2010; Hesse, 2010). This, however, only indirectly addresses domains of urban policy. Rather, the decisive domains of design and action lie with companies or the emergence of their interactions in value chains (Yeung, 1994).

To ascertain the root causes of global un-sustainability, we fundamentally identify that the urban pressures on the planet, are strongly associated with industrial – corporate-driven – value creation as a functional urban-industrial amalgamation (Krumme, 2016; Liu et al., 2015; McHale et al., 2015). Globalized industrial value and supply chains are caused by a largely urban demand system, which requires structures and services for bridging global teleconnections and actually built up the "nervous system" of the urbanization progress.

While the GCC framework provides models for describing and understanding the space of flows and the specific dominance effects of globalization and urbanization, it still does not adequately exploit the role of modern operations-design services in their value-added relationships (Coe et al., 2008). The role of modern supply chain management (SCM) and logistics services in particular has been underrepresented as a conditional performance factor (Rodrigue & Hesse, 2006).

12.2.2 Taking a Supply Chain View on Urban Sustainability

In addition to the need for innovation in order to develop the functional capacities for the interaction between cities and the nested organizations of the biosphere, developed by Sassen and Dotan (2011), further approaches are needed. Sassen and Dotan contextualize shifted cycles of production and consumption, among other things, in ecological economics. This combinatorial strategy is helpful but needs to be extended with other essential elements. These elements refer in particular to the fact that in the modern economic system, the interaction of production and consumption alone is not sufficient to fully explain the resulting demand for resources (Melkonyan & Krumme, 2020).

Rather, the emergent system effect is co-generated by the nature of the structures and services of the intermediate "translating" supply chain system (Krumme, 2020; O'Rourke, 2014). A good example of this is the digitalized interaction of buying and trading and of such marked product life cycles. The growth of e-commerce, with all its implications and partly unsustainable new consumption trends, is made possible only through the power of (digital) supply chain structures and services (flexible "on demand" services, fast home delivery, supply chain tracing, returns, etc.).

The connections between and operationalizations of urban-industrial value-added functions, on different scale levels, are therefore represented by industrial supply chains, which represent a variety of services connected with a flow of goods that connect industrial sources with mostly urban demand and consumption systems. It does not matter if industrial sources and production sectors are urban or rural. They are planned and operationalized not by cities but by companies worldwide in order to operate and develop supply systems based on mainly urban demand systems. This generates "on the ground" feedbacks in the sense of global un-sustainability, as the operationalized levels of value creation, transportation, storage, transshipment, information flow, and energy flow are linked to enormous emissions and resource consumption. The supply chain is a major trigger for the energy consumption and ecological footprints (water, carbon) that accompany the product (Hoekstra, 2015; Hoekstra & Wiedmann, 2014). Product life cycles are thus underpinned by services and structures that to a large extent become anchored in spatial forms in cities and metropolitan areas.

Given the global space of flows and the role of urbanization in overstating and controlling production and consumption patterns, alternative constellations of products, energy, materials, information, and cash flows must be integrated into supply services and structures (Krumme, 2020; O'Rourke 2014) and be considered in reference to urban-industrial source-sink relationships.

However, on the demand side, especially for cities, this requires sustainable reversal in the commercial and consumer systems, deeply rooted in the sphere of lifestyle transformations (Melkonyan & Krumme, 2020). Changing lifestyles necessitate a significant qualitative behavioral shift and place the collective societal interest alongside individual needs (Jackson, 2005; Lorek and Spangenberg, 2014; Moore, 2015). Extensive recent research shows a strong interaction between lifestyles and supply chain (including logistics) services with respect to unsustainable effect and also potential sustainability gains (Melkonyan & Krumme, 2020). Further conceptual progress makes it necessary to take a closer look at sustainable supply chain strategies.

12.2.3 Sustainable Supply Chains Revisited

Supply chains connect sources and sinks. When it comes to the role of urban systems in the global displacement of source-sink structures, as discussed, a supply chain strategy must provide the necessary coordinates for sustainable urban-industrial supply systems.

Generally, the concept of the supply chain describes complex structures and processes of contracting companies/customers as a network of suppliers: manufacturing plants, retailers, supporting companies involved in various design, procurement, storing, shipping, selling, or servicing processes (Sheffi & Rice, 2005). Defined in this way, supply chains basically consist of physical elements – i.e., infrastructures, production facilities, distribution facilities, etc. – and integrated management, services, and flows of information, finance, and energy (Figure 12.2). Very generally, supply chain management (SCM) describes integrated, coordinated, and cooperative activities of design, planning, execution, control, and monitoring along supply chain structures and flows with the objective of effectively synchronizing demand and supply (Cooper et al., 1997).

In the context of this chapter, supply chain businesses integrate strongly urbanized global patterns and contextualize the supply chain as a mediator between the (consumptive) city and its markets and retailing system as terrains within the dispersed worldwide pattern of production and product-service distribution.

Principally, there are manifold potential starting points for sustainability in SCM. By definition, modern SCM integrates flows of goods, information, energy, personnel, and financial value into economic and social systems. With respect to the challenge of sustainability, the paradigms of SCM have been expanded to develop sustainable SCM (SSCM) (Carter & Rogers, 2008; Seuring & Müller, 2008). Central performance indicators to be addressed by effective SSCM are those that display and modify "co-flows" of resources (e.g., water, energy, carbon, or further ecosystem-dependent assets) that support sustainable economic value creation (Krumme, 2020; Linton et al., 2007). Notwithstanding, the "proactive" role of transformative supply chains in bringing about changes in the overall socioeconomic system – for example, based on concepts from GCCs – has so far been under-examined (Krumme & Melkonyan, 2020).

In this respect, Krumme (2020) has analyzed some shortcomings of state-of-the-art SSCM, which are believed to be primarily due to SSCM being founded on "weak sustainability."[1] He proposes strategical improvements based on strong sustainability, particularly the integration of *principles of nested systems organization* as well as

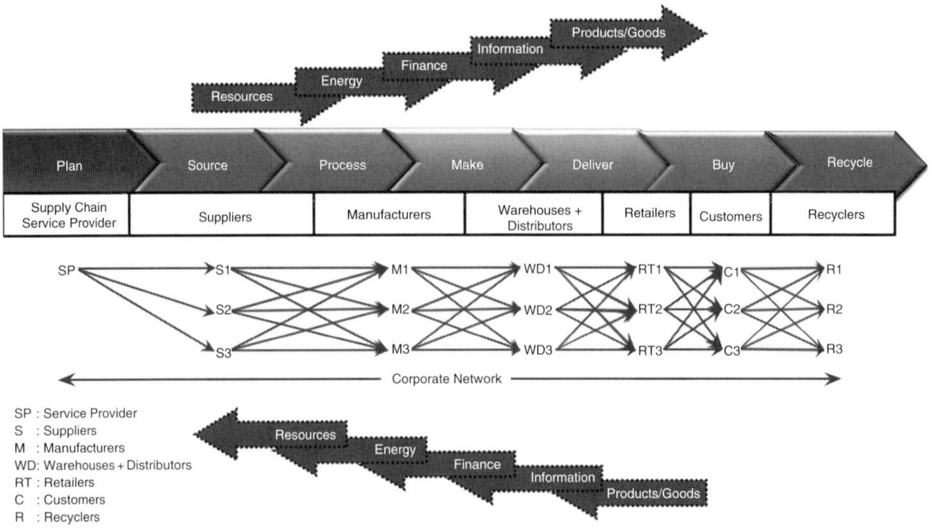

Figure 12.2 Structural elements, operational networks, and flows of a supply chain, including information, energy, and finance. Source: Krumme, 2020

conceptual bonds from ecological economics: (1) the assessment of *critical capital*, (2) the *distributive equity* of capitals within and along the entire supply chain, and (3) the *shared responsibility* of supply chain stakeholders. He also advocates an advanced definition of SSCM that takes account of externalized environmental and social costs in order to balance the service-level requirements of individual customers with societal interests. This results in advanced business and service archetypes at different levels of supply chain planning, management, and controlling as "*lead sustainability service provider*" (Gruchmann et al., 2018; Krumme & Melkonyan, 2020).

The above explanation is relevant in the context of this chapter, since in this way, SSCM would represent the missing link between the network nodes of GCC and the needed transformative sustainability orientation. Since a reduction of the urban ecological footprint depends ultimately on the altered qualities, quantities, and constellations of resource consumption in the form of imported material and energy, and on the quality and quantity of correlated outflows (including all waste deposits), SSCM is needed to implement modified compositions as well as changed spatial and temporal patterns of product-service life cycles and respective material-resource and energy flows. Moreover, SSCM is capable of communicating between strategical levels of governance in value-creating networks to downscale operations and decision-making. It can be shown that any form of sustainable change in modes of production – e.g., the modularization of products and product components – in the fundamental structural and temporal extension of product life cycles, and in effective circularity depends on their implementation by supply chain services (Krumme & Melkonyan, 2020).

12.2.4 Taking an Ecological Economics View of Urban-Industrial Supply

Against the understanding of worldwide dispersed network flows of resources, energy, and data, certain capacities would have to be incorporated into improved concepts, namely those that are not typical industrial capacities but also act as "sources for the sources" in the form of ecosystem goods and services (EG&S). According to ecological economics (EE), industrial production would be seen as the consumption of natural capital (Costanza et al., 1992; Wiedmann et al., 2006).

The importance of EE for urban sustainability, as a counterpoint to neoclassical socio-economic theories, has already been indicated by Sassen (2009; 2010a; 2010b). EE is based on the essential idea that the evolution and survival of complex systems is critically connected to nested systems hierarchies (Costanza et al., 1993). Following this, Costanza and Patten (1995) argue that a nested hierarchical organization of systems must be considered in sustainable development in order to avoid failures, costs, and further risks.

EE recognizes the overall design of desirable sustainable systems as a nested organization of distinct capitals, understood as stocks and flows (natural, human, social, financial, technological/manufactured capital), where natural capital plays an ultimate role as the conditioning and limiting factor for other capital forms. As the basis of the central paradigm of "strong sustainability," natural capital is therefore classified as "critical capital" for sustainable development and not substitutable through other capital forms (e.g., technology) (Daly, 1997). This contrasts sharply with the "weak sustainability" models, which are much more popular and in principle assume equivalence (and hence substitutability) between less differentiated categories of sustainability (as social, ecological, and economic).

However, aspects of strong sustainability offer high conceptual compatibility with the terms of SSCM (Krumme, 2020). Beside the notion of critical capitals, this is based on the sub-concepts of the *shared* and (to all) *transparent responsibility* in and along value chains and of the *distributive equity* of capitals among the value chain's share- and stakeholders (Kestemont, 2015; Krumme, 2020).

12.3 Strong Sustainability Frameworks of Urban-Industrial Supply

12.3.1 Metabolism Models and Sustainable Urban-Industrial Supply

Principally, source-sink relations of demand and supply have been central to the urban metabolism (UM) of the "ecology of cities" (Pickett et al., 1997) since the 1970s. UM describes holistic budgets that can help visualize the flow of material resources and energy and rearrange in- and outflows and circulations (Chrysoulakis et al., 2013; Kalmykova et al., 2015; Newman, 1999; Thomson & Newman, 2018). UM can serve as a modeling tool to make cities more resource- and energy-efficient, to provide indicators for alternative urban design, to introduce information and control levels, and to strengthen the physical and technological aspects of the city as a circular resource system (Thomson & Newman, 2018). Although metabolic references of the UM may be essential to sustainable cities, the limits of the concept have so far lain in its fundamentally spatial foundation. The UM is essentially unable to integrate teleconnections and globalized supply chains into the global sustainability impact of the urban demand system.

In terms of visualization, control, and modification, as well as a consistent idea of establishing dynamic flow, UM shows many intersections with the concept of the supply chain. One could say that UM is a clear concept that, initially, seems very clear within named system boundaries, while the supply chain is primarily defined functionally against the background of planning, management, and controlling tasks. Of course, every supply chain is reflected spatially. Within this section of the chapter, a conceptual fusion of both approaches is shown.

The "urban-industrial nexus" (Krumme, 2016) represents a conceptual shift from a structural/spatial approach toward a functional redrawing of system boundaries to reveal the inseparability of the "urban" and the "industrial" spheres as the two planetary drivers for (un)sustainability. Krumme (2016) presented an EE-based metabolism model of "urban-industrial supply and demand systems" (Figure 12.3). A recent refinement integrates supply chain thinking and illustrates sustainability gains through transformative SSCM (Figure 12.4) (Krumme, 2020).

In accordance to the "full world" economy models of EE (Daly, 1973; Daly, 2005), the general concept (see Figure 12.3) considers natural capital as a limited system environment in which the structures, processes, and functionalities of the economy are embedded, determined to a large extent by "laws" of physics (thermodynamics) and ecology in particular. The economic system, expressed here in terms of the urban-industrial nexus, is seen as a subsystem as part of a nested organization within planetary boundaries (critical natural capital), but puts pressure on the functioning of the surrounding system through economic activity resulting in economic growth. Thus, the ties between industrial production, supply, and (urban) consumption systems can be interpreted as the expenditure of natural capital. Besides the typology of the sinks as "urban," a source-based view then incorporates those capacities which are the "sources of the sources," linked as *eco-industrial sources*. The expansion of the urban-industrial, economic subsystem is driven by demand and supply between source and sink. The environmental impact is determined by supply and demand, combined with the turnover of resources, the effects on the eco-industrial source (in terms of conversion of natural capital into human or industrial capital), and all kind of wastes/emissions from the urban sink, including nonrecyclable deposits of degraded resources.

On this basis, future sustainability functions can be captured by SSCM (Figure 12.4 below). Once the relationship between the eco-industrial source and the urban sink is further qualified by a supply chain, the relationship can be embedded into a more comprehensive *sustainable supply systems model* (SUSY) (Figure 12.4). A supply chain perspective is linked conceptually to the EE and UM framework and the main drivers of (un) sustainability. The scope of the supply chain is contextualized with the ultimate meaning of ecosystem goods and services as a direct form of how critical natural capital becomes "valuable" in the economic system.

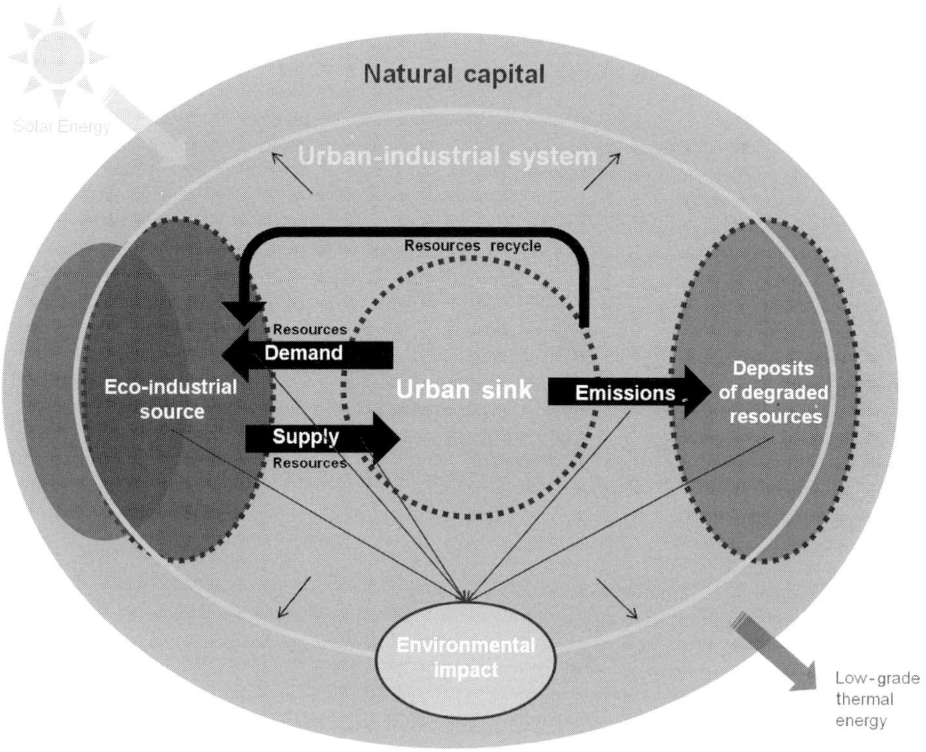

Figure 12.3 Advanced urban-industrial metabolism model. Source: Krumme, 2016

Principles of strong sustainability, particularly with respect to critical capital, shared responsibility, and distributive equity, are implemented at all stages of the supply chain: *S* (sourcing of materials), *P* (production and manufacturing), *D* (distribution, storage, transshipments), *R* (retailing), and *B* (buying). Direct further effects on sustainability are addressed by nonclassical elements of SSCM in the (urban) after-sales area. This is related to sustainable forms of consumption and people's lifestyles, as well as indirectly to the redesigning of product life cycles and associated supply chain services. Within the urban system, at least three different forms of consumption and use are shown: *U1* (primary consumption), *U2* (further circulation of used products; sharing economy), and *U3* (product modification or modularization, including upcycling into other forms of use; extended circular economy). *U2* and *U3* take advantage of the high degree of network density and interdependence (physical/social infrastructure as well as high variability of available product-service systems) to effectively extend product life cycles (Krumme & Melkonyan, 2020). *C* describes the conventional recycling of materials (simple circular economy) after the previous stages have been fully implemented. Closed loops in relation to the eco-industrial source (e.g., via remanufacturing or refurbishment) are linked to all segments in the after-sales area. This also applies to deposits, whose integration into the

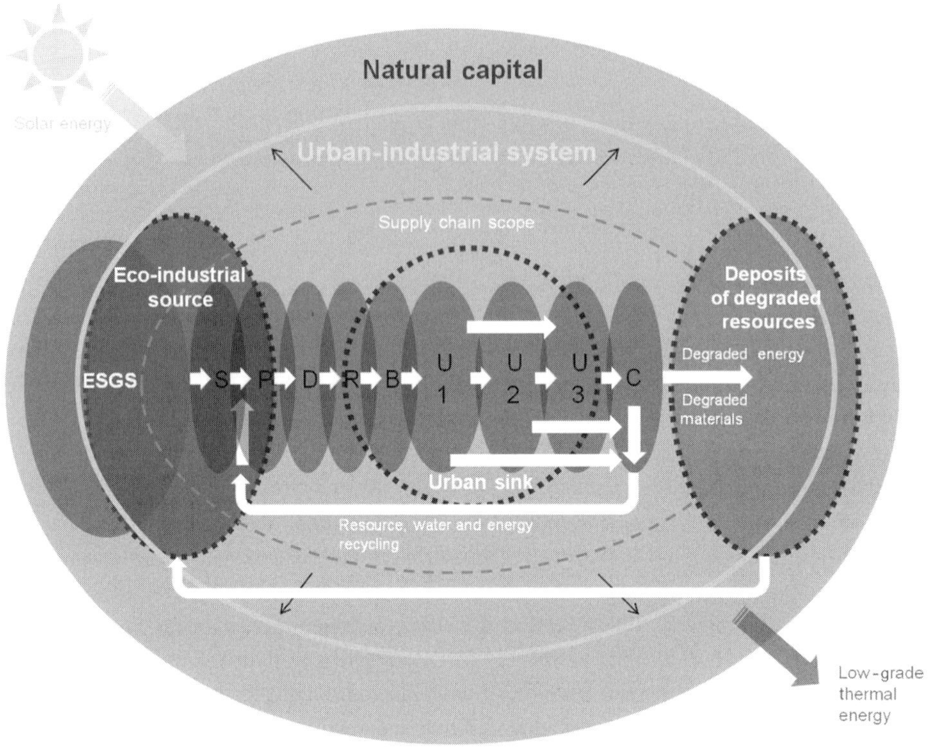

Figure 12.4 SUSY (sustainable supply systems) based on the urban-industrial metabolism. Source: Krumme 2019

closed loop has to be intensified, or their emission must be avoided by upstream "precaution" qualities of the supply chain.

It becomes obvious that realizing such a transformative supply chain would involve innovated logistics skills as part of the business and service portfolios of a green (urban) economy. The service model of the "lead sustainability service provider" (Gruchmann et al., 2018; Krumme & Melkonyan, 2020) represents a recently published framework for innovation that can support the needed transformations on the operational service level.

In its development, this business and service model is based on the evolution of system-oriented, knowledge-intensive archetypes of logistics and supply chain services, which are characterized by comprehensive digitization of the supply chain and its corresponding systems (e.g., internet of things, internet of services in "Industry 4.0," or newer "smart city" concepts) (Krumme & Melkonyan, 2020). The lead sustainability service does not focus on urban metabolism, but rather on necessarily sustainable supply chains, which, as explained, are characterized by urban-industrial systems on different scale levels. The lead sustainability service provider is capable of integrating different scales for operating such supply chains and refers to the need for telecoupling (e.g., between eco-industrial sources and urban sinks), as well as for innovation in the (often structurally urban) last or first mile of the supply chain.

12.3.2 Multi-Domain Framework of Sustainable Urban-Industrial Supply

The earlier explanations have made clear that the inversion of the contradictory relationship between urbanization, a globalized urban system, and global sustainability is a multi-layered problem. To create solutions, state-of-the-art concepts must be linked to new approaches in a nested system context. The paradigm shifts toward a focus on the global space of flows, such as those represented by WCN or GCC, raise the question – beside the already existing problem of the multiple and overlapping dimensions to be tackled – of what kind of transformation mechanism can take account of the interdependence of modern urban systems and global teleconnections (Liu et al., 2015, Seto et al., 2017). A first sketch of a framework therefore has to represent and connect the concrete levels of action domains and strategic tasks. It is important to understand that, based on the nested systems organization theory, tasks and domains do not operate discretely on different scales. Rather, the levels of domains and tasks integrate different scales to achieve emergent network effects.

To perceive problems correctly in their comprehensiveness and to cope with complexity, systems thinking is a possible basis (Bossel, 2007; Meadows & Wright, 2008). In a systems-thinking approach the entities being investigated and their environment are seen as (sub)systems in relationships with other systems, placed at higher organizational levels. The features of this "system of systems" can be detected in its subsystems and it is described using the principles of nested systems hierarchies or nested systems organization (Bossel, 2007; Findeisen et al., 1980; Mesarovic et al., 1970). All the interconnected systems, then understood as subsystems within a greater complex system, are part and parcel of a dynamic environment.

Thus, our perception should turn toward principles of organization with regard to analyses and transformation as the vital correlated parts of sustainability science (Wiek et al., 2012). The focus should not be primarily on whether specific system factors are included in assessment, planning, and management, but rather on the way in which the comprehensiveness of factors is organized to produce a sustainable (with regard to transformation) or unsustainable (with regard to analysis) interplay and performance.

The multi-domain framework proposed here responds to the complexity of the targeted real-world systems, as well as to the interfaces between the levels of organization therein. The framework represents different analysis, understanding, and design levels of the nested organization, which is connected to the urban "space of flows." Dedicated to a sustainability transformation process, the framework takes up several innovative conceptual elements, as discussed (1. social-ecological-technological systems, 2. urban metabolism, 3. urban-industrial networks, 4. ecological economics, 5. sustainable supply chain management, 6. lead sustainability service provider). The goal is to outline action domains and strategy task levels for a comprehensive approach to increasing the sustainability of urban systems

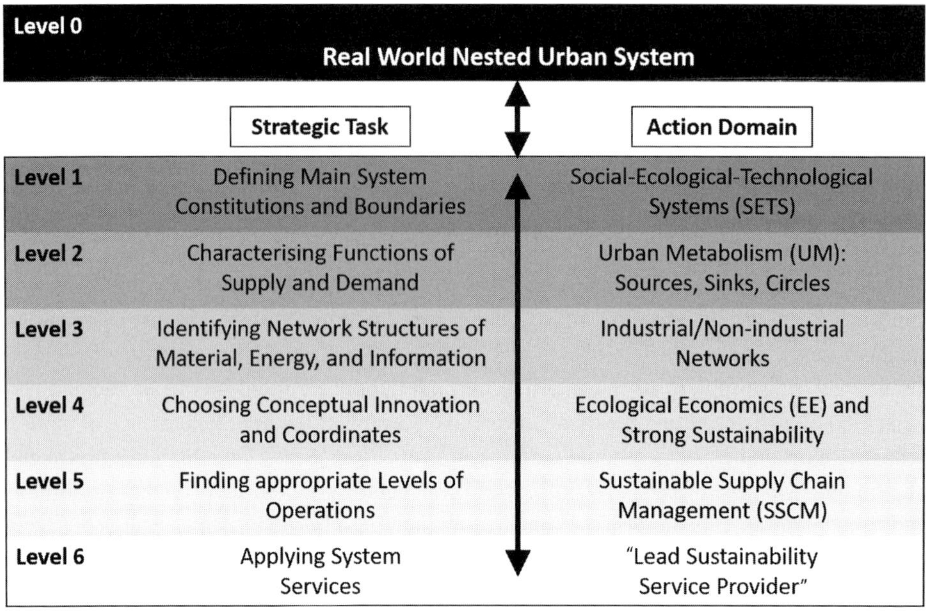

Figure 12.5 Multi-domain framework of sustainable urban-industrial supply systems

through a multi-domain analytical lens and a transformational governance structure. This chapter offers a first orientation in this regard. Detailed future conceptual work and research are needed in order to expand this approach with further details.

To explain the multilevel framework for sustainable urban-industrial supply systems outlined for the first time here, action domains, strategic tasks, the macroscale, and the microscale are connected on seven (0 to 6) levels (see Figure 12.5):

1 First of all, all real problem constellations exist across scales and are extremely complex (level 0). Levels 1 to 6 serve to break these down into actionable and necessarily coherent action and transformation levels.
2 Level 1 deals with the qualitative differentiation of system constitution and system boundaries in order to be able to recognize general system effects (the strategic task). The associated action domain, which is a tool in itself, contains frameworks such as social-ecological-technological systems (SETS, Krumme, 2016), which can map the impact dimensions and their interaction. The integration of technological-organizational dimensions is particularly important in relation to urban systems (Krumme, 2016) and this level connects them in the sense of "third natures" (Sassen & Dotan, 2011).
3 Level 2 identifies the interaction between demand and supply in integrated considerations of production, supply, and consumption. It identifies sources and sinks of material and energy flows. The urban metabolism (UM) concept loses its narrow city-related context due to the incorporation of global teleconnections, but henceforth, functionally

refers to the global space of flows with respect to WCN and GCC. It thus corresponds to the extended metabolism models presented in this chapter (Figure 12.3 and Figure 12.4).

4 Level 3 deals with the network structures responsible for material, energy, and correlated information flows. In addition to industrial networks, nonindustrial networks (for example, at the local or regional level, networks of small-scale and micro-production for local/regional consumption) can be included.

5 Level 4 combines the aforementioned levels of analysis with value-based normative strategies for a desired sustainability transformation. These are influenced, in particular, by using the strong sustainability models of ecological economics to determine a value and reference system (Costanza et al., 1992; Pelenc & Ballet, 2015).

6 Level 5 combines the strategic and operational management of material, energy, and information flows (or cycles) at the level of the expanded understanding of SSCM. In doing so, local, regional, and global chains in the sense of telecoupling (Liu et al., 2015) are all operationalizable.

7 Level 6 fills the supply chain structures with services, in the sense of business capabilities of "lead sustainability service providers." It is important to note that these services work within the framework of the parent levels. Thus, business is not detached, but acts in a broader environment of tasks and stakeholders in order to be "transformative" and sustainable. Since the urbanized interplay of production, supply and demand, and consumerism is implemented through business rather than municipal institutions, the framework offers a different, more realistic focus than the state-of-the-art urban sustainability transformations.

12.4 Conclusion and Outlook: New Pathways in Urban Sustainability Science

Previous approaches to urban sustainability research have been predominantly city-centered without regard for complex teleconnections, understood as globalized network structures and flows, which are responsible for the global manifestation of urban unsustainability. In principle, the established exploration of urban systems as a phenomenon of globalized networks (WCN, GCC), especially through the application of the organizational principle of nested systems, offers interesting starting points for mapping different strata of problem description (analysis) and finding solutions (transformation).

What is needed are frameworks and tools that can describe very precisely the respective network structures and flows in their unsustainable effects. The proposed integration of supply chains as a concept can be particularly powerful here. Conversely, supply chains can also be operationalized for urban sustainability transformations if their conceptual framework and methods are related to established sustainability-science strategies (Krumme, 2020). One such opportunity is the integration of SSCM with alternatives to neoclassical economics, namely ecological economics.

The multi-domain framework outlined at the end of the chapter relates several domain levels to each other, but it is a preliminary sketch. Research and experimental applications need to be rapidly developed in the face of the urgency of global sustainability issues. Based on the outlined multi-domain framework, it is important to think and act within complex transdisciplinary research and transformation programs, beyond individual projects. This includes several stakeholder groups in joint knowledge production, bringing together urban public authorities, civil society groups, business, politics, and academia. This would facilitate a more comprehensive view of cities in the context of global change, while integrating societal, economic, and ecological dimensions to generate a complex transformational process.

For academic stakeholders, there are two sides to this coin: to better understand needs and options for sustainable urban solutions through transition research, and to take part in promoting these by exploring new transdisciplinary methodological settings and experimental innovation designs as part of transformative research.

Following this idea, there is much reason to ask the "mindset of planning" question of Castells (1992) again, but contextualized in a new form: "The world has changed – can planning change?" As Castells says, "[W]e are living in the midst of a fundamental process of historical change that is affecting the intellectual and social foundations of planning and its practice. The main elements of this multidimensional change are identified. The chances of the planning field responding to this historical mutation are evaluated and suggestions are offered about possible intellectual orientations."

One important issue, however, remains open: in addition to intellectual orientation and the strengthening of transdisciplinary capacities, it is above all urgent to implement alternative system patterns for sustainable multi-level urban development in a concrete way.

Note

1. See this article for a more detailed explanation.

References

Ahern, J. (2011). From fail-safe to safe-to-fail: Sustainability and resilience in the new urban world. *Landscape and Urban Planning*, 100(4), 341–343.

Amin, A., & Thrift, N. (2002). *Cities: Reimagining the Urban*. Cambridge. Polity Press.

Bai, X. (2007). Industrial ecology and the global impacts of cities. *Journal of Industrial Ecology*, 11 (2), 1–6.

Bettencourt, L., & West, G. (2010). A unified theory of urban living. *Nature*, 467 (7318).

Bossel, H. (2007). *Systems and Models: Complexity, Dynamics, Evolution, Sustainability*. Norderstedt, Germany: BoD–Books on Demand.

Bugliarello, G. (2006). Urban sustainability: Dilemmas, challenges and paradigms. *Technology in Society*, 28(1–2): 19–26.

Cajot, S., Peter, M., Bahu, J.-M., Koch, A., & Maréchal, F. (2015). Energy planning in the urban context: Challenges and perspectives. *Energy Procedia*, 78: 3366–3371.

Carter, C. R., & Rogers, D. S. (2008). A framework of sustainable supply chain management: Moving toward new theory. *International Journal of Physical Distribution & Logistics Management*, 38(5), 360–387.

Castells, M. (1992). The world has changed: Can planning change? *Landscape and Urban Planning* 22(1): 73–78.
Castells, M. (2002). Urban sociology in the twenty-first century. *Cidades, Comunidades e Territórios*, (5).
Chrysoulakis, N., Lopes, M., & San José, R., et al. (2013). Sustainable urban metabolism as a link between bio-physical sciences and urban planning: The BRIDGE project. *Landscape and Urban Planning*, 112, 100–117.
Coe, N. M., Dicken, P., & Hess, M. (2008). Global production networks: realizing the potential. *Journal of Economic Geography*, 8(3), 271–295.
Costanza, R., Daly, H. E., & Bartholomew, J. A. (1992). Goals, agenda and policy recommendations for ecological economics. *Ecological Economics*, 1–12.
Costanza, R., Wainger, L., Folke, C., & Mäler, K. G. (1993). Modeling complex ecological economic systems: Toward an evolutionary, dynamic understanding of people and nature. *BioScience*, 43(8), 545–555.
Costanza, R., & Patten, B. C. (1995). Defining and predicting sustainability. *Ecological Economics*, 15(3), 193–196.
Cooper, M. C., Lambert, D. M., & Pagh, J. D. (1997). Supply chain management: More than a new name for logistics. *The International Journal of Logistics Management*, 8(1), 1–14.
Daly, H. E. (1973). *Toward a Steady-State Economy*. San Fransisco: WH Freeman.
Daly, H. E. (1997). *Beyond Growth: The Economics of Sustainable Development*. Boston: Beacon Press.
Daly, H. E. (2005). Economics in a full world. *Scientific American*, 293(3), 100–107.
Derudder, B., & Witlox, F. (2010). World cities and global commodity chains: An introduction. *Global Networks*, 10(1), 1–11.
Ekins, P., Simon, S., Deutsch, L., Folke, C., & De Groot, R. (2003). A framework for the practical application of the concepts of critical natural capital and strong sustainability. *Ecological Economics*, 44(2–3), 165–185.
Findeisen, W., Bailey, F. N., Brdys, M., Malinowski, K., Tatjewski, P., & Wozniak, A. (1980). *Control and Coordination in Hierarchical Systems*. London: Wiley.
Friedmann, J. (1986). The World City hypothesis. *Development and Change*, 17(1), 69–83.
Gereffi, G., & Korzeniewicz, M. (Eds.) (1994). *Commodity Chains and Global Capitalism*. Westport: Praeger Publishers.
Girardet, H. (2000). Cities and the culture of sustainability. In *Earth Summit 2002: A New Deal: Earthscan*. New York: Routledge, pp. 202–211.
Grimm, N. B., Pickett, S. T., Hale, R. L., & Cadenasso, M. L. (2017). Does the ecological concept of disturbance have utility in urban social-ecological-technological systems? *Ecosystem Health and Sustainability*, 3(1).
Grimm, N., Faeth, S., Golubiewski, N., et al. (2008). Global Change and the ecology of cities. *Science*, 319(5864), 756–760.
Gruchmann, T., Melkonyan, A., & Krumme, K., (2018). Logistics business transformation for sustainability: Assessing the role of the lead sustainability service provider (6PL). *Logistics*. 2018, 2(4), 25.
Hashemian, B., Massaro, E., Bojic, I., Arias, J. M., Sobolevsky, S., & Ratti, C. (2017). Socioeconomic characterization of regions through the lens of individual financial transactions. *PLoS ONE*, 12(11), e0187031.
Harvey, D. (1996). *Justice, Nature and the Geography of Difference*. Oxford: Blackwell Publishers.
Held, D., McGrew, A., Goldblatt, D., & Perraton, J. (2000). *Global transformations: Politics, Economics and Culture*. Stanford: Stanford University Press, pp. 1–28.
Hesse, M. (2010). Cities, material flows and the geography of spatial interaction: Urban places in the system of chains. *Global Networks*, 10(1), 75–91.
Hoekstra, A. Y. (2015). The sustainability of a single activity, production process or product. *Ecological Indicators*, 57, 82–84.
Hoekstra, A. Y., & Wiedmann, T. O. (2014). Humanity's unsustainable environmental footprint. *Science*, 344(6188), 1114–1117.

Seto, K. C., Dhakal, S., Bigio, A., et al. (2014). Human settlements, infrastructure and spatial planning. In O. Edenhofer, R. Pichs-Madruga, Y. Sokona et al. (eds.), *Climate Change 2014: Mitigation of Climate Change: Working Group III Contribution to the IPCC Fifth Assessment Report*. Cambridge and New York: Cambridge University Press, pp. 923–1000.

Jackson, T. (2005). Live better by consuming less? Is there a "double dividend" in sustainable consumption? *Journal of Industrial Ecology*, 9(1–2), 19–36.

Jacobs, J. (1984). *Cities and the Wealth of Nations*. New York: Random House.

Kalmykova, Y., Rosado, L., & Patrício, J. (2015). Urban economies resource productivity and decoupling: metabolism trends of 1996–2011 in Sweden, Stockholm, and Gothenburg. *Environmental Science & Technology*, 49(14), 8815–8823.

Keivani, R. (2010). A review of the main challenges to urban sustainability. *International Journal of Urban Sustainable Development*, 1(1–2), 5–16.

Kestemont, B. (2015). The conditions for strong sustainability. *Cosmopolis – A review of cosmopolitics*, 1, 35–43.

King, A. (2009). Postcolonial cities. In R. Kitchin & N. Thrift (eds.), *International Encyclopedia of Human Geography*. Amsterdam: Elsevier, pp. 321–326.

Krumme, K. (2016). Sustainable development and social-ecological-technological systems (SETS): Resilience as a guiding principle in the urban-industrial nexus. *Journal of Renewable Energy & Sustainable Development*, 2(1).

Krumme, K. (2020). Supply chains and systems of sustainability: An attempt to close the gap. In A. Melkonyan & K. Krumme (eds.), *Innovative Logistics Services and Sustainable Lifestyles: Interdependencies, Transformation Strategies and Decision Making*. Cham: Springer Nature, pp. 21–60.

Krumme, K., & Melkonyan, A. (2020). Research and innovation perspectives for integrated supply chains in a sustainable economy. In A. Melkonyan & K. Krumme (eds.), *Innovative Logistics Services and Sustainable Lifestyles:Interdependencies, Transformation Strategies and Decision Making*. Cham: Springer Nature, pp. 289–307.

Linton, J. D., Klassen, R., & Jayaraman, V. (2007). Sustainable supply chains: An introduction. *Journal of Operations Management*, 25(6), 1075–1082.

Liu, J. Q., Hull, V., Batistella, M., et al. (2013). Framing sustainability in a telecoupled world. *Ecology & Society* 18(2), 26.

Liu, J., Mooney, H., Hull, V., et al. (2015). Systems integration for global sustainability. *Science*, 347 (6225), 1258832.

Lorek, S., & Spangenberg, J. H. (2014). Sustainable consumption within a sustainable economy: Beyond green growth and green economies. *Journal of Cleaner Production*, 63, 33–44.

Marchal, V., Dellink, R., Van Vuuren, D., et al. (2011). OECD environmental outlook to 2050. *Organisation for Economic Co-operation and Development*, 8, 397–413.

McHale, M., Pickett, S., Barbosa, O., et al. (2015). The new global urban realm: Complex, connected, diffuse, and diverse social-ecological systems. *Sustainability*, 7(5), 5211–5240.

McPhearson, T., Pickett, S. T., Grimm, N. B., et al. (2016). Advancing urban ecology toward a science of cities. *BioScience*, 66(3), 198–212.

Melkonyan A., & Krumme K. (2020). Integrating perspectives of logistics and lifestyles for a sustainable economy. In A. Melkonyan & K. Krumme (eds.), *Innovative Logistics Services and Sustainable Lifestyles: Interdependencies, Transformation Strategies and Decision Making*. Cham: Springer Nature, pp. 3–20.

Meadows, D. H., & Wright, D. (2008). *Thinking in Systems: A Primer*. White River Junction: Chelsea Green Publishing.

Mesarovic, M. D., Takahara, Y., & Macko, D. (1970). *Theory of Hierarchical, Multilevel Systems*. Cambridge, MA: Academic Press.

Moore, J. (2015). Ecological footprints and lifestyle archetypes: Exploring dimensions of consumption and the transformation needed to achieve urban sustainability. *Sustainability*, 7 (4), 4747–4763.

Moser, S. C., & Hart, J. A. F. (2015). The long arm of climate change: Societal teleconnections and the future of climate change impacts studies. *Climatic Change*, 129(1–2), 13–26.

Neumayer, E. (2003). *Weak Versus Strong Sustainability: Exploring the Limits of Two Opposing Paradigms*. Cheltenham: Edward Elgar Publishing.
Newman, P. (1999). Sustainability and cities: Extending the metabolism model. *Landscape and Urban Planning*, 44(4), 219–226.
Newman, P. (2006). The environmental impact of cities. *Environment and Urbanization* 18(2), 275–295.
Newman, P., & Jennings, I. (2012). *Cities as Sustainable Ecosystems: Principles and Practices*. Washington, DC: Island Press.
O'Rourke, D. (2014). The science of sustainable supply chains. *Science*, 344(6188), 1124–1127.
Ostrom, E. (2009). A general framework for analyzing sustainability of social-ecological systems. *Science*, 325(5939), 419–422.
Pelenc, J., & Ballet, J. (2015). Strong sustainability, critical natural capital and the capability approach. *Ecological Economics*, 112, 36–44.
Pickett, S. T., Burch, W. R., Dalton, S. E., Foresman, T. W., Grove, J. M., & Rowntree, R. (1997). A conceptual framework for the study of human ecosystems in urban areas. *Urban ecosystems*, 1 (4), 185–199.
Rees, W. E. (1992). Ecological footprints and appropriated carrying capacity: what urban economics leaves out. *Environment and Urbanization*, 4(2), 121–130.
Rees, W., & Wackernagel, M. (1996). Urban ecological footprints: Why cities cannot be sustainable – and why they are a key to sustainability. *Environmental Impact Assessment Review* 16(4–6): 223–248.
Rodrigue, J. P., & Hesse, M. (2006). Global Production Networks and the role of logistics and transportation. *Growth and Change*, 37(4), 499–509.
Sassen, S. (1991). *The Global City: New York, London, Tokyo*, Princeton University Press.
Sassen, S. (2002). Locating cities on global circuits. In S. Sassen (ed.), *Global Networks, Linked Cities*. New York: Routledge, pp. 1–37.
Sassen, S. (2009). Human settlement development: The central role of cities in our environment's future: Constraints and possibilities. UNESCO: Encyclopedia of Life Support Systems (EOLSS). www.eolss.net/
Sassen, S. (2010a). Global inter-city networks and commodity chains: Any intersections? *Global Networks* 10(1): 150–163.
Sassen, S. (2010b). Cities are at the center of our environmental future. *S.A.P.I.EN.S*, 2(3).
Sassen, S., & Dotan, N. (2011). Delegating, not returning, to the biosphere: How to use the multi-scalar and ecological properties of cities. *Global Environmental Change*, 21(3), 823–834.
Sassen, S. (2015). Cities: Capital, global, and world. In J. D. Wright (ed.), *International Encyclopedia of the Social & Behavioral Sciences*. Amsterdam: Elsevier, pp. 585–592.
Schandl, H., Fischer-Kowalski, M., West, J., et al. (2018). Global material flows and resource productivity: forty years of evidence. *Journal of Industrial Ecology*, 22(4), 827–838.
Seitzinger, S. P., Svedin, U., Crumley, C. L., et al. (2012). Planetary stewardship in an urbanizing world: Beyond city limits. *AMBIO: A Journal of the Human Environment*, 41, 787–794.
Seto, K. C. , Golden, J. S., Alberti, M., & Turner, B. L. (2017). Sustainability in an urbanizing planet. *Proceedings of the National Academy of Sciences*, 114(34), 8935–8938.
Seto, K. C., Reenberg, A., Boone, C. G., et al. (2012). Urban land teleconnections and sustainability. *Proceedings of the National Academy of Sciences*, 109(20), 7687–7692.
Seuring, S., & Müller, M. (2008). From a literature review to a conceptual framework for sustainable supply chain management. *Journal of Cleaner Production*, 16(15), 1699–1710.
Sheffi, Y., & Rice Jr., J. B. (2005). A supply chain view of the resilient enterprise. *MIT Sloan Management Review*, 47(1), 41.
Steffen, W., Richardson, K., & Rockström, J., et al. (2015). Planetary boundaries: Guiding human development on a changing planet. *Science*, 347(6223), 1259855.
Taylor, P. (1995). World cities and territorial states: The rise and fall of their mutuality. In P. L. Knox & P. J. Taylor (eds.), *World Cities in a World System*. Cambridge and New York: Cambridge University Press, pp. 48–62.

Taylor, P. (1997). Hierarchical tendencies amongst world cities: A global research proposal. *Cities*, 14 (6), 323–332.
Taylor, P. (2004). *World City Network: A Global Urban Analysis*. New York: Routledge.
Taylor, P., & Csomós, G. (2012). Cities as control and command centres: Analysis and interpretation. *Cities*, 29(6), 408–411.
Taylor, P., & Derudder, B. (2015). *World City Network: A Global Urban Analysis*. New York: Routledge.
Thomson, G., & Newman, P. (2018). Urban fabrics and urban metabolism: From sustainable to regenerative cities. *Resources, Conservation and Recycling*, 132, 218–229.
Torreggiani, D., Dall'Ara, E., & Tassinari, P. (2012). The urban nature of agriculture: Bidirectional trends between city and countryside. *Cities*, 29(6), 412–416.
Ullman, E. L. (1953). Human geography and area research. *Annals of the Association of American Geographers*, 43(1), 54–66.
United Nations. (2017). *World Population Prospects: The 2017 Revision*. United Nations.
Wackernagel, M., Kitzes, J., Moran, D., Goldfinger, S., & Thomas, M. (2006). The ecological footprint of cities and regions: Comparing resource availability with resource demand. *Environment and Urbanization*, 18(1), 103–112.
Worldwatch Institute (2016). *State of the World: Can a City Be Sustainable?* Washington, DC: Island Press.
Weber, M. (1921). Die Stadt. *Archiv für Sozialwissenschaft und Sozialpolitik*, 47: 621ff.
Wiedmann, T., Minx, J., Barrett, J., & Wackernagel, M. (2006). Allocating ecological footprints to final consumption categories with input–output analysis. *Ecological Economics*, 56(1), 28–48.
Wiedmann, T. O., Schandl, H., Lenzen, M., et al. (2015). The material footprint of nations. *Proceedings of the National Academy of Sciences*, 112(20), 6271–6276.
Wiek, A., Ness, B., Schweizer-Ries, P., Brand, F. S., & Farioli, F. (2012). From complex systems analysis to transformational change: A comparative appraisal of sustainability science projects. *Sustainability Science*, 7(1), 5–24.
Yeung, H. W. C. (1994). Critical reviews of geographical perspectives on business organizations and the organization of production: Towards a network approach. *Progress in Human Geography*, 18 (4), 460–490.
Zasada, I., Loibl, W., Berges, R., et al. (2013). Rural–urban regions: A spatial approach to define urban–rural relationships in Europe. In K. Nilsson, S. Pauleit, S. Bell, C. Aalbers & T. S. Nielsen (eds.), *Peri-urban futures: Scenarios and models for land use change in Europe*. Berlin: Springer, pp. 45–68.

13

Indicators for Assessing the Sustainability of Cities

*Anne Boesch and André de Montmollin**

13.1 Introduction

There are a number of initiatives aiming at assessing the sustainability of entities at the local level. While initiatives at the international and national levels had emerged as early as the end of the 1980s, those pertaining specifically to the local level began to emerge some years later, in the mid-1990s, and grew in importance at the end of the 2000s, as exemplified in Figure 13.1.

It is impossible to conduct an exhaustive review of all the initiatives dealing with sustainability assessment at the local level, among other reasons because such initiatives tend not to be described and published in academic papers, and also because, even if one broadens one's search to the entire worldwide web, they are very probably described exclusively in the language spoken in the country or region they are implemented in, rendering them invisible to a general search, e.g., in English only. Searching for sustainability assessment initiatives through different channels, however, yields the result that most published initiatives pertaining to the measurement of sustainability – or of dimensions of sustainability, such as quality of life, well-being, or environmental issues – were launched in the second half of the 2000s, thus confirming the trend obtained by searching for peer-reviewed academic papers.[1]

Sustainability assessment instruments designed for use at the local level are not all equally broad regarding the definition of sustainable development they rely on. Some are very comprehensive and incorporate the classical dimensions of sustainable development directly derived from the Brundtland definition (WCED, 1987), including aspects of intragenerational ("here and elsewhere") and intergenerational ("now and later") equity. Other instruments restrict themselves to one or two aspects. All-encompassing instruments designed to assess sustainability at the local level are few. This is exemplified by the fact that Zoeteman et al. (2016) and Singh et al. (2012), for example, cite instruments restricted to either the environmental dimension or the socioeconomic dimension of sustainability as "current efforts to monitor city sustainability," or "sustainability indices for cities" respectively. Among the all-compassing instruments are the Sustainable City Index (SCI), developed by the Sustainable Society Foundation (2014) with the methodological support of the

* The opinions expressed in this chapter do not necessarily reflect the official views of the Swiss Federal Statistical Office.

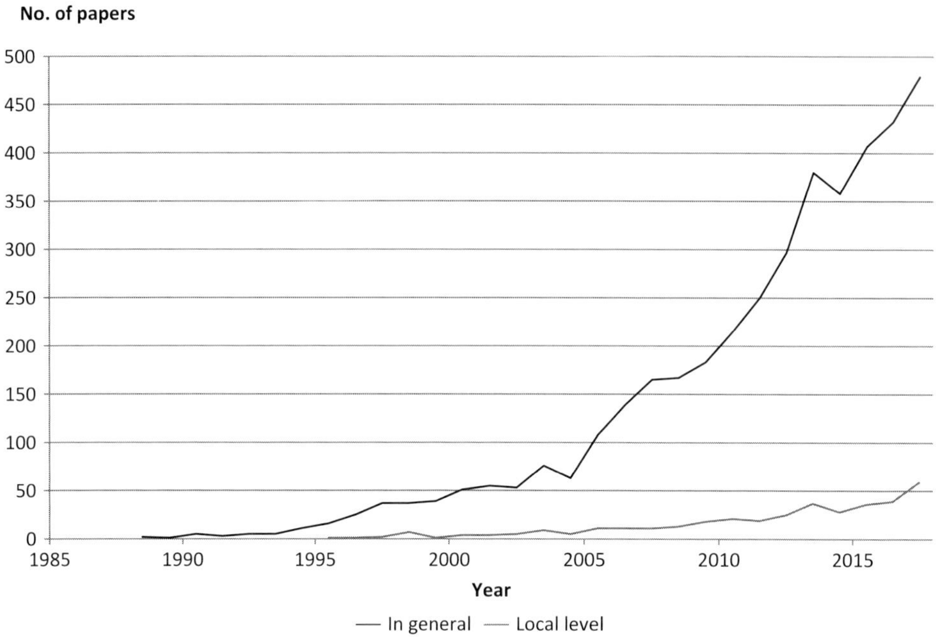

Figure 13.1 Papers relating to sustainability assessment, in general and at the local level. Number of papers published corresponding to the search equation "TITLE(sustainability OR 'sustainable development') AND TITLE(assessment OR indicator* OR monitoring) *AND TITLE(city OR cities OR urban OR local OR municipal*)*"; (the italicized part in the search equation is used to restrict the search to the local level). Based on the Scopus database, March 31, 2018.

Joint Research Centre (JRC) of the European Commission for Dutch municipalities; the Global Power City Index (GPCI) developed by the Mori Memorial Foundation in Japan for 40 major cities around the world (Yamato et al., 2017); and the UrBes (*Il benessere equo e sostenibile nelle città*) instrument developed by the Italian Statistical Office Istat in collaboration with Italian cities (Istat, 2015). There are more instruments dealing with one or several aspects of sustainable development, such as the "Quality of Life Project" supported by several city councils in New Zealand[2] or "Understanding Glasgow" on health and well-being in the city, developed by the Glasgow Centre for Population Health (GCPH).[3]

Sustainability assessment can take different forms. However, indicators are very frequently at the heart of an assessment (Ramos, 2009). The term "indicator" itself can be understood in many different ways depending on the context in which indicators are used and the scientific discipline in question. Definitions of indicators range from very general ones such as "We have many words for indicator – sign, symptom, omen, signal, tip, clue, grade, rank, data, pointer, dial, warning light, instrument, measurement" (Meadows, 1998) to very specific ones such as "a statistical variable presented in the form of a time series and chosen to monitor the evolution of a specific aspect of the issue dealt with … towards a desired direction or a target value" (Boesch et al., 2014). In this chapter, we will adopt a definition suggested by Maggino (2017), which is slightly more general: "an indicator is not simple crude statistical information but represents a measure organically connected to a conceptual model aimed at describing different aspects of reality. In other words, a generic index value becomes an 'indicator', when its definition and measurement occur in the ambit of a conceptual model and [when it] is connected to a defined aim." This definition calls on the notion of "purposeful statistics" coined by Horn (1993) and is also in line with the idea that indicators are developed for a specific purpose and have a "significance that extends beyond the properties directly associated with the parameter value" (OECD, 1993). In addition, indicators can also be considered as boundary objects, "an analytic concept of those scientific objects which both inhabit several intersecting social worlds . . . and satisfy the informational requirements of each of them" (Star & Griesemer, 1989), and that "facilitate discussion, negotiation and decision making" (Turnhout et al., 2007).

Setting up and using indicators for measuring sustainable development is associated with additional challenges such as the multitude of perspectives on what sustainable development actually is, and the strong interconnections between the observed phenomena. The interdisciplinary perspective it requires is also a challenge for the policy relevance of the assessment, since it goes beyond sectoral programmes or policies. Such challenges are addressed by the Bellagio Principles that were first published in 1997 as a synthesis by international practitioners and researchers of practical efforts in the development of sustainability indicators. These principles were updated in 2012 and published as the *Bellagio Sustainability Assessment and Measurement Principles* (Bellagio STAMP) (Pintér et al., 2012). The rationale behind the Principles is the recognition that guidance and harmonization are needed at the stage of developing and analyzing indicators. The Principles address: the need for a guiding vision of sustainable development (Principle 1); the importance of adopting a holistic view that takes into account the interdependencies, risks, and uncertainties within the socioecological system (Principle 2); the definition of an appropriate time horizon and geographical scope (Principle 3); the fact that the assessment should rely on a conceptual framework that determines the domains for which indicators should be selected and reference values for the indicators (Principle 4); the importance of transparency about the data, the assessment methods, and the assumptions made (Principle 5); the importance of effective communication (Principle 6); the importance of broad participation, engaging early on with the users of the assessment (Principle 7); and the importance of continuity and capacity that allows for the stability of the indicator systems, as well as periodic reviews to ensure their relevance over the long term (Principle 8).

This chapter aims to illustrate the diversity of sustainability assessment tools that were developed at the local level and their different and complementary uses by presenting two instruments in use throughout Switzerland: Cercle Indicateurs, which is an all-encompassing tool for sustainability monitoring and benchmarking at the level of cantons and cities, and the Swiss implementation of the Europe-wide City Statistics (formerly Urban Audit), with specific developments for ensuring compatibility with the concept of quality of life as defined by the OECD for its "How's Life" initiative (OECD, 2011). The development and use of these two instruments will be analyzed through the lens of the Bellagio STAMP, which we will group into the following five categories: (1) Conceptual framework (STAMPs 1, 2, and 4), (2) Time and spatial scale (STAMP 3), (3) Participation (STAMP 7), (4) Transparency and communication (STAMPs 5 and 6), and (5) Continuity and capacity (STAMP 8). The analysis will also take into account the suggested definition of indicator that implies the relation with a conceptual model and the definition of a specific aim.

13.2 Indicators Developed for Swiss Cities

13.2.1 Cercle Indicateurs

The initial developments that led to Cercle Indicateurs date back to the end of the 1990s, when several Swiss cities and cantons were developing their own sustainable development indicator systems in parallel, following the initial inputs given by the Brundtland Report in 1987 and the Earth Summit in 1992.[4] The cantons of Aargau, Bern, Basel-Landschaft, Graubünden, and Zurich, together with the cities of Baden, Bern, Chur, Langenthal, Lausanne, Rheinfelden, Schaffhausen, and Winterthur, had come together and were beginning to establish sustainable development indicators. At the same time, several other cantons (Geneva, Vaud) and cities (Zurich, Basel) started their own sustainability assessment initiatives. The Federal Office for Spatial Development (ARE), which has been in charge of sustainable development at the federal level since 2000 and also supports the cantons and cities in implementing it at the regional and local level, approached all these cantons and cities with the aim of bringing them together in one common initiative, Cercle Indicateurs, in order to work in a collaborative manner, share efforts and knowledge, and exploit synergies. They established what was known as the "responsible body" (the decision-making body), in which each participating canton and city, as well as the ARE, the Federal Office for the Environment (FOEN), the Federal Office of Public Health (FOPH), and the Federal Statistical Office (FSO), were represented, with the ARE having general responsibility for the project. Cantons and cities participate on a voluntary basis and contribute financially to the project. They are represented in most cases by delegates from their territorial planning, environmental protection, or central services units. Between 2003 and 2005, an indicator framework was built and indicators selected; the indicators were first published in 2005. Since then, the data has been updated every two years for the cantons and every four years for the cities. At the time of writing, seven updates had been made for the cantons and four for the cities (during the period 2005–2017). The data source for the indicators is either the federal statistical system (FSO or other federal offices that provide data on specific topics) or the participating cantons and cities themselves. In rare cases, the data has to be bought from the private sector. The share of the data that is provided in a decentralized manner – i.e., by the participating cantons and cities – is higher for the cities (about 35 percent, compared to 20 percent, for the cantons) since there is less data from the federal statistical system available at this geographical level.

The number of participating cantons and cities increased over time (see Figure 13.2 for a map of the current participants), and the involvement of the federal offices has also changed. At the time of writing, 25 cities of various sizes,[5] 19 cantons (out of 26), and three federal offices (ARE, FSO, and FOEN) were represented in the responsible body of Cercle Indicateurs. The role of the FSO also evolved over time. It initially had an advisory function as a member of the responsible body. Since 2008, the ARE (which has global responsibility for the project) and the participating cantons and cities have given the FSO a mandate to carry out methodological developments, as well as data collection and dissemination (called the Secretariat). For a couple of years, the FSO has also acted more and more as an advisor to the cantons and cities when they interpret their data.

The indicator framework used in Cercle Indicateurs was defined by taking the three classical "pillars" of sustainable development (environment, economy, and society) as the three main dimensions to be measured. Between 10 and 12 topics ("target areas" when translated literally from German) were defined for each of the three dimensions. Subsequently, one indicator was selected to measure each topic (two in some rare cases). The selection of the topics and of the related indicators reflects the preoccupations of the participants at that time and their (political) interpretation of Agenda 21 (UNCED, 1992). They wanted to showcase the efforts made at their level toward sustainable development and compare them with those of the other participants. The indicator framework itself has not changed much since its creation in 2003. Several indicators were revised but the topics are still the same (see Figure 13.4 for an overview of the topics and indicators). The framework evolved, however, in the sense that it was made more robust a posteriori, by harmonizing and completing the description of the links between the topics and sustainable development in a first phase, and by harmonizing and completing the justification of the choice of the indicators to measure the topics in a second phase. Both the description of the links between the topics and sustainable development, and the justification of the choice of the indicators, were carried out in a participatory manner and are described in the form of short texts of about 100 words that are integral parts of the "indicator sheets" (documents with conceptual and technical information on each indicator, publicly available online, described in more detail in Box 13.1).[6] An indicator typology based on the one used for the monitoring of sustainable development at the national level in Switzerland (the MONET system) is also being introduced (see Willi et al., 2012, pp. 63–65, for a description of the typology). Carrying out the exercise of attributing one of the six indicator types (level, capital stocks, input/output, distribution, efficiency, and response) to each indicator is meant to help the participating cantons and cities identify (and avoid) potential pitfalls in the interpretation of the indicators used to measure the topics. An indicator selected to measure one topic may indeed only give a partial picture and other "sensors" may well be necessary to ensure an interpretation that is as comprehensive and neutral as possible regarding the topic. The indicator chosen to monitor a topic may, for example, reflect capital stocks or inputs to/outputs from the capital stocks, whereas distributional or efficiency aspects may also be relevant for the topic. The use of the typology helps identify the missing information that should be referred to in order to avoid a biased interpretation. The topics from Cercle Indicateurs were also mapped onto the targets of SDGs of the Agenda 2030 for Sustainable Development (UNGA, 2015) in order to ensure

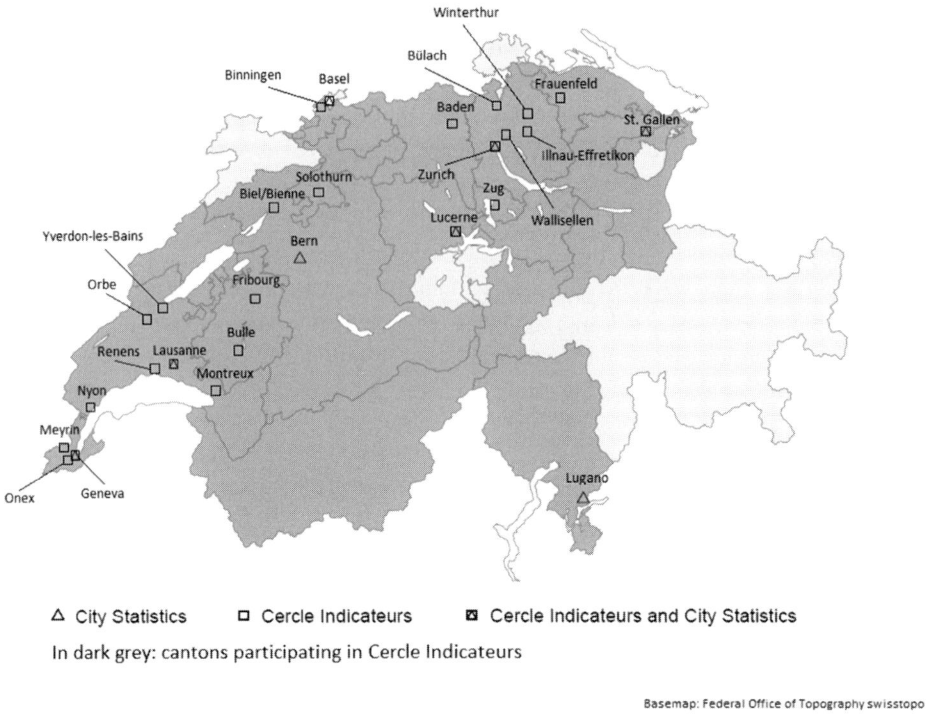

Figure 13.2 Cantons and cities participating in Cercle Indicateurs and in City Statistics Switzerland (as of September 2018)

the compatibility of Cercle Indicateurs with this new frame of reference, which can be seen as an update of Agenda 21 on which the Cercle Indicateurs framework is based.

13.2.2 City Statistics

City Statistics (formerly Urban Audit) was created at the end of the 1990s by the Directorate General for Regional and Urban Policy at the European Commission (DG Regio), in cooperation with Eurostat (the Statistical Office of the European Union), with the aim of describing quality of life in cities in the European Union. The data collected was the basis for the two "State of European Cities Reports" that were published in 2007 and 2010 and that aimed at describing and analyzing urban dynamics, as well as developing a typology of cities in Europe (Neumann & Seidel-Schulze, 2010). City Statistics is coordinated at the European level by DG Regio, Eurostat, and the National Urban Audit Coordinators (NUAC), who are generally representatives of the national statistical offices and who form the link with the participating countries.

In Switzerland, the impetus for taking part in City Statistics came from the ARE. A pilot phase was conducted between 2006 and 2008 with the cities of Zurich, Geneva,

Box 13.1 **Generic structure of the indicator sheets of Cercle Indicateurs**

- Description of the topic
  Description of the topic and its link to the concept of sustainable development
- Indicator name, definition, and unit
- Justification of the choice of the indicator
  Description of the relevance of the indicator as a means for measuring the topic, i.e., the extent to which the selected variable indicates something about sustainable development in the context of the topic and thus is an indicator
- Desired evolution of the indicator (increase or decrease)
  Direction in which the indicator should evolve for sustainable development
- Indication on transversal comparisons
  Description of the aspects that should be paid attention to when comparing the indicator values of different cities or cantons (due, e.g., to data collection method or to known variability of local situations that directly influence the indicator value)
- Indication for the interpretation of time series
  Description of the aspects that should be paid attention to when interpreting the evolution of the indicator values
- Technical information
  Data source(s), frequency of update by Cercle Indicateurs, time gap between year of data validity and update by Cercle Indicateurs, lower and upper bounds (used for the standardization of values for the "strengths and weaknesses profile" graph)

Bern, and Lausanne. The ARE and the FSO then conducted City Statistics with the 10 most populated Swiss cities between 2009 and 2015, with the FSO leading the project.[7] In 2016, the FSO and the ARE were joined by the State Secretariat for Economic Affairs (SECO) and all three work with eight of the most populated Swiss cities. The participating federal entities and cities form the City Statistics steering committee. As with Cercle Indicateurs, the cities participate on a voluntary basis and contribute financially to the project. Unlike Cercle Indicateurs, however, most cities are represented by their statistical unit or office.

When it was created by DG Regio, City Statistics was a collection of around 300 variables structured into nine main domains (demography, social aspects, economic aspects, civic involvement, training and education, environment, travel and transport, information society, and culture and recreation). The vast majority of the variables stem from the official statistical system and are coherent with its nomenclatures (e.g., for the definition of households, business units, economic activity). The variables are collected not only at the city level (according to municipal boundaries) but also at the agglomeration and neighborhood levels. Not all variables are available at the neighborhood level, however. The number of variables was reduced over time to about 180, yet the communication of the large amount of information they contain remained a challenge. Switzerland made various efforts to improve communication, such as by producing city portraits and atlases, and in particular, in 2014, by implementing the OECD's "How's Life" concept as part of the measurement of well-being in City Statistics. This concept, described in OECD (2011), draws on a long tradition of work on the measurement of quality of life by the OECD, as well as on the so-called Stiglitz Report (Stiglitz et al., 2009) that is based on the acknowledgment that GDP is not a good proxy for well-being. Unlike previous measures of well-being, the "How's Life" framework distinguishes between current and future well-being (see Figure 13.3). It stresses the importance of distributional aspects of current well-being and addresses future well-being in terms of preservation of capital stocks (natural, economic, human, and social capitals). The latter relies on conceptual work carried out by a UNECE/OECD/Eurostat Working Group and is described in the report "Measuring Sustainable Development" published by the United Nations Economic Commission for Europe (UNECE, 2009). An overview of the quality of life dimensions selected for Switzerland, and of the related indicators, is presented in Figure 13.4. Compared to the OECD "How's Life" concept, the version implemented in Switzerland does not include the "social connections" and "subjective well-being" dimensions. On the other hand, three additional dimensions were defined to take into account the specificities of Swiss cities, namely "infrastructure and services," "mobility," and "culture and leisure" (Lautenschütz

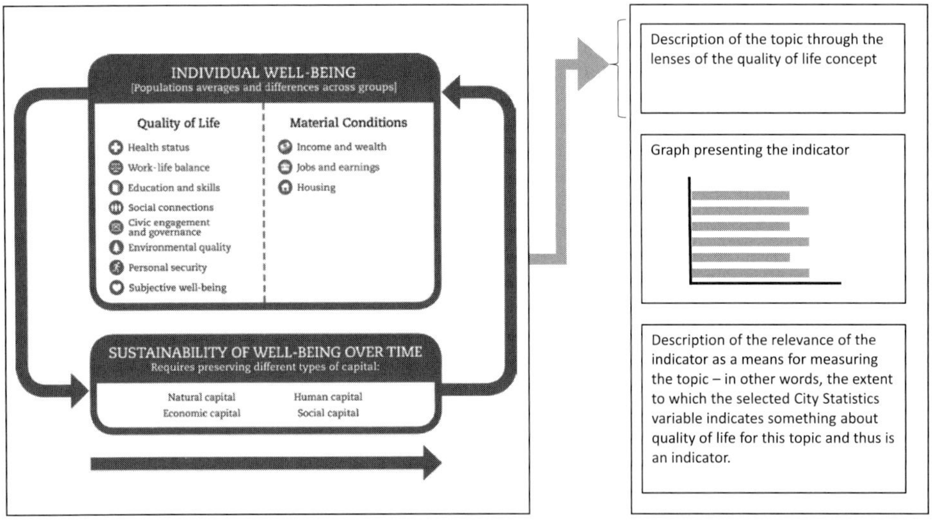

OECD "How's Life" conceptual framework

Adaptations for implementation as part of the Swiss City Statistics quality of life indicators:

- Topics *Social connections*, *Subjective well-being*, and *Natural*, *Economic*, *Human* and *Social capital* not considered
- Topics *Income and wealth* and *Jobs and earnings* merged
- Topics *Infrastructure and services*, *Mobility*, and *Culture and leisure* added

Swiss City Statistics quality of life indicators

As presented in Schneeberger & Jeanneret (2018)

Figure 13.3 Implementation of the OECD "How's Life" framework as part of the Swiss City Statistics quality of life indicators. Source for OECD "How's Life" conceptual framework: OECD (2015)

& Pedrini, 2016). The existing nine domains and variables of City Statistics were analyzed according to the concepts underlying each quality of life dimension and subsequently attributed to one of these dimensions. The link between each relevant variable and the dimension it was attributed to was made explicit and described in the form of a short text of about 40 words. These texts are published in a "pocket statistics" booklet entitled *Quality of Life in the Cities* that has been released every two years since 2014 (see Schneeberger and Jeanneret (2018) for the most recent version). They are also presented online as part of the quality of life indicators.[8] This step of making the link between the variable and its dimension explicit gives the variables the same status as indicators according to the definition of the term used in this chapter.

13.3 Conceptual Frameworks

Sustainable development is a broad, multifaceted concept that can be interpreted in many different ways. It is therefore of crucial importance that, during the interpretation process that is necessary to make the sustainable development concept measurable, one follows a guiding vision (STAMP 1) and adopts a holistic view that takes into account the interdependencies between the social, economic, and environmental components (STAMP 2), in order to establish a conceptual framework that "defines the issues to be measured, the priorities for the reference community whose actions are to be assessed, and the specific domains that core indicators have to cover" (STAMP 4). In the case of Cercle Indicateurs and City Statistics, however, there is no intent to assess the specific actions of a given community, as they are meant to be general measurement systems. Many other authors acknowledge the need for setting up a conceptual framework (de Vries & Petersen, 2009; Pope et al., 2017; Ravetz, 2000; Sala et al., 2015), which is also called a "measurement framework," "analytical framework," or "indicators framework." The last two formulations are used by Gallopín (1997), who also notes that "closely related to the question of frameworks are the linkages between indicators and various models," which relates to STAMP 2.

The conceptual frameworks adopted by Cercle Indicateurs and the framework resulting from the implementation of the OECD "How's Life" approach to City Statistics in Switzerland are admittedly very similar. However, they rely on different guiding visions. As described in Section 13.2.1, the Cercle Indicateurs framework was defined by taking the three classical pillars of sustainable development (environment, economy, and society) as the three main dimensions to be measured, within which about 10 "target areas" were defined. These "target areas" cover the "here and elsewhere" and "now and later" axes that are at the heart of the official understanding of the concept of sustainable development at the Swiss federal level.[9] As for City Statistics, Section 13.2.2, the original focus lies on current well-being or quality of life, to which the "here and elsewhere" and "now and later" axes were added in Switzerland through the implementation of the "How's Life" framework in 2014. These different guiding visions have a direct effect on the implementation: although both conceptual frameworks ultimately cover the same elements (economic, social, and environmental dimensions; here and elsewhere, now and later), City Statistics places more emphasis on the determinants of current well-being, whereas Cercle Indicateurs has a less detailed but more overarching approach to the three dimensions of sustainable development. For example, the Swiss City Statistics quality of life indicators provide more information on various aspects of housing, health, mobility, and culture and leisure than Cercle Indicateurs. There are also differences regarding how intergenerational equity ("now and later") and intra-generational equity ("here and elsewhere") are approached. Cercle Indicateurs broaches both intergenerational and intra-generational equity. It measures, by means of proxies, various natural, economic, and human capital stocks (e.g., biodiversity, qualification level, public debt) or the efficiency of their use (e.g., renewable electricity). It also tackles inequities within the current generation through indicators such as those relating to low-income taxpayers or relief actions. These aspects are less prominent in the Swiss City Statistics quality of life indicators, where there are only a few indicators addressing either inter- or intra-generational equity. This lack of indicators measuring intra-generational equity is due to a lack of appropriate data for the distribution of well-being that is in line with the statistical concept of households used in City Statistics. Concerning intergenerational equity, this concept was added to the quality of life concept by OECD for the "How's Life" initiative. However, although the OECD "How's Life" concept was applied to City Statistics in Switzerland, the focus was on the well-being of the current generation. The different approaches used for setting up the two conceptual frameworks have an influence on this matter. Indeed, the application of the "How's Life" concept to City Statistics in Switzerland was very pragmatic and data-driven (attribution of the existing variables to the quality of life dimensions). For Cercle Indicateurs, much more emphasis was placed on the definition of the topics or target areas and their relation to the concept of sustainable development. The search for relevant indicators that could measure the target area took place only in a subsequent step.

Both City Statistics and Cercle Indicateurs adopt a holistic view and address interactions between the selected indicators and other dimensions within their respective conceptual framework. No attempt is made to measure the interactions; however, the user is made aware of them in the introduction and in the boxed texts in the City Statistics publication (Schneeberger & Jeanneret, 2018) and in the "description of the topics and its links to the concept of sustainable development" in the indicator sheets of Cercle Indicateurs (see Box 13.1). The latter also encourages the users to adopt a holistic view by presenting, among other things, all the indicators pertaining to a canton or city in graphs called "strengths and weaknesses profiles", which is made possible by means of the standardization of the values so that indicators with different units can be presented on a common scale (see Figure 13.5a).

13.4 Time and Spatial Scales

The Bellagio STAMP 3 introduces the importance of selecting both an appropriate time horizon and an adequate geographical scope. Finding an appropriate time horizon is an

Cercle Indicateurs Framework		
Topic (target area)	**Indicators for cantons**	**Indicators for cities**
Environment dimension		
Env 1: Biodiversity	Diversity of plant species	City breeding bird index
Env 2: Nature and landscape	Valuable natural areas	Valuable natural areas
Env 3: Energy quality	Renewable energy (placeholder)	Renewable electricity
Env 4: Energy consumption	Total energy consumption (placeholder)	Electricity consumption
Env 5: Climate	CO_2 emissions	Greenhouse gas emissions
Env 6: Material consumption	Municipal waste	Municipal waste
	Rate of separate waste collection	Rate of separate waste collection
Env 7: Water regime	Water flow through wastewater treatment plant	Water flow through wastewater treatment plant
Env 8: Water quality	Nitrate content in groundwater	Polluting substances emitted after wastewater treatment
Env 9: Land use	Built-up area	Built-up area
Env 10: Soil quality	Soil pollution by heavy metals (placeholder)	No indicator
Env 11: Air quality	Long-term air pollution index	Long-term air pollution index
Economy dimension		
Econ 1: Income	Cantonal GDP	Taxable income of natural persons
Econ 2: Cost of living	Rent level	Rent level
Econ 3: Labour market	Unemployment rate	Unemployment rate
Econ 4: Investments	Extension, transformation, and maintenance works	Extension, transformation, and maintenance works
Econ 5: True costs	No indicator	Implementation of the “polluter pays” principle
Econ 6: Resource efficiency	No indicator	No indicator
Econ 7: Innovations	Jobs in innovative sectors	Jobs in innovative sectors
Econ 8: Economic structure	Jobs in sectors with high labour productivity	Jobs in sectors with high labour productivity
Econ 9: Know-how	Qualification level	Qualification level
Econ 10: Public finances	Net debt ratio	Net debt ratio
Econ 11: Taxes	Index of the exploitation of tax potential	Tax burden of natural persons
Econ 12: Production	No indicator	No indicator
Society dimension		
Soc 1: Noise / housing quality	Traffic noise pollution	Traffic calming zones
Soc 2: Mobility	Access to the public transport system	Access to the public transport system
Soc 3: Health	Potential years of life lost	Potential years of life lost
Soc 4: Security	Road traffic accidents with victims	Road traffic accidents with victims
	Serious violent offenses	Burglaries
Soc 5: Income and wealth distribution	Low-income taxpayers	Low-income taxpayers
Soc 6: Participation	Participation in elections and in voting	Participation in elections and in voting
Soc 7: Culture and leisure	Expenditure on culture and leisure	Expenditure on culture and leisure
Soc 8: Education	Young people in training	Break in the training path (placeholder)
Soc 9: Social assistance	Social assistance recipients	Social assistance recipients
Soc 10: Integration	Naturalizations	Naturalizations
Soc 11: Equal opportunities	Women in management positions	Childcare services
Soc 12: Interregional solidarity	Relief actions	Relief actions

Swiss City Statistics Quality of Life Framework	
Quality of life dimension	**City indicators**
Income and jobs	Economic activity rate
	Part-time employment
	Social assistance rate
	Unemployment rate
Housing conditions	Traffic noise
	Single-family houses
	Overcrowded dwellings
	Dwelling vacancy rate
Health	Practising doctors
	Mortality rate <65 years
	Suicide rate
Education	Educational attainment
Environmental quality	Land use
	Air quality
Personal security	Violence
	Burglaries
	Car theft
	Road accidents
Civic engagement	*Placeholder*
Work-life-balance	Infant day care
	Duration of commute
Infrastructure and services	*No specific indicators (in other dimensions)*
Mobility	Price of monthly public transport ticket
	Choice of transportation mode to work
	Public transportation stops
Culture & leisure	Cinema seats
	Museums, theatres, cinemas
	Demand of museums and theaters

Figure 13.4 Swiss City Statistics quality of life and Cercle Indicateurs frameworks. Status as of 2018. Cercle Indicateurs framework: translated into English by the authors from the original French version (FSO and ARE); City Statistics framework: available in English on the FSO website

unrelenting challenge since the concept of sustainable development implies a long-term perspective, while the policy- and decision-making processes that the sustainable development indicators inform are short term by nature. In this respect, the Cercle Indicateurs framework addresses a mixture of relevant short-, medium-, and long-term phenomena. Capital stocks – or proxies for capital stocks (e.g., investments in or depreciation of capital stocks[10]) – such as biodiversity or public debt are indicators relating to intergenerational equity and are relevant over the long term, whereas rent levels or burglaries, which pertain to the quality of life of the current generation, can be assessed over shorter time periods. In addition, some "target areas" and their related indicators are closely linked to current policies pertaining to sustainable development, such as the share of waste collected separately for recycling or the implementation of the causality principle, whereas others, such as the biodiversity indicators or potential years of life lost, have a certain distance from policy- and decision-making, with no single public policy having a decisive impact on their evolution. Such a mixture of short-, medium-, and long-term indicators does not facilitate interpretation. The City Statistics quality of life indicators are, generally speaking, of a more short-term nature because they pertain to the well-being of the current generation. In addition, City Statistics presents the indicators in the form of graphs comparing the values of the different cities for one or two specific years (see Figures 13.6a and 13.6b), whereas for Cercle Indicateurs, time series graphs are published for each indicator and city (or canton) next to graphs that allow a comparison between cities/cantons or between one city/canton and the average value of all cities/cantons (see Figure 13.5b and 13.5c). These observations on the time scales adopted by Cercle Indicateurs and City Statistics are closely related to their original guiding visions that, as discussed in Section 13.3, have an impact on how the conceptual frameworks are implemented in the form of measurable indicators.[11]

Concerning geographical scope, Cercle Indicateurs is restricted to the political boundaries of the municipalities (cities) and cantons. Some of the Swiss City Statistics quality of life indicators (resulting from the implementation of the OECD "How's Life" framework) allow for comparisons between the core city and the agglomeration (see Figure 13.6a). In addition, City Statistics in Switzerland has enhanced its offering and publishes maps, portraits, and graphs that allow for comparison between neighborhoods, the core cities, and their agglomeration. For the cities of Basel and Geneva, a cross-border exercise is even carried out with data from Germany and France in the case of Basel, and from France in the case of Geneva, allowing the realization of detailed analyses that reflect the reality of these cities better than adopting a purely national perspective would.

Neither Cercle Indicateurs nor City Statistics, however, really address global interdependencies (long-distance impacts of actions) – with the notable exception of the Cercle Indicateurs' "relief actions" and "greenhouse gas emissions" indicators, although the latter are hardly measurable by the participating cities due to a lack both of comparable regional and local energy statistics and of national standards for the inventory of greenhouse gases at these geographical levels.

(a)

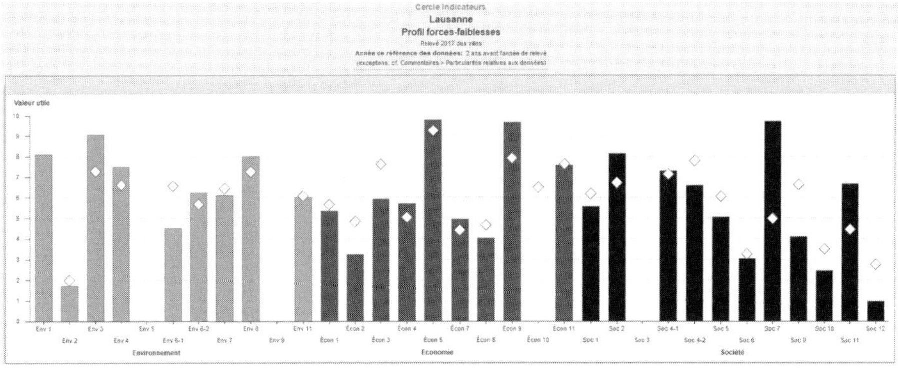

Figure 13.5a Example of a "strengths and weaknesses" profile graph (for the city of Lausanne) (Valeur utile: standardized value; Environnement: Environment; Economie: Economy; Société: Society). Source: FSO website (graphs retrieved in January 2020)

(b)

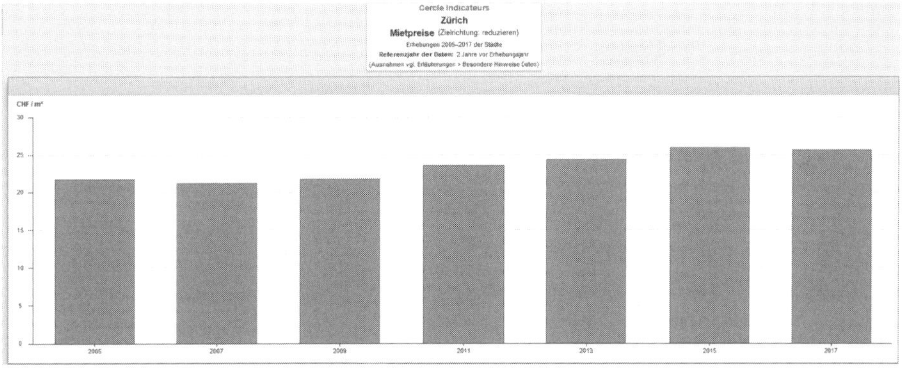

Figure 13.5b Example of a monitoring graph (for the city of Zurich) (Mietpreise (Zielrichtung: reduzieren): Rent level (desired evolution: decrease)). Source: FSO website (graphs retrieved in January 2020)

(c)

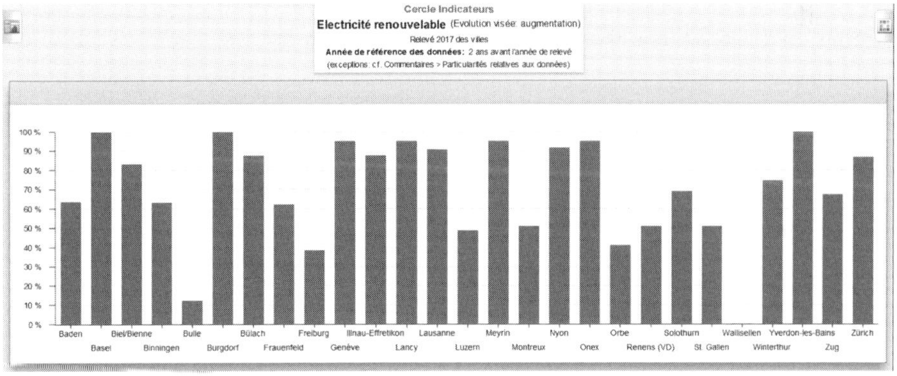

Figure 13.5c Example of a comparison graph (for the indicator "Renewable electricity", i.e., share of renewable electricity in the total electricity consumption of the city). Source: FSO website (graphs retrieved in January 2020)

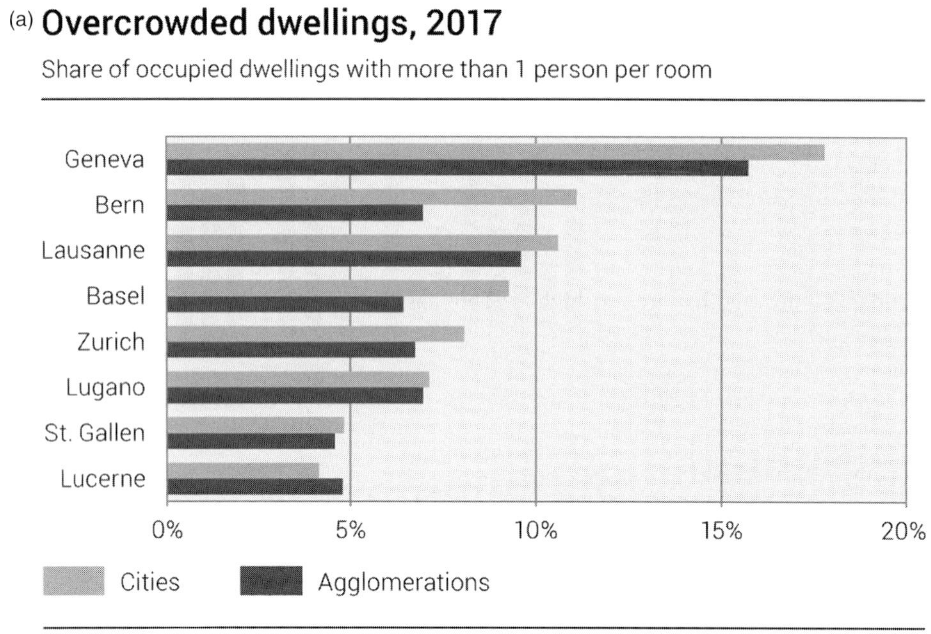

Figure 13.6a Example of a graph presenting core city and agglomeration values (indicator "Overcrowded dwellings"). Source: Schneeberger & Jeanneret (2018)

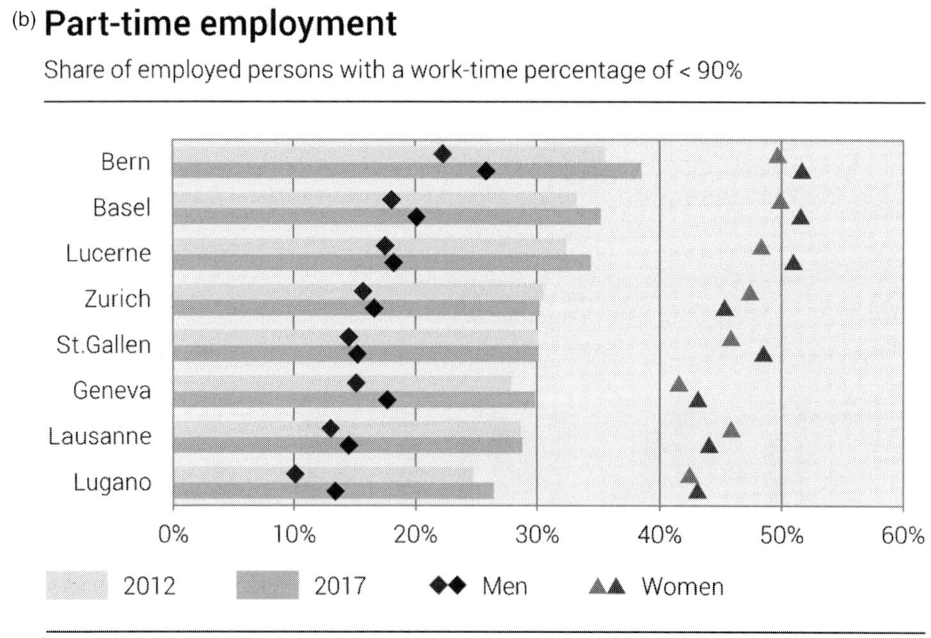

Figure 13.6b Example of a graph presenting values for two years and according to gender (indicator "Part-time employment"). Source: Schneeberger & Jeanneret (2018)

In a more general manner, City Statistics and Cercle Indicateurs are anchored in the official statistical system, which implies that high standards in terms of data quality have to be followed (CORSTAT & FSO, 2012), (Eurostat & European Statistical System Committee, 2017). However, the FSO and the other actors in the federal statistical system do not have the obligation to produce data at the municipal level, which can therefore often be seen as by-products of the federal statistics. Specific exploitations of survey data with data pooling over several years may, for example, be necessary to obtain some variables at the municipal level, and the data may anyway not be available for small cities due to confidence intervals that are too high.[12]. This has the consequence that finding data for building indicators for certain dimensions of quality of life (City Statistics) or certain target areas of sustainable development (Cercle Indicateurs) is a challenge.

There are two main ways to circumvent the problem of the lack of centralized data. The first is the use of proxies, i.e., data that is not measuring exactly what was defined but a related phenomenon. The second consists of obtaining data by collecting it in a decentralized manner, i.e., by asking the participating cities to provide the data directly. This is, for example, the case for most data on environmental aspects (biodiversity, valuable natural areas, water regime and quality), as well as extra-familial childcare (infant day care).

13.5 Participatory Aspects

The Bellagio STAMP 7 entitled "Broad participation" recommends, on the one hand, to "find appropriate ways to reflect the views of the public" and, on the other hand, to "engage early on with the users of the assessment so that it best fits their needs." The first point is hardly implemented by Cercle Indicateurs or City Statistics, among other reasons because it has traditionally not been considered the task of the federal statistical office to engage in a dialogue with the general public. For the second aspect, however, things are different. First of all, for both Cercle Indicateurs and Swiss City Statistics, participatory processes are enshrined in the general governance rules of the projects that are defined in the contracts between the participating federal offices, cantons (for Cercle Indicateurs), and cities.

Concerning Cercle Indicateurs, it is broadly based on a bottom-up, participatory approach that engages the participating cantons and cities. Back in the beginning of the 2000s, a working committee composed of the participating cantons and cities defined the topics (target areas) that were then validated by the responsible body. The same occurred for the selection of indicators. Cercle Indicateurs is therefore a joint product built by the participating cantons, cities, and federal offices, and not solely by the ARE or the FSO. This participatory and collaborative approach is still in the DNA of the project. Each further development of the indicator framework, be it the revision of an indicator or a conceptual development such as the introduction of an indicator typology, is discussed and decided upon during the meetings of the responsible body on the basis of documents prepared and sent in advance by the project team at ARE and FSO. The representatives of the cantons and cities are regularly involved in these developments themselves before a decision is taken.

This happens either in the form of workshops as part of meetings of the responsible body, or of ad hoc meetings in smaller working groups.

The participating cantons and cities are also required to publish a short comment (one A4 page) about their results when they are published, which happens every two years for the cantons and every four years for the cities. It is actually during this step that the boundary object nature of the indicators becomes tangible, for two reasons. The first reason is that it is during the comment-writing phase that the representatives of the cantons and cities – who for the most part belong to territorial planning, environmental protection, or central services units – enter the world of official statistics that requires exercising caution when interpreting the indicators, paying attention, among other things, to their exact definition, as well as avoiding establishing causal links, e.g., between an observed trend and a given public policy measure that cannot be proven. A dialogue opens between the users (in the policymaking sphere in the cantons and cities) and the representatives of the official statistics body (FSO) in the form of comments by the official statistics representatives on the comments about the results written by the users in the policymaking sphere, which can lead to the organization of a coaching session for the users by the official statistics body. The second, and probably more important reason, is that the comment-writing phase brings about a dialogue about sustainable development within the municipal or cantonal administration and – potentially – with the municipal or cantonal government, because the writing process requires, at least in some cantons and cities, that representatives of several units across the administration work together on the comment and that a member of the municipal or cantonal executive approves the document. The exercise does not stop after writing the comment on the results for all cantons and cities. According to an internal analysis, about 50 percent of the participating cantons and cities in Cercle Indicateurs use the indicators for own communication purposes, such as using the structure of the system and the indicators to write a report on sustainable development (city of Winterthur, among others) or presenting the indicators in an annex to the legislative programme (city of Lucerne).

City Statistics has a different organization that relies on a more top-down approach, with participatory aspects being less prominent. The catalogue of variables was defined and is regularly updated in a formal but nevertheless participatory manner at the European level, during the meetings of the National Urban Audit Coordinators (NUACs). The steering group of the project in Switzerland, which brings together delegates of the participating Swiss cities and representatives of the federal bodies (ARE, FSO, and SECO), decides upon the technical aspects of how variables are specified and upon dissemination at the national level. A working group exclusively constituted of representatives of statistical offices and services develops the specifications of the variables. The implementation of the OECD "How's Life" concept to City Statistics, which is specific to Switzerland, was undertaken in a more participatory manner, within a support group involving members of the municipal administration, who are considered to be the direct users of City Statistics. The participating cities are, however, not required to comment on their results as part of the project.

13.6 Transparency and Communication

As stated in Section 13.3, sustainable development can be understood in many different ways, and its interpretation into measurable dimensions that are structured in a conceptual framework is a normative exercise that is inevitably imbued with subjectivity. In this regard, the Bellagio STAMP 5 on transparency is of crucial importance; among other things, this states that it is essential to "explain the choices, assumptions and uncertainties determining the results of the assessment."

The other elements stated in Bellagio STAMP 5 (ensuring that "the data, indicators and results of the assessment are accessible to the public," and disclosing "data sources and methods" and "all sources of funding and potential conflicts of interest") and in Bellagio STAMP 6 on effective communication (such as presenting "information in a fair and objective way that helps to build trust" and making "data available in as much detail as is reliable and practicable") are in line with the quality standards and the principles of official statistics that are set out in the Charter of Swiss Official Statistics (CORSTAT & FSO, 2012) that itself is in line with the European Statistics Code of Practice (Eurostat & European Statistical System Committee, 2017). The following principles of the Charter of Swiss Official Statistics are particularly relevant: Principle 3 describes statistical information as a public good that "shall be publicly accessible and published while guaranteeing statistical confidentiality and sufficient quality"; Principle 4 on transparency states that "statistical information shall be well documented to ensure that it is easily understood and used correctly"; according to Principle 6 on professional independence, "statistical agencies shall enjoy professional independence in the performance of their tasks, particularly from political authorities and interest groups"; finally, Principle 7 on impartiality and objectivity specifies that "statistical information shall be collected, analyzed, presented and commented on impartially."

Both City Statistics and Cercle Indicateurs, as projects anchored in the Swiss official statistical system, follow these principles. However, as is elaborated in the STAMP 6 principle, it may be necessary to use proactive communication and "recognize the value of dynamic engagement between the producers and consumers in a process of joint information and knowledge construction." This is what was attempted with the Swiss version of City Statistics, which changed its focus from a collection of about 180 variables grouped into nine main domains to a framework focused on quality of life in cities, in collaboration with the users of the statistics in the administrations of the participating cities.

STAMP 6 also underlines the importance of presenting "not only statistical data, but broader contextual information in different forms." This is what is attempted in the publicly available indicator sheets produced within the scope of Cercle Indicateurs (see Box 13.1), that include, along with classical technical information on the indicators such as definition, unit, and data source, the texts describing the link between the target area and sustainable development, the justification for the selection of an indicator for measuring the target area, as well as information on the elements that should be taken into account while interpreting the indicators, such as known structural differences between, for example, large cities and small towns.

13.7 Continuity and Capacity

According to STAMP 8, sustainability assessment requires repeated measurement, responsiveness to change, investment to develop and maintain adequate capacity, and continuous learning and improvement. Official statistics have a long-term perspective and produce data that is coherent across space and time. This is undoubtedly a strength of City Statistics and Cercle Indicateurs, which are anchored in the official statistical system and rely on such data. In addition, both projects have been in place for 10 to 15 years at the time of writing and, in addition to regular updates of the data (every year for City Statistics, every two to four years for Cercle Indicateurs), they have evolved over time and allowed their participants to gain insight into and knowledge about data, indicators, and the operationalization of the concepts of quality of life and sustainable development, respectively, into measurable dimensions or target areas. STAMP 8 is, however, a challenge for both Cercle Indicateurs and City Statistics, since they are co-financed by the participating federal entities, cities, and (for Cercle Indicateurs) cantons for periods of three to four years, which leads to uncertainties about their existence over the medium and long term, and which is not coherent with the long-term perspective of official statistics.

13.8 Conclusion

The scientific literature mentions various instruments pertaining to sustainability assessment at the local level. However, little attention is paid to their specificities, to the reasons behind the variety of these instruments, and more importantly, to the variety of information that these instruments deliver. This variety of information shows that sustainability and sustainability assessment can be understood in many different ways, which of course has an influence on the result of the assessment. On the basis of the two cases presented in this chapter for the Swiss context and using the Bellagio STAMPs, we suggest that the rationale for the setup of any sustainability assessment instrument and the way it is actually implemented should be documented and published alongside the results.

The Cercle Indicateurs framework reflects the political priorities for sustainable development at the local and regional level in Switzerland at the beginning of the first decade of the twenty-first century, while City Statistics reflects the understanding of the concept of quality of life in Western Europe in the same period. This is exemplified by the detailed consideration of the environmental dimension within Cercle Indicateurs or of the economic aspects of quality of life in City Statistics, which should be contrasted with the lack of target areas or dimensions pertaining, for example, to social cohesion or to subjective well-being. Both conceptual frameworks can thus be classified as "policy-based," as opposed to "conceptual-based" according to the UNECE (2009: p. 27ff.).

With its bottom-up, participatory approach, the Cercle Indicateurs framework may encourage the representatives of the cities and cantons to identify more closely with the project; however, it also entails certain inertia due to the consensus-based decision-making processes, and therefore a certain resistance to change. City Statistics has a rather top-down approach that allows the project managers to rapidly react to change and, for example, develop new communication channels. The associated drawback is that there is less support by the participating cities, who are less involved in the setting up, evolution, and communication of the indicators.

Due to the Swiss national context, both City Statistics and Cercle Indicateurs operate in a trilingual environment. This entails, on the one hand, a translation effort in the literal sense (e.g., for internal documents and communication of the results) and represents a difficulty for the rollout of the discussion during the meetings of the participating cities (and cantons for Cercle Indicateurs). There are, however, indications that such a multilingual setting may also produce a culture of mutual listening and a collaborative attitude.

Indicators can be considered as "shuttles" that make statistical information more accessible, or as "boundary spanners" between science and statistical information on the one side and policy- and decision-makers on the other. City Statistics and Cercle Indicateurs play different roles in this respect. City Statistics makes a lot of data available for analysis, which was originally presented in the form of variables and not of indicators according to the definition we use here. The implementation of the OECD "How's Life" concept is a step toward a facilitated interpretation for the user. Cercle Indicateurs offers less data but more help for interpretation is available. However, there is a lack of additional, easily accessible data that could support the interpretation of the indicators.

The conceptual frameworks underlying City Statistics (for the measurement of quality of life) and Cercle Indicateurs depend on the context in which they were developed and cannot therefore be transposed as such to any other geographical and/or temporal context. However, the participatory and collaborative processes and the communication tools they offer could be very useful for the development of indicators for the sustainability assessment of cities in other regions of the world.

Acknowledgments

We would like to express our gratitude to Ms. Barbara Jeanneret of the Swiss Federal Statistical Office, who provided us with valuable information about City Statistics, and to Dr. Daniel Wachter, head of the Department for Municipalities and Regional Development Planning of the canton of Bern, Switzerland, for his constructive comments on the chapter.

Notes

1. The sources: the professional networks of the authors, the Brainpool project (https://ec.europa.eu/eurostat/cros/content/brainpool_en), www.wikiprogress.org, Singh et al. (2012).
2. See www.qualityoflifeproject.govt.nz/(accessed 28.05.2018).
3. See www.understandingglasgow.com/(accessed 28.05.2018).
4. A description of the project and how it is situated in the Swiss political context is available in English in Wachter (2012).
5. Among these are eight of the ten most populated Swiss cities, but also cities as small as Orbe with about 7,000 inhabitants (state 2016).
6. The indicator sheets are published online as PDF documents in French ("Fiches d'indicateurs") and German ("Indikatorenblätter") on both the FSO (www.cercleindicateurs.bfs.admin.ch) and

ARE websites (www.are.admin.ch/cercleindicateurs). They are published separately for the cantons and the cities.

7. The most populated cities have a minimum of 50,000 inhabitants.
8. See www.bfs.admin.ch/bfs/en/home/statistics/cross-sectional-topics/city-statistics/indicators-quality-life.html.
9. See the "three-dimensional model" described online (www.are.admin.ch/are/en/home/sustainable-development/strategy-and-planning/understanding-of-sustainability-in-switzerland/three-dimensional-model.html, last accessed on 22.05.2018).
10. Corresponding to the type "input/output" in the MONET typology (see Willi et al., 2012).
11. City Statistics offers data for both core cities and their agglomeration in the form of time series available through an interactive tool. However, they are not directly related to the quality of life indicators.
12. There is, therefore, more data available for the cities participating in City Statistics, since the lower limit to be a project partner is set at 50,000 inhabitants (Cercle Indicateurs includes cities with fewer than 7,000 inhabitants), which allows for more possibilities in terms of representative data based on surveys.

References

Boesch, A., de Montmollin, A., Kulig, A., Palm, V., Willi, V., & Zuinen, N. (2014). *Getting Messages across Using Indicators: A Handbook Based on Experiences from Assessing Sustainable Development Indicators, 2014 edition*. Luxembourg: Eurostat (Statistical Office of the European Union).

CORSTAT (Swiss Conference of regional statistical offices) & FSO (Swiss federal statistical office) (2012). *Charter of Swiss Official Statistic*, 3rd revised version.

de Vries, B. J. M., & Petersen, A. C. (2009). Conceptualizing sustainable development. *Ecological Economics*, 68(4), 1006–1019.

Eurostat (Statistical Office of the European Union) & European Statistical System Committee. (2017). *European Statistics Code of Practice*, revised edition 2017.

Gallopín, G. C. (1997). Indicators and their use: Information for decision-making. In B. Moldan and S. Billharz (eds.), *Sustainability Indicators: Report of the Project on Indicators of Sustainable Development*. Chichester: Wiley, pp.13–27.

Horn, R. V. (1993). *Statistical Indicators for the Economic & Social Sciences*. Cambridge: Cambridge University Press.

Istat (Italian National Institute of Statistics) (2015). *UrBes 2015 – Il benessere equo e sostenibile nelle città*. www.istat.it/it/archivio/153995.

Lautenschütz, A.-K., & Pedrini, S. (2016). Indicateurs de qualité de vie dans les villes de l'Audit urbain. In *Développement durable et qualité de vie dans les quartiers*. Bern: ARE (Federal Office for Spatial Development), pp. 16–22.

Maggino, F. (2017). Developing indicators and managing the complexity. In F. Maggino, (ed.), *Complexity in Society: From Indicators Construction to their Synthesis*. Social Indicators Research Series, 70. Cham: Springer, pp. 87–114.

Meadows, D. (1998). *Indicators and Information Systems for Sustainable Development: A Report to the Balaton Group*. Hartland Four Corners: The Sustainability Institute.

Neumann, U., & Seidel-Schulze, A. (2010). *Urban Audit Analysis II*. Presented at the Statistische Woche 2010, SCORUS-Session, Munich.

OECD. (1993). *OECD Core Set of Indicators for Environmental Performance Reviews. A Synthesis Report by the Group on the State of the Environment*. Paris: Organisation for Economic Cooperation and Development (OECD).

OECD (2011). *How's Life? Measuring Well-Being*. Paris: OECD Publishing.

OECD (2015). *How's Life? 2015: Measuring Well-Being*. Paris: OECD Publishing.

Pintér, L., Hardi, P., Martinuzzi, A., and Hall, J. (2012). Bellagio STAMP: Principles for sustainability assessment and measurement. *Ecological Indicators*, 17, 20–28.

Pope, J., Bond, A., Hugé, J., and Morrison-Saunders, A. (2017). Reconceptualising sustainability assessment. *Environmental Impact Assessment Review*, 62, 205–215.

Ramos, T. B. (2009). Development of regional sustainability indicators and the role of academia in this process: The Portuguese practice. *Journal of Cleaner Production*, 17(12), 1101–1115.

Ravetz, J. (2000). Integrated assessment for sustainability appraisal in cities and regions. *Environmental Impact Assessment Review*, 20(1), 31–64.

Sala, S., Ciuffo, B., and Nijkamp, P. (2015). A systemic framework for sustainability assessment. *Ecological Economics*, 119, 314–325.

Schneeberger, Y., & Jeanneret, B. (Eds.) (2018). *Quality of Life in the Cities: Pocket Statistics 2018*. Neuchâtel: FSO (Swiss Federal Statistical Office).

Singh, R. K., Murty, H. R., Gupta, S. K., & Dikshit, A. K. (2012). An overview of sustainability assessment methodologies. *Ecological Indicators*, 9(2), 189–212.

Star, S. L., & Griesemer, J. R. (1989). Institutional ecology, "translations" and boundary objects: Amateurs and professionals in Berkeley's Museum of Vertebrate Zoology, 1907–39. *Social Studies of Science*, 19(3), 387–420.

Stiglitz, J. E., Sen, A., & Fitoussi, J.-P. (2009). *Report by the Commission on the Measurement of Economic Performance and Social Progress*.

Sustainable Society Foundation. (2014). Sustainable City Index, SCI-2014. Retrieved from www.ssfindex.com/

Turnhout, E., Hisschemöller, M., & Eijsackers, H. (2007). Ecological indicators: Between the two fires of science and policy. *Ecological Indicators*, 7(2), 215–228.

UNCED (United Nations Conference on Environment & Development) (1992). *Agenda 21*. Rio de Janeiro: United Nations.

UNECE (United Nations Economic Commission for Europe) (2009). *Measuring Sustainable Development*. New York and Geneva: United Nations.

UNGA (United Nations General Assembly) (2015). *Transforming our World: The 2030 Agenda for Sustainable Development*. New York: United Nations.

Wachter, D. (2012). Benchmarking sustainable development in the Swiss confederation. In A. Fenna & F. Knüpling (eds.), *Benchmarking in Federal Systems*. Canberra: Productivity Commission and Forum of Federations, pp. 123–143.

Willi, V., Wachtl, J., de Montmollin, A., Boesch, A., et al. (2012). *Sustainable Development Report 2012*. Neuchâtel: FSO (Swiss Federal Statistical Office).

WCED (World Commission on Environment and Development), (1987). *Report of the World Commission on Environment and Development: Our Common Future*. United Nations.

Yamato, N., Hamada, Y., Matsuda, M., Dustan, P., & Taki, N. (2017). *Global Power City Index 2017: GPCI 10th Anniversary Special Edition*. Tokyo: Institute for Urban Strategies, The Mori Memorial Foundation.

Zoeteman, K., Mommaas, H., & Dagevos, J. (2016). Are larger cities more sustainable? Lessons from integrated sustainability monitoring in 403 Dutch municipalities. *Environmental Development*, 17, 57–72.

14

Ontology-Based Integration of Urban Sustainability Indicators

Emanuele Massaro, Aristide Athanassiadis, Achilleas Psyllidis, and Claudia R. Binder

14.1 Introduction

The complexity, structure, and dynamics of cities and urban systems are multi-scalar in nature. In a similar way, data and information about how cities perform involve a range of spatial scales, from a disaggregate level (e.g., individual activities, events at specific locations) to an aggregate level (e.g., neighborhoods, census tracts, entire cities as single entities) (Berry 1964; Singleton et al., 2017). This has an impact on how we measure, evaluate, and understand the problems facing contemporary cities. Examples of the latter include population growth or, in some cases, shrinkage in urban areas, the use of energy resources to sustain urban populations and infrastructure, as well as the circulation of goods and people across the urban fabric, to name a few. In response to the aforementioned problems, modern-day urban policies call for increased sustainability, resilience, and circularity of materials and resources in order to improve the overall quality of life. Despite the importance of these in assuring greater well-being for urban populations, the lack of a coherent and shared understanding regarding what defines the sustainability and resilience of an urban system results in ambiguous interpretations and, further, makes the quantitative and qualitative evaluation of these policies rather cumbersome.

To better understand what makes an urban system sustainable, a wealth of indicators and indicator sets, structured in the form of standards (e.g., ISO, OECD, SDG Index), have been developed and proposed over recent decades (Griggs et al., 2013; Hiremath et al., 2013; Organisation for Economic Co-operation and Development, 2008). These standards aim to disassemble the concept of sustainability and take different approaches to understanding the dimensions that contribute to sustainable cities and urban systems. The indicators comprising the standards mentioned above are primarily based on measured or empirical data, derived from a variety of sources. The multiplicity of existing indicator sets reveals a lack of consensus among the various standards and relates to their normative perspective (see Chapter 1 (Halla & Binder, 2020)). For instance, similar indicators are described using different terms, or similar terms refer to different indicators (for instance CO_2 or CO_2 Emissions). The current lack of consensus among the various standards poses challenges for the measurement, evaluation, and comparison of urban sustainability performance across cities, especially when data from heterogeneous sources are used. It is, therefore, imperative to provide a framework that enables links and comparisons among the various existing standards and their corresponding indicators to be made.

An approach to fostering interoperability among the different urban sustainability standards could involve the use of ontologies (Psyllidis, 2015, 2016). Ontologies play a pivotal role in semantic integration and data interoperability, by accounting for shared vocabularies and formal definitions of domain concepts and their interrelationships. These concepts represent real-world entities, which are expressed in a machine-processable format, meaning that they can be further interpreted by computing systems. Ontology concepts are most frequently represented as classes. These are subsequently organized into hierarchies or taxonomies, connecting the different concepts together through explicitly defined relationships. Other essential features of ontologies include attributes, which enrich concepts with data types (e.g., integers, strings, Booleans) and values, as well as axioms, which constitute logical statements (e.g., a class is *equal to* another class, or a class is *different from* another class) that enrich the knowledge about the domain in question. At the data level, ontologies are further characterized by instances – also referred to as individuals – which constitute specific objects belonging to more generic classes (e.g., a train station is an instance of a generic class representing all types of buildings) (Figure 14.1). Being built on these components, ontologies constitute prominent repositories for sharing, interpreting, and reusing knowledge about a domain.

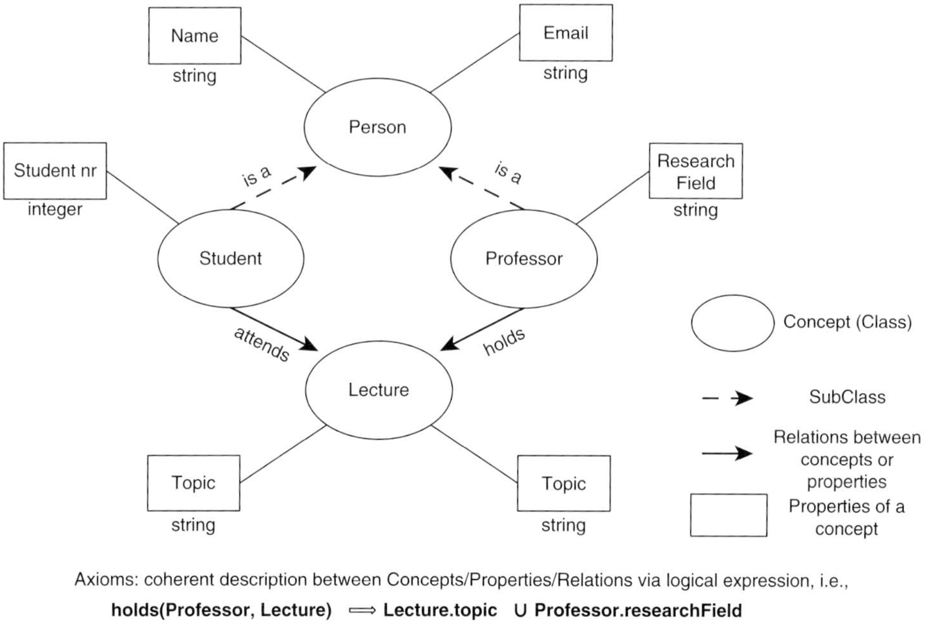

Figure 14.1 Representation of an ontology showing concepts (classes), hierarchical relationships (subclass), properties, relations between concepts and properties, and axioms that define coherent description between concepts, properties and relations through logical expressions. Source: own illustration

We propose that ontologies could offer support in dealing with the problem of the different indicator standards we have mentioned. Therefore, this chapter introduces an ontology-driven framework for the semantic interoperability of urban sustainability indicators. It presents and describes a formal representation of knowledge about sustainability indicators and their interrelationships, through the development of a domain ontology. Given the dynamic redefinition of sustainability indicators, we demonstrate how the proposed ontology-driven framework offers a more flexible approach – compared to predefined vocabularies – to documenting and semantically representing urban sustainability standards. To increase its adaptability and potential for reuse, as well as to facilitate its continuous redevelopment, we have made the developed ontology available online, through a dedicated web portal.[1]

The remainder of this chapter is organized as follows. First, we present a set of prevalent standards and their corresponding indicators, used in urban sustainability studies. Next, we introduce the proposed ontology-driven framework and describe the ontology for urban sustainability. We specifically focus on how the ontology allows for semantic linkages among the indicators included in the numerous existing standards. Finally, we discuss the limitations of our framework, summarize the conclusions, and describe future lines of research.

To select the relevant classes for assessing sustainability of the urban system, Brundtland's concept of sustainability was chosen (Holden et al., 2014). This definition of sustainability consists of three pillars: economic, ecological, and social. Similar to the sustainability solution space – i.e., Chapter 8 (Binder et al., 2020) – we choose indicators that fulfill the following requirements:

- They represent the concept of sustainability chosen, i.e., they consider the three pillars.
- They allow for comparison among different cities and different countries.
- Data should be available for several cities, to be able to perform a comparative analysis.

This is a clear limitation, as discussed in Chapter 1 (Halla & Binder, 2020): however, our methodological approach can be applied to any definition of sustainability. The goal of this chapter is to provide a generic approach for defining an ontology of urban sustainable indicators.

14.2 Indicators of Urban Sustainability

Indicators are a key element in assessing the sustainability of cities, defining quantitative objectives, and monitoring the progress made toward them, as well as in supporting communication between different stakeholders (Shen et al., 2011). In fact, a number of researchers, private companies, and consultants, as well as international administrations, have worked on developing sustainability indicators for specific cities or groups of cities. Yet, at this stage, there is no consensus on urban sustainability indicators, which in turn results in findings that are unconsolidated and difficult to compare (Kahn, 2007). The lack of consensus on the choice of indicators is very closely related to the fact that there is no

Table 14.1 *Total number of indicators and source of information for the different frameworks*

Name	N	Source
OECD	41	https://stats.oecd.org/
ISO 37120	133	www.dataforcities.org/wccd/
SDG	48	http://unsdsn.org/resources/publications/us-cities-sdg-index/
CI	34	www.bfs.admin.ch/bfs/en/home/statistics/sustainable-development.html
UMI	83	Reference (Kennedy et al., 2015)

common definition as to what urban sustainability or a sustainable city is (Alberti et al., 1996). Due to the numerous and multi-faceted ways in which cities impact and are impacted by the environment, both locally and globally, describing this complex relationship through a limited amount of indicators can be an extremely difficult (or even vain) exercise.

This subsection presents a number of indicator standards focusing on urban sustainability. We analyze the motivation to build the indicator standards, the similarities and differences amongst them, as well as how they treat certain aspects of sustainability. The indicator standards, summarized in Table 14.1, that will be presented in this part are as follows:

- International Organization for Standardization (ISO): ISO standard 37120 on the sustainable development of communities (Zdaveski et al., 2017);
- CI: Cercle Indicators from the Swiss federal office of statistics;
- OECD: the OECD indicators;
- UMI: the urban metabolism indicators;
- SDG: US Cities SDG Index (Prakash et al., 2017).

14.2.1 ISO Standard 37120

The ISO standard 37120 for sustainable development of communities provides a standardized set of indicators of city services and quality of life that is claimed to be "comparable over time . . . [and] across cities." The standard brings together more than 100 indicators, clustered in three main types of indicators: *profile indicators* provide more context about a city and enable its comparison with others, including generic information about demography, economy, climate, etc.; *core indicators*, for which cities need to provide data in order to receive a certification; and finally *supporting indicators*, which are highly recommended indicators but not mandatory. Core and supporting indicators are classified into 17 broad themes: economy, education, energy, environment, finance, fire and emergency response, governance, health, recreation, safety, shelter, solid waste, telecommunication and innovation, transportation, urban planning, wastewater, and water and sanitation. As can be seen, the indicator framework covers a wide range of aspects of urban life that are not necessarily linked to urban sustainability per se, but to the capacity of a city to provide specific services to its inhabitants. Nevertheless, by combining profile indicators and other indicators (core and supporting), this standard assists cities to learn one from another when comparing their data and local initiatives to similar cities, in terms of size, population, GDP, etc.

14.2.2 The Cercle Indicators

The Cercle Indicators are sustainability indicators for Swiss cantons and municipalities, developed by the Swiss Federal Office for Territorial Development (Office fédérale du développement territorial (Meier & Wachter, 2005)). This indicator set was developed to serve as a benchmark for the evolution of Swiss cities toward sustainability as shown in Chapter 13 (Boesch & de Montmollin, 2020). Urban sustainability is accounted for under its three dimensions, namely environment, economy and society. Within each dimension, 11 to 12 themes are considered (more details about the themes are provided in Table 14.1) and one central indicator is used to represent each theme. The Cercle Indicators (like most other indicators sets) claim to help decision-makers to develop and implement action plans, as well as to communicate more effectively on urban sustainability. Yet, as the indicators remain quite vague, they don't enable the assessment of specific policies or projects. This indicator set is structured around traditional elements of sustainability and attempts to realize these on urban territories. Yet, it does not necessarily take into account the specificity and context of urban systems.

14.2.3 OECD Regional and Metropolitan Databases

The Organisation for Economic Co-operation and Development's (OECD) aim is to "promote policies that will improve the economic and social well-being of people around the world." To do so, they work with governments to measure and analyze economic data, in order to understand what drives economic, social, and environmental change. To streamline the comparison between countries, cities, and policies, the OECD has also developed numerous international standards, including indicators standards. More specifically, the OECD has developed an indicator set that has comparable data for about 2,000 regions and 281 OECD metropolitan areas (urban areas with 500,000 or more inhabitants). The 41 indicators relevant to metropolitan areas cover economic factors (GDP and patent activities), geographic and administrative forms, environmental factors, social factors (income and inequality), the labor market, and demographic indicators.

14.2.4 Urban Metabolism Indicators

Urban metabolism is a developing topic in the scientific community comparing the functioning of cities to a living organism (Kennedy et al., 2015). While there are different disciplinary vantage points within the community, an essential element of urban metabolism is the assessment of material, energy, water, and other flows that enter and exit urban systems. A number of studies have characterized the flows of cities across the globe (Athanassiadis et al., 2017; Barles, 2009; Hoekman & Blottnitz, 2017; Niza et al., 2009; Voskamp et al., 2017). Depending on data availability, authors choose different types of accounting methods, and therefore different indicators and data to characterize the metabolisms of cities. A number of cases have used economy-wide material flow accounting, which was initially developed for national economies, due to its set accounting method and enabling of comparability. Some authors have brought in modifications to the existing method to better encompass what happens at an urban level (Barles, 2009; Voskamp et al., 2017). Other researchers have simply compiled data on metabolic flows with no particular methodology, mostly dependent on data availability. The inconsistency of the indicators used by researchers to measure the metabolic flows represents one of the main challenges facing the community, as the result is a juxtaposition of assessments that makes it impossible to develop a robust theoretical and methodological framework. Kennedy et al. (2014) proposed an indicator set for urban metabolism that was later applied to 27 megacities, which is the largest sample of comparable cities from a metabolic perspective (Kennedy et al., 2015). The indicator list proposed is divided into four layers of information that provide quantitative and qualitative information about the metabolisms of megacities. The first layer covers the definition of a megacity, or in other words the spatial and administrative delimitation of the city, as well as information on population and GDP. The second layer presents biophysical characteristics of megacities including climatic and building area details. The third layer focuses on the characterization of metabolic flows per se, meaning the quantification of energy, water, waste, and materials flows and of the material stock. The final layer provides qualitative information about the utilities that circulate and metabolize the flows quantified in the previous layers. The main objective of urban metabolism indicators is to help understand the mechanisms that are behind urban resource use and pollution emissions in order to develop mitigation strategies. From that perspective, this set of indicators is focused on the environmental aspect of urban sustainability and offers an academic perspective on it.

14.2.5 US Cities SDG Index

The indicator set presented here is derived from the 17 Sustainable Development Goals (SDGs) developed by the United Nations, as applied to US cities. In 2015, the SDGs replaced the Millennium Development Goals (and their 60 indicators) and included goals relating to poverty, hunger, health, or sustainable cities and communities, among others. Based on these goals, an SDG index with 79 indicators and using data from international organizations (such as the World Bank, Food and Agriculture Organization, etc.) was developed to track countries' progress toward or performance on the SDGs (Sachs et al., 2016). The US Cities SDG Index transposes the aforementioned Global SDG Index onto the 100 most populous cities of the United States of America, or more specifically onto metropolitan statistical areas, as they offer better data availability. This urban index consists of 49 indicators and its main objectives are to provide a database to monitor sustainable development in American cities, to better understand where US cities stand on SDG implementation, as well as to identify potential actions to accelerate this implementation, and finally to identify data gaps that hinder cities in monitoring the implementation of SDGs. Most of the data required to satisfy the 49 indicators of the index are provided by the American Community Survey, yet they do not always reflect the full extent of each goal. In addition, as one of the 17 goals specifically focuses on cities and communities (SDG 11), the question is raised as to whether the rest of the goals should be also be inquired into (as is done currently in the index) or whether more indicators should be included for SDG 11 in order to develop a truly city-based index. As with most of the other indicator sets (and especially the Cercle Indicators), the US Cities SDG Index covers a wide array of aspects of urban sustainability but remains quite superficial, and thus hinders a deeper understanding of the urban system and does not necessarily enable the development of mitigation action plans.

14.3 Ontology Design and Development

In this section, we describe the methods and the phases we used in order to aggregate and combine different sustainability indicators extracted from the five different frameworks in the form of an *ontology*.

The goal of this ontology is to (i) share a common understanding of the structure of information among scholars and stakeholders, (ii) enable the reuse of domain knowledge, and (iii) analyze domain knowledge in the field of urban sustainability assessment. We aggregate the different sustainable indicators proposed by the five different frameworks previously described in the form of ontology by defining a hierarchical structure and links between different classes and indicators.

14.3.1 What Is an Ontology?

The literature contains many definitions of ontology; many of these contradict one another (Guarino et al., 2009).[2] For the purposes of this research, we define an ontology as a formal explicit description of concepts in a domain of discourse (classes), properties of each concept describing various features and attributes of the concept (properties), and (relations) between classes and individuals (Noy & McGuinness, 2001). An ontology, together with a set of individual instances of classes, constitutes a knowledge base. Classes are the focus of most ontologies. Classes can be defined as an extension or an intension. According to an extensional definition, they are abstract groups, sets, or collections of objects. According to an intensional definition, they are abstract objects that are defined by values of aspects that are constraints for being a member of the class. The first definition of class results in ontologies in which a class is a subclass of a collection. The second definition of class results in ontologies in which collections and classes are more fundamentally different. It is clear that the conception of the classes needs to be known before the term/class can be properly defined in an ontology (Kuhn, 1996). Classes may classify individuals, other classes, or a combination of both. Some examples of classes are the following:

- *Person*, the class of all people, or the abstract object that can be described by the criteria for being a person.
- *Vehicle*, the class of all vehicles, or the abstract object that can be described by the criteria for being a vehicle. A car can be a subclass of *Vehicle*.
- *Class*, representing the class of all classes, or the abstract object that can be described by the criteria for being a class.
- *Thing*, representing the class of all things, or the abstract object that can be described by the criteria for being a thing (and not nothing).

Importantly, a class can subsume or be subsumed by other classes; a class subsumed by another is called a subclass (or subtype) of the subsuming class (or supertype). For example, *Air Pollution* subsumes *CO_2 Emissions*, since (necessarily) anything that is a member of the latter class is a member of the former. Relationships (also known as relations) between objects in an ontology specify how objects are related to other objects. Typically, a relation is of a particular type (or class) that specifies in what sense the object is related to the other object in the ontology. For example, in the ontology that contains the concept *OECD* and the concept *GHG* (greenhouse gas emissions), these might be related by a relation of the type ***isDefinedBy***. The full expression of that fact then comes in the form of a semantic triple:

GHG	isDefinedBy	OECD
Subject	Predicate	Object

An important type of relation is the subclass relation (**is-a-subclass-of**). This defines which objects are classified by which class. For example, we have already seen that the class *GHG* **is-a-subclass-of** *Air Pollution*, which in turn **is-a-subclass-of** *Air*. The addition of the is-a-subclass-of relationships creates a taxonomy: a tree-like structure (or, more generally, a partially ordered set) that clearly depicts how objects relate to one another. In such a structure, each object is the "child" of a "parent class." (Some languages restrict the is-a-subclass-of relationship to one parent for all nodes, but many do not.)

An example of the taxonomic hierarchy of classes and subclasses is shown in Figure 14.2. In practical terms, developing an ontology includes:

- defining classes in the ontology,
- arranging the classes in a taxonomic (subclass–superclass) hierarchy,
- defining slots and describing allowed values for these slots,
- filling in the values for slots for instances.

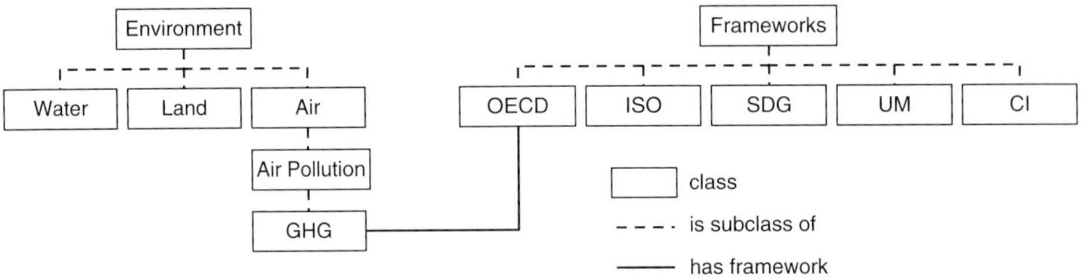

Figure 14.2 The figure shows the ontology scheme. White boxes represent classes, dashed lines (--) show the links to the subclasses, while the solid line represents the connection between the data and the framework that describes the data point. In this ontology, we have two super classes, Environment and Frameworks, with different subclasses (e.g., water, land, air). The indicator GHG (which represents Green House Emissions) is a subclass of Air Pollution. At the same time, it is a property defined by the framework OECD. Source: own illustration

14.3.2 Ontology for Urban Sustainability Assessment

In order to create an ontology of urban indicators from the frameworks we described in Section 14.2, we define a hierarchical structure based on the three pillars of sustainability: economy, environment, society (Brundtland, 1987). As explained in the introduction Section 14.1, in this chapter we only focus on the methodological approach of defining an ontology of urban sustainable indicators, without discussing the definition of sustainability based on the aforementioned three pillars, which has already been extensively discussed in Chapter 1 (Halla & Binder, 2020).

We first collected 334 sustainability indicators from the five frameworks described in Section 14.2. Given the indicators, the frameworks, and the sustainability definition based on the three pillars, we designed a hierarchical taxonomy in order to conceptualize our domain of interest. The first two layers of our hierarchical taxonomy are (1) Sustainability Indicators and (2) Frameworks, as shown in Figure 14.2. For the Sustainability branch, we performed an in-depth analysis of the indicators in order to relate them to the three main pillars of sustainability. For each of the three main classes, we defined subclasses. For example, we defined the classes *GDP* and *Employment* as subclasses of the class *Economy*. Or *Crime* and *Deaths* as subclass of the *Social* class, or, for instance, *Air* and *Climate* as subclasses of the *Environment* class. The complete list of the subclasses for each class are reported in Table 14.3. For the complete list of the class relations see the ontology online.[3] In Table 14.3, we report the subcategories we defined for each of the three pillars, where, for instance, *GDP* is a subclass of the category *Economy*. Following this procedure, we defined a three-layer hierarchical taxonomy for the *Sustainability* branch, where *GDP per Capita* is a subcategory of *GDP*, which is a subcategory of *Economy*. Some of the indicators could not be clearly allocated to a subcategory of the three main categories and for this reason, for each category we defined a subcategory *Others*: some examples of those indicators are *Cost of Living* under the *Economy* section, *Racial Segregation* in the *Social* domain, or *Biodiversity* in the *Environmental* one. The ontology was built using the Protégé ontology development platform (*Protégé Software*, n.d.). According to the hierarchical taxonomy defined above, the top level of our ontology, summarized in Figure 14.2, is composed of two classes: Sustainability Indicators and Frameworks. The Frameworks class contains five subclasses corresponding to the frameworks we analyzed in this research and described in Section 14.2, such as: SDG, OECD, ISO 37120, UMI, and CI that correspond respectively to *US Cities SDG Index*, *OECD regional and metropolitan database*, *ISO standard 37120*, *Urban Metabolism Indicators* and *Cercle Indicators*.

Furthermore, for each of the sustainability indicators, we created a hierarchical taxonomy for each class. While the Frameworks subclasses are defined just by a short description of the framework itself, the subclasses of the *Sustainability Indicators*, such as *Economy*, *Society*, *Environment* have a sub-structure containing the information for the 334 indicators we collected. A comparison of the different frameworks for the different indicators is reported in Figure 14.4 and in Table 14.2 and Table 14.3.

Moreover, each class defining an indicator has the property *isDefinedBy* and the property *comment* that contains the information of the framework that defined the indicator itself and the original name. For instance, the class ***heartAttackDeaths*** has the following properties:

- *comment*
  - Heart Attack Deaths per 100,000 Inhabitants
- *isDefinedBy*
  - SDG

Another important property of the ontology is the property *EquivalentTo* that allows us to define equivalent indicators among the set of the data points we collected. For instance, the OECD framework defines the indicator "*Estimated average exposure to air pollution* "(PM2.5) based on imagery data OECD that corresponds to the class estimatedAverageExposure ToAirPollution of our ontology. While, the SDG framework defines the indicator "$_{P}M_{2.5}$ *Average Levels* (Population Weighted), " that corresponds to pM2.5AverageLevels of our ontology. Then for those classes we set the property *EquivalentTo*:

estimatedAverageExposureToAirPollution – EquivalentTo – $_{p}M_{2.5}$*AverageLevels*

14.4 Comparing the Indicator Standards for Urban Sustainability

In this section, we discuss the results of our methodological approach. Our ontology shows that, while all the selected frameworks focus on (urban) sustainability, they address different aspects of sustainability. Furthermore, they don't show a clear and common structure; rather each reflects its own underlying normative views. This implies that an assessment of urban sustainability is likely to differ depending on the framework chosen. This restates the importance of making and differentiating normative and systemic perspectives (as proposed in Halla & Binder, 2020), as the choice of indicators for comparing different cities is a critical issue, both for the efficacy of a stakeholder-driven approach, and for reaching and monitoring the goals set.

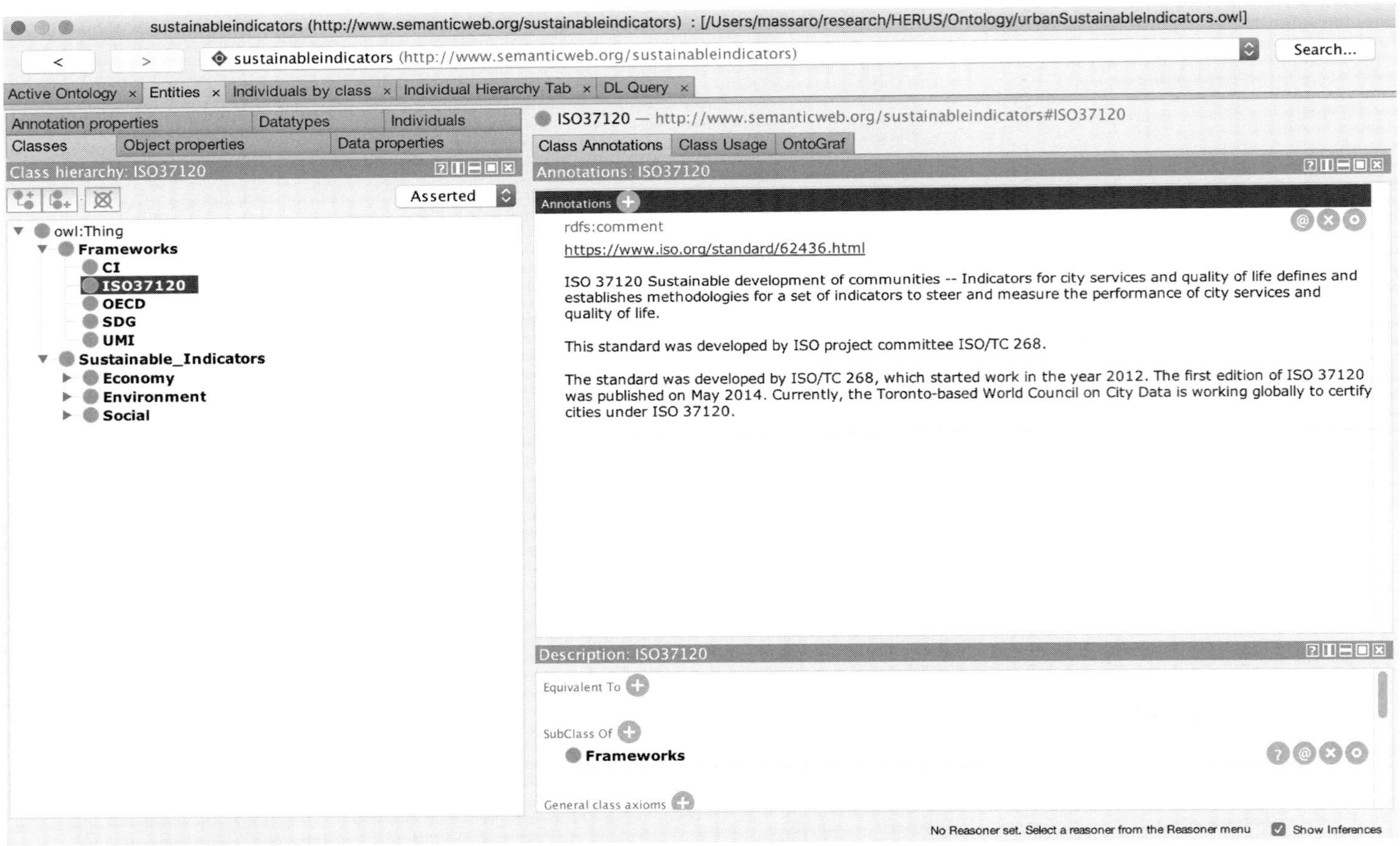

Figure 14.3 Screenshot of the Protégé software for the description of the class ISO 37120 that is subclass of the class Frameworks. For each framework we added a comment providing information about the framework itself. The complete structure of the ontology can be downloaded online.[4]

To illustrate these statements, we show how the indicators from the different frameworks relate to the three pillars of sustainability. In this case, we take the perspective that the definition of sustainability based on the three pillars of sustainability means that a balanced approach should take into account all three aspects in equal distribution.

In Figure 14.4 we present the percentage of indicators falling under each of the three classes of sustainability for each of the different frameworks and calculate how balanced they are across the three classes. We notice that the most *balanced* frameworks are the Cercle Indicators and the OECD indicator framework, where the three pillars are more or less equally distributed (see Table 14.3). This can be also evaluated by computing the Shannon Entropy Index of diversity, $S = -\sum_i p_i \log p_i$ where p_i for the different frameworks are the percentage values reported in Table 14.3. The values of the Shannon Entropy are 1.09, 1.07, 1.06, 0.97, and 0.41 respectively for CI, OECD, ISO, SDG, and UMI, as shown in Figure 14.4. These values give us a ranking from the most *balanced* framework (CI) to the most *unbalanced* one (UMI). The ISO 37120 is the framework with the largest number of indicators, i.e., 133 (see Table 14.1). The SDG, OECD, and UMI frameworks could be utilized for a sustainability assessment that was focused on society, economy, and environment (energy) respectively.

Similarities and differences between the indicator sets. The single indicator that is present across all five frameworks is *GDP per Capita*. However, indicators such as *unemployment rate*, *urbanized area*, and *green area* are common to several indicator

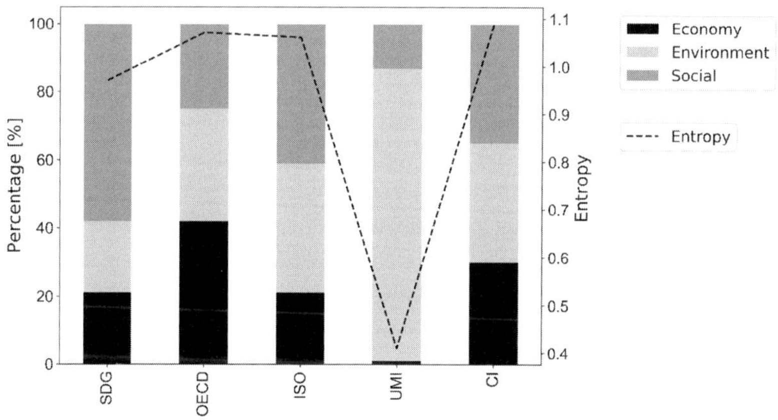

Figure 14.4 (Left y-axis) Comparison of the percentage of indicators relating to the different classes in each framework. As we can see, the most balanced frameworks are the Cercle Indicators (CI) and the OECD frameworks, while the most unbalanced – with a strong environmental focus – is the Urban Metabolism Framework (UMI). (Right y-axis) The dashed line corresponds to the value of the Shannon Entropy of diversity for each framework. Source: own illustration

Table 14.2 *Comparison of the frameworks for the indicators chosen. The indicators are consistent across the different frameworks. For example, in the SDG framework, the value of the GDP is not per capita but the total GDP of the city; however, it is possible to calculate the GDP per capita from the total population.*

Frameworks	SDG	OECD	ISO	UMI	CI
Indicators					
Economy					
1) GDP per Capita	△	•	•	•	•
2) Unemployment Rate	•	△	•		•
3) Patent Application	•	•			
Environment					
4) PM 2.5	•	•	△		
5) CO_2 per Capita	△	•			
6) Urbanized Area		•	•	•	△
7) Green Area	△	△	△	•	
Social					
8) Violent Crimes	•		•		•
9) Internet Connections	•		△	△	
10) Population Density		•	•	△	

•: exact same indicator value; △: values that can be extracted from the dataset.

frameworks, although they might be defined differently, which can hinder comparability between frameworks or case studies. For instance, the ISO standard 37120 accounts for energy use with three main indicators: *Total Residential Electrical Energy Use per Capita*, *Energy Consumption of Public Buildings per Year*, and *Total Electrical Energy Use per Capita*. UMI accounts for energy use (from different sources) in tons and excludes electricity use. In Kennedy et al. (2014), the authors distinguish between stationary and mobile energy use, and then further disaggregate by fuel type. In addition, they add the sectoral use of energy (residential, commercial, industrial, and transportation). By disaggregating their indicator set as much as possible into numerous individual indicators, they enhance comparability with other indicator sets, as they all use different individual indicators for similar themes (for instance, energy use). The three main subclasses (*Economy*, *Environment*, and *Society*) are discussed in the following subsections.

14.4.1 Economy

The indicators under the *Economy* class were divided into the following subclasses: *Employment*, *GDP*, *Labor*, *Patent*, and *Others*. Table 14.3 presents the economic indicators (63 in total) and their distribution across frameworks. The most detailed framework for an economic analysis would be the OECD with 42 percent of indicators fitting into the

Economy class. The OECD framework includes 15 indicators, which are equally distributed throughout our subclasses; moreover, all the indicators in the dataset can be well classified and there are no indicators in the *Others* subclass. The Urban Metabolism Indicators framework (UMI) has only one indicator in total, also reflecting the preferences of the analysis of urban metabolism.

14.4.2 Environment

The *Environment* indicators subclasses are *Air*, *Climate*, *Energy*, *Land*, *Materials*, *Waste*, *Water*, and *Others* (see Table 14.3). The strength of the Urban Metabolism Indicators framework (UMI) is in the environmental pillar, which is reflected by the 71 indicators in total that represent 85 percent of the total dataset. Most of the data relate to the *Energy* sector with 46 indicators for sustainability assessment of energy. In the UMI dataset, we were not able to detect indicators characterizing air quality or air pollution. At the same time, it was possible to find a subclass for all the indicators. In fact, the subclass *Others* is empty for the UMI: it implies that the chosen environmental subclasses completely satisfy the UMI framework. The environmental indicators represent more than 30 percent of the ISO, UMI, and CI frameworks, while only 20 percent of the OECD dataset.

14.4.3 Social

Crime, *Deaths*, *Education*, *Health*, *ICT*, *Mobility*, *Others*, *Population*, *Poverty*, and *Quality of Service* are the subclasses of the last pillar of sustainability indicators. Table 14.3 gives a detailed representation of *social* indicators in each framework. For the *Social* class, we collected 115 indicators in total. As in the previous sections, the ISO standard 37120 (ISO) has the greatest number and diversity of indicators, as we can see from Table 14.3. However, this framework doesn't include indicators for poverty or information and communications technology (ICT). The US Cities SDG Index framework consist of 28 indicators in the *Social* class, which were spread across almost all the subclasses, except *ICT* and *Population*. The OECD framework includes the smallest number of indicators for social sustainability assessment, with nine in total: seven for *Population* and two in *Others*. Finally, the most representative framework for the social pillar is reflected by the SDG with 58 percent of social indicators in its framework. The SDG is followed by ISO and Cercle Indicators, with 41 percent and 35 percent of social indicators each. The OECD and UMI are the frameworks with the smallest percentage of social indicators, 25 percent and 13 percent respectively.

14.5 Concluding Remarks

This study proposes an ontology for conceptualizing and comparing different sustainability assessment frameworks and indicator sets. It provides a new overarching principle to bring

Table 14.3 *The number and the percentage of indicators for the different the sustainability subclasses: Economy, Environment, and Social*

Frameworks	SDG	OECD	ISO	UMI	CI
Indicators					
Economy					
1) Employment	1	5	5	-	1
2) GDP	1	3	4	1	1
3) Labor	-	4	4	-	2
4) Patent	1	3	1	-	-
5) Other	7	-	13	-	6
Total	10	15	27	1	10
Percentage	21%	42%	21%	1%	30%
Environment					
1) Air	3	4	7	-	1
2) Climate	-	-	3	4	1
3) Energy	1	-	7	46	2
4) Land	4	8	9	3	3
5) Materials	-	-	-	4	2
6) Waste	-	-	15	6	-
7) Water	1	-	6	8	2
8) Others	1	-	4	-	1
Total	10	12	51	71	12
Percentage	21%	33%	38%	86%	35%
Social					
1) Crime	4	-	3	-	1
2) Deaths	3	-	4	-	1
3) Education	4	-	7	-	1
4) Health	7	-	2	-	1
5) ICT	-	-	-	3	-
6) Mobility	3	-	7	-	1
7) Population	-	7	14	1	-
8) Poverty	2	-	-	-	-
9) Quality of Service	1	-	1	7	1
10) Others	4	2	16	-	6
Total	28	9	55	11	12
Percentage	58%	25%	41%	13%	35%

together two distinct aspects, namely (i) the sustainability indicators, structured as environment, social, and economic and (ii) frameworks.

We analyzed five sustainability frameworks which are widely used in policy-making to measure the sustainability of cities on a national and regional level. In order to make these different sustainability frameworks comparable we created an ontology-based model of 334 sustainability indicators, which were collected from the five different frameworks: US cities SDG index (SDG); OECD regional and metropolitan databases (OECD); ISO standard 37120 (ISO); urban metabolism indicators (UMI); and the Cercle Indicators (CI). We classified these indicators into three main classes, considering the standard definition of sustainability based on the Brundtland Report: *Economy*, *Environment*, and *Society*. In order to navigate through the indicators, we defined a hierarchical taxonomy.

Each class has properties and relationships with other classes, thus transforming the system into an ontological framework (Noy & McGuinness, 2001). We used the Protégé software (*Protégé Software*, n.d.) to develop the ontology, and to analyze and compare the different frameworks and indicators to each other.

Our results show that while all the indicators frameworks focus on (urban) sustainability, they address different aspects of it, and none of them addresses even the similar aspects in the same way. Each of them has its own specific perspective on what the sustainability of urban systems is concerned with. That is, we can observe a very clear normative perspective for each indicator framework and set (see also Chapter 3 (Meinherz et al., 2020)). For example, UMI focuses on the environmental perspective, and SDG puts an emphasis on societal issues. This implies that the results obtained in an urban sustainability assessment by applying each of these indicator sets is likely to differ, as different priorities and underlying normative values determine the structure of the indicator set and the indicators selected, and thus the assessment. This reaffirms that the choice of indicators for comparing different cities is a critical issue both for the efficacy of a stakeholder-driven approach and for reaching and monitoring the goals set.

The ontology as presented in this chapter provides a way to make these underlying perspectives explicit. On the one hand, by bringing the indicators proposed in the different frameworks together, it makes it possible to develop a perspective that includes all three pillars of sustainability. Thus, the overarching set of indicators reflects the three pillars of sustainability as broadly as possible. When assessing a city or an urban system, the ontology can provide a supporting mechanism for looking beyond established frameworks and can expand perspectives toward a broader and more systemic view of the system. This is crucial for an overall assessment of urban sustainability.

Finally, in the literature, a broad range of different processes are described utilizing the heading of sustainability assessment. As presented in Chapter 1 (Halla & Binder, 2020), sustainability assessment requires a robust framework in order to overcome concerns that have been put forward in the scientific community. One of the key concerns is the issue of how indicators for the assessment should be selected in order to be representative of the system and allow the best representation of the problem. Our analysis showed that many institutes have adopted sets of sustainable development indicators to track progress toward a sustainable society. While these initiatives have helped to put sustainable development on the agenda of national and international institutions, significant differences between the approaches remain. Our analysis suggests that a conceptual framework is needed to harmonize the different ways in which sustainable development has been measured by different organizations.

Notes

1. https://github.com/emanuelemassaro/focus.
2. Part of this subsection uses material from the Wikipedia article Ontology Components (https://en.wikipedia.org/wiki/Ontology_components\#cite_note-2), which is released under the Creative Commons Attribution-Share-Alike License 3.0.
3. https://github.com/emanuelemassaro/focus
4. https://github.com/emanuelemassaro/focus/tree/master/OnToology/urbanSustainableIndicators.owl.

References

Alberti, M., et al. (1996). Measuring urban sustainability. *Environmental Impact Assessment Review*, 16(4), 381–424.

Athanassiadis, A., Fernandez, G., Meirelles, J., Meinherz, F., Hoekman, P., & Cari, Y. B. (2017). Exploring the energy use drivers of 10 cities at microscale level. *Energy Procedia*, 122, 709–714. Elsevier.

Berry, B. J. (1964). Cities as systems within systems of cities. *Papers in Regional Science*, 13(1), 146–163.

Binder, C. R., Baldi, M. G., Gex, B., & Massaro, E. (2020b). The sustainability solution space. In C. R. Binder, E. Massaro, & R. Wyss (eds.), *Sustainability Assessment in Urban Systems*. Cambridge University Press, pp. 181–208.

Barles, S. (2009). Urban metabolism of Paris and its region. *Journal of Industrial Ecology*, 13(6), 898–913.

Boesch, A., & de Montmollin, A. (2020). Indicators for assessing the sustainability of cities. In C. R. Binder, E. Massaro, & R. Wyss (eds.), Binder, C. R., Massaro, E., Wyss, R. (eds), *Sustainability Assessment in Urban Systems*. Cambridge University Press, pp. 181–208.

Brundtland, G. H. (1987). *Our Common Future: Brundtland Report*. Oxford: Oxford University Press.

Griggs, D., Stafford-Smith, M., Gaffney, O., et al. (2013). Sustainable development goals for people and planet: Policy. *Nature*, 495(7441), 305–307. https://doi.org/10.1038/495305a.

Guarino, N., Oberle, D., & Staab, S. (2009). What is an ontology? In *Handbook on Ontologies*. Dordrecht/ Heidelberg/ London/ New York: Springer, pp. 1–17.

Halla, P., & Binder, C. R. (2020). Sustainability Assessment: Introduction and Framework. In C. R. Binder, E. Massaro, & R. Wyss (eds.), *Sustainability Assessment in Urban Systems*. Cambridge University Press, pp. 7–29.

Hiremath, R. B., Balachandra, P., Kumar, B., Bansode, S. S., & Murali, J. (2013). Indicator-based urban sustainability: A review. *Energy for Sustainable Development*, 17(6), 555–563.

Hoekman, P., & Blottnitz, H. (2017). Cape Town's metabolism: Insights from a material flow analysis. *Journal of Industrial Ecology*, 21(5), 1237–1249.

Holden, E., Linnerud, K., & Banister, D. (2014). Sustainable development: Our Common Future revisited. *Global Environmental Change*, 26, 130–139. https://doi.org/10.1016/j.gloenvcha.2014.04.006.

Kahn, M. E. (2007). *Green Cities: Urban Growth and the Environment*. CITY: Brookings Institution Press.

Kennedy, C. A., Stewart, I., Facchini, A., et al. (2015). Energy and material flows of megacities. *Proceedings of the National Academy of Sciences*, 112(19), 5985–5990.

Kennedy, C., Stewart, I. D., Ibrahim, N., Facchini, A., & Mele, R. (2014). Developing a multi-layered indicator set for urban metabolism studies in megacities. *Ecological Indicators*, 47, 7–15.

Kuhn, T. S. (1996). *The Structure of Sscientific Revolutions* (3rd ed). Chicago, IL: University of Chicago Press.

Meier, A., & Wachter, D. (2005). Indicators centraux pour le développement durable des villes et cantons. *Rapport Du Cercle Indicateurs. Berne, Switzerland: Office Fédéral Du Développement Territorial*.

Meinherz, F., Fritz, L., & Schneider, F. (2020). How Values Play into Sustainability Assessments: Challenges and a Possible Way Forward. In C. R. Binder, E. Massaro, & R. Wyss (eds.), *Sustainability Assessment in Urban Systems*. Cambridge University Press, pp. 65–86.

Niza, S., Rosado, L., & Ferrao, P. (2009). Urban metabolism. *Journal of Industrial Ecology*, 13(3), 384–405.

Noy, N. F., & McGuinness, D. L. (2001). *Ontology development 101: A guide to creating your first ontology*. www.corais.org/sites/default/files/ontology_development_101_aguide_to_creating_your_first_ontology.pdf.

Organisation for Economic Co-operation and Development. (2008). *OECD factbook 2008*. Paris: OECD Publishing. http://dx.doi.org/10.1787/factbook-2008-en.

Prakash, M., Teksoz, K., Espey, J., Sachs, J., Shank, M., & Schmidt-Traub, G. (2017). Achieving a Sustainable Urban America. SDNS – United Nations. *Protégé Software*. (n.d.). https://protege.stanford.edu/products.php.

Psyllidis, A. (2015). Ontology-based data integration from heterogeneous urban systems: A knowledge representation framework for smart cities. In *14th International Conference on Computers in Urban Planning and Urban Management (CUPUM 2015)*, Cambridge, MA: MIT, pp. 240–241.

Psyllidis, A. (2016). *Revisiting Urban Dynamics through Social Urban Data: Methods and tools for data integration, visualization, and exploratory analysis to understand the spatiotemporal dynamics of human activity in cities* (PhD dissertation). Delft University of Technology.

Sachs, J., Schmidt-Traub, G., Kroll, C., Durand-Delacre, D., & Teksoz, K. (2016). *SDG Index & Dashboards: A Global Report*. Gütersloh: Bertelsmann Stiftung.

Shen, L.-Y., Ochoa, J. J., Shah, M. N., & Zhang, X. (2011). The application of urban sustainability indicators: A comparison between various practices. *Habitat International*, 35(1), 17–29. https://doi.org/10.1016/j.habitatint.2010.03.006.

Singleton, A. D., Spielman, S., & Folch, D. (2017). *Urban Analytics*. Sage.

Voskamp, I. M., Stremke, S., Spiller, M., Perrotti, D., Hoek, J. P., & Rijnaarts, H. H. (2017). Enhanced performance of the Eurostat method for comprehensive assessment of urban metabolism: A material flow analysis of Amsterdam. *Journal of Industrial Ecology*, 21(4), 887–902.

Zdraveski, V., Mishev, K., Trajanov, D., & Kocarev, L. (2017). ISO-standardized smart city platform architecture and dashboard. *IEEE Pervasive Computing*, 16(2), 35–43.

Part IV
Focal Points of Urban Sustainability

Cities are home to the most consequential current attempts at human adaptation and they provide one possible focus for the flourishing of life on this planet. However, for this to be realized in more than an ad hoc way, a substantial rethinking of current approaches and practices needs to occur. In the last part of this book we show practical solutions in which different methodologies are applied to different case scenarios. This part argues the need to find models and solutions in order to design the urban sustainable cities of the future in light of the complexity of urban social life. The authors focused on different aspects of urban sustainability from energy to housing, to mobility and health covering social, economic, and environmental aspects.

Chapter 15 focuses on urban energy systems: The authors propose a solution that integrates a "multi-energy vision" that will allow cities to become self-sufficient in energy by relying on locally available renewable energy resources, mainly environmental heat and solar energy.

Chapter 16 is dedicated to urban housing: This chapter focuses on the housing sector as a relevant component of the urban system. It explores the complex interplay between the material system (materials and energy resources used in housing systems) and the social system (decision-making rules used in housing systems). The authors combine different methodological approaches, which allow them to couple the material perspective with the decision-making processes of different actors. Thereby, they provide a holistic view of the housing sector, supporting an integrative sustainability assessment.

In Chapter 17 we analyze the sustainability effect of the so-called urban agriculture: This chapter discusses the critical points of urban agriculture and then suggests some opportunities to move the practice of sustainability assessment of urban agriculture forward. These include the adoption of inter- and transdisciplinary research strategies, and a critical approach to urban agriculture practices, power relations, social norms, and institutional conditions that have developed over time in specific contexts.

Chapter 18 shows an agent-based model (ABM) in order to clarify the role of cities in the coordination of actions and the reduction of social entropy. One expected result from the model is that space matters for coordinating actions, but simulations surprisingly showed that space is a necessary but not sufficient condition for the reduction of entropy.

In Chapter 19, the authors presented a case study applied to the city of Stockholm. They show a model called Eco-Cycle Model 2.0 that attempts to be much more than an overview of the functions and flows that characterize a city district.

Chapter 20 is dedicated to one of the most critical aspects of modern cities: mobility. The author shows the application of the shareability network model to the city of Santiago de Chile. The authors show that ride-sharing potential is substantial, with nearly 100 percent of the trips shareable with current public transportation. This benefit comes with reductions in service cost and emissions, and with split fares, hinting toward a wide passenger acceptance of such a shared service.

The last chapter shows a model to study the interplay between urban mobility and mosquito-borne disease. The main innovation of the proposed modeling framework is to improve the current compartmental epidemiological models proposed in literature by considering not only the vector-to-human transmission at fixed cells, but also the probability of transmission along different mobility pathways.

15

Energy Challenges in Urban Systems

François Vuille and François Maréchal

Box 15.1 authored by Sébastien Cajot

15.1 Energy-Use Patterns in Cities

Energy is the fuel of cities, as it provides various key services such as comfort, health, and mobility, and drives industrial production. For the energy sector, cities represent the major final-energy users. Today, the building and service sectors worldwide consume about 30 percent of final energy and 55 percent of electricity globally, and are responsible for nearly 40 percent of the world's CO_2 emissions (International Energy Agency, 2017a). Developing energy-efficient cities that rely on renewable energy sources is therefore paramount for the global transition toward sustainable low-carbon economies. Hence, it is no surprise that this corresponds to goal 11 of the United Nations Sustainable Development Goals (United Nation Secretary-General, 11 May 2017).

Although densification can prove beneficial in terms of efficient energy use (Rode et al., 2014), urban development also presents major energy challenges with regard to energy supply infrastructure. In the past, dense megacities and spatially concentrated industrial sites have relied on fossil fuels (oil, coal, natural gas), the high energy density of which makes them easy to distribute and to store. However, growing concerns about climate change and air pollution in city centers (UN-HABITAT, 2011) are driving efforts to shift consumption away from fossil fuels and toward reliance on renewable energy sources (International Energy Agency, 2015). This challenge will be particularly acute for cities, which will have to develop and adapt their infrastructures to keep ensuring a high degree of energy-supply security while phasing out reliance on fossil fuels. It is likely that as cities adapt to new ways of harvesting, distributing, storing, and consuming energy, this will fundamentally change not only the way their energy system is structured but also the relationship that urban citizens will have with their energy consumption. Promoting a rational use of energy, which concerns both the supply and demand for energy services, will become increasingly important, alongside the efforts to increase the share of renewable energy sources in the energy mix (European Commission, Directorate-General for Energy, 2016).

15.2 Assessing the Sustainability of an Urban Energy System

To optimize energy flows in the city, one has to consider the complete supply chain of energy in reverse order, starting from the delivery of energy services to the population, all the way up the chain to the harvesting of energy resources. This implies identifying and characterizing the different energy services needed and the renewable resources available, as well as defining the optimal energy harvesting technologies and conversion pathways and the associated distribution systems that will maximize efficiency and minimize waste and unwanted emissions. This analysis needs to be done with attention to the three pillars of sustainability: economic, environmental, and social. In a generic way, the following formula details the contributions of different driving factors for consumption and the impact of emissions by considering the entire energy supply chain. It is expressed as the product of factors that define energy flows and their impacts. Each factor can be understood as the inverse of the efficiency of the conversion step and can be associated with a specific investment when one wants to express the economic value of it or an employment rate if one wants to calculate its social effect.

$$I = H_{cap} \cdot S_{ser,cap} \cdot N_{n,ser} \cdot D_{x,n} \cdot E_{d,x} \cdot R_{r,d} \cdot F_{p,r} \cdot I_{i,p} \quad (15.1)$$

Where:

- H_{cap} is the vector of the population of the city, the population can be divided into different classes [cap].
- $S_{ser,cap}$ is the matrix of the services per inhabitant [ser/cap]. This can be, for example, the available floor area, hot-water demand, mileage.
- $N_{n,ser}$ [kJ_s/ser] is a matrix that represents the energy need per unit of energy services (e.g., mobility [kJ/km], heating requirements [kJ/m^2])
- $D_{x,n}$ [kJ_x/kJ_s] is the exergy value of the energy needs (e.g., exergy of the heat in the building's hydronic system). The exergy value allows us to compare different types of energy systems. This expression is particularly useful when comparing heat and electricity.
- $E_{d,x}$ [kJ_d/kJ_x] is the amount of distributed energy used in the conversion device to produce one unit of exergy value of a need. This represents the exergy conversion efficiency in devices that convert the distributed energy to meet the energy needs (e.g., energy of natural gas to the exergy value of the energy distributed by the hydronic system).
- $R_{r,d}$ [kJ_r/kJ_d] is the amount of energy resources used per unit of distributed energy. This value considers the entire life cycle of the energy consumed per unit of distributed energy (e.g., amount of natural gas from the well needed to supply the natural gas in the building, or the energy from the coal in the mine needed to deliver one unit of electricity to the building).
- $F_{p,r}$ [e_p/kJ_r] represents the flows of emissions or extractions associated with an energy resource. This factor transforms energy consumption into its associated emissions (e.g., CO_2 emissions of the natural gas boiler over its life cycle, including manufacturing, extraction, and end of life).
- $I_{i,p}$ [IP/e_p] is the impact factor associated with each of the emission flows (e.g., global warming effect of CO_2 emissions). Impact factors are used to generate global impact indicators that aim at aggregating in single indicators the impacts of different emissions on health, climate, and the environment. This is the role of the life-cycle impact assessment indicators as described in Frischknecht and Jolliet (2016).

- For the indices, x refers to exergy, ser to service, n to needs, d to distributed, r to resources, p to pollutant, and i to impact.

Equation 15.1 offers a holistic approach to assessing the sustainability of urban energy flows and their related system. The lower the impact, the higher the level of sustainability. Each contributing factor to the equation then represents a partial assessment of the sustainability of the city, and efforts can be made on each factor to reduce the overall impact. The matrixial form of the equation also expresses the potential synergies of system integration, allowing for the joined production of different services, such as jointly producing heat and electricity in a single cogeneration device.

The decomposition approach of the energy supply chains has the great advantage of showing explicitly the relative impact of the different contributing factors on the overall energy system, which is paramount for decision-makers if they are to prioritize efforts and take informed, efficient actions. As the formula is a multiplication of factors greater than one, it also shows the importance of acting at the end of the conversion chain – that is, on the demand side. This gives the following priority chain for actions:

1) People -> 2) Sobriety -> 3) System integration -> 4) Efficiency -> 5) Resources

Although expressed with energy in mind, this formula needs to be considered in a matrix form involving various flows, therefore considering not only energy but other material flows like water, food, etc., and considering their possible synergies. Hence, this equation can actually serve to assess the overall sustainability of a city.

With the exception of the emission factor F and the impact factor I, each contributing factor in this equation represents a driver of consumption, but also a potential for mitigation. In the coming sections, we will discuss each of these drivers and illustrate the formula by applying it step by step to the energy services in buildings. The same exercise could be done for the industrial and transport sectors which are also discussed, although in less detail, later in this chapter.

15.3 The Building Sector

15.3.1 Population (H [cap])

The number of inhabitants of a city is the first driver of energy demand. Although marginal energy consumption can, for certain services such as public transport or the heating of buildings, be decoupled from population growth much more than it can in non-urban areas, thanks to the better mutualization of equipment, it nonetheless remains that the higher the population, the higher the energy needs, primarily related to the increasing number of dwellings.

Yet, the increase of the building stock may represent an opportunity to lower national consumption if proper sustainable development principles are applied when constructing new urban areas. In those districts, high efficiency standards have to be applied and integrated designs that look at the various criteria for sustainable development can be applied or imposed by authorities. Certifications can also be applied, like the One Planet

Living methodology (Bioregional Development Group, October 2017), that aim at engaging all the stakeholders involved in the development.

However, it is not always possible to develop new districts in response to demography. Often, the densification of existing areas has to be preferred, e.g., by increasing the height of buildings or by reallocating land to different uses. Hence, renovation strategies play a crucial role in mitigating the energy impact of cities (Ecofys, 2012).

15.3.2 The Service of Comfort: Floor Area (S [m^2/cap])

The floor area per capita is a metric of comfort. There is a wide disparity in floor area per person, both between continents and within continents. In Europe, for example, floor area per person ranges from 24 to 77 m^2/cap (ENTRANZE consortium, 2014). There is a general trend toward the increase in floor area per person (Odyssee consortium, 2018), resulting from economic growth and the demand for greater comfort. According to the International Energy Agency (2017b), the total surface area per capita is increasing at a pace of 2 percent per year. This translates into an increase in energy demand as several services are correlated with floor area, in particular heating and cooling.

15.3.3 Need for Energy Services (N [MJ/year/m^2])

Demand for energy services is driven by thermal comfort, water supply, electrical appliances, lighting, and cooking. Figure 15.1 shows the average repartition of energy services in the residential and service sectors (International Energy Agency, 2016). Thermal comfort is

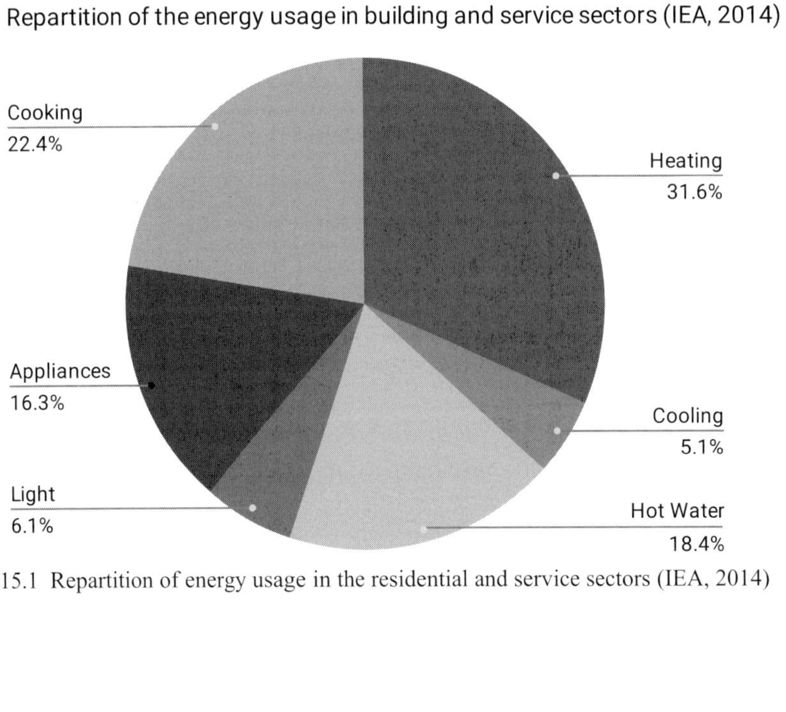

Figure 15.1 Repartition of energy usage in the residential and service sectors (IEA, 2014)

the main driver for energy demand and is the most impactful factor in the overall energy chain. Hence, we will spend a bit more time on this section.

Thermal comfort, and its perception, is typically defined as a given room temperature or hot water temperature. The preferred room temperature depends on the perception of the occupants, their activities, and the clothes they wear. In addition to temperature, humidity and air quality (typically measured by levels of CO_2 or volatile organic compounds) are also important components of comfort. These define the need for air renewal flows in a confined environment, which is also a driver of energy consumption.

Figure 15.2 presents the energy flows of a building, used to calculate its thermal energy balance. Energy demand to reach the preferred comfort temperature is met by the heat gains from solar irradiation, lighting, appliances, and human presence, with the remaining needs supplied by the heating/cooling distribution system, which also compensates for heat losses through the walls and the air-conditioning/handling system.

The heating or cooling needs essentially depend on the following factors:

- The internal gains coming from the devices and the people in the building;
- The air flows entering and leaving the building to control humidity and air quality;
- The difference between the comfort temperature and the outdoor temperature, which depends on meteorological conditions as well as the physical form of the city;
- The gains from solar irradiation, highlighting the importance of urban features like shading, color, and reflection;
- The thermal losses of the building, which depend on the quality of its envelope.

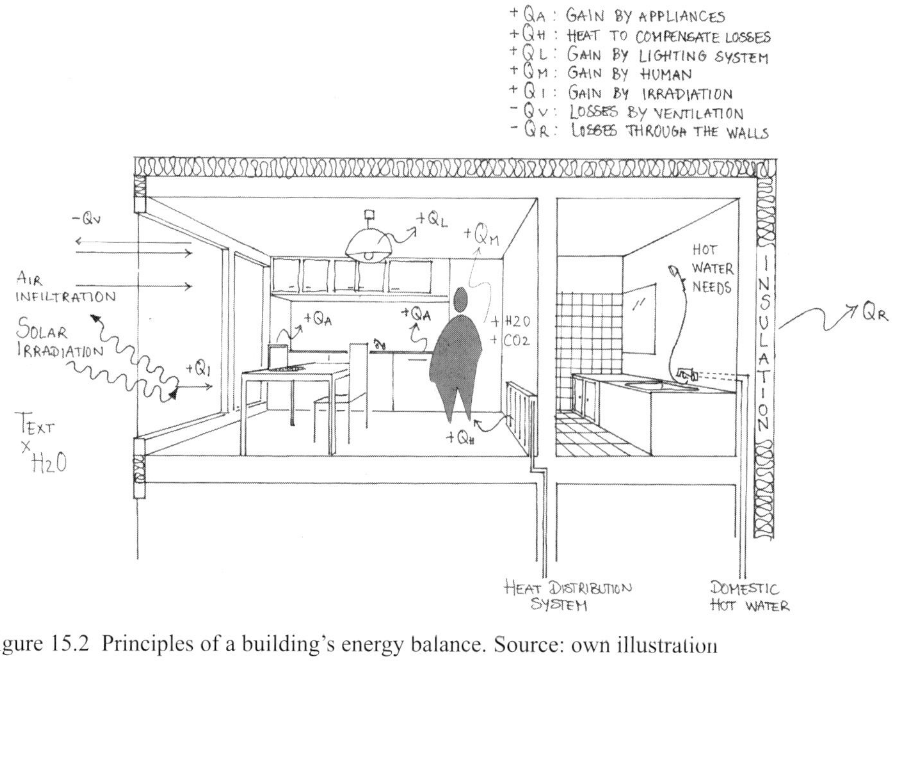

Figure 15.2 Principles of a building's energy balance. Source: own illustration

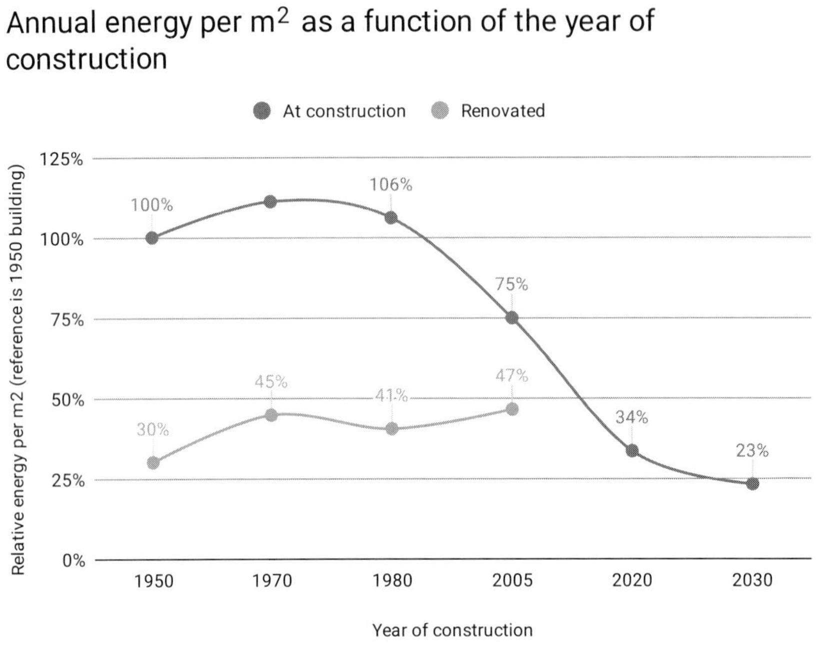

Figure 15.3 Evolution of the energy demand of buildings (Girardin et al., 2012)

Since the outdoor and comfort temperature can hardly be modified, the energy efficiency of the building design – limiting thermal losses and maximizing the use of the gains – is the sole factor that has a direct impact on the heating demand of a building. Limiting the losses is done by adequately insulating the envelope and by ensuring the airtightness of the building. Building efficiency, which defines the factor N, has drastically improved in the past years thanks to the implementation of increasingly strict building standards and norms which specify energy consumption targets to be reached per square meter of heated surface. Figure 15.3 shows, for example, the evolution of building quality with time. It shows that new buildings may consume 70 to 80 percent less final energy than old buildings from the 1950s to 1980s. It also shows that renovation can drastically improve building quality, but renovation cannot reach the energy-efficiency standards of new builds.

Renovation will play a crucial role in reducing the energy demand of cities in the coming decades (Boermans et al., 2012). But energy renovation is challenging as it often entails the modification of the exterior architecture (e.g., the width of pavements might be reduced due to thickening of the insulation), which may prove incompatible with urban requirements and regulations on buildings protected for heritage reasons.

The choice of construction and insulation materials is also a key parameter in the analysis of building efficiency. This is because gray energy – that is, the energy spent to produce these materials – can become more important than the energy saved by the increased building efficiency over its lifetime: the thicker the insulation, the higher the building efficiency, but the higher its gray energy (International Institute for Applied Systems

Analysis (IIASA), 2012). The gray energy will therefore add a new line in the N factor of the energy formula and will affect the subsequent steps. Hence, to minimize the impact of building construction materials, the use of biomass-based or recyclable materials should be favored.

Besides the envelope, there is a second dimension to energy efficiency in buildings: the thermal management of air and water flows defines specific terms in the N matrix. Not only should these flows be managed so that they can satisfy the comfort conditions, but they should also be optimized so that their heating/cooling content can be recovered when they exit the building. For air flows, infiltration should be minimized by making the buildings airtight, while heat should be recovered by a counter-current heat exchanger between the inlet and outlet air flows. This means having controlled ventilation units and ventilation pipes. The same applies to wastewater leaving the building, the heat content of which can serve to preheat hot water, while the remaining wastewater can still serve as a source for the heat pump in a cascading approach.

The third dimension of building efficiency is energy management. Using sensors combined with learning algorithms, smart buildings will learn their occupancy profile and optimize comfort based on occupants' presence and preferences regarding humidity, air quality, temperature, and light, while minimizing energy consumption by limiting services in unoccupied rooms. Using smart algorithms with predictive capabilities, the energy management system will define the operating strategies necessary for the heating/cooling system to stay in the comfort zone, considering the inertia of the air-conditioning system, the forecasted demand, and the availability of energy sources.

15.3.4 Exergy Value of the Energy Needs (D [MJx/MJth])

The energy needs in a building are supplied either by electricity (e.g., for lighting and appliances) or by the heating or cooling of heat-transfer fluids, typically air or water. As the different energy services are supplied by different forms of energy, it is important to compare them on an equal footing. Exergy is a useful thermodynamic concept that can be used to quantify the value of different forms of energy. For thermal needs, the exergy value is defined as the theoretical demand of work needed to supply the heating/cooling energy needed and is calculated

$$D=N*(1-Ta/Td) \tag{15.2}$$

where N is the thermal heat needed to close the energy balance, Ta is the environmental temperature (typically the outside air temperature), and Td the mean temperature of the heat distribution system (Ta and Td are measured in °K).

The ratio Ta/Td represents the maximum fraction of the heat that can be directly harvested in the environment. It highlights the importance of the heat distribution – the value of D varies, for example, from 0.1 for floor heating systems to 0.2 for radiator-based systems – as Td needs to be significantly higher for radiators (55°C compared to 30°C) at equivalent exterior temperature Ta. The value of D will be 1 for an electrical heater. This means that the minimum work needed can double when using a high-temperature distribution system (such as radiators) compared to a low-temperature one (such as floor heating) and can be 10 times larger when an electrical heater is used. We can also conclude from thermodynamic theory that an efficient heating system should use the heat from the environment, hence the key role of heat pumps.

15.3.5 Exergy Efficiency of the Energy Conversion System (E [MJe/MJx])

The energy conversion system of a building is a set of equipment which encompasses the heating/cooling system, the lighting system, as well as the electric and electronic appliances (fridge, washing machine, dryer, electronics, etc.). This equipment converts the energy distributed via the energy infrastructure of the city (electricity, natural gas, heating oil, wood pellets, environment heat) into useful energy to supply the needs of buildings. The factor E of the energy conversion system is defined as the amount of distributed energy used to satisfy the energy demand expressed by unit of exergy D.

The conversion efficiency of lighting systems, electric appliances, and electronic devices can vary widely between similar pieces of equipment. For instance, the conversion efficiency of an LED light is five times greater than that of a halogen lamp, and 10 times greater than an incandescent light bulb for the same lighting power delivered. Similarly, a high-efficiency fridge or dishwasher consumes two to three times less electricity than low-efficiency models for the same service.

For heating and cooling, the energy conversions can be classified into four categories, the exergy performance of which is shown in Figure 15.4:

- Boilers that produce heat only;
- Cogeneration units that produce both heat and electricity;
- Resistive electric heaters that use electricity to produce heat;

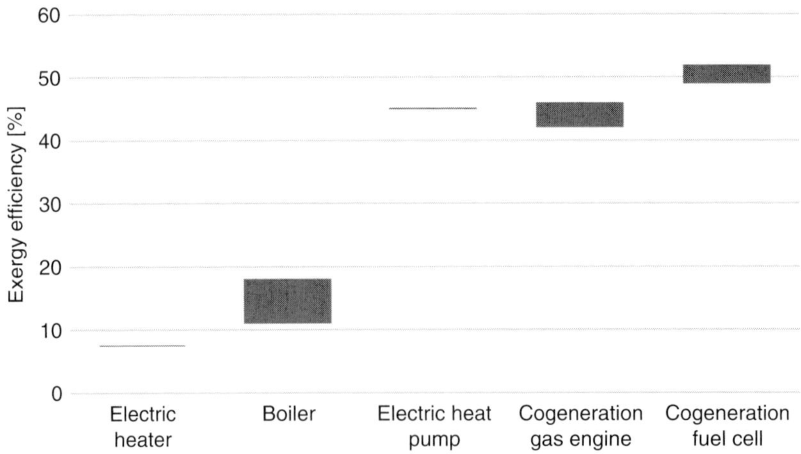

Figure 15.4 Exergy efficiency of a building plant (Favrat et al., 2008)

- Heat-pump systems that use high-quality energy (e.g., electricity or high-temperature heat) to harvest ambient heat from various sources, such as outdoor air, rivers, lakes, or under the ground, in order to supply heat or cold to the distribution system. One considers free cooling as an extreme case of heat pumps.

The exergetic efficiency of a heater represents the ratio of the heat effectively supplied to the maximum heat that could have been supplied with the same energy input. In other words, it represents how close to the best case the performance of the unit is. This notion highlights, for instance, the poor performance of electrical heaters and boilers in comparison to modern heating systems such as heat pumps and fuel cells, in spite of the fact that their energy conversion is close to 100 percent. This apparent paradox lies in the fact that boilers and radiant electric heaters significantly degrade their high-quality energy –high-temperature heat and electricity respectively – even though this could provide much more energy. Typically, high-temperature heat can be used to produce heat and electricity jointly in cogeneration units, and electricity can produce about four times more heat if it operates a heat pump instead of simply being radiated in a resistive electric heater. Of course, Figure 15.4 reflects only the exergy performance of the conversion units. A holistic view must be adopted that encompasses the entire supply chain, in particular reflecting when electricity is used, as this electricity must first be produced, which may generate high exergetic losses if done with thermal power plants. But this does not change the key messages discussed here. In the case of cogeneration (of heat and electricity), as it concerns different distributed energy vectors, the matrix E will have positive and negative terms.

Sustainable cities must ensure that the most efficient equipment is used in order to minimize the energy wasted and thus meet the energy demand with minimum energy input. In many countries, compulsory labels will indicate the energy efficiency of equipment to guide consumers in their choices. However, energy-efficient equipment tends to be more expensive than the low-efficiency equipment – due to higher system complexity – which hampers their adoption. While regulations in modern societies tend to ban the least efficient solutions (e.g., incandescent light bulbs, low-efficiency fridges), governments can hardly force consumers to purchase the best, and hence the most expensive, technologies. However, high-efficiency appliances often have the benefit of a lower total lifetime cost of ownership, thanks to reduced energy bills. Efforts to communicate such economic advantages should be made alongside communicating their energy-efficiency advantages, so as to trigger good consumer habits and speed up the transition to a sustainable economy.

It is worth noting that certain cities, such as Geneva, Switzerland, require exergy analyses to be carried out for industrial or real-estate projects (Favrat et al., 2008).

The different heating/cooling technologies are connected by multiple grids: for example, a cogeneration unit is connected to the gas grid, the electrical grid, the heat distribution system, and the data grid. It produces, in a coordinated way, both heat for a building and electricity, whereas the latter can be used either by a heat pump in another building or a refrigeration system. Modern (sustainable) cities will increasingly become integrated multi-energy systems in order to mutualize resources and infrastructures, while

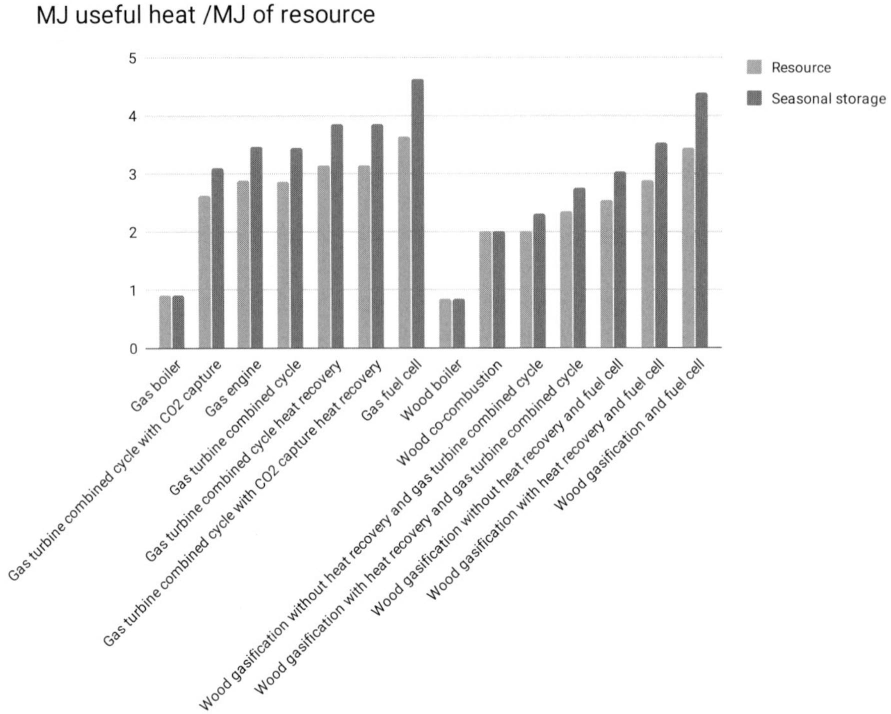

Figure 15.5 Useful heat supplied per unit of energy resource for different types of boilers (Suciu et al., 2018)

homogenizing demand. For instance, new houses could be equipped with heat pumps, while old ones might have biogas-fed cogeneration units that would power the heat pumps elsewhere.

Figure 15.5 presents the amount of heat supplied to the building per unit of energy from the resource. In addition to boiler solutions, the other solutions considered are the use of heat pumps and advanced conversion devices. Figure 15.5 shows that advanced options are up to four times more resource-efficient than the boiler options. Extending the approach with the extensive use of fifth-generation district heating/cooling grids can generate autonomous cities (Suciu et al., 2018).

15.3.6 Distributed Energy Infrastructure (E [MJe/MJx])

The term $E_{d,x}$ defines the amount of distributed energy consumed by the energy conversion system in order to meet the energy needs of the buildings. Hence, we introduce a second section for this factor, in which we discuss the role of energy infrastructure in cities, which encompasses different networks that distribute energy vectors: electricity, gas, oil, heating, and cooling.

15.3.6.1 Electricity Distribution Network and Micro-grids

Electricity was first used at the beginning of the twentieth century, essentially for lighting; user-friendliness was seen as its major advantages over gas and oil. In order to enhance the electricity load factor by filling "demand valleys," other applications (electrified public transport such as electric trams, household equipment, etc.) were encouraged from 1920, when electric lighting became mainstream. Small, local grids started to become interconnected, first at the regional level and later at the national and international level, in order to further smooth demand and improve reliability while limiting the need for spinning reserves that are required to capture peak demand.

In the coming decades, it is likely that more and more cities will turn back to local grids, or so-called micro-grids, in order to better integrate local electricity production. Micro-grids will enable cities to increase the electricity supply security and the resilience of electricity distribution, while significantly increasing their energy autonomy by allowing local electricity production, essentially from solar photovoltaics (PV), to cover a high share of the electricity demand.

When looking at PV integration, two parameters are important: the self-sufficiency that defines the amount of the need that can be covered by local production, and the self-consumption that defines how much of the production can be directly used to meet these needs.

Figure 15.6 shows the excess electricity that many cities will experience in summer. To avoid curtailment, this excess must either be stored (e.g., in batteries or electrochemical systems) or be absorbed by demand-response measures. The objective of demand response is to shift the times when certain appliances (e.g., dishwashers) are operated or to use the

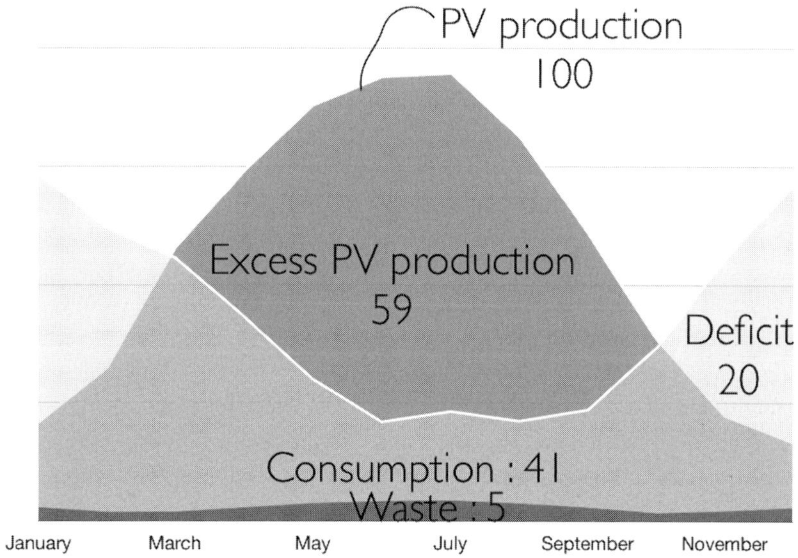

Figure 15.6 Photovoltaic (PV) production and the energy needs of a city. Source: own illustration

thermal inertia of buildings and hot-water storage to operate heat pumps in a way that better matches the production profile of intermittent renewables (wind and PV). Demand response is also part of smart grid operation, which is based on predictive control techniques.

The scale at which micro-grids can be applied ranges from individual buildings to the entire city. The larger the scale, the higher the potential for self-sufficiency, as demand-side management options can be mutualized, while supply and demand profiles become less "peaky."

Changing the scale (going from the single building to the neighborhood) will also give greater importance to multi-energy grids (i.e., grids that are not only electrical but also gas and thermal) and their management. This offers synergies between systems by mutualizing PV surfaces and high-quality heat sources (data centers, geothermal, etc.). While buildings can, in some circumstances, be zero-energy – i.e., PV panels producing, on an annual accounting basis, the energy consumed by the building – the daily and seasonal variations of solar irradiation do not allow the buildings to be isolated from energy grids. Typically, there will be periods of excess production and periods of energy deficit.

Buildings in hot climates can typically offer a better match between supply and demand as electricity is used primarily for air conditioning, unlike those in cooler climates in which electricity is used to operate heat pumps during the winter season when solar irradiation is lowest.

Battery storage and demand response can only smooth out the daily supply and demand, not the net summer electricity surplus, for which other solutions must be adopted. The excess of electricity in the summer period necessitates so-called seasonal storage solutions, by which electricity is converted into a storable form for reconversion into final energy later in the year, on the principle of power-to-gas (PtG). To date, only (pumped-)hydro storage has been used for seasonal storage, as it can handle large storage volumes. In the future, it is expected that solar electricity can be stored as synthetic liquid fuels. Excess electricity is used to first produce hydrogen (H_2) via a water electrolysis process. The produced H_2 can then be combined via thermo-chemical processes with carbon dioxide (CO_2) to form various kinds of storable fuels such as methane or methanol. The CO_2 can either be captured from thermal power plants or from the CO_2 that is the by-product of biomass conversion.

15.3.6.2 Gas Distribution Network

In cities, natural gas is distributed by pipes. The low-pressure gas distribution grid is fed by the main gas transportation grid that is fed by gas supply units or distribution hubs. Gas distribution needs gas storage facilities to manage the seasonal variations of demands and to coordinate these with a more constant flow of gas supply. Energy management by the gas grid may become a critical asset for many cities in the future for two reasons: first, it is expected to increasingly store and distribute gas of renewable origin (biogas, synthetic natural gas, hydrogen); second it can provide fossil-fuel natural gas to compensate for the seasonality of renewable energy sources. This may be the last form of reliance on fossil fuels in sustainable cities.

15.3.6.3 Oil Distribution Network

In the city, oil distribution typically uses the road system and a multitude of small-scale local storage tanks. In today's cities, the oil system is a well-organized multi-scale energy storage management system. As with the gas grid, the oil system aims at reducing the impact of the seasonality by smoothing demand to reach a more or less constant supply, though this system offers less integration with renewable sources and is expected to disappear in cities that benefit from a gas grid.

15.3.6.4 Heating/Cooling Distribution Networks

District heating/cooling (DHC) systems are attractive in dense urban environments as they benefit from (i) the proximity of consumers, which minimizes distribution losses, (ii) centralized, and hence more efficient, conversion technologies, (iii) a high baseload and a relatively homogeneous demand profile throughout the year, in particular in mixed cities that combine households, industries, and services, and (iv) the possibility of sharing energy resources, in particular environmental heat sources and waste heat. In addition, district heating/cooling systems are operated centrally by professionals, which allows for technologies with a higher level of technicity to be implemented, offering a high degree of flexibility for energy management at the district level (United Nations Environment Programme (UNEP), 2015). In compact cities, DHC is the most effective approach for unlocking the potential of energy efficiency and renewable energy (UNEP, 2015).

In the past, district heating and cooling have been typically considered as separate networks, while the temperature of district heating systems was significantly higher than that of the actual heat demand. Such systems are highly inefficient from an energy point of view. Modern networks are increasingly based on low-temperature heating systems (fourth-generation) which allows for tapping into waste heat sources and combining heating and cogeneration units (Lund, et al., 2014). Fifth-generation systems distribute the heat/cold from the environment (Suciu et al., 2018). They are closer to theoretical need by separating heat harvesting in the environment and the heat supply with a distribution network at intermediate temperature (15–20°C) that can supply both heating and cooling. The heat-transfer fluid can be water with a small temperature difference and therefore a high flow, or CO_2 (in both gas and liquid form) that uses the latent heat of vaporization/condensation and has the advantage of needing much smaller pipes, significantly enhancing its implementation potential in dense cities.

Both heat harvesting and supply will use heat pumps, the former being centralized in a location where attractive resources can be found, and the latter being decentralized systems in buildings, supplying the heat at exactly the temperature it is needed. In such hybrid systems, waste heat can be harvested and either reused or released into the environment. The system distributing the heat and cold at a temperature near to that of the surrounding environment even allows for waste heat to be converted into electricity before being distributed to users. In such systems, the heat excess can even be stored and reused with a view to managing seasonal variation in supply and demand.

15.3.7 From Energy Sources to Distributed Energy (R [MJr/MJd]) and their Environmental Impact (F [ep/MJr]) and (I [Impact/ep])

Distributed energy has to be harvested, transported, and transformed from energy resources. Those operations require energy and will produce emissions. The transformation from energy resources to distributed energy will therefore be discussed below, considering the complete system.

15.3.7.1 From Fossil Fuels to Renewable Sources of Energy

In the nineteenth century, cities primarily relied on coal as an energy source for heating and cooking and oil for lighting. Gas was used as a secondary energy source, produced from coal and distributed via a gas network, with one of the major applications being lighting, as an alternative to smelly, smoky petroleum lamps.

While many cities have so far focused their efforts primarily on energy efficiency, the next step toward a sustainable energy system will require a significant increase in the use of renewable energy to substitute products of fossil-fuel origin.

Renewable energy may significantly reduce CO_2 emissions and air pollution, but it also increases energy security and resilience, while bringing economic empowerment through an improved balance of payment, reduced public health costs, and job creation (International Renewable Energy Agency, 2018).

Cities can rely on three main renewable energy sources that are available within the city limits: solar, heat from the environment, and biomass wastes. Cities that are on rivers may also use hydropower. Other renewable resources – such as woody biomass, wind energy, or hydroelectric dams – have footprints that are largely incompatible with a dense urban environment. However, since cities are connected to electrical grids, they will be able to use these other resources to make up any deficit in their energy needs that cannot be met with their own production.

15.3.7.2 Heat from the Environment

A heat pump is a device that moves thermal energy in the opposite direction of spontaneous heat transfer, by absorbing heat at low temperature and releasing it at a higher temperature, or the other way around. To do this, heat pumps use a small amount of distributed energy (typically electricity) to accomplish the work of extracting energy from the heat source to meet the heat demand. Fridges and air-conditioning systems are typical examples of heat pumps. Heat pumps are becoming increasingly popular options to heat buildings by extracting heat from a cold source in the environment (outdoor air, river, lake, underground) and transferring it to the heat distribution system in a building.

Environmental heat is a key resource for cities. The denser the city, the more likely it is that environmental heat represents the renewable energy source with the highest potential, as the footprint of heat pumps is low in comparison to other renewable energy resources such as solar, wind, or biomass. Cities must therefore rely on environmental heat to reach a high level of sustainability.

A detailed inventory of the cold/heat sources needs to be established, starting with sources in the building itself such as wastewater (in particular hot water from showers, washing machines, and dishwashers), exhaust air, or solar thermal panels. In addition to ambient air, the potential of heat from under the ground (in the form of water or geothermal energy) or from surface water (lakes, seas, or rivers) will be mapped. When available, shallow geothermal sources (<200 m) are also attractive, in particular for cities that need both heating and cooling in different seasons, as these can offer heat storage for a hybrid heat pump that offers both heating (winter) and cooling (summer) modes. Cities offer the advantage of heterogeneous usages: household heating, air conditioning or refrigeration in shopping malls, cooling of data centers, or industrial activities that could produce waste heat. In such systems, a proper integration of heat pumps to harvest the highest-quality sources first needs to be realized in order to ensure the highest efficiency.

15.3.7.3 Solar Energy

Besides environmental heat, solar energy is the other key renewable energy source that is directly available in cities. However, the power density of this resource is low compared to what is needed. The denser the city, the lower the ratio of solar harvesting to floor area (International Energy Agency, 2016). This underlines the importance of reducing demand, so as to increase the extent to which solar energy can meet energy needs. Typically, rooftop solar panels can meet the annual electricity demand of a two-storey house, but can only cover a small portion of that of a skyscraper. The higher the building, the more the potential for harvesting solar energy through facades using Building Integrated Photovoltaics (BIPV). However, the BIPV potential of a building might be limited in dense city centers by shading from neighboring buildings. There may also be significant potential harvest solar energy from infrastructure as well as from buildings. Solar panels can be placed on parking lots or stadiums, or beside highways or railways.

Should solar thermal or solar photovoltaics be preferred? This is a recurring question, which does not have a universal answer. Solar thermal systems for the production of hot water have a rated efficiency of about 60 percent. Using photovoltaic panels to produce electricity with an efficiency of 18 percent to then heat water in an electrical boiler seems less efficient. However, if a photovoltaic system is coupled with a heat pump, then its overall efficiency exceeds 60 percent, as the electricity can always be injected into the grid when heat demand is low and the heat pump is at rest. This analysis shows the importance of managing energy in storage systems in order to combat the intermittency and seasonality of solar resources. With the fast learning curve of photovoltaic units cost, these systems will become increasingly cheaper and simpler to install than solar thermal systems, which require dedicated water distribution systems. Now, hybrid panels that combine photovoltaic cells at the front and a thermal collector at the back may represent the most energy-efficient solution not only because it collects the most energy from solar irradiation, but also because it keeps the photovoltaic cells cool and avoids a drop in efficiency. Although these systems remain expensive today, they will have the advantage of reducing the footprint of renewable energy harvesting.

The variability of solar electricity production is a challenge for the grid, which will increase as photovoltaics penetrate further. However, there are many ways to ensure grid stability in the future. Smart-grid technologies and micro-grid architecture, including decentralized storage and demand response, are part of the solution.

The seasonal variations of solar energy present another important challenge in non-tropical cities. As shown in Figure 15.6, those cities will have to manage an excess of solar electricity in summer while having to compensate for a deficit in winter. This will require seasonal storage strategies and a mix of technologies like wind/solar, pump storage facilities, or chemical storage (power to gas, power to liquid, or more generically Power-to-X).

15.3.7.4 Biomass

Biomass, essentially wood, is still far from being the principal renewable energy source in the global energy mix, covering just above 10 percent of world demand, and mainly used for heating and cooking purposes. Although biomass is of renewable origin, it is often used in an unsustainable way and with poor efficiency (5–10 percent); open stoves lead to dangerous levels of indoor air pollution and the resource is often overused, with significant impacts on public health and deforestation. About 18 percent of urban populations in developing countries still use fuelwood and charcoal for cooking, and in the least developed countries, it is close to 70 percent (United Nations, Department of Economic and Social Affairs (DESA), 2013).

Biomass is a versatile resource in the sense that it can be converted into many different energy carriers, such as solid, liquid, or gaseous fuels, as well as electricity. Biomass therefore has the unique potential amongst renewable energy sources of providing any energy service. Yet besides the health issue, combusting biomass to produce low-temperature heat for space heating is the least interesting option available, as it does not exploit the high exergetic potential of the resource, while space heating can be supplied from other, more adequate sources, in particular heat pumps.

There is no universal answer to the question of what the best use of biomass is for cities. This will depend on the type and volume of biomass available, on the potential of other renewable energy sources, as well as on the demand profile for different energy services (high-/low-temperature heat, electricity, transport fuels). Generally speaking, biomass should be converted into final energy carriers in large centralized thermochemical plants in order to benefit from economies of scale, and be brought into the city using gas, heat, road, or electricity networks. Biomass conversion pathways include anaerobic digestion, gasification, and methanation for the production of synthetic gas to be injected in the gas grid, as well as pyrolysis and Fischer-Tropsch synthesis for the production of liquid biofuels. The possibility of integrating the biomass conversion process in order to supply the heat needs of industrial processes must not be neglected.

If access to modern thermochemical conversion technologies is not possible, then the combustion of biomass in cities remains a reasonable option provided the following rules are applied: As a priority, biomass should be used in centralized cogeneration units for the joint production of heat and electricity, in order to take advantage of the high temperature of the combustion. Filters should be applied to capture harmful particulate emissions. After cogeneration of electricity, the heat is then injected into district heating networks. As a last resort, biomass should be combusted in high-efficiency (>90 percent) stoves, such as pellet boilers, for heat-only production. However, importing the biomass as solid fuels (chips, pellets) into the city with trucks is the least sustainable option, from an energy and CO_2 point of view, as compared to converting the biomass to gaseous biofuels or bio-electricity and importing it using the gas or the electricity network (see Section 15.3.6).

Cities will also produce a lot of bioenergy waste, in the form of sludges from wastewater treatment plants and the biomass portion of municipal and industrial solid wastes. These wastes have significant energy content which should be exploited to meet urban energy demand with local resources.

Different types of biomass will be classified as a function of their water content and their capacity to be treated by biological processes (digestibility). Dry and woody biomass can be directly used as fuel in a boiler to supply heat with an efficiency of 85 percent, but with a poor exploitation of its potential to provide energy services (its exergy efficiency is below 20 percent, see Figure 15.4). It can also be converted into electricity either by co-combustion in a conventional power plant to reach an electrical efficiency of 40 percent, or through gasification and final conversion by an advanced system (e.g., fuel cells) to reach efficiencies above 65 percent.

The conversion of biomass into final energy generates carbon dioxide. This biogenic CO_2 can be either sequestrated or used in a Sabatier reaction to produce renewable natural gas using hydrogen produced with excess electricity. Biomass therefore becomes a key player in the energy system not only by supplying energy but also by supplying a biogenic carbon source to store intermittent forms of renewable energy (Codina Gironès, 2018).

15.3.7.5 Other Renewable Energy Sources

Onshore and offshore wind farms, hydropower plants, ocean energy plants, and deep geothermal plants are renewable power production options that will produce electricity outside cities. Electricity networks will continue to bring electricity to the cities as they do today (see Section 15.3.6). With the advent of intermittent solar and wind energy, increasing amounts of excess electricity might be produced.

It should be noted that small wind turbines for rooftop installation are hardly competitive, while also being noisy and detrimental to bird life due to their high rotation speed. Hence, this technology is a priori not to recommend for city environments.

15.3.7.6 Non-renewable (Fossil) Energy Sources and CO_2 Emissions

Should cities have no other choice but to rely on fossil-fuel resources to complement their energy mix, then a certain number of rules apply to minimize the CO_2 impact:

- Natural gas should be favored over petroleum products, and in particular over coal, as natural gas emits less CO_2 per unit of energy.

Table 15.1 *CO_2 emissions in g CO_2-eq./kWh per unit of distributed energy (Bauer et al. 2008, Ecoinvent, 2013).*

	Fuel preparation [g CO_2/kWh]	Fuel combustion	Fuel total	Electricity
Natural gas[1]	26	200	226	432
Coal[2]	37	323	360	914
Gasoline[3]	60	241	301	602

1) Natural gas from conventional sources: power plant 57% efficiency + 8% grid losses. 2) Hard coal: power plant 43% efficiency + 8% grid losses. 3) Gasoline, power plant being an internal combustion engine 50% efficiency (no grid losses).

- Cogeneration of heat and electricity should be favored over large centralized thermal power plants as this makes it possible to increase overall production efficiency.
- Carbon capture, utilization, and storage (CCUS) should be implemented wherever possible. When fossil fuels are used, carbon dioxide emissions can be reduced by capturing CO_2 for sequestration or reuse. This creates a penalty in the electricity production efficiency that can be compensated for by connecting the power plant to a district heating system to allow waste heat recovery.

It should be recalled that the emissions associated with fossil fuels are not only those from the direct combustion of the fuels, but those produced over their entire life cycle, including through the extraction, transformation, and transport of fossil resources, which are unequally distributed around the globe. Based on data from the ecoinvent (2013) database, Table 15.1 gives the energy consumed and the related emissions of the fossil-fuel supply chain. The generation of electricity from fossil-fuel resources includes the conversion efficiency of the power plant in addition to the supply chain of the fuel.

15.3.7.7 The Positive Socioeconomic Impact of Renewable Energies

In addition to decreasing the CO_2 emissions and environmental impacts associated with energy provision, it is important to mention that increasing the share of renewable energy harvested in the city implies that the investments in the harvesting, distribution, and management of renewable energy resources, as well as in increasing efficiency, will generate local jobs and improve the balance of payment. For the cost of the energy services being directly injected into the local economy, this will create an important side benefit of renewable energy penetration.

In addition, renewable energy resources are much more evenly distributed around the globe than fossil resources. As a result, increasing reliance on renewable sources and improving energy efficiency to reduce demand is likely to enhance energy supply security. In this sense, sustainable cities will be more resilient to geopolitical issues.

15.3.8 Summary

In the above sections, we have discussed each contributing factor to a sustainable energy system in buildings, as provided by Equation 15.1. In Table 15.2, we provide quantitative figures for each of these factors in the form of minimum and maximum bounds for space heating, together with the corresponding range of overall CO_2 impact when multiplying all the factors.

In other words, Table 15.2 indicates the CO_2 emissions per inhabitant from space heating for buildings by providing an indicative range from best to worst practices for each factor assessed. The best case corresponds to a high-efficiency building with high-density occupation, using a combination of photovoltaic panels, heat pumps, and fuel cells fed by biomass gasification. The worst case corresponds to a low-density, inefficient house heated by a gas boiler. Life cycle CO_2 emissions between these two extreme cases differ by more than three orders of magnitude, from 2 to 4,200 kg CO_2-eq/person/year.

Finally, a key question is how these insights can be integrated in the spatial planning process of a city. That is, how and to which extent can spatial planning and energy planning be combined? Box 15.1 presents SAGESSE (Systematic Analysis, Generation, Exploration, Steering, and Synthesis Experience), which was developed specifically to address large-scale problems such as those encountered in urban and energy planning for an interactive optimization for urban energy system planning.

15.4 Industrial Sector

Equation 15.1 applies to the industrial sector just as much as it does to the building sector. The service industry's offer is manufacturing the products that society needs. Industry has a large untapped potential for reducing energy consumption and greenhouse gas emissions by means of the following actions:

- Realizing energy audits and developing process models that aim at understanding and characterizing the energy needs of the production processes, i.e., understanding the role of energy for industrial production.
- Recovering waste heat either directly through heat exchangers or indirectly by heat pumping or transfering heat between processes. It has been demonstrated that potential for heat recovery can be as high as 30 percent of the heat requirement of a process, and even 50 percent in combination with heat pumps.
- Improving the conversion efficiency of heat production systems, in particular introducing combined heat and power or combined heat and fuel production from biomass-based thermochemical conversion units.
- Considering the use of renewable energy as an alternative to fossil fuels. This usually implies increasing the electrification of the industrial processes and developing integrated energy management and storage approaches.
- Considering renewable resources as alternatives to fossil-fuel- and mineral-based materials, especially substituting plastics of fossil-fuel origin with biomass- or waste-based resources.

Box 15.1 (cont.)

2 To accelerate the exploration process, the quasi-random "Sobol" sampling sequence, developed by the mathematician Ilya Sobol, is adopted. This sampling approach provides a quick way to gain an overview of the solution space, in the areas preferred by the decision-maker.

3 Multi-attribute decision analysis, cluster analysis, and linked data visualization techniques are a combination of methods that facilitate the interpretation of the Pareto-optimal results in real time (Figure 2). Their complementarity with the parallel coordinates chart improves the decision process by making key information more accessible, and by focusing the attention of the decision-maker on the most relevant solutions.

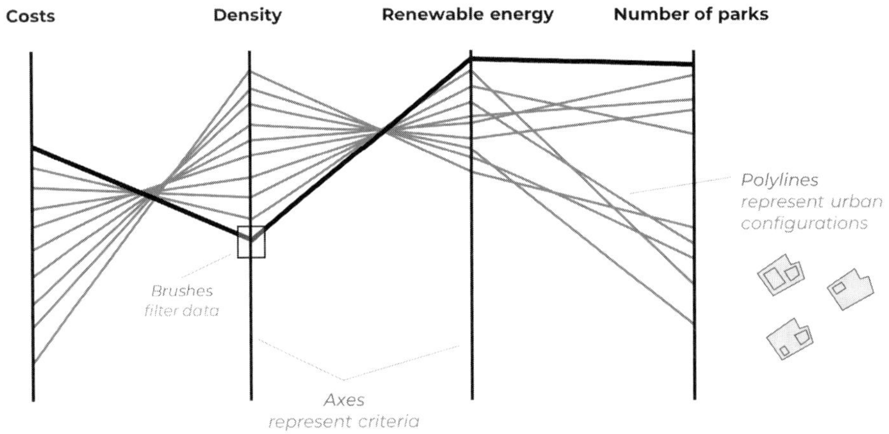

Figure 1 (Box 15.1) Illustration of a parallel coordinates interface, displaying a few urban configurations generated by an optimization approach and their corresponding criteria. The spatial representation of each configuration can also be visualized separately. Source: Cajot (2018)

Coupled with mixed integer linear programming models of urban and energy systems, this methodology led to development of the planning support system URBio (http://www.urbio.ch), which has been applied to support the planning of both greenfield and brownfield development projects in the Swiss canton of Geneva (Cajot et al., 2020; Schüler et al., 2018). By interacting with parallel coordinates, planners can directly specify the preferred values to be achieved for each criterion, while the computer provides them with feasible urban configurations, whose key performance indicators can be explored and compared. This searching and learning process not only helps identify efficient plans which satisfy the various stated objectives, but also help the decision-maker understand and gain confidence in justifying their chosen (or discarded) solutions.

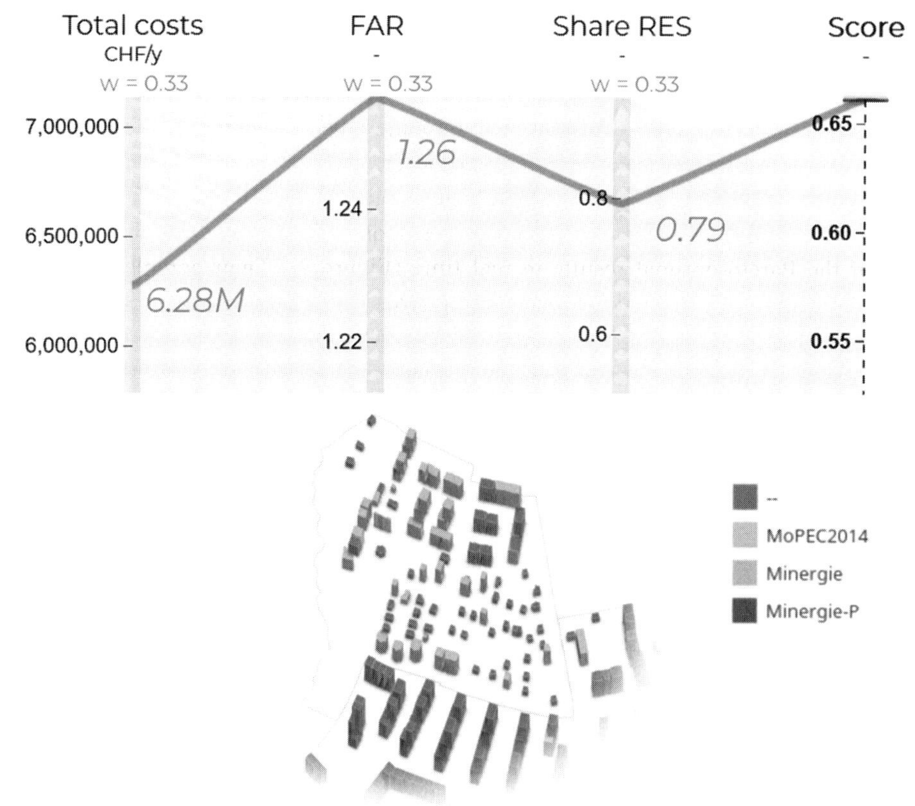

Figure 2 (Box 15.1) Illustration of the parallel coordinates interface, highlighting one of the calculated Pareto-optimal urban configurations, and its spatial representation. Source: Cajot (2018)

Industrial sites have traditionally been built outside cities to minimize their burden on populations, such as through noise, traffic, and pollution. Today, the expansion of cities is bringing industry closer and closer to urbanized zones. This growing urban mixing offers new opportunities for reducing the energy consumption and environmental impacts of both cities and industry. Industry currently consumes about 30 percent of the final energy demand in industrialized countries. This demand is mainly in the form of high-temperature heat for industrial processes. The medium- or low-temperature heat that comes out of these processes is typically released in the environment as waste heat. Hence there is a growing potential for using this waste energy to meet the heat demand of cities using district heating integration and possibly to jointly produce electricity in cogeneration units. In such cases, cities become a sort of cooling utility for industry.

The underlying concept behind this actually extends beyond energy to include material wastes and wastewater. In particular, industries will increasingly organize themselves into clusters sharing equipment and resources, including waste streams, developing as an industrial symbiosis, following the model of industrial ecology (Erkmann, 1997). This will include the development of bio- and waste refineries.

Thus, the proximity of industry to cities offers new opportunities for an integrated approach to waste management, through which the reuse, recycling, and conversion of wastes into usable materials or final energy make waste into an asset. This is the concept of the circular economy (Tukker, 2015), in which cities, including their industries, would increasingly evolve toward zero energy and zero waste, hence minimizing their impact on climate and the environment. The quest for the circular economy is not, however, a purely technical challenge – socioeconomic and governance dimensions are equally important to ensure the right enabling conditions (Moreau, 2017).

Finally, increasing the efficiency of the industrial sector and the eco-design of its products will have the systemic benefit of reducing the environmental footprint and the impacts of the production of materials, including those used to build and develop the city (insulation materials, efficient cars, and recyclable batteries).

15.5 Transport Sector

Three options have to be considered to render the transport sector more sustainable: (i) improving the efficiency of the technologies used, (ii) fostering a shift toward more sustainable technologies, and (iii) reducing the demand for transport. Today, transport accounts for just over a third of global energy use in cities and this figure could grow to nearly 50 percent by 2030 (IRENA, 2016). In this context, reducing the demand for transport is likely to be challenging. This option will be partly addressed in the Chapter 20 (Massaro, 2020), together with issues related to soft mobility and autonomous vehicles. In the present chapter, we focus instead on the technology aspect of transport, in particular on fuel and the motorization of vehicles, discussing the technical options available to lower their carbon, particulate, and noise emissions.

The transport sector may prove harder to decarbonize than the building sector as it currently relies almost entirely on fossil fuels, where there are well-established distribution infrastructures, and fewer renewable options exist. Passenger transportation is especially inefficient, accounting for more than 60 percent of the energy consumption of the transport activities yet with only 12–30 percent of this energy truly converted into momentum (Rodrigue, 2017). Vehicles can be made more sustainable by improving their fuel efficiency, and by switching from fossil fuels to renewable energy sources, which could be green electricity used in electric vehicles, biofuels used in conventional internal combustion engines, or synthetic fuels (e.g., hydrogen) used in fuel-cell vehicles.

$$ImpactCO2 = \sum\nolimits_{service\,i} SiNiDiEiRiFi \qquad (15.1.1)$$

Equation 15.1 can be applied to assess the transport sector in the very same way that we illustrated the building sector. Again, the assessment will follow the supply chain of transport fuels (or electricity in the case of electric vehicles), all the way from the extraction of the primary energy resources to the delivery of motive power through the different energy-conversion steps of the supply chains. In the sections below, we focus the discussion on comparing the efficiency and emissions of different motorization systems, without detailing the different steps of Equation 15.3.

15.5.1 Fuel Efficiency

Gasoline and diesel vehicles are particularly inefficient in urban environments, as internal combustion engines (ICE) operate at below 20 percent efficiency when used at low speed and when continuously starting and stopping in traffic, i.e., in typical urban driving conditions. Electric motors that offer 90 percent efficiency are far better suited to these operations. Hence, the deployment of battery electric vehicles (BEVs) and plug-in hybrid vehicles (PHEVs) is a necessary step toward making urban transport more sustainable.

Private vehicles are also particularly inefficient because they have a very poor weight-to-service ratio. In other words, cars are very heavy in comparison to the weight of the passengers they transport, in particular given the low rate of occupancy (1.6 passengers/car (Papadimitriou, et al., 2013)). The average vehicle weight has kept on increasing in the past 30 years (ICCT, 2017) in order to offer incrementally higher levels of comfort and safety, while the actual transport service rendered has remained unchanged. There is a critical need to reduce the weight of vehicles by increasing the use of lighter materials, such as plastics and advanced composites. This is perfectly possible with modern techniques without compromising on safety, in particular with the advent of intrinsically safer autonomous vehicles. The life cycle impact of using novel materials will depend on their nature. Eco-design approaches should be preferred so as to minimize the impact of manufacturing and maximize the potential for recycling.

15.5.2 Electric Vehicles (EVs)

In addition to their unbeatable fuel efficiency, electric vehicles can contribute to the reduction of pollution in city centers. This is actually the main driver behind support schemes for EVs in many cities that suffer from smog, e.g., Beijing and Shanghai. Of people living in urban areas, more than 90 percent deal with air quality levels exceeding World Health Organization limits (WHO, 2016). In low- and middle-income countries, this rises to 98 percent. IRENA estimated the cost of outdoor air pollution at USD 1.8–6.0 trillion in 2010, or about 3–10 percent of global gross domestic product (GDP) (Markandya et al., 2016). Under a business-as-usual scenario, this will rise to USD 2.4–8.8 trillion per year by 2030.

However, the decarbonization potential of EVs will depend on the carbon intensity of the grid electricity. Although EVs do not generate any direct emissions, the emissions of the power plants that produce the electricity consumed by EVs should be considered as indirect emissions attributable to the EVs. Should the electricity be produced largely from coal plants, then the switch from petroleum vehicles to EVs is likely to increase overall carbon emissions (Hill et al., 2014). The greener the grid, the lower the indirect emissions from EVs.

Also, EVs are much quieter than petroleum vehicles. An estimated 65 percent of EU citizens living in major urban areas are exposed to high noise levels, with 1–2 million disability-adjusted life years (DALYS) lost to environmental noise in the EU each year (European Commission, 2015). In cities in the developing world with high population densities, the effects are likely to be even more severe.

EVs are particularly well suited to private mobility in urban environments, as individual city cars typically operate short mileages every day (of the order of 20–40 km), which is perfectly compatible with the limited range offered today by electric vehicles compared to ICE vehicles.

Electrification is also possible for fleet vehicles, such as taxis, delivery vans, or buses, providing the battery recharge time can be fast enough to minimize impact on operations. Usually, the longer the daily mileage, the more economical it is to drive electric, as the higher vehicle purchase price is offset by a lower fuel cost and higher fuel efficiency. Economics and the desire to reduce pollution are driving the adoption of electric buses worldwide, in particular in China, where 20 percent of all city buses are already electric. Beijing is aiming for 80 percent of buses to be electric by 2020 (International Renewable Energy Agency, 2016).

The charging of electric vehicles in urban environments remains to date an unsolved challenge, which is probably the most critical barrier to mass-market adoption of this technology. The vast majority of car owners in urban environments have to park in the street. Customers with no access to private parking with a plug are unlikely to opt for an electric vehicle, as relying exclusively on public fast-charging stations would increase the "fill-up" time by a factor of 3 to 10 compared to petroleum cars for an equivalent range – and it could even be much longer if no plugs are available. No clear solutions to the urban charging challenge have yet emerged, as installing charging units at each and every public parking spot is unlikely to be an option in the absence of systematic grid reinforcement, which is hardly a large-scale solution for cost reasons. Rather, it is likely that future EV owners will rely on a range of options for charging their car, combining public and private infrastructure, of different speeds (slow, semi-fast, and fast units) and types (fixed, mobile, contactless induction systems, etc.).

15.5.3 Biofuels

Biofuels represent the simplest way to increase the share of renewable energy sources in the transport sector, as they capitalize on the existing vehicles and fuel distribution infrastructure. Biofuels can be blended with gasoline, diesel, and natural gas to various extents, depending on their nature, with minimal or no modification to vehicle engines (Bauen, 2014). However, merely substituting fuels with alternative fuels does not solve the fundamental issue of the poor energy efficiency of internal combustion engines.

In addition, ensuring the sustainability of biofuels remains a challenge. First-generation biofuels, such as bioethanol and biodiesel, have long been criticized for three main reasons: first, they are produced from edible crops (soy beans, corn, palm oil, rape seed, etc.), thus competing with the food supply; second, they have a relatively poor carbon-emission-reduction potential compared to fossil fuels, due to the high level of indirect emissions from intensive agricultural practices; and third, they are associated with both direct and indirect changes in land use and hence deforestation (IEA Bioenergy, 2009).

Biofuels that are based on non-food crops usually benefit from a lower CO_2 footprint, as well as lower overall environmental and social impacts as compared to first-generation biofuels. However, they are still not commercially viable at large scale and their economic and environmental sustainability remains to be demonstrated (IEA Bioenergy, 2009).

To meet the current transport-fuel needs of a city in a temperate climate with biofuels, an area equivalent to three to five times the size of the city would be required to grow the bioenergy crop. In comparison, only about 3 percent of the surface of the city would be required for the amount of photovoltaic panels needed to power the transport services of that city, should its vehicle fleet be 100 percent electric.[1] This difference of two orders of magnitude is due essentially to the higher resource-to-tank conversion efficiency of photovoltaics compared to photosynthesis, as well as to the higher efficiency of electric motors compared to internal combustion engines. Hence, unless the land used to grow biomass can offer additional benefits – such as habitat for biodiversity, soil protection, climate stabilization, and recreational areas, which are services that can be offered by natural forest, but hardly by intensive monoculture crops – biofuels are unlikely to represent a genuine sustainable solution.

15.5.4 Fuel Cell Vehicles

Fuel cell drivetrains benefit from a fuel efficiency of about 40 percent, which is significantly higher than that of diesel/gasoline cars in city environments (<20 percent). However, electricity should, as far as possible, be fed directly into battery electric vehicles, which offers a fuel efficiency of about 70 percent, rather than used to produce hydrogen in an electrolyser (50 percent efficiency including compression) that is then used in a fuel cell (50 percent efficiency), which thus offers a mere 25 percent overall efficiency (Transport & Environment, 2017). However, hydrogen mobility will make great sense if based on excess electricity that is converted into hydrogen instead of being curtailed. Fuel cell vehicles (FCVs) also represent a meaningful sustainable option for heavy-duty vehicles traveling long distances because hydrogen tanks offer a much higher energy density per mass than batteries. FCVs are in particular relevant for fleets, as they can rely on a dedicated hydrogen refuelling infrastructure. The deployment of a large-scale hydrogen network remains a key barrier to the mass deployment of private hydrogen cars. Therefore, it is usually agreed that fuel cell and battery electric vehicles are not directly competing against each other, but are rather addressing complementary market segments.

15.6 Conclusion

Sustainable cities will be integrated into larger-scale food, energy, waste, and water systems by way of interconnected multi-energy grids, as illustrated in Figure 15.7. Adopting and

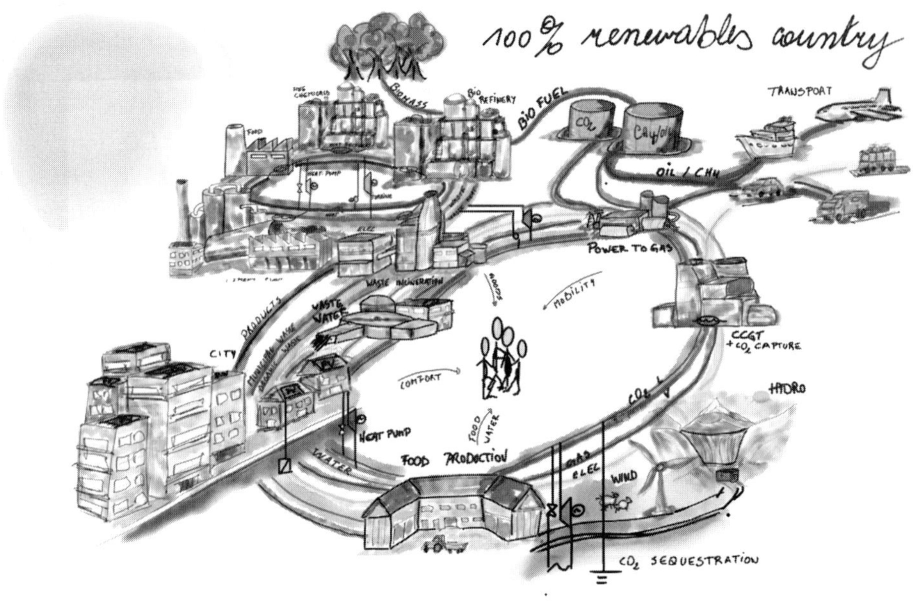

Figure 15.7 Multi-energy system integration in sustainable cities. Source: own illustration

implementing this integrated multi-energy vision will allow cities to become self-sufficient in energy by relying on locally available renewable energy resources (mainly environmental heat and solar energy) or by using renewable energy harvested outside cities and transported via the multi-energy grids. Operating this system in a dependable way will require a high level of smart energy management in order to balance supply and demand in real time, combining techniques of artificial intelligence, forecasting, and big data.

Assessing the sustainability level and the potential for improvement of urban energy systems can be done using Equation 15.1. For a given impact category, e.g., CO_2 emissions, the overall impact of an urban energy system per inhabitant is given by the product of the individual factors summed over the different energy services (space heating, appliances, lighting, process heating, etc.), as illustrated in Equation 15.1. This analytical approach is universal in the sense that it is applicable to any energy system (industry, transport, building) in any urban and climatic context. Also, its simple way of breaking down energy supply chains from the extraction of energy resources to the delivery of energy services into multiple conversion steps makes it possible to clearly identify those steps where most sustainability is lost, which helps prioritize improvement efforts.

Designing sustainable cities will require two complementary approaches to be used: thermodynamics-based thinking and multi-criteria analysis. Thermodynamics-based thinking will enable systems to be designed considering the efficiency of the energy conversion steps along the entire energy conversion chain, from the exploitation of resources to the delivery of energy services. This approach reveals the synergies made possible by system integration, such as cascading heat, reusing waste heat, connecting heat sources and sinks, and managing storage capacities.

With the help of modeling and optimization techniques, decision-support methods will enable the application of multi-criteria decision-making strategies so as to meet the needs of all stakeholders while minimizing energy demand. This method for multi-energy system design is universal and can thus be applied to any typology of cities and climatic conditions. It allows for the integration of different demand profiles (comfort cooling and heating) and local resources (sea, rivers, solar, geothermal), as well as industrial activities.

As a co-benefit, sustainable cities will have more local jobs, both on the energy supply side, but more importantly in the development and operation of sustainable infrastructures (buildings, transport systems, waste and water management systems). However, the scale of the challenge depends on the city considered, in particular on its legacy infrastructure, on its level of urban mixed use, on the energy quality of its building stock, as well as on the availability of local energy resources. Transforming cities to include more mixed-use districts in order to better exploit internal resources is likely to be the greatest challenge ahead in moving toward sustainable cities, as it may, in certain cases, require a profound overhaul of their urbanism.

Note

1. Based on EPFL Energy Center calculation: Considering the city of Warsaw, daily travel 40 km/day/car, energy intensity 0.2 kWh/km for EV and 6L/100km for gasoline cars.

References

Bauen, A. (2014). EU Auto-Fuel Biofuels Roadmap. *European Biofuels Technology Platform.* Brussels: E4tech.

Bioregional Development Group. (October 2017). *One Planet Goals and Guidance for Cities and Regions 2017.* London: Bioregional.

Boermans, T., Bettgenhäuser, K., Offermann, M., & Schimschar, S. (2012). *Renovation Tracks for Europe up to 2050.* Technical report. ECOFYS Germany GmbH on behalf of European Insulation Manufacturers Association.

Cajot, S., 2018. Interactive optimization for supporting multi-criteria decisions in urban and energy system planning (Doctoral thesis). EPFL, Lausanne, Switzerland. DOI:10.5075/epfl-thesis-8925.

Cajot, S., Schüler, N., Peter, M., Koch, A., & Maréchal, F. (2020). Interactive Optimization with Parallel Coordinates: Exploring Multidimensional Spaces for Decision Support. Front ICT 2019. DOI:10.3389/fict.2018.00032.

Bauer, C., Heck, T., Dones, R., Mayer-Spohn, O., & Blesl, M. (2008). Technical data, costs, and life cycle inventories of advanced fossil power generation systems. *NEEDS Project final report.*

Codina Gironès, V. P. (2018). On the assessment of the CO_2 mitigation potential of woody biomass. *Frontiers in Energy Research*, 5, 37.

ecoinvent. (2013). Swiss Centre for Life Cycle Inventories, Overview and methodology: Data quality guideline for the ecoinvent database version 3, 2013.

ECOFYS. (2012). *Renovation Tracks for Europe up to 2050: Building renovation in Europe – What Are the Choices?* European Insulation Manufacturers Association (Eurima). Köln: ECOFYS Germany GmbH. www.eurima.org/publications/90/146/Renovation-Tracks-for-Europe-up-to-2050.html.

ENTRANZE Consortium. (2014). ENTRANZE Online database. *An in-depth analysis of the structure and dynamics of buildings and related energy systems in EU-27 (+Croatia and Serbia).* Enerdata. www.entranze.enerdata.eu/.

Erkmann, S. (1997). *Industrial Ecology: A Historical View.* Industrial Ecology.

European Commission. (2015, Jan). Thematic Issue: Noise Impacts on Health (Issue 47) (S. C.-U. (UWE), Ed.) Bristol.

European Commission, Directorate-General for Energy. (2016). *An EU Strategy on Heating and Cooling.* http://eur-lex.europa.eu/legal-content/en/TXT/?uri=CELEX:52016DC0051

Favrat, D., Marechal, F., & Epelly, O. (2008). The challenge of introducing an exergy indicator in a local law on energy. *Energy,* 33(2), 130–136. DOI:10.1016/j.energy.2007.10.012.

Frischknecht, R., & Jolliet, O. (2016). Global Guidance for Life Cycle Impact Assessment Indicators. *Publication of the UNEP/SETAC Life Cycle Initiative, Paris,* DTI/2081/PA, ISBN, 978–992.

Girardin, L., Maréchal, F., & Favrat, D. (2012). *A GIS-based Methodology for the Evaluation of Integrated Energy Systems in Urban Area.* Lausanne: EPFL. DOI:10.5075/epfl-thesis-5287.

Hill, J. D., Marshall, J. D., & Tessum, C. W. (2014). Life cycle air quality impacts of conventional and alternative light-duty transportation in the United States. *PNAS.*

ICCT. The International Council on Clean Transportation. (2017). *European Vehicle Market Statistics, Pocketbook 2017/2018.* http://eupocketbook.org/wp-content/uploads/2017/11/ICCT_ocketbook_2017.pdf.

IEA Bioenergy. (2009). *Bioenergy – a Sustainable and Reliable Energy Source.* www.ieabioenergy.com/publications/main-report-bioenergy-a-sustainable-and-reliable-energy-source-a-review-of-status-and-prospects/ (accessed 30.1.19).

International Energy Agency. (2014). *Energy Efficiency Indicators: Fundamentals on Statistics, 2014.* France: IEA.

International Energy Agency. (2015). *WEO-2015 Special Report: Energy and Climate Change.* France: IEA.

International Energy Agency. (2016). *Energy Technology Perspectives 2016: Towards Sustainable Urban Energy Systems.* France: OECD/IEA.

International Energy Agency. (2017a). *Energy Technology Perspectives 2017: Catalysing Energy Technology Transformations.* France: OECD/IEA. www.iea.org/etp2017.

International Energy Agency. (2017b). *Market Report Series: Energy Efficiency 2017.* France: IEA. DOI:10.1787/renew-2017-en.

International Institute for Applied Systems Analysis (IIASA) (2012). *Global Energy Assessment: Toward a Sustainable Future.* T. Johansson, N. Nakicenovic, A. Patwardhan, & L. Gomez-Echeverri (eds.). Cambridge University Press. www.globalenergyassessment.org.

International Renewable Energy Agency. (2016). *Renewable Energy in Cities.* Abu Dhabi: IRENA. www.irena.org.

International Renewable Energy Agency. (2018). *Renewable Energy and Jobs: Annual Review 2018.* United Arab Emirates: IRENA.

Lund, H., Werner, S., Wiltshire, R., et al. (2014). 4th Generation District Heating (4GDH). *Energy,* 68, 1–11. DOI:10.1016/j.energy.2014.02.089.

Markandya, A., Saygin, D., Miketa, A., Gielen, D., & Wagner, N. (2016). *The True Cost of Fossil Fuels: Saving on the Externalities of Air Pollution and Climate Change.* International Renewable Energy Agency (IRENA). IRENA. ISBN: 978–92–95111–87–5.

Massaro, E. (2020). A study of ride sharing opportunities in the city of Santiago de Chile. In C. R. Binder, E. Massaro, & R. Wyss (eds.), *Sustainability Assessment in Urban Systems,* pp. 480–488, Cambridge University Press.

Moreau, V. (2017). Moreau, V., Sahakian, M., van Griethuysen, P., & Vuille, F. (2017). Coming full circle: Why social and institutional dimensions matter for the circular economy. *Journal of Industrial Ecology,* 21(3), 497–506.

Odyssee Consortium. (2018). Odyssee: European energy efficiency and demand database. Enerdata. www.odyssee-mure.eu.

Papadimitriou, G., Ntziachristos, L., Wüthrich, P., et al. (2013). *Transport data collection supporting the quantitative analysis of measures relating to transport and climate change (TRACCS).*

Rode, P., Keim, C., Robazza, G., Viejo, P., & Schofield, J. (2014). Cities and energy: Urban morphology and residential heat-energy demand. *Environment and Planning B: Planning and Design*, 41(1), 138–162. DOI:10.1068/b39065.

Rodrigue, J.-P., Comptois, C., & Slack, B. (2017). *The geography of transport systems*. London: Routledge, Taylor & Francis Group.

Schüler, N., Cajot, S., Peter, M., Page, J., & Maréchal, F. (2018). The Optimum Is Not the Goal: Capturing the Decision Space for the Planning of New Neighborhoods. Front Built Environ 2018. DOI:10.3389/fbuil.2017.00076.

Suciu, R., Girardin, L., & Maréchal, F. (2018). Energy integration of CO_2 networks and power to gas for emerging energy autonomous cities in Europe. *Energy*. DOI:10.1016/j.energy.2018.05.083.

Transport & Environment. (2017). *Roadmap to climate-friendly land freight and buses in Europe*. www.transportenvironment.org/sites/te/files/publications/Full_%20Roadmap%20freight%20buses%20Europe_2050_FINAL%20VERSION_corrected%20%282%29.pdf (accessed 30.1.19).

Tukker, A. (2015). Product services for a resource-efficient and circular economy – a review. *Journal of Cleaner Production*, 97, 76–91.

UN-HABITAT. (2011). *Cities and Climate Change: Global Report on Human Settlements 2011*. United Nations Human Settlements Programme. London, Washington, DC: Earthscan. https://unhabitat.org/books/cities-and-climate-change-global-report-on-human-settlements-2011/.

United Nation Secretary-General. (11 May 2017). *Progress towards the Sustainable Development Goals: Report of the Secretary-General*. New York: UN. DOI:E/2017/66.

United Nations Environment Programme (UNEP) (2015). *District Energy in Cities: Unlocking the Potential of Energy Efficiency and Renewable Energy*. Tech. rep., United Nations Environment Programme, Paris. https://europa.eu/capacity4dev/file/23122/download?token=i3wTZfTk.

United Nations, Department of Economic and Social Affairs (DESA) (2013). *World Economic and Social Survey 2013: Sustainable Develoment Challenges*. New York: UN.

World Health Organization (WHO) (2016). *World Health Statistics 2016: Monitoring Health for the SDGs, Sustainable Development Goals*. Geneva: WHO.

16

Sustainability Assessment of the Housing System: Exploring the Interplay between the Material and Social Systems

Anna Pagani, Rafael Laurenti, and Claudia R. Binder

Box 16.1 authored by Stefanie Hellweg and Niko Heeren

16.1 Introduction

In a rapidly changing and urbanizing world, the demand for housing and city infrastructure, and the related use of natural resources, are continually increasing. Whereas, in 1900, a mere 10 percent of the global population were urban dwellers, in 2010, that percentage exceeded 51percent, and by 2050, 66 percent of the world's population is projected to be living in cities (IRP, 2018; United Nations, 2018). This indicates that the housing sector is likely to face increasing challenges if it is to meet the needs of the growing urban population. Furthermore, cities emit 75 percent of all carbon dioxide equivalent from energy use (IPCC, 2014), and globally the energy use by the residential sector is expected to double by 2050 from its 2010 level.

Housing is a central and interconnected part of an urban system (Waddell, 2002), and thus of fundamental importance in a transition toward a more sustainable society over the years (Hondo et al., 2006). Since the early 1970s, several initiatives on sustainable housing have appeared around the globe, characterized by deep green environmental values and beliefs. At that early stage, citizens developed several practical demonstration projects and made individual sustainable lifestyle choices but this had little influence upon government policy (Lovell, 2004). During the 1990s, governments and other mainstream institutions became interested in sustainable housing as a solution to a range of policy problems (Lovell, 2004). During those initial efforts in the area of sustainable urban environments, the term "sustainable housing" was widely used to describe housing with a lower environmental impact (i.e., with enhanced energy-efficiency features) and economic gains drove progress toward reducing natural-resource use (Seyfang, 2010). Around 2010, new technologies in building construction, standards, regulations, and ICT tools started to be widely adopted and used for improving natural-resource efficiency of buildings in all stages of their life cycle (Mateus & Bragança, 2011). More recently, greater attention has been given to other factors that contribute to sustainability than just environmental factors, namely social (including health and well-being, as well as segregation), economic, and cultural factors (Prochorskaite et al., 2016).

Arriving at a win-win-win situation, in which an increase in overall natural-resource efficiency yields both economic benefits and improvements in quality of life, has been observed only within certain conditions and contexts.[1] This is because material- and energy-resource allocation in housing is indirectly affected by context-dependent variables, such as the type of dwelling (house or apartment), tenure status (owner-occupied home or rented dwelling), housing affordability (percentage of income spent on housing), size of the dwelling, and housing quality (e.g., sanitary facilities and general condition, thermal/ acoustic insulation, presence of natural light).

Identifying strategies for reconciling urban development and sustainable development requires, in addition, an adequate understanding of how individuals' housing preferences relate to and affect the environmental impacts of dwellings. However, while environmental impacts from housing life cycle are well understood, little knowledge about how actors' decisions and behavior affect material and energy flows and resource allocation is available (Froemelt et al., 2018).

The aim of this chapter is therefore to advance a broader understanding of the complex interplay between the material system (material and energy resources used in housing systems) and the social system (social norms, traditions) as a part of an integrative sustainability assessment of housing.

We apply the heuristic for material-flow management developed by Binder (2007) to guide our analysis, highlighting how the material system (demand and supply) is affected by the social system and vice versa. More specifically, the research questions (RQs) pursued in this chapter are:

RQ1. What key variables and technical measures for the material system are important for the environmental performance of housing?

RQ2. What are the relevant variables of the social system that affect these variables and technical measures?

RQ3. Which indicators enable the material and social systems to be considered when assessing the sustainability of housing systems?

RQ4. What is the interaction between the selected indicators and what role do the indicators play within the housing system?

16.2 Methods

16.2.1 Structural Agent Analysis

To understand the mechanisms and linkages between material flows and the drivers that affect these flows, we applied structural agent analysis (SAA) (Binder, 2007). SAA combines material flow analysis (MFA) with its related social system (Binder, 2007). The fundamental premise is that a material system affects and is affected by a social system and this feedback loop interaction is governed by decision-making rules (see Figure 16.1).

MFA is a systematic assessment of the flows and stocks of materials within a system defined in space and time (Baccini & Brunner, 2012; Brunner & Rechberger, 2005, 2017). It

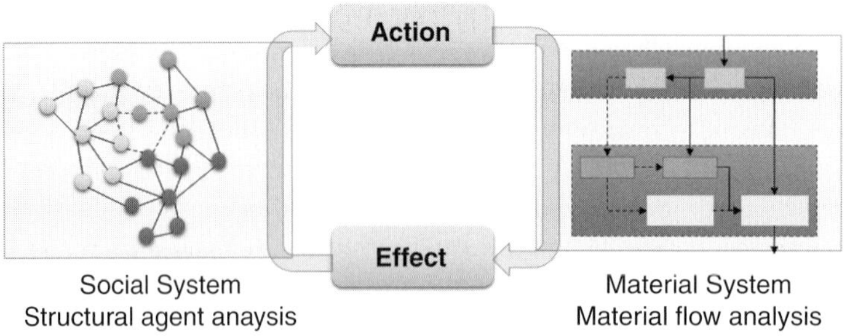

Figure 16.1 Interaction between the material system and the social system governed by feedbacks of action-effect and components of Binder's (2007) heuristic (MFA1–3 and SSA1–3). The dashed lines represent new connections between agents (left-hand side of the figure) and processes (right-hand side of the figure) for each iteration of action-effect (center of the figure).

is a commonly used method in the research field of industrial ecology to study anthropogenic systems (i.e., human-made systems such as an urban system), comprising in-use stocks and the processes and flows that maintain and operate these stocks, from the extraction of primary materials to the disposal of waste and emissions (Fischer-Kowalski et al., 2011).

The analysis of the social system is grounded on Giddens's (1978) structuration theory, in which social structures (e.g., legislation, culture, and economic systems) affect human action, but human action itself also changes or perpetuates (intentionally or unintentionally) the social structures (Binder, 2007).

According to Binder (2007), the basis of SAA is an already-performed MFA of the system at hand. Based on this, the material system should include (i) material management goals (MFA1); (ii) identification of the main variables for changing the system (MFA2); and (iii) potential technical measures for improving the material system (MFA3) (see Figure 16.1). Similarly, the analysis of the social system consists of (i) elicitation of the agents affecting main MFA variables (SAA1); (ii) the structural factors affecting agents' decisions (SAA2); and (iii) agents' options for and constraints on change (SAA3) (Figure 16.1). Understanding interaction and feedbacks between these two systems improves material-resource management.

16.2.2 Causal Loop Diagram (CLD)

Following the definition of the key agents (SAA1), the identification of the structural factors affecting their decisions and the causal links between them makes it possible to target the "deficient" actor, factor, or process (Binder, 2007), and eventually to develop more effective management strategies. Therefore, to depict the interrelation between the structural factors affecting agents' decisions (SAA2), we developed a causal loop diagram (CLD, Figure 16.4).

CLD is a system modeling technique utilized to qualitatively explore the variables and interrelationships in a system of interest (Bala et al., 2017). It makes it possible to both analyze the current state of a system and make assumptions about its dynamic behavior. Feedback loops occur when the effect of a change propagates around the variables in a system through cause-and-effect chains, and evokes a response ("feedback") to the original change (Meadows, 2008). This response can either reinforce or oppose the original perturbation. If it reinforces the original change, it is a reinforcing loop; if it opposes the original change, it is a balancing loop. Reinforcing feedback loops generate (exponential) growth or self-reinforcing decline, amplify deviations, and reinforce change (Meadows, 2008); balancing loops lead to stabilization. System behavior is generated through the interaction of these loops and delays, the latter being responsible for making prediction difficult (Bala et al., 2017).

According to Bala and colleagues (2017), these four basic steps are followed when constructing a CLD:

1. relevant variables (explaining events, influencing problems) are identified;
2. relationships between variables are determined and connected with arrows indicating the direction of influence (positive correlation: *positive causal link* [+] / inverse correlation: *negative causal link* [–]);
3. a closed loop is formed and its type determined by the addition of the negative causal link: *Reinforcing loop* when the sum is even or 0 (marked with R), *Balancing loop* when the sum is odd (marked with B);
4. delay between variables is represented with a double line.

Among the many guidelines to follow when drawing a CLD, the definition of boundaries is key. The number of possible connections being very large, only the significant variables associated with the selected theme investigated are drawn. In the CLD proposed in this book chapter (Figure 16.4), the boundaries of the system were drawn according to the need to depict the role played by the users in the supply and demand system, and the mutual relationship between environment and society.

16.2.3 Identification of Relevant Indicators for Sustainability Assessment

In order to assess the sustainability of the housing sector, we complemented the system analysis – performed by means of the methods described above – with the selection of indicators (see Chapter 8 (Binder et al., 2020b)). To do so, we relied on the sustainability solution space methodology, steps 2 and 3 (Binder et al., 2020).

Based on our conceptualization of the housing system (Figure 16.5), we conducted a brainstorming session; we derived 40 indicators and divided them into environmental, social, and economic dimensions of sustainability. We classified them as follows:

- Indicators that affect specific actors
- Indicators that are affected by specific actors
- Life cycle (LC) stage the indicators impact (i.e., operate, construct, demolish)

To reduce their number, we ranked the indicators according to their relevance from a sustainability perspective (based on literature), on a scale of high, medium, and low. A total of 18 indicators were ranked as highly relevant. Then, a workshop with five experts from different disciplines in the area of sustainability assessment, life cycle assessment, architecture, social sciences, and economics was organized in order to validate the relevance of these indicators for the sustainability assessment of housing. Experts chosen were partners of the Swiss National Research Programme (NRP73) Shrinking Housing's Environmental Footprint (SHEF) project. As a result, 2 of the 18 indicators were replaced by other indicators not previously considered (Table 16.3).

Following the definition of the indicators, the desirable development of each from a sustainability perspective was elicited (i.e., increase ↑, decrease ↓, and stay in a range). Furthermore, the material management goals and technical measures were associated with the indicators, in order to display to what extent the indicator could monitor, influence, and/ or be influenced by their realization.

The 18 indicators were subsequently divided into the groups "operation" and "other phases" – as the operation phase is the longest and most important from an energy and carbon footprint perspective (Heeren et al., 2015) – in order to explore the interaction between the material and social systems.

16.2.4 Impact Analysis

To analyze the interrelation and trade-offs between the indicators for the material and social systems, two impact matrixes were developed (Appendix 16.A and Appendix 16.B) based on formative scenario analysis (Mißler-Behr, 1993; Scholz & Tietje, 2002) presented hereafter.[2]

The strength of the mono-directional influences between indicators was assessed for each indicator according to a predefined scale – 0 meaning no influence, 1 meaning a moderate influence, and 2 meaning a strong influence; inverse influence is indicated by a minus sign (Gordon & Hayward, 1968; Knoeri et al., 2011; Scholz & Tietje, 2002).

The resulting matrix was analyzed by summing the absolute values of the rows and columns: the sum of the absolute values of the rows indicates the activity of the indicator (influence value), and the sum of the absolute values of the columns indicates its passivity (dependence value).

The absolute activity and passivity sum for each indicator was plotted in influence grids (Figure 16.6 and Figure 16.7). Based on their position in the quadrant of the influence grid, the indicators were then classified into active, ambivalent, indifferent, and passive indicators (see Table 16.1). This classification refers to their strength and role in sustainability assessment of housing systems – the details of this procedure can be found in see Chapter 8 (Binder et al., 2020b).

Table 16.1 *Indicator types in sustainability assessment – after Knoeri, Binder, and Althau (2011) and Wiek and Binder (2005)*

Indicator type (role)	Influence value (activity sum)	Dependence value (passivity sum)
Active (driving)	High	Low
Ambivalent (key connected)	High	High
Passive (indicating)	Low	High
Indifferent (disconnected)	Low	Low

16.3 Sustainability Assessment of Housing

16.3.1 Housing and the Material System

16.3.1.1 Material Flows of Housing

In the preliminary phase of the SAA, we conceptualize the housing system as a material flow system using an MFA. Thereby, we consider that the demand for housing and city infrastructure is met by transforming raw material resources into housing stocks. Figure 16.2 presents the key processes involved in housing. Extracting raw materials and constructing refer to the *construction phase*; maintaining, operating, and refurbishing the housing stock in use refer to the *use phase*; and demolishing, recovering, and landfilling to the *end-of-life phase*. These phases drive the use of materials and energy in an urban system (Chen & Graedel, 2015; Krausmann et al., 2017). Recently, research has sought to determine material and energy use and the greenhouse gas emissions of long-lived stocks of housing and city infrastructure globally (Müller et al., 2013).

Housing demands several different types and quantities of materials. Figure 16.3 shows the development of global material stocks and flows from 1900 to 2010 for constructing, maintaining, operating, and refurbishing housing and city infrastructure stocks (solid wood, plastics, iron/steel, aluminum, copper, other metals, concrete, asphalt, bricks, and sand and gravel). The data reflect the intense period of rapid urbanization that started in the 1920s in high-income countries, when in-use stocks of materials started to accumulate. This trend is currently taking place in emerging economies, hence saturation at the global level is not in sight for at least the next 50 years (Krausmann et al., 2017). Furthermore, a higher rate of material extraction and disposal is likely to undermine environmental sustainability efforts in the future (see Box 16.1). Thus, it is of paramount importance to understand what drives the flows in the different phases and what measures might be adequate to minimize the potential negative environmental impacts of increasing demand for housing.

16.3.1.2 Material Management Goals

From an environmental sustainability perspective, the overarching goal for the material system of housing is to minimize resource consumption and environmental impacts caused by the provisioning of housing's functions,[3] in other words, the material and energy inputs

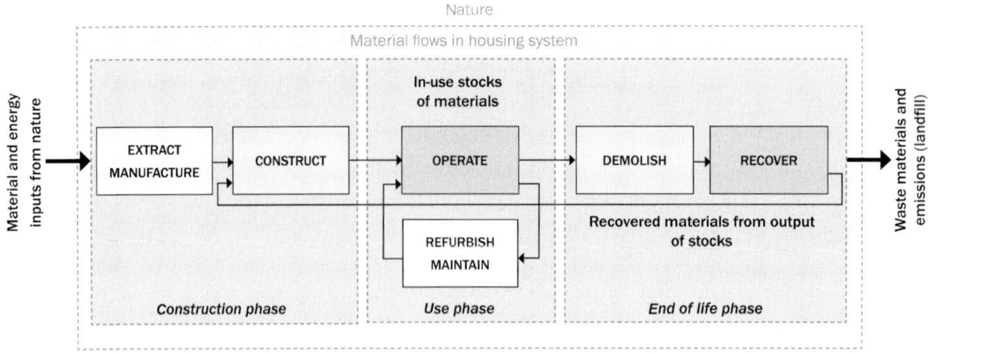

Figure 16.2 Aggregated material flows in housing system. Source: authors

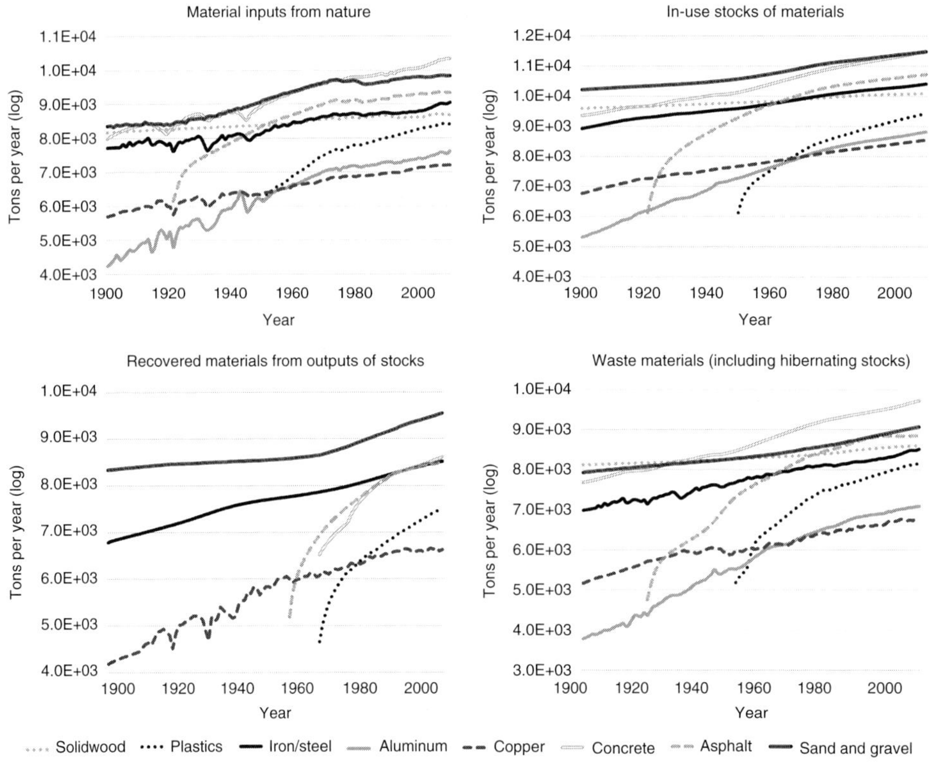

Figure 16.3 Global material extraction to satisfy the demand for services in urban systems (upper left-hand side), global in-use material stocks (upper right-hand side), recovered materials from outflows of stocks (bottom left-hand side) and waste materials (e.g., landfilled materials) (bottom right-hand side) from 1900 to 2010. Data source: Krausmann et al. (2017)

Box 16.1 **A model of the housing stock development in Switzerland**

Due to the long lifetimes of buildings and long investment cycles, decisions taken in the building sector have long-term implications, often lasting for decades or even centuries. This also affects the environmental impacts of buildings. A well-known example is heating systems: once the investment is made, the system will not be changed for many years. For example, the lifetime of an oil-heating system is between 10 and 20 years, and during this time it is very unlikely that the fuels will be switched (e.g., to renewables). Construction materials in the building sector often even have longer lifetimes. This means that materials influence the properties of a building for a long time, and the recycling or treatment of these after the use phase occurs in the far future, by which time new technological developments will have occurred and information about the building's material composition may have been lost. Efforts to reduce operational energy often involve a trade-off against the impacts of the materials used, due to the increased demand for additional insulation and other materials. As a consequence, the impacts of construction materials have steadily increased and are projected to continue doing so in the future, reaching a similar level of magnitude as energy-driven impacts from heating and cooling. Therefore, while reducing the operational energy of buildings has rightfully been a political priority in the past, the environmental impacts of materials require more attention.

To represent the long-term dynamics of decisions regarding materials and understand the inertia of the building stock, a dynamic material flow model was developed for the complete residential building stock in Switzerland (Heeren & Hellweg, 2018). This model combines three-dimensional and geo-referenced building data with information about building properties and material composition (Heeren & Hellweg, 2018). As output, the model delivers quantitative data on mass flows and stocks. Additionally, life-cycle assessment indicators were applied to quantify and assess the environmental impacts. The results show that population development is the main driver of material flows in the building stock. While currently more material is used (inflow into the building stock) than discarded (outflow), it is projected that a steady-state situation will be reached by 2050. The reason for this is reduced demand for new construction while the aging building stock leads to the constant generation of material waste due to demolition and refurbishment. Converging in- and outflows offer great potential for material recycling. A large amount of construction waste is already recycled, but this often represents a down cycling with small impact savings, which depend mainly on the substituted materials. Therefore, the proactive development of circular technologies – allowing, for example, the reuse of building components through better product design – as well as better documentation of the material composition of buildings are needed to obtain maximal environmental benefits.

Insulations materials are of particular relevance here. An important wave of first-generation insulation is expected to be discarded in the next few decades as a result of renovation activities. Around the 1970s, Switzerland experienced a construction boom and the buildings built during that period were among the first that were subject to energy-saving regulations. Although the mass flows are rather small in comparison to other construction materials, the environmental impacts are projected to account for roughly half the total greenhouse gas emissions from the production and disposal of building materials by 2050 (Heeren & Hellweg, 2018). One reason for the large impact is that flammable insulation materials are equipped with flame-retardants in trace amounts, some of which are hazardous and prevent any reuse/recycling of the entire material stream. A prominent example is the substance HBCD in expanded and extruded

Box 16.1 (cont.)

polystyrene insulation, which now falls under the Stockholm Convention on Persistent Organic Pollutants and therefore requires by law that the entire insulation material is incinerated. This example illustrates that decisions many decades ago can make it impossible to close cycles and make optimal environmental use of materials today. It is important not to repeat the mistakes of the past, but rather to develop and use materials that are low in production impacts, have energy-saving properties, and can ideally be reused or recycled after the use phase. Dynamic building models can help evaluate the future environmental benefits from such measures.

from nature and the waste and emissions to nature should be minimized as much as possible. Based on these, we derived the following three material management goals (MMGs) for the housing system:

MMG1) Reducing material use

Reducing consumption of material resources and related environmental impacts should be one of the highest priorities for the building sector. This goal starts during the design and planning phase; which is essential, since the decisions made in this phase may "lock in" the performance of the dwelling for its entire lifetime.[4] In this sense, promoting better design that weighs resource use against the needs and functionality of dwellings and considers scenarios for deconstruction is a proactive target. Project planning can ensure greater use of material-efficient products by, for example, using recycled materials, reusing existing materials, and using waste as a fuel.[5] See the discussion about material efficiency in Allwood et al. (2011).

MMG2) Decreasing GHG emissions related to energy use from a life-cycle perspective

Reducing the consumption of energy from fossil sources leads to decreasing GHG emissions. To achieve this, policies generally allocate efforts toward increasing the share and provision of renewable energy (e.g., solar, wind, hydro). It has been shown that policies focusing on energy supply to buildings are more effective than strategies focusing on energy demand from buildings. Overall, both are required to reach sustainability targets, such as those envisioned by the "2000-watt society" (Heeren et al., 2013).

MMG3) Reducing construction and demolition waste

It is traditionally recognized that construction and demolition (C&D) waste is the debris generated during the construction, renovation, and demolition of buildings, roads, and bridges, such as concrete, wood, metals, glass, and salvaged building components (Youcai & Sheng, 2017). C&D waste has come to comprise a large part of municipal solid waste since the 1990s: construction and demolition activities represent 34 percent of waste generated in the European Union according to economic activities, and mineral and solidified wastes account for 76 percent of the waste generated according to waste category (Silva et al., 2014). In Switzerland, C&D waste accounts for by far the largest fraction of total waste (around 70 percent), 85 percent of which is composed of mineral waste (FOEN, 2001; Knoeri et al., 2011).

C&D waste is the largest waste stream in the EU (European Commission, 2014). The European Commission Waste Framework Directive 2008/98/EC set the target that, by 2020, 70 percent of the construction and demolition waste should be recycled in the EU countries (European Parliament, 2008). Currently, a large number of countries in Europe recycle only about 50 percent of their C&D waste, and only a few countries (including Switzerland) have already developed and implemented a framework which leads to a recycling rate of up to 90 percent (European Commission, 2016; Hügi et al., 2008; Knoeri et al., 2014; Spoerri et al., 2009).

16.3.1.3 Technical Measures

Finally, technical measures (TMs) are set. These relate to the means (mechanisms) used to pursue the material management goals and aim to influence the main variables for changing housing systems. Here, we present a set of technical measures based on the seminal work of Allwood et al. (2011) for addressing the MMGs. These measures are applicable in the three main phases of housing shown in Figure 16.2 (construction, use, end-of-life).

Construction (MMG1, MMG2)

TM1. Using tools to estimate energy demand and environmental impacts in the planning phase. For example, one such tool is building information modeling (BIM), a 3D model-based process that helps professionals improve decision-making, as well as the performance and efficiency of buildings and infrastructures across their life cycles. Various integrated LCA solutions using BIM are being developed (Hollberg et al., 2018; Soust-Verdaguer et al., 2017). These tools are essential when the planner is required (e.g., by the Swiss label Minergie ECO) to calculate the material-related environmental impact of the building.

TM2. Applying sustainable construction methods (e.g., pre-fabrication) to avoid construction waste, emissions (dust), and general discomfort (noise, dirt), and to ensure the safety of workers (i.e., reduction of the construction waste by storing, reusing, or recycling materials or assembling prefabricated material on site; use of local construction techniques requiring less specialized expertise and enabling final users to intervene in the process, as well as reducing costs) (Akadiri et al., 2012).

TM3. Adopting efficient technologies for the extraction and processing of raw materials (energy use, CO_2 emissions etc.), which reduce the amount of embodied energy, or the energy required for mining, processing, manufacturing, and transporting (IRP, 2017).

TM4. Using recovered materials and components from output of stocks (i.e., reuse). This means using materials and building elements that have been recovered or diverted from C&D waste in the construction of new buildings (Allwood et al., 2011).

Use (MMG2)

TM5. Intensifying the use of existing stocks. This means increasing the number of residential building units within a zoned and largely constructed area. In this measure, more people will be using an existing unit of services, by, for example, sharing common spaces (Grams, 2018).

TM6. Increasing the service lifetime of the building stock. This measure actually starts in the planning phase and affects the use phase. It can relate, for example, to designing the building in a modular way to ensure that the internal layout can be modified according to changing building use over time, hence avoiding demolition (OECD, 2012).

End-of-life (MMG3)

TM7. Using sustainable demolition techniques (i.e., techniques that reduce energy consumption and emissions during the demolition phase while ensuring the recyclability of the structure and materials) (Jin et al., 2020).

TM8. Adopting separation and recovery technologies for handling C&D waste. Traditional disposal and recycling are the two pathways of C&D waste treatment nowadays, including backfilling, stacking, landfilling, sea reclamation, and road paving. No sorting or source separation is needed, and very coarse and simple crushing processes can meet the requirements of these ways of disposal. Recycling commonly includes the manufacturing of various products, which aims at turning C&D waste into regenerated resources (Youcai & Sheng, 2017).

16.3.1.4 Housing Size as a Key Variable for Changing the System

The material and energy resources used in housing systems can be influenced by a large number of variables, including housing size, design, building physics, source of energy supply, and type of construction material (Heeren et al., 2015). In this chapter, we have chosen to focus on housing size.

Housing size is a key variable encompassing both the material system (in relationship to material and energy resource use (Heeren et al., 2015)) and the social system (see Section 16.3.2.2). Three interdependent phenomena have resulted in greater attention being paid to housing size:

- As shown in Table 16.2, the size of new dwellings has been constantly increasing. Increasing dwelling size can be observed in countries like Germany, the United States, and Switzerland (Moura et al., 2015; Swiss Federal Statistical Office, 2011).
- As housing size has increased, the average household size has been decreasing, resulting in greater per capita floor space (Fries et al., 2017). In Switzerland, for instance, the number of occupants per dwelling went from 2.9 in 1970 to 2.2 in 2017 (Federal Statistical Office (FSO) data).
- While dwellings are home to smaller households, population keeps increasing (e.g., in Switzerland the population grew by more than one-third between 1970 and 2017 (UN – DESA, 2017), resulting therefore in a greater need for housing.

Table 16.2 *Comparison of historical average dwelling size in selected countries. Data source: Evans and Hartwich (2005), Swiss Federal Statistical Office (2018), United States Census Bureau (2018).*

Country	Year of construction	Average sqm	Year of construction	Average sqm
Austria*	≤ 2002	90.6	2002	96
Germany*	≤ 2002	86.7	2002	109.2
France*	≤ 2002	88	2002	112.8
Denmark*	≤ 2002	108.9	2002	137
Switzerland**	1946–60	84	2001–2005	131
USA***	in 1973	154.2	2010	226

* Average floor space of all dwellings built up to 2002 and of newly built dwellings in 2002; ** Average floor space by period of construction; *** Average floor space by period of construction of single-family dwellings.

In this context, it has been argued that the growth of one-person households will lead to an increase in the resource consumption for domestic use (energy, land, and household goods), as well as in waste production (Williams, 2006). Therefore, decreasing dwellings' size has strong potential to reduce material use (MMG1), energy use and emissions (MMG2), and C&D waste (MMG3) (Clune et al., 2012; Williams, 2006; Wilson & Boehland, 2008).

16.3.2 Housing and the Social System

The residential environment has been defined as a "complex set of physical structures and processes that are mutually defined by sets of supply and demand factors" (Lawrence, 2004, p. 6). Following the structural agent analysis (SAA) method (Binder, 2007), this section presents the relevant actors as well as their relationships (SAA1), the factors influencing their decisions (SAA2), and hypotheses regarding the path to change, including options and constraints (SAA3). It focuses on housing size, this time in relationship to the social system.

16.3.2.1 Agents Affecting Main Variables (SAA1)

As multidisciplinary assemblages (Berardi, 2012), buildings are today the result of the interaction between a multiplicity of actors such as engineers, architects, and constructors (what Knoeri and colleagues (2014) define as a "complex socio-technical system"). Being responsible for decisions regarding the demand and supply of dwellings, these actors affect, at different stages, the key variables of the housing sector presented in Section 16.3.1.4. Their diversity, as well as the degree of complexity of their interactions, has increased over time. If, in pre-industrial societies, "unspoken" but "rigidly maintained" rules used to govern the construction of vernacular houses, after the Industrial Revolution explicit design intentions were directly translated into material forms. Supported by the ease of using new materials and technologies, this translation required more specialized professions

(Lawrence, 1987a): the once "user-client-designer-builder" became a multiplicity of actors such as the client (represented by different institutions or committees – i.e., governments, private corporations, companies, benevolent societies); the designers (architects, engineers, and other related professions); the building contractors; and the users (who range from the owners to the landlords, tenants, and occupants).

Because of this large fragmentation, the requirements and expectations of these actors do not always coincide (Lawrence, 1987a). However, to promote socially acceptable planning, the setup of alternatives by architects and the choices made by clients tend to be subordinated to the representations of users' needs. Furthermore, by choosing to move in or out, users' preferences and needs still shape the demand and, consequently, the supply. Therefore, given the dominant role of housing size in the material system, it is critical to study final users, their relationships and exchanges with other actors in the building sector, and their demand for living space (Heeren, 2017).

16.3.2.2 Structural Factors Affecting Agents' Decisions (SAA2)

If we are to acknowledge the current complexity of interactions between agents and their networks, and also to understand the relationship between these interactions and resource use and sustainability, it is necessary to think with a systems perspective. In this context, previous research has been carried out on the role played by cultural, societal, and socioeconomic factors in the regulation of the design patterns of houses (Belcher & Vazquez-Calcerrada, 1972), and more specifically on the way certain structural factors affect the decision-making processes of architects and civil engineers (Knoeri et al., 2011; Knoeri et al., 2014; Spoerri et al., 2009). Starting from these premises, the following section focuses on understanding the dynamics of different factors affecting housing size.

Figure 16.4 explains the user's decision about the size of their dwelling, considering the social structure, households' behavior, and environmental responses. Following the method presented in Section 16.2.2, the main causal links between structural factors are displayed in a CLD where the key actors are inscribed into a system of relationships (with clients, architects, and experts through information, markets, and technical measures).

Users decide on the size of their dwelling according to what is available and according to trends. On the one hand, the existing offer limits the range of options that actors can choose from. On the other hand, the market shapes the expectations of the households, who consider a dwelling "large" or "small" according to the context they live in (e.g., in an American town with a large number of individual houses, what is considered a large house in Hong Kong might appear very small). Therefore, the larger the available dwellings, the larger the size of the chosen house will be. Considering the reciprocal relationship between demand and supply, the size of dwelling chosen by households will, after a time lag and above a certain threshold, have an impact on the market, increasing the offer of large houses to meet the needs of stakeholders (reinforcing loop R1).

Aside from the market, different "situational factors" (Friege et al., 2016) affect the expectations that households have about the size of their future dwelling.

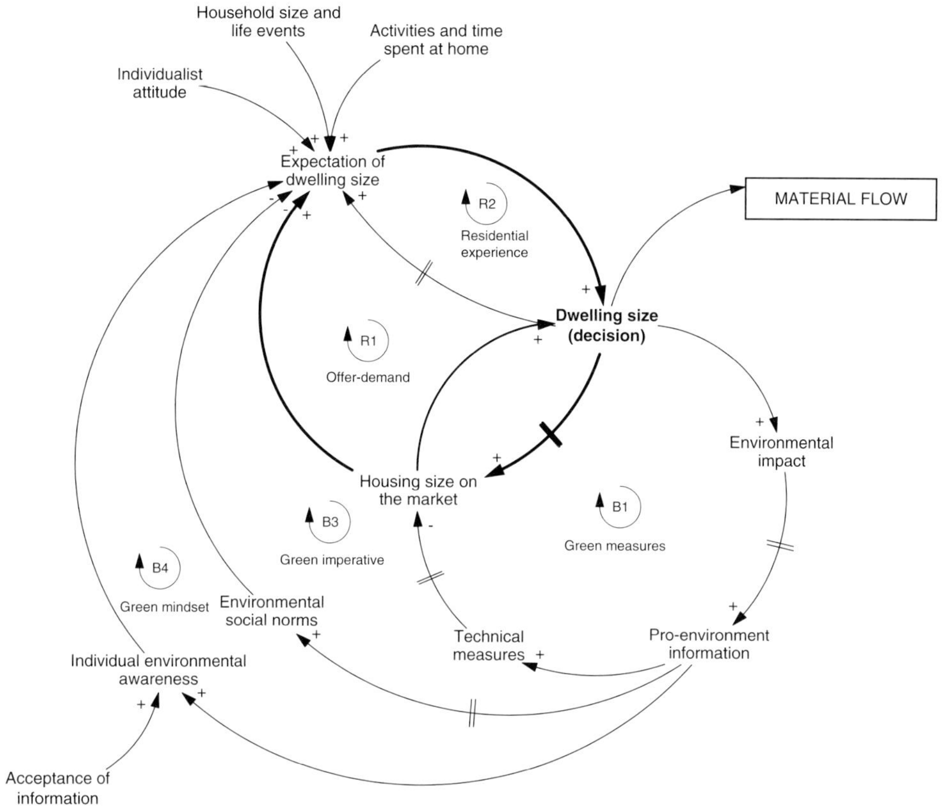

Figure 16.4 Causal loop diagram representing the structural factors affecting actors' decision regarding the size of their house, and their relationships. Source: authors

First, the number of people in a household often determines the space needed: life events such as divorces or the loss of the partner, together with long-term plans such as the preparation for ageing, might result in people moving (if possible) to smaller apartments, while the arrival of a new family member, or plans to expand the family, can lead to the opposite (e.g., in order to have a room for the newborn).[6]

Second, postmodern individualist culture – based on wealth, the economic capability to live alone, an ageing population, and market adaptations – is supporting an increment in the share of single-person households (Williams, 2006) (e.g., the number of these households is projected to increase by 34 percent between 2005 and 2030, according to the Bundesamt für Statistik (2008)).

Last, the increasing number of desired functions that dwellings should fulfill (Belcher & Vazquez-Calcerrada, 1972) also results in a greater need for space: in poorer countries the lack of technology prevents the privatization of domestic life, encouraging the use of shared facilities and increasing the time spent in communities, while in developed countries 80–90 percent of the day is spent in built environments, mostly at home (World Health

Organization (WHO), 2010). As an example, in the US, the lower classes entertain mostly in bars or outside locations, while the upper classes distinguish themselves by opening their doors to friends (Belcher and Vazquez-Calcerrada (1972)). Through domestication (or the integration of technology into households) (Støa & Aune, 2012), the diffusion of the internet, and the rise of social networks, interactions, sports activities, gaming, and even studying and working now happen in private dwellings. The more activities are carried out at home, the larger the space needed to conduct them. An increase in household size, in individualist attitudes, and in the number of activities and time spent at home eventually cultivate the expectation of a larger dwelling and determine the appliances, the furniture, and therefore the space needed.

With a time delay, when making a new choice, a household will reshape its expectations based on past residential experience (Lawrence, 1987b) (reinforcing loop R2): as with the market, past residential experience has an influence on how a "large" or "small" dwelling is defined.

The chosen dwelling size – which is related to the social and economic factors previously presented – has direct consequences on the environment in terms of energy consumption and land use: compared to an equivalent-quality space, a larger dwelling increases the need for lighting or heating, while the reduction of housing size represents a good opportunity to reduce sprawl (EEA & FOEN, 2016).

The increasing need for energy and land shape the outcomes of scientific research and concerns: the more relevant environmental concerns are, the more information on pro-environmental measures will be spread. It can be assumed that such information reaches three distinct sectors: institutions, society, and individuals. First, the technical measures adopted as a consequence of this information are aimed at regulating housing size through standards (e.g., the Swiss system of housing evaluation SEL[7] reflects changes in floor-space trends over time, recommending minimum and maximum areas). These "green measures" affect the dwellings available on the market, both by suggesting a preferable choice (assigning a greater value to more sustainable dwellings) and by imposing constraints. These changes will happen with a delay in time, related to construction, renovation, and large-scale diffusion, but will ultimately reduce the environmental impact of housing (balancing loop B1).

Second, the production and diffusion of pro-environmental information can lead to the reshaping, in time, of social norms: a green imperative raises public awareness and inculcates the responsibility to contribute to the well-being of the planet (Lovell, 2004). These new social norms change expectations of house size, and eventually housing design, through a balancing loop (B3).

Last, environmental concerns can increase individual awareness, leading to the shaping of a green mindset (B4). However, this happens only if the information campaign is socially accepted, and in line with status quo development and aspirations. In that case, expectations will be recalibrated, leading to more sustainable decisions.

In summary, housing size affects and is affected by a multiplicity of factors (standards, markets, dwelling characteristics, users' characteristics, and expectations). These structural factors are themselves shaped by the interactions between users, clients, architects, and all the actors involved in the process. The final decisions made by users will eventually impact the design, construction, use, and end-of-life of the dwelling: in other words, the material flow.

16.3.2.3 Options and Constraints for Change (SAA3)

Based on the analysis of the role of key actors, as well as the structural factors determining final decisions (Figure 16.4), we reflect on the constraints and options that restrict or enable the reduction of housing's environmental footprint.

Options – Awareness

Information plays an important role in shaping users' expectations. Normative messages, social media, advertizing, knowledge, and training, together with "awareness occasions" (occasions that offer the possibility to spread knowledge and, conversely, to learn) represent crucial phases for the acceptance of new solutions and the reshaping of expectations. The relevance of knowledge diffusion goes in two directions: on the one hand, to raise awareness of environmental issues; on the other hand, to identify and propose new options that might be unknown (e.g., the Swiss micro-apartments of *iLiveSchweiz* or *MICRO*). On this matter, as shown in the work of Knoeri and colleagues (2014), the scenarios simulating the effect of increased awareness on the part of actors (i.e., the probability of considering certain options based on information campaigns) have proven to lead to the highest reuse of construction and demolition waste (Knoeri et al., 2014). However, information needs to be socially acceptable and coherent and not interfere with people's values and culture: sometimes campaigns (e.g., informing people about laws and standards, or promoting sustainable behaviors or the adoption of new solutions) might even increase the undesirable behaviors and misperceptions they aim at decreasing (Schultz et al., 2007).

Constraints – Failure of system thinking

Preferences are the outcomes of decision-making processes, which engage system thinking and the consequent systemic errors: action-oriented, stability, perception, judgment, or framing-of-alternatives biases call for broader thinking (Beshears & Gino, 2015). As an example, the tendency to adopt quick satisfactory decisions (requiring less effort and less information) can lead, as reported by Sterman (2006), to the confusion of the size of a home with its quality. Neglecting to understand the relationships between factors, and especially the delayed impact – in other words, the failure of system thinking – represents a constraint in a sector whose outcomes have a long life, but also a long incubation period (from the programming phase to demolition).

To conclude, a deeper understanding of system elements and their interconnections (i.e., the key actors (SAA1), the structural factors (SAA2), and the way they affect housing size (CLD Figure 16.4) is crucial to achieving the material management goals (MMG1, MMG2, MMG3). More specifically, action could be taken by, for example, housing providers, offering smaller but flexible layouts that are able to accommodate changing lifestyles and offer shared spaces for activities while preserving privacy (e.g., in the cooperatives *Mehr als Wohnen, Kraftwerk*, or *CODHA* (Pattaroni & Marmy, 2016)). These solutions would need to be combined with greater information concerning the environmental impact of housing size in terms of material use (MMG1), energy use and emissions (MMG2), and

C&D waste (MMG3). Furthermore, the computer simulation of the dynamics of the social system would allow for the simulating of scenarios of change, based on which tools could be designed and provided to decision-makers and stakeholders to assess the feasibility and acceptability of future technical measures (TMs).

16.3.3 An Integrated System Model

Based on these analyses, we present an integrated system model for the sustainability assessment of housing (Figure 16.5), following the structured analysis and design technique (SADT) notation (Marca & McGowan, 1988). In this system model, the role played by each actor (the social system) is linked to each phase of the dwelling's life cycle (the material system). This life cycle starts long before construction begins.

First, needs or opportunities for new housing and housing services are identified in the programming phase (*Program* – see Figure 16.5). This phase falls under the responsibility of the owner, who represents the main decision-maker. However, the "client-owner" may not have enough expertise to set the goals, and may need a consultant (programmer). Furthermore, sometimes "client-users" (Cherry & Petronis, 2016) are involved in a so-called participatory process.

Once objectives, requirements, and strategies (i.e., flexibility, security, functions, space) have been formulated, the development of a plan can start: the plan contains specifications for construction, or in some cases refurbishment (*Plan*, *Refurbish / Maintain*). Plans need to follow codes and standards that have been acknowledged during the programming phase (minimum floor area per person, facilities, etc.). The growing use of new technologies and software (like building information modeling, or BIM) by architects, engineers, and other experts allows for an interactive process and the making of predictions regarding energy, costs, schedule, and materials, in line with the client's requirements. Depending on these specifications, different quantities and types of materials and semi-finished products are extracted from the earth's biosphere (*Extract*, *Manufacture*), involving different companies according to the desired material (or product).

The dwelling is then built by, for example, construction companies or building contractors according to codes and standards that regulate the construction process (*Construct*). Different construction methods are employed according to geographical location, type of project, company, material requirements, and the desires of the client.

The dwelling is then occupied (*Operate*) by the final users, sometimes through an intermediary, such as the owner or a building management agency. It receives regular maintenance (through users' independent interventions, or after the approval of the building manager) and is eventually refurbished according to the client-owner's decisions, based on long-term plans and projections.

Once the dwelling becomes obsolete, owners, experts, and demolition contractors are responsible for its demolition, retrofitting, or conversion (*Demolish*, *Recover*). Building materials and elements are recovered when possible to be reused in new constructions by

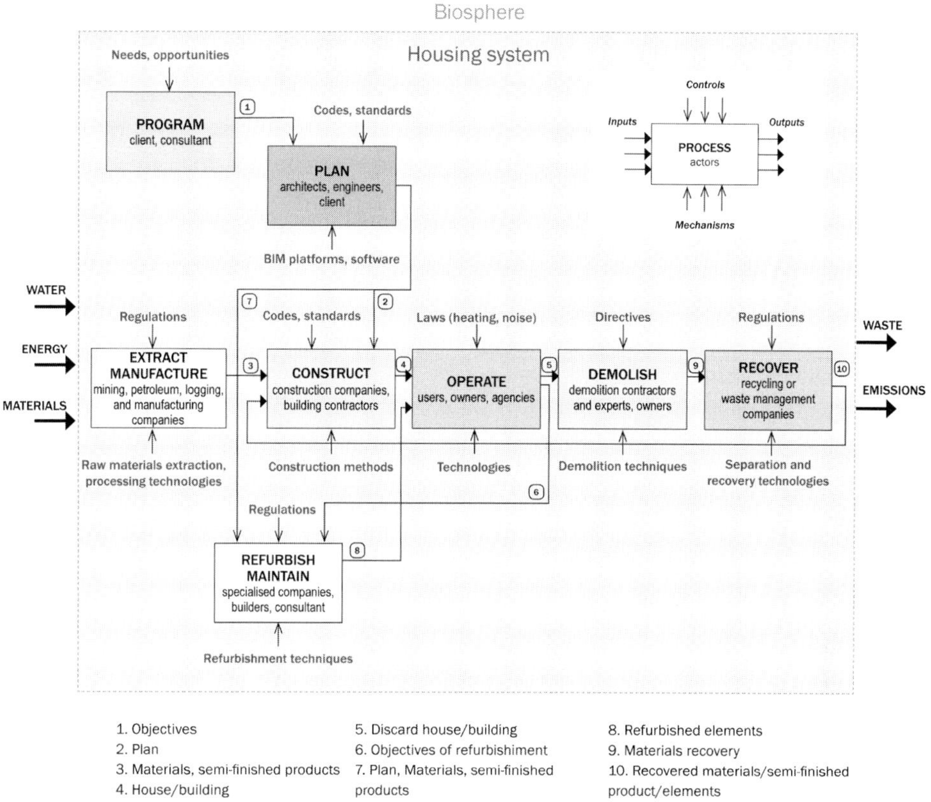

Figure 16.5 System model showing main activities, material flows, and actors in a housing system. Each activity in the diagram is divided into five parts: (1) inputs of materials to an activity; (2) controls, which are factors that constrain and orient an activity toward a specific direction; (3) mechanisms, as tools (also human resources) used to produce outputs; (4) outputs, that represent the result(s) of an activity; (5) actors involved in the activities. Energy, water, and materials coming from the earth biosphere enter the system, are used, and exit the system, returning to the biosphere in form of waste (solid, liquid, gaseous, heat) and emissions (to soil, air, water). This diagram follows the structured analysis and design technique (SADT) notation (Marca & McGowan, 1987). Source: authors

recycling companies, or sent to landfills or to incineration by waste-management companies. All these processes are individually regulated by controls (e.g., codes, standards, regulations, directives) and enabled by mechanisms (e.g., platforms, technologies, methods).

As shown in Figure 16.1, energy (electricity and fuels) and water are consumed and emissions and waste produced in varying amounts during all of the processes (phases). The production and use of energy, water, and materials and the discharge of waste and emissions into the natural environment (biosphere) to fulfill the different demands of users in each of these phases cause some sort of disturbance (impact) on the natural environment.

16.4 Indicators and Their Interaction in the Housing System

Based on and embedded into a systemic view, indicators make it possible to monitor the progress of the housing sector and anticipate potential sustainability problems. In line with the system model displayed in the previous section (Figure 16.5), we propose a list of 18 indicators (Table 16.3). Each of the indicators is relevant to one or more life-cycle stages (i.e., *Construct, Operate, Demolish, etc.*).

16.4.1 The Operation Phase

Figure 16.6 shows the influence grid depicting the relevance of the selected indicators related to the operation phase. *Attitudes towards sustainability measures*, *Information and awareness*, *Shared space*, *Flexibility and adaptability*, and *Indoor comfort* are the social indicators driving the system in the operation phase. On the environmental side, the indicator *Share of renewable energy* also has an influence on the other indicators in the

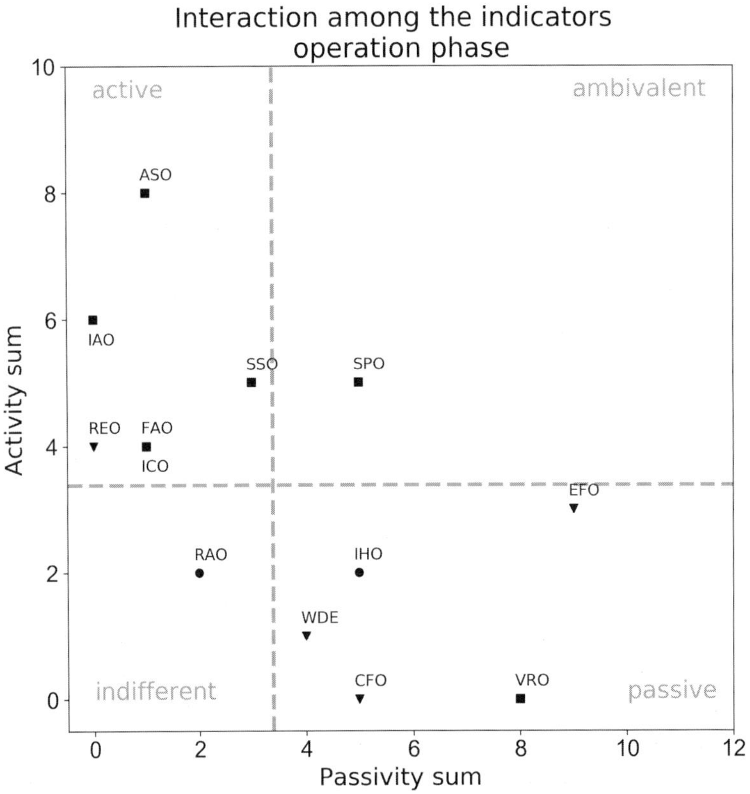

Figure 16.6 Influence grid of the indicators related to the operation phase. Codes correspond to the indicators as shown by Table 16.3. Triangle symbols represent environmental indicators, dot symbols economic indicators, and square symbols social indicators. The two dotted-lines axes cross at the average value of the activity and passivity of the indicators. Source: authors

Table 16.3 *Selected indicators for sustainability assessment of housing. DD: desired development. Source: authors' investigation*

ACTIVE AND PASSIVE ACTORS	SUST. DIMENSION	CODE	INDICATORS	LC STAGES	MMG/TM	UNIT	DEFINITION	DD
Client	Economic	ROI	Return on investment	All phases	All MMG	%	(Gain from investment – Cost of investment) / Cost of investment	↑
Users, agencies	Economic	RAO	Rent affordability	Operate	None	%	(Household income / Qualifying income) x100	↑
Users, architects, engineers	Economic	IHO	Income spent on housing operation and maintenance	Operate	None	%	% of income spent by the final users on the operation (rent, consumption) and maintenance	↓
Client, architects, engineers	Environmental	LUC	Land use	Construct	MMG1	m^2 / pp	Size of parcel including dwelling complex / Size of household	↓
Users, clients, architects, engineers	Environmental	EFO EFM	End energy footprint	Operate Materials	MMG1–2	MJ x pp / yr	Operation: energy (for heating) and electricity consumption per person per year. Materials: energy used to produce and manufacture the building materials	↓
Users, clients, architects, engineers	Environmental	REO REM	Share of renewable energy	Operate Materials	MMG1–2	%	Operation and materials: Renewable energy / Total energy used	↑
Users, clients, architects, engineers	Environmental	WDE	Water demand	Operate	None	liters x pp / yr	Liters of fresh water used per person per year in a household in the operation phase	↓
No actors (output)	Environmental	CFO CFM	Carbon footprint	Operate Materials	MMG2	kg CO_2 eq.	Operation: greenhouse gas emissions from the energy used in the operate phase. Materials: greenhouse gas emissions from the energy consumed in producing the building materials	↓
Users, architects, engineers	Environmental	RMC	Use of recovered materials and components	Construct	MMG1, TM4	%	Percentage of recovered materials and elements used in a new dwelling	↑
Construction and demolition contractors	Environmental	MFR	Materials for recycling	Demolish	MMG3, TM7–8	%	Percentage of materials of a demolished dwelling sent for recycling	↑

clients) and in turn influence the passive indicators such as *End energy footprint* and *Carbon footprint* (Appendix 16.B). There are several indifferent indicators that are relevant for the respective phases but are not well integrated into the system itself. These are *Stakeholder participation*, *Return on investment*, and *Materials for recycling*.

16.4.3 Comparison of Phases

When comparing the two influence grids of Figure 16.6 and Figure 16.7, we observe the following:

- The environmental indicators are predominantly passive in all phases. They are therefore useful for monitoring the system (e.g., the choices made in housing design). However, the indicator *Share of renewable energy* drives the system in the operation phase with an activity sum score of 4. In fact, this indicator has been selected to capture how variations in the choice of heating systems can influence the energy and carbon footprint.
- Social indicators are predominantly active. *Information and awareness* as well as *Attitudes towards sustainability measures* are drivers of the system in all phases. Strategies which focus on these indicators therefore have the potential to influence the system. Furthermore, in the operation phase, the active indicators *Flexibility and adaptability, Indoor comfort*, and *Shared spaces* influence a set of other relevant variables related to users' satisfaction. Therefore, it becomes clear that the dwelling design also ensures the social sustainability of the housing system.
- Similarly to *Carbon footprint, Vacancy rate* is a passive indicator in the operation phase (score of 8 in the passivity sum). In fact, comfort, price, and affordability (the active indicators) determine whether the household will rent the dwelling or not. Strategies to reduce vacancies must therefore focus on the drivers of the system and, as mentioned, the dwelling design.
- From the operation to the other phases, the indicator *Space per person* changes from ambivalent (score of 5 for activity and 5 for passivity) to passive (3 for activity and 1 for passivity). This shift is related to the importance that space per person plays in the operation phase, in relation to the rent paid and the percentage of income spent on housing, as well as the services that can be shared. In the other phases, space per person only influences *Land use*, and is influenced by environmental concerns, which, as presented earlier, might impact the reduction of housing size.
- All the economic indicators are mostly indifferent (activity and passivity sum between 0 and 2), with the expectation of *Income spent on housing operation and maintenance* (2 for activity and 5 for passivity). However, these indicators play an important role in the decisional process of investors and users and therefore in both the achievement of the MMG and the implementation of the TM. Their low systemic relevance brings about further reflection on potential strategies that integrate economic factors in the conceptualization of the housing system.
- Last, since the average influence value of the indicators differs for each matrix, the activity, ambivalence, passivity and indifference of the indicators are defined by different

threshold values. The location of the indicator on the grid needs therefore to be considered in relationship to the system. For most of the indicators, the influence is rather weak compared to the potential that information and awareness have in driving the system (e.g., during the construction or demolition phases).

16.5 Implications for Sustainability Assessment

This section summarizes the analyses presented above and sets out their implications for sustainability assessment. For doing so, we use the assessment framework presented in Chapter 1 (Halla and Binder, 2020) and show how this can be implemented for the case of housing. Thereby, we include the three key dimensions of the sustainability assessment process: the normative, systemic, and procedural dimensions as proposed in the SSP (Binder, et al., 2020; Halla & Binder, 2020). Table 16.4 illustrates the different steps and methods to be taken when performing a sustainability assessment of the housing sector. It can be seen that the different steps are interrelated and that some methods might be applied within different steps.

Table 16.4 *Translation of the assessment framework presented in Chapter 1 (Halla & Binder, 2020) to housing focusing on the assessment process itself*

Dimension	Topic	Application to housing
Normative	Concrete goals	• Set the material management goal based on the heuristic of Binder (2007)
	Trade-offs and synergies	Identify trade-offs at different scales: • in the material system (e.g., shifting from use to the material impact) • in the social system (e.g., individualist culture *versus* environmental awareness) Identify synergies: • drivers that influence similar indicators and variables (see influence matrix) • actors with similar goals and time frames for action
	Assessment process	• Identify the sustainability ranges (upper and/or lower boundary) or targets for each indicator • Analyze which group of actors should be included in the assessment process • Develop weighting schemes reflecting the normative perspective of groups of actors
Systemic	Conceptualization	• Apply the heuristic of Binder (2007) to understand the feedbacks between material and social systems • Follow the SADT to identify the processes, inputs, outputs, controls, and mechanisms in a system model, and in addition SSA to identify actors involved and the relevant institutional settings • Apply a causal loop diagram (CLD) to identify the relationship between the determinants of decisions

Table 16.4 (*cont.*)

	Choice of tools and/ or indicators	• Select the indicators based on the conceptual framework, the causal loop diagram, and the material management goals. • Set up an impact matrix to represent the relationship between indicators • Model the relevant processes (Box 16.1), depending on the need of the analysis
	Technical management of tools/indicators	• Classify the indicators into active, ambivalent, indifferent, and passive indicators referring to their strength and role in the sustainability assessment of housing systems
Procedural	Stakeholder participation	Think of a participatory process when: • Critically reflecting on the material management goals • Defining the indicators • Filling in the impact matrix • Setting the weights of the indicators for a multi-criteria assessment
	Design of process	In the designing the process, we suggest drawing on different methodologies depending on the focus of the assessment. Thus, we suggest including the SAA heuristics (Binder, 2007), the structured analysis and design technique (SADT) notation (McGowan & Marca, 1988), and last, the impact matrix (Scholz & Tietje, 2002), including stakeholders depending on the goal of the assessment
	Feedback and learning	Information for policymakers and social learning should be facilitated by the identification of the key actors involved in the process and the structural factors affecting the material flow (as well as the mechanisms and controls facilitating or preventing the achievement of goals)

16.5.1 Conditions of the Assessment, Context, and Trade-Offs

When assessing the sustainability of housing, the system context has to be considered and may play a crucial role in setting targets and sustainability ranges (see Chapter 2 (Binder et al., 2020)). This becomes clear when one analyses the indicators identified. For example, the indicator *Space per person* can monitor increasing spaciousness as well as a desire to decrease crowdedness. This results in two very different goals: on the one hand, shrinking floor space per person, and on the other hand, providing populations with *adequate* housing (UNHCR & UN-Habitat, 2012). In this context, what might be considered sustainable space per person from a social point of view is highly dependent on the boundary conditions: the customs, codes, and regulations, as well as the meanings assigned to housing (e.g., social status, shelter, uniqueness of the occupant, affiliations with community) which might differ from country to country (Belcher & Vazquez-Calcerrada, 1972; Gauvain & Altman, 1982; Lawrence, 1987b).

The different uses and values also imply contrasting definitions of comfort (Støa & Aune, 2012). Furthermore, when studying the energetic needs of a dwelling, one could also argue that how warm or how cold a place should be is dependent on the external climatic conditions (see discussion in Yang et al., 2014).[8] Thus, including the boundary conditions of the assessment is relevant for the interpretation of the results obtained (Table 16.4).

16.5.2 Stakeholder Involvement

The conceptual approach – looking at the life cycle of a building – presented in this chapter, scrutinizes the different activities, material flows, and actors involved across the lifetime of a building. When carrying out the sustainability assessment of either the use phase or the planning phase, different actors should be involved. What becomes clear from our analysis is that including potential users at a very early stage might increase the *social sustainability* and the *acceptability* of the building.[9] This is because users can bring their specific needs and values into the planning and design process itself. When coupling this with an in-depth knowledge of construction and resource use, as well as the potential technical measures that can be taken, a building can be planned, built, and hopefully used in a more sustainable way.

16.5.3 Dynamics of the Material and Social Systems: Systemic View

The central feature of the housing system lies in its dynamics. Our analysis showed that initial decisions in planning might lead to lock-ins with regard to the consumption of materials and energy resources. This is shown more precisely by Box 16.1, where a dynamic material flow model is developed to represent the long-term dynamics of decisions about materials and to understand the inertia of the building stock. Understanding the dynamics of the system thus supports the evaluation of the achievement of the material management goals.

Regarding the social dynamics, other tools such as the causal loop diagram in Figure 16.4 make visible the delays between decisions and their implications and potential changes. Thus, if we are to assess the sustainability of the housing sector, we need to consider these aspects (see also Chapter 2 (Binder et al., 2020) and Chapter 5 (Schilling et al., 2020)). Our indicators *Information and awareness* and *Attitudes towards sustainability measures* allow us to grasp social dynamics and conceptualize them over time. However, it has to be considered that the indicators themselves deliver only a snapshot. Models looking at the dynamics of the system over time as presented in Box 16.1 will be essential for assessing the development of housing over time. This means that these models should allow for the assessment of ex-ante potential sustainability issues that might emerge in the planning stage of the housing sector. A typical question that should be considered is *how can we consider path dependencies (historic developments) when interpreting the sustainability of the present situation and possible future system states?*

16.5.4 Policy Relevance: Drivers

The set of indicators proposed in this chapter already includes the related actors and is structured into the drivers of the system, interlinked indicators, monitoring indicators, and the buffering ones. This enables the design of policy measures specifically addressing the responsible actors, who drive the system. Thus, aspects related to policy are already included and we can increase the capacity of system actors to adapt and manage the transition process toward a more sustainable housing system (see also Chapter 5 (Schilling et al., 2020)). We also have to study the system context when designing the different policies, as the latter might be more or less effective depending on the social, cultural, and climatic contexts. A question to be considered would be *how can the indicators flow back into the decision-making system?*

16.6 Conclusion

This chapter focused on the housing sector as a relevant component of the urban system. It *explored the complex interplay between the material system (materials and energy resources used in housing systems) and the social system (decision-making rules used in housing systems)*. We combined different methodological approaches, which allowed us to couple the material perspective with the decision-making processes of different actors. Thereby, we provided a holistic view of the housing sector, supporting an integrative sustainability assessment.

By representing the relationships between the material and social systems we explored the interdependencies between the material management goals and the social options and constraints that affect whether these are achieved, in the context of shrinking housing size.

Our analyses showed that decisions in the early stages of the life cycle of buildings – i.e., the programming and planning phases – determine not only the future environmental performance of a building, but also social aspects such as comfort and acceptability (addressing RQ1 and RQ2).

Furthermore, our results suggest that indicators related to the social system, such as *Information and awareness* and *Attitudes towards sustainability measures* tend to drive the system, whereas environmental indicators such as *Carbon footprint* and *End energy footprint* are passive indicators showing the impact of the overall system on the environment. They are adequate for monitoring the system development (addressing RQ3 and RQ4).

Finally, when aiming to interpret the sustainability assessment itself, we consider that the following aspects are essential: (i) an underlying knowledge of the system, including the dynamics of physical and social processes as well as the actors affecting them; (ii) an understanding of the context and boundary conditions of the system; and (iii) an understanding of the different normative views of the actors involved.

Future studies are needed to further develop and validate the applicability and effectiveness of the proposed approach and to better combine the social with the material dynamics. Furthermore, we propose to use the presented approach not only for analyzing and assessing the current state of the housing system, but also for governing it. This represents an important contribution toward addressing the pressing need for shrinking the environmental footprint of housing in a rapidly changing and urbanizing world.

Notes

1. Examples are the buildings designed according to the Swiss Sustainable Building Standard SNBS of the NNBS (Sustainable Construction Network Switzerland) and the Certification System of the DGNB (German Sustainable Building Council), which place equal emphasis on the environmental, social and economic aspects of sustainability.
2. For more details, see Chapter 8 (Binder et al., 2020b).
3. Referring to system thinking, the system's *function* or *purpose* plays a crucial role: despite the *elements* and *interconnections* remaining unchanged, a change in the system's function can profoundly affect its behavior (Meadows, 2008). In the context of housing, dwellings can have different functions that go from the basic provision of a *shelter* to a *status symbol* (Belcher & Vazquez-Calcerrada, 1972). Just as systems can be nested within systems, additional functions are nested in the presented functions (e.g., sleeping, eating, having friends at home, playing an instrument), whose provision results in environmental impacts as presented in the paragraph.
4. Examples of lock-ins would be, for instance, a façade orientation that inhibits the energy-efficient operation of a building, or the adoption of a particular technology that, over time, becomes obsolete and whose replacement might not be financially feasible – see Box 16.1.
5. Material efficiency means providing the same unit of service with less material and energy input.
6. Non-profit owners have been applying apartment occupancy rules, which match the size of households with the size of dwellings (Blumer, 2012).
7. Système d'évaluation de logements, www.wbs.admin.ch/fr.
8. In this regard, the so-called adaptive thermal models are implemented in a number of building codes.
9. It is important to note that we are discussing here the "social sustainability" of the dwelling. In fact, the indicator *Stakeholder participation* is identified as neither passive nor active (see Figure 16.6 and Figure 16.7). The participation of users in the design of building does not necessarily imply a reduction of energy consumption or a choice of recycled materials, which is rather fostered by the diffusion of information and awareness. Therefore, it is the combination of information and user participation that can have a strong influence on a building's sustainability.

References

Akadiri, P. O., Chinyio, E. A., & Olomolaiye, P. O. (2012). Design of a sustainable building: A conceptual framework for implementing sustainability in the building sector. *Buildings*, 2(2), 126–152. https://doi.org/10.3390/buildings2020126.

Allwood, J. M., Ashby, M. F., Gutowski, T. G., & Worrell, E. (2011). Material efficiency: A white paper. *Resources, Conservation and Recycling*, 55(3), 362–381. https://doi.org/https://doi.org/10.1016/j.resconrec.2010.11.002.

Baccini, P., & Brunner, P. H. (2012). *Metabolism of the Anthroposphere: Analysis, Evaluation, Design* (2nd edition). Cambridge, MA: MIT Press.

Bala, B. K., Arshad, F. M., & Noh, K. M. (2017). Causal Loop Diagrams, 37–51. https://doi.org/10.1007/978-981-10-2045-2_3.

Belcher, J. C., & Vazquez-Calcerrada, P. B. (1972). A cross-cultural approach to the social functions of housing. *Journal of Marriage and Family*, 34(4), 750–761. www.jstor.org/stable/350328.

Berardi, U. (2012). Sustainability assessment in the construction sector: Rating systems and rated buildings. *Sustainable Development*, 20(6), 411–424. https://doi.org/10.1002/sd.532.
Beshears, J., & Gino, F. (2015). Leaders as decision architects. *Harvard Business Review, 2015*(May). https://doi.org/102262149.
Binder, C. R. (2007). From material flow analysis to material flow management. Part II: the role of structural agent analysis. *Journal of Cleaner Production*, 15(17), 1605–1617. https://doi.org/10.1016/j.jclepro.2006.08.017.
Binder, C. R, Hutter, M., Pang, M., & Webb, R. (2020). System science and sustainability assessment. In C. R. Binder, E. Massaro, & R. Wyss (eds.), *Sustainability Assessment in Urban Systems*. Cambridge University Press, pp. 30–64.
Binder, C. R., Baldi, M. G., Gex, B., & Massaro, E. (2020b). The sustainability solution space. In C. R. Binder, E. Massaro, & R. Wyss (eds.), *Sustainability Assessment in Urban Systems*. Cambridge University Press, pp. 181–208.
Blumer, D. (2012). Vermietungskriterien der Gemeinnützigen Wohnbauträger in der Schweiz. Eine Studie zur Anwendung von Belegungsvorgaben und Einkommenslimiten bei 1000 gemeinnützigen Wohnbauträgern. BWO. www.bwo.admin,ch/dokumentation.
Brunner, P. H., & Rechberger, H. (2005). *Practical Handbook of Material Flow Analysis*. New York: Lewis Publishers.
Brunner, P., & Rechberger, H. (2017). *Handbook of Material Flow Analysis: For Environmental, Resource, and Waste Engineers* (2nd edition). Boca Raton: CRC Press.
Bundesamt für Statistik. (2008). Haushaltsszenarien – Entwicklung der Privathaushalte zwischen 2005 und 2030. *BSF Aktuell*, 1–12.
Chen, W.-Q., & Graedel, T. E. (2015). In-use product stocks link manufactured capital to natural capital. *Proceedings of the National Academy of Sciences*, 112(20), 6265–6270. https://doi.org/10.1073/pnas.1406866112.
Cherry, E., & Petronis, J. (2016). Architectural Programming. www.wbdg.org/design-disciplines/architectural-programming.
Clune, S., Morrissey, J., & Moore, T. (2012). Size matters: House size and thermal efficiency as policy strategies to reduce net emissions of new developments. *Energy Policy*, 48, 657–667. https://doi.org/10.1016/j.enpol.2012.05.072.
EEA & FOEN. (2016). *Urban Sprawl in Europe*. https://doi.org/10.1002/9780470692066.
European Commission. (2014). *Communication from the Commission to the European Parliament, the Council, the European Economic and Social Committee and the Committee of the Regions on resource efficiency opportunities in the building sector*. Brussels.
European Commission. (2016). *EU Construction and Demolition Waste Protocol*. Brussels.
European Parliament. (2008). Directive 2008/98/EC of the European Parliament and of the Council of 19 November 2008 on Waste and Repealing Certain Directives (Text with EEA relevance). *Official Journal of the European Union*.
Evans, A. W., & Hartwich, O. M. (2005). *Unaffordable Housing: Fables and Myths*. London.
Fischer-Kowalski, M., Krausmann, F., Giljum, S., et al. (2011). Methodology and indicators of economy-wide material flow accounting: State of the art and reliability across sources. *Journal of Industrial Ecology*, 15(6), 855–876. https://doi.org/10.1111/j.1530-9290.2011.00366.x.
FOEN. (2001). *Bauabfälle Schweiz – Mengen, Perspektiven und Entsorgungswege. Band 1: Kennwerte [Construction and demolition waste in Switzerland – amounts, perspectives and disposal routes. Volume 1: Statistical values]. Umwelt-Materialien*. Bern: Federal Office for the Environment (FOEN).
Friege, J., Holtz, G., & Chappin, É. J. L. (2016) . Exploring homeowners' insulation activity. *Jasss*, 19 (1), 1–20. https://doi.org/10.18564/jasss.2941.
Fries, D., Hasenmaile, F., Hürzeler, F., et al. (2017). Tenants wanted. *Investment Solutions & Products: Economic Research, Swiss Real* (March).
Froemelt, A., Dürrenmatt, D. J., & Hellweg, S. (2018). Using data mining to assess environmental impacts of household consumption behaviors. *Environmental Science & Technology*, 52(15), 8467–8478. https://doi.org/10.1021/acs.est.8b01452.

Gauvain, M., & Altman, I. (1982). A cross-cultural analysis of homes. *Architecture & Comportement*, 2(1), 27–46.
Giddens, A. (1978). *New Rules of Sociological Methods*. London: Hutchinson.
Gordon, T. J., & Hayward, H. (1968). Initial experiments with the cross impact matrix method of forecasting. *Futures*, *1*(2), 100–116. https://doi.org/https://doi.org/10.1016/S0016-3287(68)80003-5.
Grams, A. (2018). *Playing with Density: the Compass for Inward Development as a Problem-Focused Methodology for Densification in Small and Medium-Sized Communes* (Vol. 8). Zürich: vdf Hochschulverlag.
Halla, P., & Binder, C. R. (2020). Sustainability Assessment: Introduction and Framework. In C. R. Binder, E. Massaro, & R. Wyss (eds.), *Sustainability Assessment in Urban Systems*. Cambridge University Press, pp. 7–29.
Heeren, N. (2017). *Modelling environmental impacts of building: Energy, material, and dynamics*. ETH Zurich. https://doi.org/10.3929/ETHZ-B-000225616.
Heeren, N., & Hellweg, S. (2018). Tracking construction material over space and time: Prospective and geo-referenced modeling of building stocks and construction material flows. *Journal of Industrial Ecology*, 23(1), 253–267. https://doi.org/10.1111/jiec.12739.
Heeren, N., Jakob, M., Martius, G., Gross, N., & Wallbaum, H. (2013). A component based bottom-up building stock model for comprehensive environmental impact assessment and target control. *Renewable and Sustainable Energy Reviews*, 20, 45–56. https://doi.org/https://doi.org/10.1016/j.rser.2012.11.064.
Heeren, N., Mutel, C. L., Steubing, B., Ostermeyer, Y., Wallbaum, H., & Hellweg, S. (2015). Environmental impact of buildings – What Matters? *Environmental Science and Technology*, 49 (16), 9832–9841. https://doi.org/10.1021/acs.est.5b01735.
Hollberg, A., Tschetwertak, J., Schneider, S., & Habert, G. (2018). Design-integrated LCA using early BIM. In E. Benetto, K. Gericke, & M. Guiton (eds.), *Designing Sustainable Technologies, Products and Policies: From Science to Innovation*. Cham: Springer International Publishing, pp. 269–279. https://doi.org/10.1007/978-3-319-66981-6_30.
Hondo, H., Moriizumi, Y., & Sakao, T. (2006). A method for technology selection considering environmental and socio-economic impacts: Input-output optimization model and its application to housing policy. *International Journal of Life Cycle Assessment*, 11(6), 383–393. https://doi.org/10.1065/lca2006.03.245.
Hügi, M., Gerber, P., Hauser, A., et al. (2008). *Abfallwirtschaftsbericht 2008. Zahlen und Entwicklungen der schweizerischen Abfallwirtschaft 2005–2007*. Bern: Federal Office for the Environment (FOEN).
IPCC. (2014). *Climate Change 2014: Mitigation of Climate Change. Contribution of Working Group III to the Fifth Assessment Report of the Intergovernmental Panel on Climate Change*. (O. Edenhofer, R. Pichs-Madruga, E. F. Y. Sokona, S. Kadner, K. Seyboth, A. Adler, . . . J. C. Minx, eds.), *Working Group III Contribution to the Fifth Assessment Report of the Intergovernmental Panel on Climate Change*. Cambridge, UK, and New York: Cambridge University Press. https://doi.org/10.1017/CBO9781107415416.
IRP. (2017). *Green Technology Choices: The Environmental and Resource Implications of Low-Carbon Technologies*. Suh, S., Bergesen, J., Gibon, T. J., Hertwich, E., Taptich M. A report of the International Resource Panel. Nairobi, Kenya: United Nations Environment Programme.
IRP. (2018). *The Weight of Cities: Resource Requirements of Future Urbanization*. Swilling, M., Hajer, M., Baynes, T., Bergesen, J., Labbé, F., Musango, J. K., Ramaswami, A., Robinson, B., Salat, S., Suh, S., Currie, P., Fang, A., Hanson, A. Kruit, K., Reiner, M., Smit, S., Tabory, S. A Report by the International Resource Panel. Nairobi, Kenya: United Nations Environment Programme
Jin, R., Yuan, H., & Chen, Q. (2020). Science mapping approach to assisting the review of construction and demolition waste management research published between 2009 and 2018. *Resources, Conservation and Recycling*, 140(May 2018), 175–188. https://doi.org/10.1016/j.resconrec.2018.09.029.
Knoeri, C., Binder, C. R., & Althaus, H.-J. (2011). An agent operationalization approach for context specific agent-based modeling. *Journal of Artificial Societies and Social Simulation*, 14(2). https://doi.org/10.18564/jasss.1729.

Knoeri, C., Binder, C. R., & Althaus, H. J. (2011). Decisions on recycling: Construction stakeholders' decisions regarding recycled mineral construction materials. *Resources, Conservation and Recycling*, 55(11), 1039–1050. https://doi.org/10.1016/j.resconrec.2011.05.018.

Knoeri, C., Nikolic, I., Althaus, H.-J., & Binder, C. R. (2014). Enhancing recycling of construction materials: An agent based model with empirically based decision parameters. *Journal of Artificial Societies and Social Simulation*, 17(3), 10. https://doi.org/10.18564/jasss.2528.

Krausmann, F., Wiedenhofer, D., Lauk, C., et al. (2017). Global socioeconomic material stocks rise 23-fold over the 20th century and require half of annual resource use. *Proceedings of the National Academy of Sciences*, 114(8), 1880–1885. https://doi.org/10.1073/pnas.1613773114.

Lawrence, R. J. (1987a). *Housing, Dwellings and Homes: Design Theory, Research and Practice*. Chichester: John Wiley & Sons.

Lawrence, R. J. (1987b). What makes a house a home? *Environment and Behavior*, 19(2), 154–168. https://doi.org/10.1177/0013916587192004.

Lawrence, R. J. (2004). Housing and health: From interdisciplinary principles to transdisciplinary research and practice. *Futures*, 36(4), 487–502. https://doi.org/10.1016/j.futures.2003.10.001.

Lovell, H. (2004). Framing sustainable housing as a solution to climate change. *Journal of Environmental Policy and Planning*, 6(1), 35–55. https://doi.org/10.1080/1523908042000259677.

Marca, D., & McGowan, C. L. (1987). *SADT: Structured Analysis and Design Technique*. New York: McGraw-Hill.

Mateus, R., & Bragança, L. (2011). Sustainability assessment and rating of buildings: Developing the methodology SBToolPT–H. *Building and Environment*, 46(10), 1962–1971. https://doi.org/https://doi.org/10.1016/j.buildenv.2011.04.023.

Meadows, D. H. (2008). *Thinking in Systems: A Primer*. (D. Wright, ed.). London: Chelsea Green Publishing. https://search.library.wisc.edu/catalog/9910100084402121.

Mißler-Behr, M. (1993). *Methoden der Szenarioanalyse*. Deutscher Universitätsverlag. https://books.google.ch/books?id=_486AAAACAAJ.

Moura, M. C. P., Smith, S. J., & Belzer, D. B. (2015). 120 years of U.S. residential housing stock and floor space. *PLoS ONE*, 10(8), 1–18. https://doi.org/10.1371/journal.pone.0134135.

Müller, D. B., Liu, G., Løvik, A. N., et al. (2013). Carbon emissions of infrastructure development. *Environmental Science and Technology*, 47(20), 11739–11746. https://doi.org/10.1021/es402618 m.

OECD. (2012). *Compact City Policies: A Comparative Assessment* (OECD Green). OECD Publishing.

Pattaroni, L., & Marmy, V. (2016). *Les coopératives de logements dans le canton de Vaud*. Lausanne: Département des institutions et de la sécurité (DIS), Service des communes et du logement (SCL).

Prochorskaite, A., Couch, C., Malys, N., & Maliene, V. (2016). Housing stakeholder preferences for the "soft" features of sustainable and healthy housing design in the UK. *International Journal of Environmental Research and Public Health*, 13(1). https://doi.org/10.3390/ijerph13010111.

Schilling, T., Mühlemeier, S., Wyss, R., & Binder, C. R. (2020). A Concept for Sustainability Transition Assessment (STA): A Dynamic Systems Perspective Informed by Resilience Thinking. In C. R. Binder, E. Massaro, & R. Wyss (eds.), *Sustainability Assessment in Urban Systems*. Cambridge University Press, pp. 123–138.

Scholz, R. W., & Tietje, O. (2002). *Embedded Case Study Methods: Integrating Quantitative And Qualitative Knowledge*. Thousand Oaks: Sage Publications.

Schultz, P. W., Nolan, J. M., Cialdini, R. B., Goldstein, N. J., & Griskevicius, V. (2007). The constructive, destructive, and reconstructive power of social norms. *Psychological Science*, 18 (5), 429. https://doi.org/10.1111/j.1467-9280.2007.01917.x.

Seyfang, G. (2010). Community action for sustainable housing: Building a low-carbon future. *Energy Policy*, 38(12), 7624–7633. https://doi.org/10.1016/j.enpol.2009.10.027.

Silva, R. V., De Brito, J., & Dhir, R. K. (2014). Properties and composition of recycled aggregates from construction and demolition waste suitable for concrete production. *Construction and Building Materials*, 65(August), 201–217. https://doi.org/10.1016/j.conbuildmat.2014.04.117.

Soust-Verdaguer, B., Llatas, C., & García-Martínez, A. (2017). Critical review of BIM-based LCA method to buildings. *Energy and Buildings*, 136, 110–120. https://doi.org/10.1016/j.enbuild.2016.12.009.

Spoerri, A., Lang, D. J., Binder, C. R., & Scholz, R. W. (2009). Expert-based scenarios for strategic waste and resource management planning: C&D waste recycling in the Canton of Zurich, Switzerland. *Resources, Conservation and Recycling*, 53(10), 592–600. https://doi.org/https://doi.org/10.1016/j.resconrec.2009.04.011.

Sterman, J. D. (2006). Learning from evidence in a complex world. *American Journal of Public Health*, 96(3), 505–514. https://doi.org/10.2105/AJPH.2005.066043.

Støa, E., & Aune, M. (2012). Sustainable housing cultures. In *International Encyclopedia of Housing and Home* (Vol. 7). Elsevier Ltd. https://doi.org/10.1016/B978-0-08-047163-1.00556-7.

Swiss Federal Statistical Office. (2011). Living, building: Switzerland's built environment. *Values*, (2), 28.

Swiss Federal Statistical Office. (2018). Building and Dwelling Statistics. Neuchâtel, Switzerland:

UN – DESA. (2017). *World Population Prospects: The 2017 Revision*. United Nations, Department of Economic and Social Affairs. https://population.un.org/wpp/

UNHCR & UN-Habitat. (2012). *The Right to Adequate Housing*, 21(21). https://doi.org/10.1017/CBO9781107415324.004.

United Nations. (2018). *World Urbanization Prospects: The 2018 Revision*. United Nations, Department of Economic and Social Affairs, Population Division.

United States Census Bureau. (2018). *Highlights of Annual 2017 Characteristics of New Housing. Office of Policy Development and Research* (PD&R) US Department of Housing and Urban Development.

Waddell, P. (2002). UrbanSim: Modeling urban development for land use, transportation, and environmental planning. *Journal of the American Planning Association*, 68(3), 297–314. https://doi.org/10.1080/01944360208976274.

Wiek, A., & Binder, C. (2005). Solution spaces for decision-making: A sustainability assessment tool for city-regions. *Environmental Impact Assessment Review*, 25(6), 589–608. https://doi.org/10.1016/j.eiar.2004.09.009.

Williams, J. (2006). Innovative solutions for averting a potential resource crisis: The case of one-person households in England and Wales. *Environment, Development and Sustainability*, 9 (3), 325–354. https://doi.org/10.1007/s10668-006-9068-x.

Wilson, A., & Boehland, J. (2008). Small is Beautiful: U.S. house size, resource use, and the environment. *Journal of Industrial Ecology*, 9(1–2), 277–287. https://doi.org/10.1162/1088198054084680.

World Health Organization (WHO) (2010). *Developing guidance for health protection in the built environment: Mitigation and adaptation responses Meeting report. International Workshop on Housing, Health and Climate Change*.

Yang, L., Yan, H., & Lam, J. C. (2014). Thermal comfort and building energy consumption implications: A review. *Applied Energy*, 115, 164–173. https://doi.org/https://doi.org/10.1016/j.apenergy.2013.10.062.

Youcai, Z., & Sheng, H. (2017). *Pollution Control and Resource Recovery: Industrial Construction and Demolition Wastes*. Oxford: Butterworth-Heinemann. https://doi.org/https://doi.org/10.1016/B978-0-12-811754-5.00001-4.

Appendix

		ENV				ECON		SOC							
		EFO	REO	WDO	CFO	RAO	IHO	FAO	SPO	SSO	VRO	ICO	IAO	ASO	Activity
ENV	EFO. End energy footprint		0	0	2	0	1	0	0	0	0	0	0	0	3
	REO. Share of renewable energy	0		0	-2	0	-2	0	0	0	0	0	0	0	4
	WDO. Water demand	1	0		0	0	0	0	0	0	0	0	0	0	1
	CFO. Carbon footprint	0	0	0		0	0	0	0	0	0	0	0	0	0
ECON	RAO. Rent affordability	0	0	0	0		0	0	0	0	-2	0	0	0	2
	IHO. Income spent on housing operation and maintenance	0	0	0	0	0		0	0	0	2	0	0	0	2
SOC	FAO. Flexibility and adaptability	0	0	0	0	0	0		-1	0	-2	1	0	0	4
	SPO. Space per person	2	0	0	0	-1	1	0		-1	0	0	0	0	5
	SSO. Shared space	-1	0	-1	0	1	-1	0	1		0	0	0	0	5
	VRO. Vacancy rate	0	0	0	0	0	0	0	0	0		0	0	0	0
	ICO. Indoor comfort	2	0	0	0	0	0	0	0	0	-2		0	0	4
	IAO. Information and awareness	-1	0	-1	-1	0	0	0	-1	1	0	0		1	6
	ASO. Attitudes towards sustainability measures	-2	0	-2	0	0	0	1	-2	1	0	0	0		8
	Passivity	9	0	4	5	2	5	1	5	3	8	1	0	1	

Appendix 16.A Impact matrix of the selected indicators related to the operation phase

		ENV						ECON	SOC				
		EFM	REM	LUC	CFM	RMC	MFR	ROI	SPP	SQP	IAP	ASP	Activity
ENV	EFM. End energy footprint		0	0	2	0	0	0	0	0	0	0	2
	REM. Share of renewable energy	0		0	-2	0	0	2	0	0	0	0	4
	LUC. Land use	1	0		0	0	0	0	0	0	0	0	1
	CFM. Carbon footprint	0	0	0		0	0	0	0	0	0	0	0
	RMC. Use of recovered materials and components	-2	0	0	-2		0	0	0	0	0	0	4
	MFR. Materials for recycling	0	0	0	0	0		0	0	0	0	0	0
ECON	ROI. Return on investment	0	0	0	0	0	0		0	0	0	0	0
SOC	SPP. Stakeholder participation	0	0	0	0	0	0	0		0	1	0	1
	SQP. Space per person	1	0	2	0	0	0	0	0		0	0	3
	IAP. Information and awareness	-1	2	-1	-1	2	1	0	1	-2		2	13
	ASP. Attitudes towards sustainability measures	-1	2	-2	-1	2	1	0	0	-2	0		11
	Passivity	6	4	5	8	4	2	2	1	4	1	2	

Appendix 16.B Impact matrix of the selected indicators related to phases other than the operation phase

17

Sustainability Assessment of Urban Agriculture

Giuseppe Feola, Marlyne Sahakian, and Claudia R. Binder

Box 17.2 authored by Patricia Zundritsch

17.1 Agriculture in Urban Systems

Urban agriculture has attracted the attention of academics, policy-makers, and practitioners alike as a potential measure to support the food needs of growing urban populations and contribute to addressing some of the negative environmental and economic effects of urbanization (De Bon et al., 2010; Mougeot, 2005; Orsini et al., 2013; van Veenhuizen, 2006). Urban agriculture can be defined as "[a]gricultural production (crops and livestock) in urban and peri-urban areas for food and other uses, the related transport, processing and marketing of the agricultural produce and non-agricultural services provided by the urban farmers (water storage, agro-tourism, urban greening and landscape management, among others)" (de Zeeuw, 2004, p. 2). Urban agriculture may occur within the city boundary (intra-urban agriculture) or in the spaces immediately surrounding it (peri-urban agriculture). It is also highly diverse, and can appear in many different forms, from community gardens, home gardens, rooftop gardens, urban farms, guerrilla gardens, and backyard gardening to livestock farming, and aquaponics systems (de Zeeuw, 2004; Lin et al., 2015).

Urban agriculture can make positive contributions to food security and nutrition (Eigenbrod & Gruda, 2015; FAO, 2007; Orsini et al., 2013; Poulsen et al., 2015; Zezza & Tasciotti, 2010). However, land availability in and around cities is often a constraint (Badami & Ramankutty, 2015) and the actual food produced may be minimal in some contexts (Warren et al., 2015; Zezza & Tasciotti, 2010). Nevertheless, between 100 and 800 million people worldwide are estimated to earn part of their income directly from urban farming, or to be actively engaged in urban agriculture for subsistence including from the exchange or sale of surpluses (FAO, 1996; FAO, 1999). In cities in the Global South, up to 32 percent of dwellers can be full- or part-time farmers (de Zeeuw & Dubbeling, 2009; the percentage can be higher in certain contexts – see Drechsel & Keraita (2014) who estimated 60 percent of dwellers in Accra, Ghana). Urban agriculture also contributes to economic development. Various studies have shown that urban farmers in the Global South earn incomes significantly higher than the minimum subsistence income, while urban farms also generate additional income from related activities such as agro-tourism (De Bon et al., 2010; de Zeeuw & Dubbeling, 2009; FAO, 2007; Orsini et al., 2013; Poulsen et al., 2015; Zezza & Tasciotti, 2010). Urban agriculture initiatives have often been initiated by local authorities or non-governmental organizations (NGOs) with the aim of fostering social and gender integration, and poverty reduction. Moreover, urban agriculture can promote community-building, civic engagement, empowerment of youth and minorities, physical and psychological relaxation, environmental education, and the provision of care for people with psychological disorders (Poulsen, 2017; van Veenhuizen, 2006). Furthermore, food production in an urban context can strengthen the symbolic connection between people and their food culture (Sahakian et al., 2016).

Finally, urban agriculture can contribute to urban environmental management. On the one hand, agricultural production can reuse composted urban organic waste. In addition, it can have a positive impact upon the greening of the city, for example through the creation of green belts, the improvement of the urban microclimate (wind breaks, dust reduction, shade, sequestration of CO_2 and other pollutants), the conservation of soil, water, biodiversity, and the cultural landscape, and the provision of ecosystem services (pollination, pest control, and climate resilience) (Drechsel & Keraita, 2014; Galluzzi et al., 2010; Lin et al., 2015; Pearson et al., 2010). Notably, due to the proximity of production to consumers, urban agriculture may entail a low ecological footprint and a reduction of "food miles" and the associated carbon footprint (but see Goldstein et al., 2017).

On the other hand, urban agriculture has also been associated with health and environmental risks. First, it can be impacted by contaminants emitted by other urban activities (e.g., uptake of heavy metals in soils, or air and water pollution). Second, urban agriculture, especially when not conducted according to best practices, can contaminate the urban environment (e.g., agrochemical residues or excess nitrate in water courses and water supplies) (Rabinovitch & Schmetzer, 1997). Certain diseases, such as bovine tuberculosis, pork and beef tapeworm, trichinosis, anthrax, salmonella, and campylobacter, can also be transmitted from domestic animals to people, with the risk being high in urban contexts in which agriculture is contiguous to densely populated residential areas. Finally, urban agriculture is also associated with occupational health risks (e.g., handling of agrochemicals), and with possible conflicts with non-farming neighbors who may raise concerns about dust, smell, and noise created by the urban farms (de Zeeuw, 2004).

Urban agriculture is increasingly seen as a viable policy option to increase urban food security and sustainability. Governance is central to ensuring that positive nutritional, economic, social, and environmental outcomes are maximized, while minimizing or avoiding potentially negative impacts. Considerable advances have been made at the research-policy interface to derive lessons, best practices, and guidelines for the implementation of urban agriculture initiatives (de Zeeuw & Dubbeling, 2009; van Veenhuizen, 2006). However, urban agriculture has traditionally raised governance issues that remain largely unresolved. First, urban agriculture's sheer diversity implies that no one-size-fits-all policy is effective for governing it. Second, as borderlands, peri-urban spaces are economically multifunctional, socially diverse, and ecologically complex, but theories of the persistence of agriculture in and around cities have had difficulties in grappling with the hybrid nature of these spaces (Lerner & Eakin, 2011; Madaleno & Gurovich, 2004; Mendez et al., 2005; Pérez-Martinez, 2016). Third, competing policy narratives often misinterpret urban agriculture – for example, as a purely male or female activity (Mougeot, 2005). Similarly, urban agriculture has been leveraged differently by institutional actors (e.g., local authorities, international organizations), which have privileged particular discursive framings (e.g., the socially inclusive city, the environmental/sustainable city, economic development) to pursue different policy objectives (van Veenhuizen, 2006). Fourth, local planning processes have often failed to integrate different themes (i.e., health, environment, social, economy), or to institutionalize the incorporation of different types of knowledge in the governance of urban and peri-urban spaces (Marshall et al., 2017). Therefore, governance approaches have usually failed to create institutional, policy, and planning arrangements that are conducive to sustainable urban agriculture (de Zeeuw & Dubbeling, 2009; Drechsel et al., 2006; Lerner et al., 2013; Olsson et al., 2016; Pearson et al., 2010).

Sustainability assessment can play an important role as part of a broader governance strategy to support sustainable urban agriculture (de Zeeuw, 2004; Lang, 2014; Pearson et al., 2010; Quon, 1999). As noted by de Zeeuw and Dubbeling, an "urban food policy should be based on a systematic multi-actor assessment of the actual food system in the metropolitan or city region and an integrated and comprehensive plan on how to strengthen the urban food system, looking into regional/local food production and other supply chains, distribution (effective, equitable), health, economic and environmental and resilience aspects" (2009, p. 32). Indicators for sustainability assessment, if appropriately embedded in local governance systems, can usefully contribute to policy decisions and be meaningful to urban planners and local community gardeners (Beilin & Hunter, 2011). Yet Lang (2014) warns against the risk of an excessive focus on indicators per se, and further calls for better understanding of how urban sustainability initiatives might work with, but also move beyond, indicators, which may offer guidance in moving toward wider visions of sustainable urban life.

This chapter engages with the existing literature on urban agriculture and with concrete case studies to examine current challenges and ways forward for the sustainability assessment of urban agriculture. The chapter identifies current conceptualizations of urban agriculture, and sustainability assessment methods, and discusses them in the light of normative, systemic, and procedural dimensions of sustainability assessment (Binder et al., 2010). The diversity of urban agriculture and its presence in very different urban contexts worldwide, represent challenges for sustainability assessment. It increases the need to carefully select distinct sustainability assessment methods that may be appropriate for different contexts and purposes (Binder et al., 2010; Gasparatos, 2012), and to practice caution and self-criticism in adapting methods developed elsewhere to new contexts (Barrett et al., 2017). Specifically, this chapter asks the following questions:

- How can urban agriculture be conceptualized? In particular, are there important conceptual differences between urban agriculture in the Global North and South, or between distinct forms of urban agriculture?
- How can the sustainability of urban agriculture be assessed? What methodological differences, if any, should be taken into consideration in assessing different forms of urban agriculture in distinct urban contexts?

- What are the current challenges and what are the opportunities for improving the sustainability assessment of urban agriculture?

17.2 Conceptualizing Agriculture in Urban Systems

Scholars have approached the diversity of urban agriculture from a range of perspectives (Table 17.1). For example, the extension of cultivated land, and the degree of access to irrigation resources and infrastructure can vary substantially across locations (Thebo et al.,

Table 17.1 *Sources of diversity in framing urban agriculture. An asterisk denotes the sources that are particularly relevant in urban as opposed to rural agriculture.*

Sources of diversity	Descriptor
Goal	
Purpose	Subsistence, commercial, multifunctional
Main function	Food production, ecotourism, educational services, care services
General geographical characteristics	
*Location	Intra-urban/peri-urban; ground/rooftop
Land extension	Small to large farms
*Resource-use profile	Integration in the built environment, energy for space conditioning (light and temperature)
Infrastructure	Access to irrigation, transport, electricity, etc.
Farming characteristics	
Agricultural system	Crop, livestock, mixed
Produce	Type of crop or animal product
Management	Individual/family/collective
Institutional/social characteristics	
Formality	Formal/informal
Farming philosophy	Conventional or alternative (e.g., organic, permaculture)
*Values	Reconnect with nature, poverty alleviation, civic protest or political activism, food justice
*Social groups involved	Male/female/mixed, urban poor/affluent/mixed, local residents/immigrants/mixed
*Institutional integration	Degree and forms of collective association (e.g., cooperatives)

2014). Similarly, urban agriculture is characterized by differing levels of integration into formal markets and institutions such as farmer and producer organizations, or planning or consultative committees (FAO, 2007; Schmidt et al., 2015). The Food and Agriculture Organization of the United Nations (FAO), proposed a tripartite typology – multifunctional, commercial, and subsistence agriculture – based on the purpose and livelihood structure of urban farmers (van Veenhuizen, 2006). These types of urban agriculture may also be related to different motivations for engaging in food production (e.g., saving on food expenditures or making a profit from the sale of produce) and to different contextual conditions (e.g., access to land, personal skills). Goldstein et al. (2016a), instead, used a taxonomy based on resource-use profiles. They identified two variables, namely building integration (physical embedding of urban agriculture within the built environment) and space conditioning (degree of interaction between urban agriculture and the ambient environment), and on this basis, developed a matrix of four urban agriculture types. Mendez et al. (2005) proposed an urban agriculture typology based on the motivation for its emergence: (i) economic necessity), (ii) absorption in the expanding urban system, (iii) external or internal institutional intervention, (iv) exploitation of available resources (e.g., space), or (v) expression of rural antecedents.

Important differences can also be noted in the way urban agriculture has been framed in debates and political action in different contexts (Table 17.1). By and large, urban agriculture in the Global North has often been associated with progressive movements promoting sustainable lifestyles and reconnection with nature, in the context of civic and political struggles, as in the food justice and food sovereignty movements (Goodman et al., 2012; McClintock, 2014), or in relation to educational or social integration programs (Saldivar-Tanaka & Krasny, 2004; Savoie-Roskos et al., 2017; Shinew et al., 2004). Thus, in the Global North urban agriculture has mostly been a terrain for political and social change, while the potential for actual food production and income generation has been marginal (perhaps with the exception of some "food deserts") (Hashim, 2015; Tornaghi, 2014). In the Global South, in contrast, urban agriculture has often been framed in terms of development, which brings to the forefront the potential of urban agriculture to favor social integration, providing employment and contributing to poverty reduction, and to produce food both for subsistence and for the market (Sahakian et al., 2016). Agriculture in cities in the Global South has also often been an arena for social struggles and the empowerment of marginal groups, as in the agroecology and food sovereignty movements. It can further be argued that many of those struggles have come about as part of counter-development movements, and as such they have been influenced, if only as counterpoints, by developmentalist discourses (Chappell et al., 2013). Such framing does not fully capture other trends that may relate to urban agriculture, such as changing diets and practices among the urban middle classes, which impact the demand for particular types of food (dairy, meat), food waste, and food circulation associated with changing food habits (e.g., eating out) (Sahakian et al., 2016). Understanding food consumption practices in urban spaces in the Global North and South is a growing area of study, linking the sociology of consumption with urban and environmental studies (see also Box 17.1).

Box 17.1 Perceptions of "local and seasonal" food among urban consumers in Switzerland

Households have an important role to play in transitions towards "healthy and sustainable food," which relates to how people represent notions of health and sustainability in their day-to-day diets. A recent study in Switzerland set out to uncover "food prescriptions," or all of the diverse guidelines around what and how one should eat (Plessz et al., 2016). Through qualitative research, involving discourse analysis, observations, in-depth interviews, and focus groups, the more dominant prescriptions related to healthy and sustainable diets were identified, revealing overlaps and tensions between them (Godin & Sahakian, 2018). The main finding was that health is a more prominent concern than environmental responsibility. All of the prescriptions relate to healthy people, while concerns about a healthy planet are much less dominant. The notion of a "balanced meal" is the more prominent prescription, along with the idea that food and eating should be "pleasurable." Increasingly, "local and seasonal" food production is normalized as contributing to "healthy and sustainable" diets, thus prompting increased interest in alternative food networks, including urban agriculture. Guidelines that encourage eating "local and seasonal" products overlap with "organic and natural" food consumption, while prescriptions to "eat less meat of higher quality" are in tension with prescriptions around "vegetarian and vegan diets." These prescriptions are set forth by different types of actors, from the Swiss nutritional society to retailers or citizen associations, but also friends and family. The media represent an important site for prescriptions to be vocalized, be it in the general press or in the blogosphere. Prescriptions exist at the level of discourse and representations, but also play out in practice; in this respect, they can either be a resource for or an obstacle to healthy and sustainable eating habits. For the latter, the sheer amount of prescriptions and tensions between them seem to suggest that people are burdened by making the right choice in relation to health and sustainability: "Too much choice kills choice," as one interviewee declared. Placing the responsibility for transitioning to healthy and sustainable diets on consumers alone disregards the different ways food consumption plays out in practice, and changing this would involve tackling three main elements: the social norms and prescriptions around food; people's skills and competencies when it comes to preparing meals or urban gardening; and the availability of and access to certain products, or retail or gardening spaces. Guidelines or prescriptions are therefore not enough, in and of themselves, to shift people's diets. Other factors that must be taken into account include time availability, the links between mobility and food preparation in urban centers, and the social relationships built around food and eating.

17.3 Approaches and Methods for Assessing the Sustainability of Agriculture in Urban Systems

The number of methods specifically developed to assess the sustainability of urban agriculture is limited. Furthermore, the "literature reveals various approaches to and indicators for measuring the sustainability of [urban agriculture], but to date, few systematic attempts have been made through monitoring its presence and impacts over a longer period of time in a given city or cities" (FAO, 2007, p. 70).

Box 17.2 **A geographic information system to estimate the potential of urban agriculture**

The development of urban agriculture requires suitable surfaces in cities. Thereby, conflicting interests play a role when deciding upon the use of a specific piece of land. A geographic information system (GIS)-based land inventory and yield estimates can support policy-makers in the development of urban agriculture zones and in weighing the benefits of using land for agriculture against other possible uses. Baker (2012), Saha and Eckelmann (2017), and Zundritsch (2018) propose a methodology using GIS to develop an inventory of feasible urban agriculture sites.

The criteria for determining suitable areas for urban gardening depend on whether we are dealing with ground level or rooftop urban agriculture. On the ground, high-resolution maps of green spaces are needed, which might be available from city cadastre data. Alternatively, a detailed layer of vegetation can be derived from the intensity of reflection of a laser beam that is used in LIDAR surveying technology (Teo & Wu, 2017). For rooftop mapping, layers of building footprints and elevation models are required. In addition, economic factors such as ownership of parcels (public or private) and land use determine whether the area can be developed. Including vacancy in GIS models is difficult, due to its dynamic nature and the fact that there are few reliable or accessible data sources. Tax data or real estate assessors' databases may be used if available (Baker, 2012).

For estimating the potential harvest, environmental factors such as the slope of a site, light exposure, site pollution, soil quality, and water access have to be considered. Quality limits and suitability classes vary depending on a site's location and the type of urban gardening. Sizes of plots and their proximity and accessibility to interested citizens are two additional factors influencing behavior and harvest.

The Swiss city of Lausanne has about 150,000 inhabitants and an area of 46.22 km^2. A spatial analysis for the geographic data layers of public and private ownership, vegetation type, area solar radiation, and slope was performed for different combinations of the criteria and for various minimum plot sizes. The potentially suitable ground area was found to be between 5 km^2 and 10.16 km^2, representing 11 percent and 22 percent respectively of the total land area in Lausanne (Zundritsch, 2018). This area is split almost evenly between public and private parcels. However, public parcels are often more exposed to sunlight and less sloped than private parcels. The resulting potential corresponds to research in US cities where a range of 2.3–7.8 percent of total municipal land areas was found suitable according to the same criteria and additionally including whether the land was currently vacant (Grewal & Grewal, 2012; McClintock et al., 2013).

Yet, the range of existing sustainability assessment methods is relatively large. While indicator-based assessment methods are very common, the sustainability of urban agriculture has been assessed also via methods relying, for example, on geographic information systems (Box 17.2; see also Ghosh (2014) on the use of GIS to estimate available land for agriculture), and life-cycle analysis (Box 17.3).

Indicators have often been used to assess the sustainability of urban agriculture. The FAO (2007) identified commonly addressed sustainability criteria, which included productivity, land security, protection of environment and people, economic viability, social and political

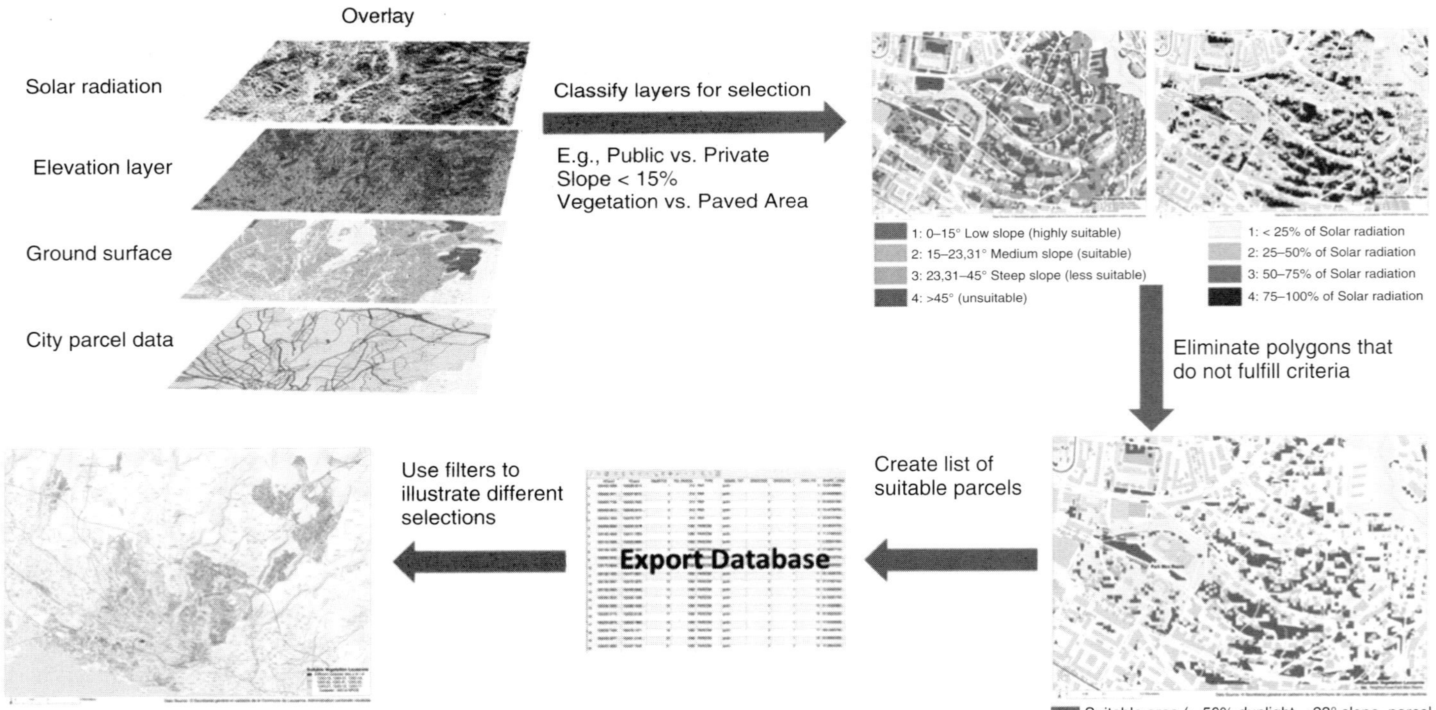

Map extents show the Commune of Lausanne, CH (left: in full), (right: Parc Mon Repos).
Data Source: © Secrétariat général et cadastre Commune de Lausanne, OTI Vaud

Figure 1 (Box 17.2) Geographic information systems methodology (inspired by Ringenbach, Valcourt and Wang, 2013)

Box 17.3 Life-cycle assessment of urban agriculture

Some sustainability assessment methods based on life-cycle assessment (LCA) have been proposed as alternatives to indicators. LCA quantifies the environmental impacts associated with a product, service, or activity throughout its life cycle. Goldstein et al. (2016b) performed an LCA to assess the environmental performance of lettuce and tomato production in urban farms in Boston, USA. Environmental performance was defined in this study as a composite measure of (i) supply-chain efficiency (reduced distance from farm to consumer attenuating "food miles" and carbon footprint); (ii) urban symbiosis (interactions with a city's material and energy fluxes, reduction of a farm's operational inputs, absorption of urban waste flows such as food waste, lowering building energy demand, and other local environmental benefits such as tempering storm water runoff); (iii) ex-situ environmental benefits (reductions in agricultural land occupation, carbon sequestration). Goldstein et al. (2016b) adopt a cradle-to-shelf approach that includes cultivation, harvesting, and distribution of food to market, but not post-purchase transport and preparation.

Similarly, Kulak et al. (2013) used LCA to quantify the potential savings of food-related GHG emissions that may be achieved with the establishment of an urban community farm in London, UK. Their analysis assumed that fruit and vegetables produced by the community farm would substitute for the same commodities available at the local supermarket and supplied through the conventional food chain. Data for development of the LCA inventory, as well as future scenarios for the community farm, were collected through interviews and field visits.

Sustainability assessment methods based on LCA may hold potential for providing a detailed analysis of environmental sustainability. However, they tend to be limited to the environmental dimension of sustainability, and as shown by these examples, require numerous assumptions, as do indicator-based methods. Furthermore, to the authors' knowledge and in contrast to indicator-based methods, to date LCA-based methods have not been used in actual governance of urban food systems.

acceptability, and ability to form cooperatives (FAO, 2007). A higher number of studies, though, appear to have specifically addressed the profitability of urban agriculture (FAO, 2007). Based on existing experiences of sustainability assessment, the FAO (2007, p. 27) proposed that the "sustainability of [urban agriculture] basically implies its ability to continue in the future and operate at the current or increased levels. In order to be sustainable, [urban agriculture] should be profitable and economically viable, environmentally sound, socially just and culturally acceptable." While the FAO does not propose a specific assessment method, it puts forward a general indicator list comprising 25 economic, environmental, and social indicators, variably measured at household, city, or macro level (FAO, 2007).

Soler Montiel and Rivera-Ferre (2010; see also Ortega-Cerdá & Rivera-Ferre, 2010) depart from a notion of urban agriculture sustainability that is rooted in an agroecological and food sovereignty perspective. In this view, urban agriculture conducted according to agroecological and food-sovereignty principles can be a tool for urban sustainability with deep implications not only at the ecological level, but also at the social level. According to this perspective, urban farms can help reorient current urban development models from an individualist model to a more equitable one, in which citizens can play a more active, participatory role in the definition of public policies. Based on these premises, Soler Montiel and Rivera-Ferre (2010) identify five areas for assessment: (i) access to resources, (ii) production model, (iii) transformation and commercialization, (iv) food consumption and the right to nutritious food, (v) agricultural policies and civil society organization (Ortega-Cerdá & Rivera-Ferre, 2010). While Soler Montiel and Rivera-Ferre (2010) do not identify an indicator list, they specify the criteria for the selection and operationalization of their assessment areas, which include their simplicity and low measurement cost, their participatory nature (i.e., whether stakeholders participate in the process of knowledge-generation), and their flexibility (i.e., their applicability to a wide range of regions and contexts).

Participation processes are central in other indicator-based assessment methods. For example, the Farming Concrete Data Collection Toolkit (Farming Concrete, 2015) is a protocol developed by the community-based research project Farming Concrete in New York, USA. This tool is intended to support local communities to measure the outcomes and impacts of community gardens and urban farms. The toolkit enables measurement of food production (crop and harvest count), environmental data (landfill waste diversion, compost production, rainwater harvesting), social data (participation, skills and knowledge creation, outreach), health data (attitude change, emotions, healthy eating, aesthetics of the garden), and economic data (market sales, donations of food). The toolkit has an explicit aim of enabling communities to measure the positive impacts of their urban agriculture projects, and therefore empowering them as local agents of change.

Participation plays an important role also in the approach proposed by Blixen Magariños et al. (2007). Basing their approach on the MESMIS framework (López-Ridaura et al., 2002), these researchers stress the highly context-specific nature of sustainability assessment, which requires a participatory process for the adaptation of the assessment methodology to the local context. They also focus on five sustainability attributes of agroecosystems: (i) productivity, (ii) stability, (iii) resilience, (iv) adaptability, (v) autonomy. In their application of the approach to the evaluation of a community program for food production in Montevideo, Uruguay, they identified 36 indicators, which were measured through 67 wide-ranging variables (e.g., to capture farm management, soil quality, land tenure, labor management, work culture, dependency on external inputs, among others).

Similarly, Beilin and Hunter (2011) developed a participatory approach for scientists, community gardeners, and local authorities to co-produce indicators to assess the sustainability of urban gardens in Sydney. The approach resulted in three sets of (i) social, (ii) ecological, and (iii) local food production indicators. These were highly place-specific and highly relevant to the governance of urban agriculture in the city. The development of indicators improved the relations among community gardeners, local authorities, and other community groups, and also enabled the monitoring and revising of the governance system in order to smooth factors that were limiting urban agriculture's potential (e.g., official registration of gardening sites).

Stakeholder participation and expert opinions also play an important role in the method developed by Landert et al. (2017). This sustainability assessment method for urban-food-system governance explicitly aims to be holistic (i.e., to cover all relevant aspects of an urban food system), and to enable comparison between cities. This method has a specific focus on the extent to which the urban food system is governed sustainably by local politics and administration, and is informed by the guidelines for Sustainability Assessment of Food and Agriculture Systems proposed by the FAO. Accordingly, the method defines sustainability in terms of good governance, environmental integrity, economic resilience, and social well-being. "These four dimensions are divided into 21 themes with 58 subthemes in total. . . . For each of the 58 subthemes, a goal is defined to evaluate the sustainability of farms or businesses along the food value chain" (Landert et al., 2017). Indicators are defined for each subtheme based on stakeholder participation, relevance, and data availability, and are then weighted through an expert-informed process. In an application of the method to the Swiss city of Basel, Landert et al. (2017) used a total of 97 indicators.

In other cases, the assessment is based on a set of indicators that is predefined and not developed with stakeholders. For instance, Losada et al. (2001) evaluated the economic productivity and sustainability of growing the nopal vegetable (*Opuntia ficus-indica*) in Mexico City. For this purpose, they used three sets of economic, social, and environmental indicators and collected data through a survey of 100 urban farmers. Economic indicators included a gross margin analysis, commercialization strategies, and provision of employment. Social indicators were the education level, family size, and origin of laborers; plot size, which provided a measure of equity; and social self-organization. Environmental indicators were soil nutrient content and fertilizer application, technological management, and crop and natural biodiversity. For each farm, the results of the assessment were scored on a scale from zero to 100.

Finally, some researchers have transferred and adapted general sustainability assessment methods to the urban context. For example, Drechsel and Dongus (2010) used an adapted version of the Framework for Evaluating Sustainable Land Management (FESLM) developed by the FAO to assess the sustainability of urban agriculture in Dar es Salaam, Tanzania. According to the FESLM, sustainable land management relies on five pillars: (i) maintenance or enhancement of production/services, (i) reduction of the level of production risk, (iii) protection of the potential of natural resources and prevention of degradation of soil and water quality, (iv) economic viability, (v) social acceptability. Drechsel and Dongus (2010) used mostly secondary data (interviews, official statistics, maps, and remote sensing data) available from previous studies. Like Soler Montiel and Rivera-Ferre (2010), Drechsel and Dongus (2010) did not predefine any specific indicators. Instead, they adopted a more descriptive, data-driven approach that attempted to capture the dynamics of urban agriculture regarding the five pillars, whereby further insight is provided by the comparison with other African cities where similar data were available.

17.4 Sustainability of Urban Agriculture: Challenges and Opportunities

The previous two sections have presented conceptualizations of urban agriculture (see Section 17.2) and illustrated the range of sustainability assessment methods that have been employed in the Global North and South (see Section 17.3). These sections have shown that urban agriculture is not only highly diverse socially, environmentally, technically, economically, institutionally, and culturally, but also highly contested. Urban agriculture has been, in cities in the North as well as in the South, an arena of political struggle, and of governmental and non-governmental intervention. It has been used to promote various and often contradictory visions of sustainability, health, food, citizenship, and development. To reiterate: the diversity of urban agriculture forms, the multifunctionality of peri-urban spaces where urban agriculture largely takes place, contested framings of urban agriculture, and the difficulties involved in integrating and incorporating different types of knowledge and land use into urban planning often result in the failure to create institutional, policy, and planning arrangements that are conducive to sustainable urban agriculture (de Zeeuw & Dubbeling, 2009; Lerner et al., 2013; Olsson et al., 2016; Pearson et al., 2010). Furthermore, our discussion has illustrated the absence of established formalized methods for assessing the sustainability of urban agriculture specifically. While a sophisticated toolbox for the assessment of agricultural sustainability in general exists, not many methods have been specifically developed for urban agriculture although, as shown (see Section 17.2), urban agriculture presents crucial differences from agriculture in rural contexts.

This section develops the above analysis to identify some key challenges that the theory and practice of sustainability assessment of urban agriculture pose to researchers. The analysis is structured according to three dimensions of sustainability assessment as defined by Binder et al. (2010) (and see Chapter 1 (Halla & Binder, 2020)), namely normative, procedural, and systemic (Table 17.2).

17.4.1 Normative Dimension

Urban agriculture is often the object of, or even a tool for the contestation of, divergent visions of sustainable development. From political gardening to resistance to land appropriation for urban expansion, from debates around the supposedly inherent sustainability of local

Table 17.2 *Main challenges faced in the sustainability assessment of urban agriculture*

Normative	Procedural	Systemic
Sustainability concept, goal-setting, and assessment type	Preparatory/setup phase, indicator selection; measurement, assessment, application, follow-up	Systemic representation and indicator interaction
Setting assessment goals Mediating potentially conflicting stakeholder interests Defining sustainability Defining indicator weightings	Need for dedicated investigation strategies Sustaining participation	Identifying the system's boundaries Establishing indicator interactions, especially with non-agricultural system components (built environment, buffer zones)

production to debates about the regeneration of urban systems, urban agriculture is often interrelated with deep-seated cultural meanings, socioeconomic objectives, and political imaginaries (Certomá & Tornaghi, 2015; Goodman et al., 2012; Sahakian et al., 2016; Tornaghi, 2014). Ultimately, the different ways in which urban agriculture has been conceptualized, can be traced back to fundamentally different notions of human well-being (see Chapter 3 (Meinherz et al., 2020)). For example, anthropocentric and technocentric worldviews, as opposed to organic ones, are reflected in varying combinations of market, subsistence, or agroecological models of urban agriculture (see Chapter 3 (Meinherz et al., 2020)).

This has important implications (Table 17.2) for the normative dimension of the sustainability assessment of urban agriculture, which is only compounded by the striking diversity of urban agriculture, the presence of a relatively mobile and diverse population, and the proximity and complementarity of agricultural and non-agricultural activities, all of which extend the range of possible stakeholders and blur the boundaries of the system to be assessed.

The high number and diversity of stakeholders, and the fact that urban agriculture may be a part-time income-generating activity, suggests that the assessment's goal-setting may be challenging and that it may be necessary to mediate among conflicting interests, not only across but also within the farming and non-farming populations. While many sustainability assessment methods assume that the local authority will set up the assessment, most methods entail some form of public participation, which may involve the definition of the assessment goal. Nevertheless, most methods reviewed in the previous section also predefine sustainability to a significant extent, for example identifying specific dimensions or pillars of sustainability (Table 17.3). It is unclear to what extent these definitions of

Table 17.3 *Sustainability dimensions in selected methods for sustainability assessment of urban agriculture*

Source	Dimensions
Beilin & Hunter (2011)	Social, ecological, local food production
Blixen Magariños et al. (2007)	Productivity, stability, resilience, adaptability, autonomy
Drechsel & Dongus (2010)	Maintenance or enhancement of production/services, reduction of the level of production risk, protection of the potential of natural resources and prevention of degradation of soil and water quality, economic viability, social and political acceptability
FAO (2007)	Productivity, land tenure security, protection of environment and people, economic viability, social and political acceptability, and ability to form cooperatives
Landert et al. (2017)	Good governance, environmental integrity, economic resilience, and social well-being
Losada et al. (2001)	Economic, social, environmental
Soler Montiel & Rivera-Ferre (2010)	Access to resources, production model, transformation and commercialization, food consumption and right to nutritious food, agricultural policies, and civil society organization

sustainability may fit different purposes and contexts of urban agriculture, if they are compatible with the underlying worldviews of different stakeholders, and how they may be received by diverse populations and by policy-makers.

Moreover, while some methods take an explicitly normative position, for example by adopting an agroecology perspective (Soler Montiel & Rivera Ferre, 2010), others are presented as less normatively charged. However, the latter too, by defining and operationalizing sustainability, take strong normative positions that implicitly exclude other possible understandings of sustainable urban agriculture (e.g., Drechsel & Dongus, 2010; see also Goldstein et al., 2016b). More subtly, indicator weightings reflect normative notions of sustainability. They may raise further challenges not only in a given context, where different stakeholders may disagree on attributed weightings, but also regarding the use of a selected assessment method in contexts where urban agriculture may have different purposes (e.g., income generation) from the context in which the method was originally developed (e.g., social inclusion). These issues, and more broadly the question of the transferability of the assessment method to distinct urban contexts, are hardly addressed in the methods reviewed in this chapter, and therefore represent an important area for future research (see also Barrett et al., 2017).

Furthermore, the above-mentioned implications underscore the importance of a careful contextualization of the sustainability assessment by which the conditions for the assessment are explicitly identified (see Chapter 1 (Halla & Binder, 2020)). These include how sustainability is conceptualized by different stakeholders, which underlying worldviews have shaped these conceptualizations, how these worldviews are rooted in the socioeconomic and socio-ecological context in which they are expressed, and how the assessment would feed into the governance process itself. By making these assumptions and their socioeconomic and socio-ecological embeddedness explicit, a common definition of sustainability could potentially emerge, which would then serve to inform the research design and assessment tools.

17.4.2 Procedural Dimension

Two main challenges can be identified with respect to the procedural dimension of the sustainability assessment of urban agriculture, namely the need for what Certomá and Tornaghi (2015) call "dedicated investigation strategies," and the difficulties in defining the user group and in sustaining participation (Table 17.2).

First, and in relation to the previous discussion, the often contested and political nature of urban agriculture raises questions about the role of the researchers in the sustainability assessment process. While it is out of the scope of this chapter to discuss in detail the possible forms of scientist-activism configurations in sustainability and critical scholarship (see for example: Pickerill, 2008; Tornaghi & van Dyck, 2015), it is important to highlight that the sustainability assessment of urban agriculture may, even more than for agriculture in rural spaces, challenge the position of the researchers and their practices (Tornaghi & van Dyck, 2015). The political nature of urban agriculture makes it difficult to escape the normative basis and implications of research practice, and therefore not only "poses methodological questions and calls for dedicated investigation strategies, it also requires an understanding of the reasons for, and effects of, their personal engagement, far beyond their mere commitment to reciprocity" (Certomá & Tornaghi, 2015 p. 1127). The methods illustrated in the previous section take distinct approaches to this issue along a broad spectrum from a critical but active engagement (Soler Montiel & Rivera-Ferre, 2010) to substantially neutral positions (Beilin & Hunter, 2011; Losada et al., 2001). Nonetheless, these examples suggest that the urgency of the questions regarding the researcher's political and normative position, and therefore the need to develop appropriate "dedicated investigation strategies," may depend not only on the researcher's own beliefs and approach to investigation, but critically on the level of political struggle and contestation in the specific system under investigation.

A second procedural challenge relates to sustaining participation. This issue may arise from the often higher mobility of the urban population, and especially in peri-urban spaces, as compared to people living in rural areas and settlements. Peri-urban areas are often spaces of temporary immigration in which people may engage in farming activities. Moreover, urban agriculture may often be only one of a number of income-generating activities for urban residents. More generally, urban citizens may show less attachment to place than rural ones (Anton & Lawrence, 2014). Therefore, for example, a mobile urban population may make it difficult to identify a community of interest, and to secure community participation especially in a lengthy participatory process. Moreover, even when participation may be secured, it is more likely that those who participated in the preparation and selection of the indicators may not be the same participants who may be called upon to follow up on them, or who reap the benefits of any sustainability-enhancing intervention. In fact, the characteristic of a mobile population may be relevant even for sustainability assessment methods that do not entail stakeholder participation but, for instance, rely on other forms of data collection such as surveys or interviews. In those cases, the assessment may be based on data related to farming activities or participants that are not those who will benefit or be influenced by any follow-up interventions.

A further challenge to sustaining participation in the sustainability assessment of urban agriculture is posed by the more heterogeneous population of urban as compared to rural systems. First, urban farmers may have other jobs or activities and therefore differential time pressures, may be spatially unevenly distributed, and may be subject to different social responsibilities and expectations, as in the case of female versus male farmers in different ethnic or cultural groups, or social classes. Second, given the proximity of agricultural and non-agricultural activities that is typical of urban systems, non-farmer stakeholders are also more diverse than in many rural contexts. Therefore, devising participatory strategies that encourage and enable the participation of such a diverse farmer and non-farmer population may be difficult logistically as well as at a normative level (as discussed). However, none of the approaches and methods illustrated in the previous sections address, in a substantial manner, the potential issue raised by mobile, heterogeneous urban populations with little attachment to place. This is an important area of methodological development for sustainability assessment of urban agriculture.

One possibility to address some of the challenges outlined may consist in employing transdisciplinary sustainability assessment approaches, which entail the engagement of relevant stakeholders in defining a given problem, and the participatory codesign of an approach for research and action (Binder et al., 2010; de Zeeuw & Drechsel, 2015). Transdisciplinary approaches are not immune from power dynamics (see Chapter 4 (Fritz & Meinherz, 2020)) but offer ways to recognize and deal with them in designing and conducting the assessment.

17.4.3 Systemic Dimension

Urban agriculture is often spatially and socially interstitial: it is not necessarily practiced in open fields, but in vacant lots, on rooftops as well as in backyards (Certomá & Tornaghi, 2015). Moreover, it is often spatially and socially porous: it is practiced by professional farmers as well as by citizens in their free time, in private as well as in public spaces. Thus, urban agriculture often has soft boundaries and strong interactions and complementarity with its non-agricultural context; due to such proximity and interactions, both the positive (e.g., psychological benefits from a greener urban landscape) and the negative (e.g., water pollution) effects of urban agriculture can easily spill over. On account of this, it is often difficult to clearly identify the unit of analysis or any separations between a garden or urban farm and the system in which it is environmentally, infrastructurally, and socially embedded. For example, many urban and peri-urban farms are parts of short food supply chains in which consumers purchase the produce directly on the farm, sometimes actively participating in field maintenance and harvesting, as in community-supported agriculture schemes. These experiences not only shorten food supply chains, but also blur the boundaries between production, retail, and consumption. This has important implications for sustainability assessment. However, as illustrated by the diversity of methods presented in the previous section, there appears to be no established approach that can deal with this aspect of urban agriculture, since assessment methods may (Landert et al., 2017) or may not (Goldstein et al., 2016b; Losada et al., 2001) include system components beyond the farm.

It is also important to note that the examples of assessment methods presented do not include interactions among the indicators. This may be a sign of a lower level of sophistication of these methods compared to other sustainability assessment methods that do consider those interactions (Binder et al., 2010). The lack of consideration for interactions among indicators may reflect an emphasis on the social rather than the environmental dimension, as discussed previously regarding the normative dimension. On the other hand, it could also reflect the difficulty of representing mathematically or computationally the interactions between environmental, agronomic, and infrastructural (built environment) components of the system, thus again underscoring the challenge posed by the mixed nature of urban and peri-urban systems for the assessment of urban agriculture.

Interdisciplinary approaches offer a way forward to understand system complexity in sustainability assessment. Methods from the social and environmental sciences, as well as interpretivist and positivist approaches, can be fruitfully combined to build awareness and understanding of the interrelationship between the different elements and processes, as well as their hierarchical relations. For example, interpretivist methods can help identify system boundaries through thick descriptions of the different and interrelating elements that make up an urban or peri-urban system, while being sensitive to multiple and possibly conflicting views of the system (see Chapter 8 (Binder et al., 2020a)). This can then lead to a quantification and qualification of material and energy flows (e.g., Karg et al., 2016; Leray et al. 2016), while the drivers of these flows can then be determined through social science approaches (e.g., Binder, 2007).

17.5 Conclusions

Governance is central to ensuring urban agriculture's nutritional, economic, social, and environmental positive outcomes are maximized, while its potential negative impacts are avoided or minimized. Sustainability assessment can play an important role as part of broader governance strategies to support sustainable urban agriculture and sustainable urban food systems more broadly. However, this chapter has shown that there is a paucity of assessment methods that have been developed specifically for urban agriculture and are flexible enough to be immediately applicable for different forms of urban agriculture in different contexts.

Sustainability assessment of agriculture has usually focused on agriculture for market production in relatively stable rural contexts. However, urban agriculture poses challenges that many existing sustainability assessment approaches and methods fail to address. The diversity of urban agriculture forms, the multifunctionality of peri-urban spaces where urban agriculture largely takes place, contested framings of urban agriculture, and the difficulties involved in integrating and incorporating different types of knowledge and land use into urban planning often result in the failure to create institutional, policy, and planning arrangements that are conducive to sustainable urban agriculture.

Some of the challenges identified in this chapter are not unique to urban agriculture. Agriculture is often contested regardless of whether it occurs in an urban or rural system, and rural farmers often have multiple employments and can be mobile, e.g., seeking seasonal employment in different places and economic sectors. Nevertheless, as has been amply discussed in the literature and in this chapter, these characteristics manifest more acutely in urban and peri-urban spaces due to the specific nature of urban systems.

This chapter has suggested some opportunities to move the practice of sustainability assessment of urban agriculture forward. These include the adoption of inter- and transdisciplinary research strategies, and a critical approach to urban agriculture practices, power relations, social norms, and institutional conditions that have developed over time in specific contexts. A reflexive research approach and "dedicated investigation strategies" may also go a long way in supporting the sustainability assessment of urban agriculture. But there are no silver bullets or predetermined solutions to the challenges identified in this chapter. Ultimately, sustainability assessment of urban agriculture may be a litmus test for governance arrangements to support agriculture in urban and peri-urban spaces, and for research approaches that can contribute to sustainable development.

Acknowledgments

Giuseppe Feola acknowledges support by the Royal Geographical Society (with IBG) through the Environment and Sustainability Research Grant 01/17. Claudia R. Binder and Marlyne Sahakian recognize support from the Swiss National Science Foundation, "Healthy nutrition and sustainable food production" (NRP 69). Claudia R. Binder acknowledges, in addition, the support of Swiss Mobiliar.

References

Anton, C. E., & Lawrence, C. (2014). Home is where the heart is: The effect of place of residence on place attachment and community participation. *Journal of Environmental Psychology*, 40, 451–461.

Badami, M. G., & Ramankutty, N. (2015). Urban agriculture and food security: A critique based on an assessment of urban land constraints. *Global Food Security*, 4, 8–15.

Baker, S. E. (2012). *Evaluating the Feasibility of Urban Agriculture on Oakland's Private Land.* (Bachelor's thesis). University of Berkeley.

Barrett, T., Feola, G., Krylova, V., & Khusnitdinova, M. (2017). The application of Rapid Appraisal of Agricultural Innovation Systems (RAAIS) to agricultural adaptation to climate change in Kazakhstan: A critical evaluation. *Agricultural Systems*, 151, 106–113.

Beilin, R., & Hunter, A. (2011). Co-constructing the sustainable city: How indicators help us "grow" more than just food in community gardens. *Local Environment*, 16, 523–538.

Binder, C. R, Hutter, M., Pang, M., & Webb, R. (2020). System science and sustainability assessment. In C. R. Binder, E. Massaro, & R. Wyss (eds.), *Sustainability Assessment in Urban Systems*. Cambridge University Press, pp. 30–64.

Binder, C. R., Feola, G., & Steinberger, J. K. (2010). Considering the normative, systemic and procedural dimensions in indicator-based sustainability assessments in agriculture. *Environmental Impact Assessment Review*, 30, 71–81.

Binder, C. (2007). From material flow analysis to material flow management Part I: social sciences modeling approaches coupled to MFA. *Journal of Cleaner Production*, 15, 1596–1604.

Blixen Magariños, C., Colnago Vieyto, P., González Jiménez, N., Márquez Scotti, C., & Chiappe Hernández, M. (2007). Indicadores de sostenibilidad para la agricultura urbana. I seminario de cooperación y desarrollo en espacios rurales iberoamericanos. *Sostenibilidad e indicadores. Almeria*, 16–17 Octubre, 2007

Certomá, C., & Tornaghi, C. (2015). Political gardening: Transforming cities and political agency. *Local Environment*, 20(10), 1123–1131.

Chappell, M. J., Wittman, H., Bacon, C. M., et al. (2013). Food sovereignty: An alternative paradigm for poverty reduction and biodiversity conservation in Latin America. *F1000Research*, 2, 235.

De Bon, H., Parrot, L., & Moustier, P. (2010). Sustainable urban agriculture in developing countries. A review. *Agronomy for Sustainable Development*, 30, 21–32.

de Zeeuw, H. (2004). The development of Urban Agriculture; some lessons learnt. Keynote presented at the conference Urban Agriculture, Agro-tourism and City Region Development, Beijing, 10–14 October.

de Zeeuw, H., & Dubbeling, M. (2009). Cities, food and agriculture: Challenges and the way forward. Presented at the technical consultation Agriculture, Food and Cities, Rome, 24–25 September.

de Zeeuw, H., & Drechsel, P. (Eds.) (2015). *Cities and Agriculture: Developing Resilient Urban Food Systems*. London: Routledge.

Drechsel, P., Graefe, S., Sonou, M., & Cofie, O. O. (2006). Informal Irrigation In Urban West Africa: An Overview. Research Report Series. Colombo, Sri Lanka: International Water Management Institute.

Drechsel, P., & Dongus, S. (2010). Dynamics and sustainability of urban agriculture: examples from sub-Saharan Africa. *Sustainability Science*, 5(1), 69.

Drechsel, P., & Keraita, B. (Eds.) (2014). *Irrigated Urban Vegetable Production in Ghana: Characteristics, Benefits and Risk Mitigation*, 2nd edition. Colombo, Sri Lanka: International Water Management Institute (IWMI).

Eigenbrod, C., & Gruda, N. (2015). Urban vegetable for food security in cities: A review. *Agronomy for Sustainable Development*, 35, 483–498.

FAO (1996). *The State of Food and Agriculture*. Rome: FAO.

FAO (1999). Committee on Agriculture – COAG/FAO. Urban and peri-urban agriculture. OAG/99/10. Presented at the Fifteenth Session of the COAG. 25–29 January. Rome: FAO.

FAO (2007). Profitability and sustainability of urban and peri-urban agriculture. *Agricultural Management, Marketing and Finance Occasional Paper*. Rome: FAO.

Farming Concrete (2015). *Farming Concrete Data Collection Toolkit*. New York: Design Trust for Public Space

Fritz, L., & Meinherz, F. (2020). The politics of participatory sustainability assessments: An analysis of power. In C. R. Binder, E. Massaro, & R. Wyss (eds.), *Sustainability Assessment in Urban Systems*. Cambridge University Press, pp. 87–122.

Galluzzi, G., Eyzaguirre, P., & Negri, V. (2010). Home gardens: Neglected hotspots of agro-biodiversity and cultural diversity. *Biodiversity and Conservation*, 19, 3635–3654.

Gasparatos, A., & Scolobig, A. (2012). Choosing the most appropriate sustainability assessment tool. *Ecological Economics*, 80, 1–7.

Ghosh, S. (2014). Measuring sustainability performance of local food production in home gardens. *Local Environment*, 19(1), 33–55.

Godin, L., & Sahakian, M. (2018). Cutting through conflicting prescriptions: How guidelines inform "healthy and sustainable" diets in Switzerland. *Appetite*, 130, 123–133.

Goldstein, B. P., Hauschild, M. Z., Fernández, J. E., & Birkved, M. (2017). Contributions of local farming to urban sustainability in the northeast United States. *Environmental Science & Technology*, 51, 7340–7349.

Goldstein, B., Hauschild, M., Fernández, J., & Birkved, M. (2016a). Urban versus conventional agriculture, taxonomy of resource profiles: A review. *Agronomy for Sustainable Development*, 36(1), 9.

Goldstein, B., Hauschild, M., Fernández, J., & Birkved, M. (2016b). Testing the environmental performance of urban agriculture as a food supply in northern climates. *Journal of Cleaner Production*, 135, 984–994.

Goodman, D., Du Puis, M., & Goodman, M. K. (2012). *Alternative Food Networks: Knowledge, Practice, and Politics*. London: Routledge.

Grewal, S. S., & Grewal, P. S. (2012). Can cities become self-reliant in food? *Cities*, 29(1), 1–11.

Halla, P., & Binder, C. R. (2020). Sustainability Assessment: Introduction and Framework. In C. R. Binder, E. Massaro, & R. Wyss (eds.), *Sustainability Assessment in Urban Systems*. Cambridge University Press, pp. 7–29.

Hashim, N. (2015). Reversing food desertification: Examining urban farming in Louisville, Chicago and Detroit. *Local Environment*, 20(6), 611–636.

Karg, H., Drechsel, P., Akoto-Danso, E. K., Glaser, R., Nyarko, G., & Buerkert, A. (2016). Foodsheds and city region food systems in two West African cities. *Sustainability*, 8(12), 1175.

Kulak, M., Graves, A., & Chatterton, J. (2013). Reducing greenhouse gas emissions with urban agriculture: A life cycle assessment perspective. *Landscape and Urban Planning*, 111, 68–78.

Landert, J., Schader, C., Moschitz, H., & Stolze, M. (2017). A holistic sustainability assessment method for urban food system governance. *Sustainability*, 9(4), 490.

Lang, U. (2014). Cultivating the sustainable city: Urban agriculture policies and gardening projects in Minneapolis, Minnesota. *Urban Geography*, 35, 477–485.

Leray, L., Sahakian, M., & Erkman. S. (2016). Understanding household food metabolism: Relating micro-level material flow analysis to consumption practices. *Journal of Cleaner Production*, 125, 44–55.

Lerner, A. M., & Eakin, H. (2011). An obsolete dichotomy? Rethinking the rural-urban interface in terms of food security and production in the Global South. *The Geographical Journal*, 177, 311–320.
Lerner, A. M., Eakin, H., & Sweeney, S. (2013). Understanding peri-urban maize production through an examination of household livelihoods in the Toluca Metropolitan Area, Mexico. *Journal of Rural Studies*, 30, 52–63.
Lin, B. B., Philpott, S. M., & Jha, S. (2015). The future of urban agriculture and biodiversity-ecosystem services: Challenges and next steps. *Basic and Applied Ecology*, 16, 189–201.
López-Ridaura, S., Masera, O., & Astier, M. (2002). Evaluating the sustainability of complex socio-environmental systems: The MESMIS framework. *Ecological Indicators*, 2, 135–148.
Losada, H., Vieyra, J., Soriano, R., Bennett, R., Cortés, J., & Zavaleta, P. (2001). Assessing the sustainability of a terraced agroecosystem for production of nopal vegetable (Opuntia ficus-indica) in metropolitan Mexico City. *American Journal of Alternative Agriculture*, 16(3), 98–105.
Madaleno, I. M., & Gurovich, A. (2004). "Urban versus rural" no longer matches reality: An early public agro-residential development in periurban Santiago, Chile. *Cities*, 21, 513–526.
Marshall, F., Dolley, J., Randhawa, P., et al. (2017). Why Peri-urban Ecosystem Services Matter for Urban Policy (Policy Briefing). ESPA briefing. Brighton: STEPS Centre.
McClintock, N. (2014). Radical, reformist, and garden-variety neoliberal: Coming to terms with urban agriculture's contradictions. *Local Environment*, 19(2), 147–171.
McClintock, N., Cooper, J., & Khandeshi, S. (2013). Assessing the potential contribution of vacant land to urban vegetable production and consumption in Oakland, California. *Landscape and Urban Planning*, 111, 46–58.
Meinherz, F., Fritz, L., & Schneider, F. (2020). How Values Play into Sustainability Assessments: Challenges and a Possible Way Forward. In C. R. Binder, E. Massaro, & R. Wyss (eds.), *Sustainability Assessment in Urban Systems*. Cambridge University Press, pp. 65–86.
Mendez, M., Ramirez, L., & Alzate, A. (2005) La práctica de la agricultura urbana como expresión de emergencia de nuevas ruralidades: reflexiones en torno a la evidencia empírica. *Cuadernos de Desarrollo Rural*, 55, 51–70.
Mougeot, L. J. (2005). *Agropolis: The Social, Political and Environmental Dimensions of Urban Agriculture*. IDRC/London: Earthscan.
Olsson, E., Kerselaers, E., Søderkvist Kristensen, L., Primdahl, J., Rogge, E., & Wästfelt, A. (2016). Peri-urban food production and its relation to urban resilience. *Sustainability*, 8, 1340.
Orsini, F., Kahane, R., Nono-Womdim, R., & Gianquinto, G. (2013). Urban agriculture in the developing world: A review. *Agronomy for Sustainable Development*, 33, 695–720.
Ortega Cerdà, M., & Rivera-Ferre, M. G. (2010). Indicadores internacionales de Soberanía Alimentaria. Nuevas herramientas para una nueva agricultura. *Revibec: revista de la Red Iberoamericana de Economia Ecológica*, 14, 53–77.
Pearson, L. J., Pearson, L., & Pearson, C. J. (2010.) Sustainable urban agriculture: Stocktake and opportunities. *International Journal of Agricultural Sustainability*, 8, 7–19.
Pérez-Martinez, M. E. (2016). Las territorialidades urbano rurales contemporaneas: un debate epistémico y metodológico para su abordaje. *Bitácora*, 26(2), 103–112.
Pickerill, J. (2008). The surprising sense of hope. *Antipode*, 40(3), 482–487.
Plessz, M., Dubuisson-Quellier, S., Gojard, S., & Barrey, S. (2016). How consumption prescriptions affect food practices: Assessing the roles of household resources and life-course events. *Journal of Consumer Culture*, 16(1), 101–123.
Poulsen, M. N. (2017). Cultivating citizenship, equity, and social inclusion? Putting civic agriculture into practice through urban farming. *Agriculture and Human Values*, 34, 135–148.
Poulsen, M. N., McNab, P. R., Clayton, M. L., & Neff, R. A. (2015). A systematic review of urban agriculture and food security impacts in low-income countries. *Food Policy*, 55, 131–146.
Quon, S. (1999). *Planning for Urban Agriculture: A Review of Tools and Strategies for Urban Planners*. Cities Feeding People series, report 28. Ottawa: International Development Research Centre.
Rabinovitch, J., & Schmetzer, H. (1997). Urban agriculture: Food, jobs and sustainable cities. *Agriculture and Rural Development* 4(2), 44–45.

Ringenbach, J., Valcourt, M., & Wang, W. (2013) Mapping the Potential for Urban Agriculture in Worcester: A Land Inventory Assessment. Interactive Qualifying Projects (All Departments). 2644. Worcester Polytechnic Institute.

Saha, M., & Eckelman, M. J. (2017). Growing fresh fruits and vegetables in an urban landscape: A geospatial assessment of ground level and rooftop urban agriculture potential in Boston, USA. *Landscape and Urban Planning*, 165, 130–141.

Sahakian, M., Saloma, C., & Erkman, S. (Eds.) (2016). *Food Consumption in the City: Practices and Patterns in Urban Asia and the Pacific*. Oxford: Routledge.

Saldivar-Tanaka, L., & Krasny, M. E. (2004). Culturing community development, neighborhood open space, and civic agriculture: The case of Latino community gardens in New York City. *Agriculture and Human Values*, 21(4), 399–412.

Savoie-Roskos, M. R., Wengreen, H., & Durward, C. (2017). Increasing fruit and vegetable intake among children and youth through gardening-based interventions: A systematic review. *Journal of the Academy of Nutrition and Dietetics*, 117(2), 240–250.

Schmidt, S., Magigi, W., & Godfrey, B. (2015). The organization of urban agriculture: Farmer associations and urbanization in Tanzania. *Cities*, 42, 153–159.

Shinew, K. J., Glover, T. D., & Parry, D. C. (2004). Leisure spaces as potential sites for interracial interaction: Community gardens in urban areas. *Journal of Leisure Research*, 36(3), 336.

Soler Montiel, M., & Rivera Ferre M. (2010). Agricultura urbana, sostenibilidad y soberanía alimentaria: hacia una propuesta de indicadores desde la agroecología. Actas del X Congreso Español de Sociología FES (Federación Española de Sociología), Sociología y sociedad en España.

Thebo, A. L., Drechsel, P., & Lambin, E. F. (2014). Global assessment of urban and peri-urban agriculture: Irrigated and rainfed croplands. *Environmental Research Letters*, 9(114002).

Teo, T. A., & Wu, H. M. (2017). Analysis of land cover classification using multi-wavelength LiDAR system. *Applied Sciences*, 7(7), 663.

Tornaghi, C. (2014). Critical geography of urban agriculture. *Progress in Human Geography*, 38, 551–567.

Tornaghi, C., & Van Dyck, B. (2015). Research-informed gardening activism: Steering the public food and land agenda. *Local Environment*, 20(10), 1247–1264.

Van Veenhuizen, René (Ed.) (2006). *Cities Farming for the Future: Urban Agriculture for Green and Productive Cities*. RUAF Foundation, IDRC and IIRR.

Warren, E., Hawkesworth, S., & Knai, C. (2015). Investigating the association between urban agriculture and food security, dietary diversity, and nutritional status: A systematic literature review. *Food Policy*, 53, 54–66.

Zezza, A., & Tasciotti, L. (2010). Urban agriculture, poverty, and food security: Empirical evidence from a sample of developing countries. *Food Policy*, 35, 265–273.

Zundritsch, P. (2018). Cartography of Potential Sites for Urban Gardening in Lausanne. Semester project, École Polytechnique Fédérale de Lausanne.

18

Cities and Entropy: Assessing Urban Sustainability as a Problem of Coordination

Vinicius M. Netto, João Meirelles, and Fabiano L. Ribeiro

18.1 Introduction: Sustainability as Self-Maintenance

The central challenge associated with urban sustainability is that of finding *means* to put it into practice (see Cohen, 2017). Even though definitions of urban sustainability may vary tremendously (Singh et al., 2012), it seems safe to acknowledge that assessing urban sustainability is a major issue, and a crucial step toward solving the challenges we face today. With climate breakdown looming large on the horizon, we need to find ways to reduce damage to environmental systems. Cities have the power to lead the way toward sustainability, given the fact that the majority of the world's population and economic transactions are concentrated in urban centers, and as we hope to show, they are key agents in the continuity of societies as complex systems (Hashemian et al., 2017).

While cities could be a major force in effecting a move toward sustainability, they also lie at the center of anthropogenic environmental impacts. With footprints that extend far beyond their political boundaries, cities are home to 54 percent of humanity and are responsible for 70 percent of all CO_2 emitted on the planet (United Nations, 2011). These figures suggest urgent changes are needed in social behavior, such as shifting production processes toward less material-intense configurations or reducing consumption to levels compatible with the environment's capacity for regeneration. Solutions to these and other issues are likely to demand new and impressive levels of *coordination*: massive numbers of people will need to change their habits and learn to focus their actions in certain sustainable directions.

But the need for people's actions to be coordinated is not something that began with the sustainability crisis we face today. It is instead an anterior requirement, perhaps even an elementary feature of sustainability related to *continuity* and *self-maintenance*. A living system must develop the ability to maintain itself, alongside coexisting systems and its environment. One way of ensuring self-maintenance is precisely through mechanisms for creating internal and external connectivity, allowing entities to relate to each other and coordinate their actions. For any system to exist and reproduce itself, it has to evolve into a state in which connections between entities and coordination of their behaviors become possible. For instance, human societies are formed by large numbers of people and contexts and technical objects potentially behaving in different ways. It is interaction and coordination that enable such diverse sets of agencies to somehow emerge as a single, working system (cf. Luhmann, 1995).

These questions feel more crucial if we think of the increasing challenges faced by contemporary urban societies and the urgent need to coordinate our actions in sustainable ways. The deeper nature of such challenges may be clarified through a classic concept from information theory and thermodynamics: *entropy*. As we shall see, entropy is both a measure of probability in the face of uncertainty (Shannon, 1948), and a measure of disorder (Prigogine and Stengers, 1984). In one way or another, humans face entropy all the time. Our daily actions are riddled with uncertainty, from the daily choices we make to the way our actions will play out once they merge with those of others. If entropy relates to trends toward uncertainty and disorder, and if social systems face entropy all the time, continuity and self-maintenance become significant issues. Self-maintenance requires that the system can keep itself in a low-entropy state (Kolchinsky and Wolpert, 2018; cf. Ayeni, 1976; Purvis et al., 2017; Xuan et al., 2012). We need means of increasing coordination as a way into self-maintenance – ways of reducing the entropy triggered by our own uncertainties and by the unintended consequences of our actions. We will argue that the reduction of entropy brings together issues of sustainability of *social* and *urban* systems. In fact, we hope to show that cities play a crucial role in our conscious and unconscious efforts to cooperate with each other, connecting people's actions into systems we call "societies."

Perhaps one analogy might clarify how cities can be a part of that process. A well-known experiment involves the synchronization of *metronomes*, the century-old tool used by musicians to keep time (tempo) as they perform. The experiment begins with dozens of metronomes oscillating at different times. The metronomes are spaced regularly on a board. As they oscillate in time, the energy of each individual metronome is transmitted through the board. These oscillations spread energy in the form of rhythmic vibrations, triggering mutual alterations between metronomes. This transmission operates very much like waves in the air or on the surface of bodies of water: at times reinforcing a trend as peak meets peak (the encounter with vibration waves from other metronomes) or as valley meets valley (the absence of vibrations at that moment and in that position); at times, nullifying differences as peak meets valley in vibrations across the board (cf. Pantaleone, 2002). As these individual exchanges progress, a pattern begins to appear: converging vibrations progressively "capture" and change the behavior of individual metronomes. The collective result is total synchrony. Synchronization is enabled by the board, which serves as an "interaction medium" between metronomes (Strogatz, 2012).

As a medium, the built environment would adopt a similar role in the coordination of our actions. Cities and their spatiality are capable of expressing and supporting multiple agencies. We propose in this chapter that *self-maintenance can be stimulated by cities that enable us better to coordinate our actions* – like moving around more efficiently, meeting more widely, interacting more diversely, mutually understanding each other, and changing our actions and orientations as we interact with the environment. Cities can reduce the entropy of actions that might otherwise disperse and lead to social fragmentation and instability.

But how might coordination work in real cities and societies? How can individual actions unfold into something like a working system of interactions? Well, quite differently from metronomes on boards. The energy exchanged between social entities in an urban context takes a rather specific form: *communication*, the transmission of information as meaningful content that is mutually understandable by people interacting. The board here is more than just material support: urban space would serve both as a form of *environmental information* and as a means for exchange of information between people. In other words, we suggest that among all the systems of communication created to give us information about what is available out there, one of them is crucial and quite old: *the city*. Possibilities for interaction are presented to us and to some extent preselected for us by our own environment, shaped in the form of cities. Environmental information will allow for the coordination of individual actions at the heart of collective life, and cities have historically played that role.

In short, we are interested in knowing how seemingly chaotic actions together amount to coherent interaction systems, and how these systems reduce their own entropy through the urban environment. Essentially, we will track these transitions and the variation of entropy that they entail. We suggest that by carefully looking into the place of cities in those transitions, the constant ordering/disordering of action will be clarified, helping to explain self-maintenance more clearly. We do so arguing that urban spaces have the effect of reducing uncertainty and unpredictability in actions.

Now that the problem has been set out, Section 18.2 establishes cities as informational environments, while Section 18.3 advances the city as a frame of reference for actions and explores how these coevolve into systems. In turn, Section 18.4 hypothesizes how the reduction of entropy mediated by the city becomes an essential part of the coordination of actions. Since the coordination of actions in our daily lives transcends local contexts and is largely beyond observation, we designed simulations *in silico* to try and clarify the effect of cities on coordination. We examine this process in Section 18.5, proposing an agent-based model (ABM) capable of assessing the role of different social and spatial factors in entropy, such as personal orientation and an extensive space creating friction for mobile agents able to change and retrieve information from their environment. In the final section, we discuss what our theory and model say about the role of cities in sustainability as a problem of coordinating actions.

18.2 The City as Informational Environment

Niklas Luhmann (1995) shows that social systems are immersed in semantic production: meaning becomes their environment. We wish to further develop this idea by exploring urban space as part of such an environment. In fact, the idea of space as an environment able to contain social information has gained great support recently. From Vygotsky (1978) to Wilson (2002) and Haken and Portugali (2015), a number of cognitive properties of space and spatial properties of cognition have been identified (Table 18.1).

This non-discursive knowledge includes spatial properties and heterogeneities, and enables us to build inferences, for example, when we try to imagine a street where we are likely to find a certain activity taking place. In turn, Lakoff and Johnson (1999)

Table 18.1 *Cognitive properties of space and spatial properties of cognition*

Relation environment-cognition	Cognitive and spatial properties
Cognition Is Situated and Extended	Our cognitive activity occurs in the context of a real environment and inherently involves perception. Our cognitive activity is linked to our continuous interaction with the environment (Clark & Chalmers 1998; Vygotsky, 1978; Wilson, 2002). Order and systematicity in human cognition and action derive in part from the stability of our environment (Michaelian & Sutton, 2013).
We Load the Built Environment with Information	Certain cognitive processes trigger associations with elements of the environment through the incorporation of socially acquired information (Kintsch, 1970; Passini, 1992; Rosch, 1978). Environmental elements (say, buildings or places) are interpreted through such socially shared meanings (Neisser, 1994). The probability of a building or place evoking a shared mental representation among people is enhanced by its physical appearance and visual identity, along with its visibility and location in the environment and the social information associated with activities performed there (Faria & Krafta, 2003; cf. Portugali, 2011).
Spatial Information Relieves Our Cognitive Work	We deal with the environment also through memory. However, our short-term memory is constrained in its capability to process information (Haken & Portugali, 2015). Luckily, our knowledge of spatial properties and patterns can integrate semantic, visual, and configurational aspects projected into an urban environment as symbolic off-loading. The spatial environment becomes an external memory carrying information about activities and agencies found in it for future retrieval (Kirsh & Maglio, 1994; Kosslyn, 1994; Wilson, 2002). Environmental information is a means of reducing the effort of memorization.
Cognition Is Pressed for Time	Daily life requires response capacity. More cognitive capacity can be built up from successive layers of real-time interaction with our spatial context. We create mental models of the environment from which we create action plans. Sophisticated forms of situated cognition happen in any activity that involves the continuous updating of plans in response to changing conditions of action. Time pressure demands spatial decisions (Brooks, 1999; Clark, 1997; Pfeifer & Scheier, 1999).
Spatial Information Serves Action	Cognition serves action through a flexible and sophisticated strategy, where information is stored for future use without firm commitments on what the future use may be (Franklin, 1995; Gibson, 1979; Glenberg & Robertson, 1999; Iverson & Goldin-Meadow, 1998; Krauss, 1998;). Spatial information can be absorbed through a variety of uses for which it was not originally encoded. This means that new uses may be derived from a stored representation of space. Environmental representations, either schematic or detailed, appear to be largely free of a particular purpose, or at least contain information beyond what is necessary for a specific action. This is certainly an adaptive cognitive strategy. The fact that humans encode the physical world using spatially and semantically structured mental models offers a huge advantage in solving problems.

argue that mental models are based on a modeling of the physical world and bolster analogies between abstract and concrete domains. Other works tie semantics with imagetic schemes capable of incorporating knowledge of the physical world as a way to encode relationships between events. In perceiving something, we perceive not only its observed form, but also the potential information enfolded in it (Haken & Portugali, 2015). This very property is crucial to the presence of urban space in the selection of actions to be performed.

Thus, our actions encode space with social information, and this informationally differentiated space plays a part in easing the representational bottleneck in our memories. We are able to retrieve information from this semantic arrangement that takes the form of the city before and during our actions and experiences. This semantic layer is stored in activity places and in the spatial relations between them and may be related to physical and functional heterogeneities, such as accessibility and centrality patterns (Faria & Krafta, 2003). Such layers of spatial information can be evoked in our memories and used when we need to make inferences, such as where we could find a particular social situation or place. However, most theories of situated cognition still do not recognize how this informational environment is part of the way we create action systems. Let us see how this could be the case.

18.3 The City as a Frame of Reference

We propose to explore the informational role of urban space in how agents build connections as a step toward coordination and toward keeping an interaction system in a low-entropy state, as elementary conditions of sustainability. We know that urban space is produced to express human activity. But theories of cognition suggest much more: space would be semanticized by our actions. That means that activity places are informationally differentiated and acquire a level of semantic definition similar to types of action (Netto, 2008, 2017). This differentiation is enacted in and associated with the very structure of urban space. Space is differentiated on at least three levels: (i) its physical properties of extensity and configuration, such as accessibility and centrality patterns in a city; (ii) recognizable shapes in its visual and three-dimensional form (Haken & Portugali, 2015); and (iii) the semantic content of activities performed in buildings and places (cf. Faria & Krafta, 2003; Portugali, 2011) (Figure 18.1).

How can this informational space become a part of action? There is a remarkable lack of theoretical and empirical work on this problem. First, we seem to retrieve meanings associated with our actions in architectural and urban spaces. We arguably grasp useful information about the activity performed in a place not only by means of visual features, but also by inferring what people do there. Space does not only represent activity: it is enacted and thus loaded with meanings related to performance. This is a semantic dimension of space: space "means" as much as our actions, precisely because it is semanticized by our actions. This enacted information is very important (Netto et al., 2018). Action is temporally related to spatial locations.

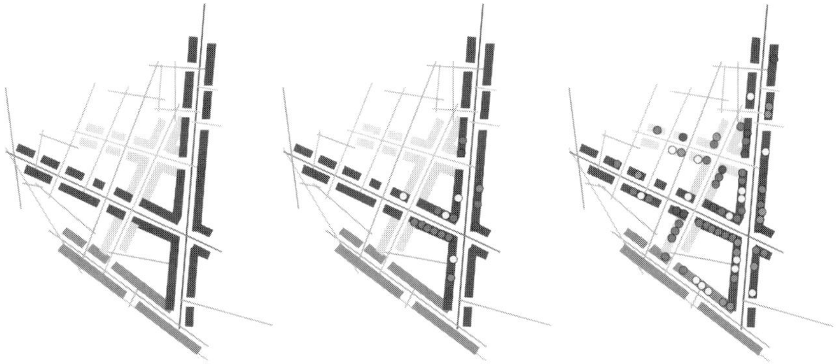

Figure 18.1 Like a code of instructions for collective action, urban space finds differentiation both physically, as hierarchies of accessibility and distribution of built form (left), and semantically, through actions performed in buildings and places (center, right)

Second, these locations allow us to access potential interacting agents. As we shall see, knowing a city means that we can find places where certain activities are performed. Recognizing spatial differences and patterns allows us to infer where such locations might be. Apart from other sources of information such as linguistic exchanges, we do so because we can retrieve environmental information about activities and location patterns.

Third, places are means of connection: we can actualize connections with certain people or activities during a period of time. These spatial links allow us to create complexes of interaction. In practice, places "draw" courses of action with different orientations and contents, and tie them together momentarily. Flows of convergent and divergent actions happen all the time: when people leave their homes to work, to seek services, or to go about to socialize, often without prior knowledge of the activities, agents, or places they wish to visit. Urban space becomes what Parsons (1968) would call an "action frame of reference," a connective fabric that both enables and constrains choices, materially and socially.

18.4 The Reduction of Entropy as a Way into Sustainability

The concept of entropy, a term derived from the Greek word *tropos*, "transformation," and introduced by the German physicist Rudolf Clausius in 1865, originated in the context of physical systems, specifically the second law of thermodynamics, which describes the irreversible process of energy dissipation. The concept was advanced by Ludwig Boltzmann's connection of entropy and probability in 1877, addressing nonequilibrium processes and linking the macroscopic properties of a system to its microscopic disorder. There are more possible disordered states than ordered ones, so systems are likely to move toward disorder. From the infinite variety of dynamic states, entropy is a measure of the propensity for certain states. It characterizes each macroscopic state in terms of the number of ways of achieving this state (Prigogine & Stenger, 1984). We also argue that entropy can be used to assess how successful social and urban systems can be in dealing with their own self-maintenance and sustainability (cf. Marchettini et al., 2006; Purvis et al., 2017).

Societies are interaction systems. People's actions are mediated by information: they have meanings, from personal orientation (Weber, 1978) to informational (Luhmann, 1995) and practical content (Wittgenstein, 2001). Meanings produce informational difference. We recognize actions through such informational differences – say, in the contents of utterances or in the tasks we perform with someone. In principle, the greater the diversity of orientations and actions, the harder it is to predict what someone's next action will be. But there is more to this temporal condition. A state of high entropy surrounds actions in a potential state, before they come into being, when a number of possibilities for action lie ahead. Bringing Shannon's (1948) and Luhmann's insights together, the problem of coordinating actions is, at its heart, a problem of selecting actions and reducing entropy.

We experience entropy whenever we deal with uncertainty, options, decisions, unpredictable situations, or too much information, but we rarely realize we do so. Entropy is a phenomenon "beyond observation": we cannot see or touch entropy, even though we experience it on a daily basis. We are not used to thinking about the challenges we face in order to make choices or put our actions together in any workable sense. The key question here is how such a heightened field of choices and the taken-for-granted process of selection involve our environment. We need to understand how cities are part of the semantic exchanges that constitute collective action. And the first step here is to understand urban space as information in its own right.

In order to be a part of the selection and coordination of actions, the urban environment needs to be informational enough, and not just to suggest particular options but to allow unforeseen changes in the course of our actions. Luhmann suggests that a desired social activity must be within reach. "Because complete interdependence is unattainable, however, interdependencies only come about by selection.... Successfully established interdependencies then serve as perspectives for and constraints on the structural selections that connect onto them" (Luhmann, 1995, p. 284). As a social event, this connection is produced through communication. But before communication comes into being, certain conditions have to be met spatially. Places must be chosen as conjunctive pieces that materialize connections.

Could cities stimulate connections? If they could, and given the fact that they are formed by space and that space is not fully malleable, is it reasonable to suppose that certain spatial formations could facilitate such momentary connections? We know that proximity increases the intensity of interaction (Allen, 1977; Ribeiro et al., 2017). But what form should urbanized space take in order to meet such systemic expectations? We may understand such spatial conditions through a counterfactual scenario. Imagine a fully chaotic urban formation with no recognizable concentrations or paths. Visual elements could not convey information, as spatial differences would not develop into structures emerging out of absolute heterogeneity. References to activities of interest would have to rely only on our memory. Selection of actions would become dependent on very detailed mental representations of such a chaotic formation. Inferences about more likely places to find particular activities would be very hard to make. We would be immersed in a spatial environment without patterns to guide our choices, reduce our efforts, and amplify our interactions. In a world of unstructured spaces, actions would face a lack of information, noise, and relentless entropy. The possibility that space may have an informational presence in interaction expresses the possibility that the physical environment may have informational properties and that the world is rich in information.

Now, it is not only our daily experience that denies that cities are such completely chaotic, structureless places – spatial economics and urban studies also offer plenty of theories and evidence to show that, as complex as they may be, cities are (at least partially) structured places. From location patterns described since Alonso (1964) and accessibility patterns described from Hansen (1959) to Hillier (1996), we know that urban patterns matter: they imply that activities can be arranged in ways that are recognizable and accessible. And from the point of view of selection, the realization that activities are somehow arranged according to a spatial structure is a form of preselection. Activities tend to be distributed according to levels of accessibility, land values, and practical dependencies, facilitating complementary actions. Intentionally or not, and however subject to contingencies, urban space is also structured (physically and informationally), which allows possibilities for action to be more easily known, more easily selected, and more viable. In short, at first, the urban structure affords a range of possibilities for selection. In addition, the structure itself suggests gradients of attractive possibilities.

In view of social systems constituted by connections between actions, this means that space can be part of the constant transition from individual acts to complexes of actions (individual act → places as connections → action systems). Our hypothesis here, to be tested in computational experiments in the following section, is that cities become a crucial part of this connectivity. They would reduce risks such as the lack of information or courses of action too costly to emerge.

What does this say about the effect of cities on entropy? Beginning with Luhmann, interactions have structural value because they represent selections from combinatorial possibilities. If we relate this to Shannon entropy, the very emergence of urban structures eliminates spatial scenarios where every possible connection would have the same probability. Another counterfactual scenario might help here. Entirely homogeneous cities (or entirely heterogeneous, for that matter), free from structure, would present even probabilities of choice between actions. Of course, this would be a problem for social systems: connections that were potentially interesting to most people would be as difficult to find as any other single connection. If urban space was purely homogeneous or purely random, the probability of finding an activity would be distributed homogeneously in space (cf. Batty et al., 2014; Wilson, 1970). That is a scenario of maximum entropy. The spatial environment would be useless for stimulating certain sought-after connections which could otherwise exist – say, when we concentrate activities like final supply or input-output exchanges in production. Effort, time spent, and economic costs involved in finding activities of interest would rise.

On the other hand, when urban space finds differentiated contents and structures – say, location patterns along accessible paths – it naturally creates differences in the probability of interaction and decreases in entropy. Location patterns are in fact material and informational expressions of interaction systems. The differences engendered by such patterns generate differences in the chances of finding an agent, a service, or commerce. If a city did not have recognizable internal formations such as centralities or high streets, agents would have more difficulties in knowing where they are most likely to find what they are after. A partially structured environment allows us to build inferences about the actions and agencies available in a social system. When these agencies are also related temporally through proximity and functional complementarity, there is an even greater potential for differences in probability to emerge, suggesting new connections and sequences. What all this means is that cities, internally differentiated yet far from absolutely heterogeneous, have the effect of reducing social entropy.

Before experimenting with these relationships *in silico*, let us attempt an introductory description of what these differences in probability entail for the way social systems handle entropy (Figure 18.2). Linearizing, for the sake of simplicity, processes that in fact occur simultaneously, the reduction of social entropy would take the following form. (a) In an initial state, free of space, think of the actions as lines moving in time. Agents can do anything, and we cannot foresee what they will do – a potential state of high entropy. (b) Then agents start selecting actions and converging into different positions in a spatial system, arranged as places or buildings (represented by colors in the vertical strip), in order to connect with others. Action lines might have subtle differences in relation to the places they approach, so they converge into places through informational proximity (Claudel et al., 2017). Connections can only happen if all other possibilities of connection are

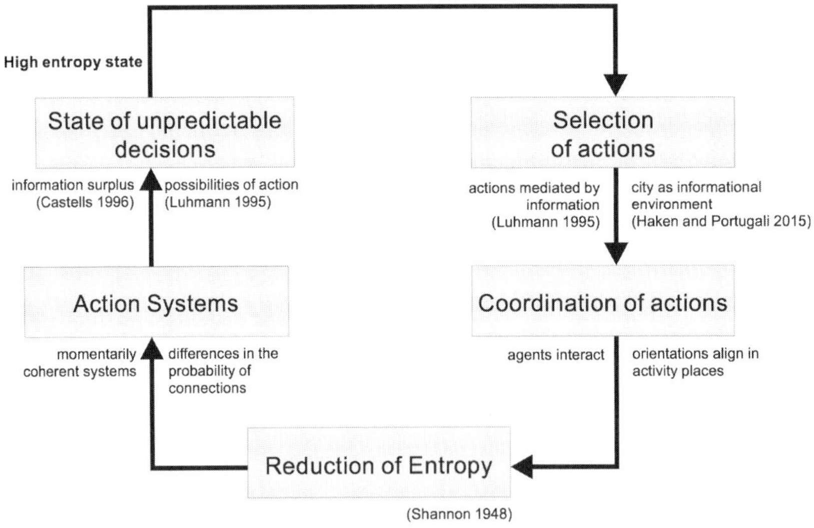

Figure 18.2 Recursive process that conducts interaction systems from chaotic states (high entropy) into cooperation and coordination in action systems (low entropy)

excluded. (c) As these convergences happen, the initially chaotic maze becomes a momentarily coordinated system, where agents cooperate. The overall entropy of actions is reduced. (d) After each event, actions may change again, according to changing orientations. Accordingly, the colors of the lines change. Entropy increases as actions go into another momentary state of unpredictability, as new possibilities are presented to agents and some must be selected if actions are to be actualized. (e) And then actions "refer" again to meanings and positions in space, starting a new cycle of entropy.

These distinct moments are theoretical, of course. In reality, recalling Prigogine and Stengers (1984), this "multitude of events" takes place simultaneously and may render any clearly emergent cycle invisible. But that neither means that individual cycles do not happen or aggregate in bunches, nor that they compensate one another like peaks and troughs in colliding sound waves. In fact, routinization in daily life leads to rhythms and cycles unfolding from or folding over the seemingly chaotic maze of actions. But even if actions were far from synchronic, the fabric of interaction still faces the challenge of entropy, that is, the challenge of producing differences in the probability of connections as a way to facilitate coordination whenever agents feel compelled to create new interactions, and this process is remarkably recursive. We converge in places to act with others and do so on a daily basis. Once engaged in an activity place, interaction requires levels of cooperation. We may bring our own distinct tendencies or latent orientations, in the form of long-term memories of how to act, along with short-term memories of a previous action, both of which shape our next actions. As we act socially, we bring our orientations into contact in the communication process, regulating collective action. A result of this coordination is to reduce initial differences. Our actions "align" within an activity place.

All this suggests that social reproduction involves a continuous although unconscious handling of entropy, a vital oscillation between unpredictability and predictability that is at the heart of processes of self-maintenance and sustainability. As this process engages an enormous number of agents and events and transcends places and contexts, and therefore cannot be observed as a whole, entropy can only be fully grasped in theoretical representations. A useful way to examine space as an informational environment for action is through a computational model, a means to examine a counterfactual world where other steering media such as language or social rules are "switched off," keeping only the properties of space active, along with agents' cognitive abilities to align orientations with activities. Once we abstract from other media, we may assess whether space could have any presence in the coordination of actions. Let us examine this possibility through some experiments.

18.5 Digital Experiments: Unidimensional Model

18.5.1 Design Concepts

An agent-based model (ABM) is proposed. Agents perform actions in different places at different time-steps. The decision of which action to perform next may be influenced by three different conditions: (i) Latent orientation $\sigma_i^{in}(t)$, representing the tendency of a single agent to act around a particular type of action, initially randomly distributed; this condition remains constant over time. (ii) Current action $\sigma_i(t)$ performed by agents as they select an activity place in order to perform a new action; this means the current action influences the new action, while allowing gradual changes of orientation in time, influenced by other agents and activities. (iii) Types of activity places $\sigma_{x'}^{in}(t)$ where agents perform actions, which support specific types of action. Agents follow simple rules, selecting their activity places closer to their latent orientations and current actions, while being influenced by those activities. Activity places are also influenced by visiting agents, but they change at a slower rate. In short, agents coevolve with their spatial and social environment. The model simulates different situations under this basic structure. Differences in the weight of these factors over the next action may lead to quite different levels of social entropy, suggesting new possibilities for understanding the phenomenon. Although there is a tradition of modeling daily activities, including a growing literature using digital locational data (e.g., Farber et al., 2015), our ABM is not designed to represent empirical sequences of actions or actual routines. Instead, it focuses on trends that might emerge from the interfaces of simplified systems of action, information, and space.

18.5.2 Variables and Scale

Consider a unidimensional city formed by agents and places. Places form a ring with length (or perimeter) L. Our choice for representing the city as a ring is justified by the minimal sufficient representation of spatial distance as a factor whose role in social coordination is to be assessed. This is allowed by a unidimensional model (e.g., Krafta et al., 2011; Lanchier & Scarlatos, 2013; Schelling, 1971). The ring form allows continuous movement across a linear sequence of locations, eliminating centrality factors while taking into account periodic boundary conditions in order to reduce border effects, eliminating the role of topology while isolating the problem of distance (see Ribeiro, 2015; Ribeiro & Ribeiro, 2015; dos Santos et al., 2015). This stylized city houses agents, which in each time-step select and visit a specific place located at the position x within the city. Consider that the position of the agent at the time is represented by $x_i(t)$. The position of agents can assume the integer values *1,2, . . . , L*, according to the place that they choose to visit. This means that, at every time-step, each agent will choose one activity place in which to perform their next action.

We considered $\sigma_i(t)$ as the current action of the *i*-th agent and $\sigma_x(t)$ the activity performed in a place located at the position $x = (1, 2, \ldots, L)$ of the city, both in time *t*. We quantify action orientations weighting the three variables (latent orientation, current action, and activity place). First, variables are translated into different numeric values. Let us assume that an orientation is an integer number between 0 and 1,000, each number represents a particular type of action, and numbers in their vicinity mean similar actions. The resulting orientation in time *t* for each agent is the weighted average of those three parameters. The difference $|\sigma_i(t) - \sigma_x(t)|$ gives us the *difference in orientation* between an agent and the activity place. At every time-step, each agent assesses the difference between their orientation and every activity place in the city. An agent chooses a specific place based on their orientation affinity with this place.

As we have hypothesized, the urban structure plays a role in this selection. In this experiment, we reduced "urban structure" to distance. In order to investigate how distance may or may not interfere in this selection, we propose two scenarios. In the first scenario, agents select their next activity based only on the similarity in orientations between themselves and the activity place. Agents can move across a space free of friction. Space is not a constraint. This scenario considers only differences in orientation. The parameter $E_i(x, t)$ estimates the interaction between agent i and the place located at x at the time t. That is, the agent selects activity locations that minimize the quantity:

$$E_i(x, t) = |\sigma_i(t) - \sigma_x(t)| \tag{18.1}$$

In the second, more realistic scenario, space imposes friction on movement. The agents take into account the physical distance between their current location in the city and the location of their next activity and opt to minimize this distance along with the difference between their orientation and that of the activity place. That is, an agent i selects at time t a particular activity place located at x that minimizes the function:

$$E_i(x, t) = |(x_i(t) - x)(\sigma_i(t) - \sigma_x(t)| \tag{18.2}$$

In the first scenario, agents will choose activity places that are closer to their orientation. In the second, they will choose activity places that are closer in both orientation and physical distance. This brings a form of "energy cost" into the factors considered. Space takes on a function role because of the energy used in "visiting." Agents move around this linear city seeking to minimize this cost, while searching for social information latent in places close to their changing orientations. Changes in entropy levels are derived from this energy function. In its spatial version, the model assesses the effects of the effort to reduce energy in action minimizing informational differences (between orientations and activity places) and spatial distances (between agents and activity places).

18.5.3 The Evolution of Action Orientations

Orientation evolves in time according to the following rule: when an agent chooses, and goes to a particular place, both agent and place become a little closer in terms of orientation. This means that activity places are not immune to the actions that agents perform within them, and that the urban activity system also changes in time. To illustrate how orientations are constantly updated, consider that agent i selects an activity place located at x'. Orientations will be updated according the rule

$$\sigma_i(t+1) = \frac{1}{\alpha + \beta + \gamma}\left(\alpha\sigma_i^{in}(t) + \beta\sigma_i(t) + \gamma\sigma_{x'}(t)\right) \tag{18.3}$$

Selection also depends on three additional parameters: latent orientation $\sigma_i^{in}(t)$ weighted by parameter α; current orientation $\sigma_i(t)$ weighted by parameter β; and type of activity place $\sigma_{x'}(t)$ weighted by parameterγ. This means that agents will consider the three factors previously described $(\sigma_i^{in}(t), \sigma_i(t), \sigma_{x'}(t))$ with different weights (α, β, γ) to estimate which activity they want to perform in the next time-step.

The latent orientation evolves from an initial, randomly distributed behavior, σ_i^0. We consider that $\sigma_i^{in}(t)$ is normally distributed around σ_i^0, meaning that every agent has an "average" latent orientation, whose value will be derived at each time-step from a normal distribution peaking at the agent's average orientation. If α is sufficiently small in relation to β and γ, then the latent orientation does not play a role in the agent's action. However, if α is sufficiently large (once again in relation to β and γ), then the action becomes strongly dependent on the latent orientation. This would lead to a pretty conservative city where inhabitants are not open to changes in behavior.

An agent's current action may influence a new action with an intensity that depends on parameter β. If this parameter is small in comparison to α and γ then the agent has no memory of an ongoing orientation. However, if β is sufficiently large, then the new action is strongly dependent on a previous one (a Markovian behavior).

The intensity of the activity place's influence on the agent's action depends on the value of γ. If this parameter is small in comparison to α and β, then the activity place does not affect the agent's next action, meaning that the place does not change behaviors. However, if this parameter is sufficiently large, then the place has a strong influence on future actions. The activity place will be updated according to the rule

$$\sigma_{x'}(t+1) = \sigma_{x'}(t) + \theta \sum\nolimits_{i \epsilon x'} \sigma_i(t) \tag{18.4}$$

where θ is a parameter that is sufficiently small. That is, places are less influenced by agents than the other way round. This means that, at every time-step, a place's type of activity would be closer to the average orientation of its visitors. Therefore, the main activity of the place will change slightly according to visiting agents, while also changing their orientations.

18.5.4 Frequency of Orientations and Entropy Levels

We calculate entropy by assessing the distribution of resulting orientations of all agents in the social system at each time-step, using Shannon entropy. Our quantitative interpretation of information removes ambiguities from the relation between Shannon information and semantic information, as different orientations, actions, and types of activity places are represented by numerical values. This allows us to estimate social entropy through Shannon ideas. The entropy of actions is calculated as follows: consider $N(\sigma, t)$ as the number of agents with orientation at the time (note that the total population is $N = \sum_\sigma N(\sigma, t)$). We compute the frequency (or density) $\rho(\sigma, t)$ of this orientation within a population with

$$\rho(\sigma,t) = \frac{1}{N}N(\sigma,t) \tag{18.5}$$

which calculates the probability of an orientation. We compute the entropy level for any distribution of orientations with

$$S(t) = \sum\nolimits_{\sigma} \rho(\sigma,t) ln\left(\rho(\sigma,t)\right) \tag{18.6}$$

which describes how uneven the probability of finding different orientations is. Higher values mean that different orientations have almost the same probability of happening, while lower values indicate a system with clear orientation trends. The reduction of entropy implies that the probability of certain actions increases – that is, actions grow in similarity. In the limit, as entropy falls to zero, all agents in the system would reach the same orientation.

18.5.5 Model Procedure

The model performs the following procedures:

1. The city is created by generating the following:
   a. The type of activity in places: that is $\left(\sigma_{x=1}(t=0), \sigma_{x=2}(t=0), \ldots, \sigma_{x=L}(t=0)\right)$, also generated from a random distribution. This step creates activity places in the ring-shaped city and assigns them randomly distributed activity values $\sigma_{x'}(t)$.
   b. The initial position of N agents: that is $(x_1, \ldots, x_N)$, and their respective orientations $\left(\sigma_1(t=0), \sigma_2(t=0), \ldots, \sigma_N(t=0)\right)$, generated from a random distribution. This step creates moving agents in random locations and assigns them latent orientations based on the initial, randomly distributed orientation $\sigma_i^{in}(t) = \sigma_i(0)$.
2. At each time-step every agent chooses a place to act. This place should minimize the function $E_i(x,t)$. Suppose that the chosen place by i is defined as x'. Then agent and place update their orientations σ_i and $\sigma_{x'}$.
3. Update the distribution of orientations $\rho(\sigma,t)$.
4. Compute Shannon entropy $S(t)$.

18.5.6 Results

We have developed a number of observations of the behavior of social systems working under different parameters.

Entropy reduction is only found in scenarios where space imposes friction on movement; that is, where the spatial distance between agents and activity places is considered as an active factor in selection. Entropy requires an extensive space in order to be reduced. But space cannot do it alone. Surprisingly, space is a necessary, but not sufficient, condition. Figure 18.3 compares two scenarios. In one scenario, agents attempt to minimize distance

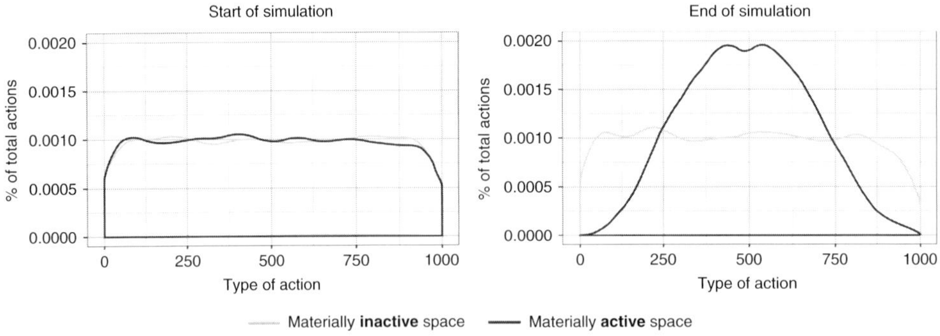

Figure 18.3 Histogram of probability distribution of agents performing different types of action at the start (left) and at the end (right) of simulations in scenarios where distance is not considered (gray line) and distance is considered (black line). Results are averaged over 30 runs for 125 parameter combinations.

in the selection of activities (black line). In another, agents do not take distance as a criterion for selecting activities (gray line). The distribution of orientations changes from a homogeneous one at the start of simulation (left) to a nearly normal distribution at the end of the simulation (right), where certain kinds of action are more likely to happen. Informational content in extensive space helps to align content into actions. In the second scenario, agents move free of spatial friction (gray line). Orientations are initially randomly distributed (left) and continue to be so at the end of the simulation (right), as a similar number of agents are distributed along different orientations. This result suggests that a materially active space becomes a means for increasing the probability of certain interactions, facilitating the collective coordination of actions.

Now, assessing the influence of spatial and personal factors – namely, activity places, latent orientation, and current action – on the selection of a next action (Figure 18.4), we can say the following:

1. There is structure in the relation between selection factors and the reduction of entropy. Entropy begins to fall and fluctuate around specific values, according to different combinations of factors. For some combinations, there is a large reduction of entropy. For others, the reduction is minimal, almost negligible. Fluctuations derive from the random component in the decision-making of the agent (under the influence of latent orientation).
2. A strong latent orientation (α sufficiently large) leads to increasing entropy (Figure 18.4, left), since agents cannot align their actions with other agents and activity places. Like long-term memory, systems whose actions are dictated by latent orientations are likely to preserve initial orientations, which were randomly distributed and, therefore, homogeneous. This condition is responsible for limiting the reduction of entropy.
3. Current action alone does not shape new actions in any specific way (Figure 18.4, center). It just preserves what is already happening, working as "reinforcement

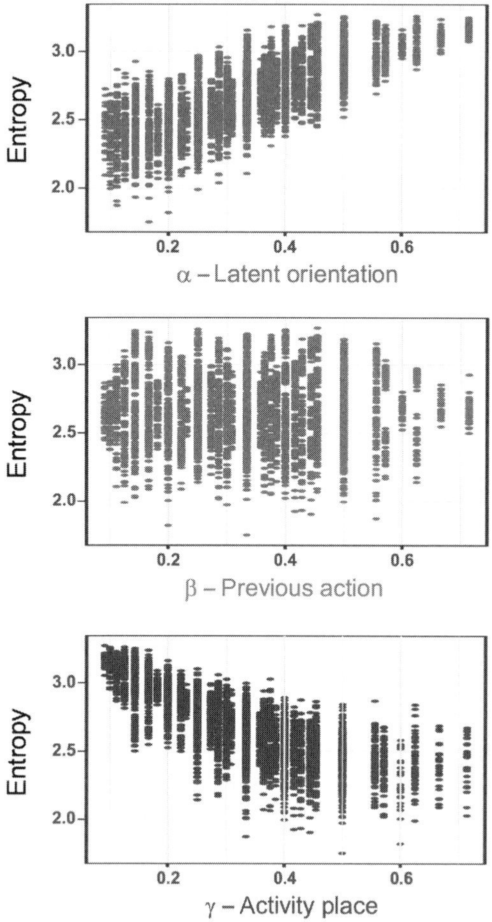

Figure 18.4 Parameter exploration: isolated importance of each parameter in entropy (under the friction of distance). Each vertical set of dots represents one fixed value for the highlighted parameter, with the two other parameters assuming every possible combination within the tested range. Each dot corresponds to the entropy value when a sufficiently large time frame is used.

feedback" for whichever direction the agent (and the system) is going in. Current actions are a means to conserve tendencies in the system.

4. Activity places play a key role in the reduction of entropy (Figure 18.4, right). The social information in space "contaminates" agents: they align their actions through the social contents of places. We have seen that physical space (measured as distance) matters to coordination. Now we see that space also has a very active informational presence.
5. Different combinations of factors have different effects on entropy. When agents do not keep information from previous selections (i.e., $\beta \approx 0$), the action system reduces more entropy than in other parameter combinations. A strong short-term memory leads the

system to conserve itself and to a poorer capability to coordinate actions. Also, when current actions β and activity places γ share a similar weight over the next action, the social system does not experience a great reduction of entropy as agents tend to reproduce their actions.

6. Finally, the reduction of entropy implies that the probability of certain actions and interactions increases. In practical terms, this means more alignments between agents and more connections between actions (interactions). However, if all agents in the system reached the same orientation and entropy dropped to zero, the system would lose internal differentiation. Agents would behave in the same way, say, in a world with no personal differentiation, specialization, or division of labor. New orientations (therefore, entropy) are necessary if the social system is to maintain differentiated agencies. On the other hand, a system with maximum entropy would create difference in actions to a point where no coordination of actions or interaction would be possible. Clearly this situation cannot be the case. A social system requires balance: neither full entropy nor total predictability.

These results also suggest that we are dealing with distinct "social memories": long-term memory is active in what we call latent orientations. Short-term memory is active in the influence of a current orientation over a new action. In turn, the social information latent in activity places is a result of social arrangements (say, as firms, a local economy, and so on) that find a certain stability, changing much more slowly than actions. It is an extension of the social system projected onto urban space, stabilizing the system to some extent.

We explored one last feature through our model: population density (Figure 18.5). By changing the number of activity places while keeping the number of agents the same, we simulated the evolution of entropy over time in cities with different population densities. Our results suggest that denser cities experience a stronger reduction of entropy. Population density leads to higher levels of interaction between agents, which end up coordinating actions in a sharper way.

18.6 Cities and Entropy: Concluding Remarks

What conclusions can we draw from our theoretical and computational model of social entropy in cities? First of all, we expect to have contributed to clarifying the role of cities in the coordination of actions and the reduction of social entropy. One expected result from the model is that space matters for coordinating actions, but *simulations surprisingly showed that space is a necessary but not sufficient condition for the reduction of entropy.* Neither material cognitive resources nor the individual powers of agents are enough. Information present in activity places and, to some extent, agents' personal histories also plays a role in the way social systems deal with their own entropy. That would mean a causal but nondeterministic presence of space.

Substantively, this approach explores a subtle but fundamental presence of cities in the coordination of actions. We argue that urban space materializes gradients of difference in

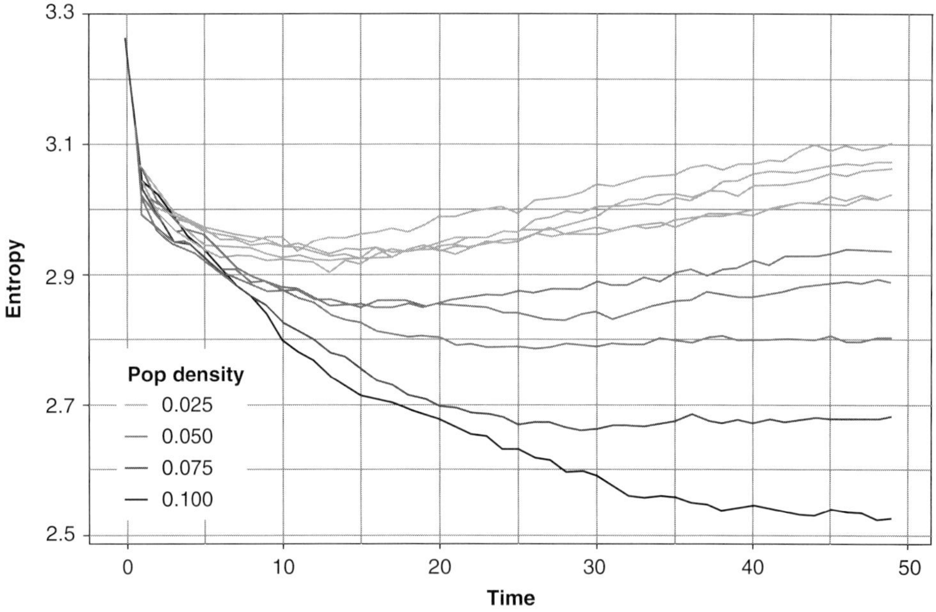

Figure 18.5 The importance of density: isolated importance of population density in social entropy (under friction of distance). Each line represents the evolution over time of social entropy under different population density values. Results are averaged over 30 different runs for each density value.

potential interactions, from less to more recognizable, costly, or likely. Placing simple criteria, including distance, as factors in selecting activities, our ABM showed that *space becomes a means for producing differences in the probabilities of interaction*, increasing the chances of certain selections and convergences in collective action.

In reality, people recognize the social information of activity places, along with the uses of busy streets or local centralities. We are able to retrieve these differences from the built environment and relate to them. One of the key points of our argument is that these differences help us make selections. Every time we move through the city and select places to perform, we participate in the large-scale coordination of actions. We enact space as a "referential system" (Netto, 2008, 2017), a set of semantic pieces indexing social activities and informing and guiding daily decisions. Space becomes inherently part of the conversion of orientations into interactions, that is, connections that crisscross sequences of actions, (re)creating the interaction system. By means of *a structure that both materializes and restricts the quasi-endless combinatorial possibilities of interaction*, this system can acquire sufficient internal guidance to make its own reproduction possible. By distributing sufficiently recognizable differences in the probability of interaction, cities express and release local forces that reproduce social systems. The interfaces of action, cognition, and spatial systems transform entropic complexity into structured complexity, constantly reordering actions in time (see Netto et al., 2018).

Another important path to be followed explores the role of different factors in the coordination of actions in a city. Further work may include the relational roles of culture, language, social norms, and other steering media, along with explorations of possibly similar effects of communication technologies on entropy. At this stage, we attempted to integrate a social dimension (agents engaged in coordination), a spatial dimension (an extensive environment), and an informational dimension (as differences in action and in the environment itself), a demanding interdisciplinary effort. The approach identifies a central role for coevolving agents actualizing aims as they coordinate (cf. Hodges & Baron, 1992), and a central role for the environment, exterior but responsive to agents, leading to cumulative changes over time. The model also identifies roles for cognition and memory in the ways agents deal with their own orientations and choose their actions and activity places, changing their spatial environment, with consequences for the overall levels of entropy. Finally, density seems to matter: denser cities (as opposed to rarefied ones) seem to further reduce social entropy. All this suggests that the behavior of the model cannot be reduced to or fully predicted from the behavior of individual variables, which is a key aspect of complexity.

Should we conclude from all this that entropy is a problem for social systems? Our approach suggests that it is not. Entropy is a necessary force. It means that novel orientations are entering the interaction system and must be dealt with. Entropy only becomes a problem if it is not converted into coordination – only if numerous potential actions are not converted into smaller sets of actual interactions. The effects of new actions over entropy would be positive once actualized, having to do with the diversity of agency. Conservative systems are likely to face less entropy, but also likely to produce less novelty, having homogeneity as a problematic horizon. Fluctuations of entropy seem vital to complex societies.

This does not mean that the coordination of actions enabled by cities will necessarily lead to *sustainable states* in the sense of positive configurations of production or consumption in our societies. If we look at actions qualitatively, it could rather lead to the opposite, as coordination may point toward less sustainable, unintended collective consequences (see Schelling, 1978). As to whether this trend toward coordination allowed by cities will lead us into sustainability or accelerate its breakdown, that will depend on the direction it takes. The point we make in this chapter is that, at a fundamental level, cities will allow coordination and the emergence of interaction systems, in the form of the transmission of information and efficiencies in exchanges and cooperation, which could potentially lead to more sustainable configurations of society.

Given such findings, this chapter proposes that cities work as a coordination platform for society and suggests that sustainability assessment methods should take that into account in order to monitor *entropy levels as a dimension of sustainability*. In future work on this topic, we expect to focus on how societies trigger specific types of action, from sustainable to unsustainable, and how such qualitative mechanisms would allow us to promote the former and avoid the later. By adopting this view in the sustainability assessment of urban systems, we might be able to evaluate how effectively actions are coordinated and behaviors are adopted in cities, focusing on promoting regenerative communities. Our approach attempts to throw light on the deep processes through which cities could catalyze transitions that our society may endeavor to bring about in the coming decades.

Acknowledgments

A previous version of this chapter was published as “Social Interaction and the City: The Effect of Space on the Reduction of Entropy,” in *Complexity*, Vol. 2017, Article ID 6182503, https://doi.org/10.1155/2017/6182503.

A companion article with a three-layered model of information in cities, namely (1) environmental information in physical space, (2) environmental information in semantic space, and (3) the information enacted by interacting agents can be found as “Cities, from Information to Interaction” in *Entropy* 2018, 20, 834, www.mdpi.com/1099–4300/20/11/834.

F.L.R. acknowledges *Coordenação de Aperfeiçoamento de Pessoal de Nível Superior* (CAPES) (process number 88881.119533/2016–01), CNPq (process number 405921/2016–0) and Fundação de Amparo à Pesquisa de Minas Gerais (FAPEMIG) for their financial support.

References

Allen, T. (1977). *Managing the Flow of Technology*. Cambridge, MA: MIT Press.

Alonso, W. (1964). *Location and Land Use: Toward a General Theory of Land Rent*. Cambridge, MA: Harvard University Press.

Ayeni, M. A. O. (1976). The city system and the use of entropy in urban analysis. *Urban Ecology*, 2 (1), 33–53.

Batty, M., Morphet, R., Masucci, P., & Stanilov, K. (2014). Entropy, complexity, and spatial information. *Journal of Geographical Systems*, 16(4), 363–385.

Brooks, R. (1999). *Cambrian Intelligence: The Early History of the New AI*. Cambridge, MA: MIT Press.

Clark, A., & Chalmers, D. (1998). The extended mind. *Analysis*, 58(1), 7–19.

Clark, A., (1997). *Being There: Putting Brain, Body, and World Together Again*. Cambridge, MA: MIT Press.

Claudel, M., Massaro, E., Santi, P., Murray, F., & Ratti, C. (2017). An exploration of collaborative scientific production at MIT through spatial organization and institutional affiliation. *PLoS ONE*, 12(6), e0179334.

Cohen, M. (2017). A systematic review of urban sustainability assessment literature. *Sustainability*, 9 (11), 2048.

dos Santos, R. V., Ribeiro, F. L., & Martinez, A. S. (2015). Models for Allee effect based on physical principles. *Journal of Theoretical Biology*, 385, 143–152.

Farber, S., O’Kelly, M., Miller, H. J., & Neutens, T. (2015). Measuring segregation using patterns of daily travel behavior: A social interaction-based model of exposure. *Journal of Transport Geography* 49, 26–38.

Faria, A., & Krafta, R. (2003). Representing urban cognitive structure through spatial differentiation, in *Proceedings of 4th Space Syntax International Symposium*, pp. 531–518, London: UCL Press.

Franklin, S. (1995). *Artificial Minds*. Cambridge, MA: MIT Press.

Gibson, J. (1979). *The Ecological Approach to Visual Perception*. Boston: Houghton-Mifflin.

Glenberg, A. M., & Robertson D. A. (1999). Indexical understanding of instructions. *Discourse Processes*, 28(1), 1–26.

Haken, H, & Portugali, J. (2015). *Information Adaptation: The Interplay between Shannon Information and Semantic Information in Cognition*. New York: Springer.
Hansen, W. G. (1959). How accessibility shapes land use. *Journal of the American Institute of Planners*, 25(2), 73–76.
Hashemian, B., Massaro, E., Bojic, I., Arias, J. M., Sobolevsky, S., & Ratti, C. (2017). Socioeconomic characterization of regions through the lens of individual financial transactions. *PLoS ONE*, 12(11), e0187031.
Hillier, B. (1996). *Space Is the Machine*. Cambridge, UK: Cambridge University Press.
Hodges, B. H., & Baron, R. M. (1992). Values as constraints on affordances: perceiving and acting properly. *Journal for the Theory of Social Behaviour*, 22(3), 263–294.
Iverson, J. M., & Goldin-Meadow, S. (1998). Why people gesture when they speak. *Nature*, 396 (6708), 228.
Kintsch, W. (1970). *Memory and Cognition*. New York: John Wiley and Sons.
Kirsh, D. & Maglio, P. (1994). On distinguishing epistemic from pragmatic action. *Cognitive Science*, 18(4), 513–549.
Kolchinsky, A., & Wolpert, D. H. (2018). Semantic information, autonomous agency and non-equilibrium statistical physics. *Interface Focus*, 8: 20180041. http://dx.doi.org/10.1098/rsfs.2018.0041.
Kosslyn, S. M. (1994). *Image and Brain: The Resolution of the Imagery Debate*. Cambridge, MA: MIT Press.
Krafta, R., Netto, V. M., & Lima, L. (2011). Urban built form grows critical. *Cybergeo: European Journal of Geography*, 565. DOI:10.4000/cybergeo.24787.
Krauss, R. M. (1998). Why do we gesture when we speak? *Current Directions in Psychological Science*, 7 (2), 54–60.
Lakoff, G., & Johnson, M. (1999). *Philosophy in the Flesh: The Embodied Mind and Its Challenge to Western Thought*. New York: Basic Books.
Lanchier, N., & Scarlatos, S. (2013). Fixation in the one-dimensional Axelrod model. *The Annals of Applied Probability*, 23(6) 2538–2559.
Luhmann, N. (1995). *Social Systems*. Stanford University Press.
Marchettini, N., Pulselli, F. M., & Tiezzi, E. (2006). Entropy and the city. *WIT Transactions on Ecology and the Environment*, 93. DOI:10.2495/SC060251.
Michaelian, K., & Sutton, J. (2013). Distributed cognition and memory research: History and current directions. *Review of Philosophy and Psychology*, 4, 1–24.
Neisser, U. (1994). Multiple systems: A new approach to cognitive theory. *European Journal of Cognitive Psychology*, 6(3) 225–241.
Netto, V. M. (2008). Practice, space, and the duality of meaning. *Environment and Planning D: Society and Space*, 26(2), 359–379.
Netto, V. M. (2017). *The Social Fabric of Cities*. New York: Routledge.
Netto, V. M., Brigatti, E., Meirelles, J., et al. (2018) Cities, from information to interaction. *Entropy*, 20(11), 834. https://doi.org/10.3390/e20110834.
Pantaleone, J. (2002). Synchronization of metronomes. *American Journal of Physics*, 70(10), 992–1000.
Parsons, T. (1968). *The Structure of Social Action*. New York: The Free Press.
Passini, R. (1992). *Wayfinding in Architecture*. New York: Van Nostrand Reinhold.
Pfeifer, R., & Scheier, C. (1999). *Understanding Intelligence*. Cambridge, MA: MIT Press.
Portugali, J. (2011). *Complexity, Cognition and the City*. New York: Springer.
Prigogine, I., & Stengers, I. (1984). *Order out of Chaos: Man's New Dialogue with Nature*. New York: Bantam Books.
Purvis, B., Mao, Y., & Robinson, D. (2017). Thermodynamic entropy as an indicator for urban sustainability? *Procedia Engineering*, 198, 802–812.
Ribeiro, F. L. (2015). A non-phenomenological model of competition and cooperation to explain population growth behaviors. *Bulletin of Mathematical Biology*, 77(3), 409–433.
Ribeiro F. L., & Ribeiro, K. N. (2015). A one dimensional model of population growth. *Physica A. Statistical Mechanics and Its Applications*, 434, 201–210.

Ribeiro, F. L., Meirelles, J., Ferreira, F. F., & Neto, R. C. (2017). A model of urban scaling laws based on distance-dependent interactions. *Royal Society Open Science*, 4, Article ID 160926.
Rosch, E. (1978). *Principles of categorization*. In E. Rosch and B. Lloyd (eds.), *Cognition and Categorization*. Hillsdale: Lawrence Erlbaum, pp. 28–49.
Schelling, T. C. (1971). Dynamic models of segregation. *Journal of Mathematical Sociology*, 1(2), 143–186.
Schelling, T. C. (1978). *Micromotives and Macrobehavior*. New York: Norton.
Shannon, C. E. (1948). A mathematical theory of communication. *Bell System Technical Journal*, 27 (4), 623–656.
Singh, R., Murty, H., Gupta, S., & Dikshit, A. (2012). An overview of sustainability assessment methodologies. *Ecological Indicators*, 15(1), 281–299.
Strogatz, S. (2012). *Sync: How Order Emerges from Chaos in the Universe, Nature, and Daily Life*. Hachette, UK: Hachette Books.
United Nations. (2011). *Cities and Climate Change: Global Report on Human Settlements 2011*. London: Earthscan.
Vygotsky, L. (1978). *Mind in Society: The Development of Higher Psychological Processes*., Cambridge, MA: Harvard University Press.
Weber, M. (1978). *Economy and Society*, vol. 1. Berkeley: University of California Press.
Wilson, A. G. (2013/1970). *Entropy in Urban and Regional Modelling* (Routledge Revivals). London: Routledge. [Original: 1970, London: Pion] .
Wilson, M. (2002). Six views of embodied cognition. *Psychonomic Bulletin & Review*, 9(4), 625–636.
Wittgenstein, L. (2001). *Philosophical Investigations*, 3rd edition. Oxford, London: Blackwell Publishers.
Xuan, W., Jieqiong, S., Shan, S., & Yan, Z. (2012). Urban ecological regulation based on information entropy at the town scale. *Procedia Environmental Sciences*, 13, 1155–1164.

19

Conceptualizing Urban Systems for Ecologic Sustainability Assessments: Case Study of the Stockholm Royal Seaport City District

Ulf Ranhagen and Björn Frostell

19. 1 Introduction

In 2010, the City of Stockholm received authorization from the Delegation for Sustainable Cities in Sweden to go ahead with five sub-projects that would help the Stockholm Royal Seaport (SRS) city district become a world-leading urban area from a sustainability perspective. One of these sub-projects was the development of the Eco-Cycle Model 2.0. In 2012, the KTH School of Architecture and the Built Environment was invited to participate, through Adjunct Professor Ulf Ranhagen and Professor Bjorn Frostell, in the city's development by working on the scientific basis for the model. This model was intended to reflect the ambition to make SRS a world-class example of an attractive, sustainable, and climate-positive city district.

The Eco-Cycle Model 2.0 attempts to be much more than an overview of the functions and flows that characterize a city district, which the Hammarby Model was (cf. Hammarby Model, 2018), here referred to as the Eco-Cycle Model 1.0. The ambition was that the model should be seen as a tool for learning about, understanding, illustrating, communicating, discussing, and influencing the metabolic behavior of a city district, with the underlying aim of contributing to sustainability.

This chapter reports on the practical development of the Eco-Cycle Model 2.0 and recent additional work to implement the ambitions of the model. Although reflecting work in a single city, we believe many of the challenges and opportunities encountered in this work are of a generic character and thus would be of interest to a wider audience.

19.1.1 Purpose and Delimitation

As a first step, in 2012, a feasibility study was conducted with the following aims:

- To contribute to the development of an eco-cycle model that captures more dimensions than the Hammarby Model (Eco-Cycle Model 1.0; cf. Hammarby Model, 2018; Ranhagen & Frostell, 2014) and that allows for more detailed analyses of energy, materials/waste, and water resource flows;
- To create a model that allows for both conceptual and detailed descriptions of the relevant resource flows and their interaction;

- To enable descriptions of functions and flows associated with different scales and levels of planning;
- To develop a model that can be used as an aid for transdisciplinary, triple-helix collaboration between city officials, representatives of the private sector (developers, technology companies, suppliers, and consultants), as well as researchers and other experts in academia;
- To propose a model that may be used as a basis for the further development of a communication platform for collaboration and dialogue between the City and the public, visitors, and others;
- To develop a model that is so dynamic and flexible that it can adapt to new information and facts over time due to new innovations and changes in demand and desires.

Models and concepts for urban development may provide valuable insight and highlight important aspects and challenges. An example of this – connected to ambitions to achieve ecological sustainability – is the Hammarby Model, which will be briefly presented in Section 19.3.1. The Eco-Cycle Model 2.0 for SRS is an attempt to combine two lines of intellectual approach to ecologically sustainable urban development: (i) visualization of complex built structures rooted in architecture and urban planning and (ii) metabolic thinking about physical resource flows and stocks based on industrial ecology. It is a life-cycle-thinking-based (cf. Frostell, 2013) attempt to grasp and illustrate the complexity of a modern urban structure and its functioning.

19.2 Environmental Challenges

A range of global and local challenges served as a starting point for the work. Recent studies illuminate the use of physical resources (energy and materials) relevant to urban development. From a global perspective, we have been influenced by three main concepts: the concept of planetary boundaries, the ecological footprint, and the carbon footprint. Planetary boundaries (the planet's limits) is an approach to defining the conditions for human development and was first introduced in a now well-known article by Rockström et al., 2009 and with a follow-up article by Steffen et al. (2015). According to the planetary boundaries approach, basic biophysical boundary conditions have already been exceeded to a significant extent, as a result of human actions and activities that have affected the environment since the Industrial Revolution. According to Steffen et al. (2015), two boundary conditions are especially critical: (i) biosphere integrity, especially the accelerating loss of genetic biodiversity that will lead to the extinction of certain species, and (ii) negative impacts on nitrogen and phosphorous cycles. These two factors are linked to the seven other boundary conditions discussed: climate change, novel entities, stratospheric ozone depletion, atmospheric aerosol loading, ocean acidification, freshwater use, and land-system change.

The **ecological footprint (EF)** is an overall measure of the consumption-related requirement for fertile land, which was first coined by the Canadian scientists Wackernagel and Rees (1998). The EF shows how much biologically productive area is required to produce everything we consume and to absorb the waste – including the surface area required for the absorption of carbon dioxide emissions. We were inspired by the great pedagogic value of expressing our human pressure on the biosphere in the way the EF does.

The **carbon footprint** (cf. Global Footprint Network, 2018) shows more specifically the issues of climate impact, in the form of gases (CO_2, CH_4, NO_x, halogens) from accommodation, transportation, food, and other consumption. This includes emissions driven by consumption within a municipality and takes into account whether these emissions occur within or outside the municipal boundaries.

19.3 Previous Work

19.3.1 Models that Visualize Functions, Flows, and Synergies in the Cycle in a Qualitative Way

The Hammarby Model (cf. the Hammarby Model, 2018) is an important base for the present work, since for many years it has served as a foundation for describing eco-cycle intentions in Hammarby Sjöstad, the first urban area in Stockholm to be environmentally profiled. The Hammarby Model shows, in a two-dimensional graphical picture, the main resource flows of energy, water, and waste that can be connected together to create a resource-efficient district, with a focus on housing. The model was developed in the late 1990s in a collaboration between the City of Stockholm and three resource-management companies in order to reach the overall goal of reducing the environmental load by 50 percent. The ambition was to design and build Hammarby Sjöstad as a resource-efficient and environmentally sound district, based on strict eco-cycle thinking. The Swedish Government also gave financial support to the development as a part of their climate mitigation program and local investment program (KLIMP and LIP).

Although the model is only a rough illustration of resource flows without actual quantification, it has been of great importance – especially internationally – in explaining a city's or a district's systems approach. It shows the importance of visualization for teaching and explaining complex systems synergies and potential solutions. There are a number of conceptual, pedagogical descriptions of the model in the information booklets developed for Hammarby Sjöstad's information center, GlasHusEtt, although there was no ambition for these to be rooted in and linked to conceptual or generic scientific models. Nevertheless, the Hammarby Model is an important source of inspiration for the Eco-Cycle Model 2.0, where we had the ambition to embed the ideas in sustainability and industrial ecology concepts. One reason for this is that it allows a more profound analysis of resource flows in an urban context, as well as better-supported proposals for the future.

The conceptual model for urban sustainability presented in the SymbioCity Approach (Ranhagen & Groth, 2012) builds on established theories of sustainability and centers people/humans/humankind in their/its interactions with environmental, sociocultural, and economic issues. The necessary synergies between all urban systems including energy, water, and materials/waste are emphasized. The spatial dimension is given great weight, as well as institutional factors. In connection to the SymbioCity Approach, a number of practical examples of spatial eco-cycle models have been developed around the world, for example in Ireland, Russia, Canada, and China.

19.3.2 Material, Energy, and Water Accounts that Quantify Functions and Flows in Cycles

Life cycle assessment (LCA) has become an increasingly important approach for discussing environmental issues at all levels of society. Simply put, LCA seeks to identify and quantify all the potential environmental impacts that occur in a product's or a service's life cycle. Life cycle thinking is an even broader concept than LCA. Although there is not yet an accepted definition of it, it is possible to say that life cycle thinking strives to apply holistic and global thinking to ecological, social, and economic aspects of social activities, such as products, processes, and services.

A review of life cycle thinking and life cycle assessment was conducted by Frostell (2013). A conclusion of this work was that it is becoming increasingly important to apply life cycle thinking in environmental accounting and report the total energy and material flows of a particular product, service, or process, whether used or provided in the SRS, for example, in Sweden, or elsewhere in the world.

19.4 Methodology

19.4.1 Multi-stakeholder Process Based on Workshops and Back-Casting

In the planning of the practical approach needed to develop an Eco-Cycle Model 2.0, it was judged necessary to involve relevant actors from city departments and other influential actors in city governance and development. This was in order to bring in as much as possible of their practical knowledge and experience in handling environmental issues in a large modern city. Since there are so many important actors involved in physical resource handling and management in a big city (e.g., planning departments, builders, energy companies, water and waste companies, environmental departments, business development agencies), the process of arriving at a mutually accepted approach is very challenging. Thus, there was not one single obvious solution to how the model should be designed; rather it was a question of creating a process of interaction for further development inspired by the action-oriented participatory research approach performed in the Swedish sustainable municipality project (see Ranhagen, 2012 and Ranhagen et al., 2017). This type of approach has the advantage that it mobilizes the creativity, knowledge, and experiences of the participants in a systematic way, which contributes to a rich pool of ideas that can be compiled and aggregated to give a comprehensive result.

In order to involve different local stakeholders, two workshops were organized in collaboration with the city, both of which were documented in separate reports. A basic idea of the entire feasibility study, and also of the workshops, was to work with a relatively long-term perspective (to 2030) and use a back-casting approach. This means that the main focus of the workshops was to find possible ideas and solutions for the year 2030. This was achieved by using a vision for 2050 as a basis. In the workshops, concrete solutions that could be expected to be realized by 2030 were defined.

In **Workshop 1** (held on 31 May 2012), about 20 people representing different departments within the SRS project organization as well as representatives from the Port of Stockholm and the exergy company FORTUM participated.

In the first stage of the workshop, the participants – divided into four groups – were given the task of formulating the main objectives of the Eco-Cycle Model 2.0. The results of the four groups' work were brought together and processed further within the city into a coherent picture of the targets (see Figure 19.1). In the second stage of Workshop 1, the four groups were asked to develop ideas regarding resource flows that it would be important to account for in the new model. The third part of the workshop was devoted to brainstorming ideas on how an integrated model in which all types of resource flows – energy, materials/waste, and water – could be illustrated at different geographical systems levels.

During Workshop 2 – held on 23 October 2012 – again about 20 people participated, of whom 12 had also attended Workshop 1. The first step in Workshop 2 was to continue the work initiated during Workshop 1: to come up with ideas of what resource flows could look like in 2030, using the material developed in Workshop 1 as a starting point. Ideas that were

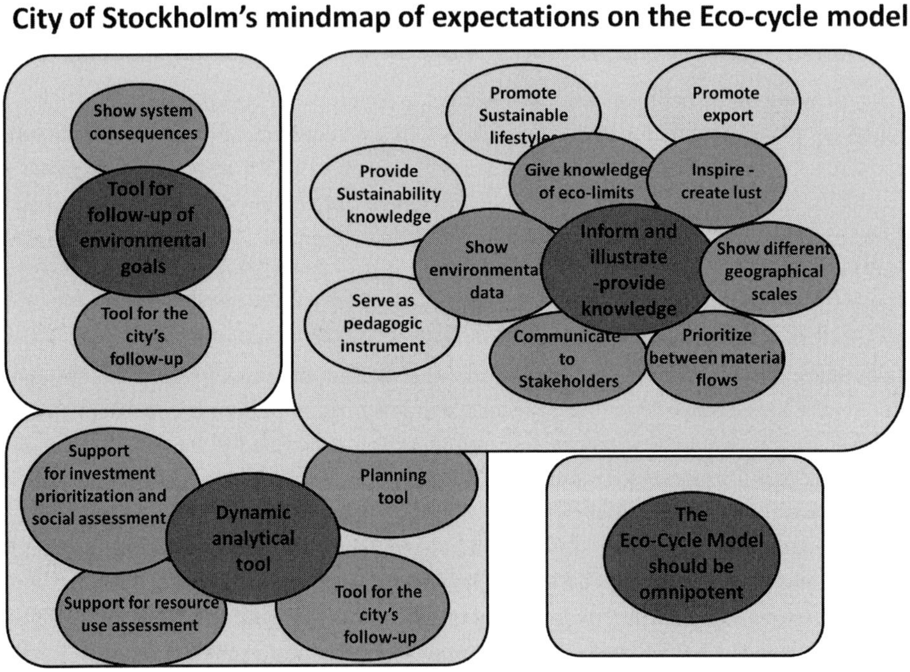

Figure 19.1 Mind map showing the City of Stockholm's expectations of the Eco-Cycle Model 2.0 as developed during the first workshop

generated regarding the different steps in the flow model (resource extraction/production – distribution/treatment – use – reuse/recycling) have been documented in two separate workshop reports by the research team. These materials were used to support the design of the flow models included in the Eco-Cycle Model 2.0 that was ultimately proposed, and in producing the final report (Ranhagen & Frostell, 2014).

In January 2013, it was decided by the steering group of the City of Stockholm that one comprehensive future scenario for 2030 (looking ahead to 2050) would be developed to reflect the ongoing planning within the SRS. This decision was anchored in discussions with the researchers, as it was not realistic to explore a number of scenarios in detail due to the time schedule for the whole city development project. During spring 2013, the draft model was gradually refined to produce the proposed Eco-Cycle Model 2.0, as further described in the results section. During the final phase, the development work followed a non-formalized Delphi process, in which a core project team from SRS with the three city representatives and the two researchers revised parts of the proposed model successively in several exercises until a common understanding was reached. The critical but constructive discussion that took place in this part of the project contributed significantly to the proposed Eco-Cycle Model 2.0 and gave it considerably more depth and consistency relative to the provisional proposals.

Although developed for an urban development project in a single city (Stockholm) – and thus representing a single case – the physical resource metabolisms of larger cities are principally of a similar character, such that the model should be able to give valuable insights into challenges of generic character for larger cities.

19.5 Results

19.5.1 The Eco-Cycle Model 2.0 – Conceptual Approach

The model is based on systems thinking in a broad sense that we have divided into the following levels:

- Level 0 – Established theories and concepts for sustainable social and urban development
- Level 1 – The Eco-Cycle Model 2.0 rooted in a broader sustainability context
- Level 2 – Overview of functions, actors, and flows in the model
- Level 3 – Material and energy flow accounts, starting with energy, carbon, and water

Each of them will be briefly presented in Figure 19.2.

19.5.1.1 Level 0 – Established Theories and Concepts for Sustainable Social and Urban Development

The Eco-Cycle Model 2.0 is designed based on an ethos of sustainable development that is in line with the Brundtland Commission's proposal in the report *Our Common Future* to divide sustainable development into ecological, social, and economic aspects of sustainability, but also its so-called generation principle. The basic definition of sustainability in

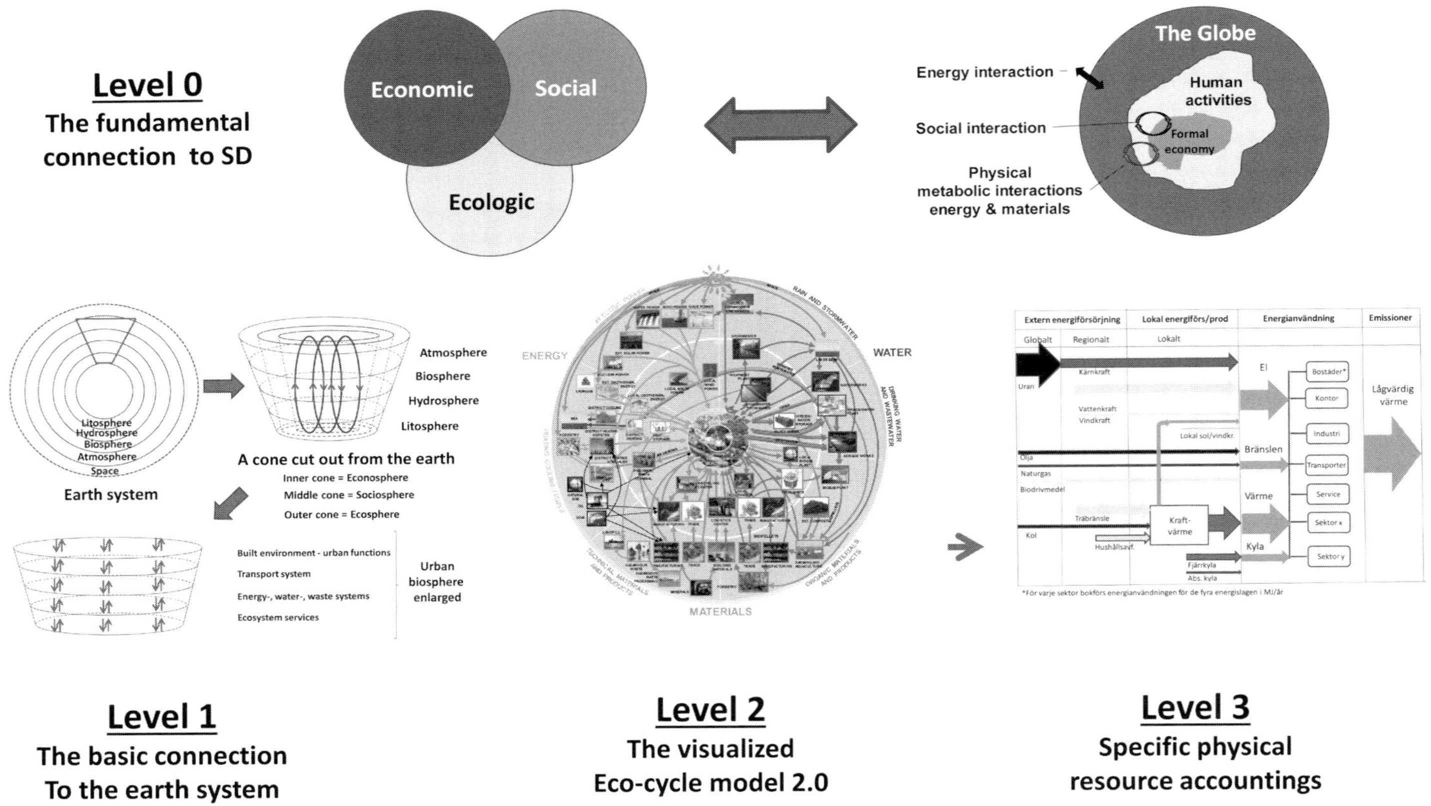

Figure 19.2 Illustration of the fundamental and practical approach used in constructing the Eco-Cycle Model 2.0 – overview of systemic levels

the Brundtland Report has stimulated the emergence of a number of different ways to look at sustainability, research that could be described as development discourses.

There are strong reasons for setting the ecological aspects in focus here, since ecosystem functioning and ecosystem capacity (planetary boundaries), to our current knowledge, set the limits for demographic and economic growth (cf. Steffen et al., 2015). Martinez-Alier and Muradian (2015) convincingly argue that that ecological services cannot be replaced by other resources such as financial or social capital and are essential for sustainability. This would imply that the interpretation on the right-hand side in Figure 19.2 should become the preferred illustration of relations between economic, social, and ecological aspects of sustainability.

An important environmental discourse – deep ecology – originates with the Norwegian philosopher Arne Naess. In a paper presented in Bucharest in 1972, he made an attempt to formulate an alternative way of thinking that was deeper than what he called shallow ecology (nowadays often referred to as reform ecology). Naess argued that shallow ecology was too human-centered and only ascribed one-dimensional quantitative values to the environment. On the contrary, deep ecology would view humanity as inseparable from the environment and would try to maintain a non-anthropogenic bias. For more information on the deep ecology discourse, please see Naess, 1989.

The discourse of ecological modernization (Ayres & Simonis, 1994; Mol & Sonnenfeld, 2000) looks primarily at the limitations of human, social, organizational, and technological creativity as a threat to our survival and not the lack of natural resources. It is assumed that environmental problems can be solved by scientific achievements and innovation linked to techno-economic measures without the need to sacrifice economic growth.

Global justice is a young, socially oriented discourse seeking answers to questions such as those concerning the ethics and morals connected to the distribution of global resources. For an early discussion of these aspects, see Singer, 1972.

19.5.1.2 Level 1 – The Eco-Cycle Model 2.0 Rooted in a Broader Sustainability Context

Based on the global discourses and concepts that were presented at Level 0, we deepened the discussion on how to anchor the Eco-Cycle Model 2.0 in a more fundamental sustainability context. This resulted in an explanatory model as shown in Figure 19.3. The figure shows that we illustrate the reality with a number of concentric rings in a hypothetical cross section of the earth and in the vicinity of this section we cut out a cone, representing the ecosphere. If one were to be very complete, one would also need to illustrate the fact that solar radiation enters the ecosphere, since the sun is essential for life on earth. Our entire existence is dependent on how the earth was formed from materials in space over billions of years. Although there is a central dimension of an overall discussion of the cycles, we leave this here.

The ecosphere is here subdivided into four partial spheres:

- The lithosphere, which consists of the bedrock and the top 10 kilometers of the earth's crust
- The hydrosphere, which consists of water in bedrock, seas, lakes, rivers, glaciers, and the atmosphere

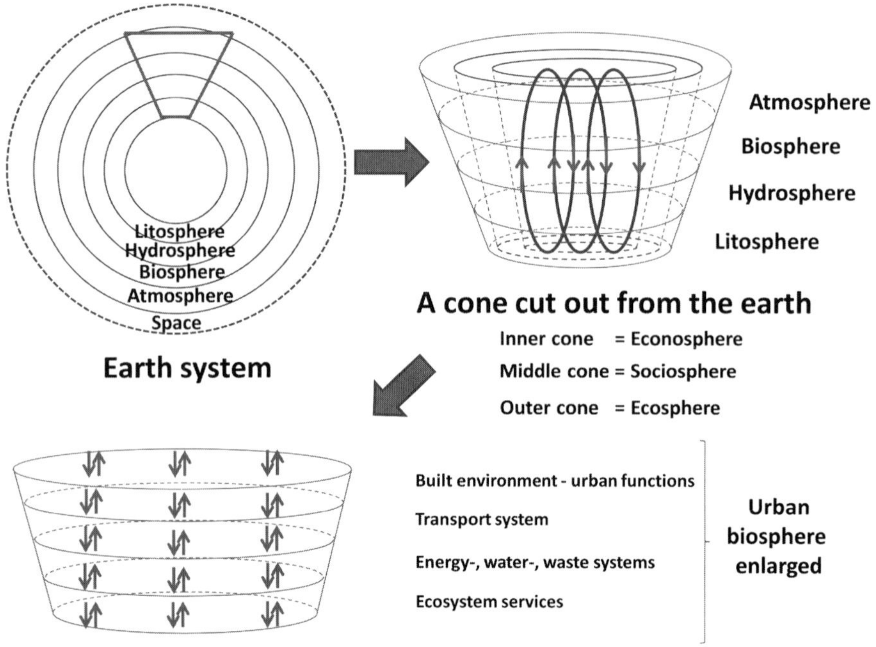

Figure 19.3 Level 1 – Illustration of the basic connection of the Eco-Cycle Model 2.0 to the earth system, as developed in discussions between the researchers, the city's steering group, and workshop participants, and based on the sustainability theories and concepts presented in Section 19.5.1.1 (Level 0)

- The biosphere, which is made up of living organisms in the form of animals and plants on earth
- The atmosphere, which consists of the air we breathe and its connection to the earth's other metabolism

19.5.1.3 Level 2 – Overview of Functions, Actors, and Flows in the Model

Level 1 gave us a base from which to move forward in the concretization of the Eco-Cycle Model 2.0, by presenting its construction in a series of explanatory pictures connected to the anticipated situation in SRS by the year 2030, with an outlook to 2050 (as brainstormed during the two workshops). Several of these pictures are presented in the project report (Ranhagen & Frostell, 2014), but are left out here. Instead we present the final visualization of the Eco-Cycle Model 2.0 Level 2 in Figure 19.4. However, the final model includes also a Level 3 with accountings for energy, materials and water presented below in Section 19.5.1.4. The model Level 2 shows flows and synergies of the SRS at local, regional, and global levels. The people and systems that the cycle will serve are contained in the middle of Figure 19.4 (the users). Urban functions in the form of housing, work and services, resource-efficient buildings, and transport are shown in the center of Figure 19.4 and may be found in enlarged pictures in Ranhagen and Frostell (2014).

A basic idea of the Eco-Cycle Model 2.0 is to visualize the links between life in SRS and the rest of the world (to create a connection), in order to create an understanding of the complexity of a modern urban area and create incentives to understand and manage the resource flows and stocks of the city area. In the practical application of the Eco-Cycle Model 2.0, it will be important to both minimize resource requirements and to try to maximize resource recycling and renewable supplies of materials, energy, and water.

In the model shown in Figure 19.4, there appear four concentric rings (three of them green and the outer one light blue). The concentric rings delimit different geographical scales connected to life in SRS. The innermost circle highlights the people (the households) living in SRS. The next circle illustrates the local neighborhood in SRS and the third the outer boundary of SRS (the one marked NDS). Here it is illustrated that important physical metabolic functions take place within the boundaries of SRS itself, while others are located outside the SRS (from a national or regional scale to a global scale). The outermost ring delimits the world. We emphasize in the full report from the project (Ranhagen & Frostell, 2014), and demonstrate in practical work with the model, that we foresee the necessity of working with a multitude of spatial system scales, including the municipal, provincial, national, international regional (e.g., Europe), and global scales.

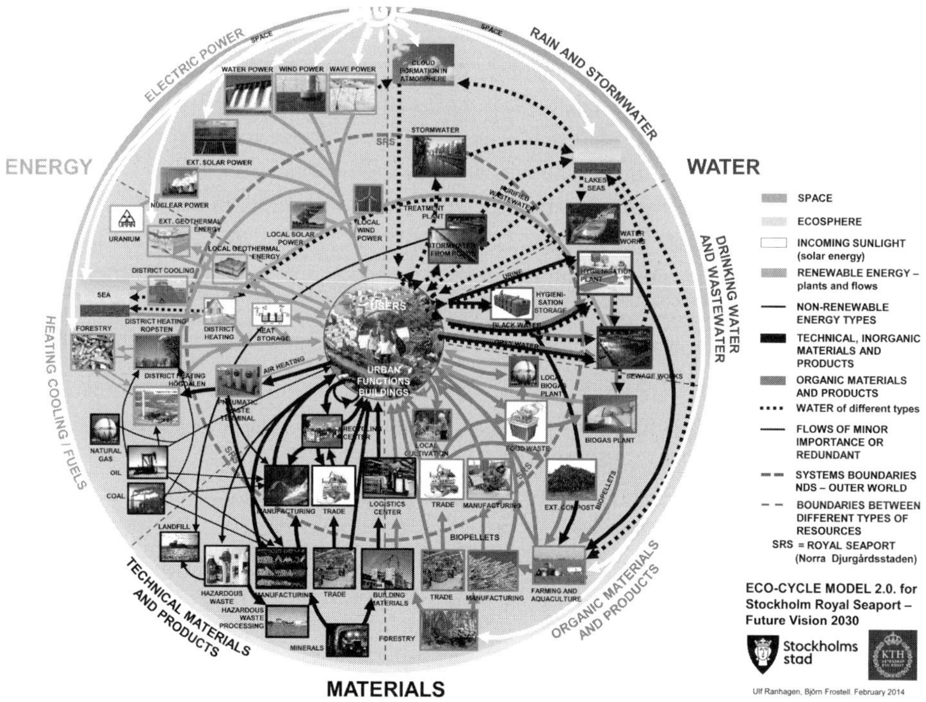

Figure 19.4 Level 2 – The visualized Eco-Cycle Model 2.0

Figure 19.4 also illustrates both local and global dependencies of three main physical-resource systems (energy, water, and materials), each divided into two sub-systems that are the most detailed resolution that we see as being possible at this level:

- Energy – divided into the sub-forms (i) electricity and (ii) heating/cooling and different fuels for these purposes and for transport. Fossil fuels that include a non-desirable use of stock resources from the material system are marked with distinctive black narrow arrows.
- Water – divided into (i) rainfall and storm water and (ii) drinking water and wastewater.
- Materials – divided into stock resources and renewable resources.

19.5.1.4 Level 3 – Flow Analyses Related to Accounting for Energy, Materials, and Water Cycles

Level 3 of the proposed Eco-Cycle Model 2.0 includes annual accounts of key parameters for ecological sustainability. As a first step, it is proposed that the accounts be developed for at least three different parameters, namely energy, carbon, and water. In the longer term, it will be necessary to establish accounts for additional parameters such as nitrogen, phosphorus, sulphur, key metals, and possibly POPs (Priority Organic Pollutants). The pace at which new parameters are introduced must be discussed in the further development of the Eco-Cycle Model 2.0 and based on experience from a pilot demonstration of accounts and their effectiveness in environmental work.

Reasons to start introducing accounts for energy, carbon dioxide, and water are as follows. Energy is a key resource for all social and economic development. This is regardless of the degree to which the global community has the ability to move to a climate-neutral energy system or not. Thus, there is a very strong incentive to follow both the total energy consumption as well as different types of specific energy consumption, such as energy per produced good or service unit, or energy use per person per year.

Carbon (dioxide equivalents): The most discussed environmental issue in a global context is climate impact. It is focused on four different substances/groups of substances, namely carbon dioxide, methane, nitrogen oxides (NO_x), and halogens. To facilitate the discussion, the total climate impact is normally expressed as CO_2 equivalent, focussing specifically on climate impact. The largest contributions come from carbon dioxide and methane emissions and they in turn are mainly linked to the following human activities:

- Use of fossil fuels, coal, oil, natural gas, peat, in the global energy system;
- Deforestation and land-use change;
- Emissions from food production, particularly beef cattle and poultry.

Implementing parallel accounts for energy and carbon (dioxide) provides a unique opportunity both to better monitor desired energy-efficiency development and to follow climate work efficiency.

Water is a key resource for life and in many parts of the world an even more basic resource than energy (at least with the current material standard level). In Sweden – with ample water resources in an international perspective – one could argue that water is not among the most limited natural resources and therefore need not be recorded. Seen in an international perspective, however, water is a crucial limitation for continued social and economic development and the globalization of the economy means that consumption in Sweden has an influence on the global water cycle. This justifies the inclusion of water as a key essential parameter to accompany the accounts even in a Swedish context and from an SRS perspective.

An important issue in the practical implementation of the accounting is how it will be linked to physical and administrative reality. By choosing administrative boundaries, it is, in our opinion, easier to connect the management of physical resource flows to political power. It is, however, not entirely certain that this is always the best system boundary. As an example, water management in Europe is linked to watersheds and not to administrative boundaries (i.e., water management in Europe and Sweden uses a physical basis for system boundary division). It may be noted that with modern ICT it would be possible to overcome such challenges. As an example, it would be possible to use a natural system boundary for water, and then by means of modern ICT transform the results into administrative boundaries through appropriate allocations.

Visual models are powerful tools in bringing out a message and/or conveying complex interactions effectively. An example of how accounts based on, for instance, input-output analysis can be converted to effective communication is the use of Sankey diagrams. These diagrams are based on illustrating flows of, for example, energy, water, or materials with arrows, where the thickness of an arrow is directly proportional to the magnitude of the flow: see, for example, Miller and Blair (2009). Such an approach was suggested for the physical resource accountings in the Eco-Cycle Model 2.0 (cf. Figure 19.5).

19.6 Discussion

19.6.1 Conceptual Improvements over the Hammarby Model

The Eco-Cycle Model 2.0 contains several conceptual improvements compared to the Hammarby Model and represents a considerably higher level of ambition (cf. the expectations on the Eco-Cycle Model 2.0 shown in Figure 19.1). The most important difference is the introduction of physical resource accountings in the Eco-Cycle Model 2.0, allowing both a qualitative (visualizing) and quantitative representation of the important resource flows in a city district or a municipality. Another major difference is that the Eco-Cycle Model 2.0 uses a life cycle representation of the physical resource flows, and not only local flows; it also emphasizes system boundaries as part of the model. In Table 19.1, we have compared the Hammarby Model and the Eco-Cycle Model 2.0 for a few key aspects.

19.6.2 Possibilities to Use the Model Generally and in Other Contexts

The Eco-Cycle Model 2.0 has been developed mainly in relation to a specific case, the Stockholm Royal Seaport city district. However, in the course of our work we have

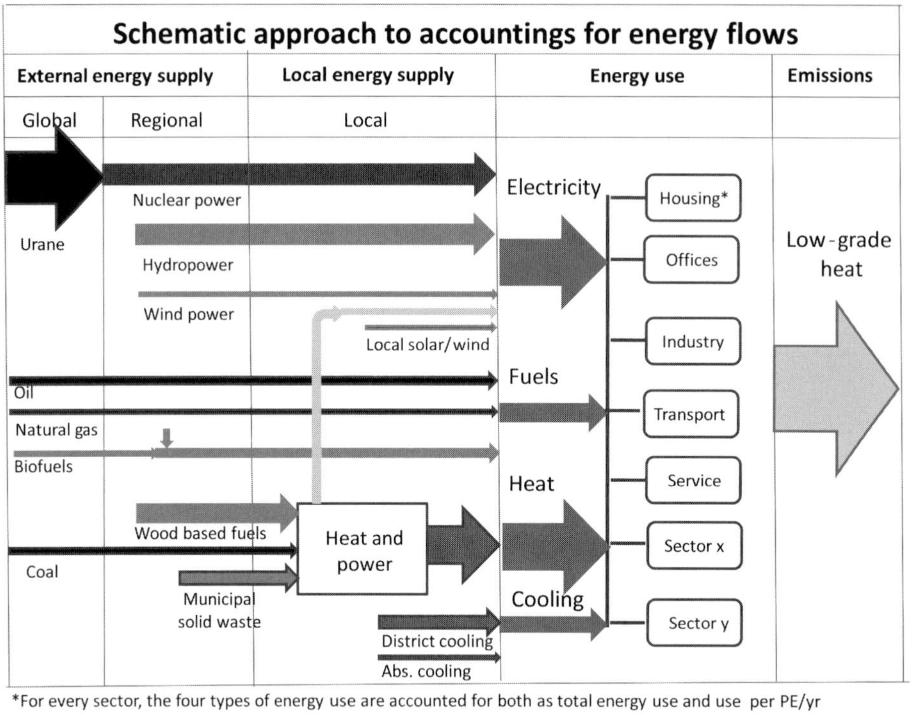

Figure 19.5 Schematic diagram showing the principal layout of the proposed physical-resource accounting approach for energy in the SRS area. Corresponding principal Sankey diagrams for water and materials flows (carbon) can be found in the full report by Ranhagen and Frostell, 2014.

successively discovered the options for presenting the different levels of the model as general "layers" that have the potential to be useful in other contexts, such as small towns, mid-sized cities, and different kinds of urban areas (industrial areas, commercial areas, etc.). We have had the opportunity to conduct some rough testing of the principles of the model in some other cases.

The basic principles of the Eco-Cycle Model, further described in the full report (Ranhagen & Frostell 2014), have been used as a basis for the development of an eco-cycle model in two medium-sized cities in Sweden (Falun-Borlänge), a collaboration between participants from the two cities and KTH Royal Institute of Technology. Stakeholders representing different parts of the organization of the energy and water companies – district heating, waste, electricity net, loading infrastructure – together with planners and project strategists, participated in the discussion, creation, and documentation of ideas for measures, systems solutions, and synergies regarding energy, materials, and water. The enlarged principal diagram (Figure 19.6) was used as a template on which the stakeholders could write down and illustrate ideas. The result of the work has been integrated into the planning program work for a housing area (Västra Jakobsgårdarna),

Table 19.1 *A comparison between the characteristics of Eco-Cycle Model for Hammarby Sjöstad and the Eco-Cycle Model 2.0 for the Stockholm Royal Seaport*

Aspect	The Hammarby Sjöstad Model	The Eco-Cycle Model 2.0 for the Stockholm Royal Seaport
Sets humans in the center	Yes, to a certain extent	Yes, in depth
Visualizes connections and synergies between physical resource flows	Yes	Yes, but in a more specific and detailed way
Aims at covering all physical resource flow in a city district/municipality	No	Yes, but has a more elaborated view on waste as a resource
Uses a life cycle perspective	No	Yes
Contains physical resource accounting	No	Yes
Differentiates between different system boundaries	No	Yes
Emphasizes the importance of actor dialogues as instruments for the development of the model	No	Yes, the model has been developed by interdisciplinary co-creation among stakeholders from academia, the public sector, and the business sector

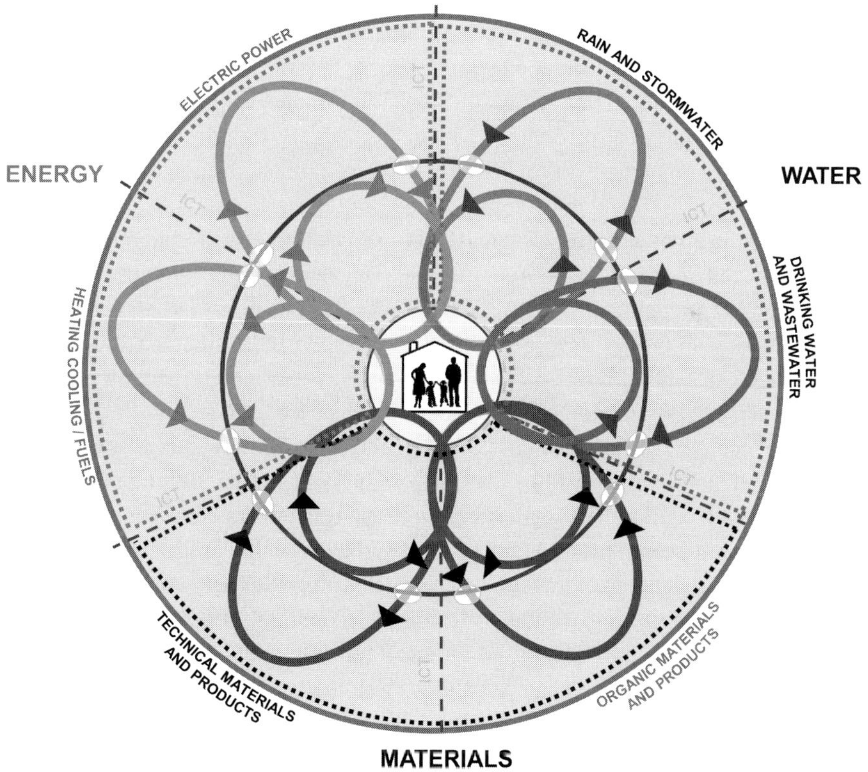

Figure 19.6 Example of principles for the final draft of the eco-cycle model shown in Figure 19.4 (cf. Ranhagen & Frostell, 2014)

that forms part of a sustainability program for the whole municipality following the Swedish process for certification of City Districts (a City Lab Action launched by the Sweden Green Building Council, www.sgbc.se). The conceptual eco-cycle model for Borlänge has also been used as the basis for a master's thesis project on an eco-cycle building being proposed as a sustainability center in the Jakobsdalen city district. This process has been documented in a Swedish R&D project "Sustainable Region," which aims to analyze and develop principles, methods, and tools for actor-oriented processes for sustainable urban development in more sparsely populated regions outside the city regions in Sweden (Svensson et al., 2018).

19.6.3 Further Developments in the City of Stockholm

In the City of Stockholm, the focus for the further development of the eco-cycle model approach has been (i) the development of the communication platform Reflow (2018) and (ii) an effort to develop a demonstration of physical resource accounting for the Stockholm Royal Seaport. Both these efforts are rooted in the work that was carried out to shape demands for and create the Eco-Cycle Model 2.0. In the City of Stockholm's own words (Reflow, 2018), "Reflow visualizes how the city is interlinked with nature and our planet. Global and local flows of energy, water and material keep the city going and makes it flourish. Explore the hidden flows of the city. Go Reflow!" Reflow is currently aiming to provide systems-oriented information on the urban physical resource metabolism to the public and will gradually be developed and expanded. In 2017, the Swedish Environmental Protection Agency granted the City of Stockholm money for a project to develop a demonstration of physical resource accountings in the Stockholm Royal Seaport area. This demonstration is currently (as of 2018) under development in cooperation between the City of Stockholm, KTH, and the company Ecoloop AB.

Visualization is a powerful tool, increasingly used as a means of communicating complex structures and interconnections (compare Pettit et al., 2011 and Salter et al., 2009). It is also very useful in strengthening participatory processes in planning (Salter et al., 2009). In the current work with the Eco-Cycle Model 2.0, we used visualization as a tool to make the best possible illustration of how the Stockholm Royal Seaport could function in 2030. The road map to achieve the aim comprised (i) merging ideas from the fields of urban planning and industrial ecology, (ii) discussing, analyzing, and brainstorming during two workshops with a total of approximately 30 experts from various urban development fields in Stockholm, and (iii) iteration of suggestions from the researchers with city representatives in a non-formalized Delphi process (approximately 10 iterations) until a mutual agreement on the structure and detailed expression of the model was reached.

An essential part of the model is the inclusion of accounting for physical resource flows. This contribution to the model is based on metabolic life cycle thinking for energy and materials, rooted in the young science of industrial ecology (Graedel & Allenby, 1995). A person living in the Royal Seaport will not only use locally or regionally produced goods and services, but will, through his or her consumption pattern, cause metabolic activity and emissions in different parts of the world. Thus, the project considered it essential to include both direct metabolic activity in the local Stockholm Royal Seaport area as well as all indirect metabolic activities in other parts of the world in the suggested accounting. In this way, we believe the accounting will represent the best possible illustration of the potential environmental impacts all over the world caused by life in the Royal Seaport. Having been developed for the Stockholm Royal Seaport district, the Eco-Cycle Model 2.0 is anchored in the local reality of Stockholm. However, the model is in many ways very generic in nature and may, with modifications related to different urban contexts, be applied in any city area of the world.

The generic character of the model is mainly developed for the following reasons:

- Urban physical resource metabolisms (flows and stocks of energy and materials) are of a similar principal character in cities all over the world (infrastructure construction, energy supply, food provision, transport of goods and persons, industrial production processes), although they may vary in detail and in magnitude from city to city.
- Global economic development is currently concentrated to a great extent in cities, which increasingly represent hubs in the global economy where differences in lifestyle are gradually disappearing and being replaced by a "global culture."
- Globalization of the economy has resulted in increased standardization and homogeneity in the means of industrial production, construction, and everyday activities in cities.

The proposal requires further work and gradual updating in collaboration with various stakeholders in order to remain in line with its stated intentions and to stay up to date with stringent environmental targets for the district. According to the back-casting methodology, the Eco-Cycle Model 2.0 can be related to different time periods; the chosen target of the feasibility study was a proposal concerning the desirable situation in 2030, with an outlook to 2050.

The Eco-Cycle Model 2.0. has been designed in such a way that the ICT component may be further investigated using the different components of the model as a base. All of the many internal linkages and synergies between (i) water, material, and energy resources and (ii) the users and the urban functions in the core of the model and their use of resources from an ICT perspective may be further analyzed in depth in R&D and practical applications. One of several starting points for such work would be to relate the 14 ICT solutions and their potential to reduce the amount of energy used for travel, heating, and the consumption of food, as proposed by Kramers et al. (2014) in the article "Smart Sustainable Cities." All the resource flows defined in the model can also be discussed in relation to ICT as a tool for (i) increased awareness among stakeholders, (ii) reduction of use of resources, and (iii) innovation of new systems solutions for efficiency, comfort, and quality of life.

19.6.4 International Perspectives

Further development efforts should be formulated for different stakeholders – city officials, politicians, academics and experts, residents and visitors, etc. The international perspective is important because interest in SRS is broad in a rapidly urbanizing world, where many cities are facing challenges and are planning neighborhoods with bold environmental and sustainability ambitions. A network of European academic institutions in the field of urban planning and industrial ecology was initiated in 2016, consisting of institutions in England, Holland, Germany, and Sweden and aiming to further develop the concept of "circular cities." The Eco-Cycle Model 2.0 has been judged as an excellent basis for this further collaboration, which aims to facilitate the exchange of experiences from the different countries involved, but also look at applications for a deeper development of eco-cycle models with specific consideration of the institutional and spatial context of each country.

19.7 Concluding Remarks

There is great potential to develop more holistic approaches to sustainable urban development and the eco-cycle model represents one possible way of achieving more advanced systems solutions and synergies between energy, materials/waste, and water in both an urban planning and an institutional context. However, there is still a gap between different academic and professional cultures, as well as between different disciplines, which may cause barriers and time lags in the process of designing and implementing the systems solutions identified in the conceptual eco-cycle model.

In the Stockholm case, the model has been accepted as a basic philosophy and an umbrella for more tangible and specific projects, such as the development of household waste systems and state-of-the-art accounting of physical resources. But there is also a need to develop the holistic model in itself, including more advanced digital visualization and simulation modules. This is a prerequisite if the model is to be used for more advanced systems solutions that bridge different sectors. It seems difficult to identify a clear and responsible owner for the holistic model as the organization is divided between municipal departments responsible for planning and different municipal companies responsible for energy, water, and waste.

In the Falun-Borlänge case, where a small test of the conceptual model presented in Section 19.5.1.3 was carried out for two medium-sized cities, it was easier to initiate the process and bring together the stakeholders, and also easier for the results to be implemented in some policies and programs. At the same time, there is lack of resources for investment compared to Stockholm, so it will take longer to implement some of the systems solutions than in Stockholm. In summary, the principles formulated in the eco-cycle model are powerful when it comes to finding new pathways for sustainable urban development.

Thus there is a short-term need to find a number of possible test-beds for site-specific, applied developments. Development projects should be formulated for each test-bed, including organization, delimitation, expectations, etc., and the preparation of follow-up and evaluation research. From a medium-term perspective, valuable experiences can be drawn from analyses across the different cases. From a long-term perspective, it is possible that a number of successful, full-scale applications will be implemented and will inspire many committed researchers, practitioners, politicians, and citizens to adopt the holistic approach when striving for sustainable societies, cities, and towns locally and globally.

Important challenges for further work in the effort to understand and master physical resource flows and stocks in urban areas can be divided into three main areas:

1. The need to understand and master the complexity of the urban metabolism
2. The need to develop holistic and transdisciplinary approaches
3. The need of integrated urban planning and resources management

19.7.1 The Need to Understand and Master the Complexity of the Urban Metabolism

- Modern urban metabolism is so complex, with so many products and services involved and being so interlinked with other areas in the world through globalization, that it is almost impossible to fulfill an ambition to account for them all in a detailed way.
- Perhaps the most imminent need for Swedish local governments in striving for ecologic sustainability is to bridge the gaps between different administrative departments and start a dialogue on this issue.
- How can we establish a common mutual picture of the physical resource metabolism in our municipality (city, city district)?
- How is the metabolism in our municipality linked to the rest of the world?
- What parameters and parameter flows and stocks should be monitored in this effort to understand our physical resource metabolism?
- How do we establish a concerted approach to gather the information needed?
- Where do we find the most important contributors to our municipality's physical resource metabolism (in a life cycle perspective)?
- What flows and stocks represent the most important impacts on the local, regional, and global environment?
- What magnitudes of flows and stocks do we foresee as sustainable in the local, regional, and global context?
- How do we approach the challenge of keeping physical resource flows (under our command) within sustainable limits?
- How can integrated resources management be a key issue in comprehensive and detailed planning from the regional scale to the scale of individual blocks?
- How can the synergies identified when visualizing functions, flows, and synergies in an eco-cycle model be used as a basis for the planning of resource-management centers where plants for water treatment, materials and waste treatment, and energy production are colocated and designed as an attractive element in the urban structure?
- How can the interplay between urban areas and the surrounding rural areas be further developed by using nutrients produced in resource-management centers to replace artificial nutrients, etc.?

19.7.2 The Need to Develop Holistic and Transdisciplinary Approaches

- The Swedish and international research systems are still very discipline oriented, which means that many researchers have rather narrow interest areas and that funded research projects – despite strong efforts from the government and funding bodies to broaden research efforts – still focus on rather isolated parts of the complex urban system.
- Business interests are – by definition – mainly focused on selling existing products and services rather than solving future challenges. When such interests interact with discipline-oriented research environments, broader and overarching issues are not considered to the extent needed in order to solve overarching socioeconomic challenges.
- Current urban administrations in Sweden are divided into many different departments, all with their own dominant values, cultures, and practices. They represent bubbles of thinking and practices that will have to be opened up to a great extent and they will have to cooperate with other departments in order to be able to implement an overarching comprehensive approach such as the physical resource accounting system based on the eco-cycle model.
- When isolated research and business interests meet city administrations lacking a comprehensive overview, there is a risk that the focus of research and innovation efforts will be too isolated in comparison to the overarching challenges, and that demands on the research-innovation system will be suboptimal.

Acknowledgments

The formal client of the feasibility study was the Stockholm City Development Administration and the financial support is gratefully acknowledged. The work was carried out by the authors in collaboration with a working group composed of Ingmarie Ahlberg, environmental manager at the SRS development office, Christina Salmhofer, environmental coordinator at SRS, and environmental expert Maria Lennartsson.

The work was also carried out in cooperation with Miljösamordningsgruppen för Norra Djurgårdsstaden (the environmental coordination group for Stockholm Royal Seaport) and its six focus groups, in total involving 45 persons. These focus groups were invited to the two workshops organized during the project and have been given the opportunity to comment on and influence the outcome of the work. Architect Jessica Agoes contributed to the documentation of the workshops and in the presentation of the final draft we had great help from architect Olav Heinmets; both were active at Sweco Architects at the time of the implementation of the study.

References

Ayres, R. U., & Simonis, U. E. (1994). *Industrial Metabolism: Restructuring for Sustainable Development*. New York: United Nations University.

Frostell, B. (2013). Life cycle thinking for improved resource management: LCA or? In J. Kaufman & K. M. Lee (eds.), *Handbook of Sustainable Engineering*, Dordrecht, Springer Verlag, pp. 837–857.
Global Footprint Network (2018). Carbon footprint. www.footprintnetwork.org/our-work/climate-change/ (accessed 20.4.18).
Graedel, T. E., & Allenby, B. R. (1995). *Industrial Ecology*. Englewood Cliffs, NJ: Prentice Hall.
Hammarby Model (2018). www.hammarbysjostad.eu/2-hammarby-sjostad-the-full-story-the-hammarby-model/ (accessed 20.4.18).
Kramers, A., Höjer, M., Lövehagen, N., & Wangel, J. (2014). Smart sustainable cities: Exploring ICT solutions for reduced energy use in cities. *Environmental Modelling & Software*, 56, 52–62.
Martinez-Alier, J., & Muradian, R. (2015). Taking stock: the keystones of ecological economics. In J. Martinez-Alier & R. Muradian (eds.), *Handbook of Ecological Economics*. Cheltenham: Edward Elgar, pp. 1–25.
Miller, R. E., & Blair, P. D. (2009). *Input-Output Analysis: Foundations and Extensions*. Cambridge University Press.
Mol, A. P., & Sonnenfeld, D. A. (2000). *Ecological Modernisation around the World: Perspectives and Critical Debates* (Vol. 11, No. 5). Bingley, West Yorkshire, UK: Emerald Group Publishing, pp. 475–476.
Naess, A. (1989). *Ecology, Community, Lifestyle: Outline of an Ecosphy*. Translated and revised by David Rothenberg. Cambridge: Cambridge University Press.
Pettit, C. J., Raymond, C. M., Bryan, B. A., & Lewis, H. (2011). Identifying strengths and weaknesses of landscape visualisation for effective communication of future alternatives. *Landscape and Urban Planning*, 100(3), 231–241.
Ranhagen, U. (2012). *4 big leaps and 20 small steps. Conceptual guidelines on sustainable spatial planning*. Swedish Energy Agency.
Ranhagen, U., & Frostell, B. (2014). *Eco-cycle Model 2.0. for Stockholm Royal Seaport City District: Feasibility Study Final Report*. Stockholm: Royal Institute of Technology, Dept of Architecture and the Built Environment: Urban and Regional Studies. TRITA-SoM 2014-10.
Ranhagen, U., & Groth, K. (2012). *The SymbioCity Approach: A Conceptual Framework for Sustainable Urban Development*. Stockholm: SKL International.
Ranhagen, U., et al. (2017). Co-creation in urban station communities. *Mistra Urban Futures Report*, 2.
Reflow (2018). Reflow. http://reflow.stockholm.se/#/water/home/hotspot–6 (accessed 28.4.18).
Rockström, J., Steffen, W., Noone, K., et al. (2009). Planetary boundaries: Exploring the safe operating space for humanity. *Ecology and Society*, 14(2): 32. www.ecologyandsociety.org /vol14/iss2/art32/.
Salter, J. D., Campbell, C., Journeay, M., & Sheppard, S. R. (2009). The digital workshop: Exploring the use of interactive and immersive visualisation tools in participatory planning. *Journal of environmental management*, 90(6), 2090–2101.
Singer, P. (1972). Famine, affluence, and morality. *Philosophy & Public Affairs*, 229–243.
Steffen, W., Richardson, K., Rockström, J., et al. (2015). Planetary boundaries: Guiding human development on a changing planet. *Science*, 347(6223), 1259855.
Svensson, T., Ranhagen, U., Håkansson, M., et al. (2018). Den uthålliga regionen – Energifrågans hantering i samhällsplanering utanför större tillväxtområden (in Swedish with English summary), Swedish Energy Agency, E2B2 report 2018:15.
Wackernagel, M., & Rees, W. (1996). *Our Ecological Footprint: Reducing Human Impact on the Earth*. Gabriola Island, BC: New Society Publishers.

20

A Study of Ride-Sharing Opportunities in the City of Santiago de Chile

Emanuele Massaro

20.1 Introduction

Today, 54 percent of the world's population lives in urban areas, a proportion that is expected to increase to 66 percent by 2050. Projections show that urbanization combined with the overall growth of the world's population could add another 2.5 billion people to urban populations by 2050, with close to 90 percent of the increase concentrated in Asia and Africa, according to a United Nations report launched in 2014.[1] Migration from the cities to the suburbs is leading to settlement structures that involve long travel distances. This phenomenon of urban expansion goes hand in hand with an increase in the number of cars owned and in commuter traffic. At the same time, many countries have the goal of reducing CO_2 emissions (in Europe, the goal is to reduce emissions by 60 percent, compared to 1990 levels, by 2050[2]). In order to meet this challenge, it will be necessary to increase mobility and reduce traffic, accidents, and pollution through local mobility policies. Digitization, urbanization, globalization, and demographic changes are changing the fabric of our society, and therefore it is necessary to change the current paradigms of transport policy in order to face the challenges of the future. The theme of urban mobility is crucial not only because it is directly and immediately connected to the quality of life of citizens, but also because it is the component most responsible for polluting emissions. It is important to intervene to improve energy efficiency, with an emphasis on electric mobility and electric public transport systems, so as to promote the diffusion of new forms of mobility. The European Parliament, for instance, has paid great attention to the issue of public transport in urban areas, underlining the need to give more emphasis to this topic and proposing to add another objective to the 10 already stated in the strategy outlined in the White Paper 3, which would consist of doubling the use of public transport in urban areas by 2030. Another central aspect is the behavior of transport users, increasingly active and protagonist, crucial for the development of a more sustainable system. In order to reverse the trend of the current mobility system, it is necessary to provide citizens with the motivation for, and the possibility of, using safer and more sustainable means of transport (walking, cycling, bike sharing and rental), public transport, car sharing, or carpooling, which should be used within a secure infrastructure. Here we introduce the notion of the shareability network (Santi et al., 2014) to model trip-sharing in a simple, static way, and apply classical methods from graph theory to solve the taxi trip-sharing problem in a provably efficient way in the city of Santiago de Chile (Massaro, 2017).

Santiago is one of the most prosperous and advanced Latin America capitals, but also one of the most polluted cities in the region. The Santiago metropolitan area has experienced fast growth in recent decades, from about 4 million inhabitants in 1992 to the current 6.7 million. Fast growth and urban sprawl have caused increasing environmental concerns and, among these, air pollution represents a severe issue. The geographic position of the city, lying in a valley surrounded by high mountains, makes the air pollution problems particularly acute, with periods of very high concentration of PM_{10} and $PM_{2.5}$. Thus in recent years, many measures have been implemented in Santiago to better understand and subsequently reduce air pollution in the city, and there is clear evidence that transportation represents one of its main causes. The goal of this study is to provide a quantitative estimation of the potential benefits of ride sharing in the extended Santiago metropolitan area (Massaro, 2017). The study will also assess the potential environmental benefits arising due to shared mobility.

20.2 Data Description

The study is based on data extracted from an extensive mobility survey conducted in 2012 and made publicly available by SECTRA (Secreteria del Planificacion de Transporte – Ministerio de Transporte y Telecomunicacion) through their website.[3] The survey has been conducted over an area of the Santiago Metropolitan Region (or simply Metropolitan Region) one of Chile's 15 first-order administrative divisions. The surveyed area includes the full Santiago Metropolitan Area, (32 *comunas*, or municipalities) and the neighboring areas populated by a significant number of commuters, for a total number of 45 comunas. The area has a population of approximately 6.8 million people, representing more than 90 percent of the population of the Santiago Metropolitan Region, with an estimated 1,160,000 private vehicles, 6,300 urban buses, 27,000 taxis, 11,000 *taxis colectivos* (sharing taxis), and 5 metro lines totaling more than 104 km in length. The main aim of the survey was to collect detailed information on the trips performed daily in the selected area considering an appropriately selected sample of 18,000 households. The collected information includes timing of the trips, path, and mode of transportation (public/private).

The mobility survey comprises records of 113,591 trips performed in the above-described extended Santiago metropolitan area. The area is divided into zones, corresponding to a zonification process based on different urban and socioeconomic parameters. Each trip record reports, among other things, information about the origin and destination of each trip, characterized by the granularity of the zones, the starting time of the trip, and the transport mode. This latter information is used to select the subset of trips relevant for our study, namely, trips performed using either a private vehicle or a taxi. These amount to about 31,376 trips, which are still a representative sample of mobility in Santiago. In particular, I consider only the categories 1, 4, 5, 6, 8, 11, and 12 of the *Modo Agregado* field, as reported in Table 20.1.

Table 20.1 *Different categories of means of transportation in our database. The dataset is composed of 18 sub-categories for the categories* Modo *and* Modo Agregado, *6 for the category* Modo Difusion, *and 3 for the category* Modo Motor.

Category	Modo	Modo Agregado	Modo Diffusion	Modo Motor
1	Private driver	Car	Car	Yes
2	Urban bus	Bus TS	Bib!	No
3	General bus	Bus no TS	Sharing taxi	Other
4	Metro	Metro TS	Taxi	
5	Sharing Taxi	Sharing Taxi TS	Bib!-Other Public	
6	School bus as passenger	Taxi	Bib!-Other Private	
7	Taxi or radiodataxi	Bus TS-BUS no TS	Other	
8	Walk	Auto-Metro	Walk	
9	Bicycle	Bus TS-Metro	Bicycle	
10	Motorbike	Bus no TS-Metro		
11	Institutional bus	Sharing taxi-Metro		
12	Rural bus	Taxi-Metro		
13	School bus as escort	Other-Metro		
14	Metrobus	Other-Bus TS-Metro		
15	Informal services	Other-Bus TS		
16	Train	Metro		
17	Auto escort	Sharing Taxi-Other		
18	Motorbike escort	Taxi-Walk		

Unless otherwise stated, this is the reference data set considered in the remainder of this study. These 31,376 trips are relatively short: if I observe the linear distance between the origin and destination points, 95 percent of them are in fact below 18 km, with an average length of 5.75 km. The average trip duration is 1,712 seconds, and 95 percent of the trips are below 80 minutes. When interpreted as the probability *P(r)* of finding a displacement of length *r* in a short time *dt*, the existence of a typical length scale often justifies the description of dispersal in terms of diffusion equations on large spatio-temporal scales. If, however, *P(r)* lacks a typical length scale, that is $P(r) \sim r^{-(1+\beta)}$ with $\beta < 2$ as in this case, the diffusion approximation fails. In physics, random processes with a single-step distribution are known as Lévy flights (Brockmann et al., 2006; González et al., 2008). In order to evaluate the real distance of a trip, I made use of the Google Maps APIs[4] which allow us to extract the real distance between two points, A and B, given the coordinates expressed in latitude/longitude UTM format.

In this case, I observed an average communing travel distance equal to 20.32 km, while 95 percent of the trips were below 40 km, with a median distance of 12 km. From this point on, I will make use of the distances extracted from the Google Maps API for our analysis. I observed that most of the trips appear in the same zone: in ref. (Massaro, 2017), I reported the map of the 10 zones with the highest number of internal trips – i.e., trips

Table 20.2 *Correspondence between zona (zone) and comuna (municipality).*

Zona (Zone)	737	738	760	770	783	786	785	820	821	830	831
Comuna (Municipality)	76	76	98	98	103	103	103	86	86	89	89

with an origin and destination in the same zone that are always in some comuna as reported in Table 20.2. Here I take into account only the commuting trips between two different zones.

20.3 Shareability Network

The opportunities for any two trips to be shared are determined using a zone-based approach that exploits the subdivision of the Santiago metropolitan area into non-overlapping zones. Each trip record also reports the origin and destination zone of a trip. Two trips are considered to be shareable if they have the same origin and destination zone, and if their starting times are at most T minutes apart, where T is a tunable parameter used to express user tolerance to ride-sharing. Sharing opportunities between any possible trip pair will be determined based on the approach described, with the goal of building the corresponding shareability network (Massaro, 2017) as defined by Santi et al. (2014). The shareability network is a mathematical model of ride sharing opportunities that allows efficient computation of the optimal ride sharing solution.

Once the shareability network is formed, ride-sharing opportunities will be quantified according to the following metrics:

- Percentage of shareable trips, i.e., the percentage of trips that have at least one sharing opportunity. This corresponds to the fraction of nodes in the shareability network that have a degree of at least one.
- Average number of sharing opportunities, i.e., the average number of sharing options available for each trip. This corresponds to the average node degree in the shareability network.
- Shareability, i.e., the fraction of trips that can be shared. This metric is defined by first computing the maximum matching of the shareability network, which corresponds to the maximum number of pair wise trip-sharing possible, then counting the number M of nodes that belong to the maximum matching, and finally dividing M by the total number N of nodes in the shareability network.

I count 17,860 distinct locations A and B where at least one trip was made. However, in order to build the shareability network, I need to take into account only the possible combinations with more than one trip: 5,167 possible combinations contain at least two trips. Then, in order to take into account the effect of shareability, I consider all the possible combinations for a shared trip between a zone A and a zone B.

In particular, let us say that if we have four shareable trips between A and B, so $t^{r}_{a,b} = 1, 2, 3, 4$, then all the possible combinations are $c_{a,b} = [(1,2),(1,3),(1,4),(2,3),(2,4),(3,4)]$.

In general, the total number of combinations $t^{c}_{a,b}$ between two zones A and B is given by:

$$t^{c}_{a,b} = \frac{1}{n_{a,b}} n_{a,b}(n_{a,b} - 1) \qquad (20.1)$$

I counted 58,611 possible combinations, but there are only 11,596 if we consider a shareability time $T = 30\ min$. In order to detect the most interesting shareability zones, I consider zones that share more than 10 trips with a sharing frequency of at least 50 percent. The sharing frequency between two zones A and B is computed as the fraction between the shareable and the total trips. As result of this assumption, I detect 20 zones, as reported in Figure 20.1, where I show the comparison between shareable trips and sharing frequency of the aforementioned zones.

20.4 Quantifying Emission Reduction

Here I show the effect of shareability in terms of emission reduction. In particular, I estimate the total number of kilometers from all the trips in our database. In doing so I count all the possible trips among the 5,167 coupled ones. In total, I count 19,139 trips and 143,749 km. If we consider a shareability time of 30 minutes, we can count 2,510 shareable trips that allow us to save more than 20,587 km, which represents 14 percent of the distance

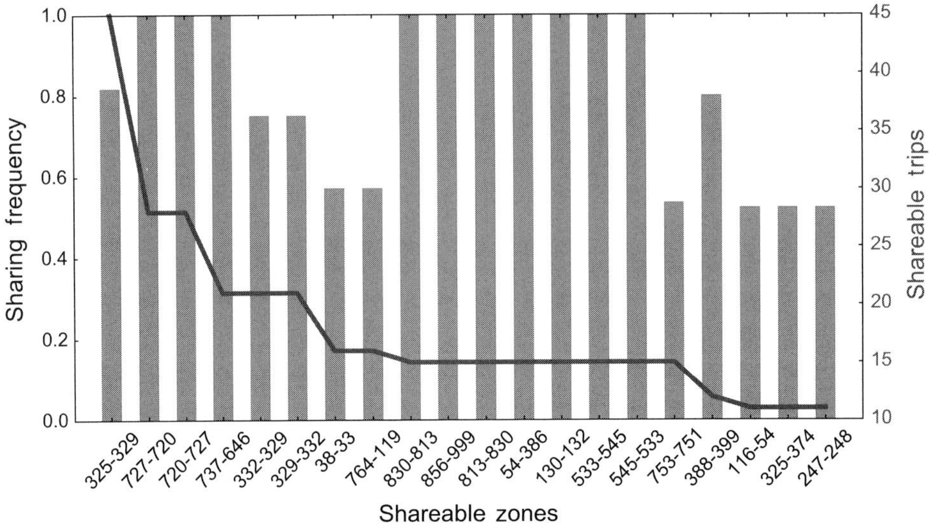

Figure 20.1 Comparison between sharing frequency (blue) and shareable trips (red) in the zones with more than 10 shareable trips and at least 50 percent of sharing frequency. Source: own illustration

among the possible shareable coupled zones ($29.10^4 km$). To translate this distance reduction into emission reduction, I consider the following well-to-wheels emission factors for gasoline vehicles (Huo et al., 2009): 0.05 g/km for PM_{10}, 0.024 g/km for $PM_{2.5}$, and 2.25 g/km for carbon dioxide CO_2. Total daily emission reductions then amount to 1.029 kg of PM_{10}, 0.494 kg of $PM_{2.5}$, and 46.32 kg of CO_2, summing up to 375.58 kg, 180 kg, and 16,906 tons, respectively, for the whole year.

Even more substantive emission reductions could be achieved if shared trips were served by a fleet of shared electric vehicles. In this case, the total traveled kilometers of the 2,510 shared trips would imply zero emissions for those travelled distances and a yearly emission reduction of 14.5 tons of PM_{10}, 6.96 tons of $PM_{2.5}$, and 652 tons of CO_2, respectively. Please note that these emissions savings, already substantial, account only for the trips included in the mobility survey, which represent a small fraction of the actual trips in the city of Santiago. We can then expect that much larger savings would be made if ride sharing coupled with electric mobility was extended to the entire mobility demand in Santiago. However, due to lack of suitable data sets, it is not currently possible to quantify these reductions using a scientifically sound methodology.

20.5 Sustainability Assessment and Feasibility of Mobility Sharing

A transportation system based on personal car use is inefficient and unsustainable. Can a future with more shared and active mobility mean cleaner, happier cities? Governments at all levels are mulling over how to regulate a highly transformed transportation landscape, while also encouraging innovation. For many advocates of the future of mobility, the expected societal benefits of these changes are self-evident: less congestion, lower emissions, greater efficiency, lower costs, and – most compelling – saved lives.

But even if we accept these advantages, the speed with which this future vision will arrive likely hinges not only on technological and regulatory advances, but also on how quickly consumer expectations and behavior shift. How we get from point A to point B is ultimately an individual, rather than a collective, choice that is influenced by a multitude of factors, from the obvious (cost, convenience) to the obscure (perceived prestige, peer pressure). Just because a new technology offers benefits on paper does not mean that customers will ultimately embrace it. This is especially true with something as deeply ingrained in our individual and collective consciousness as the automobile. According to Dixon et al. (2018), people may be hesitant to change their consumer habits even though they are familiar with the potential benefits and gains. The basis of this action is rooted in psychological perception. Specifically, humans inherently have cognitive biases that impact their decision-making. In the context of new mobility offerings, there is a tendency to accept and prefer the status quo, whether that means choosing to drive a personal vehicle or take public transportation. There is a barrier to accepting new products and services because of the endowment effect, which is when individuals prefer what is already in their possession. As a result, a new mobility option would not be seriously considered unless an individual had a negative experience with their personal vehicle, such as having high insurance rates or an old vehicle that cost a lot to maintain (Fugiglando et al., 2018).

For mobility operators, there remains the challenge of framing the benefits of technology in ways that the consumer will not just understand, but accept as well. While it is hard to get people to adopt new habits, embracing new mobility options will be beneficial to individuals and the greater community. Shared mobility is an opportunity to reduce congestion in cities, improve quality of life for individuals, and create a greater sense of community among citizens – i.e., building sustainable urban systems. Without shared mobility, roads will not be able to accommodate the projected population growth, and individuals' health will be at risk due to pollution. Shared mobility providers, governments, and other stakeholders need to overcome the biases built into society in order to pave the way for the future of mobility. Technology adoption is typically characterized by an S-shaped distribution: a relatively small number of early adopters initially use the new technology, followed by a rapid proliferation until a point of saturation is approached and adoption rates taper off. The speed of adoption can vary dramatically. It took 25 years for the telephone to reach 10 percent of American households, and just five years for the tablet to do the same. By understanding and paying attention to consumers' cognitive biases and the special role the automobile plays in many cultures, companies, governments, and others at the leading edge of changes in the mobility ecosystem can help ensure that the adoption of shared mobility and autonomous vehicles more closely resembles a "skinny S."

20.6 Conclusions

In this study, I analyzed the effect of public ride sharing in the city of Santiago. I quantified the reduction in terms of traveling and in terms of emission. The mathematical tool I used to draw optimal sharing routes is called "shareability networks" (Santi et al., 2014). The key idea was to express the shareable resource – in this case, a taxi trip – as a node in a network, and to draw links between two nodes if the corresponding resources – trips – could be shared. A recent study has shown that taxi ride shareability – i.e., the fraction of taxi trips that can be shared – can be well approximated by knowing a number of city parameters (Tachet et al., 2017).

These parameters are, namely, city area, average speed of traffic, and taxi demand. With a city area of approximately 641 km^2 and an average traffic speed of 31 km/h, the taxi ride-sharing potential in Santiago is reported in Figure 20.2. As seen from the figure, the ride-sharing potential is substantial, with nearly 100 percent of the trips shareable with current taxi trip demand (Massaro, 2017). This benefit comes with reductions in service cost and emissions, and with split fares, hinting toward a wide passenger acceptance of such a shared service. The accompanying reductions in car numbers would dramatically lower the cost of our mobility infrastructure and the embodied energy associated with building and maintaining it. Fewer cars may also mean shorter travel times, less congestion, and a smaller environmental impact (Massaro et al., 2017). Future studies should see the development of

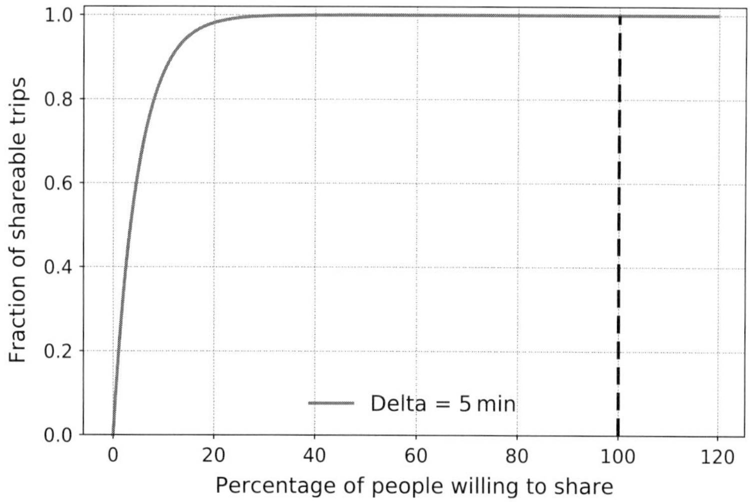

Figure 20.2 Taxi ride-sharing potential in the city of Santiago, estimated according to Tachet et al. (2017), assuming that shared rides incur a delay Δ of at most five minutes. With current taxi demand (dashed line), nearly 100 percent of the trips can be shared. Ride-sharing potential remains high even if one in five customers opts for sharing a taxi ride. Source: own illustration

a model that includes more social and economic factors in shareability, such as safety (whether riding with a stranger might be perceived as dangerous) and pricing. Moreover we should take into consideration the possible unintended consequences, such as lost jobs for taxi drivers or cuts in bus services (Martin, 2016). Already, some US cities are reportedly considering cuts to the availability of public transportation, under the assumption that stranded customers can instead use a ride-hailing company.

Notes

1 www.un.org/en/development/desa/news/population/world-urbanization-prospects-2014.html.
2 https://ec.europa.eu/clima/policies/strategies/2050_en.
3 www.sectra.gob.cl/index.htm.
4 https://developers.google.com/maps/

References

Brockmann, D., Hufnagel, L., & Geisel, T. (2006). The scaling laws of human travel. *Nature*, 439 (7075), 462–465.

Dixon, S., Irshad, H., Pankratz, D. M., and Bornstein, J. (2018). The 2019 Deloitte city mobility index: Gauging Global Readiness for the Future of Mobility. www2.deloitte.com/content/dam/Deloitte/br/Documents/consumer-business/City-Mobility-Index-2019.pdf.

Fugiglando, U., Massaro, E., Santi, P., et al. (2018). Driving behavior analysis through can bus data in an uncontrolled environment. IEEE Transactions on Intelligent Transportation Systems, 99, 1–12.

González, M. C., Hidalgo, C. A., & Barabási, A.-L. (2008). Understanding individual human mobility patterns. *Nature*, 453(7196), 779–782.

Huo, H., Wu, Y., & Wang, M. (2009). Total versus urban: Well-to-wheels assessment of criteria pollutant emissions from various vehicle/fuel systems. *Atmospheric Environment*, 43(10), 1796–1804.

Martin, C. J. (2016). The sharing economy: A pathway to sustainability or a nightmarish form of neoliberal capitalism? *Ecological Economics*, 121, 149–159.

Massaro, E., Ahn, C., Ratti, C., et al. (2017). The car as an ambient sensing platform [Point of View]. *Proceedings of the IEEE*, 105(1), 3–7.

Massaro, E. (2017, November). A study of ride sharing opportunities in the City of Santiago de Chile. In S. S. Bodrunova (ed.), *International Conference on Internet Science*. Cham: Springer, pp. 159–173.

Santi, P., Resta, G., Szell, M., Sobolevsky, S., Strogatz, S. H., and Ratti C. (2014). Quantifying the benefits of vehicle pooling with shareability networks. *Proceedings of the National Academy of Sciences*, 111(37), 13290–13294.

Tachet, R., Sagarra, O., Santi, P., et al. (2017). Scaling law of urban ride sharing. *Scientific Reports*, 7(1).

21

Mosquito-Borne Disease and Human Mobility in Urban Environments

Emanuele Massaro, Damiano Pasetto, Andrea Rinaldo, and Claudia R. Binder

21.1 Introduction

The world is becoming increasingly urbanized by the day, and the process has been ongoing since the Industrial Revolution began in the eighteenth century.[1] The United Nations estimates that 3.9 billion people currently live in urban centers (United Nations, Department of Economic and Social Affairs, & Population Division, 2014). The rapid influx of residents to urban areas, however, is not universal: the developed countries are already highly urbanized, while a big rise in urban population is expected in the next 30 years in Asia and Africa. Urbanization leads to many challenges for global health and in particular for the epidemiology of infectious diseases (Neiderud, 2015). New megacities can be incubators for new epidemics, and zoonoses can spread more rapidly and become worldwide threats. Adequate city planning and surveillance can be powerful tools to improve global health and decrease the burden of communicable diseases. Different risk factors (World Health Organization & United Nations Human Settlements Programme, 2010) in the urban environment can be, for example, poor housing, which can lead to proliferation of insect- and rodent-vector diseases and geohelminthiases, low risk perception from the social layer, as well as human mobility patterns.

Target 3.3 of Sustainable Development Goal (SDG) 3 (World Health Organization 2016), states: "By 2030, end the epidemics of AIDS, tuberculosis, malaria and neglected tropical diseases and combat hepatitis, water-borne diseases, and other communicable diseases." Thus it becomes necessary to develop solutions in order to better understand, predict, and contain mosquito-borne diseases in urban environments (Ajelli, 2017). Diseases that were once mostly confined to tropical regions are now becoming real threats in temperate countries – for instance, the chikungunya outbreak in northern Italy in 2007 (Rezza et al., 2007), the chikungunya epidemic in the Americas and the Caribbean beginning in late 2013 (Fischer & Staples, 2014), the major Zika virus epidemic in 2015 (Lessler et al., 2016), which also led to local transmission in the United States (Likos et al., 2016), and the recent surge of yellow-fever cases in new areas of Brazil (Paules & Fauci, 2017). The ongoing globalization process that favors the spread of pathogens and the dramatically increasing mobility of human populations – including of susceptible and/or asymptomatic infected individuals – are likely among the main factors leading to this change. For example, such processes favor the arrival of invasive mosquito species in new areas of the globe, tend to increase contacts between humans and mosquitoes because of an increased flux of travelers and tourists, and may increase the contact rate between susceptible humans and mosquitoes carrying certain diseases because of migratory fluxes of individuals. One thing that is certain is that the population exposed to the risk of infection from mosquito-borne diseases is dramatically increasing (Kraemer et al., 2015). This poses a series of new challenges for public health and urban sustainability.

Modeling analyses can help in guiding the response to emerging vector-borne diseases by evaluating the cost-effectiveness of a wide spectrum of possible intervention options, ranging from mosquito-control strategies to advising against pregnancy during an outbreak, as in the case of the Zika virus (Ferguson et al., 2016; Griffin et al., 2010; Poletti et al., 2011). Modeling should not be considered only as a tool for testing control strategies *in silico* and projecting future trends; it is also instrumental for filling data gaps, estimating key epidemiological parameters, providing optimal control of emergency management, and explaining the mechanisms behind observed patterns of disease spread. The changing epidemiology of mosquito-borne diseases, however, is posing new challenges to the modeling community, especially when it comes to the estimation of the risk of exposure (Ajelli, 2017).

The risk of transmission of mosquito-borne pathogens depends on cross-species contact – i.e., contact between a human host and a mosquito vector – and on the probabilities of infection in hosts and vectors given such contact. Indeed, the disease spread represents a prototypical complex system, where the behaviors of human hosts and of mosquito vectors mutually interplay and affect each other. Clearly, this feedback cycle encompasses non-linear dynamical aspects, emergent phenomena, and critical points that describe how each process affects the other both microscopically and macroscopically. Given the limited mobility of mosquito species, from a macroscopic perspective, only individuals living or traveling to areas where a certain virus is circulating are exposed to the risk of infection. However, from a microscopic perspective, there exists a strong variability in the exposure risk even among individuals of the same population (Ajelli et al., 2017). Indeed, the biological characteristics of the mosquito vector (e.g., flight range, host preferences, survival rate) and of the natural environment (e.g., presence of breeding sites, resting spots, sugar sources for feeding) greatly contribute to high local variability.

These days, mosquito-borne diseases are also becoming more frequent in the urban setting, which means that the infection transmission process is moving to a new stage of complexity: the modern-day city. There, the transmission of diseases such as dengue and chikungunya, which were traditionally linked to the household setting (Mammen et al., 2008; Salje et al., 2016), might follow completely new trajectories (Grubaugh et al., 2017). Measuring mosquito-bite exposure is also becoming more and more challenging. Research on mosquito vector biology in urban environments is lagging behind by 20 years. Characteristics such as mosquito biting rate, biting periodicity, rate of emergence of adult mosquitoes, and so on are shaped by the urban landscape itself. The presence of public green space or standing water could be key in providing resting spots and breeding sites; the intensity and direction of the wind and the formation of urban heat islands are shaped by streets and buildings as well, and may affect the dynamics of the mosquito population. These data will be essential to generating background knowledge at the level of city neighborhoods on mosquito-vector presence and abundance, and on their characteristics – a sort of "vector landscape." In modern cities, especially in temperate countries, individuals may be exposed to mosquito bites mainly (if not only) when they spend time outdoors. The duration, time of day, and specific location in the city where individuals are outdoors are in turn shaped by human activity patterns – daily commuting from places of residence to workplaces and schools, running errands, spending time in typical leisure areas such as parks, restaurants, and so on. Such complex patterns determine how human hosts interact with the vector landscape, their exposure to mosquito bites, and thus the transmission dynamics of the pathogen.

New mosquito-borne threats are emerging along with the re-emergence of old enemies. In 2016, local Zika transmission occurred for the first time in an urban area with high population density in the United States – Miami-Dade County (Likos et al., 2016). In Brazil, worries are now emerging about the possibility for "urban transmission" (i.e., human-to-human transmission through *Aedes aegypti* mosquitoes) of yellow fever, once thought to be under control (Paules & Fauci, 2017). In 2015–2016, a yellow-fever outbreak started in Angola and subsequently crossed the border into the Democratic Republic of Congo and began spreading there; this could be just a small taste of what might happen if urban transmission starts in Brazil. In an age of widespread air travel, the possibility that an epidemic emerging in Brazil could scale up to the international level cannot be ignored (Dorigatti et al., 2017), and in that case the possible consequences in terms of global health and economic impact could be huge (Yamey et al., 2017).

If the modeling community wants to contribute to urban sustainability, it has to keep pace with mosquito-borne diseases, and thus it must evolve. Developing a new generation of "data-hungry" mathematical and computational models will require the collection (and the analysis) of micro-scale data on the biology of the vector(s) and of human activity and mobility. The target is to achieve an understanding both of the biology of the vector and of human activity and mobility at the level of city neighborhoods, and to combine this microscopic knowledge with the broader picture of possible international spread (Balcan et al., 2009; Zhang et al., 2017). Moreover, next-generation sequencing technologies are opening up a new era in the characterization of infectious pathogens. The integration of these new kinds of data with traditional surveillance methods is becoming a valuable source of information. How to bridge these data and use them in computational modeling in order to contribute to public health and thus to urban sustainability is a new challenge. At the end of the day, modeling could prove to be a powerful tool for understanding the hidden links that the complex urban environment and human behavior have with the ecology of mosquito vectors, and an important instrument for policymakers to use in developing preparedness and response plans aimed at hindering the surge of mosquito-borne diseases.

In this chapter, we study the interplay between human mobility and the spread of the mosquito-borne dengue virus in urban environments through agent-based and compartmental SIR models (Keeling & Rohani, 2008). The models presented here investigate, for example, the variability of the mosquito (Esteva & Vargas, 1998), the variability of the human population (Esteva & Vargas, 1999), the vertical transmission between mosquitos (that is, the transmission between mosquito generations) (Esteva & Vargas, 2000), as well as seasonal patterns (Hartley et al., 2002). Otero, Schweigmann, and Solari (2008) presented a dengue model that takes into account the evolution of the mosquito population. As the flight range of mosquitoes is limited to a few hundred meters (Stoddard et al., 2013), it is generally assumed that humans carry the dengue virus to previously dengue-free areas and infect local mosquitoes. There is evidence that the spread of mosquito-borne diseases is related to human mobility (Stoddard et al., 2009). Various agent-based simulations suggest that the mobility of humans could be the main driving force behind the spread of the dengue virus (Barmak et al., 2011). Teurlai et al. (2012) showed that human mobility, estimated using the road network, influences the spread at a national scale in Cambodia. House-to-house human movements in particular seem to play a key role in Iquitos, Peru (Stoddard et al., 2009). Related malaria studies show that human mobility, which is estimated from cell-phone networks (ownership of cell phones proves less socially biased than one may think, even in developing countries), drives the dissemination of malaria parasites as well (Wesolowski et al., 2012). Recently Wesolowski et al. (2015) studied the impact of human mobility on the emergence of dengue epidemics in Pakistan using mobile-phone-based mobility tracking of relevant fluxes.

21.2 Epidemiological Model

Epidemiological models aim to estimate the number of infected individuals at different stages of the disease over time (Bagnoli et al., 2012; Massaro et al., 2018): in the case of urban systems, this is done by taking into account the probability of transmission of the infection depending on the individual's daily path and the spatial distribution of mosquitoes in an urban setting. Two different approaches can be used to reach this goal: on the one hand, agent-based models track the position and the epidemiological stages of each individual human and vector in the area of interest; on the other, compartmental models consider the average variations in the number of individuals in the different compartments. Although agent-based models need to simulate the behavior of hundreds of thousands of agents, a clear advantage of these models is that it is simple to estimate the instantaneous exposure of each agent based on its position. Compartmental models, conversely, cannot track the movements of single individuals and an average daily exposure must be considered for those individuals that commute during the day. Here we propose a novel spatially explicit compartmental model for mosquito-borne disease epidemics where individuals are subject to different exposure rates depending on their possible commuting pathways. The functional dependence of the exposure risk on the mobility pathway is arguably relevant to urban epidemiology in general, and is formalized here for the first time. Moreover, here we shall highlight the main differences with the corresponding agent-based model.

The compartmental model is based on an epidemiological model developed for dengue epidemics, where female mosquitoes of the species *Aedes aegypti* and *Aedes albopictus* become infected by biting infected humans, and then transmit the infection to other people (for more details see e.g., Barmark et al., 2011; Otero et al., 2011). The spatially explicit model subdivides the region of interest (e.g., the city) into n cells, and estimates the local number of susceptible, infected, and recovered humans and mosquitoes. Disease spreading among cells is then a consequence of human mobility, for example due to individuals who daily commute between the home node and the work node.

Focusing on a single cell i, female adult mosquitoes are subdivided into three compartments, susceptible (S_i^V), exposed (E_i^V), and infected (I_i^V). Note that the symbol V in the exponent denotes variables and parameters associated with the vector. Susceptible mosquitoes can contract the disease by biting an infected human, thus becoming exposed (Figure 21.1). The force of infection governing the transition rate from susceptible to exposed individuals in the vector population, indicated with λ_i^V, is proportional to the density of infectious humans and the biting rate b: $\lambda_{i,t}^V = \beta^V b I_{i,t}^H / N_i^H$, where $I_{i,t}^H$ is the number of infected humans at time t, N_i^H is the total human population in the cell, and β^V is the probability of transmission from an infected human to a mosquito, which typically needs to be calibrated. The incubation period, determining the transition between exposed and infectious individuals, has a mean duration of $1/\varepsilon^V$.

The described population dynamics of the adult female mosquitoes is modeled first by sampling the number of mosquitoes that change category (new susceptible S_i^{VN}, new exposed E_i^{VN}, and new infected I_i^{VN}) and that die (S_i^{VD}, E_i^{VD}, and I_i^{VD} in the susceptible, exposed, and infected compartments) during a time-step of size δ:

$$S_{i,t}^{VN} \sim Bin\left(Pu_{i,t}, \delta p_{H,t}\right); \tag{21.1a}$$

$$\left(E_{i,t}^{VN}, S_{i,t}^{VD}, -\right) \sim Multinom\left(S_{i,t}^V; \delta\lambda_{i,t}^V, \delta a_D^V, 1 - \delta\lambda_{i,t}^V - \delta a_D^V\right); \tag{21.1b}$$

$$\left(I_{i,t}^{VN}, E_{i,t}^{VD}, -\right) \sim Multinom\left(E_{i,t}^V; \delta\varepsilon^V, \delta a_D^V, 1 - \delta\epsilon^V - \delta a_D^V\right); \tag{21.1c}$$

$$I_{i,t}^{VD} \sim Bin\left(I_{i,t}^V, \delta a_D^V\right); \tag{21.1d}$$

where $Bin(k,p)$ represents a binomial random variable associated with k repetitions with probability p, and $(x_1, x_2, \ldots, x_l) \sim Multinom(k; p_1, p_2, \ldots, p_l)$ is a multinomial random variable for k events repartitioned in categories $x_1, x_2, \ldots, x_l$ with probabilities $p_1, p_2, \ldots, p_l$ (Robert et al., 2016). The parameter a_D^V is the death rate for adult mosquitos and can be time dependent as a result of environmental factors. The parameter $p_{H,t}$ is the rate governing the passage from *Pupae* (Pu_t) to adult mosquitoes. The number of mosquitoes per compartment at the new time-step is then given by the following stochastic equations:

$$S^V_{i,t+1} = S^V_{i,t} - E^{VN}_{i,t} - S^{VD}_{i,t} + S^{VN}_{i,t}; \tag{21.2a}$$

$$E^V_{i,t+1} = E^V_{i,t} + E^{VN}_{i,t} - I^{VN}_{i,t} - E^{VD}_{i,t}; \tag{21.2b}$$

$$I^V_{i,t+1} = I^V_{i,t} + I^{VN}_{i,t} - I^{VD}_{i,t}. \tag{21.2c}$$

In simplified approaches, the mosquito population is considered to be in equilibrium (the total mosquito population N^V_i is constant in each node) and deaths are replaced by an equal number of new susceptible mosquitoes. In more detailed models, the number of mosquitoes changes seasonally according to a specific stochastic mosquito-population model that differentiates between immature mosquitoes and adult mosquitoes. Only the latter actively contributes to the spreading of the disease. Immature mosquitoes can be categorized within one of three compartments: eggs, *Eg*, that develop into larvae, *La*, and then pupae, *Pu* (Figure 21.1). Environmental factors such as local temperature and precipitation (as a proxy for water availability) can play an important role in the determination of the rates governing the transition between these compartments, the duration of the gonotrophic period, the location of the breeding sites, and the environmental maximum capacity to sustain mosquito larvae (see, e.g., Focks et al., 1993; Otero et al., 2008).

The human population at each cell (N^H_i) is considered to be at demographic equilibrium (total population constant in time) and the individuals are subdivided into four compartments: susceptible (S^H_i), exposed (E^H_i), infected (I^H_i), and recovered (R^H_i). The dynamics of these compartments is similar to those described for the mosquitoes, with the following main differences: (1) the infectious period has an average duration of $1/\mu^H$; (2) after healing, infected human individuals acquire immunity to the disease and enter the compartment R^H_i. The stochastic equations that describe this dynamic are

$$S^H_{i,t+1} = S^H_{i,t} + S^{HN}_{i,t} - E^{HN}_{i,t} - S^{HD}_{i,t}; \tag{21.3a}$$

$$E^H_{i,t+1} = E^H_{i,t} + E^{HN}_{i,t} - I^{HN}_{i,t} - E^{HD}_{i,t}; \tag{21.3b}$$

$$I^H_{i,t+1} = I^H_{i,t} + I^{HN}_{i,t} - R^{HN}_{i,t} - I^{HD}_{i,t}; \tag{21.3c}$$

$$R^H_{i,t+1} = R^H_{i,t} + R^{HN}_{i,t} - R^{HD}_{i,t}; \tag{21.3d}$$

where the random number of individuals that change category (new exposed E^{HN}_i, infected I^{HN}_i, and recovered R^{HN}_i) and the deaths (S^{HD}_i, E^{HD}_i, I^{HD}_i, R^{HD}_i) are sampled at each time-step of size δ:

$$(E^{HN}_{i,t}, S^{HD}_{i,t}, -) \sim Multinom\left(S^H_{i,t}; \delta\lambda^H_{i,t}, \delta a^H_D, 1 - \delta\lambda^H_{i,t} - \delta a^H_D\right); \tag{21.4a}$$

$$\left(I^{HN}_{i,t}, E^{HD}_{i,t}, -\right) \sim Multinom\left(E^H_{i,t}; \delta\varepsilon^H, \delta a^H_D, 1 - \delta\epsilon^H - \delta a^H_D\right); \tag{21.4b}$$

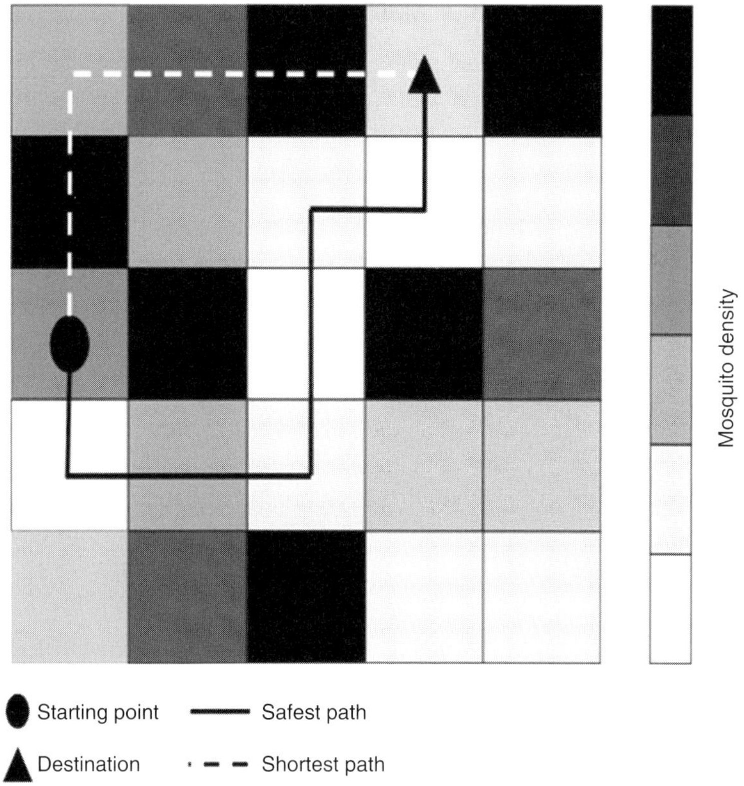

Figure 21.1 Schematic representation of the vector-borne model in a single block: the model is similar to previous studies (Karl et al., 2014) in which mobility of humans, growth of mosquitoes, and epidemiological dynamics are implemented.

$$\left(R_{i,t}^{HN}, I_{i,t}^{HD}, -\right) \sim Multinom\left(I_{i,t}^{H}; \mu^{H}, \delta a_{D}^{H}, 1 - \delta\mu^{H} - \delta a_{D}^{H}\right); \tag{21.4c}$$

$$S_{i,t}^{HN} = S_{i,t}^{HD} + E_{i,t}^{HD} + I_{i,t}^{HD} + R_{i,t}^{HD} \tag{21.4d}$$

where a_D^H is the demographic death rate and ε^H is the analogous of ε^V. The force of infection $\lambda_{i,t}^H$ is proportional to the percentage of infectious mosquitoes with respect to the humans in the cell, $I_{i,t}^V/N_i^H$, to the mosquito's biting rate, b, and to the probability of transmission from an infectious mosquito to a human, β^H:

$$\lambda_{i,t}^{H} = \beta^{H} b \frac{I_{i,t}^{V}}{N_{i}^{H}}. \tag{21.5}$$

Equation (21.4d) is a consequence of our assumption of demographic equilibrium.

21.3 Mobility Model

The compartmental model presented in the previous section describes the local disease dynamics for vectors and humans without considering mobility. We are here interested in adapting these equations in such a way as to consider the impact that human mobility has on the spreading of the disease. In fact, the population of individuals moves through the geographical space of the model where daily activities are performed. A common modeling approach to consider mobility is to assign two preferred cells to each agent, denominated as Home and Work cells, where individuals spend most of their day. Then, the probability that an individual living in cell i (Home cell) becomes infected is related to the mosquito's concentration in both Home and Work (cell j) cells and to the time spent in the two cells. In the following we assume that individuals' daily commutes outside their home cell has the probability m. Then, the probability of daily commuting from i to j is indicated with q_{ij}, which can be estimated empirically using a gravity-based model (q_{ij} is proportional to the reference populations N_i^H and N_j^H and inversely proportional to the cell's distance d_{ij}) and/or from data, e.g., using mobile-phone data to track human mobility. The mobility matrix q_{ij} satisfies the conditions $\sum_j q_{ij} = 1$ and $q_{ii} = 0$. Assuming that τ_h and τ_w are the number of hours of the day spent at home and work ($\tau_h + \tau_w = 1$ day, and usually $\tau_w = 8$), commuting individuals are subject to a force of infection $\lambda_{i,t}^H$ for a period τ_h and of $\lambda_{j,t}^H$ for a period τ_w. With an agent-based model, one can simply track the movement of individual agents in the domain using a sufficiently small time-step, δ, and assign the force of infection depending on the agent's position. In the compartmental model, however, we cannot track the movement of single individuals; thus we need to consider a constant rate of infection for those people who are moving. The probability that individuals commuting between cells i and j become infected during a time-step of size δ is now given the probability that they become infected, thus:

$$p_{ij,t} = 1 - \left(1 - \delta\tau_h\lambda_{i,t}^H\right)\left(1 - \delta\tau_w\lambda_{j,t}^w\right) = \delta\tau_h\lambda_{i,t}^H + \delta\tau_w\lambda_{j,t}^w - \delta\tau_h\lambda_{i,t}^H\delta\tau_w\lambda_{j,t}^w \tag{21.6}$$

The last term in this expression takes into account that individuals cannot be infected both at work and at home. Using this probability and the assumption that susceptible individuals stay in the home cell all day, defined by probability $(1 - m)$, eq. (21.4a), which samples the number of newly exposed individuals during a time-step δ in cell i, becomes:

$$(E_{ii,t}^{HN}, E_{i1,t}^{HN}, \ldots, E_{in,t}^{HN}, S_{it}^{HD}, -) \sim Multinom\left(S_{i,t}^H; \delta(1 - m)\lambda_{i,t}^H, mq_{i1}p_{i1,t}, \ldots, mq_{in}p_{in,t}, \delta a_D^H, r_i\right) \tag{21.7}$$

where $E_{ii,t}^{HN}$ are the newly exposed individuals derived from the portion of susceptible individuals who do not move, while $E_{ij,t}^{HN}$ are those derived from the portion of the population that moves from i to j ($j = 1, \ldots, n$; $j \neq i$). Probability r_i represents the probability of remaining in the compartment $S_{i,t}^H$ and is given by one minus the other probabilities in the multinomial distribution. Finally, the number of newly exposed individuals in the node i (used in eq. 21.3b) is obtained by summing the sampled exposed, $E_{i,t}^{HN} = \sum_j E_{ij,t}^{HN}$.

Note that the multinomial distribution in (21.7) has $n+2$ categories, with most of the categories having a very low probability. It is thus necessary to use a large number of iterations of the model to reproduce the variability associated with the epidemic. The probability space can be restricted by assuming that m and q_{ij} represent fixed rates. In this case we can sample the new exposed individuals from the subset of the population moving from i to j:

$$(E_{ii,t}^{HN}, S_{ii,t}^{HD}, -) \sim Multinom\Big(\lfloor(1-m)\rfloor S_{i,t}^{H}; \delta\lambda_{i,t}^{H}, \delta a_{D}^{H}, r_{ij,t}\Big); \tag{21.8a}$$

$$(E_{ij,t}^{HN}, S_{ijt,}^{HD}, -) \sim Multinom\Big(\Big\lfloor mq_{ij}S_{i,t}^{H}\Big\rfloor; p_{ij,t}, \delta a_{D}^{H}, r_{ij,t}\Big); \tag{21.8b}$$

where the brackets $\lfloor\ldots\rfloor$ represent the integer part and $S_{ij,t}^{HD}$ are the dead individuals among the portion of the population that moves between cells i and j. Although this second formulation samples from simpler probability distributions, there are two main disadvantages with respect to eq. (21.7): First the rounding of the population might lead to zero individuals traveling from i to j, thus excluding the possibility of an individual being infected in j after coming from node i. This event, conversely, still has a chance of occurring in (21.7) when $q_{ij}p_{ij,t}$ is greater than zero. Second, one has to ensure that the total number of susceptible individuals considered in (21.8a–b) is unchanged by the rounding, with the possibility of randomly redistributing the missing individuals.

Finally, note that, owing to human mobility, the denominator in (21.5) might change over time. This can be easily taken into account using an agent-based model by counting the human agents in each cell. In the compartmental model we approximate this step by computing the force of infection using the reference population of the cell, i.e., only counting the humans living in the cell.

21.4 Transmission along Pathways

In this section we extend the impact of the mobility model by also considering the probability of transmission along the pathway between home and work cells. In fact, commuting time can represent an important fraction of the daily routine and there exists a definite possibility that susceptible individuals cross cells occupied by infected mosquitoes while commuting, should exposure be possible. Pathways between home and work cells are randomly selected in accordance with the road network and available public transportation (see Figure 21.2). In the following, we indicate with γ_k $(k = 1, \ldots, K)$ the possible K pathways between cells i and j (the dependence of the pathway γ_k and of the total number of pathways K with respect to the starting and finishing cells is neglected for the sake of clarity). We assume that the time necessary to travel along a singly pathway γ_k is constant each day and equal to τ_k, and the

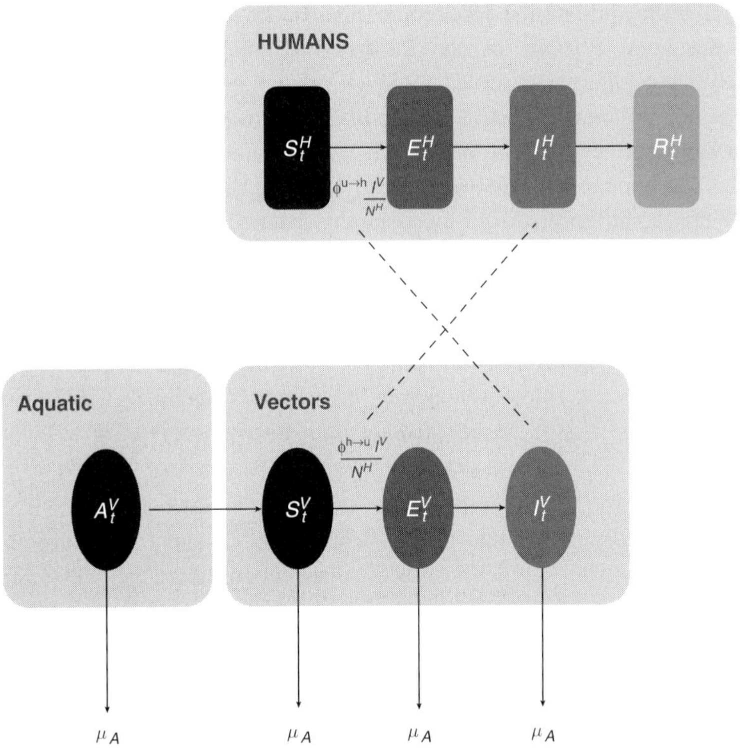

Figure 21.2 Humans can move in the city from a starting point (home) to a destination point (work): they can decide to take the shortest path or the safest one, avoiding zones with a high concentration of mosquitoes. The optimization control tools should select the path having the best the trade-off between length of travel time and risk of getting the disease. Source: own illustration

probability of being infected during this travel is π_k. The following section presents a possible way to compute τ_k and π_k on the basis of the force of infection associated with the cells along the pathway. Each day, individuals moving along pathway γ_k spend a time 2 τ_k commuting, then τ_w at work (usually fixed at $\tau_k = 8$ hours) and the rest of the day at home, $\tau_{h,k} = 1 - 2\tau_k - \tau_w$ (the time passed at home becomes dependent on the time necessary to travel along the particular pathway). Again, if using an agent-based model with a sufficiently small time-step, it is sufficient to keep track of the agent movements along the pathway and of their possible change of status from susceptible to exposed due to the local force of infection. With a compartmental model, however, the impact of the different pathways should be considered in the daily rates of transmission. Similar to eq. (21.6), the probability of passing from the susceptible to the exposed compartment during a time-step δ for an individual who commutes along the pathway λ_k is:

$$p_{ijk,t} = 1 - \left(1 - \delta\tau_{h,k}\lambda^H_{i,t}\right)\left(1 - \delta\tau_w\lambda^H_{j,t}\right)\left(1 - \tau_k\lambda\pi^H_{j,t}\right) \tag{21.9}$$

Let $c_1, \ldots, c_K$ be the probabilities of choosing a particular pathway among $\gamma_1, \ldots, \gamma_K$ with $\sum_k c_k = 1$. These probabilities can be, for example, inversely proportional to the path length. Then, the number of newly exposed among the individuals traveling from i to j, which was before computed in eq. (21.8b), now becomes:

$$\left(E^{HN}_{ij1,t}, \ldots, E^{HN}_{ijK,t} S^{HD}_{ijt}, -\right) \sim Multinom\left(\left\lfloor mq_{ij} S^{H}_{i,t} \right\rfloor; c_1 p_{ij1,t}, \ldots, c_K p_{ijK,t}, \delta a^{H}_{D}, r_{ij,t}\right) \quad (21.10)$$

where $E^{HN}_{ijk,t}$ are the newly exposed individuals arising from pathway γ_k. A similar expression can be used in eq. (21.7), by exchanging the probabilities of each destination ($mq_{ij}p_{ij,t}$) with the probabilities of each pathway ($c_1 mq_{ij} p_{ij1,t}, \ldots, c_K mq_{ij} p_{ijK,t},$). Considering the fact that for a given cell i there are $n-1$ possible destinations and K_{ij} pathways for each destination, the number of different categories in the multinomial of eq. (21.7) rapidly rises. Since this distribution should be sampled for each node i and at each time-step of the simulation, it is reasonable to consider only a subset of the possible work destinations and pathways for each node.

21.5 Force of Infection along Pathways

An important step for the model presented is the computation of the time necessary to travel along a pathway γ_k, τ_k, and the associated probability of infection, π_k. First of all, the possible pathways considered here are constituted by a sequence of single moves from the centroid of one cell to a neighborhood one along cardinal directions (for an example of a pathway, see Figure 21.2. Needless to say, it is possible to conceive of more realistic models of contact – for example, eight nearest neighbors). Each pathway can be written as the sequence of L cells along the pathway, indicated in the following as $\gamma_k = \left(\gamma_{k,1}, \ldots, \gamma_{k,l}, \ldots, \gamma_{k,L}\right)$, where the first cell, $\gamma_{k,1}$, is the home cell i and the work cell j is $\gamma_{k,L}$. If the average times necessary to cross each cell are $\tau_{k,1}, \ldots, \tau_{k,l}, \ldots, \tau_{k,L}$, assuming that individuals are using the same means of transportation, then the total time associated with the pathway is $\tau_k = 0.5\tau_{k,1} + \tau_{k,2} + \ldots + 0.5\ \tau_{k,L}$. The probability of becoming infected while crossing the l-th cell along the pathway is $\tau_{k,l}\lambda^{H}_{l,t}$. Thus, the probability of becoming infected in a time-step λ due to the travel along γ_k is one minus the probability of not becoming infected:

$$\pi^{H}_{k,t} = 1 - \left(1 - 0.5\delta\tau_{k,i}\lambda^{H}_{i,t}\right)\left(1 - \delta\tau_{k,2}\lambda^{H}_{2,t}\right) \cdot \ldots \cdot \left(1 - 0.5\delta\tau_{k,j}\lambda^{H}_{j,t}\right) \quad (21.11)$$

This expression relates the probability of becoming infected along a pathway γ_k to the local forces of infection (i.e., local mosquito concentrations) in the cells crossed.

21.6 Final Considerations

This chapter contributes to urban sustainability by providing a modeling approach that can be used to improve public health. The main innovation of the proposed modeling framework is to improve the current compartmental epidemiological models by considering not only the vector-to-human transmission at Home and Work cells, but also the probability of transmission along mobility pathways. In fact, exposure to the disease strongly increases for the commuters whose pathways have a high probability of crossing vector-infested areas where exposure is possible. This is achieved by considering the contribution to the daily force of infection by the probability of infection along the single pathways. In this way, the model is able to evaluate the risk of transmission associated with different choices of commuting pathways.

The risk of infection computed for the different pathways can be used within decision-support tools in order to identify the best choice for the commuters. In this framework, the optimal control problem is formulated as the research for the pathway that minimizes the trade-off between the risk of disease transmission and the commuting times. The results proposed by this modeling endeavor can be used for improving urban design, specifically of urban green spaces and mobility pathways within the city. It also suggests that current indicators of urban sustainability, such as green spaces within a city, might not be sufficient for assessing urban sustainability. Two additional aspects have to be considered: First, spatial location is crucial when looking into the health component of sustainability, since as shown for the case of mosquitos, the location of green spaces and water bodies within parks might significantly alter the contamination pathways. Second, dynamics and transmission pathways cannot be neglected when looking into sustainability issues in urban planning, as they can be influenced through specific policies during an epidemic outbreak.

Future research should aim to prove the efficacy and stability of this conceptual model by comparing the solutions of the optimal control problems obtained with machine-learning tools and nonlinear programming to further contribute to spatial urban planning.

Acknowledgments

The authors acknowledge the EPFL-ENAC Exploratory Grant 2018 via the project "Risk evaluation of mosquito-borne disease transmission through urban commutes pathways." DP and AR acknowledge funds provided by the Swiss National Science Foundation (www.snf.ch), via the projects: "Dynamics and controls of large-scale cholera outbreaks" (DYCHO CR23I2 138104) and "Optimal control of intervention strategies for waterborne disease epidemics" (200021–172578).

Note

1. Part of this chapter belongs to "M. Ajelli, Modeling mosquito-borne diseases in complex urban environments. Acta Trop. 2017 Dec;176:332–334. DOI: 10.1016/j.actatropica.2017.08.026. Epub 2017 Aug 30" under license to reuse in a book ordered through Copyright Clearance Center's RightsLink® service, Order Number 4504110660463 on 8 January 2019.

References

Ajelli, M. (2017). Modeling mosquito-borne diseases in complex urban environments. *Acta Tropica*, 176, 332–334. https://doi.org/10.1016/j.actatropica.2017.08.026

Ajelli, M., Moise, I. K., Hutchings, T. C. S. G., et al. (2017). Host outdoor exposure variability affects the transmission and spread of Zika virus: Insights for epidemic control. *PLoS Neglected Tropical Diseases*, 11(9), e0005851. https://doi.org/10.1371/journal.pntd.0005851.

Bagnoli, F., Massaro, E., & Guazzini, A. (2012). Community-detection cellular automata with local and long-range connectivity. In *International Conference on Cellular Automata*, pp. 204–213. Berlin/ Heidelberg: Springer.

Balcan, D., Colizza, V., Goncalves, B., Hu, H., Ramasco, J. J., & Vespignani, A. (2009). Multiscale mobility networks and the spatial spreading of infectious diseases. *Proceedings of the National Academy of Sciences*, 106(51), 21484–21489. https://doi.org/10.1073/pnas.0906910106.

Barmak, D. H., Dorso, C. O., Otero, M., & Solari, H. G. (2011). Dengue epidemics and human mobility. *Physical Review E*, 84(1). https://doi.org/10.1103/PhysRevE.84.011901.

Dorigatti, I., Hamlet, A., Aguas, R., et al. (2017). International risk of yellow fever spread from the ongoing outbreak in Brazil, December 2016 to May 2017. *Eurosurveillance*, 22(28). https://doi .org/10.2807/1560–7917.ES.2017.22.28.30572.

Esteva, L., & Vargas, C. (1998). Analysis of a dengue disease transmission model. *Mathematical Biosciences*, 150(2), 131–151. https://doi.org/10.1016/S0025-5564(98)10003–2.

Esteva, L., & Vargas, C. (1999). A model for dengue disease with variable human population. *Journal of Mathematical Biology*, 38(3), 220–240. https://doi.org/10.1007/s002850050147.

Esteva, L., & Vargas, C. (2000). Influence of vertical and mechanical transmission on the dynamics of dengue disease. *Mathematical Biosciences*, 167(1), 51–64. https://doi.org/10.1016/S0025-5564 (00)00024–9.

Ferguson, N. M., Cucunuba, Z. M., Dorigatti, I., et al. (2016). Countering the Zika epidemic in Latin America. *Science*, 353(6297), 353–354. https://doi.org/10.1126/science.aag0219.

Fischer, M., & Staples, E. (2014). Chikungunya virus spreads in the Americas – Caribbean and South America, 2013–2014. *Morbidity and Mortality Weekly Report*, 63(22), 500–501.

Focks, D. A., Haile, D. G., Daniels, E., & Mount, G. A. (1993). Dynamic life table model for *Aedes aegypti* (Diptera: *Culicidae*): Analysis of the literature and model development. *Journal of Medical Entomology*, 30, 1003–1017.

Griffin, J. T., Hollingsworth, T. D., Okell, L. C., et al. (2010). Reducing *Plasmodium falciparum* malaria transmission in Africa: A model-based evaluation of intervention strategies. *PLoS Medicine*, 7(8), e1000324. https://doi.org/10.1371/journal.pmed.1000324.

Grubaugh, N. D., Ladner, J. T., Kraemer, M. U. G., et al. (2017). Genomic epidemiology reveals multiple introductions of Zika virus into the United States. *Nature*, 546(7658), 401–405. https:// doi.org/10.1038/nature22400.

Hartley, L. M., Donnelly, C. A., & Garnett, G. P. (2002). The seasonal pattern of dengue in endemic areas: Mathematical models of mechanisms. *Transactions of the Royal Society of Tropical Medicine and Hygiene*, 96(4), 387–397. https://doi.org/10.1016/S0035-9203(02)90371–8.

Karl, S., Halder, N., Kelso, J. K., et al. (2014). A spatial simulation model for dengue virus infection in urban areas. *BMC Infectious Diseases*, 14(1). https://doi.org/10.1186/1471-2334-14-447.

Keeling, M. J., & Rohani, P. (2008). *Modeling Infectious Diseases in Humans and Animals*. Princeton: Princeton University Press.

Kraemer, M. U., Sinka, M. E., Duda, K. A., et al. (2015). The global distribution of the arbovirus vectors *Aedes aegypti* and *Ae. albopictus*. *ELife*, 4. https://doi.org/10.7554/eLife.08347.

Lessler, J., Chaisson, L. H., Kucirka, L. M., et al. (2016). Assessing the global threat from Zika virus. *Science*, 353(6300), aaf8160–aaf8160. https://doi.org/10.1126/science.aaf8160.

Likos, A., Griffin, I., Bingham, A. M., et al. (2016). Local mosquito-borne transmission of Zika virus: Miami-Dade and Broward Counties, Florida, June–August 2016. *MMWR. Morbidity and Mortality Weekly Report*, 65(38), 1032–1038. https://doi.org/10.15585/mmwr.mm6538e1.

Mammen, M. P., Pimgate, C., Koenraadt, C. J. M., et al. (2008). Spatial and temporal clustering of dengue virus transmission in Thai villages. *PLoS Medicine*, 5(11), e205. https://doi.org/10.1371/ journal.pmed.0050205.

Massaro, E., Ganin, A., Perra, N., Linkov, I., & Vespignani, A. (2018). Resilience management during large-scale epidemic outbreaks. *Scientific Reports*, 8(1).

Neiderud, C.-J. (2015). How urbanization affects the epidemiology of emerging infectious diseases. *Infection Ecology & Epidemiology*, 5(1), 27060. https://doi.org/10.3402/iee.v5.27060

Otero, M., Schweigmann, N., & Solari, H. G. (2008). A stochastic spatial dynamical model for *Aedes Aegypti*. *Bulletin of Mathematical Biology*, 70(5), 1297–1325. https://doi.org/10.1007/s11538-008–9300-y.

Otero, M., Barmak, D. H., Dorso, C. O., Solari, H. G., & Natiello, M. A. (2011). Modeling dengue outbreaks. *Mathematical Biosciences*, 232, 87–95.

Paules, C. I., & Fauci, A. S. (2017). Yellow fever: Once again on the radar screen in the Americas. *New England Journal of Medicine*, 376(15), 1397–1399. https://doi.org/10.1056/NEJMp1702172.

Poletti, P., Messeri, G., Ajelli, M., Vallorani, R., Rizzo, C., & Merler, S. (2011). Transmission potential of chikungunya virus and control measures: The case of Italy. *PLoS ONE*, 6(5), e18860. https://doi.org/10.1371/journal.pone.0018860.

Rezza, G., Nicoletti, L., Angelini, R., et al. (2007). Infection with chikungunya virus in Italy: An outbreak in a temperate region. *The Lancet*, 370(9602), 1840–1846. https://doi.org/10.1016/S0140-6736(07)61779–6.

Robert, M. A., Christofferson, R. C., Silva, N. J., Vasquez, C., Mores, C. N., & Wearing, H. J. (2016). Modeling mosquito-borne disease spread in US urbanized areas: the case of dengue in Miami. *PLoS ONE*, 11(8), e0161365.

Salje, H., Lessler, J., Paul, K. K., et al. (2016). How social structures, space, and behaviors shape the spread of infectious diseases using chikungunya as a case study. *Proceedings of the National Academy of Sciences*, 113(47), 13420–13425. https://doi.org/10.1073/pnas.1611391113.

Stoddard, S. T., Forshey, B. M., Morrison, A. C., et al. (2013). House-to-house human movement drives dengue virus transmission. *Proceedings of the National Academy of Sciences*, 110(3), 994–999. https://doi.org/10.1073/pnas.1213349110.

Stoddard, S. T., Morrison, A. C., Vazquez-Prokopec, G. M., et al. (2009). The role of human movement in the transmission of vector-borne pathogens. *PLoS Neglected Tropical Diseases*, 3 (7), e481. https://doi.org/10.1371/journal.pntd.0000481.

Teurlai, M., Huy, R., Cazelles, B., Duboz, R., Baehr, C., & Vong, S. (2012). Can human movements explain heterogeneous propagation of dengue fever in Cambodia? *PLoS Neglected Tropical Diseases*, 6(12), e1957. https://doi.org/10.1371/journal.pntd.0001957.

United Nations, Department of Economic and Social Affairs, & Population Division. (2014). *World urbanization prospects: the 2014 revision*.

Wesolowski, A., Eagle, N., Tatem, A. J., et al. (2012). Quantifying the impact of human mobility on malaria. *Science*, 338(6104), 267–270. https://doi.org/10.1126/science.1223467.

Wesolowski, Amy, Qureshi, T., Boni, M. F., et al. (2015). Impact of human mobility on the emergence of dengue epidemics in Pakistan. *Proceedings of the National Academy of Sciences*, 112(38), 11887–11892. https://doi.org/10.1073/pnas.1504964112.

World Health Organization & United Nations Human Settlements Programme (Eds.) (2010). *Hidden Cities: Unmasking and Overcoming Health Inequities in Urban Settings*. Kobe, Japan: World Health Organization; UN-HABITAT.

World Health Organization. (2016). *World Health Statistics 2016: Monitoring Health for the SDGs Sustainable Development Goals*. World Health Organization.

Yamey, G., Schäferhoff, M., Aars, O. K., et al. (2017). Financing of international collective action for epidemic and pandemic preparedness. *The Lancet Global Health*, 5(8), e742–e744. https://doi.org/10.1016/S2214-109X(17)30203–6.

Zhang, Q., Sun, K., Chinazzi, M., et al. (2017). Spread of Zika virus in the Americas. *Proceedings of the National Academy of Sciences of the United States of Americas*, 114(22), E4334–E4343. https://doi.org/10.1073/pnas.1620161114.

Index